DISCARDED
WORTHINGTON LIBRARIES

ROME
CITY IN TERROR

OSPREY
PUBLISHING

This book is dedicated to my wife of 49 years,
Patricia A. Failmezger

VICTOR FAILMEZGER

ROME
CITY IN TERROR
THE NAZI OCCUPATION 1943-44

OSPREY PUBLISHING
Bloomsbury Publishing Plc
Kemp House, Chawley Park, Cumnor Hill, Oxford OX2 9PH, UK
1385 Broadway, 5th Floor, New York, NY 10018, USA
E-mail: info@ospreypublishing.com
www.ospreypublishing.com

OSPREY is a trademark of Osprey Publishing Ltd

First published in Great Britain in 2020

© Victor Failmezger, 2020

Victor Failmezger has asserted his right under the Copyright, Designs and Patents Act, 1988,
to be identified as Author of this work.

For legal purposes the Acknowledgments on pp.8–11 constitute an extension of this copyright page.

All rights reserved. No part of this publication may be reproduced or transmitted in any form or
by any means, electronic or mechanical, including photocopying, recording, or any information
storage or retrieval system, without prior permission in writing from the publishers.

A catalog record for this book is available from the British Library.

ISBN: HB 978 1 4728 4128 5; PB 978 1 4728 4129 2; eBook 978 1 4728 4127 8;
ePDF 978 1 4728 4125 4; XML 978 1 4728 4126 1

20 21 22 23 24   10 9 8 7 6 5 4 3 2 1

Maps by www.bounford.com
Index by Fionbar Lyons

Typeset by Deanta Global Publishing Services, Chennai, India
Printed and bound in Great Britain by CPI (Group) UK Ltd, Croydon, CR0 4YY

Front cover: A Panzer VI Tiger I in front of the Vittorio Emanuele II Monument, Rome, February 1944. (Bundesarchiv,
Bild 101I-310-0880-34, Fotograf(in): Engel)
Back cover: An atmospheric view over the rooftops of the Eternal City. (Photo by David Lees/Corbis/VCG via Getty Images)

Osprey Publishing supports the Woodland Trust, the UK's leading woodland conservation charity.

MIX
Paper from
responsible sources
FSC
www.fsc.org   FSC® C020471

To find out more about our authors and books visit **www.ospreypublishing.com**. Here you will find extracts, author
interviews, details of forthcoming events and the option to sign up for our newsletter.

Key to military symbols

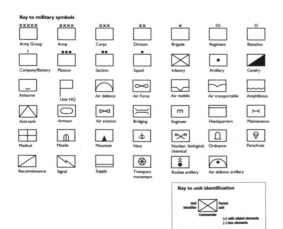

Contents

List of Maps

Acknowledgments

Many friends, colleagues, and others helped make this book come to fruition. First, thanks must go to my wife, Patricia, who helped at every stage. Then thanks to my first line reviewer, fact checker, and longtime friend, Chief Petty Officer Peter R. Knight, Royal Navy Retired. Pete and I were stationed together in Castel Volturno, outside of Naples, 50 years ago and he still lives in the Naples area.

Thanks also to Mr. Malcolm Barr, a veteran of The Associated Press. He read two early drafts of the book and made significant comments on the manuscript. He has earned my gratitude as he assisted with style and consistency.

Special thanks to my brother-in-law, Father Robert L. Grant, professor at Saint Ambrose University, Davenport, Iowa. Bob studied in Rome at the North American College during our tour of duty at the American Embassy and his enthusiasm for this book and his knowledge of Rome and Roman Catholic institutions together with his critical comments were most welcome.

Sometimes luck and the internet reunite old friends. The best man at our 1971 Naples, Italy wedding was Fred Bullock who contacted me out of the blue after almost 47 years. Fred volunteered to proofread the book and a wonderful proofreader he is. Fred, as an ex-corporal, Survey, Corps of Royal Engineers, British Army, also provided a much-appreciated double check on my use of British Army terms.

If this book begins to tell the very complicated story of the Nazi occupation of Rome with any degree of clarity, it is because of my learned friend Mr. Howard Klein. Howard was formerly a critic for the *New York Times* and a director of the Rockefeller Foundation in New York. His assistance with the pace and flow of the story allowed these characters to come to life and tell their stories.

While stationed at the American Embassy Rome, I had the pleasure to work with a friend from SMU college days, Mr. Joe B. Johnson. Joe was our Embassy press attaché. I convinced him to not only read the book but to give me his comments for which I am very grateful.

For research assistance I am in debt to Pier Paolo Battistelli and Piero Crociani, co-authors of Osprey Publishing's *World War II Partisan Warfare in Italy.* Pier Paolo provided me with material from the British National Archives detailing organization and personnel at the *Aussenstelle Rom,* material from the *Archivio Ufficio Storico dell'Esercito, Roma,* and the *Bundesarchiv* in Germany. Pier Paolo warned that I might face criticism from locals as, even 70 years later, some of these events remain controversial. Piero lent me books from his extensive library and made recommendations for further reading. He also allowed me to copy parts of the daily reports for both German Kommandants of Rome. He thoroughly checked the manuscript and corrected many errors and was extremely helpful in the selection of photos for the book.

Dr. Lutz Klinkhammer, of the *Deutsches Historisches Institut in Rom,* graciously spent time with me, provided copies of his extensive writings on the period, and assisted with my access to the Institute's collection and entry to the *Bundesarchiv* photo collection.

Through Dr. Klinkhammer I was introduced to Amedeo Osti Guerrazzi, who many consider the Italian expert on the period. Amedeo gave me copies of several of his books, which proved invaluable. Further he helped me obtain electronic copies of more than 1,200 pages of research documents.

Dr. Alessia A. Glielmi at the *Museo Storico della Liberazione* is a wonderful researcher and historian. She has helped me with a wide variety of issues and assisted in obtaining permission to reproduce photographs and other items from the Museum's collection.

In total, during the course of this research, I obtained more than 3,700 pages of documents and photographs, many from the US National Archives. I have made electronic versions of most of them available to the *Museo Storico della Liberazione* and to the *Deutsches Historisches Institut in Rom.*

Other individuals who provided guidance and assistance were:

Dr. Silvia Haia Antonucci at the *Archivio Storico della Comunità Ebraica di Roma* (ASCER);

Professor Allan Ceen, Professor of History of Urban Development at *Studium Urbis*, who helped with the Vatican maps of 1939–1945;

Katy Gorman, Dr. Mario Setta, and Patricia Chandler for their assistance in the Italian town of Sulmona;

Dr. Antonio Parisella, President of the *Museo Storico della Liberazione*;

Ann Pulver, friend, longtime resident of Rome, geography lecturer at Penn State, Rome campus, and our Borgo Pio landlady;

Dr. Riccardo Sansone, a historian of the period and an expert in what happened in the Quadraro area of Rome in April 1944;

Dr. Andrea di Stefano who provided important documents and is associated with the North American College.

I am also thankful to the following archives, libraries, and organizations:

Archivio Centrale dello Stato, Roma;

Archivio Ufficio Storico dell'Esercito, Roma;

Biblioteca di storia moderna e contemporanea, Roma;

Georgetown University Manuscripts Library which holds the Harold H. Tittmann, Jr. Papers;

The National Archives, College Park, Maryland (NARA);

The US Army Military Heritage and Education Center, Carlisle, Pennsylvania;

The US Holocaust Memorial Museum, Washington DC.

Finally, special thanks to the entire Osprey team: Marcus Cowper, publisher; Kate Moore, editor extraordinaire; and Gemma Gardner, senior desk editor, for their help and guidance with this and my previous book, *American Knights*. And finally, to Allison Davis of Osprey/Bloomsbury in New York City for her suggestions and work in publicizing this book; the Osprey team made this book a reality.

ACKNOWLEDGMENTS

Every effort has been made to use correct Italian and German words and grammar; however, the reader is asked for indulgence as neither of these languages is my native tongue. Any errors, omissions or other mistakes are mine and mine alone.

Victor "Tory" Failmezger
Middletown, Virginia and Rome, Italy, 2019

Author's Introduction

Rome is a city of amazing clear, impossibly blue skies, its ancient buildings flanked by tall umbrella pines. Double and triple arched windows reach to the high open loggias crowned by penthouses with green gardens of trees and plants. Its ancient streets are lined with block upon block of churches, palaces, and apartments, whose stone reflects the light which changes with every angle of the sun. Statues of angels abound, including one that causes a lop-sided effect on the high façade of the church of Sant'Andrea della Valle, recalling scene one of *Tosca*, the story of a previous occupation of Rome.

Then there are the feral cats of Rome. Proud, arrogant, aristocratic, and secure in the knowledge that some of their ancestors fed the populace during hard times. Street markets are full of fruits and vegetables so fresh you can taste them with just the smell. Coffee-scented air wafts from a thousand bars, stacked with pastries so beautifully displayed that you want one of each. Small tables and chairs outside these bars face narrow ancient streets of foot-aching cobblestones.

Walking through the city you continually catch glimpses of interior courtyards with fountain, statues, and flowering plants. Around a corner, you hear before you see it, the splash and glitter of an unexpected fountain stacked with naked gods and sometimes turtles, like the Fontana delle Tartarughe, at the entrance to Rome's Jewish Ghetto. Banks of flowers of every color line the windows and flower stalls while old women in black and men in suit jackets sporting caps from another time sit outside doorways. Boys zip by on motorcycles with slender, dark-haired, beautiful girls riding behind them. They enjoy their youth but are destined to become plump matrons and aging lovers. Interspersed throughout the city are the big open piazzas filled with people meeting friends and going about their business. This is Rome; beautiful, magnificent, magical Rome, the Rome that was subjected to abject terror during the Nazi occupation.

I have long had a love affair with Rome. Before I knew anything about the Eternal City, I knew about the power of ancient Rome. Brought up as a Roman Catholic, I was fascinated by the Roman legionaries depicted on the Stations of the Cross around Our Lady of Lourdes parish church in Milltown, New Jersey. As I grew older, I became a fan of the 1960s crop of ancient sword and sandal movies, especially *Ben Hur* and *Cleopatra*. During my 1968 Grand Tour of Europe between my junior and senior years at university, a highlight was my visit to Rome. Returning to Texas and spending some time with my World War II veteran uncle, Tommy Welch (1st Lt Thomas Peter Welch, 601st Tank Destroyer Battalion), I learned of his own visit to Rome as one of the first soldiers to enter and liberate the city during the war.

In 1969, at the height of the Vietnam War, I enlisted in the US Navy and requested duty in Europe. Needless to say, I was delighted when I received orders to NATO, Naples, Italy. That meant I could return to Rome from time to time and explore the city. Within a year I had met and married a US Navy Nurse, Patricia Grant. She too has loved Rome from the first moment we visited there together in February 1971.

Several tours of duty later I found myself a lieutenant working as the special assistant to the Director of Naval Intelligence, Admiral Sumner Shapiro. The admiral, needing an assistant naval attaché in Rome, asked if Patricia and I were willing to serve in Rome. We jumped at the chance. Those three plus years in Rome were our favorite assignment. We explored the city at every opportunity. While I escorted senior naval officers to official meetings and acted as interpreter, Patricia escorted their wives around Rome. The result was that we both learned our way around the city.

My interest in the World War II history of Rome was piqued on June 4, 1984. On that date I participated in the celebration of the 40th anniversary of the liberation of Rome in full naval uniform. I was impressed by the number of surviving Italian partisans and US Fifth Army veterans who had come to Rome for the ceremony. Wreaths were laid at the Porta San Paolo by those partisans and surviving veterans of General Frederick's 1st Special Service Force near the 1st-century white marble pyramid tomb of Caius Cestius. Scars from this battle were pointed out to me and can still be seen to this day on the ancient white marble. Later at a special reception for partisans, Allied wartime veterans and others, I was privileged to meet and spend some time with many of these veterans, including the famous former US *Stars and Stripes* cartoonist Sgt. Bill Mauldin.

After my retirement from the Navy in 1990, we continued to visit Italy frequently and always spent time in Rome. One catalyst for my new efforts at writing was the discovery of Uncle Tommy's 150 letters to my grandmother and mother. Included among them was his account of entering Rome on June 4, 1944. Although Tommy had passed on, I realized that I had enough material to write a book and was grateful when Osprey Publishing agreed to publish it in 2015. The result was *American Knights*, the story of Tommy and the 601st Tank Destroyer Battalion.

In the summer of 2014, I received an email from Frank Billecci. Frank reminded me that he had met Patricia and me in 1971 when he visited Naples and that we had shown him the ancient sights of the *Campi Flegrei* in the Bay of Naples. He added that he had used the photos he took during his visit throughout his subsequent career as a teacher and educator and just wanted to reconnect. In a series of emails, I learned that Frank had served as secretary and driver to Brother Robert Pace who had been instrumental in hiding escaped Allied servicemen in Rome during the nine-month-long Nazi occupation of the city. Frank felt Brother Robert's story should be told and, looking for a new project, I decided to investigate.

We thought we knew the history of the city, but in exploring what happened during the German occupation Patricia and I discovered that familiar streets held terrible World War II secrets. I quickly learned that there was much more to the story and it would involve discovering an aspect of the Eternal City that I knew little about. I was encouraged in this effort by Kate Moore, my editor at Osprey.

Rome is the major character of this book. The war affected all who lived in the city and caused everyone to constantly live in fear. From time to time this fear turned into stark terror. Hitler's Wehrmacht, the SS, and the diplomatic corps in Rome were formidable forces. Mussolini's Fascist government carried out its mission of repression with ardor. Against the steel reality of its armaments, weaker entities, hardly equal to the demands of this fight, stood in opposition: the monarchy of Vittorio Emanuele III; the Vatican under Pope Pius XII; the scattered aristocracy; the resistance among the Romans (from ardent anti-fascists to militant communists); pockets of infiltrators; foreign diplomats; Allied ex-POWs; and ordinary citizens, especially women, who were active but barely hidden from view. These disparate entities conspired to bring Rome out from under the clouds of war while preventing the destruction of the priceless buildings, artifacts, and art that is the soul of the city.

As I completed this manuscript, the Vatican announced that the secret archives of Pope Pius XII from World War II would be released to researchers on March 2, 2020. Getting access for non-university researchers to the Vatican Archives is nearly impossible and, given the interest that this announcement generated, it would take years for me to get access to them. I will have to rely on third parties for any relevant facts that might change this narrative. Having said that, I believe that my comments about the Pope and the Vatican during World War II will stand the test of time.

In writing this book we were obliged to return to Rome six times. We visited every scene of action described; even timing the walking distances from one place to another. It is amazing how much of wartime Rome is still intact and can be visited today. The reader is invited to make this journey with us and reflect on what it was like to live among the terror that abounded in the city.

Dramatis Personae

ALLIED SERVICEMEN WHO HID IN ROME

Buchner, Bruno, Yugoslav, soldier, ran the Escape Line apartment on Via Cellini

Byrnes, Captain Henry Judson, Royal Canadian Army Service Corps, responsible for Escape Line records and books

Cedomir, Lieutenant Ristic, Yugoslav, worked for the International Red Cross in Rome

Derry, Major Sam I., British, Territorial Royal Artillery, ran the Escape Line in Rome

Dukate, Captain Elbert L. Duke, USAAF, hid in Sulmona

Fane-Hervey, Hugh, British Army Officer, captured in North Africa

Furman, Lieutenant John, British, key member of the Escape Line

Garrad-Cole, Pilot E., British, RAF, captured in North Africa

Mander, Captain D'Arcy, British, Green Howards Regiment, worked with "A" Force in Rome

Newman, 1st Lieutenant William Loring, US, 3rd Ranger Battalion, Baker Company, hid in Rome

Pollak, Private Joseph, British Palestinian Pioneer Corps, Czech Jew, member of the Escape Line

Rendell, Captain Dennis, British 2nd Parachute Regiment, hid in Sulmona and Rome

Simpson, Lieutenant William C., British, Royal Artillery, key member of the Escape Line

Smith, Captain Gil, British, 4th Royal Tank Regiment, escaped from the Sulmona hospital

Tompkins, Major Peter, US, spy and the head of the OSS in Rome during the Nazi occupation

Wilson, RCAF Captain Glenn Pat, American Flying Officer, hid in Sulmona
Wilson, Captain R. Tug, British, trained saboteur

CLERGY

Benedetto, Father Maria, French, head of DELASEM, Jewish Assistance
 Organization
Hérissé, Monsignor Joseph, French, priest at the Vatican who helped the Jews
Hudal, Bishop Alois, German, rector of the German Catholic Church in Rome,
 ODESSA member
McGeough, Monsignor Joseph, US, director of the North American College
Montini, Monsignor Giovanni Battista, Italian, Vatican Under-Secretary of
 State
Mother Mary, Jane Scrivener, US, Vatican Information Bureau, Rome diary
 publisher
O'Flaherty, Monsignor Hugh, Irish, started the efforts to help Allied ex-POWs,
 the Escape Line
Pace, Brother Robert, Maltese, Christian Brother, key Escape Line organizer
Perfetti, don Pasqualino, Italian, a former priest who betrayed the Escape Line
Pfeiffer, Pancrazio, German, Abbot General Salvadorian Order, unofficial Gestapo
 liaison
Pius XII, Pope, Italian, the Bishop of Rome and worldwide leader of the Roman
 Catholic Church

DIPLOMATS

Mackensen, Hans Georg von, German Ambassador to Italy until 1943
Möllhausen, Consul Eitel Friedrich, German, senior diplomat, German Embassy
 in Rome
Montgomery, Hugh, secretary to Sir D'Arcy and Escape Line assistant
Osborne, Sir D'Arcy, British, Ambassador to the Holy See, force behind the
 Escape Line
Rahn, Rudolf, German Ambassador to Italy, replaced Mackensen
Salazar, Count Sarsfield, Swiss Embassy member of the Council of Three
Tittmann, Harold H., Jr., US, Chargé d'Affaires at the Holy See, force behind
 the Escape Line
Trippi, Count Captain Leonardo, Swiss, Military Attaché, key Escape Line helper
de Vial, François, Vice Consul, French, Embassy to the Holy See, key Escape Line
 supporter
Weizsäcker, Baron Ernst von, German, Ambassador to the Holy See

ESCAPE LINE CIVILIAN HELPERS; NON-ITALIAN

Almagiá, Esmé (nee Simpson), English, widow of an Italian Jew
Chevalier, Henrietta, Maltese, hid many escapees in her tiny apartment
Lucidi, Adrienne, French, a key Escape Line helper
Lucidi, Renzo, half Danish-Italian, husband of Adrienne and a key Escape Line helper
May, John, British, valet to Sir D'Arcy and a key Escape Line helper

GERMANS

(For a complete listing of the SS and Gestapo, see Appendix C.)
Dannecker, SS-Hauptsturmführer Theodor, Eichmann's Jewish troubleshooter sent to Rome
Dollmann, SS-Obersturmbannführer Eugen, SS-Chief Heinrich Himmler's man in Rome
Elling, SS-Obersturmbannführer Georg, Vatican spy
Harster, SS-Gruppenführer Generalleutnant der Polizei Wilhelm, head of police activities in Italy
Himmler, Heinrich, the German Interior Minister and Chief of German Police and SS
Kappler, SS-Obersturmbannführer Herbert, head of the Gestapo in Rome
Kesselring, Field Marshal Albert Konrad, Wehrmacht Commander-in-Chief, South
Mälzer, General Kurt, second Stadtkommandant (city commander) of Rome, self-styled King of Rome
Priebke, SS-Hauptsturmführer Eric, SS-Chief of Counterespionage, Rome
Skorzeny, SS-Hauptsturmführer Otto, the man who rescued Mussolini
Stahl, General Rainer, first Stadtkommandant of Rome
von Hohenberg, Carl F. Clemm, Graf (Count), head of the Abwehr in Rome
von Ribbentrop, Joachim, German Foreign Minister
Wolff, SS-Obergruppenführer Karl F., head of the SS in Italy

ITALIANS

(See also Appendix E for more people of Sulmona.)
Ambrosio, General Vittorio, the Chief of the Italian General Staff (*Comando Supremo*)
Badoglio, Pietro, Marshal of Italy, head of government after Mussolini
Buffarini-Guidi, Guido, the RSI (Fascist) Minister of the Interior
Calvi di Bergolo, General Count Giorgio, Vittorio Emanuele III's son-in-law and commandant of Rome

Carboni, General Giacomo, commander of the Italian Motorized Armored Corps in Rome

Caruso, Pietro, Rome Fascist Police Chief

Castellano, General Giuseppe, assistant to General Ambrosio, negotiated the armistice

Cipolla, Ubaldo, an Italian SS officer and important double agent for the Germans

Colonna, Vittoria, Duchess of Sermoneta, lady-in-waiting to Italy's queen

Costantini, Secondo, an Italian employee of the Swiss Legation

Crespi, Lele, an Italian Air Force officer (aviator) and a close associate of Peter Tompkins

Giglio, Lieutenant Maurizio, OSS agent, in control of Radio Vittoria 2

Graziani, Marshal Rodolfo, RSI (Fascist) Minister of War

Imperoli, Iride, from Sulmona, courier between the escaped Sulmona POWs and the Vatican

Koch, Pietro, head of the Special Fascist Police Unit (*Reparto Speciale di Polizia*), Banda Koch

Lousena, Major Umberto, Italian Army parachute officer, SIM, SOE Number One Special Force

Malfatti, Franco, SIM, OSS agent and Via Veneto bookstore owner

Menicanti, Clemente, OSS agent, in control of Radio Vittoria 1

Montezemolo, Colonel Giuseppe Cordero Lanza di, FMCR Resistance leader, head of Rome SIM

Nebolante, a Communist partisan who assisted the Escape Line

Secco-Suardo, Palatine Count Baldo, a close associate of Peter Tompkins

Vassalli, Giuliano, member of the Socialist Party and a close associate of Peter Tompkins

Vittorio Emanuele III, King of Italy

THE ROMAN PARTIGIANI (PARTISANS)

Bentivegna, Rosario, third year university medical student, partisan, boyfriend of Capponi

Blasi, Guglielmo, the partisan who betrayed his comrades

Calamandrei, Franco, GAP Vice Commander and university law graduate

Capponi, Carla, university student, partisan, and girlfriend of Bentivegna

Cortini, Giulio, physics department at the University of Rome, head of the GAP bomb-making team

Fiorentini, Mario, a one-time university student who was not allowed to finish as he was a Jew

Musu, Marisa, 19-year-old university chemical student

Ottobrini, Lucia, 20-year-old Treasury Ministry employee

Salinari, Carlo, GAP Central Commander and university literature student

Prologue

War had come to Italy; Allied armies hammered their way across Sicily and bombs rained down on the country's industrial cities. It was 1943 and so far Rome had been spared; but would the Eternal City be next? Italy's Fascist government under Benito Mussolini kept a tight grasp on power over the populace and their institutions and edifices. What Edgar Allan Poe called the grandeur of Rome, was balanced on the brink of destruction.

Allied long-range, full-scale bombing operations of Italy had started in the early fall of 1942, principally over the industrial triangle of Genoa, Milan, and Turin. Then the Allies had landed in North Africa on November 8, 1942. The Italian king, Vittorio Emanuele III, concerned about the inevitable consequences of that landing, and perhaps looking for a lifeline, directed Count Galeazzo Ciano, the Foreign Minister, to preserve any remaining contacts he might still have with London and Washington in case they could prove useful. Ciano, son of a recently made count, had been a minor official in the Italian Ministry of Foreign Affairs who had married Mussolini's daughter Edda, thus providing him with a fast track to the upper echelons of government. The king didn't trust the Nazis and he believed that eventually Italy would have to join the Allies to fight the Russians and communism. The king understood that by and large the Italian people had simply had enough, and it was now clear to many that the Axis could not win the war. Germany's armies were bogged down in Russia, and Japan was being challenged in the Pacific Islands. The year 1943 would prove to be the turning point in the war.

Shortly after the New Year, the king sent his cousin, Prince Aimone, the Duke of Aosta, to Switzerland with a peace feeler for the British. The duke, through the Italian consul general, passed on to the British government the message that if Britain came to Italy as an ally and not a conqueror; if it left the Italian fleet intact; and if it promised to preserve the monarchy, the duke would raise an army against Mussolini. The British declined. At the same time, the Vatican, with the approval of Pope Pius XII, sent a secret delegation to retired Marshal Pietro Badoglio to see if he would be willing to ultimately replace Mussolini.

Meanwhile, a new German Ambassador was appointed to the Holy See: Ernst Baron von Weizsäcker, a white-haired, blue-eyed, former World War I naval officer who had joined the German Foreign Service in the 1920s. By 1936, after several European assignments, he had been appointed as head of the Third Reich's Foreign Office Political Department in Berlin. In fact, German Foreign Minister Joachim von Ribbentrop wanted to get rid of him as he felt Weizsäcker was not a committed Nazi. Nevertheless, Ribbentrop believed that, as a former naval officer, Weizsäcker would obey orders, and so he named him as Ambassador to the Vatican. In Rome, Weizsäcker headed a staff of four. One of the smallest embassies assigned to the Holy See, it was considered the most professional. Weizsäcker was in an ideal position to gather information on the Pope and the Vatican but, due to the closeted nature of the Holy See, he was frequently frustrated in his attempts to penetrate its maze.

Between January 14 and 24, 1943, as the Allies battled with Italian troops and Germany's Afrika Korps for control of Tunisia, Prime Minister Winston Churchill and President Franklin D. Roosevelt met in the newly liberated Moroccan city of Casablanca. The Casablanca Conference affirmed the principle of unconditional Axis surrender and planned the immediate strategy for the conduct of the war. However, one key question that was not resolved during the negotiations was whether Italy could be considered an ally if it left the Axis and joined the war effort against the Third Reich.

Shortly after the conference adjourned on February 2, 1943, the German 6th Army at Stalingrad collapsed and more than 91,000 German soldiers were taken prisoner.* With the fall of Stalingrad and

---

* Of that number, only 6,000 would eventually return home after the war.

the earlier loss of thousands of Italian Eighth Army troops in Russia, the pressure on Mussolini was enormous.

Like most dictators, Mussolini, when faced with bad news, took revenge on his cronies. He had controlled all policy and operations, he had constrained the king and influenced the Pope, but his grip was slipping. On February 5, he fired all of his government ministers, including his son-in-law, Ciano.

Soon, however, Ciano was back in the government as Ambassador to the Holy See. Vittoria Colonna, the Duchess of Sermoneta, ascribed it to the rumor that Mussolini's lover, Claretta Petacci, had influenced the dismissal of Ciano because he blocked one of her brother's associates from being appointed Ambassador to Spain.

Others speculated that Ciano had been moved to the Holy See to start peace negotiations with the Allies through the good offices of the Vatican. The real reason may have been that Ciano had been caught expressing his dissatisfaction with Mussolini. This indiscretion was reported in a US Office of Strategic Services (OSS) cable sent from Switzerland to the US. The Germans intercepted the OSS cable and broke the code. Hitler, with a certain amount of schadenfreude, forwarded the intercept to Mussolini and Ciano was summarily dismissed as Foreign Minister. If true, it is uncertain why Mussolini subsequently allowed him back in power; perhaps it was pressure from his daughter or the growing realization that an individual previously critical of Mussolini may be in a better position to approach the Allies for peace.

Meanwhile, March 1943 saw widespread strikes inside the armament factories across northern Italy threatening vital wartime production. The workers demanded increases in pay, shorter working hours, and increases in food rations. In Turin, for example, an astonishing 100,000 workers from more than 200 factories went out on strike. Further antagonizing the Italian people was the fact that the bombing of Italian factories and military installations intensified as soon as North Africa was in Allied hands. The bishops of Milan, Turin, Genoa, Naples, and Palermo, anguished at the devastating effects, complained to the Pope about the Allied destruction of their cities. The Pope formally responded that he had requested that the Allies spare the civilian populations of the warring nations. The Pope then asked Sir Osborne D'Arcy, British Ambassador to the Holy See, for an explanation of the Allied bombing policy in Italy. British military planners were unsympathetic and, in reply, Sir D'Arcy sent the following memo:

1. The purpose of the bombing is to weaken the enemy's capacity for war and is directed against war-industries, communications and ports.
2. Damage to civilian and church properties is not and was never an objective, although such damage is inevitable.
3. The total loss of all Italian civilians throughout the country is less than single cities such as Warsaw, Rotterdam and Belgrade and less than any British city.
4. It is not possible to distinguish between Italian Fascists who declared war on Great Britain and those who were not responsible for it.
5. The Italian people should remember that Mussolini asked Hitler to participate in the air attacks on Britain.*

Despite the curt official response, so far Rome herself had been spared. Allied planning staffs did consider two risks involved in bombing Rome before any operations were to be launched. First there was the risk of possible outrage from the Catholic populations in Britain, the US, and the still neutral but predominately Catholic countries of Spain and Portugal. Extensive care was to be taken to avoid damage to the Vatican and other religious institutions. As a result, Churchill and Roosevelt agreed that the Pope must be assured that Allied pilots were ordered not to bomb the Vatican itself. Second, since Rome was seen as the cradle of European civilization, any damage to the city and its artworks would be roundly condemned.

True to their word, an Allied Military Bombing Map of Rome, produced in 1943 and before bombing began, lists only 15 targets. A note at the top of the list asks pilots to provide updated bombing pinpoints for accuracy. The 15 targets to be bombed included the downtown Palazzo Venezia where Mussolini had his office, two electric power stations, a refinery, the gasworks, two munitions depots, a fuel depot, the wireless (radio) transmitter station, the Centocelle Airfield,

---

* Mussolini had sent an Italian Royal Air Force (*Regia Aeronautica*) expeditionary force to support the Luftwaffe during the Battle of Britain.

the San Lorenzo Marshalling Yard, and the Termini railway station. The map carried the notation that Vatican City was not to be bombed; Allied pilots would subsequently quip that if they hit the Colosseum or the Vatican it would be better not to return to their air base.

By April it had become clear to all that neither the Italian military nor industry could sustain the war. Time was simply running out. The Chief of the Italian General Staff (*Comando Supremo*), General Vittorio Ambrosio, informed the king that Italy was on the verge of a military collapse. With the king's approval, Ambrosio organized a plan to arrest Mussolini and his chief lieutenants. In early May, the Allies had defeated German and Italian forces in Tunisia and more than 250,000 Axis soldiers became prisoners of war. Clearly, Sicily, Sardinia or mainland Italy was to be next.

I

Bombing the Cradle of Christianity

At 11:00 on the hot morning of July 19, 1943, the USAAF bombed Rome for the first time. The thud of bombs hitting the ground punctuated the wail of air raid sirens and the pop-pop of the few antiaircraft guns that responded. The targets, as planned and agreed in advance, were exclusively military: railway marshalling yards and airfields in the north and east of the city. The bombs of course did not always follow the plan.

Amid the din of aircraft engines and explosions, many bombs fell far from their assigned targets. Bombs rained on the *Policlinico Umberto I*, the University of Rome teaching hospital, causing many civilian casualties. This hospital had first opened in 1903 and is spread over many buildings. A 21-year-old bespectacled, dark-complexioned medical student, Rosario Bentivegna, was making his normal rounds at the *Policlinico* when the first bombs fell. He and fellow medical students immediately gave first aid to the wounded. Smashed windows and littered broken glass added to the confusion and injured many more. Soon more victims were rushed in from the surrounding residential quarter. Later Bentivegna recalled the harrowing scene:

> I ran up and began to collect patients and carry them to the ward in the cellars; and then the wounded and dead began to arrive ... each room in the Policlinico had been turned into an operating room. And those rags filled with plaster and blood, torn, piling up on the floor in layers of ooze, of blood, of dirt, of vomit, and it was a hellish thing.[1]

Bentivegna and the others worked all afternoon and long into the night. He blamed Mussolini for the Allied destruction of his city and vowed to become even more outspoken in his resistance to Fascism.

Bentivegna's family was Sicilian and had been active supporters of the national hero Giuseppe Garibaldi during the unification of Italy in the 1860s. Bentivegna himself had joined a communist youth group in 1938. In 1941, he joined 4,000 other students to protest a military call-up that would interrupt their university exams and studies. Bentivegna, one of the leaders, was noticed by the so-called Italian Gestapo, OVRA, the Organization for Vigilance and Repression of Anti-Fascism (*Organizzazione per la Vigilanza e la Repressione dell'Antifascismo*). He was arrested and spent two years in prison before being released through the influence of a friend, Leto Disma, the son of the director of OVRA. He resumed his studies and continued in his opposition to the Fascist regime by joining the PCI, the Italian Communist Party (*Partito Comunista Italiano*).

OVRA had been created by Mussolini with the express purpose to monitor his own citizens. It was, in reality, the Italian Secret Police with its headquarters in the Palazzo Viminale in Rome, an impressive neo-classical building located two blocks from the Rome Opera House. OVRA was responsible only to the Ministry of the Interior and Mussolini himself. Organized in early 1924, OVRA relied upon volunteers to provide information on anti-fascist activities and individuals. It was also active against anti-fascists abroad with some of the volunteers transitioning to become paid informers who reported to Italian embassies and consulates. Some suggest that such individuals occasionally carried out acts of sabotage. According to a US FBI report there were four OVRA agents in the United States from January 1935 until April 1941.

In Italy, OVRA had relatively few paid agents but a large number of volunteers with offices in most major Italian cities. It may have had as many as 1,800 members in Rome and was overseen by the chief of police (*Questura*). Agents opened and photocopied letters from abroad while riding in railway mail cars. During its heyday, OVRA sent secret reports to the Special Tribunal (TS – *Tribunale Speciale*), a special court at the ornate late-19th-century *Corte Suprema di Cassazione*, often referred to as the Palace of Justice, in Piazza Cavour. The tribunal had

12 members who acted as judges, only two of whom were lawyers and the rest were either military officers or appointed civilians.[*]

In the face of such unremitting control of all aspects of civilian life it is admirable that Bentivegna and others dared to risk further retribution and greater prison terms to defy Mussolini's iron rule.

Some distance from the epicenter of that first Allied air attack, Vittoria Colonna, the Duchess of Sermoneta, wrote of the bombing:

> Then on the morning of July 19th the sirens hooted and we heard the drone of many engines. I was watering my garden when the first bombs dropped, and it was curious to see all the birds – swallows, pigeons, sparrows, even the wrens and the blackbirds – whirling around in a great circular flights [sic], terror-stricken by the flying monsters that had invaded their skies. Soon thick smoke rose from the Portonaccio quarter of Rome [eastern part of the city], and later we heard that the marshalling yards of the station had been destroyed, together with a good many houses belonging to the working classes. The beautiful old basilica of San Lorenzo was much damaged.[2]

Vittoria Colonna was aristocratic, elegant and a part of Rome's highest society. A lady-in-waiting to Queen Elena of Italy, she came from one of Rome's oldest families and married into another, the Caetani, although her marriage effectively ended when her husband emigrated to Canada with his lover. Vittoria was born in London of Italian parents, had an English grandmother, and spoke and wrote English. An adventurous trendsetter prewar, she had embarked on a dangerous safari to Abyssinia (modern-day Ethiopia) by car. Possibly it was her previous adventures which ensured that she commented on the first bombing raid of Rome in such a cool manner.

But this first bombing raid was to be followed by many more. Indeed, there would be more than 50 Allied bombings of Rome.[†] Approximately

---

[*] After Mussolini was removed, OVRA was officially dissolved by the National, formerly Fascist, Chief of Police, Carmine Senise. It never really went away, however, and the Badoglio government retained many of its informers during their 45 days in power from Rome. Badoglio used OVRA to investigate illegitimate Fascist wealth. After the establishment of the Salò Republic it was reconstituted on a smaller scale in October 1944, and was called the Inspectorate for Public Security (*Ispettorati di Pubblica Sicurezza*).

[†] See Appendix B.

80 percent of all north/south railway traffic in Italy passed through Rome and the German Wehrmacht had begun to use the railway which transected the city to move huge amounts of weapons and supplies to Sicily, which had been invaded on July 10 by the Allies in Operation *Husky*. South of the yards were secondary targets, an industrial zone with a steel mill and a chemical plant. There was, as Sir D'Arcy had so succinctly pointed out, no way Allied planners would fail to include the city on the list of targets. Certainly, the bombing was not unexpected by the general populace. International Law had long called for warnings to be issued several days in advance of an action or bombardment if an attack might involve civilian populations. Prior to The Hague Convention of 1907, and throughout the 20th century, the concept of such warnings was written into the laws of most countries so, during World War II, warnings were regularly issued. In keeping with those laws, during the night of May 4/5, British RAF bombers had dropped leaflets over Rome encouraging the Italians to declare peace with honor and reading:

> As long as Italy remains an instrument of Germany, your industrial cities will be bombed without respite … Allied planes will pulverize the ports, railroads, and industrial centers of Italy. Today the war is at the gates of Italy. Peace is within the hands of the Italian people. The choice is up to you! If you still want war, we shall wage a *total war*. Africa is ours. Our naval vessels are able to bombard the Italian coastal cities along a 2,500-mile front. Our soldiers can land anywhere in Italy.[3]

A senior Vatican official, likely Monsignor Montini, Vatican Under-Secretary of State, requested clarification on the matter of complying with this demand. Sir D'Arcy was in London for consultations, so Hugh Montgomery, Sir D'Arcy's secretary, sent an urgent and confidential report to the British Foreign Office concerning the leaflet bombing. The leaflets suggested that deposing Mussolini alone might be enough to end Italian participation in the war. Montgomery was told that unconditional surrender meant that there could be no negotiations of the conditions of Italian surrender. Further, there would be no Allied territorial or economic promises prior to the receipt of surrender.

Next the Pope appealed to Washington and sent a personal letter to President Roosevelt dated May 18. The letter implored him to spare the

Italian people and the patrimony of Italy for the world.[4] The president's response of June 16 was cordial, but he gave the Pope no assurance that Rome would not be bombed. On June 30 the RAF dropped more leaflets again calling on the Italian people to denounce Fascism.

On the ground, these leaflets had some effect. Local resistance was growing and, on July 7, several Roman anti-fascist parties joined to form a Committee of Opposition which demanded the end of the Fascist Party and agitated for a free press and the release of all political prisoners.

On July 15, eight B-25 Mitchell bombers dropped 120,000 warning leaflets over the city. The bombers were neither intercepted nor fired upon. The leaflets, written in large black letters, screamed:

> Romans! Leave your houses if they are near to railway stations, airports, or caserns [military posts]. Get away from military objectives that the Allies could bomb. Romans! This is an urgent warning. Don't believe Mussolini's propaganda. Save yourselves.[5]

During the evening of July 18, the BBC (British Broadcasting Corporation), which was covertly listened to by everyone in Rome who understood English, warned Romans that airfields, railway stations, railway yards, and other military infrastructure would be bombed the next day. In the midnight hours the RAF again dropped thousands of leaflets repeating the same warning although this time the bombers received a far from warm welcome. The American diplomat Harold Tittmann, who was the US Chargé d'Affaires to the Holy See and resident in the Vatican, reported on this nighttime leaflet raid:

> [It was] an extraordinary spectacle, guns could be heard from every direction as the anti-aircraft batteries opened up, while red rocket flares and tracer bullets streamed brilliantly across the sky. Whenever the din faded, we could hear the voices of the Santa Marta nuns as they prayed continuously in their chapel …[6]

The first actual bombing raid, called Operation *Crosspoint*, lasted two and a half hours. The weather that fateful summer's day was perfect. The attack, an all-American affair, included 662 bombers initially escorted by 268 P-38 Lightning fighters, all from the Northwest African Strategic

Air Force (NASAF), whose commanding officer was Major General James H. Doolittle, the same Jimmy Doolittle who had conducted the American raid on Tokyo on April 18, 1942. The attack, led by a B-17 Flying Fortress nicknamed "Lucky Lady," was composed of four waves of B-17s and five waves of B-24 Liberators. Taking off from airbases in North Africa, the aircraft headed north and climbed to 20,000 feet, overflew Naples, hugged the coast, and then went inland to the north of Rome. Among the bomber crew of the B-17 "Delta Rebel 2" was the Hollywood star Clark Gable.*

Once the aircraft were aloft, Allied Forces Headquarters at Algiers sent a message to London and Washington confirming the military necessity of destroying the railway lines running through Rome. The major objectives were the San Lorenzo Railway Marshalling Yard, the Littorio Railway Marshalling Yard, and the Ciampino Airfield, home to a Luftwaffe unit. Targets were selected to minimize damage to non-military targets. The message stressed that these targets were clearly marked on maps and their bomb trajectories calculated so as to avoid prohibited or populated areas. It further averred that the pilots had been specially selected for their bombing expertise and that bombing during daylight hours would guarantee precision. The target bombing sequence was so arranged that smoke from previous bomb drops would not obscure follow-on bombing runs.[7]

The aircraft overflew the Littorio Railroad Freight Marshalling Yard and the adjoining Littorio Airfield. As it was the first target overflown, it would be the last to be bombed so the resulting smoke would not interfere with subsequent bombing runs. Then the bombers flew to the southwest, passing over the Tiburtina Railway Marshalling Yard: it too would be hit by successive waves. Finally, the first aircraft reached the San Lorenzo Freight Marshalling Yards, their most important target. Simultaneously two waves of B-25 Mitchell bombers and three waves of B-26 Marauder bombers attacked the Ciampino Airfield to the southeast of the city.

---

* Clark Gable, the film star, at this point a US Army captain, volunteered to join the air corps shortly after his wife, Carole Lombard, was killed in an airplane crash. He was assigned to supervise the making of training films and was sent to Italy to gain some experience before going to Britain to start production. Normally he held a camera, but on one occasion he in fact manned a gun. Gable also flew several missions against targets in Northern Europe.

Rome's meager antiaircraft defenses fired rapidly, but were not accurate. The Italian Breda-produced antiaircraft guns could reach a maximum altitude of 16,000 feet; the American bombers flew at 20,000 feet. Only two bombers were lost, a B-25 and a B-26. Great billows of smoke rose from the city. Across town the residents of the Vatican could smell the smoke. There were false rumors that several planes had descended to 30 feet and their crews had machine-gunned civilians but this was quickly disproved as Fascist propaganda.

Harold Tittmann's family were living with him inside the Vatican and were witnesses to this first Allied bombing raid. On July 19, his eldest son, Harold III, then 15 years old, wrote in his diary:

> At about a quarter past eleven in the morning, we heard a droning of planes. Suddenly the alarm sounded and the flak opened up simultaneously. We grabbed our field glasses and rushed downstairs. We could see puffs of smoke as the anti-aircraft shells exploded, and then we saw the planes. They were wonderful to see. Flying in perfect formations of three, they swept toward their objectives, gleaming in the bright sunlight … The anti-aircraft defenses made a lot of noise but we then climbed to the top floor of the Palazzo Santa Marta [where they were living] and looked out of a window. We had at first thought that they were bombing places around Rome, but when we saw huge clouds of smoke rising in the direction of the station, we knew that it was Rome's turn to suffer the horrors of war.[8]

Young Tittman's father, attending a meeting with Vatican officials, viewed the attack from the Loggia di Raffaello, a corridor space in the Apostolic Palace with windows overlooking the city. He reported that the raid angered at least one young Italian monsignor who exclaimed: "It doesn't matter. We will win – perhaps not now, but soon!" (*Non fa niente. Vinceremo – forse non addesso, ma nel futuro!*)[9] Tittmann wrote to the State Department that bombing the Eternal City might provoke a popular uprising against the diplomats residing in the Vatican, whom the Germans and their Fascist allies regarded as a nest of spies. Sir D'Arcy Osborne, for all his curt official correspondence, was appalled by the devastation caused in the city he loved and wrote his own letter of concern to the British Foreign Office.

Indeed, precision bombing had proved to be a vain promise. Early release from high altitude caused bombs to drop on the ancient Basilica of Saint Lawrence Outside the Walls (*San Lorenzo Fuori le Mura*) built in 579 by Pope Pelagius II. San Lorenzo was the resting place of the 19th-century Pope Pius IX, informally known as Pio Nono. Bombs also fell on the adjacent Campo Verano Cemetery, tearing up and splitting open graves including those of family members of the current pope, Pius XII.

Some 1,500 civilians were killed with perhaps as many as 2,000 injured. One reason for the high number of casualties was the concentration of trams packed with passengers in the square directly in front of the Basilica of San Lorenzo as the bombing commenced.

The bombers had dropped more than 4,000 500lb bombs. After the last plane flew over the city at 14:00, the code word "Dunit" was broadcast, signifying the attack had been a success. Despite the many stray bombs, the intended damage to military targets was significant. Although the photo interpretation reports and pilot debriefs could not account for lost lives, the reports listed the physical damage to the targets. Summarized from the official reports, this was as follows:

A. The San Lorenzo Marshalling Yards: extreme damage to rolling stock, tracks, railway infrastructure and nearby industrial establishments including a steel plant and a chemical plant. The yards are at least temporarily blocked.

B. The Littorio Marshalling Yards: at least 80 bombs fell on the yards and corresponding railroad tracks. The heaviest damage was done in the center of the yard with many direct hits on the tracks and rolling stock. Principal arteries in and out of the yard have been destroyed. At the nearby Littorio Airfield there was extensive damage to hangars and the entire facility.

C. Ciampino Airfield: the airfield was made temporarily unusable. The runway was cratered and many support building (administration, hangars, and sheds) were damaged. Twenty-four aircraft were observed on fire or damaged in the north part of the airfield; in the south of the airfield at least 14 aircraft were damaged.

Three hours after the July 19 bombing, in a bid to win the public relations war, reconnaissance photos were taken and published to prove that Vatican City and the Basilica of Santa Maria Maggiore had remained untouched.

For the first time since the summer of 1940, Pope Pius XII left the Vatican to visit the site of the bombing. Accompanied by Monsignor Montini, the Vatican Under-Secretary of State, they carried with them more than two million lire in cash for the victims. Montini turned the funds over to the Capuchin monks of the Basilica of San Lorenzo to be distributed among those most affected. At the scene, the Pope stayed for several hours, praying and comforting the people. Returning to his Mercedes, his white cassock stained with blood, some in the crowd demanded he prevent any further bombing raids. Returning to the Vatican, the Pope immediately wrote a letter of protest to President Roosevelt.

King Vittorio Emanuele III also visited the site of the San Lorenzo bombing in the immediate aftermath. According to the contemporary diary of the Swiss female journalist M. de Wyss, the king with the Prince and Princess of Piedmont was received poorly by the crowd:

They were hissed and insulted. People shouted at the king *"cornuto"* (the word usually applied to a deceived husband), the worst Italian offense, and at the Princess Marie José *"putana"* (whore). They also screamed: "You are guilty!" One woman tried to spit at them.[10]

The royal party also traveled to the military airfield at Ciampino. With its cratered runways, and destroyed hangars and facilities, it had already been abandoned by the Italian airmen stationed there.

———

As Rome was being bombed and its citizenry terrified, Mussolini, who was ultimately responsible for it all, was not there to witness the attack. The Allied forces had now established a foothold in Sicily and Mussolini knew it was only a matter of time before mainland Italy was invaded. Amidst this deteriorating situation tensions between the two European Axis powers grew and Hitler had summoned Mussolini to a meeting in northern Italy on the very same morning that the Allied bombing raid had been scheduled. Mussolini's health, which had begun to deteriorate with the Allied invasion of North Africa, continued to worsen. It was noted that:

> Mussolini began to suffer from nausea, retired to bed, and became very thin. In terrible pain, he could barely reach his desk. A fellow fascist hierarch described him as "gray, ashy, with sunken cheeks, troubled and tired eyes; his mouth revealing a sense of bitterness." Many around him believed he would die.[11]

Before he left for the meeting, key figures in the Italian government, as well as the king, had urged Mussolini to tell Hitler that Italy had to make a separate peace with the Allies or risk untold destruction and loss of life. General Ambrosio bluntly told Mussolini that he had got them into this, so he had to get them out. The king had secretly decided that Mussolini would have to go if he could not convince Hitler that Italy could no longer continue the war.

The two dictators flew separately to Treviso and then shared a train to Belluno, transferring to a car for the one-hour drive to a remote countryside villa outside the small town of Feltre. For more than three hours Hitler lectured Mussolini about how to wage war, hardly letting Mussolini utter a word. Mussolini, not using an interpreter but relying on his mediocre German, barely understood that Hitler was ordering Italy to stay in the war, supply its own men and materiel, and wait for the arrival of powerful and secret weapons. There was no other course. In the midst of this tirade, an Italian aide rushed in with an urgent message for Mussolini: the Allies had bombed Rome!

Three days later, Palermo, Sicily, fell to the troops of US General George S. Patton. Italians were distraught. Mussolini had promised that the enemy would never set foot on Italian soil; now his rash promises were increasingly proved hollow. Reacting to the capture of Palermo, Mussolini asked the Vatican to issue a passport to Luigi Fummi, a Roman banker with ties to the J.P. Morgan Bank of New York. Fummi's mission was to make contact with the British Foreign Secretary, Anthony Eden, in London and tell him that Italy wished to sue for peace. However, he only got as far as Lisbon where the British Ambassador refused to see him. In any case Gestapo agents in Rome were well aware of his mission and SS-Obersturmbannführer Eugen Dollmann, SS-Chief Heinrich Himmler's man in Rome, had alerted the German Ambassador, Rudolf Rahn, that Mussolini was under increasing pressure from his government to capitulate to the Allies.

In great distress, Mussolini knew he needed to act. Now back in Rome and for the first time in years, Mussolini called a meeting of the full 26 members of the Fascist Grand Council. In theory, the council had the duty to direct the course of the nation; however, up to this point Mussolini had considered it merely an advisory body. But Mussolini clearly needed to share the blame for his mismanagement of the war. His solution was to empower the council's ministers to run their departments without his interference.

The council meeting started at 17:00 on July 25 at the Palazzo Venezia's *Sala del Pappagallo.* The palazzo was a magnificent building built of stone quarried from the ancient Roman Colosseum and was the former residence of the Venetian Ambassador to the Holy See. Count Ciano opened the meeting by stating that the Germans, by refusing to send arms and men sufficient to defend the country, had abandoned the Italian people and Italy was therefore no longer under any obligation to continue the war. He reinforced his argument by stating that Germany had reneged on its agreement to delay a war in Europe until 1942, in order to give the Italian armed forces time to recover from its adventures in Ethiopia and Spain.

Count Dino Grandi, former Italian Foreign Minister and Ambassador to Britain, argued passionately that Italy must break all ties with Hitler and seek peace with the Allies. The debate raged for ten hours. Early the next morning Grandi called for a vote of confidence on Mussolini's policies. It was 19 against Mussolini, seven in favor. Furious at this betrayal Mussolini would later write in his 1944 memoirs that "The enemies of Fascism all began to raise their heads; the traitors came out from the shadows."[12] News of the meeting quickly reached SS-Hauptsturmführer Kappler, head of the Gestapo in Rome, who was told of what took place by an unidentified intelligence source in the office of the Ministry of the Interior.

The next day, a Sunday, Mussolini carried out a normal routine ignoring the results of the vote. This included receiving the departing Japanese Ambassador to Italy, Shinrokuro Hidaka, in the morning and later he visited the quarters of Rome that had been bombed. But soon, nothing would be normal for Mussolini.

———————

Informed of the Grand Council vote, the king knew that Mussolini must go. Usually he and Mussolini met for a weekly meeting on a Monday, but the king summoned Mussolini to an unusual Sunday audience at the Villa Savoia, now called the Villa Ada. At 17:00 on July 26, Mussolini met the king for what he assumed was a routine session. He noted that there appeared to be a large number of Carabinieri present; the Italian Military national police force, known for their fierce loyalty to the king and the House of Savoy. Instead of being dressed in civilian attire, the diminutive 5-foot-tall king was in the full uniform of an Italian field marshal, signaling that this indeed would be a momentous occasion. In his memoirs Mussolini recalled, perhaps with a selective memory, the king's choice of words:

> My dear Duce, it can't go on any longer. Italy is in pieces. Army morale has reached the bottom and the soldiers don't want to fight any longer. The Alpine regiments have a song saying that they are through fighting Mussolini's war. ... The result of the votes cast by the Grand Council is devastating. Nineteen votes in favor of Grandi's resolution and four of them cast by holders of the *Collare dell'Annunziata* [Order of the Annunciation, Italy's highest decoration, with the right to call the king "cousin"]. Surely you have no illusions as to how Italians feel about you at this moment. You are the most hated man in Italy; you have not a single friend, except for me. You need not worry about your personal safety, I shall see to that. I have decided that the man of the hour is Marshal Badoglio. He will form a cabinet of career officials in order to rule the country and go on with the war. Six months from now we shall see. All Rome knows about what went on at the Grand Council meeting and everyone expects drastic changes to be made.[13]

The audience lasted only 20 minutes. The king escorted Mussolini to the front door of the villa, took his hand and said his farewells. As Mussolini walked to his limousine, a Carabinieri Captain, Paolo

Vigneri, stopped him and pointed instead to a military ambulance. The captain said it had been provided for his safety and he should climb in. In fact, Mussolini was under arrest and was sped off to a Carabinieri cadet barracks for the night.

That evening Radio Rome, to the public's astonishment, announced that the king had accepted Mussolini's resignation. According to de Wyss:

> Hearing the news, people rushed into the streets just as they were: in night-gowns, night-shirts, pyjamas, some in trousers and bare above the waist, some in slippers; some barefoot, all howling, yelling, screaming. Disheveled, gaping, panting, they laughed and wept and threw themselves into each other's arms. They shouted *"Abbaso Mussolini"* ... They hurled down the Duce's pictures and trampled and spat on them.[14]

Fascist symbols were hacked from public buildings, Fascist offices and newspapers were looted, and jubilant bonfires lit the sky.

Compassionate prison guards allowed 1,466 prisoners (416 women and 1,050 men) to escape from Rome's Regina Coeli Prison.* Built on the banks of the Tiber River, the prison was constructed to hold 900 inmates, but frequently held as many as 2,500. It consisted of five arms which led out of a communal hall where religious services were held. Each arm had two upper stories with cells that looked on open lattice metal platforms so guards could see what went on below. By January 1944, the third arm was used exclusively by the Gestapo for political prisoners. Now freed were leaders of opposing parties and even citizens who had merely been arrested for tearing down pictures of Mussolini, painting slogans on city walls, and other such minor offenses.

---

*The Regina Coeli (Queen of Heaven) Prison, named after a convent originally on the site, is on the right bank of the Tiber River below the Janiculum hill and not far from the Vatican. The entrance to the prison is about one story below the level of the more modern street, the Lungotevere. That is because one of the first major construction works in Rome when it became the new capital after 1870 was the building of a high embankment along the Tiber River to contain the periodic flood waters. It remains Rome's main prison today.

The celebrations were short lived, however, and confusion soon reigned as Marshal Pietro Badoglio formed a new, non-fascist government. Badoglio was a World War I veteran who had played a controversial role in the tremendous Italian losses in the battle of Caporetto in 1917 and had been Italian Military Chief of Staff between 1925 and 1940. He had also commanded the Italian forces in the Second Italo-Abyssinian War (1935–1937), where he had employed poison gas against musket-equipped tribesmen. Seemingly this was the man to replace Mussolini.

Outside of the capital, euphoria at the announcement was swift as was its repression. In Milan 300 factory workers celebrating in the streets were fired upon by Carabinieri. Making things worse, the RAF dropped 4,000lb blockbuster bombs on the city, effectively ending the pro-Allied demonstrations. In Bari on the southern Italian Adriatic coast, 23 celebrants were killed by the police firing into the throng. The newly installed Badoglio regime imposed country-wide martial law.

Furthermore, Badoglio astonished many by declaring that Italy would carry on the war. Worried by the rapid turn of events and fearful of a German military reaction, Badoglio hoped to stall for enough time to allow him to bring Italian troops back from France and the Balkans to oppose a German attempt to occupy Italy. It was to be a case of too little too late.

2

The Frantic Effort to Leave the Axis

Contingency planning for the German invasion of Italy, codenamed Operation *Alaric*, had in fact started in May 1943 as Hitler's mistrust of the Italian commitment to continue the war grew. Planning activities intensified upon Mussolini's arrest on July 26, 1943. Hitler was furious when the news was conveyed to him. He referred to the king as "the little traitor" and threatened to occupy Rome, seize the Pope, and loot the Vatican. With Mussolini under guard, it had been the king's intention to calm the Germans by letting them assume that Italy would meet its obligations to the Axis partnership, while clandestinely suing the Allies for a separate peace.

For his part, Hitler gave the appearance of cooperating with the Badoglio regime in order to gain time to move German troops into Italy. And he hoped, perhaps naively, that the now-dissolved Italian Fascist Party would rise up and demand that Italy continue the fight on the Axis side.

The Germans' mistrust of the Italians was justified when on July 29 German codebreakers intercepted a trans-Atlantic telephone conversation between Churchill and Roosevelt where an Italian armistice was discussed. From that moment, the Germans were on the lookout for secret negotiations between the Allies and the Italians. Planning for Operation *Alaric*, now renamed Operation *Achse* (Axis), intensified and would include the disarmament of the entire Italian armed forces as well as the seizing or sinking of the Italian Navy.

Tensions ran high at the Vatican as well. US Chargé d'Affaires Tittmann was summoned to the office of Cardinal Luigi Maglione, the Vatican Secretary of State, on July 30. There he was introduced to Francesco Babuscio Rizzo, the chief of cabinet at the Italian Foreign Ministry. Introduction over, the cardinal left the room, and Rizzo, soon to be named Italian Ambassador to the Holy See, replacing Ciano, informed Tittmann that the Italian government was seeking secretly to negotiate an armistice with the Allies. But as Tittmann had no secure means of communicating with Washington there was little he could actually do. Meanwhile, Cardinal Maglione informed the members of the Rome Curia, the senior leadership of the church, that he was convinced that the Germans would march on Rome.

Possibly as a result of that intercepted telephone call, the Germans called a senior level meeting of both governments to take place in Tarvisio in northern Italy, close to the Austrian frontier, on August 6. German Foreign Minister Joachim von Ribbentrop, accompanied by Field Marshal Wilhelm Keitel, *Chef Oberkommandos der Wehrmacht* (OKW), arrived via a special, heavily armored train. Representing the Italians was Raffaello Guariglia, the newly appointed Italian Foreign Minister and General Vittorio Ambrosio, chief of the *Comando Supremo*, Keitel's Italian counterpart. Ribbentrop was assisted by Rome-based SS-Obersturmbannführer Eugen Dollmann, as interpreter.

The meeting took place on an Italian train surrounded by SS troops. To say that trust was not on that train is to put it mildly. The Germans even refused to eat or drink anything during the course of the meeting. There was no real practical outcome as a result of the conference. The German party proposed that the king meet with Hitler in Berlin for further talks, a ploy summarily rejected by the Italians. The only course of action agreed upon was that a further meeting, this time without diplomats, would convene in Bologna on August 15. Meanwhile the German Ambassador to Italy, Hans Georg von Mackensen, and the German Military Attaché, General Emil (Enno) von Rintelen, were both recalled from Rome. Their crime was that both had painted too rosy a picture of a still pro-German Rome after Mussolini's removal.

After a lull of some 24 days, Rome was bombed a second time on August 13. Again the target bombed was the San Lorenzo Marshalling Yards and other military targets. A massive American force of 106 B-17

Flying Fortresses was escorted by 45 P-38 Lightning fighters. A second force of 102 B-26 Marauder and 66 B-25 Mitchell bombers concentrated on the Littorio Marshalling Yards. But this time the American pilots did not only face the somewhat ineffective Italian antiaircraft fire. The Luftwaffe stalked the skies as well. Counterattacking with a force of approximately 75 fighters, the Luftwaffe shot down two B-26s. But the American escorting force of P-38s downed at least five German aircraft and the bombers still successfully dropped 500 tons of bombs. Tittmann's son, Harold Tittmann III, described the bombing as much smaller than the July 19 bombing while Swiss diarist M. de Wyss wrote:

> Happening to be near St. Peter's Square, I hurried there to have a look. It was a quite unique sight – people huddled like chickens under the colonnade; long files of cars parked all over the place; cabs with steaming horses obviously driven here at a great speed; and people still pouring in from every direction, in cars, on bicycles and on foot. Each stops with the expression: "Now finally I am safe!"[1]

Once again bombs went astray. At least 380 people were killed, and in the city center the German communications network at the Italian Ministry of War was hit. The Basilica of San Lorenzo and the *Policlinico* were hit again and the church of Saint Helena on Via Casilina was damaged. There the parish priest was killed while tending the wounded. Once again, the Pope visited the wreckage amid fears that the bombing would spark a popular uprising; it did not. The German genius for propaganda quickly got to work and declared that the bombing of Rome was the work of barbarians.

In an attempt to protect Rome from any further bombing raids the capital was officially declared an Open City by the Badoglio government on August 14 (*Città Aperta di Roma*). The government declared that military forces would not be stationed within the city; therefore, there would be no military justification to bomb the city. In response the Allies set forth the following impossible conditions to be met before recognizing Rome as an Open City:

1. Italian government agencies directly involved in the prosecution of the war must leave Rome immediately.
2. Italian and German armed forces must leave immediately.

3. Communication infrastructure, railways, roads, airways and shipping crossing Rome could not be used by military forces or to transport military supplies.
4. Airports in the vicinity of Rome must cease operations.
5. War industrial plants must cease production and military supply depots, maintenance and repair yards must close.

For the agreement to take effect, the Italian government had to notify the governments of Great Britain and the United States within seven days when these actions had been completed. Furthermore, the Italian government had to allow inspections by a neutral government to verify that these conditions had been satisfied.

The Pope endorsed the declaration, but the Allies knew that these conditions could not be implemented by the Italians nor forced on the Germans. The Allies believed, and rightly so, that the Germans would, in reality, ignore the conditions. They knew that the Germans had no intention of respecting them by rerouting their vital resupply lines around the city and the Allies knew that eventually they would have to route their men and supplies through the city using the same infrastructure in reverse. According to Tittmann, the Allies also knew that much of Badoglio's military command structure would remain in the city and many Italian and German staff officers, simply wearing civilian clothes, were already living and working in Rome. Moreover, there was a huge munitions dump a scant two miles from the city center at the Acqua Santa Springs and a huge arsenal of bombs at the Ciampino Airfield. Axis soldiers camping in the outskirts could move into the city at a moment's notice.

In an attempt to convince the Allies of the demilitarization of Rome, the Italians formed and staffed an Intra-Ministerial Committee to organize the Open City. The Italian Open City organization included many military officers and government officials. Tittmann wrote that the Committee:

ordered the immediate removal from Rome of all possible military objectives, both personnel and materiel. Military railroad trains (30 to 40 per day) passing through Rome were forbidden to stop in the Open City. The Italian government provided me [Tittmann], through Vatican channels with a map indicating the limits of the Open City, which I sent on to Washington by diplomatic pouch.[2]

Although plans were made to move Italian military commands out of the city, the demilitarization of Rome never took place. One exception was the Italian *Comando Supremo*'s order to discontinue antiaircraft defensive measures over the city. This was a hollow gesture, however, since American bombers, as we have seen, flew higher than the Italian air defense guns.

In the midst of these somewhat half-hearted preparations and just a few days before the Bologna meeting, German officials were informed that all Italian troops were to be withdrawn from the Balkans. During the meeting itself, the Germans demanded to know whether those troops were meant be used against them. Equally suspicious, the Italians wanted to know why the Germans wanted to move more troops into northern Italy, especially since the Axis evacuation of Sicily had begun. Neither side gave the other satisfactory answers. Unsurprisingly, immediately after the meeting, Germany lost no time in securing the Alpine passes into Italy.

This was simply the first move on the chessboard. Operation *Achse* now swung into action with a full 11 German divisions moving into Italy with orders to occupy the whole of the Italian Peninsula. This was a massive deployment, pulling troops from as far away as Russia. Field Marshal Erwin Rommel's Army Group B, now in Austria, was among those prepared to move into northern Italy while his 44th Infantry Division would occupy the crucial Brenner Pass, the lowest Alpine pass that demarcated the border between Italy and Austria. The 24th Panzer and 71st Infantry Divisions would move from the Balkans, to Tarvisio in northern Italy. From the west, spearheaded by an assault group of the 60th Panzergrenadiers, the German 305th Infantry Division would move to the Franco–Italian frontier at Ventimiglia.

Still officially allies, the Germans requested assistance for these movements. The *Comando Supremo* of the Italian armed forces stalled. The Germans had requested Italian transportation for their 305th Infantry Division but they were falsely told that no transportation was available and they must wait several days. The Italians also successfully delayed the German 44th Infantry Division transit of the Brenner Pass by citing bureaucratic issues.

Hitler also ordered the crack 1st SS-Panzer Division, *Leibstandarte SS Adolf Hitler*, commanded by SS-Obergruppenführer Josef Sepp Dietrich, to leave the Russian front for Italy. To hasten things, they left their old panzers behind and picked up new ones en route. Rommel, remaining in the north, would join Field Marshal Albert Kesselring in command of

German troops in Italy. Kesselring would command central and southern Italy. His mission was to halt the Allies in Sicily and prevent them from landing on the Italian mainland. By August 11, most of Rommel's troops were in northern Italy and now each field marshal had eight divisions. Kesselring stationed 36,000 first-class troops from two of his divisions to surround Rome. Her days as a free city were numbered.

Meanwhile other German plans were underway. Back on July 27, the day after Mussolini was arrested, Field Marshal Kesselring, Luftwaffe General Kurt Student, SS-Obersturmbannführer Eugen Dollmann, and Herbert Kappler, head of the Gestapo in Rome, dined with a special guest from Germany, SS-Hauptsturmführer Otto Skorzeny. Skorzeny's secret mission, personally directed by Hitler, had two distinct elements with General Student to oversee both operations.

The first element, called Operation *Eiche* (Oak), was to rescue Mussolini, Italy's once mighty Il Duce. Kappler resented the fact that Berlin had sent Skorzeny for this mission; he felt that he was more than capable of carrying out a rescue operation. Kappler had immediately started to look for Mussolini following his arrest and started to buy information on his whereabouts with his special war chest of fake British pounds. But laying hands on Il Duce was not going to be easy. First they had to find him, then overwhelm his guards, and then spirit him out of the country.

The second element, which was ultimately stillborn, was the mass arrest of King Vittorio Emanuele III, the Italian Royal Family, Marshal Badoglio, his cabinet ministers, senior military officers, and those members of the Fascist Grand Council who had voted against Il Duce, some 50 persons in all. It was called Operation *Student*. This operation was even more complicated. Both Kappler and Dollmann had grave reservations about the rounding up of so many prominent people. Dollmann took the lead on this mission, showing Skorzeny the ministries, offices, and residences where the subjects might be found. The German Embassy in Rome helped to compile the list of those to be kidnapped.

Dollmann, a most colorful character, had courted Rome's social elite, the aristocracy and Rome's creative and artistic personalities. He gathered gossip and scandalous information from the beautiful women who vied for his attention. On social occasions he would insulate himself by bringing along a girlfriend, Marie Celeste Rossi, nicknamed Bibi. She was the very attractive daughter of the woman who operated the Pension Jaseli-Owen near the Spanish Steps where he lived. Dollmann used Bibi as a cover for his preference for the company of younger male aristocrats and artistic friends whom he often entertained at his favorite restaurant, Scarpone, located in a secluded area behind the Janiculum Hill on the western edge of the city. Dollmann was especially attached to his devoted Italian chauffeur, Mario, and to Lupo, his giant Alsatian dog.

But Dollmann played a dual role. Believing that Operation *Student* was destined to fail, and ever the schemer, he secretly sabotaged it. He warned the wife of Consul Eitel F. Möllhausen, a senior-ranking German diplomat in Rome, that the king and others were to be arrested and he asked Frau Möllhausen to pass this information on to her dear friend, Carmine Senise, the Chief of the National Public Security Police (*Pubblica Sicurezza*). Senise was appalled that the Germans planned to kidnap the entire government, so he summoned his friend Dollmann to his office and told him of the plot, not knowing that Dollmann himself had set the affair in motion. Now Dollmann could inform Kesselring that the secret was out. He suggested that the plan be postponed or, better yet, abandoned. Kesselring called in Kappler ordering him to tell SS-Reichsführer Heinrich Himmler, the German Interior Minister and Chief of German Police, that since the Italians knew of the plan he should simply concentrate on finding Mussolini. Later Dollmann, the serial manipulator, would claim to have convinced General Sepp Dietrich, Otto Skorzeny's superior, to abandon plans for kidnapping the king and others over a fine lunch at the restaurant Scarpone.

On August 3, Kappler was rushed to Germany to meet with his Führer. Hitler praised Kappler for his intelligence network, for his extensive contacts and his expertise. Then he ordered Kappler to remain in Rome and continue his efforts to find Mussolini.

Energized by his meeting with his Führer, Kappler doubled down on his search for Mussolini. He received some unsolicited help from Himmler who rounded up a gaggle of psychics, astrologers, and other practitioners of the supernatural arts and sent them to Rome to help find Mussolini! Somewhat predictably they contributed nothing of value to the hunt for Mussolini but ate and drank rather well during their sojourn in Rome.

Amidst this background of intrigue and despite rising tensions, Italian authorities permitted Vatican diplomats' trips to the beach at

Fregene along the coast to the northwest of Rome. According to young Tittmann, the eldest son of Harold Tittmann, Jr., all along the way they met scores of southbound German vehicles. The German Army had set up a camp in the Fregene pine forest and, toward the end of August, had stationed artillery pieces near the beach. They removed all the beach cabins, presumably because they were in the line of fire. The boy noted in a letter that it was unnerving to swim in such close proximity to German soldiers. Swiss diarist M. de Wyss wrote:

> To-day is August 15th, a great Italian feast – Ferragosto. This brings the war home to the people more than many other things. Formerly everybody left the town, going away for at least a few days' holiday. Now all are forced to stay put for lack of transport and for fear of being unable to get back. It is worse this year than ever before, for the heat reached a degree I have never know in this country. The air seems like a thick and greasy soup. Breathing it you can almost feel a sticky pain in your lungs. Every move is a painful effort, and you hear your own sweat dropping on the floor even if you sit quiet in this furnace.[3]

Realizing they could not stop the Allied takeover of Sicily, the Germans successfully evacuated the last of their forces from the island on August 17. In phases, German soldiers had marched directly from the front line to waiting boats to take them across the narrow Strait of Messina. Remarkably the Allies did nothing to stop this removal of German forces. From August 1 to 17, the Germans evacuated a total of 39,951 troops; 14,772 wounded; 9,789 vehicles; 51 panzers; 163 artillery pieces; fuel; 1,874 tons of ammunition; and 16,791 tons of other equipment. It was a model of efficiency. During the cross-over to mainland Italy, only one soldier died and not a single German was left behind. Additionally, 59,000 Italian troops were also evacuated.[4] The Allies may have secured Sicily, but the Germans had secured the forces necessary to potentially retain Axis control of mainland Italy. The race to secure Rome was now on.

Italian troops were now on the move returning from France and the Balkans. Amidst these large-scale troop movements, on August 18, Sir D'Arcy cabled London protesting against the seemingly indiscriminate bombing of Italian cities by the Allies and requesting that the Badoglio government be given time, patience, and understanding as it greatly feared the consequences of a German invasion and occupation.

After the fall of Sicily, tensions in Rome had mounted along with the uncertainty of what would happen next. On August 23, Sir D'Arcy told Tittmann he had heard that the Germans were about to occupy Rome and invade the Vatican. Fearing his confidential papers would fall into German hands, Sir D'Arcy asked Tittmann's two sons to burn them in the Tittmanns' living room fireplace, the only working fireplace in the diplomatic apartments.* It was agreed among the Vatican's accredited diplomats that, if the Pope were to be forcibly removed from the Vatican, then foreign diplomats would attempt to go with him. As per the terms of the 1929 Lateran Treaty, the Vatican was recognized as a neutral country in international relations, and certainly up until this point had been able to continue its humanitarian efforts, despite war raging around it, and increasingly, directly overhead.

Pope Pius XII not only feared the threat of German occupation of the Vatican but he also had a deep fear of Godless communism. The Pope had served as the Papal Nuncio in Germany from 1917 until 1929. While living in Munich he witnessed what had happened when the local communist party, the Munich Soviet, took over the civil administration of the city in 1919. He witnessed social order break down and was even held captive for a while inside his residence. In the 1920s he was transferred to Berlin where he learned of the starvation of the Russian people under the new communist government and he helped arrange food shipments to a starving Russia. He was horrified by the communist rejection of religion and became a committed anti-communist. Now that the Allies included the Soviet Union, he feared that the aggression of Germany would be replaced by communist aggression and elimination of the church as a moral institution.

And so the Vatican adopted a policy of *attesismo*, the peaceful waiting for the Germans to leave and for the Allies to arrive. This was manifest by the Pope's policy of silence. He didn't want to castigate the Nazi regime openly as he feared harsh reprisals for German Catholics and,

---

* During the cold winter of 1942, Tittmann requested that Engineer Galeazzi, Director General of the Technical Services of Vatican City, install an open-hearth fireplace in his apartment to augment the scarce heat.

although he simultaneously feared the spread of communism, nor would he say anything negative about the Soviet Allies. Only a policy of silent waiting allowed him to walk this very fine line.*

The German Ambassador to the Holy See, Baron von Weizsäcker, cabled Berlin that: "In the Vatican the Italian situation is considered very threatening, no one any longer believes in an Axis victory ... Bolshevism really represents their main preoccupation." Weizsäcker followed this with a report on the Vatican's reserve toward the Badoglio government. He wrote that the Holy See believes that "the so-called freedom it promised has opened the door to Communist movements ... In reality the church today is worried. Communism is and remains its most dangerous enemy both in foreign and domestic policy."[5]

The Pope had already condemned, in general terms, all offenses against morality in war time. But he felt that he could not openly denounce the actions of Germany since as his diplomats stated they lacked the ability to both verify facts and determine guilt about specific German war crimes. Further, he believed a papal protest would only worsen the already precarious situation of Catholics in Germany.[6] By this time many Roman Catholic prelates in Germany had been arrested and sent to concentration camps; pastors who remained had to be careful with their sermons and avoid criticism of the Nazi regime.

August had heralded a mad Italian dash for peace with the Allies. It was scattered, uncoordinated and ineffectual as the Badoglio government pursued multiple channels to contact the British government.

In Lisbon on August 2, an Italian representative met with the British Ambassador to Portugal, Sir Ronald Campbell, a cousin of Sir D'Arcy; and on August 4, a different Italian envoy met with a British official in Spanish Morocco. The British were standoffish; the unidentified Italian had no official documents or proof of authority to enter into formal discussions.

A third attempt to make peace with the Allies was undertaken when Brigadier-General Giuseppe Castellano, military assistant to General Ambrosio, was sent undercover to Madrid. He left Rome on August 12

*The Vatican Under-Secretary of State, Monsignor Montini, drew up a document expressing the view that the Vatican was a neutral country and could therefore carry on its humanitarian work.

and traveled with an Italian trade delegation. Secretly he carried a written introduction from Sir D'Arcy to Sir Samuel Hoare, British Ambassador to Spain. In the letter, Hoare was asked to set up a meeting with Sir Ronald Campbell in Lisbon. Castellano was unsure if this letter would be accepted by the ambassador and he might have valued his letter of introduction more highly had he known that Sir D'Arcy had secretly sent a cable to London informing them about his mission. The cable also stated that Sir D'Arcy had a signed note from Marshal Badoglio authorizing him to enter into talks.

Castellano met with Sir Ronald in Lisbon on August 16, telling him that the Italians were ready to surrender. Telegrams were sent to London and Washington and Castellano had to wait for the Allied reaction.

President Roosevelt and Prime Minister Churchill agreed to the Lisbon meeting. US General Dwight D. Eisenhower, Commander of Allied Forces in the Mediterranean, sent his chief of staff, Major General Walter Bedell "Beetle" Smith, and the British sent Brigadier K. W. D. Strong. They were joined in the negotiations by the US Chargé d'Affaires in Lisbon, George F. Kennan, later a well-known postwar diplomat to the Soviet Union. The meeting took place on August 19. The Allied position was straightforward: unconditional surrender. This meant the immediate cessation of hostilities; the stopping of all aid to the Germans; the transfer of the Italian fleet and air force intact to the Allies; and the unrestricted use of Italian airfields by the Allies.

Castellano, having no authority to agree to these terms, entrained for Rome on August 23. He carried with him a secret radio, crystals, and codes supplied by the British. Castellano arrived in Rome on August 27; he had been away for 16 days and because he had had no access to a radio, no one in the city knew anything of his progress.

When Castellano outlined the Allies' terms to Marshal Badoglio, Badoglio was not pleased. Instead he wanted the Italian armed forces to put up a brief struggle for show and then capitulate to the Allies. This, he reasoned, would preserve Italy from the wrath of Germany. Badoglio needed to be assured that the Germans would be overwhelmed and so he made two, as it turned out, impossible conditions: the Allies must land a minimum of 15 divisions, they only had six available; and they must land north of Civitavecchia outside of Allied land-based air cover.

To communicate with the Allies, the *Comando Supremo* arranged for an English soldier and member of the secret British Special Operations

Executive (SOE), Dick Mallaby, to be released from a prison near Lake Como in northern Italy. SOE's mission, following its creation in 1940, was to develop indigenous secret armies that would, once they were strong enough to rise up, attack the German occupiers and disrupt their defenses. Relying on limited British support, these secret armies would conduct sabaotage, espionage and resistance throughout occupied Europe. In Italy, SOE's effort to arm partisans was called the Number One Special Force. Churchill's directive had been to "set Europe ablaze," and at its height SOE employed more than 13,000 agents across Europe, 3,200 of them women. When America joined the Allies after December 1941, the newly formed US Office of Strategic Services (OSS), whose missions were similar to those of the British MI-6, also had to be folded in and the two organizations started to work together. Working in the same geographical areas, these agencies needed to complement each other, and not get in each other's way. In June 1942 the OSS signed a protocol setting out ways to coordinate activities and as the war moved into Italy, coordination became even more urgent.

SOE agent Mallaby had been captured in northern Italy during a botched secret mission but was a fully trained and experienced radio operator. Taken to Rome and given the British radio equipment brought by Castellano, he was on the air by August 29, the date that the Allies had demanded that the Italians agree to continue with the discussions and confirm a second meeting.[7] With these demands in hand and now with an established communications channel, Castellano flew to Sicily on August 31. Since the Italians feared that the Germans would turn on them, he willingly gave the Allies what the *Comando Supremo* knew about the German order of battle. Further, Castellano said the Italians would need 15 days' notice to realign their forces to fight on the Allied side. Given the Italian troops in the vicinity of Rome, Castellano recommended that the Allies conduct an amphibious landing on the west coast of Italy, between Civitavecchia and La Spezia; he was sure that such a move would force the Germans to retreat north away from the capital.

Major General Bedell Smith said that an airborne division could be dropped into Rome and that anti-tank guns and ammunition could be barged up the river Tiber in support. As part of the deal, the Allies demanded extensive logistical support from the Italians: 23,000 food rations, 355 trucks, 12 ambulances, 120 tons of gasoline and oil, 12 telephone switchboards, 150 field telephones, 100 picks and shovels, and 5,000 rolls of barbed wire. On the second day they were to provide a labor pool of 500 men.[8] It was unlikely that the Italians could have provided this level of support with 15 days' notice or even longer.

Kept secret from Castellano was the fact that the British Eighth Army was to land at Reggio di Calabria, in the toe of Italy, on September 3, and that a larger Allied landing was to be at Salerno a few days later. Also kept secret from him was the British knowledge that senior Italian admirals had been in direct contact with the Allies through a naval officer in Lisbon and they intended to hand over the Italian fleet intact to the British at the first opportunity.

Allied officials, displaying a lack of trust in their Italian counterparts, had been very vague about the exact details and the timing of the landing, letting Castellano make uncorrected assumptions. By the time Castellano had returned to Rome on August 31, he had convinced himself that the landing would be at the seaside town of Anzio, 35 miles southwest of Rome and the closest beach landing site to Rome. He thought that this was reasonable because the Italians consistently overestimated the flight radius of Allied air cover and that the main objective would surely be the capital city. It was also his misimpression that the first landing of six divisions would not take place until September 12. He arrived at this conclusion on his own by extrapolating his understanding that the Allies would simply accept the 15-day requirement that he had requested. Furthermore, he convinced himself that a second and larger landing would occur shortly thereafter even though there were no such additional troops available. Castellano informed Italian General Giacomo Carboni, commander of the Italian Motorized Armored Corps, that he would have to hold off the Germans with only Italian forces and such Allied airborne troops as could be dropped until the main Allied force landed.

After his discussions in Rome, Castellano flew back to Sicily on September 2. The *Comando Supremo* had requested that he convince the Allies to postpone the invasion until September 15 when the Italians would be able to realign their troops and provide the requested supplies. Immediately after his arrival, the negotiations became more frenetic.

Castellano was now informed that the British were to cross the Strait of Messina the very next day, September 3, and that the Allies wanted the armistice to be announced in conjunction with an Allied invasion of mainland Italy in mid-September although the exact date was still kept secret. The Allies threatened that if the Italians did not agree immediately, Rome would be bombed yet again.

Messages flew back and forth to Rome. Shocked, Castellano had no choice but to sign the agreement pulling Italy out of the war. At the Vatican, Sir D'Arcy received another secret document signed by Badoglio for safekeeping. It authorized Castellano to sign the armistice document in his name, often referred to as the Armistice of Cassibile after the location in Sicily where it was signed.

Castellano had signed a short version of a much longer secret agreement, which bound the Italian government to its particulars. The long version contained political, economic, and financial dimensions of the agreement and was to be modified according to how much the Italians helped the Allies. Castellano was then flown to Algiers to coordinate activities, although the Italians continued to be kept in the dark as to both the timing of the invasion and the announcement of the armistice.

Upon arrival in Algiers, Castellano requested that he be provided with an Italian staff to assist in the coordination with the Allies. It was agreed, and a group of Italian officers were transported to the western end of Sicily before being flown to North Africa. They were unexpected and they caused quite a stir when they arrived at an Allied air base in full Italian uniform. Two of the officers wore the distinctive Bersaglieri feathered headgear and two others the distinctive Alpini hats with a feather. Castellano was not pleased as he had wished to keep the new cooperation secret, something that was now not possible.

Astonishingly, Badoglio had initiated two more Italian peace missions when he had heard no word from Castellano during his 16-day absence from Rome. The first also went to Lisbon and was headed by Italian General Giacomo Zanussi who took with him a British POW, Major General Adrian Carton de Wiart. Carton de Wiart had been captured in North Africa after his plane crashed off the coast of Libya. Although Carton de Wiart wore a business suit rather than military uniform, he was easily recognizable since he was missing an arm and wore an eye patch. They met with Sir Ronald Campbell but failed to make a deal and de Wiart was allowed to travel to England while Zanussi returned to Rome.

The second attempt was made by Count Dino Grandi, former Ambassador to Britain, who went to Spain where he too made no progress. Afterwards, he fled to South America to wait out the war. The Fascists sentenced him to death *in absentia* for his role in the Fascist Grand Council meeting and the overthrow of Mussolini.

Castellano and the Italian government continued to believe that the armistice was to be announced no earlier than September 12 and that it would coincide with an Allied airborne drop near Rome, codenamed Giant II. The *Comando Supremo* believed that the airfields to the northwest of the city could be protected from the Germans by Italian troops and would be ready for the airborne Americans. Sufficient transportation would also be ready to move the Allied troops to rallying points around Rome. General Carboni prepared a Maintenance of Public Order memo, the OP-44 memo, giving Italian commanders, either on orders from Rome or on their own initiative, the authority to defend Italy against the Wehrmacht.

On September 7, Italian reconnaissance planes spotted an Allied landing force heading directly for Salerno. The Italian high command realized that the landing was imminent and that it would in fact happen well before September 12. Too late they understood that the landing would be of no help in the defense of Rome.

The Germans, reacting quickly to news of the impending invasion, flashed the code word *Orkan* (hurricane), meaning prepare for battle. With remarkable foresight, parts of the 26th and the entire 16th Panzer Divisions had already been positioned on the plain south of Salerno. High-caliber 88mm guns were entrenched, trees removed, and strong points established. Weapons were aimed at potential landing beaches and barbed wire and mines planted. The Luftwaffe based Stuka dive bombers at local airfields and additional panzers were brought up. Rounding out his forces, Field Marshal Kesselring placed both the 15th Panzer Division and the Hermann Göring 1st Parachute Panzer Division of the Luftwaffe between Naples and Salerno. Meanwhile, further south, Kesselring's 29th Panzergrenadiers and the bulk of the 26th Panzer Division were waging a rearguard action against General Sir Bernard Law Montgomery's Eighth Army. As planned, Montgomery had landed at Calabria on September 3, after making a largely unopposed short crossing from Sicily. He commenced a slow advance up the Italian boot, hampered by blown and destroyed bridges and other infrastructure.

One of the more audacious escapades of the war occurred when American Brigadier-General Maxwell Taylor, commander of the 82nd Airborne Division Artillery, secretly entered Rome to make final arrangements with Marshal Badoglio. It was September 7, the day before the Allies planned to announce the armistice and commence a full-scale amphibious landing on the beaches of Salerno. Colonel William Tudor Gardiner of the Troop Carrier Command, later twice Governor of Maine, accompanied Taylor. Traveling from Sicily by motor torpedo boat to the tiny island of Ustica, 50 miles north of Palermo, they transferred to the Italian corvette *Ibis*. Disembarking at Gaeta, 75 miles south of Rome, they were driven to the city in a closed ambulance.

In Rome, the Italian generals misunderstood the urgency of the Americans' mission and offered amenities instead of action. The Americans were escorted by General Giacomo Carboni, the head of Italian Military Secret Intelligence (SIM) to VIP rooms in the Ministry of War. There they were served a multi-course dinner and regaled with fine wines. Finally, and only after repeated requests, they were taken in the early morning hours of September 8 to Marshal Badoglio's villa. An aide, meeting them at the door, took them to a small sitting room upstairs to wait for the marshal, who had only just been woken up. The aide insisted that Badoglio don his marshal's uniform as it was much more dignified than meeting them in his robe and slippers. Just as the situation was about to descend into a farce, Badoglio was at last officially informed of the correct timetable for the operation. Astonished, he immediately insisted that the armistice announcement be delayed until September 12. It then dawned on General Taylor how totally unprepared the Italians were to be of any help to the Allies.

Taylor agreed to return to Sicily and to try to convince General Eisenhower to postpone the landing. During the course of this meeting, Taylor could hear the bombing raid on Field Marshal Kesselring's headquarters timed to coincide with the invasion.[9] The headquarters were located just outside of Frascati, some 12 miles southeast of Rome, but as many as 6,000 civilians were killed or wounded in the attack on the town itself carried out by 130 B-17s of the 12th Air Force. After this attack, Kesselring moved his headquarters to bunkers inside the 2,267ft-high Monte Soratte, about 30 miles northeast of Rome.*

Now fully aware that his paratroopers would be unsupported by Italian troops, Taylor feared that they would be completely wiped out by the Germans so he quickly cancelled the airborne drop set for the next day and had SOE agent Dick Mallaby send the message to Allied headquarters in Sicily. With only hours to spare, the paratroopers, who were already on their aircraft waiting to take off, were recalled while Taylor and Gardiner returned to Sicily.

While Taylor was still in Rome, SS-Obersturmbannführer Dollmann was contacted by an informant. Meeting that evening in the ancient Roman Forum, Dollmann was told that General Taylor, of an Allied airborne division, was in the city. To Dollmann that meant that an airborne assault on Rome was imminent and he went to find Field Marshal Kesselring to inform him of this but, owing to the bombing of Kesselring's Frascati headquarters, he could not locate him.

General Taylor, back in Sicily, vainly argued for the postponement of the invasion, but it was too late. General Eisenhower sent a message to Marshal Badoglio that stated: "I intend to broadcast the existence of the armistice at the hour planned. If you or any of your armed forces fail to cooperate as previously agreed, I will publish to the world the full record of this affair."[10] Upon receiving the message, Marshal Badoglio inexplicably relieved key military members of their commands. They were not replaced and thus a catastrophic leadership vacuum was created.

The moment had finally come. It was at 18:30 on September 8, 1943, just as Sir D'Arcy finished a screening of the Anglo-American film *Desert Victory* about the Allied victory in North Africa, that the BBC broadcast a pre-recorded announcement by General Eisenhower that Italy had signed an armistice with the Allies and would cease hostilities. An hour later, Marshal Badoglio and, shortly thereafter, the king, made similar radio announcements. When told of the Allied–Italian armistice, Mussolini was said to have remarked that the king "was the greatest traitor in history and had invited into his country an army of Hottentots, Sudanese, mercenaries, American Negroes and

---

* Later, during the Cold War, this headquarters became the Italian government's nuclear war bunker.

other zoological specimens."[11] Tittmann's fireplace was again busy that evening as his two boys burned their father's confidential US documents.

On September 8, before the invasion fleet landed at Salerno, Admiral Raffaelle de Courten met with Field Marshal Kesselring and declared that the Italian Royal Navy (*Regina Marina*) was to sail out to meet the enemy. It was a ruse and the fleet sailed immediately for Malta and was turned over to the Allies intact.*

On the morning of September 9, Italian Naval Headquarters officially informed the *Comando Supremo* that one of their reconnaissance aircraft had spotted the huge Allied Naval Task Force in the Gulf of Salerno. General Carboni's Italian defense plan (OP-44) was ready and distributed but would never, in fact, be implemented.

The announcement of the armistice had shocked the Germans. Unlike the professional German soldiers and police, the civilian staff at the German Embassy panicked and commenced fervent packing amid the chaos. Field Marshal Kesselring's Chief of Intelligence, Colonel Carl Graf (Count) von Klinckowström, later said that if the Allies had dropped airborne troops to back up Italian forces in conjunction with a landing near Rome, German forces would have been forced north. Instead Rome quit the Axis but issued no orders to the Italian Army. It would be up to the local commanders to figure out what to do; many simply did nothing.

---

*An interesting side note is that, at the start of the war, only the Italian Navy was sufficiently prepared, with 117 submarines actively patrolling the Atlantic, the Mediterranean, the Black Sea, and the Red Sea. The Navy supported their forces in East Africa and in the Indian Ocean. Enjoying some initial superiority, Italian submarines sank 129 merchant ships totaling 668,311 tons and 13 warships totaling 24,554 tons. The Italian Navy, working with the Italian Royal Air Force (*Regia Aeronautica*), sank almost 200 merchant ships and 100 enemy warships. The most effective unit in the Italian Navy is often considered to have been the Decima MAS (*Decima Flottiglia Motoscafo Armato Silurante* – Armed Torpedo Motorboats the 10th Light Flotilla), an elite unit that employed high-speed boat-bombs, frogmen, and midget submarines called pigs (*maiale*). It sank over 130,000 tons of merchant shipping and damaged 28 warships. The most famous raid was in December 1941 when several midget submarines sneaked into the Port of Alexandria and disabled the battleships HMS *Queen Elizabeth* and HMS *Valiant*, plus an oil tanker. Later the Decima MAS became a land-based naval commando unit.

3

The Former Allies Square Off

By the beginning of September 1943, the Italian Army had seven divisions and some smaller units available to defend Rome. In theory, the total manpower to defend the city amounted to 70,700 men, 348 armored vehicles, 223 machine guns, and 534 artillery pieces. Most of these units were in the process of being re-formed or reorganized and had no recent combat experience. These forces were organized into three corps. See the map on page 61 for the disposition of both German and Italian units around Rome.

The most effective force was an armored vehicle corps (*Corpo d'armata motocorazzato*), under the command of General Giacomo Carboni. It was organized to defend the city and as a mobile unit was able to respond to any point of attack. Carboni was married to an American woman from Alabama and spoke English. During his career he also was twice head of Italian Military Secret Intelligence (SIM). In that position for less than a year, in June 1940 he was dismissed for writing reports in which he described Italian preparations for war as inadequate. After the downfall of Mussolini in July 1943 he assumed his old position as head of SIM. In that position he ordered the arrest of many Fascists still loyal to Il Duce. His corps was composed of three divisions, the Ariete II, Piave, and Centauro II.

The Ariete II was a cavalry division with a nominal strength of 9,500 men but at the time of the forthcoming battle for Rome it had 7,500 men available. The division had 176 armored vehicles (including 40 tanks), 92 antiaircraft machine guns, and 84 pieces of artillery. What it lacked, however, was fuel. It had recently been moved to Rome from

Brescia in northern Italy and was based at Lake Bracciano and along Via Cassia to the north of the city.

The Piave Motorized Division was a mobile reserve force but up to this point had had no World War II combat experience. In theory it was a highly mobile division of 6,000 men, 48 20mm antiaircraft guns, 88 pieces of anti-tank and anti-air artillery, over 2,000 vehicles, and 400 motorcycles but much of the equipment was obsolete and it too was short of gasoline. The division was deployed in a semi-circle along Via Salaria, Via Flaminia, and Via Tiburtina to the northeast of the city.

The Centauro II was a new Fascist Blackshirt division. Originally called "M" Division, it was modeled on Hitler's personal bodyguard, the *Leibstandarte SS*. It had been formed as recently as May 1943 and was still undergoing training with 40 German SS officers attached to it as advisors. After the arrest of Mussolini, it was renamed after the original Centauro Division which had been captured in Tunisia in May 1943. It was understrength with 5,500 men but had 36 tanks, eight 20mm Breda model 35 antiaircraft guns and an unknown number of 20mm Scotti antiaircraft pieces. It was based near Tivoli, on Via Tiburtina. It was commanded by General Count Giorgio Calvi di Bergolo, the son-in-law of Vittorio Emanuele III.

Part of the Centauro Division was the 18th Regiment of Bersaglieri. It consisted of four companies. There was one company of armored cars with two armored personnel carriers, one motorcycle company, one company of tracked vehicles, and one antiair company with 20mm guns. They had recently returned from southern France and were stationed near Tivoli outside of Rome, manning five roadblocks into the city.

A second armored corps, the XVII Armored Corps, manned fixed defensive positions 5–10 miles to the south and west of the city. It was under the command of General Giovanni Zanghieri, a veteran commander of the Italian Eighth Army in Russia. The corps was composed of three infantry divisions and attached units:

1 The Sardinian Grenadiers (*Granatieri di Sardegna*) was an infantry division with 12,000 men, 48 pieces of division-level artillery, 40 other pieces of artillery, 40 pieces of light artillery (anti-tank and anti-air), 24 20mm antiaircraft guns, 500 vehicles, and 80 motorcycles. It was placed within 12 miles to the south of Rome between Via Aurelia and Via Casilina.

2 The Piacenza Infantry Division had 820 men available out of an authorized strength of 8,500 men. It too was stationed to the south of the city, along Via Appia Nuova in the Colli Albani. The division suffered low morale due to the harsh conditions imposed by the commanding officer and was not considered effective.

3 The Re (King) Infantry Division had spent the last three years in Croatia, returning from there only on September 6. It had 2,500 men and 13 pieces of artillery. Stationed along Via Aurelia to the northwest of the city, it protected a military command center.

4 Attached to the Re Division was the 78th Infantry Regiment, called the Tuscan Wolves (*Lupi di Toscana*) which had recently returned to Italy from southern France. It was placed along Via Claudia from Santa Marinella to Ladispoli and was a well-disciplined force of 1,400 men. True to its name it would be the last Italian unit to actively resist the German Wehrmacht on September 12.

5 In addition, there were two coastal infantry divisions assigned to the corps. The 220th Coastal Infantry Division was spread along the coast from Tarquinia to Anzio, concentrating on the mouth of the Tiber River. The 221st Coastal Infantry Division was stationed at Anzio and to the south along the coast to the Garigliano River. Neither division was in a position to help in the defense of Rome.

6 There was a smaller force also designated as a corps stationed inside the city. It was composed of one infantry division and several attached units under General Alberto Barbieri, a veteran of the Italian war in North Africa. In addition to the available military forces, police forces augmented the corps and were nominally placed under General Barbieri's command.

7 The Sassari Infantry Division had spent two years fighting guerrillas in Yugoslavia and was designated the Garrison of Rome. It was composed of 12,000 men, had 24 20mm antiaircraft pieces, 48 pieces of divisional artillery and 32 other artillery pieces, and 24 tracked vehicles. Most of this equipment was worn out by long service.

Other assigned units to the corps were as follows:

1 The 4th Regiment of Infantry with 1,500 men, 11 20mm antiaircraft pieces, 18 assault cannons, 31 tanks, and 11 tracked vehicles, none of which were in good condition. They were augmented by Motorized Assault Battalion "A" which was assigned to guard the military caserns. There were approximately 5,000 other troops organized into various types of units and training commands attached to the regiment.

2 There were 4,000 officers and men of the Royal Corps of Carabinieri.

3 The Customs Police (*La Guardia di Finanza*) was an armed force of 1,400 men, who conducted anti-smuggling operations.

4 Metropolitan Police (*Polizia Metropolitana*) had 520 policemen and uniformed traffic police, armed with older rifles and limited ammunition.

5 Better equipped and also stationed in the city were 1,300 men from the Colonna Cheren of the Italian Africa Police (PAI – *Polizia dell'Africa Italiana*). The Colonna was divided into three motorized battalions and had one well-equipped company of light armored troop carriers and 16 other armed vehicles, including flame throwers. The PAI had originally been formed as a national police force to serve in Africa. It had been brought back to Italy from North Africa in 1942. Its barracks was at the Foro Mussolini sports complex in Rome.* Officially its loyalty was to the Fascist government; however, many individuals simply joined the PAI for a paycheck, food, and, most importantly, to avoid being sent to the regular army. Although now based only in Italy, they continued to wear tropical helmets and uniforms. After the Carabinieri, it was the most effective police force in Rome.

On paper this resembled a substantial defensive force that should have been more than capable of holding and defending Italy's capital.

---

* Designed to glorify sport and Italian youth and in an attempt to win the right to host the 1940 Olympics, which in the end were cancelled because of the outbreak of war, it was lauded as the premiere example of Fascist architecture.

DEFENSE OF ROME, SEPTEMBER 8, 1943

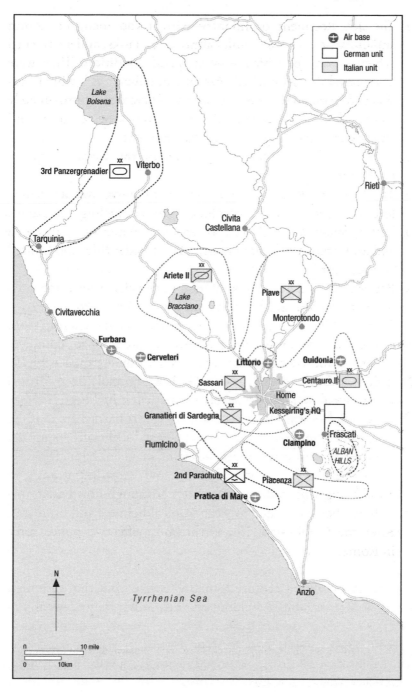

Opposing these Italian forces, the Germans had a total of 49,000 troops and 142 aircraft in the vicinity of the city. These troops included the 3rd Panzergrenadier Division with 24,000 men and 409 armored vehicles (including 150 panzers). In early September the division had started a slow movement south from Lake Bolsena, approximately 50 miles northwest of Rome.

The other division was General Kurt Student's reinforced 2nd Parachute Division (Luftwaffe). It had 12,000 men and 60 armored vehicles which had been flown into Italy without specific Italian authorization during the month of August as the Germans started to lose faith in their Italian allies. Supposedly these troops were on their way to reinforce German forces in southern Italy; instead they were deployed in a crescent from Fiumicino to the airfield at Pratica di Mare. These crack troops were there to hold Rome and were available to help free Mussolini. Most of the available German aircraft, 142 attack and fighter aircraft as well as miscelleanous transport aircraft, were also stationed there. All of these forces were called the *Fliegerkorps XI* and were under the direct control of Field Marshal Kesselring.

Although numerically inferior to the Italian troops, the German forces by and large consisted of highly experienced veterans led by capable, determined officers.

In addition there were 13,000 other armed support units. This total included the 5,000 German troops inside the city itself. They were in civilian clothes and were members of Italian/German joint staffs and military missions. They likely had access to personal weapons for self-defense.

Lacking orders from the Italian *Comando Supremo*, General Carboni, commander of the Italian Motorized Armored Corps, issued a general alarm to his three divisions on September 8. Unfortunately, with the announcement of the armistice, many Italian soldiers, both in and outside of Rome, simply abandoned their weapons and went home. Units designated to defend the city were decimated as many personnel left their barracks and shed their uniforms for civilian clothes. The entire Italian Seventh Army, stationed in southern Italy in the provinces of Apulia, Lazio, and Calabria, consisting of two corps of infantry, several coastguard divisions, and antiaircraft units, just dissolved. The Italian Fourth Army had been recalled from the south of France with the express purpose of shoring up Italian defenses in the face of an inevitable German assault, and yet it too disbanded as soon as it reached the Italian frontier.

For those Italian soldiers who remained with their units and at their posts, fighting commenced almost immediately. One of the Wehrmacht's first actions was to seize two poorly guarded Italian fuel dumps on the road between Ostia and Rome. This deprived Carboni's vehicles of gasoline and ended their utility as mobile troops.

The Royal Household had a contingency plan to whisk the Royal Family away to the south and the safety of the Allied lines. In the pre-dawn of September 9, aides woke Marshal Badoglio, the king, and others, telling them to dress. Word of the first German attacks had already come in; the king must leave the city.

Their destination was two Italian Navy ships standing off the coast at Ostia. But Via Ostiense, along with the all-important fuel dumps, was now in German hands. The only option was to head east. The royal party was bundled into waiting cars which headed into the mountains. With many high-ranking officers and government officials joining the convoy there were more than 60 vehicles in the motorcade.

In Rome, Carboni finally received orders from General Mario Roatta, the Italian Army chief of staff, to inexplicably send his units to Tivoli, 15 miles east of Rome. There, they were to regroup and prepare for the defense of the capital. Roatta's orders removed Carboni's Corps from defending the city at the most critical time for reasons that have never been clear, but it may have been to position his troops to protect the royal party as it left the capital. At noon upon learning of the departure of the king, Carboni ordered his men to return to the city, but by then it was too late as the Germans were approaching the center of Rome and active defense of the city was almost over.

With the departure of the king, Badoglio, and senior members of the *Comando Supremo*, the hierarchy of power had collapsed. All over Italy, military commanders requested instructions, but there was no one to give them. That afternoon, Carboni learned that former World War I Marshal of Italy Enrico Caviglia was already in negotiations to hand over the city to the Germans. Field Marshal Kesselring assured Marshal

Caviglia that if the troops defending Rome surrendered, the city would be spared. While the immediate capitulation of the Italian forces in and around Rome might indeed save the city, it would also allow German troops free passage to the south to confront the Allied forces now landing at Salerno. General Carboni, knowing that the Germans would now race through Rome, organized an armed defense to delay those troops and prevent their streaming to the Salerno beachhead, where he had been told the invasion was underway.

At the Vatican, the doors of Saint Peter's Basilica were firmly shut. The Swiss Guard donned fatigues and carried rifles with bayonets. Inside the Curia, officials burned sensitive papers that might have revealed the Vatican efforts to get Italy out of the war.

Meanwhile, the king and Marshal Badoglio had arrived at 10:00 at the hilltop town of Chieti, a provincial town near Pescara and the Adriatic Sea. The motorcade had been stopped by German troops several times but remarkably had been allowed to pass unmolested. Sailing northwards from Brindisi, under orders from Italian Admiral Raffaelle de Courten to pick up the royal party, were two Italian corvettes, the *Scimitarra* and the *Baionetta*. Joining later as an escort was the 6,000-ton cruiser, *Scipione l'Africano*. At 23:00, the *Baionetta* arrived at Pescara and, with the king aboard, and after a mad scramble for those wanting to embark, headed south.

As communications would be all-important, it was arranged for SOE agent Dick Mallaby to travel with the royal party. He was flown from Rome's Centocelle Airfield, just southeast of the city, to Pescara on an Italian Royal Air Force plane with his equipment. Once there he was given priority to board the *Baionetta* and became one of the 57 individuals on board. He was listed as Sgt. Major Guazzini with a notation listing him as an English Officer of the IS (Intelligence Service), Lieutenant Mallaby.[1]

While Vittorio Emanuele III and the others were being sped out of Rome to safety, British paratroopers, deployed on ships, landed at Taranto in Operation *Slapstick* on September 9. This operation was put together in haste after the Italian government offered to open the ports of Taranto and Brindisi to the Allies. Furthermore, these two ports were unlikely to be defended by the Germans. Taranto was quickly occupied and the paratroopers took the surrounding territory with minimal losses. The British aim was to capture the military airfields in the Italian heel. With these facilities in their hands they could more easily support the main Salerno landing and eventually launch long-range air strikes to northern Italy and even Germany itself.

The *Baionetta* sailed unannounced into the port of Brindisi in the heel of Italy around 14:30 the next day. The port had been taken by an unorthodox British unit nicknamed Popski's Private Army, officially called No.1 Demolition Squadron. The unit's work had been impressive in North Africa, and in the early days in Italy it provided small raiding parties moving ahead of the Eighth Army on the Adriatic side of Italy. Thanks to these efforts Vittorio Emanuele III and Badoglio were now safely ensconced in Allied-held territory.

Meanwhile, the Allied landing at Salerno, 30 miles southeast of Naples, was underway. Operation *Avalanche* began early on the morning of September 9 as 100,000 British and American troops waded ashore. The Germans were well entrenched and Kesselring was said to have remarked that the landing was God's gift to gunners. A British soldier was heard to say, "We've got them just where they want us."[2] As the Allies came under fire from the Germans, Allied ships opened fire and sent hundreds of rounds at the German defenses and gun positions, preventing the Allies from being immediately pushed back into the sea.

Some of Kesselring's troops from Sicily had been slowly retreating in advance of the British Eighth Army as it moved up from the toe of Italy. As the German troops arrived on the battlefront they were immediately sent into action against the Allied landing force. Kesselring had correctly identified the weakest point in the Allied attack as being the Sele River which separated the British and American forces.

Given the events of the last couple of days, General Giacomo Zanussi, a member of the *Comando Supremo* staff, looking back on the vacuum of command and its resulting chaos, wrote in his memoirs: "I do not think that if we had gotten together with the Allies to cook up a plan the object of which was to do the most damage to ourselves and the least to the Germans could we have concocted a better one. What we achieved was a masterpiece!"[3]

4

War in a Museum – The Battle for Rome

Carla Capponi, an attractive, petite, fair-haired University of Rome student employed as a secretary, lived with her mother, Maria Tamburri,* in a large apartment that overlooked Trajan's Column. She dressed elegantly, never leaving home without gloves. A Florentine, Carla Capponi was descended from nobility on her father's side. Her great grandmother was Viennese, Jewish, and a marchioness, but after her father died the family fell on hard times. Expensive artwork, Etruscan vases, and some of their once elegant furnishings were sold off to pay for food and rent.

Every night mother and daughter clandestinely listened to the BBC. During the early evening of September 8, 1943, they had heard US General Eisenhower broadcast the news that Marshal Badoglio and the king had signed an armistice with the Allies to pull Italy out of the war. Announcements from both Badoglio and the king had followed. Like the rest of Rome, Capponi and her mother were thrilled at the news, even though it was uncertain what would happen next. The answer came early the next morning: German troops invaded Rome.

Despite the power vacuum and lack of organization, some Italian soldiers resisted heroically. During the night of September 8/9, the German 3rd Panzergrenadier Division attacked Italian troops on the northern outskirts of Rome about 10 miles along Via Flaminia, north of the city. Italian Engineer Lieutenant Ettore Rosso, of the Ariete Division, had just completed mining a bridge and the road leading up to

---

* Women in Italy often retain and use their maiden names.

it, to prevent German troops from entering the city. Seeing the Germans approaching, he sent his men back towards Rome, while he remained with four volunteers. As the first Germans, led by an unknown colonel, crossed the mined bridge, Rosso fell on the detonator and blew up the bridge. A section of the roadway collapsed, killing the German colonel and wounding many soldiers. Lieutenant Rosso himself was killed.

Along Via Salaria to the northeast of the city, other units of the Piave Division held the German panzergrenadiers in check at Monterotondo, a small town approximately 15 miles northeast of Rome. At dawn, units from General Student's paratroops dropped on Centro A, the Italian Army Headquarters at Monterotondo and the secret headquarters for the *Comando Supremo.* There the paratroopers captured 30 generals and 150 other officers.

At the same time, the 2nd Parachute Division attacked the Piacenza Division near Frascati to the southeast. There and elsewhere during that night, the Germans employed subterfuge to disarm the Italians by waving white flags and showing false written orders.

As dawn broke on September 9, Italian forces to the southwest of the city attempted to resist the German advance at Montagnola, a few blocks east of the EUR (*Esposizione Universale di Roma*, the Rome Universal Exhibition). The fighting was fierce between the experienced Wehrmacht units and a hastily cobbled-together Italian defensive force. A monument in Piazzale dei Caduti (Square of the Fallen) today lists the toll of the fierce fighting: 26 servicemen killed – 17 named Sardinian grenadiers, six listed as unknowns, and three Carabinieri – and 11 civilians, including a mother of five, a 16-year old boy, a Catholic nun, and a war invalid.

Italian troops along the Via Ostiense streamed past the Basilica of Saint Paul Outside the Walls and fell back toward Rome and into the Mussolini-built garden suburb of Garbatella. German troops were hot on their heels. At Garbatella the Italian forces briefly delayed the Germans and then fell back to the Porta San Paolo, the ancient gate in the Aurelian wall at the 1st-century BC white marble pyramid tomb of the Roman magistrate Caius Cestius. This action would forever be named the battle of the *Piramide Cestia.* Ironically, the pyramid is across a piazza from the Ostiense train station. The station, built in an austere, fascist style, was newly completed in time to welcome Hitler's 1938 visit to Rome; now German troops were simply following in his footsteps.

By now the defenders at the pyramid were a ragtag collection of men from different units. Stragglers from the Sardinian Grenadiers were reinforced by fragments from other units. From the Sassari Division came men from the I and II Battalions of the 151st Infantry together with the III Battalion of the 152nd Infantry. These infantrymen were augmented by two companies of the XII Mortar Battalion and even a group from the 34th Artillery, although without their guns, as well as the V Battalion of sappers.

From the Ariete Division came an armored group from the Montebello Lancers (*Lancieri*) together with a battery of artillery and even a battalion of officer candidates. Other straggler units determined to join in the desperate defense included a PAI battalion from the Colonna Cheren, a Carabinieri recruitment battalion, the Carabinieri Pastrengo Squadron, and a parachute battalion. There were also several other smaller groups of soldiers. Although exact numbers are not available, there were not many defenders.

On paper the Italian Army still had at least 20,000 more men than the Germans when the attack against the city was launched. Yet this numerical advantage was merely that – theory. In reality, the Italian military was seemingly incapable of conducting any kind of meaningful defense of Rome. Theories abound as to why. The most widely accepted says the government's priority was to cover the escape of the king, Badoglio, and other military chiefs as they fled the city. Other reasons are speculative. The first cites a secret agreement with the Holy See to abandon the city and thereby spare the civilian population a bloodbath. A second cites a secret agreement between Field Marshal Kesselring and Marshal Badoglio to spare the city if he and the king left. Finally, by not formally defending Rome, General Ambrosio and Marshal Badoglio reasoned that the entire blame for any clashes or destruction in the city would fall squarely upon the Germans. However, the simplest explanation may be that with the announcement of the armistice most of the war-weary Italian soldiers simply walked away and left their units for home. There were too few soldiers left to adequately defend the city against the more experienced, better-equipped and better-led Germans.

But those Italian troops who were attempting a defense were soon augmented by enraged civilians. By mid-morning the long-suppressed citizens of Rome valiantly mobilized themselves into full battle. The anti-fascist Committee of Opposition called for civilians to take up arms and defend the city against the German invaders. All across Rome, ordinary citizens opened up hidden weapons depots in answer to the call. Anything would do: antique rifles, pistols, hand grenades, and ammunition were removed from basements and even World War I vintage weapons were broken out of their display cases at the Bersaglieri Museum at the Porta Pia City Gate.

Following the call, a reserve officer of the Sardinian Grenadiers, university professor Raffaello Persichetti, took weapons he had hidden in his apartment near Piazza Navona. Armed, he blithely boarded a public tram to the Porta San Paolo to join the group of Italian soldiers and civilians erecting barricades. But Rome's right and left hands did not know what they were doing. Local police, operating under old orders from Marshal Badoglio, dutifully arrested many civilians for openly carrying arms until they could be convinced that the Germans were now their enemy.

Hearing the call from the street for volunteers, Capponi announced that she was going to fight the Germans. Her mother, horrified, forbade her to go, but the headstrong young woman dashed out the door and raced to Porta San Paolo, toward the sound of the guns.

By the time she arrived, fighting was already fierce, the ancient Pyramid of Caius Cestius bearing the scars of stray bullets which can still be seen today on the ancient white marble. Two Italian light tanks were on the scene offering resistance. General Giacomo Carboni had additional tanks but these were unusable due to a lack of fuel.

Capponi had no military experience but she helped strengthen the barricade and joined other women rescuing and caring for the many wounded. These were taken to a Dominican convent, the church of Santa Sabina on the Aventine Hill, where a medical station had hastily been established, and to the Fate Bene Fratelli Hospital on the Tiber Island.

The Germans brought up several panzers which quickly pushed aside the flimsy barricades and swept away the two Italian light tanks. The Germans also employed artillery and flame throwers. Facing this onslaught, the small units of the Italian Army bravely fought until half of their officers and men were killed, wounded, captured, or dispersed.

Seeing that the situation was hopeless, the Italian defenders abandoned the gate and retreated to the nearby Monte Testaccio, the 100ft ceramic rubbish dump for the ancient port of Rome. There the defenders were silenced after a brief, futile attempt to stop the German advance into the city from this hilltop. Next many climbed the nearby Aventine Hill, the southernmost of the seven hills which marked the boundaries of ancient Rome, where they remained for the rest of the day.

Capponi, bypassing the Aventine, fell back to the Porta Capena, formerly a gate in the 4th-century BC defensive wall across from the broad expanse of the ancient Circus Maximus. With a great rumble and mechanical clanking, Wehrmacht soldiers drove a 62-ton Tiger I panzer along the cobblestone street from the pyramid toward the Colosseum. There, at the Porta Capena, the panzer blew up one of the few remaining mobile light tanks sent to stop the German onslaught.

Capponi watched this and could hear the screams of a trapped Italian tanker. Heedless of the flames, she rushed to pull the injured soldier from the burning wreck. Half-carrying, half-dragging him from the scene she made for the 4th-century AD Arch of Constantine, pursued by the German panzer which fired its 88mm gun into the piazza, barely missing the Colosseum. Capponi, still dragging the wounded soldier, went up the small hill to the ruins of the temple of Venus and Rome. Later she recalled:

> We were at the temple of Venus and Rome, across from the Colosseum, when a new barrage of fire opened up, bullets and shells crisscrossing just above our heads. Somehow, I stumbled on, but I couldn't help thinking that I was in the middle of a battle taking place in a museum, surrounded by all these precious monuments two thousand years old. They were shooting at the site where the ancient Romans had placed a temple to the goddess of beauty, of love and to the glory of Roman civilization.[1]

From there she headed down Via dell'Impero (now Via dei Fori Imperiali) to her apartment across from Trajan's Column, Emperor Trajan's monument to his Dacian war of the 1st century, a third of a mile away. With the help of the *portiere* (doorkeeper), she dragged the injured man up the steps to the apartment. Her mother, overjoyed that her daughter was still alive, welcomed the wounded man, a Sardinian

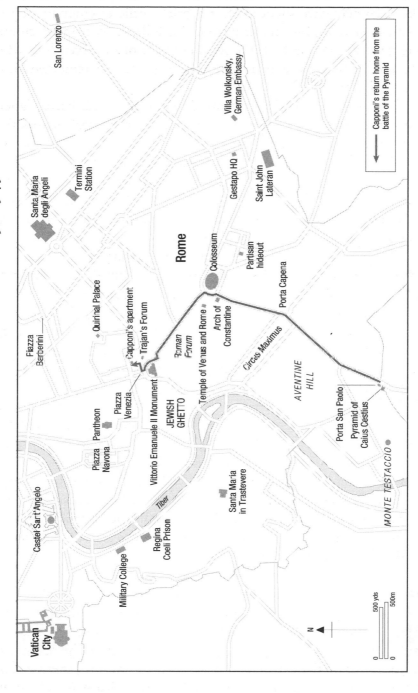

grenadier called Vincenzo Carta, into her home where she nursed him for the next several weeks.*

The Capponi apartment was soon crowded with other refugees and friends. Including the wounded soldier, five people and some weapons were now also hidden there. On the street below, Italian soldiers flooded past the apartment, discarding their uniforms as they went. Capponi and her mother emptied out her late father's closet and dropped civilian clothes to the fleeing soldiers until they had no more left.

Meanwhile General Carboni contacted the Vatican to ask the Allied diplomats to request aircraft strikes, but neither Sir D'Arcy nor Tittmann were in radio contact with the Allies in Salerno. And in any event, the range was too great for Allied aircraft to provide close air support. Bombs fell, but not in defense of Rome. Mother Mary Saint Luke was an American nun in the society of the Holy Child. Born Jessica Lynch in Brooklyn, New York, she wrote under the pen name Jane Scrivener. She worked in the Vatican Information Bureau and after the war published her diary, *Inside Rome with the Germans*. She wrote of the ongoing battle:

> At 1 o'clock, the siren again … Bombs seemed to fall close beside us. Then the whistle and thud of shells echoed over the city. It was unmistakable: they [the Germans] were using artillery and shelling the heights of Rome. Roman artillery answered from the Aventine, the Palatine, the Caelium, the Janiculum, and the Pincian [some of the hills of Rome]. A German shell screeched across Ponte Cavour and crashed into the Palazzo di Giustizia. Via Frattina, the Trinita, and Santa Maria della Pace were also hit. On the line of the Tiber, at San Gregorio, on the hills, Italian gunners were hard at work.[2]

Young Tittmann, standing by a window, witnessed the artillery bombardment of the district around the Piazza di Spagna. He later

---

* At the end of October, Carta left to return to his family in Viareggio in northern Italy. Some time later he sent word back to Carla Capponi that he had arrived home safely and his mother enclosed a bottle of French perfume as a thank you present. It was carried by a Carabinieri officer who was from Catania and was trying to work his way back home.

wrote that there were great puffs of smoke and dust where the shells from light field pieces hit the houses, apparently doing little damage. In the Palazzo Orsini, fronting the Tiber but located on a side street a short distance from Rome's central synagogue, another witness, Vittoria Colonna, the Duchess of Sermoneta wrote:

> Throughout that long afternoon it was impossible to understand exactly what was going on. I went down the drive to the gates several times and peering through the bars could see columns of black smoke billowing upwards from the direction of San Paolo. Then soldiers – our own – began to straggle in disorder through the piazza [Piazza de Monte Savello] and I called out to them to ask what was happening. They answered that there was fighting everywhere – out in the *campagna* [countryside] and now in town – that the Germans had everything, guns, ammunition, hand grenades and that they themselves had nothing, what could they do against them? They were discouraged and exhausted.[3]

The resistance could not last long. Although he only had 142 aircraft available, Field Marshal Kesselring threatened to send 700 aircraft to bomb the city if firing did not stop by 16:30. To make the point, an unidentified aircraft, likely German, dropped several bombs near the University of Rome.

By 16:00 the Italians were spent. General Count Giorgio Calvi di Bergolo, the commander of the Centauro II Division, agreed to a ceasefire. The armed citizenry melted away, hid their weapons, and went underground. Of the 597 Italians who died defending the city, 414 were soldiers and 183 were civilians, including 27 women. Nevertheless, General Carboni's troops, supported by the civilians, had managed to hold down two German divisions of 49,000 front-line soldiers for a full day, troops Kesselring could have used at Salerno.

Vengeance came with the German occupation of Rome. Members of the 2nd Parachute Division treated the populace as enemies as they robbed, raped, and looted in their advance. They tore watches off people's wrists, stripped them naked, and shot them as examples to any who dared to resist. Of this barbarity, Mother Mary wrote in her diary:

> Armored cars seemed to be everywhere at the same time, some manned by Italians, some by Germans, and all of them firing. The whole thing was a mixture of riot, civil war, real war and anarchy. Shops were shut and doors were closed, but that did not prevent looting … not only did the Germans themselves loot, but they encouraged the bewildered populace to follow their example. Some of them took photographs of the poor creatures carrying away cheeses and parcels of pasta … In rather straggling formation, they marched past the Arch of Constantine and down Via del Imperio to Piazza Venezia, where machine guns had been barking all afternoon. Another detachment of them came in by Porta San Giovanni [the city gate in the south of the city] … [4]

Swiss diarist M. de Wyss wrote that the Germans violated women and girls, including one as young as seven who had to be taken to hospital. Items looted from passersby included watches, gold bracelets, earrings, bicycles, and automobiles. She reported that, after taking the photos of the populace raiding the food stores, especially the great central market, they took the food away from them. This is her entry for September 10, 1943:

> *At night*. The usual German game began: violence, robberies, murders all over the town. The via San Saba [from the Porta San Paolo on the way to the Circo Massimo] was the most victimized. Among others the Germans broke into the apartment of the Pope's sister, Mme Rossignani, killing a paying guest who opened the door. Mme Rossignani and her brother-in-law Mgr Rossignani, a Canon of Saint Peter's, escaped death narrowly by treating the pillagers with extreme courtesy, giving them food and wine, etc. The Germans, hearing that this was the apartment of the Pope's sister, said sullenly that they meant no harm and wanted only a few souvenirs. They ate voraciously, drank deeply, bid long life to

the man they had murdered and went away, taking with them all they could lay hands on.*[5]

September 10 began what so many had feared: Rome under German occupation. It was to last 268 days. The Germans moved into the Italian War Ministry (*Ministero della Guerra*) and at 13:00 Radio Rome broadcast the harsh punitive measures that were now to be put in place against Italy: "Yesterday a truce was agreed upon by the commander of the German and Italian troops in the Rome area … It is forbidden to carry arms … Anyone killing a German soldier will be shot!"

By nightfall, Kesselring had ordered posters plastered all over Rome proclaiming:

1 The Italian territory under my command [Kesselring] is declared to be a war territory. It is subject throughout to the German Laws of War.
2 All crimes committed against the German armed forces will be judged according to the German Laws of War.
3 Strikes are prohibited and will be punished by the War Tribunal.
4 Organizers of strikes, saboteurs and snipers will be tried and executed by summary judgment.
5 I have decided to maintain law and order and to support the competent Italian authorities by all means necessary to provide for the well-being of the population.
6 Italian workers who volunteer for German labor service will be treated according to German standards and paid German wages.[†]
7 The Italian Ministers and Judicial authorities will remain in office.

---

* This incident has not been otherwise verified, but de Wyss has proved to be a highly reliable diarist. Interestingly, Mme Rossignani's daughter, Countess Elena Pacelli Rossignani, successfully sued Robert Katz, author of *Black Sabbath and Death in Rome* (see Bibliography and Resources) in 1974 for his allegations that Pope Pius XII had advance knowledge of the Ardeatine massacre. Katz was found guilty of defaming the reputation of the Pope and given a 14-month suspended sentence. The charges were set aside in 1980 after several appeals. The author is convinced that the Pope had no advance warning of the massacre.

† The Nazi Labor Minister, Fritz Sauckel, called for 1.5 million workers from Italy to come to Germany for work; only 75,000 went voluntarily.

8   Rail transport, communication and postal services will begin to function immediately.
9   Until further notice, private correspondence is prohibited. Telephone conversations, which must be kept to a minimum, will be strictly monitored.
10 Italian civil authorities and organizations are responsible to me for the maintenance of public order. They will be permitted to perform their duties only if they cooperate in an exemplary manner with the German measure for the prevention of all acts of sabotage and passive resistance.

The afternoon papers on September 11 carried the story that Germany would respect the Pope's sovereignty and protect the Vatican. Furthermore, Kesselring announced his acceptance of the Badoglio declaration that had proclaimed Rome an Open City and it would be administered by a joint German/Italian Open City organization. Kesselring offered further assurances that the city would be unoccupied and he promised that German troops would only occupy Rome's radio station, the telephone exchange, and the German Embassy, and not station troops within the city itself; German troops would be garrisoned outside of the city.

But his assurances rang hollow when ordinary Romans continued to see Wehrmacht combat troops, Luftwaffe flight officers, and paratroopers with their distinctive baggy-legged uniforms strutting through the streets, looting, sacking, and robbing stores, shops, and even banks. Government buildings and key intersections were guarded by uniformed German police and German military vehicle convoys jammed the main arteries heading south and to the Salerno front.

By the next day, the Germans had completely occupied the city. The former Axis partners had become adversaries overnight. Vittoria Colonna, the Duchess of Sermoneta, commented:

I was out early next morning, September 11th, and in crossing Piazza Venezia I saw pools of dried blood on the pavement; every policeman had vanished and all the shops were shuttered. I looked into the courtyard of my old home, Palazzo Colonna; a shell had struck the wall just over the window of what had been my bedroom as a girl, and left a gaping hole. I was told that the porter and butler had been wounded. In Via Sistina and again in Piazza di Spagna there were houses damaged, but on the whole there had been infinitely less destruction by the shelling the day before than in the air raids. What was a far worse sight were the lorries full of German soldiers roaring up the main streets. They were coming into the city from both north and south, and the crowd in silent despair stood watching them pass, for it was obvious that Rome was being occupied and that Caviglia's* attempt to keep the Germans out had been in vain ...[6]

Field Marshal Kesselring put Operation *Achse*, the plan to disarm the Italian armed forces, into effect the moment an armistice was declared. The Germans were nothing if not thorough in waging their new offensive against Italy.

In Rome, the Germans mined the water, gas, and electric installations, ready to be blown up if they had to abandon the city. And they issued an edict spelling out those violations that would be subject to the death penalty: namely, trading in the black-market, listening to enemy radio broadcasts, harboring a fugitive, disseminating enemy propaganda, possessing weapons, and violating the 21:00 curfew. Newspapers were censored, telephones tapped. Even walking in front of the hotels occupied by the Germans on Via Veneto was forbidden.

Marshal Badoglio formally issued orders to attack the Germans on September 11, but by then it was far too late. The king, now safe in Brindisi, tried to justify his flight, claiming that he hoped to spare Rome from needless fighting. His statement, which also said that Italian troops were enthusiastically fighting to push the Germans from Italy, only showed how out of touch with reality he was. In perhaps the last act of the battle for Rome, on September 13, German troops killed the commander of the Italian Piave Division and two others in front of the Hotel Flora on Via Veneto. The shooting of the Italians may have been the result of a misunderstanding. Immediately after the German takeover of Rome, the division was ordered to police the city under the command of municipal authorities. The officers, likely armed, probably went to the Hotel Flora, by now the seat of the German High Command, to coordinate activities and their presence may have been misunderstood

---

* Enrico Caviglia was the World War I Marshal of Italy who had signed the truce to end the fighting in the city.

and resulted in the shooting. The Piave Division's assignment to guard the city ended on September 23 and the unit was disbanded.

During the first week of the occupation, German paratroopers were stationed in Saint Peter's Square with orders to protect the Vatican. At least two helmeted and armed paratroopers were ordered to stand guard on the white painted line which demarked the border between Rome and the Holy City as well as connecting the outer wings of the famous Bernini Colonnade of Saint Peter's Basilica.* They would guard this border between Italy and the Vatican as long as they were in Rome. As one German officer quipped, now the Pope is nearer to Himmler than to *Himmel*; *Himmel* meaning heaven in German.

Outside Rome, the Germans were merciless to their former allies. Hitler personally ordered the officers of any Italian unit who resisted to be executed and the men sent to Germany as laborers. Italian Army General don Ferrante Gonzaga, commander of the 222nd Coast Guard Division and assigned to the XVII Armored Corps, was among the few to oppose the Germans. For this, he was assassinated in his office in Eboli (near Salerno) by a former German military comrade. Reportedly his last words were "a Gonzaga never surrenders." At the town of Aversa, north of Naples, some Italian Carabinieri were forced to dig their own graves before being shot. At the Campania town of Nola, the Germans lined up Italian military officers and murdered them by firing squad in front of their troops. Then they dumped the bodies in a latrine.

Lacking a formal war declaration from Badoglio, the Germans justified shooting Italian soldiers as deserters and traitors. At the time of the surrender, more than one million Italian soldiers were out of the country. More than 430,000 were eventually sent to Germany as workers to sustain the German wartime economy. They were not designated prisoners of war, but were termed Italian military internees. Approximately 30,000 of them died. Outside Italy, Italian and German soldiers had been stationed together as allies. Now, two German divisions

---

* This white line was in the same position as the current white line painted on the cobblestones between the arms of the colonnade which modern tourists must cross on the way to metal detectors prior to entering the Vatican and Saint Peter's Basilica.

moved into Albania and surrounded the Italian Army Group in Tirana, capturing the commanders. On the Ionian island of Cephalonia, off the coast of Greece, the Germans were brutal to their former ally. They rounded up and shot almost 5,100 Italians (341 officers and 4,750 men). In total it is estimated that at least 7,000 Italian soldiers were executed.

The Germans, anticipating invasions of Sardinia and Corsica and realizing that they did not have enough troops there to defend the islands, ordered their removal. On Sardinia, the disorganized Italian forces did nothing to stop the German retreat and some 180,000 Italian troops allowed 15,000 German troops to leave the island for Corsica. There 80,000 Italian troops, reinforced by French troops, fought for several days but eventually allowed General Frido von Senger und Etterlin and his armored brigade to withdraw.

In just two days, both at home and abroad, a total of 90 Italian divisions were dispersed, their military supplies confiscated, and their tanks and armored cars taken over intact by the Germans.

But worse news was to follow. In a daring rescue ordered by Adolf Hitler, Mussolini was freed on September 12 by German paratroopers and commandos from the Friedenthal Battalion of the 2nd Parachute Division led by SS-Hauptsturmführer Otto Skorzeny. Planning for the mission had first begun over that dinner with Field Marshal Kesselring, Luftwaffe General Kurt Student, SS-Obersturmbannführer Eugen Dollmann, Herbert Kappler and Skorzeny on July 27. What had followed had been two months of rigorous planning and intelligence work.

Marshal Badoglio had planned to use Mussolini as a bargaining chip to trade with the Allies for Italy's future. Well aware that the Germans were likely to attempt a rescue, the Italian Military Intelligence Service (SIM) kept his location secret by planting false rumors and leads for the Gestapo. SIM enjoyed a well-deserved reputation for excellence and it was soon to be a major source of Allied information on the Germans in occupied Rome. Nevertheless, it was impossible to hide Il Duce for long.

After Mussolini had been placed under protective custody in July, he was repeatedly moved between the islands off the west coast of Italy. He first spent ten days on the island of Ponza. Then he was moved by ship to La Maddalena, a small island accessible by ferry from northern Sardinia. Rome Gestapo Chief Kappler learned of these movements from two brothers from Naples who sold dried pasta to the towns along the coast.*

One of General Student's men, Captain von Kamptz, learned from a talkative Italian naval officer that Mussolini was now at a small villa on La Maddalena. The news was deemed so important that Student and von Kamptz flew to Germany to personally give the news to the Führer.

Kappler had another source, Mussolini's daughter, Edda Ciano, who had sent a letter to La Maddalena telling her father of their situation. Hitler ordered the Cianos and their three children to be flown to Germany. They believed that they would be allowed to go on to Spain, but they were held and Ciano placed under arrest.

La Maddalena was under constant surveillance, so when a seaplane with Red Cross markings took Mussolini off the island, Kappler was immediately informed. The plane landed at the Italian Royal Air Force base at Lake Bracciano amid tight security. Previously Kappler had installed a wiretap on the phone of the Minister of the Interior and was informed of an intercepted message from the Inspector General of the Interior, Giuseppe Gueli, to the chief of police, Carmine Senise. The message said that the security procedures were in place. The call was believed to be from the Gran Sasso d'Italia mountain in the Abruzzi region. Kappler now believed that he would find Mussolini at the mountain ski resort.

To verify the information, Kappler sent a three-man team to the resort. It was headed by SS-Hauptsturmführer Erich Priebke, with SS-Hauptsturmführer Gerhard Köhler and SS interpreter, Renato Ruta. They confirmed that not only was there additional security around the cable car to the mountain top, but that the staff of the Campo Imperatore Hotel had been dismissed only days before. Kappler passed on this information to Skorzeny. That Kappler was able to respond to this opportunity was all the more amazing since it was the day of the

---

* Remarkably de Wyss was told of Mussolini's whereabouts. She mentions in her diary entry of August 9 that she had heard that Mussolini was on the island of Ponza and would soon be transferred to La Maddalena (de Wyss, p. 81). Later, on September 2, she recorded that Mussolini was to be transferred to the Abruzzi Mountains (de Wyss, p. 98). Her sources were so good that on September 5 she was told by a Vatican source that the Allied landing at Salerno was imminent (de Wyss, p. 100).

battle for Rome, September 9, 1943. But he had to act fast to confirm Mussolini's whereabouts.

Gliders led by a German paratroop officer, Lieutenant Baron Georg von Berlepsch, landed on the plateau near the Campo Imperatore Hotel on the Gran Sasso. An Italian general accompanying Skorzeny ordered the 200 Carabinieri and police guarding Mussolini to lay down their weapons and Mussolini was freed. SS-Hauptsturmführer Skorzeny took the credit. Mussolini was then bundled into a tiny Fieseler Fi-156 Storch aircraft and he, Skorzeny, and the pilot, after making a hazardous short-field take-off in a dangerously overloaded plane, flew to the Italian airfield at Pratica di Mare near Rome. Mussolini was transferred to a larger aircraft and was off to Vienna and safety. After being warmly greeted by Hitler, he would soon create a new Fascist government in northern Italy, far from Rome, where he could be better protected by his German friends and away from the threat of Allied bombs.

This was no small victory and the Germans were elated. Kappler and Priebke were both promoted and presented with Iron Crosses for their part in the daring rescue of Il Duce. It may have been at the same time that SS-Reichsführer Himmler presented Kappler with a steel ring featuring a Death's Head, ancient runes, and swastikas (informally known as a *Totenkopfring*). It was intended to reinforce the wearer's German values and, rather than an official decoration, it was a personal gift bestowed by Himmler. The ring was inscribed "To Herbert from his Himmler" and Kappler proudly wore his badge of honor. Kappler's standing in the German military and SS was now greatly enhanced for he had demonstrated the thoroughness of his Roman intelligence network and his knowledge of the local situation.

After hearing the news about their Iron Crosses, Kappler and Priebke together with SS-Hauptsturmführer Eugen Haas and SS-Hauptsturmführer Gerhard Köhler got drunk to celebrate. They were accompanied by radio operator SS-Rottenführer Boehm as driver. To have some fun they went to Duke Pietro d'Acquarone's house with the intention of settling accounts with him; Kappler knew the duke was part of the group that convinced the king to oust Mussolini. Not finding the duke at home they began to ransack the house. A servant fled the building and was shot at by Boehm which alerted some nearby Italian soldiers who came to investigate. Hastily departing the scene, Boehm and Haas were left behind. Returning sometime later they ran into an Italian lieutenant who challenged the car and was shot by Kappler. Reportedly the Nazis got away with several million lire worth of goods.[7] Kappler, now officially recognized for his part in finding Mussolini, was embolded as he built his organization to place his iron grip on the city in the coming weeks.

It suited the Germans to establish a fiction that Italy was still very much an ally and, during the early days of the occupation, the Germans established an Italian military government in Rome. Italian General Count Giorgio Calvi di Bergolo was appointed Italian commandant and soon displayed his ability to adroitly handle a crisis. In the chaotic days after the battle for Rome, six Germans soldiers had been shot. Field Marshal Kesselring, suspecting civilian resistance, demanded that in retaliation 6,000 Romans be forced into the Italian labor service (*Servizio del Lavoro*) as laborers in factories, agriculture, and elsewhere. General Calvi di Bergolo cleverly placed his own name on the list along with that of Colonel Giuseppe Montezemolo, his chief of staff. General Calvi di Bergolo explained that he could not supply the other 5,998 names. Kesselring gave up.

At the same time, the Germans released Fascists from the Regina Coeli Prison who had been rounded up by General Carboni. Next, Kappler looted the Italian treasury. On September 16, he led a small convoy of trucks manned by paratroopers and SS men to the Central Bank of Italy on Via Nazionale. The troops marched into the bank and loaded the entire gold reserves of Italy into five trucks in just under an hour. The 110 metric tons of gold was transferred to two railway boxcars and sent to Berlin where it remained until it was returned to Italy after the war. Also taken were the official plates for printing lira currency notes and vast quantities of lire began to be printed.

As political and military issues were being sorted out, Hitler turned his anger on Pope Pius XII. Hoping to prove that the Pope had played a role in the armistice, Kappler ransacked the Italian Foreign Ministry on September 14. The Germans were looking for documents about peace feelers to the Allies. The 40 cartons of seized documents were sent to Germany. Although the documents did not support their suspicions, Hitler may have ordered his head of SS in Italy, Obergruppenführer Karl F. Wolff, to create a plan to abduct the Pope and loot the Vatican. The Pope and Cardinals were to be arrested and sent north to Castle Lichtenstein, a refurbished 19th-century castle in Württemberg, Germany.

The plot may have been apocryphal, but true or not it sheds light on the mood of the time. Some say the story originated as a propaganda piece by the British Political Warfare Executive broadcast on a bogus German wireless program of October 9, 1943. At any rate, the story went that the Germans would surround the Vatican with 2,000 men, seal the exits, and shut down Vatican Radio. Then they would cut off the water and electricity to the rabbit warren of rooms that is the Vatican, starving out those who were hiding. The SS would scour the Vatican for political refugees, Jews, and Allied ex-POWs. A treasure team of 50 German art experts would ransack the Vatican Museum for paintings, sculptures, gold, jewels, and foreign currency, not a small task since the papacy had been collecting artwork for centuries. They would seize the more than 500,000 manuscripts and books, including incunabula, the first printed books, from the Vatican Library. Vatican authorities, fearing such an action, walled up the Pope's personal papers and gave instructions to the Roman Curia about what to do if the Pope were in fact arrested.

On September 23, 1943 Mussolini announced the formation of the Italian Social Republic (RSI – *Repubblica Sociale Italiana*), often referred to as the Salò Republic after the small town on the shores of Lake Garda where Mussolini lived. It was merely a German puppet government. Officially, the capital remained in Rome, but government ministers were moved to the Lake Garda region near the town of Brescia. Unsurprisingly most of the state employees of these ministries found reasons why they could not leave Rome. With the announcement came a call for all military-age men to report for service in the armed forces or in labor battalions.

The resistance to Mussolini's new government was evident at many levels. Pope Pius XII refused to recognize Mussolini's government and said that Italians were under no obligation to report for military service with the regime. General Calvi di Bergolo, the German-appointed

Italian commandant of Rome who had thwarted Kesselring's demand for those 6,000 names, responded by refusing to swear allegiance to the new Italian Social Republic. In the wake of his insubordination, Calvi di Bergolo was arrested and sent to Germany. He eventually escaped to Switzerland. In a separate action, General Carboni was court-martialed *in absentia* by the new Fascist government for opposing the German occupation of Rome. The day after the announcement, Mother Mary wrote in her diary that all Italian men born between 1921 and 1925 were to be called up for labor service in Germany or to construct fortifications in Italy for the German Army on the Gustav Line which ran across Italy but was centered around the hilltop town of Monte Cassino, 80 miles southeast of Rome. "Of course, no one intends to do so."[8]

The exact number of Jews, escaped Allied POWs, political refugees, Italian ex-military, and young men avoiding Mussolini's new armed forces, the German labor camps in Germany, or the Todt Organization working on Kesselring's multiple defensive lines strung across Italy will never be known. Todt was a huge German construction company which operated in both Germany and the occupied countries. It was originally created in 1933 by Doctor Fritz Todt, of the German Armament and Supply Ministry. The major part of heavy labor was done by prisoners of war and the involuntary labor rounded up by Nazis. The defensive measures undertaken by the Todt Organization including the Gustav Line would severely hamper Allied progress.

After the Allied landing at Salerno, the Italian resistance Committee of Opposition in Rome re-formed itself as the National Liberation Committee (CLN – *Comitato di Liberazione Nazionale*). The CLN was made up of six political parties, three rightist and three leftist. Splinter groups, they had separate agendas but enough in common to work together. The groups were united only by their anti-fascism and contempt for both Badoglio and Vittorio Emanuele III; like all coalitions, it was a fragile alliance.

Understanding these parties helps to unravel the complexities of daily life under the Germans. The three rightist parties were: the Christian Democrats, headed by Alcide de Gasperi, and supported by the Vatican; the Italian Liberal Party, which looked to the great anti-fascist leader and philosopher Benedetto Croce for inspiration; and a tiny party, the Labor Democrats, headed by Ivanoe Bonomi. Croce was described as the "greatest anti-Fascist in all Italy, the living exponent of liberal philosophy whom no one had dared to silence during the long decades of the Fascist rule and was the most respected man in Italy."[9] The three leftist parties were: the Action Party (*Partito d'Azione*), headed by Count Carlo Sforza, a rigid anti-communist who favored US New Deal policies; the Italian Socialist Party, headed by Pietro Nenni; and finally, the Communists, headed by Giorgio Amendola, who was a stand-in leader for Palmiro Togliatti then residing in Moscow.*

The CLN convened a conference to decide Italy's future form of government. Specifically, it demanded that the Badoglio government restore civil and political rights, release political prisoners, and form a government with representation from all parties. For the time being, Badoglio ignored them. In reality, from his exile in Brindisi, there was little impact Badoglio could have on current Italian politics and governance, while in Rome, the German occupiers, all too aware of the attempts to establish an effective resistance, would establish an iron grip on the city.

* Togliatti was the former head of the COMINTERN (Communist International) which was founded in 1919 to organize resistance by the oppressed populations of foreign territories. It was disbanded by Stalin in March 1943 to make participation with the Allied governments more palatable to anti-communists. In March 1944, Togliatti was ordered to return to Italy where he would foster unity within the resistance and push for the eventual removal of the king. Sending him back to Italy was part of the deal that the Soviets had struck to support the Allied-influenced government of Italy. Upon his return, Togliatti became head of the Italian Communist Party of Italy (PCI) where he exerted tremendous pressure on communist and other partisans. He was to have a huge influence on post-war Italian politics as well.

The Gestapo in Rome – Kappler, Espionage, and Sabotage

Nine months of German rule in Rome began under the omnipresent eye of SS-Obersturmbannführer Herbert Kappler. His was the public face of both the Gestapo and the *Sicherheitsdienst* (SD – security service) in Rome. His management style was based on the traditional chain of command: he reported to his superior, assistants reported to him, their staffs reported to them. Duties were departmentalized and concentrated into subgroups. In a way, it was a veritable model of how to run a large operation and would have been more successful had Kappler had the zeal for detail that marks a good administrator. In fact, many responsibilities overlapped.

Kappler, then just 35, was of medium build, with cold gray eyes and an old dueling scar on his cheek. He was suave, articulate, and confident. He spoke Italian well, adored children, loved roses, and was an avid photographer and a collector of ancient Etruscan vases. He had unquestioning loyalty to the Third Reich and was committed to carrying out its orders. Like many Nazis, he loved Rome, but not Romans.

He was also intolerant, cold, and vengeful: starvation, roundups, reprisals, and murder would be the hallmarks of his reign. His will was not to be challenged. Senior German officers deferred to his knowledge and position. An unidentified postwar Allied interviewer described him as a fairly intelligent, but ruthless type who made the most of the opportunities offered to him by the Nazi regime. The same interviewer concluded that he would "be a constant menace to general security if ever he were allowed unrestricted freedom ..."[1]

Kappler was born in Stuttgart on September 23, 1907, the son of a chauffeur. He completed his secondary school education in 1925 and attended a local technical college where he studied electrical engineering. He became a certified electrician in 1929 and worked for several firms in Stuttgart. According to his debrief, Kappler, facing a choice between communism and Nazism, joined the Nazi Party, and became an SA-Mann (equivalent to a private) in the *Sturmabteilung* (SA, literally storm section or shock squad).

His rise was slow. In 1932, he joined the SS (*Schutzstaffel* – Protection Squad). After six months of probation for indoctrination and training, he was officially sworn into the SS on May 8, 1933. Initially, Kappler was assigned to the Stuttgart *Allgemeine SS* formation part-time. Later that year, he joined the State Political Police (*Politisches Landespolizei*) in the southern German state of Württemberg.*

In 1934, due to his early membership in the SA, Kappler was allowed to wear the chevron of an *Alter Kämpfer* (old fighter) on his uniform, a high honor. That same year on September 29, he married Leonora Janns from Heilbronn, Germany. It was reportedly a loveless marriage. Unable to have children, the couple adopted a son, Wolfgang, from the *Lebensborn*, the Nazi baby farm for pure Aryans. Kappler doted on the boy.

His parallel military career so far had been mediocre. During 1935–1936, Kappler was called up several times for military service where he rose to the noncommissioned officer ranks. Returning to civilian life he applied to join the SS full time. He was accepted and made an SS-Scharführer or staff sergeant,† and went to work in the SS's main Stuttgart office. In 1937, after successfully passing the difficult police examinations, Kappler, now an SS-Oberscharführer, was admitted

---

* SS men swore personal fidelity to Hitler and served in one of four branches: the *Allgemeine SS* (sometimes referred to as the Ordinary SS) performed general duties; the *Waffen SS* was the military branch which eventually had 38 divisions (some understrength); the *Totenkopfverbände SS* (Death's Head units) was responsible for murder squads and concentration camps; and the SD kept watch on just about everyone.

† See Appendix C for equivalent British and US ranks.

as the first non-Prussian to the Security Police Leadership School (*Führerschule der Sicherheitspolizei* – Gestapo) in Charlottenburg near Berlin. Upon graduation in the summer of 1937, he was appointed criminal inspector (*Kriminalkommissar*) and in 1938 he was sent in that capacity to Innsbruck, Austria, by that time a part of Germany. On November 9, 1938 he was promoted to SS-Untersturmführer (first lieutenant). At this point, he was unaware that Rome lay in his future.

In 1936, following the signing by Italy and Germany of a secret anti-communist pact, direct cooperation between Italian and German police commenced. The intention was to share information on communist activities and to exchange prisoners outside of normal extradition laws. Berlin and Rome arranged for the liaison officers to report directly to their police superiors and not through their respective foreign ministries.

Although both countries agreed they would not collect intelligence on each other, clandestinely, Germany and Italy spied on each other from the onset. They were never ideal partners. A special Hitler Order (*Führerbefehl*) had expressly forbidden espionage to be undertaken against their Italian allies. Of course, the SS ignored this order, and all through the 1930s Berlin sent covert SS agents to Rome under the cover of various Axis cooperation agreements to quietly look out for German interests.

The first German Police Liaison Officer (*Polizeiverbindungsführer*) in Rome had been Dr. Theo Helmerking, but he had been ineffectual and was described as unsuitable and uninterested in the position. His position was taken by the young Kappler.

During his postwar debriefings, Kappler stated that he had first been sent to Rome in 1939 as the chief for police liaison. Later he had been made the Police Attaché at the German Embassy with diplomatic status and in that position Kappler became a political advisor at the embassy. He reported on the activities of German citizens; exchanged information with Italian counterparts; and studied Italian police methods. He also established a direct liaison with the Italian Military Intelligence Service (SIM).

In Rome, Kappler lived with his wife and son in a secluded villa behind a wall on the tree-lined Via Salaria. Kappler's private life had its romantic intrigues though. A Fräulein Hoffman, one in a series of mistresses, was a radio operator in his SS Headquarters. Kappler had a child with her and sought Himmler's permission to divorce his wife so that they could marry, but it was not granted.

A second mistress was a Dutch national and informant, Helen Brouwer, whom he brought to Rome to work out of Gestapo Headquarters. After Holland was overrun by the Wehrmacht in 1940, Brouwer had been arrested by the SD for underground activities. Under sentence of death, she agreed to become a German agent in exchange for her life. After training, she went to Berlin where she first met Kappler and subsequently received her orders to go to Rome where she was billeted at the SS barracks in their villa on Viale Rossini.

As a sign of Kappler's growing power, in November 1939, he was recalled to Berlin to assist in the interrogation of Georg Elser, a man who had failed in an attempt to assassinate Hitler. Elser had planted a bomb at Munich's Bürgerbraükeller beer hall on the night of November 8 when Hitler was to speak. Uncharacteristically, Hitler finished his speech early and left before the subsequent explosion killed eight and injured 62. Elser was eventually executed at Dachau after being held prisoner for five years.

Working with lightning speed the Gestapo sought to blame the British for the assassination attempt, so on November 9 it kidnapped two known British Secret Intelligence Service (SIS) officers, Sigismund Payne Best and Richard Henry Stevens, outside the town of Venlo in the Netherlands. Kappler was a member of the interrogation team. Nothing was proven but Best and Stevens were held in concentration camps for the remainder of the war. It was not surprising that the Gestapo sought British intelligence officers to blame as throughout Europe the Gestapo had concentrated their counterespionage activities on the SIS, which had extensive experience and an outstanding reputation.

Kappler was determined to develop his Roman intelligence efforts so that they rivaled if not exceeded the efforts of the British.

The training essential to make German SS officers effective agents in Italy was provided by the Italian Africa Police (PAI). Under the auspices of the Minister for Italian Africa, the school was located in Tivoli, 19 miles from Rome. The course focused on how the police functioned in its African colonies – the lesson was how to handle subjugated peoples. Kappler and SS-Obersturmführer Gerhard Köhler, who was to become a key official in Kappler's Rome office, were trained there from November 18, 1940 to March 31, 1941. Over the next several months, as many as 300 SS men would attend the course. They were to spread out to all the major cities of Italy, often working undercover in German workers' organizations.*

Perhaps because of all of these activities in Rome, in 1942 Berlin sent SS-Sturmbannführer Martin Lösch to Rome, to supervise agents of the Reich Main Security Headquarters, RSHA (*Reichssicherheitshauptamt*). As a cover, Lösch was assigned to Kappler's police liaison office, relieving Kappler of some agent-support duties.

Eventually other German police officers arrived and spread out over Rome. A contingent of the Order Police (ORPO – *Ordnungspolizei*) in Rome was headquartered at the Pension Caterina on the corner of Via Po and Corso d'Italia. ORPO police officers were based at various military caserns like the Macao Barracks at the Castro Pretorio. After the German occupation, the ORPO was responsible for the uniformed German police on the streets of Rome and, most importantly, it directed German military traffic through the city. It also provided Railway Police (*Bahnschutzpolizei*), who provided both uniformed and plain clothes police at railway stations, junctions, workshops, bridges, and passenger travel control points. Further, they maintained agents on trains and monitored the teletype system along railway lines. Cooperation between Kappler and the ORPO was excellent; ORPO would prove to be a crucial cog in the impressive occupation machinery.

The second most visible SS man in Rome after Kappler was SS-Obersturmbannführer Eugen Dollmann. He was SS-Reichsführer

---

* Sabotage was high on the agenda, and sometime in 1942, Berlin sent Kappler an agent named Biersack who organized such missions. Kappler booked air passage to South America for Biersack's agents on several occasions. In one botched case, an agent left a box in his hotel room, as it was too heavy to take on the plane. It emitted a terrible stench, so Biersack had it returned to Berlin, telling Kappler that it contained bacteria which were to have been sprinkled on meat transported from South America to Britain by refrigerator ships. It is one of the very few reported instances of the Germans using biological warfare targeted against civilians during World War II.

Himmler's personal representative. Unlike most Nazis, Dollmann had had an aristocratic upbringing – his mother was a close friend of His Serene Majesty, Kaiser Franz Josef I of Austria, and Dollmann yearned for the restoration of European monarchies.

Dollmann had a sparkling wit, elegantly effeminate manners, and a genteel appearance. He had ash blonde hair, expressive eyes, tapered hands, and a rosy complexion. He was often seen strutting about Rome in his finely tailored black SS uniform. He had first gone to Rome as a student in the 1920s and stayed on.

In 1937, Dollmann served as a guide and interpreter for an Italian Fascist youth group's trip to Germany. During their meeting with Hitler he was the interpreter, the first of several times he acted in that capacity for his Führer.

During several other high-level meetings that year, Dollmann, now acting as the interpreter for Italian police officials, came to the attention of Himmler and so impressed him that he was offered a position in the SS. In November 1937, with no background screening or training, he was inducted into the *Allgemeine SS*. He now held a position of first importance.

Later when Hitler's mistress, Eva Braun, visited Italy with Hitler in May 1938, Dollmann was chosen to be her escort because, not being married to Hitler, Braun could not be part of the official German delegation. Dollmann quickly became her confidante.

After the downfall of Mussolini, he acted as the personal liaison officer between Himmler's head of the SS in Italy, SS-Obergruppenführer (General) Karl F. Wolff; Field Marshal Albert Kesselring; the Rome branch of the new Republican Fascist Party created following Mussolini's rescue; and the Vatican. Dollmann was the common denominator for this elite, rarified group.

According to Kappler, Dollmann's mission was vague. He was not directly assigned to Kappler's headquarters, but kept in touch with and entertained Himmler's Italian friends and contacts. He was given the rank of SS-Obersturmbannführer, the equivalent of lieutenant colonel, a rank senior to Kappler's at the time. Because of Dollmann's superior education and because he was a favorite of Wolff, Kappler was undoubtedly jealous of him.

Mussolini's newly created Italian Social Republic necessitated realignment between Germany and Italy. Thus, on the day of its creation, September 23, 1943, Hitler appointed Wolff as a new advisor to the Italian government for police matters. It was an important post as his rank as Senior SS and Police Leader in Italy (*Höchster Schutzstaffel und Polizeiführer Italien*) was now equal to that of a field marshal. The SS was now ready to intrude on and control every aspect of Italian life.

Wolff had joined the Nazi Party in 1931 and was commissioned in the SS in February 1932. By 1933 Wolff was Himmler's personal adjutant. Eventually he ended up managing Himmler's contacts with the SS, the Nazi Party, and state agencies. He was appointed SS liaison officer to Hitler, acting as Himmler's eyes and ears at Hitler's headquarters. After the infamous Wannsee Conference of January 20, 1942, where the Final Solution for the elimination of European Jews was discussed, Wolff initialed one of the 30 copies of the final document. The document described the genocidal actions that would be implemented. When the Jews of Poland started to be rounded up, Wolff oversaw their transportation to the death camps. He was instrumental in getting Zyklon B gas introduced at Auschwitz. Inner SS politics caused Wolff to fall out of favor with both Hitler and Himmler and in 1943 he was removed as liaison officer and sent to Italy.

Wolff, who loved Rome and had a weakness for Roman high society, now saw himself as being in position to influence events in favor of the Italians. Although a longtime Nazi, he later claimed to have had little respect for them. For example, he derisively called General Kurt Mälzer, appointed as the second Stadtkommandant (city commander) of Rome in November 1943, Mr. Bum-Bum, mocking his overweight appearance and drunkenness.

Throughout Germany and the occupied countries, SS activities were directed by the Reichsführer for the SS, Heinrich Himmler, who was also the German Interior Minister and Chief of German Police. His headquarters was in the RSHA (*Reichssicherheitshaupamt* – Reich Main Security Headquarters) in Berlin and it was there that Himmler consolidated security and police agencies, except the ORPO, the uniformed Order Police who were responsible for purely civil crimes.

As an assistant, Wolff was assigned SS-Gruppenführer Generalleutnant der Polizei Wilhelm Harster whose title was Commander of Police

Activities and the Security Service in Italy (*Befehlshaberheitspolizei und das Sicherheitsdienst Italien*). Harster had been brought from Holland to set up headquarters at Verona, Italy, in September 1943, as the Germans occupied Rome.

Harster's organization broadly mirrored the RSHA's seven bureaus called Ämter, but some bureaus were not necessary in Italy due to the active cooperation of the Fascist government. Harster obtained men and resources for these new offices and ordered his officers to collect a wide variety of intelligence, political, military, and economic. This included information on the newly re-formed Fascist Party, now called the Fascist Republican Party. They were instructed to get to know the Fascist leaders and to test the depth of their commitment to Fascism and Mussolini. Harster's officers therefore infiltrated the titled nobility, rich industrialists, bankers, intellectuals, academicians, and the professional classes of doctors, lawyers, and engineers.

When the Allies invaded the Italian mainland, Himmler ordered Harster to establish satellite SS commands throughout Italy to monitor and report on activities of interest including Rome, but also all other major cities. In Rome this was the *Aussenkommando Rom der Sicherheitspolizei* (SS-Gestapo) *und das Sicherheitsdienst* (SD) – known by its abbreviated term the AK Rom. A typical AK unit in a major city would have 450 men and was primarily responsible for suppressing anti-German elements behind the front lines, arresting undesirables, and preventing sabotage. They did this by enforcing order and security in the rear areas to protect German personnel and interests. The Rome AK was smaller as the SS still had elements of the Italian Fascist Party to do some of their dirty work for them.*

By now it was clear that what remained of Axis Italy was no longer an equal partner alongside Germany. Nevertheless, Harster continued to nurture the fiction that Mussolini mattered and had his men report on anti-fascist activities with orders to penetrate suspect organizations. They identified and then arrested those in sympathy with the Allies,

---

* Other AKs in Italy included: AK Bologna, AK Genua (Genoa), AK Mailand (Milan), AK Parma, AK Padua, AK Turin, AK Venedig (Venice). Other cities had smaller units. These commands were styled task forces and referred to as the *Einsatzkommandos* (EKs). Originally *SS Einsatzgruppen*, set up in 1941, were formed to be special SS death squads, but the term was also applied to commands such as Kappler's AK Rom.

the pro-Badoglio government of the south, and members of the CLN (National Liberation Committee).

Of high importance to Harster was his mission to deport Italian factory workers to Germany to churn out panzers, planes, and other weapons for the Nazi war machine. Germany's appetite for such workers was insatiable. Therefore the SS, working closely with Italian Fascist police forces, conducted huge roundups of men whom they sent to Germany as workers. If not to Germany these rounded-up workers were sent to work on Field Marshal Kesselring's ambitious defensive lines across Italy.

To carry out the additional responsibilities that came with occupation, Kappler was given more men, resources, and a new title, Commander of the Security Police (Gestapo) and Security Service in Rome (*Oberbefehlshaber der Sicherheitspolizei (Gestapo) und Sicherheitsdienst SD Einsatzkommando (EK) Rom*). Soon Kappler had more than 70 men and women working under him. In addition to his fiercely loyal SS, the organization included German civilians, secretaries, linguists, and Italian collaborators. Kappler was now responsible for arrests and interrogations of any who dared challenge German authority.

Kappler's headquarters was located on Via Tasso, close to the Basilica of Saint John Lateran (*San Giovanni Laterano*) and the German Embassy at the Villa Wolkonsky. It was in an ugly, five-story apartment building in a dreary street and was of typical shoddy Fascist construction. Was it not an irony that Via Tasso was named after one of Italy's greatest poets, Torquato Tasso, who wrote *La Gerusalemme liberata* (Freed Jerusalem)?

There were two front entrances; number 145, on the left, led to Gestapo offices and living quarters. The entrance at number 155 led to the prison on the right. Kappler had ordered the conversion of the former police liaison offices, at number 155, as well as the German cultural office at number 145 Via Tasso into a headquarters, prison and interrogation center when it became clear that Rome's Regina Coeli Prison could not cope with the sheer volume of prisoners. Italians who were on the SS payroll and others with business with EK Rom entered the building through the number 145 entrance which was the public entrance to Kappler's headquarters. Vincenzo Florio, an Italian racecar driver and enthusiast who was the heir of the very rich Florio family, one of the wealthiest Italian families, recorded his impression of the reception area:

> As soon as you entered the building you were ushered into a room lavishly furnished, in order to give the best impression. Couches and overstuffed chairs were covered in red Moroccan leather, the desk and chairs were mahogany and well varnished, on the floor were beautiful oriental carpets and on the wall a large portrait of Hitler in his simple uniform: on the walls were other paintings in richly decorated frames.[2]

Via Tasso became almost completely blocked off with barbed wire, machine guns, and armed guards. Pedestrians had to walk down the far side of the street in single file. Relatives of those incarcerated would stand outside the entrances of Via Tasso and attempt to pass messages, food, or a change of clothes to those inside.

Kappler had able assistants including SS-Hauptsturmführer Gerhard Köhler. Köhler had been in Rome since at least 1940. After attending a two-week PAI Italian Colonial Police School in 1941, he was sent to Tunisia as the liaison officer between the SD in Italy and Rommel's Afrika Korps.

Back in Rome, Köhler was responsible for requisitioning materials and equipment: cars, apartments, rations, anything which made life easier for his comrades. So many SS officers were driving confiscated Italian automobiles that Köhler set up a separate SS garage near Via Veneto with its own mechanics to service them. Kappler had personal use of a yellow sports car which he used for drives in the countryside with his mistress.

Kappler had four sections or *Abteilungen* (ABT) in Rome:

ABT I: Radio Communications
ABT III: Italian Political and Economic Intelligence
ABT IV: *Sicherheitspolizei*, the Gestapo
ABT VI: *Sicherheitsdienst*, Espionage and Sabotage

ABT I was responsible for long-range radio communications. In addition to running Kappler's communications with Berlin, personnel in this section trained stay-behind agents in radio communications.

Via Tasso had its own radio transmitter and an antenna on the roof gave Kappler instantaneous communications with Berlin via a direct two-way radio teletype link.

ABT III reporting on Italian political and economic affairs started even before the arrest of Mussolini. Every two weeks the nine-man staff of ABT III produced reports on German and Italian morale and the effectiveness of German and Italian propaganda. Rudolf Rahn, German Ambassador to Italy, complained that the reports presented only a negative picture of what was going on in Rome and Italy and he insisted they include positive stories as well. SS-Hauptsturmbannführer Borante Domizlaff, the head of ABT III, considered these reports of little value and he believed Berlin largely ignored them.

ABT III was located in a small, very attractive 17th-century villa, the Casino Massimo Lancellotti, part of the Villa Giustiniani Massimo, on Via Matteo Boiardo, behind Kappler's Via Tasso headquarters. The villa had an SS officers' mess and several SS officers lived there, including SS-Hauptsturmführer Carl-Theodor Schütz. It was connected to the headquarters through a door in the back-garden wall (now walled up). This door allowed Gestapo agents to enter and leave the EK Rom without being seen from Via Tasso.* Fittingly, the fresco in the central hall of the villa shows scenes from Dante's *Inferno,* depicting the devil and his minions torturing mankind.

After the German occupation of Rome, ABT III's mission changed from propaganda to intelligence collecting and identifying enemies of the Third Reich. They focused on their former Axis partners: Italian royalists and senior military officers. These men were in hiding all over Rome and were suspected of organizing resistance and reporting on Wehrmacht movements. The Germans correctly believed that many of these Italian officers were members of the FMCR (Military Clandestine Front of the Resistance) and forwarded information on Wehrmacht movements to Allied intelligence organizations. Once identified, their names were turned over to the Gestapo.

To assist in the collection of information there was a separate Italian organization directly dependent on ABT III called Group V. It was made up of Fascists, zealots, and other opportunists. Group V men

---

* This blocked-up doorway was discovered by Dr. Alessia A. Glielmi of the *Museo Storico della Liberazione* in 2010 and shown to the author in November 2017.

tracked down works of art, hidden weapons, and information on high-ranking loyal Italian military officers and Roman society elites. These agents eventually were to be part of a fifth column of stay-behind agents in Rome who reported military and other intelligence.* They were paid by Kappler from money he raised locally from his black-market activities or from his supply of counterfeit British pounds.

Kappler personally ran several ABT III Italian sources. One was a man named Pagnozzi, the private secretary to the Italian Chief of Police in Rome. He gave information to Kappler concerning the activities inside Italian government ministries. Another source was Giovanni Pastore, who ran his own group of informants and uncovered a large partisan bomb factory in Via Giulia. Rome itself was filled with foreigners and refugees; so many came that it was christened Pacelli's Refuge after the Pope. ABT III intelligence activities were directed against them as well. Needing a wide variety of information, ABT III eavesdropped on sources that provided information without knowing it. These sources were rarely of high quality. One report on this haphazard method stated for example that:

> Considerable energy was expended in trailing and attempting to arrest an "Irish Priest" suspected of being an important member of the British I.S. [Intelligence Service]. The suspect in question was in reality an ABT IV [Gestapo] Informant and penetration agent, a fact which is suggestive of some lack of coordination and skill in their following methods.[3]

The intelligence source being mentioned in the above was undoubtedly Monsignor O'Flaherty, whom we will meet later. It is highly unlikely, however, that he was ever a source for ABT III or the Gestapo. O'Flaherty, a very intelligent man but not always security conscious, may in fact have been passing false information to people he suspected of being German agents.

A third source for Jewish information was Guido Garulli, a gentile who lived in the Jewish Ghetto at an apartment across the street from

---

*The term "fifth column" had its origin in the Spanish Civil War when Madrid was besieged by four columns of troops in 1936. The Spanish nationalist leader General Emilio Mola claimed he had additional troops in the city, hence, the fifth column.

the Da Giggetto restaurant. He denounced individual Jews and told Kappler about Jewish activities. Garulli and Kappler were friendly and often had dinner together at either his home or at Da Giggetto in the heart of the historic Ghetto, also owned by a gentile; the restaurant became one of Kappler's favorites.

The Ghetto of Rome was originally established in 1555 and was controlled by the papacy until 1870 with the establishment of the Kingdom of Italy. Originally it was surrounded by a wall and the gates were locked at night. It faced the Tiber Island in an undesirable section of the city that was prone to frequent flooding from the river. In the beginning, the enclosed area was only about three hectares with 3,000 people crowded inside. The Ghetto was flanked on the southeast by the Teatro Marcello and the Palazzo Orsini, the home of the Duchess of Sermoneta. The traditional northern entrance of the Ghetto was the gate at the late Italian Renaissance Turtle Fountain (*Fontana delle Tartarughe*) across from the Palazzo Mattei. To the northwest it ran almost to Via Arenula. Inside the Ghetto was the ancient Portico of Octavia dating from c. 27 BC.

By 1888 when the Ghetto walls were destroyed eight gates were left standing. By 1943, it was no longer the exclusive residence of Jews, since they had not been required to live exclusively inside the Ghetto since the unification of Italy. More prosperous Jews moved to other parts of the city. Their vacant dwellings were occupied by poorer Christian families. The focal point of the Ghetto is the central synagogue of Rome finished in 1904 with a square aluminum dome visible from rooftops all over the city. It was, and still is, a colorful and vibrant neighborhood of central Rome. But during the nine months of the German occupation it was defined by an atmosphere of intrigue and pervasive fear, thanks entirely to the efforts of ABT III and also ABT IV.

Rome's ABT IV, the Gestapo (*Geheime Staatspolizei* – Secret State Police and often referred to as the *Sicherheitspolizei* – Security Police), was the largest SS section in Rome with over 40 men. It was the most feared of all SS organizations and SS officers had to apply to join. Originally a Prussian State Police organization, it became the national secret state police responsible for terrorizing not only Germany but all of occupied Europe. At its peak, the Gestapo had over 46,000 members in Europe. It ran 60,000 agents and a network of over 100,000 informers. In Rome, it was charged with suppressing the partisan movement and thwarting Allied intelligence organizations.

The Gestapo relied on tips provided by informers and suspects who had been identified by ABT III intelligence agents. It was kept busy arresting ex-officers of the Italian military, communists, partisans, Jews, and other enemies of the Reich. In Rome, it was also responsible for defensive security. To accomplish this its officers spied on everyone who came to their attention, conducted roundups, performed interrogations, and employed horrific tortures on prisoners. The Gestapo's efforts were pragmatic and, except for its tragic persecution of the Jews, little Gestapo activity in Rome reflected Nazi ideological bigotry.

The central force in the Gestapo, and the man who set the tone for its cruelty, was SS-Hauptsturmführer Erich Priebke who had arrived in Rome in February 1941. In 1943, Priebke was 30 years old. He spoke Italian fluently and essentially ran the Gestapo for Kappler. He also acted as Chief of Counterespionage in which he claimed to be an expert.

Priebke, born in 1913, had lost both parents when he was seven. At 14, he entered the hotel business and from 1933 on he worked in a hotel in Rapallo on the Italian Riviera. That same year he joined the Nazi Party. In 1935 he was in London working as a waiter. In 1936 he became an interpreter and translator for the political police, the precursor of the SS. In the fall of 1937, he acted as Mussolini's interpreter during his visit to Berlin. He also accompanied Göring, Goebbels, Mussolini, and Hitler on visits abroad.

When Kappler requested an assistant in 1941, Priebke was chosen. In Rome he lived in a self-described "beautiful" house with his wife, whom he had married in 1938, and child. A second child was born while in Rome. He was even presented to the Pope. As previously noted, he was involved in the rescue of Mussolini and he personally arrested Count Ciano and his wife Edda. He oversaw radio security and was responsible for radio training and obtaining radios for stay-behind agents. And he was Via Tasso's paymaster. The Kapplers and the Priebkes became close and often entertained each other at their homes.

Despite his marriage and children, Priebke had a reputation in the bedrooms of Fascist society ladies, dubbed "the white telephone set." Always impeccably attired in his jet-black SS uniform, Priebke was called the Lothario of Parioli – Parioli being the affluent neighborhood popular with high-ranking Fascist officials. Among others, Italian film star Laura Nucci became his mistress.

More importantly, Priebke was the commandant of Via Tasso Prison. An infamous prison, it housed up to 350 inmates at a time, both men and women. All told, some 2,000 people passed through the prison in just nine months. Prisoners were crowded five or eight per room with not enough space to lie down. Jewish prisoners were confined in the toilets. Reportedly some food sent over from Rome's Regina Coeli Prison would routinely be doused by the guards with the contents of dirty lavatory pans. Prisoners were often sent back and forth from Via Tasso to the Regina Coeli Prison, where the Gestapo kept a full-time warden in the German-run, third branch.

After the outset of the war, Priebke became a quick study in the interrogation arts and at Via Tasso he blossomed as an aspiring Torquemada.* His ruthless methods can be inferred by his treatment of one prisoner. On May 3, 1944, Arrigo Paladini, an OSS agent and a former Italian artillery officer, returned to Rome from northern Italy. He had contacted a Rome OSS agent who instructed him to get a radio. But before he could, Paladini was denounced to the Gestapo by Enrico Sorrentino, another OSS agent. Paladini revealed nothing, even after several weeks during which he was tortured 16 times. When the Germans retreated, he was left behind at Via Tasso and he survived. After the war, Paladini wrote about Priebke:

> I remember Captain Priebke's interrogation method perfectly … He hit me in the chest and in the testicles with his trademark brass knuckles … Priebke was never offensive or vulgar in the way he addressed me and he never lost his temper. His recurring line was, "I'm sorry, but with me you're going to have to talk. You will be shot anyway, but you can avoid needless suffering." He said this often, but then added another threat: "If you don't talk I will be forced to shoot your father." In the third interrogation, speaking in a cutting, icy tone, he told me that my father's execution had already taken place … It wasn't really true, however. My father had died in a concentration camp months earlier, but I didn't know that …[4]

Even with all his acquired skills, Priebke was not the head interrogator. That was SS-Hauptsturmführer Carl-Theodor Schütz. He conducted

---

*Tomas de Torquemada was the Grand Inquisitor during the Spanish Inquisition of the 14th century.

the most important interrogations personally and directly oversaw the others. The Gestapo interpreters who conducted the lengthy interrogation sessions were either ethnic Germans living in Italy or Italian-speaking Germans from northern Italy. Three of those known to have been torturers were SS-Hauptscharführer Walter Hotop, SS-Oberscharführer Enrico Perathoner and SS-Sturmscharführer Max August Banneck.

Schütz's interrogations usually included torture, branding, beating, and sometimes the injection of disinfectant into the urethra of a male prisoner's penis. Often it was said that the waiting to be tortured was as bad as the torture itself. Prisoners never knew when one would be called for the next agonizing session.

The aim of interrogation was naturally a full confession. When a prisoner confessed, he could be forced to collaborate. If a prisoner agreed to collaborate, he was given a cover story, and then freed. The cover story accounted for the arrest and subsequent release. If a prisoner were released soon after arrest and he showed signs of physical ill-treatment, one could be sure he had been turned into a collaborator. If a prisoner refused to collaborate, he was sent to the German Military Tribunal for a sham trial lasting mere minutes. Most were given death sentences or long incarcerations in a German concentration camp. The condemned were often sent to Fort Bravetta, one of a series of late 19th-century forts surrounding Rome where executions were carried out by Italian police. SS-Scharführer Pustowka had the duty to escort condemned men to execution sites in Rome and then report back to Priebke.

The Gestapo regularly interrogated and tortured partisans and Italians working against the Germans, but rarely tortured captured Allied servicemen, perhaps honoring the Geneva Convention. Any military information gleaned from them was passed to Field Marshal Kesselring's headquarters.

ABT IV was further subdivided into four sections:

ABT IVa: Political Section and Counterespionage
ABT IVb: Ideological and Racial Enemies
ABT IVc: Agents and Paid Informers
ABT IVd: Black-market Warehouse

Since information was power, ABT IVa, the Gestapo's largest subsection, dealt with political matters and counterespionage. Ten officers were assigned to monitor the activities of the FMCR and they learned that they were reporting Wehrmacht military movements in and around Rome. Kappler set up a large counterespionage effort to combat this.

The Ideological and Racial Enemies subsection (ABT IVb) had at least two sub-subsections manned by three agents each: the Jewish section (ABT IVb-1) and the communist section (ABT IVb-2). Their efforts were sporadic and poorly coordinated.

Section ABT IVc ran agents and paid informers. Documents dated May 1944 found at Via Tasso and the German Embassy listed Italians – men and women – whom the Germans classified as *V-Mann* agents (*Vertrauensmann*, literally a "trusted man"). Many of the 20 names listed were not spies but couriers known as letterbox agents who dropped off or picked up documents from a designated place, the letterbox.

Auskunftspersonen was the German word for informers who were told what type of information the Gestapo wanted and then went about obtaining it. They varied as to rank or profession. For example, one special informer for Priebke was an Italian colonel, described by Kappler as his most reliable agent in Marshal Graziani's (the RSI's war minister) entourage. At the opposite end of the scale was the lowly porter at the Hotel Regno in Rome who reported on the comings and goings of key individuals. There were at least 20 other recruited informers.

Other Gestapo agents and collaborators were freelance mercenaries who had their own information networks. As frequent visitors to Via Tasso, they were issued special identity cards, green with a red stripe.

Some of these agents inevitably were double agents. Ubaldo Cipolla was a one-time member of SIM. Immediately after the armistice he was arrested on suspicion of being a communist as he had a Russian wife and he spoke Russian. After intense interrogation, he agreed to work for the Gestapo and joined the newly formed Italian SS.[*][5] But he apparently continued his relationship with SIM and started to work with the British as well.[†] Later the Gestapo designated him a stay-

---

[*] It was modelled on and organized by members of the German SS. Recruits pledged their complete loyalty to Mussolini and Hitler and they revered Himmler. It never amounted to anything other than a small organization.

[†] See Chapter 10 which details his interactions with Monsignor O'Flaherty.

behind agent, charged to send intelligence to the Germans after they departed Rome. Seemingly, the Gestapo never discovered his double life.

Controlling the economy and monitoring the flow of scarce goods and food was a high priority. The Gestapo was therefore relentless in uncovering black-markets run by anyone other than itself. ABT IVd maintained their own warehouse for confiscated goods which allowed the Gestapo to run its own lucrative black-market to finance its activities and line some individual pockets. Kappler was in fact proud that, because of his black-market activities, his Gestapo was more than able to pay its own way.

The contents of the warehouse were so tantalizing that six of Kappler's men, including two radio operators, stole goods from it to sell on the black-market. They were arrested in January 1944 and sent to Verona where they served time in a Gestapo prison. They were to be sent to the Eastern Front as part of their sentence but an enraged Kappler demanded the two ABT I radiomen be sent back to Rome as they were needed.

Kappler used his black-market supplies for bribes and favors. He acquired a large supply of coffee, an unheard-of luxury in Rome, from the Italian Ministry of the Interior. He passed it out liberally to curry favor. Kappler's men were not insensible to bribes and one such man, SS-Scharführer Frühling, became a source for the US OSS.

Kappler, it turned out, was not the most efficient administrator and in March 1944, Berlin sent SS-Hauptsturmführer Johannes Max Hans Clemens to put the Rome SS in order. Instead of being offended, Kappler was impressed with Clemens, who was described as a good organizer. Going from office-to-office, checking on the staff and making suggestions, he was well-liked. Kappler was heard to say that "I am glad we had him here as I can never be bothered doing this sort of work, record keeping and paperwork, and we need it badly in Rome." Clemens, who also inspected the prisons and prisoners, left Rome on May 12, 1944, before its liberation.

With the Allies fighting north of Naples in October 1943, the German military hierarchy decided to counter with sabotage operations in Allied-occupied Italy. An order to develop these types of operations was issued by Himmler to the head of the RSHA, Dr. Ernst Kaltenbrunner, then on to SS-Obergruppenführer Wolff in Italy, and on to Harster. This section was identified as the Rome Security Service Task Force (*Das Sicherheitsdienst Einsatzkommando Rom*) and was listed as ABT VI but was essentially an extension of the German security service (*Sicherheitsdienst* – SD). It was under Kappler's direct control.

The SD's original function was investigating political activities for the Nazi Party within Germany. But the SD's role was expanded in German-occupied countries and it became an intelligence collection agency with a wider range of interests. Long before the Italian armistice, the SD had agents inside Mussolini's government ministries, institutions, and industry, gathering high-level intelligence.

Indeed, the SD had been undercover and active in Rome as early as 1942 when Berlin had first become seriously concerned about the future of the Axis alliance. The head of the SD in Rome was Hauptsturmführer Eugen Haas, a former SD undercover agent who was appointed in September 1943. Haas had been in Rome since February 10, 1935, posing as a journalist in contact with the Italian Ministry of Popular Culture. His Italian was excellent – he also spoke a number of other languages and was a well-known photographer of Italian movie stars. Allied intelligence reported that Haas was one of the most capable SS men in Italy. Sent in December 1940 on assignment to Spain and then Hungary, Haas then showed up in Berlin but, as the Allies prepared to take Tunisia, he was back in southern Italy by February 1943.

Berlin had ordered Haas to return to Rome to assist Otto Skorzeny in the hunt for Mussolini and afterwards he stayed on to assist Kappler as the head of the SD. Residing at the Grand Hotel, Haas had been so convincing an undercover agent that his Roman acquaintances never knew he was in the SS until one day when he appeared in his black SS uniform.

Haas made his headquarters in the German Embassy at the Villa Wolkonsky, a five-minute walk from Via Tasso. Like Via Tasso, the embassy had direct radio contact and an open teletype link with Berlin. Two wooden prefabricated buildings on the villa grounds had held offices used by the Military and Press Attachés. After the armistice, Kappler had use of them; Barracks IA was used for training agent radio operators, and Barracks IIB housed the SD.

As part of his new SD sabotage mission, Kappler sent 25 men to a training school near Belgrade, Yugoslavia, on October 25, 1943. The next month, he and Haas attended the Waffen SS Führer School at Bad Tölz, Germany, and, after a side trip to Berlin, toured the newly constructed SD sabotage training school at Scheveningen, Holland, near The Hague.

In late December, the first Italian agent-team was sent to Scheveningen for a month-long training course; other teams would soon follow. Joining the Italian students at the school was a special team with Arabic language skills and Middle East experience. They were to be sent into British-occupied Palestine and other Near-Eastern Muslim countries. Members of this team included four members from the retinue of the Grand Mufti, the Muslim leader of Jerusalem, Haj Amin al-Husseini, who was then living in Rome.[*]

To meet the increasing need for saboteurs, the SD opened a training school in Rome in 1944 at a villa in Viale Gioacchino Rossini 11, north of the Borghese Gardens. This school was run by an Italian named Negroni, who had selected the first group of 12 agents sent for sabotage training in Holland. He was the chief sabotage instructor and his assistant was Lt. Baldoni, a former Italian SIM officer and turncoat.

After training, the neophyte saboteurs were divided into teams of four men each. One team's mission was to cross Allied lines and sabotage gasoline dumps. They were also to gather information on antiaircraft sites, gun positions, and vehicle markings, and to obtain civilian ration cards and Allied military currency. Unexpectedly, after he crossed no-man's-land, the Italian officer in charge of his team defected and surrendered to a British outpost.

––––––––––

[*] Haj Amin al-Husseini, given the rank of SS-Gruppenführer, lent his influence to form the Bosnian Muslim Waffen SS *Handschar* Division; when deployed to Yugoslavia, it was responsible for many atrocities.

Inter-agency conflicts weakened intelligence and sabotage efforts. The German Military Intelligence Organization in Berlin, the *Abwehrdienst* (usually referred to simply as the Abwehr), the Defense Service of the Army, Navy, Air Force and the War Economics Directorate, was headed by Admiral Wilhelm Franz Canaris. It was entirely separate from the RSHA. Canaris was in constant conflict with Himmler and Ernst Kaltenbrunner (RSHA), resulting in the cool relations between the two organizations.

In Rome tension between the two organizations often erupted into personal animosity. The head of the Abwehr in Rome was Carl F. Clemm, Graf von Hohenberg, an acquaintance of the Duchess of Sermoneta. His cover was that he was an economic advisor at the German Embassy. He and Kappler did not get along. Often Kappler could be heard through his closed office door screaming at Hohenberg. With fewer resources, the Rome Abwehr office was forced to use locally recruited SD agents and the two organizations were in competition for scarce agents and equipment. For example, Rome's Abwehr unit claimed to have a mobile van equipped with frequency-detection equipment for triangulation, allowing them to detect a radio set transmission immediately. Kappler's operation also needed such equipment; he had requested it but never received it.

The Abwehr also had spies inside the Vatican run by Hohenberg. One of his agents was an impoverished Italian duke who agreed, for 50,000 lire, to provide intelligence from inside the Vatican. The duke, a friend of Cardinal Maglione, knew other cardinals and was well connected with the so-called Vatican Black Nobility, members of families ennobled by the Pope for supporting the Vatican over the centuries. Although the duke received money for his reporting, it is not certain that he didn't just make up his information.

Another Abwehr Vatican agent was Wilhelm Möhnen, a dealer in motorcycles and an art lover. He avoided conscription into the Wehrmacht by being assigned to the Abwehr office in Paris. There he met Bruno Lohse, an art buyer for Reichsmarschall Hermann Göring. Lohse urged him to go to Rome and find art for Göring's private art collection. Möhnen did so and went to work for the German Embassy's Air Attaché, Lieutenant Colonel Herbert Veltheim of the Luftwaffe, and sought art for Göring. He so ingratiated himself at the Vatican that he later served as a secret conduit for a peace feeler to the Allies.

After the liberation of Rome, Möhnen lived inside the Vatican for eight months before being expelled and turned over to the Allies.

Kappler now had at his disposal a highly efficient and effective organization to carry out his duties and responsibilities. Because of this, his power and influence in the city was much more important than his rank of lieutenant colonel would suggest. Even Field Marshal Kesselring rarely intervened in his activities.

6

First They Take the Jews[*]

The journey finally ended. In the five days since the train left Rome it had stopped multiple times, sometimes for hours, but this felt different. It was dark and in the small hours of the morning and, with the exception of some barking dogs, it was eerily silent. And then there was the smell. Not just the acrid smell of vomit, feces, urine, and human sweat that rode with them in the railway boxcar; but another strange cloyingly sweet, oily smell flavored with diesel fuel and other unidentified and unpleasant odors that sank heavily to the ground. Arminio Wachsberger tried to comfort his small whimpering daughter who shivered in the intense cold. Forced to interpret for the Nazis, he, his wife, and daughter had been loaded into the last boxcar where fewer Jews were stuffed inside. This allowed the Wachsberger family the luxury to lie down and snatch some fitful sleep during the journey.

Like other Roman Jews, Wachsberger had been rousted out of bed shortly after 06:00 on the morning of October 16, 1943. Given less than 20 minutes he collected his wife and child and they were marched by black-clad SS troops from their apartment on the Lungotevere and across the nearby Ponte Cestio to the Tiber Island. There they crossed the Ponte Fabricio, the so-called bridge of four heads after ancient sculptures adorning the bridge, to the Jewish Ghetto. Wachsberger was

---

[*] This is adapted from a poem by Martin Niemöller, a German Protestant pastor, concentration camp inmate, and postwar university lecturer. The actual quote is: "First they came for the Jews, and I did not speak out, because I was not a Jew." The poem famously concludes with the line: "Then they came for me and there was no one left to speak out for me."

almost unique in Rome's Jewish population. Born in Fiume in northern Italy, he spoke fluent German and Italian. He worked in a photographic shop on Via Volturno, across from Termini, Rome's central train station, and not far from Via Veneto – the German-occupied quarter. After the occupation the shop had been frequented by German soldiers buying film, cameras, and accessories and getting their souvenir photos of the Eternal City developed. Ultimately he became known among Rome's Jewish community as the Interpreter of Auschwitz. Wachsberger was only one of 16 on that train of more 1,000 men, women, and children who returned to Rome to tell his story:

> Through me he [Dannecker, see below] told us that we were to be transported to Germany to a camp where each of us, according to his skills, would have a job to do. Since the old, the invalid, and women with children would naturally be unable to work, and since the German government had no intention of maintaining them free of charge, all money, jewelry, and other objects of value that we had brought with us to the Collegio Militare had to be turned over to him in order to create a communal fund ... The rich Jews will have to pay for the poor Jews. "Now in your right hand you are to place all jewelry, and in your left hand, your money. You will pass in front of me and deposit everything" [this was accompanied by the injunction that if you failed to do so you would be shot. Any really nice piece of jewelry was pocketed by Dannecker].[1]

Italians were not generally anti-Semitic. Jews had been living in Rome since before the time of Christ so the repression of Jews had started slowly with the accession of Mussolini to power. The Italian government, on October 31, 1931, passed what was called the Law of the Community. It recognized the Jewish Community as a legal entity empowered to tax its own people to provide for religious instruction and other benefits. The law also required Jews carry out their religious obligations unless they formally renounced their faith. Jewish students were exempt from studying the Catholic texts of the official state religion in the public schools.

Within a year of enacting the law, Emil Ludwig, a German-Jewish biographer, published *Conversation with Mussolini*. In his book, Ludwig quoted Mussolini as saying that anti-Semitism does not exist in

Italy ... Italian Jews have always been good citizens and as soldiers they have fought courageously.

The surprising fact, in retrospect, was that Italian Jews had long supported Mussolini and Fascism. In fact, over 200 Jews participated in Mussolini's famous March on Rome, October 22–29, 1922. Italian Jews did not feel threatened by Italian Fascism because they were well integrated within society at large.

The Second Italo-Abyssinian War (1935–1937) had in fact been popular among Jews as an ancient Jewish community lived in Ethiopia. Many volunteered, others were drafted, and they contributed considerable money to the war effort. Early on, two Jews were prominent in Mussolini's government; Guido Jung was a minister of finance and Aldo Finzi was both the Under Minister of the Interior and a member of the Fascist Grand Council, although Finzi was forced to resign when the press blamed him for the murder of Giacomo Matteotti, the Socialist Party leader, who was killed on Mussolini's orders.

In the late 1930s, as Nazi influence grew in Italy, discrimination of Italian Jews increased. Mussolini and Ciano, Italy's Foreign Minister, assured German Foreign Minister Joachim von Ribbentrop that Italy had begun an intense propaganda campaign against Jews. Mussolini began removing Jews from mainstream Italian life. He even proposed that Italian Jews be deported to Palestine. Mussolini also refused to recognize the Vatican position that Jews who converted to Catholicism were no longer Jews and he directed the government not to recognize marriages of former Jews with Catholics.

This new anti-Semitism was apparent when the Ministry of Culture sponsored a conference on the Italian Race and the Jews in July 1938. During the conference scientists offered evidence that Italians were a pure race to which Jews did not belong. The conference published a paper titled *The Defense of Race* with an announcement that the Italian government had established a Bureau of Demography and Race (*La Demorazza*). One of the Bureau's first acts was to take a census of Jews which revealed that there were more than 47,000 Italian and 10,000 foreign Jews scattered across Italy.

After the conference, in September of 1938, Mussolini's government banned Jewish children and teachers from public schools. The government also ordered all foreign Jews who had immigrated to Italy after January 1, 1919 to leave the country, including naturalized Jews. This law was slightly modified in November and allowed those Jews who had married Italians and those over 65 to remain but further Jewish–Italian marriages were forbidden. By the time Italy declared war on Britain and France in 1940, 10,000 Jews had emigrated from the country, but they were quickly replaced by German Jews posing as tourists.

Next, the government restricted the rights of Jews to work in most professions or to own property. After Mussolini's return from Munich and Berlin that September, his government issued a bulletin on international Jewry which stated that the Jews were responsible for worldwide anti-fascist propaganda. Mussolini's government would therefore monitor the actions of non-Italian Jews coming to Italy. On January 5, 1939, it published a Racial Purity Law, which drew protest from an ill Pope Pius XI, who was the Pope between 1922 and 1939.

These measures rankled average Italians and exacerbated their growing doubts about Fascism. Many Jews saw the writing on the wall and left the country. From 1939 to 1943, 5,000 Italian Jews emigrated to Palestine, North Africa, and the United States. Many, if they could not leave, changed their surnames or took steps to hide their Jewish identity. Cash and other assets were hidden and bank accounts transferred to holders with non-Jewish names.

The remaining Jewish government workers were fired. However, not all Italian Jews agreed that the government was becoming anti-Semitic. One organization, the Union of Italian Jewish Communities (*Unione delle Comunità Israelitiche Italiane*) optimistically pledged the continued dedication of Italian Jews to Fascism.

Jews fleeing France, Yugoslavia, and Greece began flocking to Italy for safety. By September 1940, the government set up 15 internment camps across Italy to hold these non-Italian Jews. Mussolini, to his credit, did not deport Jews to Germany for work.

Jews interned in these camps were aided by the Hebrew Emigrant Relief Organization (DELASEM – *Delegazione per l'assistenza agli emigranti Ebrei*) based in Geneva, Switzerland. Because DELASEM provided money for food and helped meet other needs of the refugees, government officials sanctioned the organization's activities as it relieved the Italian government of the burden.

In a show of the new attitude, *Il Messaggero,* a Fascist-controlled newspaper in Rome, published a photo of 50 Jews at forced labor, digging mud along the banks of the Tiber on June 7, 1942. Outraged,

Harold Tittmann sent a letter of protest to Monsignor Giovanni Battista Montini, the Vatican Under-Secretary of State to Pope Pius XII. His letter stated in part:

> I cannot begin to tell you how degrading I consider the situation which this photograph represents. It seems all the more appalling to me that it could exist within the shadow of Saint Peter's, the fountain of Christian charity. I feel certain that the Holy See must have already approached the appropriate authorities with a view to eliminating this shameful persecution, if not from Italy, at least from the precincts of the sacred Eternal City.[2]

It is not known whether Tittmann received a formal reply to his letter; however, Cardinal Luigi Maglione, the Vatican Secretary of State, noted on June 11, 1942 that he had asked the Italian Ambassador to the Holy See to intercede for the poor Jews recruited for forced labor. The note was clearly a response to Tittmann's protest to Monsignor Montini.[3]

Tittmann had heard the rumors of the mass exterminations of Jews in occupied Europe, and he reported to the US State Department that he had spoken with the Pope about the church's silence on the Nazi treatment of the Jews. The Vatican responded that it was doing the best it could, but it lacked independent confirmation of Nazi atrocities against the Jews. This notorious failure to act became a lasting accusation against the church, perhaps never to be satisfactorily answered.

In November 1942, after Germany occupied the rest of Vichy France, Italy took over the administration of several provinces and towns on the Italian/French border. It was then that French Jews, and many other nationalities, especially from Eastern Europe, fled German-occupied France for Italian-occupied France. There Italian officials looked benignly on the refugees, identifying them as Jewish, but not deporting them. Where there had originally been between 15,000 and 20,000 Jews in the Italian Zone, by July 1943 that number had grown to 50,000, including 20,000 to 30,000 non-French Jews.

Back on June 3, 1943, a French priest, Father Benoît-Marie de Bourg d'Ire, known as Father Maria Benedetto to his Italian contacts, left

France for Italy to inform the Pope of the plight of French Jewry. At the meeting with Pope Pius XII on July 16, 1943, Father Benedetto brought an ambitious plan put forth by Angelo Donati, an Italian Jewish banker and head of the Franco-Italian Bank. Donati's plan was to transfer 50,000 Jews from the south of France to Italy from where they would board four ships for Palestine. The four ships named were *Duilio, Giulio Cesare, Saturnia,* and *Vulcania*; however, these are the names of Italian Navy warships and it is not known that Donati had worked with the Italian Navy to plan these voyages.

After obtaining the Pope's approval, Father Benedetto met with Tittmann and Sir D'Arcy on August 15. The meeting had been organized by Monsignor Joseph Hérissé who lived in the same compound as the two diplomats and was known to Father Benedetto. The voyage was to be paid for by DELASEM. On September 8, however, Donati was still in Rome soliciting support for his plan when the armistice ended all hope of such a boat lift.

The Nazis entered Rome with a high priority, the capture of Israel Zolli, the head Rabbi of Rome. The Gestapo placed a 300,000 lire price on his head. Alarmed, Zolli sent his wife and daughter to stay with friends, but finding no place for himself, he returned to his empty apartment and waited.

When the armistice was announced and the Italian Fourth Army decamped from France to Italy, some French and foreign Jews traveled with them. But thousands of Jewish refugees were not so lucky and were trapped as Germans occupied the former Italian sector of France.

After the Allied invasion of mainland Italy, DELASEM urged refugees not to stay in Rome but to go south and cross the Allied lines. Most ignored this warning even though by now there were rumors of the Final Solution and the testimony of eyewitnesses smuggled out of the Warsaw Ghetto.

Father Benedetto learned on September 13 that a train with 100 Jews had arrived in Rome from France. His informant was Lionello Alatri, a DELASEM member, who introduced Father Benedetto to two Jews who had been on the train, Stefan Schwamm, a lawyer from Vienna who carried papers identifying him as a French member of the Red Cross, and Aaron Kasztersztein. Both men went to work with Father Benedetto.

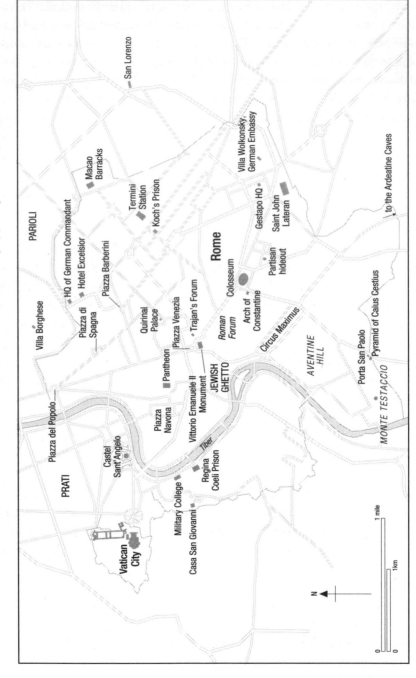

NAZI-OCCUPIED ROME, SEPTEMBER 1943 – JUNE 1944

San Lorenzo

Villa Wolkonsky,
German Embassy

Macao
Barracks

PARIOLI

HQ of German Commandant

Termini
Station

Koch's Prison

Gestapo HQ

Saint John
Lateran

to the Ardeatine Caves

Hotel Excelsior

Piazza Barberini

Rome

Partisan
hideout

Piazza di
Spagna

Villa Borghese

Quirinal
Palace

Piazza Venezia

Trajan's Forum

Colosseum

Arch of
Constantine

Roman
Forum

Circus Maximus

AVENTINE
HILL

Pantheon

Porta San Paolo

Pyramid of Caius Cestius

Piazza del Popolo

Piazza
Navona

Vittorio Emanuele II
Monument

JEWISH
GHETTO

Tiber

MONTE TESTACCIO

Castel
Sant'Angelo

PRATI

Regina
Coeli Prison

Military College

Casa San Giovanni

Vatican
City

1 mile

1 km

N

0   0

DELASEM housed the newly arrived Jews in small hotels and boarding houses, the Hotel Salus, the Pension Haeslin, and the Pension Amalfi at a cost of 40 lire per Jew per day. The International Red Cross provided what food and medicine it could but more was needed and so donations were solicited from Romans, Jews and non-Jews.

Two men who worked for DELASEM were Renzo Levi and Settimio Sorani, both Roman Jews. Like other Jews, they went into hiding after the German occupation, although Sorani continued to move about the city, hiding out in ten different locations until liberation. From his hiding places, he found places for others to hide. Starting with 100 Jews, by the end of the German occupation he had helped hide more than 2,500 Italian and 1,500 foreign Jews. He was arrested once and was tortured for ten days but he was released when his forged documents held up.

Elsewhere in Italy, the Nazi occupiers had dealt ruthlessly with the Jewish problem. In northern Italy, 54 Jews, including women and children, were murdered by the Nazis on September 15, 1943. They were mostly foreigners. The next day 35 Italian Jews were deported to Auschwitz and two days later 350 Jews were arrested across northwest Italy. This was just the beginning of Jewish roundups in Italy. Rome's Jewish population could only try to escape a similar fate. Many could not. It would be a mere four weeks after the announcement of the armistice that Arminio Wachsberger would be boarding a train with his family bound, ultimately, for Auschwitz.

———

On September 25, 1943, Himmler directed Kappler to round up Roman Jews for deportation to Auschwitz. At this point it was just two weeks after the occupation. Kappler later claimed that he objected to this order because Romans harbored no anti-Jewish feelings and many would strongly object to their arrest. He also had his own mercenary intentions.

In response to Himmler's directive, Kappler came up with a plan. On September 26, he summoned two of Rome's Jewish leaders to meet with him: Ugo Foà, the President of the Jewish Community's 15-member Board of Councilors, and Dante Almansi, formerly a Rome prefect of police and the President of the Rome-based Union of Italian

Jewish Communities. According to author Louis Newman, Foà rode around Rome with the Gestapo in the days after Rome was occupied. His purpose was to show his fellow Jews that they had nothing to fear from the Germans. He had been a Fascist municipal judge but was removed after the Italian Racial Laws were enacted.[4] They met Kappler at the Villa Wolkonsky, the German Embassy. Unbelievably, the meeting was cordial, matter-of-fact, and businesslike.

Kappler's plan was extortion. He demanded that the Jews of Rome hand over to him 50 kilos (110lb) of gold within 36 hours. If the gold was not received on time, 200 Jews would be sent to labor camps in Germany. But it was not about the gold. Kappler believed that the demand for gold would lull the Jews into a false sense of security which would make a later mass roundup that much easier.

Foà and Almansi negotiated to see if Kappler would accept lire instead of gold. Kappler reportedly replied that the German Reich had no need of lire, and if ever it should need them it could always print them. Returning to the Rome Synagogue, Almansi and Foà called a meeting of Jewish elders for the next day.

Kappler's ruse was working. By 10:30 the next morning, the elders had decided to collect the gold as Kappler demanded. Word was relayed to the Jewish community. By 11:00 they were ready to begin the voluntary collection. In the synagogue offices, a special gold team was assembled: one man assayed the purity of the gold, a second weighed each piece, and a third recorded the amount and wrote a receipt. A fourth man stood guard. Once collected, the gold was flattened so that it could be more easily placed into boxes.

Things got off to a slow start. Two hours later (by 13:00), only five kilos of gold had been collected. Many responded to the call, but either having no gold, or being reluctant to part with it, offered cash instead. Therefore, it was decided to accept the cash and then purchase gold with it, even paying a higher price than the official rate. Even so, the Jewish leaders feared they would miss the deadline.

Having learned of the gold collection that morning, Rabbi Israel Zolli, the chief rabbi of Rome, sought help from his Vatican contacts. They agreed to help and said he could pick up what gold he needed after 13:00 that day. Unaware of Rabbi Zolli's request, the collection team at the synagogue also asked the Vatican for help. At 14:00 a delegation including Levi of DELASEM met with Padre Borsarelli, the Vice Abbot at the Monastery of the Sacred Heart. After checking with the Vatican, he said that the Vatican would lend any quantity of gold they needed, although as it turned out, it was not required.

Collection efforts picked up. By late afternoon, 30 kilos of gold were in hand. Roman police arrived outside the synagogue for crowd control. Donors snaked up the staircase to the community office. By 20:00 that evening, an hour before the Nazi-imposed curfew, the Jews of Rome had 45 kilos of gold. It was necessary to end collecting for the day.

By 11:00 the next morning the goal was met. At the US official 1943 rate of $35.00 an ounce, 50 kilos of gold was worth $61,600. It was decided to add an extra 300 grams to the total in case of any mistake or disagreements, so the collection continued. Of the 50 kilos of gold now on hand, 15 kilos had been purchased. Although some have later claimed that the gold to save the Jews came from the Vatican at the direction of Pope Pius XII, it did not. To categorically prove this point, the Jewish Museum at the Rome Synagogue today displays the carbon copies of the original receipts given to donors for gold received.

Although it was not really needed, Kappler had been asked for a four-hour deadline extension. It was granted. Jewish leaders had not wanted to make it look too easy to raise the gold as they feared it was only the start of more shakedowns. Cash donations had resulted in an overage after the gold purchase of more than two million lire (about $20,000). This was kept in case there were further demands.

The gold was packed into ten small cardboard boxes holding five kilos each, plus an extra box with the remaining 300 grams. Escorted by Roman police, the Jewish delegation took the gold to the Villa Wolkonsky. Once there, Kappler declined to receive them and they were sent to the newly outfitted Gestapo Headquarters on Via Tasso, where they were made to wait. Finally, the gold was weighed before SS-Hauptsturmführer Carl-Theodor Schütz who claimed they were five kilos short and accused the Jews of cheating.

The gold was meticulously recounted and Schütz finally acknowledged that the weight was indeed correct. The Jewish delegation asked for a receipt but got none. The quibbling continued. Later, Kappler reportedly commented that to the enemy who is being relieved of his arms, one does not give receipts. He also claimed that the gold weighed in at only 48 kilos and 600 grams; the rest was gold plated and did not qualify. How he arrived at this figure is a mystery as there is no evidence of an independent assay. Seeing that the gold objects at Via Tasso were wedding rings, brooches, and other small pieces of jewelry, Kappler concluded that the gold had come from the poorer Jews and not from the rich, as he expected. Schütz crated up the gold and put it under lock and key.

Shortly thereafter, Kappler sent the gold to Ernst Kaltenbrunner, chief of the RSHA. To escort the gold, he found an SS-Sturmbannführer named Hartl, on a special assignment to the Vatican and an author of several books on Catholicism. Hartl needed a way back to Berlin and, as the gold's escort, he could be assigned transportation. He carried a letter from Kappler which explained that the Jewish gold was for the German war effort. Kappler got Hartl, and the gold, space on an aircraft to Berlin and by October 2, 1943 the crate was received by Kaltenbrunner's aide SS-Sturmbannführer Ploetz. Later propaganda inflated the hoard amount to 80 kilos of gold. The crate arrived safely but remained unopened and sat in a corner of Kaltenbrunner's office where it was eventually found in May 1945. The 50 kilos of gold was returned to the Jewish people of Rome, on whose behalf it was reportedly sent on to the new state of Israel.

The reprieve from the Gestapo lasted just one day. Foà later reported that the day after the gold was delivered, an SS-Hauptsturmführer, most probably Schütz, came to his house and escorted him to the synagogue. There he was made to open the safe. Inside were documents and the two million lire left over from the gold collection. The documents included minutes of meetings and other records and Rabbi Zolli's list with the names and addresses of Jews living in Rome. While important, the Germans already had a list of Jews that they had obtained from the Questura, Rome's police headquarters. Schütz seized both the documents and the cash. The next day, two Nazi specialists on ancient books arrived. It is believed that one of the men was Alfred Rosenberg who, in 1940, had founded the Rosenberg Project (ERR – *Einsatzstab Reichsleiter Rosenberg*). The ERR was to amass books and cultural items of Germany's enemies specifically for Johannes Pohl, director of the Hebrew Department of the Nazi Institute for Jewish Research in Frankfurt. After inspecting the Jewish main community library with its ancient and rare books, Rosenberg sealed the library and forbade further access.

On October 11, Rosenberg sent to the synagogue another SS officer, believed to be a distinguished German scholar of paleography and Semitic philology but otherwise unidentified. With an SS escort, he showed up at the Jewish community offices inside the synagogue. An expert in ancient Jewish papyri, incunabula, and rare manuscripts, parchments, and palimpsests, he was to determine what was worth stealing. He scoured both the main library and the Rabbinical School Library and knew that here indeed was a treasure. The unnamed official arranged for the Otto and Rosoni removal firm in Rome to package and transfer the thousands of volumes.

Covering well over a thousand years of Jewish history, these volumes were of immense historical and cultural value. On October 14, two large rail boxcars, brought via the tram tracks which ran nearby, were parked outside the synagogue. It took two days to load the materials, and when the boxcars were full, they were sent on their way to Munich.[5]

When next Gestapo officers returned on December 14 to see what they had missed, they found the community office abandoned, not surprisingly. They broke in and seized what was left. By this time, however, arranging transportation met with delays and the last of the books and documents were not removed until December 23. The pillaging of the libraries was now complete.*

The previous summer, Rome's Jewish leaders, fearing that things were going to get worse for their community, had hidden most of the synagogue's sacred objects, moving Torah cloths and ritual silver vessels from the synagogue to a vault in the Rome branch of the Banca di Napoli. In late November, the bank manager, learning that the Germans were going to confiscate everything in Roman bank vaults, secretly notified the Jewish leadership. In one day – and in broad daylight – the

---

* After the war, only the Rabbinical School books were found and returned to the Jewish community in Rome, but those from the main library were never found and as many as 26,568 volumes remain missing. Author Gordon Thomas claims that the books were tracked down by US Army Major Seymour J. Pomrenze, a former archivist at the National Archives in Washington. The books were shipped to the *ERR Institute der NSDP fuer Erforschung der judeneer*, in the small village of Hungen, Germany. From there Pomrenze traced them to the Rothschild library in Frankfurt and they were shipped back to Rome. Obviously Thomas was referring to the Rabbinical Library which was returned to Rome, but he does not say that.

sacred artifacts were moved to the same secure storage location where senior Nazi officials kept their own confiscated plunder!

Already bad, the Jewish predicament was about to worsen with the arrival on October 6, 1943 of SS-Hauptsturmführer Theodor Dannecker, a Nazi specialist on the Jewish problem. Known as Adolf Eichmann's troubleshooter for occupied countries, the 31-year-old Dannecker had already organized a highly effective roundup of Jews in Paris. He was accompanied by a crack detachment of Waffen SS made up of 14 officers and NCOs and 30 soldiers. He set up his headquarters at the ORPO offices on Via Po.

Because Eichmann had sent him, Kappler took Dannecker's assignment to Rome as a sign that Berlin lacked faith in him to carry out the Jewish roundup. Kappler could do nothing other than help him. Dannecker required local knowledge so Kappler assigned Köhler, Schütz, and Priebke to assist him.

Italy's new Fascist Salò Republic was a farce. Although Mussolini was nominally the head of state, Rudolf Rahn, the German Ambassador to Italy, was now the real political authority in Italy. He established his embassy in Fasano del Garda, on Lake Garda. In Rome, Consul General Eitel F. Möllhausen became the senior German diplomat. He was 30 years old, born in Turkey, and half French by birth. Postwar he described himself as not a Nazi; nevertheless, Möllhausen provided Kappler with political information and they compared notes about city regulations. Hearing that Jews were to be rounded up, Möllhausen objected, but not on humanitarian grounds. He said it would be a grave political and financial error. Möllhausen cabled his objections to Reich Foreign Minister von Ribbentrop. Unknown to the Germans, a copy of the cable was passed to the American OSS in Bern, Switzerland by Fritz Kolbe (code name George Wood), a minor official in the German Foreign Office in Berlin. Kolbe had been recruited by Allen Dulles in Geneva to send information from Berlin to Switzerland. It was a blockbuster:

> Orders have been received from Berlin by Obersturmbannführer Kappler to seize and to take to northern Italy the 8,000 Jews living in Rome. They are to be *liquidated* [author's italics]. General Stahl

[sometimes spelled Stahel], the city commandant of Rome, will permit this action only if it is consistent with the policies of the Reich Foreign Minister. It would be better business, in my opinion, to use the Jews, as in Tunis, for work on fortifications. Together with Kappler, I shall present this view through Field Marshal General Kesselring.[6]

When read in the US, the intercepted cable was considered so sensitive that the OSS made only eight copies, including one for President Roosevelt. Not surprisingly the next day, October 7, German Foreign Minister von Ribbentrop sharply rebuked Möllhausen for using the word liquidated in his cable. He was told to report to Ambassador Rahn for a personal reprimand. The Germans were not only paranoid about the Allies getting access to their cables, but also they wanted to keep the liquidation of Jews under close wraps and not let it become general knowledge.

By the end of September, some Roman Jews had gone into hiding, but many had not. A current joke ran that when tourists visiting the Basilica of San Pietro in Vincoli (Saint Peter in Chains) asked their guide where the statue of Moses (by Michelangelo) had been taken, the guide answered that for some days now he has been in the home of friends. But it was not a joke.

On October 7, 1943, the first major labor roundup was mounted. A call for 3,000 labor service volunteers had netted only 60 men. By the end of 1942 there were more than 600,000 Italian workers in Germany. Word had filtered back that these Italian workers had to work under deplorable conditions with scant food and that the working hours were excessive. So that day, hundreds of men were dragged off trams, picked up in the street and taken from apartment houses for forced labor in Germany.

It was a bloody day. Rosa Guarnieri Carducci was murdered while trying to prevent the joint German–Fascist police from arresting her son and his friends. She confronted the patrol, tempers flared, and she was shot in front of her apartment house at Viale delle Milizie 72, near the Prati military casern, about ten blocks from the

Vatican. Her courageous act gave the boys time to flee out the back of the building.[*]

On October 15, 1943, Hitler called a meeting to discuss the formation of the new Italian Fascist Army to fight alongside Germany. SS-Obersturmbannführer Dollmann, acting as an interpreter, traveled to Germany with Mussolini and Marshal Rodolfo Graziani, the RSI war minister.

During the meeting they discussed how to defend Rome against an expected Allied attack. Graziani believed that Rome should not be defended so as not to risk its destruction. He reasoned that the Allies might resume bombing, this time in the historic center, with the risk of countless precious artworks being destroyed. German and Italian prestige would never recover from that. Mussolini was committed to defending the city to the last. Dollmann suggested Rome be put under the control of the Red Cross, or even the Vatican. This would be a severe blow to the Italian king, something that Hitler desired. And, Dollmann argued, an increasingly powerful Roman resistance with the Vatican's help might hamper German forces in the city. A siege was out of the question; Rome would be impossible to feed. Hitler's reported response was succinct: we are in Rome and we shall stay in Rome. Later Dollmann claimed that he had convinced the Führer to spare the city, although it is highly likely that this was a mere postwar ploy on Dollmann's part to spare himself.

All agreed that it was vital to build up the new Italian Fascist Army. Upon his return to Italy, Marshal Graziani decreed that all male citizens born between 1920 and 1925 were subject to the draft. Refusal to comply would mean a loss of ration cards so the men would not be able to legally buy what little food was available.

Resistance to the draft was widespread all over Italy. Men went into hiding to avoid the military and labor roundups. At least 900 Italian military officers who refused to be impressed into the new army were deported to Germany as laborers. Kappler wrote in a report to Berlin

[*] There is a street in the south of Rome in the Ostiense neighborhood named for Rosa Guarnieri Carducci; formerly it had been named for Mussolini's mother, Rosa Maltoni.

that he confirmed that the ordinary Italians in principle will never collaborate with the Fascist government.

The roundups stirred ill will and backlash. Consul Möllhausen told General Mälzer, second German Stadtkommandant of Rome, that they turned Romans against Germans and, for the 500 or so men rounded up, thousands of others fled or joined the resistance. He also argued that the German-led forced labor roundups should be stopped. Even Field Marshal Kesselring saw that it was unproductive. Although a further 360 men would be sent by train to labor camps in Germany, the focus was increasingly on the Jewish population.

———

Early in the evening on October 15, Elena Di Porto from Trastevere, nicknamed *Elena la Matta* (crazy Helen), heard from her employer whose husband was a policeman that the Jews of Rome were to be rounded up. Dressed in black, she warned her friends in the Ghetto but few heeded her. That Friday, at 23:00, Montaldi Sternberg, a lawyer from Trieste, was arrested with his wife at the Hotel Vittoria on Via Campania, near the German headquarters on Via Veneto in Rome. Their only crime was that they were Jewish. It was a foretaste of what was to happen.

Besides residing in the ancient Ghetto, Jews lived all over Rome. Dannecker therefore divided the city into 26 zones and put the names and address of Jews known to be living in each zone into separate envelopes. Police squads would locate and round up those to be arrested. Squads of two or three men each were given trucks to transport the arrested Jews. Dannecker needed at least three companies for the roundup. A special SS-Police Regiment and two companies of the Order Police had recently arrived and they provided the troops. The men came from Company Three of the 20th SS-Police Regiment; Company 11 of the 12th SS-Police Regiment; and Company 5 of the 15th SS-Police Regiment. In all, 365 German police and SS men, including Dannecker's special Waffen SS team, were involved in the Rome-wide operation. No Italian police or military were involved. These men surrounded the Ghetto while others spread out across the rest of the city; especially across the Tiber in Trastevere.

Many men living in the Ghetto got up early to stand in line to buy cigarettes. It had been announced that a rare allotment of them was to be available for sale on that day. Their habit was to save them. Before 05:00 on Saturday, October 16, the streets in and out of the Ghetto were suddenly sealed and the entire area encircled by Germans.[*] A half hour later, a non-Jewish bar owner on Via del Portico d'Ottavia, the Ghetto's main street, who was preparing to open for the day, watched as two columns of Dannecker's force marched in on either side of the street.

So began the roundup of Rome's Jews, a *rastrellamento*.[†] In the Ghetto, whole families, some in their night clothes, were lined up along Via della Reginella, where it crosses the Via del Portico d'Ottavia, in front of a building that now houses a museum to the memory of Rome's Jews. There, Jews were made to wait for the German trucks that would take them to a holding area.[‡] When Germans knocked on each door, they handed the head of the family a note, in Italian, which read:

1 You and your family and all other Jews belonging to your household are to be transferred
2 You are to bring with you
  a Food for at least eight days
  b Ration books
  c Identity card
  d Drinking glasses
3 You may also bring
  a Small suitcase with personal effects, clothing, blankets
  b Money and jewelry
4 Close and lock the apartment/house. Take the key with you

---

[*] Streets blocked were Via del Tempio, Via del Progresso, Piazza delle Cinque Scole, Piazza Mattei, Via di Sant'Angelo in Pescheria, Via del Portico d'Ottavia, and Via del Teatro di Marcello.

[†] During the German occupation there were at least seven major roundups: October 7, 1943 (Carabinieri and labor); October 16, 1943 (Jews); January 31, 1944, in the central part of the city; February 3, 1944, at Saint Paul's; March 23, 1944, at Via Rasella; March 30, 1944, Quadraro quarter; and April 17, 1944, Quadraro quarter.

[‡] Next to the museum is a small excavated area six feet below street level with exposed ancient marbles. Some authors report that the Jews were made to descend into this area and wait for transportation. This is not true as this area was not excavated until after the war.

5 Invalids, even the severest cases, may not, for any reason, remain behind. There are infirmaries at the camp
6 Twenty minutes after presentation of this card, the family must be ready to depart

Regarding point number 4, later Dannecker had Wachsberger tell the Jews to surrender the keys to their apartments to the SS guards so they could collect food from their homes. Of course the real reason was to loot and ransack the now-abandoned homes.

Among those arrested were more than 200 children under the age of 15, and 190 men and women over 60. Since most of the working-age men were out buying cigarettes or had fled at the first sign of trouble, women outnumbered men two-to-one. It was thought that because the Germans were looking for men for labor gangs the women would be released. All were thrown into trucks, including children and invalids. Once emptied, the trucks returned shortly, which gave the impression that those taken were being held nearby.

The arrested Jews represented a cross section of society. In addition to laborers and second-hand-clothes sellers, there was an Italian admiral, Augusto Capon, a war invalid, who produced a personal letter from Mussolini, but it carried no weight. He was so feeble that he was carried off in a car. He was also the father-in-law of the eventual American atom bomb scientist, Enrico Fermi.

Alina Cavalieri, who had won a silver medal for nursing wounded Italian soldiers during World War I, was arrested. Also arrested was Lionello Alatri, whom we met previously, the owner of one of Rome's largest department stores and a member of the Jewish council. Even Elena la Matta, who had tried to warn others to flee, was taken.

The roundup was over by 14:00 with the arrest of 1,259 Jews comprising 689 women, 363 men, and 207 children; two individuals died shortly after they were taken.[7] They were taken by truck to the Military College (*Collegio Militare*) along the Tiber River, near the Regina Coeli Prison for sorting and screening. On the way, some of SS-Hauptsturmführer Dannecker's drivers, not knowing the most direct route, drove to Saint Peter's, which was less than a mile from the college. They stopped in front of the Vatican so the German soldiers could sightsee; the Jews remained locked in the backs of the trucks. That these trucks were close to the Basilica gave rise to the idea that

Pope Pius XII knew about the Jewish roundup since the trucks were under his very windows. There is no evidence other than this that the Pope knew about the trucks, where exactly they were parked, or who was trapped inside. Shortly after arriving at the Military College, a baby boy was born to 23-year-old Marcella Perugia and her husband Cesare di Veroli.

The scene in the college courtyard was one of incredible chaos. Babies cried and terrified parents tried to quiet them. No one knew what was going to happen to them. When a boy, taken to see a dentist, was returned after treatment, many were convinced that they were going to Germany to work and not to be killed. One man even went out a back door, bought cigarettes and returned. In spite of the injunction to bring food with them, little food had been brought to the college.

The Jews would spend two days in atrocious conditions in the college with minimal sanitation facilities. They were not loaded onto trains that day because officials at the Tiburtina railway station were busy preparing to ship 183 Italian military officers to Florence for the new Fascist Army.

Meanwhile, the sorting of prisoners continued. Non-Jews were to present themselves to the guards; the penalty for lying was death. Over the next two days, 237 non-Jews and some who were only partially Jewish were released. According to Kappler's after-action report those released included the children of mixed Jewish and Aryan marriages, Jewish spouses of Aryans, foreigners from neutral countries, illegal Aryan servants, and Italians who boarded in Jewish homes. Because SS deportation measures at the time did not apply to individuals in these categories, they were released at dawn the following day.[8] At least seven Jews also managed, by mistake, to be released as they had non-Jewish-sounding names. But the rest remained to be transported to the Reich. A Christian woman, refusing to abandon her tiny Jewish charge, remained. Legend has it that the Pope had arranged the release of the 237 prisoners from the college and issued the criteria, but Dannecker only followed the standing orders and Nazi regulations in releasing non- or half-Jews.

Word of the roundup spread quickly. Hearing of it, Princess Enza Pignatelli Aragona Cortes, one of the Pope's former students, called her friend, Gustav Wollenweber, a German diplomat assigned to the Holy See. She had no car, so asked him to take her to the Vatican to tell the Pope of the roundup. Because of her family's connections, she had an immediate audience with His Holiness, and she told Pius XII that Rome's Jews were being deported. He had not heard this news and promised to do what he could to stop the deportation. Author Susan Zuccotti, a historian of the role of the Pope during the Holocaust, wrote:

> [in the princess's] presence he made a telephone call ... There is no authoritative account of whom the pope called in the princess's presence, nor of what he said. Vatican Secretary of State Cardinal Luigi Maglione, however, recorded that he summoned Ambassador Ernst von Weizsäcker to a meeting that same day.[9]

Maglione claimed later that he had asked the ambassador to intervene in favor of those poor people. Fearful of a strong negative German reaction, Maglione left it up to Weizsäcker whether or not to report the conversation to Berlin. Maglione was apparently afraid of a veiled threat by the ambassador that he was thinking about the consequences for the papacy of such a communication. Apparently the conversation was not reported.[10]

Other German diplomats, worried that rounding up Rome's Jews would cause a riot and exacerbate problems for the city, developed a delicate stratagem. Albrecht (Teddy) von Kessel, of the German legation to the Holy See, and Gerhard Gumpert, the German Embassy's economic secretary responsible for obtaining Italian goods for Germany, decided to act. Gumpert was standing in for Consul Möllhausen who was in Fasano del Garda being reprimanded by Ambassador Rahn for using the word liquidated in his cable to Berlin.

They drafted a letter to General Rainer Stahl, German Stadtkommandant of Rome. Fearing that Hitler might retaliate against the Vatican were the letter to come directly from the Holy See, they decided that it should come instead from a German bishop. So, they arranged for Bishop Alois Hudal, an Austrian and the current rector of the German Catholic Church in Rome, Santa Maria dell'Anima, to sign and hand-deliver the letter to General Stahl. The letter ran as follows:

I must speak to you of a matter of great urgency. An Authoritative Vatican dignitary, who is close to the Holy Father, has just told me this morning that a series of arrests of Jews of Italian nationality has been initiated. In the interest of the good relations that have existed until now between the Vatican and the High Command of the German Armed Forces – above all thanks to the political wisdom and magnanimity of Your Excellency, which will one day go down in the history of Rome – I earnestly request that you order the immediate suspension of these arrests both in Rome and its environs. Otherwise, I fear that the Pope will take a position in public as being against this action, one which would undoubtedly be used by the anti-German propagandists as a weapon against us Germans.[11]

When he got the letter, Stahl called in Secretary Gumpert, who feigned surprise and then convinced the general, since it was now a diplomatic issue, to let him route the letter to Berlin.

Again, nothing happened. The deportation moved ahead. And after two days of interminable waiting, on the morning of October 18, the Jews were herded aboard black German military trucks and moved to the previously bombed Tiburtina railway station in the eastern part of the city. There they were sealed into 18 boxcars where they sat all morning and into the afternoon. Word of the transport from the Military College spread throughout the city and quickly relatives and friends crowded around the cars to speak with the prisoners through the sealed doors.

Lionello Alatri, the man who had informed Father Benedetto of the arrival of the Jews from France, was anxious to tie up loose business ends and so he wrote a detailed note and squeezed it through a hole in his boxcar, hoping that it would be found by someone and delivered. A railway employee did in fact find the note and subsequently delivered it:

We are going to Germany; my wife, my father-in-law, Anita and me! Notify our traveling salesman Mieli. Give 600 lire to my *portiere* at the end of every month and 250 lire to Irma, whom you must also reimburse for the gas and electric bills ... I don't know whether the merchandise will remain requisitioned. If we will be able to sell it, remember that the prices in the first block must be sold proportionately to the type of merchandise. If you can make currency exchanges at the Bank of Sicily, do so ... We face our departure with fortitude, though of course the presence of my father-in-law in his poor condition alarms me. Try to be brave, as we ourselves are. I embrace you all. Lionello ...

PS. Tell the baron that Ettore and Elda and her cousin Lella are with us. Tell sales representative Ricciardelli that his wife and children are with us and fine. Tell Buccellato that Vito of Via Flavia is with us and fine. Notify the *portiere* at Via Po, no 42 that his sister and sister-in-law [are] with us and fine. Notify *portiere* Via Po 162 Lello and Silvia [are] with us and fine. Notify *portiere* Via Vicenza 42 that the furrier is with us and fine. Notify *portiere* Corso Italia 106 the Di Veroli family [are] with us and fine. Raoul [is] with us and fine. Notify the *portiere* Via Sicilia 154 Clara [is] with us and fine.*[12]

The wife of one prisoner, Costanza Calò Sermoneta, returned to town on Monday morning to be shocked by the news that her husband and her five children were prisoners. Racing to Tiburtina Station, she ran along the 18 parked boxcars shouting her family's names. Recognizing a voice shouting back, she stopped and pleaded with the German guards to open the door to the boxcar. The car was unsealed and she struggled aboard. Although two of the men who survived the trip, Angelo and Isacco share the same last name of Sermoneta, it is not thought they were immediate family members of Costanza. Soon after 14:05 the cars began moving. On that train was a total of 1,022: 419 men and boys, 603 females of which 274 were younger than 15 years old.[13] Only 15 men and one woman would return.

Not knowing that Jews were on it, Allied aircraft attacked the train as it left Rome. A German guard was wounded, but the train rolled on and

---

*By October 23, 1943, most of the people mentioned in this note had been executed in the gas chambers at Auschwitz.

was not further threatened. Heading due north out of Rome, it passed through Florence and stopped at Padua. At the station, sympathetic Italians, hearing the prisoners crying out for water from inside the boxcars, pleaded with the German guards to give the prisoners much-needed water. The guards relented and the captives, a few at a time, were allowed to drink from a rail-side fountain. As the train pulled out, the guards neglected to lock one wagon door and it slid open. North of Padua, Lazzaro Sonnino jumped from the moving train and escaped. The door remained opened, but other prisoners refused to jump, fearing retaliation for those who remained. Three of the elderly died along the way.

Transiting the Reich, the train reached the infamous Auschwitz concentration camp in occupied Poland. At dawn, Dr. Josef Mengele, the notorious Nazi medical experimenter, arrived at the rail siding and, assisted by Wachsberger the Roman German-speaking Jew, made his selection. He divided the Jews into two groups. The first group consisted of 820 men, women, and children, including Wachsberger's wife and child. Mengele judged them unsuitable for work, put them on trucks and told them they were being sent to a rest camp. They were gassed that same day. After a mass incineration, only their hair and gold tooth fillings remained to mark their passage.

The second group of prisoners (201 in all: 154 men and 47 women), were walked to separate male and female work camps. Half of the men went to work in the coal mines of Jawiszowice in southern Poland, while 42 of them went to salvage bricks from the remains of the Warsaw Ghetto.* The Auschwitz log for October 23, 1943 records an official RSHA report giving the registration numbers of those admitted to the work camp, and notes that the rest were gassed. Kappler, ever the bureaucrat and policeman that he was, wrote an after-action report of the roundup. It read:

The behavior of the Italian people was clearly passive resistance which in some individual cases amounted to active resistance. In one

---

* Fifteen of the men in the second group lived to return to Rome. And a woman named Settimia Spizzichino survived Mengele's medical experiments and months of arduous labor. She was liberated when the Allies entered the Auschwitz death camp in April 1945. Still alive two days after being buried under a pile of corpses, she had been left there by the retreating guards. She believed she was spared to tell the story. She died at the age of 79.

case, for example, the police came upon the home of a Fascist in a blackshirt and with identity papers which without doubt had already been used one hour earlier in a Jewish home by someone claiming them as his own. As the German police were breaking into some homes, attempts to hide Jews were observed, and it is believed that in many cases they were successful. The anti-Semitic section of the population was nowhere to be seen during the action ... In no case was there any need to use firearms.[14]

For the Gestapo, the Roman Jewish problem was not yet over. For every Jew captured and sent to Auschwitz, 11 remained in the city desperately searching for hiding places. A very few, heeding warnings, had even left or hidden in the city before the roundup. Afterwards some found sanctuary in Roman churches, convents, monasteries, and other Catholic religious institutions, especially those near the Ghetto which threw open their doors to the refugees. Monsignor Montini directed at least two of the women-only convents to accept men so husbands and sons of the women could be hidden alongside them.

Of the estimated 200,000 to 300,000 people hiding from the Germans in Rome, about 10,500 were Jews. Most of the people in hiding were men eligible for deportation to work camps in Germany or on Kesselring's Italian defensive lines. Others were military officers fearing conscription into the new Fascist Army. Still others were known anti-fascists or political figures.

Vatican City housed at least 40 Jews, 15 of whom were baptized converts, many of whom worked at the Vatican Library. Other sources say that there were perhaps as many as 500 Jews living inside the Vatican but the smaller number is probably more realistic. Other Jews were enrolled in the Vatican's Palatine Guard, which provided security for churches and other church property across the city. The guard conferred honorary Vatican citizenship on all members which gave immunity and made them untouchable. From 1942 to the end of 1943, membership in the guard soared from 300 to over 4,000, not all of them Jews. It is not known who in the Vatican authorized this increased membership, but it would be surprising if the Pope was not aware of it.

From October until the liberation, Italian Fascists had rounded up and turned over to the Germans an additional 730 Roman Jews. These roundups increased after Pietro Caruso became Rome's Fascist Chief of Police on February 1, 1944 and ran the Questura, Rome's police headquarters. The 44-year-old Caruso, a Neapolitan, was a veteran of Mussolini's 1922 March on Rome and no newcomer to Fascist police activities. He was recommended to Mussolini by Interior Minister Buffarini-Guidi. He arrived in Rome with a list of 9,000 people to be arrested. According to Mother Mary, the American diarist nun, he was one of the original Fascists, dyed in the wool, burning to show what he could do. In January 1944, while he was head of the Questura in Verona, he witnessed the execution of Count Ciano and the others who had voted with Dino Grandi at the Fascist Gran Consul meeting on July 25, 1943 on Grandi's motion to oust Mussolini.*

Inexplicably, during the whole of the German occupation, the Gestapo never raided the Jewish Old People's Home across from the Fate Bene Fratelli Hospital on the Tiber Island. The hospital cared for Jewish patients, some of whom were not actually sick. These were identified as having K-Syndrome, a supposedly highly contagious disease which could be fatal, but was in fact an entirely fictitious disease. The ruse was created by one of the doctors, Giovanni Borromeo, who posted the symptoms, including severe coughing, in the hospital under the heading, *morbo di K* (K's disease). Of course the K stood for Kappler. It was claimed that 65 Jews suffering from *morbo di K* were saved in this manner.

For reasons that are unclear, David Panzieri, the acting head rabbi of Rome, was not arrested and was allowed to move about Rome. Panzieri replaced Isreal Zolli who was now in hiding inside the Vatican and as we have seen had a price on his head. He was often at the Fate Bene Fratelli Hospital visiting his sick congregation; but he knew the game. He served the whole city, comforting the sick, performing marriages and circumcisions.[15] After the first roundup he wrote to the Pope on October 17, begging for warm clothing for those about to be deported.[16] One morning in late April 1944, Fascist police came to see him in his apartment. While he dressed, his sister served them ersatz coffee. He prayed a last prayer, then went into the kitchen, but just as he entered, the Fascist police got up and quietly left. The Allies' arrival in Rome was

---

* Count Ciano, Emilio De Bono, Giovanni Marinelli, Luciano Gottardi, and Carlo Pareschi were executed by firing squad at Verona on January 12, 1944. One of the seven judges who condemned to death the former members of the Fascist Grand Council was murdered and the others received miniature caskets, a death threat.

imminent and the Fascists, now needing to cover up any incriminating actions, saw no reason to persist in killing Jews.

Remarkably, for a long time the Gestapo seemed unaware that Jews from France were living in the city. Father Maria Benedetto conducted DELASEM activities out of the monastery of the International Capuchin College on Via Sicilia. He helped others as well: non-Jewish refugees, ex-Allied POWs, political dissidents, and Italian draft dodgers. Hundreds came to the monastery every day to pick up food and clothing. The monastery guarded against Gestapo raids by not housing refugees at the college itself.

By early November, Father Benedetto saw that the Jewish refugees needed false documents, especially ration cards, so they could buy food. An ancient hand-operated printing press that Benedetto remembered using as a student was recovered from the bowels of the building. One refugee was a printer and he went to work making fake identity and ration cards. A quantity of blank official forms was obtained by a sympathetic Italian official. The cards identified the bearer as a foreigner but with permission to reside in Rome. To be accepted, French documents were needed, complete with official government tax stamps. Authentic French tax stamps were not available but French postage stamps would do. Stamp collectors provided these and so the forms were filled out, photographs and postage stamps affixed.

In order to protect the refugees, Father Benedetto set up the Refugee Assistance Committee (CAP – *Comitato Assistenza Profughi*) which issued identity documents certifying, in German and Italian, that the named individual was under the protection of CAP, the Swiss Consulate, and the International Red Cross. Father Benedetto had someone at the Vatican issue a separate document certifying that the CAP document was authentic. Each refugee was thus armed with a number of impressive documents that stood up under all but the most exacting review. And none of these documents mentioned that the bearer was Jewish.

Father Benedetto's support came from a reliable source of funding, Tittmann, who had requested relief funds from the American Jewish Joint Distribution Committee (the Joint), in New York. The Joint provided relief funds to Jews all over Europe whenever possible. It was originally founded in 1914 to assist Jews living in Palestine then under Turkish rule.*

Funds were granted and, on January 7, 1944, Tittmann was notified via diplomatic pouch from Switzerland that $20,000 had been deposited in a New York Bank for Benedetto's use. The funds were transferred to a London bank and Italian bankers were easily convinced by Tittmann to loan lire on promise of repayment in dollars after Rome was liberated. As lire continued to lose value, bankers and other wealthy Italians were becoming increasingly happy to loan lire for repayment in dollars or pounds sterling.

Father Benedetto met with Tittmann and Sir D'Arcy and they told him the money would be passed on to him by Monsignor Joseph Hérissé, a French priest at the Vatican. Every two weeks Benedetto received $500 in lire in cash. No more could be given as by then the package of cash became too large to be concealed.

March 1944 was a turning point for Rome and Italy. Unknown informers for the Gestapo had certainly reported on Father Benedetto's activities and the Germans realized the Hotel Salus was being used as a refuge for Jews. A raid took place on March 1, but protests from François de Vial, Vice Consul, French, Embassy to the Holy See, claimed that those arrested were French and they were released. Nevertheless, the Gestapo crackdown on the French refugees continued. Many of the refugees were not even French but had originally fled to France in the late 1930s from Eastern Europe. Approximately 500 of them now styled themselves as Hungarian refugees, not too much of a stretch since many originally had been born in the old Austro-Hungarian Empire. In response, the Gestapo conducted a raid to round up refugees with Hungarian documents, documents that had been issued by a sympathetic embassy official. When the raid started, the Hungarian Consul General, Viktor Szasz, was summoned. Unfazed he threatened reprisals against Italians residing in Hungary if his citizens were taken away.

Supporting the refugees had become expensive: 2,400 lire a month for a single refugee. By April, with Father Benedetto feeding and

*The Joint continues its work today in Israel as well as in more than 70 other countries, assisting in the rescues of Jews and providing other aid.

134

supplying approximately 2,500 Jews, he urgently needed more money. DELASEM funds had been deposited in Genoa with the local cardinal, Pietro Boetto, but Father Benedetto needed a way to get to Genoa. A friend in the French Red Cross knew an Italian Africa Policeman (PAI) who agreed to drive Father Benedetto and Stefan Schwamm, the Jewish lawyer from Vienna who had been assisting the priest, in a PAI car to Milan, a distance of more than 350 miles. It was a journey fraught with dangers and it was unclear whether Schwamm's papers identifying him as a French member of the Red Cross would hold up.

They made it safely to Milan but the Gestapo arrested Schwamm while he and Father Benedetto were having dinner on April 17 at a Milanese trattoria. Schwamm and his friend and colleague Aaron Kasztersztein, who had arrived in Rome with Schwamm, had been denounced by his two roommates at the Pension Amalfi in Rome. Escaping arrest, Father Benedetto journeyed on to Genoa, where he received a million lire for the Jews under his care. Returning to Rome with the money, he found that he too had been denounced and was forced into hiding.

Later that May, an additional $100,000 was made available through British banks, but it was difficult to transfer since even a small amount made a very large bundle of bills. By the liberation of Rome, only $36,000 had been paid out.[17] After his capture in Milan, Schwamm was sent to Germany but his eight-year-old daughter was taken to live in the Vatican with Vice Consul and Second Secretary François de Vial of the French Embassy until the liberation. It is not known if Schwamm survived.

7

The Vatican Nest of Spies

Tension between the papacy and the Italian government had its roots in the *Risorgimento* when King Vittorio Emanuele II made Rome the capital of a unified Italy in 1871. At that time, the Pope lost temporal authority over Rome and much of surrounding central Italy and moved inside the walls of Vatican City. Mussolini, early in his tenure, worked hard to resolve political issues with the Catholic Church as one way to unify the country behind him. On February 12, 1929, the Italian State and the Vatican signed a concordat, the Lateran Treaty, to resolve their differences.*

As part of the agreement, Mussolini appointed Catholic chaplains to Fascist militia units, paid the clergy a salary, and rebuilt churches. Mussolini also made Catholic education compulsory in both public and private schools, although Jews were excused, and gave the church civil power over marriages. He hoped that by supporting the church, the church would support him and he was right. Pope Pius XI called Mussolini a man sent by Providence. Although Italian Catholics represented a wide political spectrum from Fascism to communism, Pius XI urged them all to vote for Mussolini.

As part of the Lateran Treaty, Vatican City, including Saint Peter's, was recognized as an independent sovereign state. Vatican City covers only 108 acres and is home to the Pope, other clergy, police, and maintenance workers; in all, some 500 people. Those people who live and work there are called the San Pietrini (the little Saint Peters).

---

* It was not until 1984 that a new concordat was signed under which Roman Catholicism ceased to be the state religion of Italy.

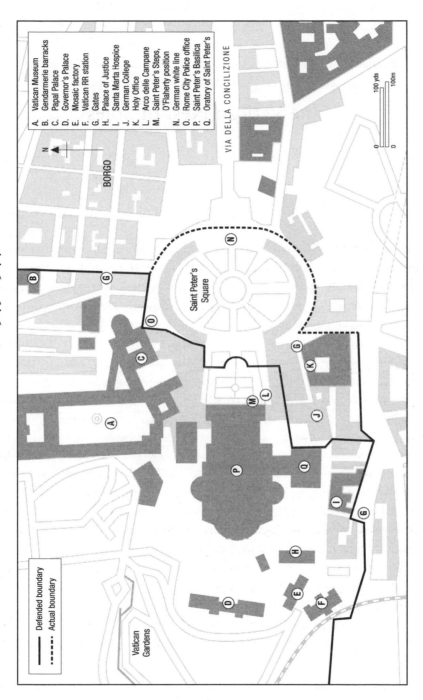

VATICAN CITY, 1943/1944

A. Vatican Museum
B. Gendarmerie barracks
C. Papal Palace
D. Governor's Palace
E. Mosaic factory
F. Vatican RR station
G. Gates
H. Palace of Justice
I. Santa Marta Hospice
J. German College
K. Holy Office
L. Arco delle Campane
M. Saint Peter's Steps,
O'Flaherty position
N. German white line
O. Rome City Police office
P. Saint Peter's Basilica
Q. Oratory of Saint Peter's

N

BORGO

Saint Peter's Square

VIA DELLA CONCILIZIONE

100 yds
100m

Vatican Gardens

Defended boundary
Actual boundary

Interestingly, the treaty authorized Rome police to guard and patrol Saint Peter's Square up to the steps of the Basilica; but the border, as is the case today, is at the end of the columns. During the German occupation neither German nor Italian police crossed that line.

In compensation for its lost secular properties, including the Quirinal Palace, the Pope's sprawling central Rome palace, Mussolini paid the Vatican the equivalent of 85 million US dollars in Italian government bonds which became worthless after the war. Outside the Vatican proper, the Holy See retained temporal control over many of their properties, including the large basilicas of Saint Mary Major (*Santa Maria Maggiore*), Saint Paul Outside the Walls (*San Paolo Fuori le Mura*), and Saint John Lateran (*San Giovanni Laterano*). These and other properties were considered extraterritorial; although outside the physical territory of the Vatican, they were treated as though they were within Vatican City. The Pope's summer residence at Castel Gandolfo in the Alban Hills was also extraterritorial. During the German occupation, signs posted outside the entrances to these properties stated, in German and Italian: Property of the Holy See, Extraterritorial Zone. This meant that it was off limits to German and Fascist authorities and could not be legitimately searched or entered for non-religious purposes. A Vatican Palatine Guard policeman stationed at the entrance ensured that the extraterritoriality was honored and, with a few exceptions discussed later, it was.

Other religious houses owned by the Vatican did not have extraterritorial status. They were however declared free from expropriation, which only meant that they could not be taken over by the government and remained Vatican owned. Each of these houses held a document signed by both Vatican and Italian authorities that it was not to be searched; however, these documents were not always honored by the Germans or Fascist authorities. The many other Catholic churches and religious institutions throughout Rome and not owned by the Vatican were not exempt from expropriation and could be searched. Many of these religious properties offered refuge to Italians, Jews, foreigners, and Allied servicemen in large numbers and under great danger.*

The temporal ruler of the Vatican was, of course, the Pope. Eugenio Maria Giuseppe Giovanni Pacelli was elected Pope on March 2, 1939.

---

* Appendix D: Vatican Extraterritoriality and Expropriation provides a listing of these properties.

The new pontiff took office as Europe was descending into another horrific conflict. To honor his immediate predecessor, Pius XI, he took the name of Pius XII. Prior to becoming Pope, Pacelli had an extensive international career with the Vatican Diplomatic Corps, including serving as the Apostolic Nuncio to Germany between 1917 and 1929. During that time, he had witnessed firsthand the disastrous economic effects of the Versailles Treaty on the German people and the subsequent rise of the Nazi Party.

Given the communist disturbances he observed in German streets, Pacelli also feared the rise of Godless communism in Europe. When he was elected Pope, the Nazi regime was pleased, thinking he would naturally be sympathetic to Germany.

In 1933, as Cardinal Secretary of State, Pacelli had worked on many treaties with European and Latin American nations; most notable was his work on the *Reichskonkordat* (Government Agreement) between the Vatican and Nazi Germany. The treaty guaranteed the rights of the Roman Catholic Church and, in return, when German bishops assumed their positions, they were required to pledge an oath of loyalty to the president of the German Reich. Further the agreement stipulated that clergy could not work for political parties. Most historians believe that the Vatican was trying to protect the German Catholic Church against Hitler's attempt to destroy what he called political Catholicism. Others claim that the *Reichskonkordat* gave legitimacy to the Nazi regime.

In the fall of 1936, while still a cardinal, Pacelli had traveled to the United States where he was greeted by large and enthusiastic crowds. He met with President Roosevelt and was royally entertained by prominent American Catholics who showered him with hospitality and gifts. These gifts included $113,000, which Pacelli had the auxiliary bishop of Boston, Francis Joseph Spellman, later a well-known American cardinal, manage for him. In addition, a wealthy American, Mrs. Nicholas Brady, who died shortly after the visit, left Cardinal Pacelli the sum of $100,000 in her will. During the war the Pope would put these funds to use for relief work.*

---

*An interesting side point is that, at the start of the war, the Vatican requested that the United States hold its gold reserves. The US Treasury agreed and on May 22, 1940, took charge of gold bars valued at $7,655,000. One portion of gold was not placed in the account, but was sold for dollars. The sum transferred consisted of nearly all the Vatican reserve. See Chadwick, p. 117.

Nazi violations occurred almost immediately after the signing of the *Reichskonkordat* and continued through the prewar period. The results were frequent protests from the Holy See, which culminated in Pope Pius XI's encyclical *Mit brennender Sorge* (With Burning Anxiety). This encyclical criticized German violations of the 1933 concordat with the Vatican about religious tolerance and Germany's preoccupation with race and state loyalty. It was read in German Catholic churches on Palm Sunday 1937. Not all Roman Catholic bishops were anti-Nazi. Bishop Alois Hudal was an Austrian, a devotee of Adolf Hitler as well as a committed anti-communist and anti-Semite. In 1937 he wrote a book called *The Foundations of National Socialism* in which he praised Hitler and indirectly attacked Vatican policies. This book was one of the reasons the Pope had published *Mit brennender Sorge*.

According to Father Bob Grant, Saint Ambrose University, Iowa, at the time of his death on February 10, 1939, Pius XI was also working on an encyclical condemning anti-Semitism. It is the so-called hidden encyclical, the *Humani Generis Unitas* and was sadly left unfinished. On October 20, 1939 Pacelli, now Pope Pius XII, borrowed from it in a *Summi Pontificatus*. In it the Pope had expressed the church's dismay over the invasion of Poland.

At the time of Pacelli's election in March 1939, the Vatican had diplomatic or other representation in 72 nations and 38 countries had diplomats accredited to the Holy See. The British delegation was headed by an ambassador already discussed in this book: Sir Francis D'Arcy Godolphin Osborne. Sir D'Arcy, as he preferred to be called, arrived in Rome as ambassador in February 1937. A descendant of the first Duke of Marlborough and a determined bachelor, he was old-style British diplomacy, elegant, suave, and with fastidious tastes. He was the driving, but usually unacknowledged, force behind what eventually became known as the Rome Escape Line, the underground Allied organization that sustained more than 4,000 escaped Allied soldiers all across Italy during the German occupation (more about this in Chapter 8).

Although a Protestant, Sir D'Arcy nevertheless had an excellent relationship with Pius XI and later developed an even closer relationship and friendship with his successor, Pope Pius XII. One of the things that endeared him to the new Pope was that Sir D'Arcy supplied him with a daily news transcript from the evening BBC broadcast. It was the only non-fascist news that reached the ears of the Pope until liberation.

On January 12, 1940, Sir D'Arcy discussed with the Pope what might happen in the event Italy declared war against Britain, which seemed highly likely. During this private audience:

> Pius XII said that he had received the visit of a German representing certain German Army chiefs. The Pope said that he knew the names of the generals but preferred not to tell Osborne [D'Arcy]. They sent a message as follows: a violent offensive was planned in the west, in the month of February, and using Holland as a route. This offensive need never happen. If the German generals could be assured of an honourable peace which would not be Wilsonian in nature [i.e. not like the Versailles Treaty, hostile to Germany], they would overthrow Hitler and negotiate a reasonable settlement in Eastern Europe – which would restore Poland and Czecho-Slovakia but keep the union with Austria.[1]

Sir D'Arcy reported the conversation to London, writing that the German generals, in return for a peace treaty, were ready to stage a coup d'état to remove Hitler. But Sir D'Arcy was not exactly sure what was being offered. "They were being offered a Germany minus Hitler, it was true; but they were also being offered the Germany of the Munich settlement, and furthermore a Germany with its armies intact."[2] This was completely unacceptable to the British and Sir D'Arcy told the Pope that peace could come only if the German military was dismantled.

February 1940 passed but these warnings continued. On March 27, 1940 Sir D'Arcy had tea with Monsignor Kaas, a German prelate who was instrumental in brokering the *Reichskonkordat* between Germany and the Holy See. At this tea the monsignor informed Sir D'Arcy that the unidentified German generals mentioned above had put aside their plans for the time being:

> Kaas also said that the coming German offensive would be carried out with every form of horror, [including] microbes, and gas. Osborne doubted even Hitler's capacity to use microbes. Kaas was sure of it. Osborne thought that someone meant to curdle his blood. And Osborne was probably right. The Nazis were well capable of seeing

that Kaas received information about the coming terror, so that he would tell the Pope, who would tell the French and the British and lower their morale in face of the coming onslaught.[3]

But was there still a way out of conflict? When war broke out, the Pope had expressed the church's dismay over the invasion of Poland in the *Summi Pontificatus*, mentioned above. Now he believed that an invasion of the Netherlands could be averted if peace were made with Britain.

In early May 1940, SIM intercepted a cable to the Vatican Nuncio in Belgium that a German attack on that country was imminent. Who passed this information to the Pope is not known, but there were suspects. This information was passed to Mussolini who, it was said, was incredulous that Hitler would not have informed him about the invasion.

It is time to speak in more detail of someone we have also discussed above: Mr. Harold H. Tittmann, Jr. Tittmann had been a 1916 graduate of Yale University. With America's entry into the war, he enlisted in the fledgling US Army Air Service. He was assigned to American Ace Eddie Rickenbacker's 94th Aero Squadron, perhaps the most well-known American air pursuit squadron of World War I. Its mission was straightforward: to clear German aircraft from the skies. The squadron's logo, Uncle Sam's red, white, and blue top hat tossed inside a ring, and the squadron's motto, "our hat is in the ring," proclaimed that America had entered the war.

In July 1918, Tittmann was set upon by five German aircraft, one of which he shot down. His aircraft riddled with bullets and himself severely wounded, he was barely able to fly back to the French lines to crash land in a wheat field. He was a long way from his aerodrome but against the odds he survived.

Tittmann spent two years in Army hospitals; first in France and later in the United States. He was the most severely injured American aviator to survive wounds received during World War I. He lost his right leg, a kidney, and half of one lung. He also suffered major bone damage to both his arms and his left leg. For the rest of his life he would walk with difficulty and often had to rely on a cane. He was decorated for bravery by both the French and American governments. Helped by his connections from Yale and his status as a distinguished war veteran, he was accepted into the US Foreign Service in 1920. First sent to the American Embassy in Paris, he was later assigned to the American Embassy in Rome, where he remained for 11 years. By 1939 Tittmann was the US Consul General in Geneva, Switzerland, but he would soon return to Rome with new duties at the Vatican.

In the 1930s, the United States had no direct representative to the Vatican. President Roosevelt, observing Mussolini moving closer to Hitler, needed to know what the Pope had to say about unfolding events; he needed his own direct channel to the Pope. Politically, Roosevelt could not appoint an ambassador to the Holy See because Americans were suspect of Catholic influence in the still largely Protestant country. His solution was to appoint Myron Taylor as his personal representative. Taylor, an Episcopalian and president of the United States Steel Corporation, was interested in the contribution that churches and churchmen made in what he called the moral order of the nation. He served without salary; and, as he owned property near Florence, he knew Italy. As Roosevelt's personal representative and not an ambassador, Taylor was exempt from all diplomatic niceties and did not require US Senate approval. Further, he could come and go as he and the president saw fit.

Since Myron Taylor did not live in Rome, the US State Department in February 1940 assigned Tittmann, still in Geneva, as Taylor's part-time assistant. If an assistant had come from the local US Embassy staff it would have been perceived as an official, diplomatic representative. In his new capacity, Tittmann was required to travel to Rome for Taylor's visits to the Vatican whenever the need arose. During one trip, between May 27 and June 23, 1940, Taylor had seven meetings with the Pope to convince him to use his influence with the Italian government to get Italy to remain neutral. The Pope tried but his pleas to Mussolini fell on deaf ears.

What Sir D'Arcy had feared finally happened on June 10, 1940, when Italy declared war on Britain and France. What prompted Mussolini's declaration of war was the defeat of the British Expeditionary Force

(BEF) in France, notwithstanding the evacuation of 340,000 British and French troops from Dunkirk. Mussolini had waited until it seemed certain that the Nazis would defeat France and invade England.

Many in the Italian Armed Services were against Italy joining the war with Germany. They, including the Italian Foreign Minister Count Ciano, believed that Italy was ill-prepared. Nevertheless, according to the German Military Attaché in Rome, General Emil (Enno) von Rintelen, many of Italy's 855 military generals and admirals stood to gain financially from their heavy investments in war production and military procurement.

By 1939, General Rintelen's German Military Attaché office had over 125 personnel assigned. All of the staff came from Germany and there were no local employees except for the doorkeeper who was not allowed inside the building. The office was located at Via Conte Rosso 25, a block away from the German Embassy at Villa Wolkonsky.* He opined that those supplying the military were largely corrupt and thought only of personal gain. Supporting this assessment was an American, Peter Tompkins, later the OSS man in German-occupied Rome, who wrote:

> By producing shoddy supplies or charging for supplies that existed only on paper, easy profits could be made quickly. Contracts were given to firms with the highest bids. For their efforts, the generals were rewarded with town houses, villas by the sea, and expensive automobiles. In the SIM, the payoff was easier with contraband imports or money from secret funds.[4]

After war was declared, British, French, Polish, and Belgian diplomats to the Holy See were moved inside the Vatican. Sir D'Arcy recorded in his diary that he had been given 36-hours' notice to move. At first, all the diplomats lived together in a small two-story Pilgrim Hostel called the *palazzina* (little house). There the British delegation had four, tiny cell-like rooms without running water. Sir D'Arcy was accompanied in his exile by his butler, John May, Miss E. K. Tindall, the legation secretary, and Sir D'Arcy's terrier Jeremy. There were mice, flies, dust, and the place smelled wet and mildewed. Comforts were to come.

---

* Villa Wolkonsky is now the residence of the British Ambassador to Italy.

The *palazzina* was attached to the main Vatican guest house, the Hospice of Santa Marta, run by the Sisters of the Order of Saint Vincent de Paul. Shortly after the diplomats moved in, a team of Vatican workmen descended on the main five-story hospice palazzo for a complete makeover. They installed running water, kitchens, bathrooms, and new flooring. Ten days later, Sir D'Arcy moved from the *palazzina* to refurbished quarters in the main hospice. The apartment had a view over the city and the Vatican Gardens. Downsides were the incessant ringing of the bells of Saint Peter's and the fact that they were virtual prisoners.

The hospice opened onto a courtyard with a large statue of the Virgin and Child overlooking a fountain. The palazzo accommodated four diplomatic missions. Sir D'Arcy and his legation occupied the top floor. The French Ambassador to the Holy See, Leon Bérard, and his wife resided on the floor below. Although appointed by the Vichy government, Bérard was inside the Vatican because the Franco–Italian armistice of June 22, 1940 had ended military activities between the two countries but not the state of war. The Polish Ambassador to the Holy See was Casimir Papée and he lived on the floor below Bérard with his wife. Below Papée lived the French First Secretary to the Holy See, Jacques de Blesson. He was secretly pro-Allied and he and Bérard argued frequently about the Vichy regime. On the ground floor the sisters of Saint Vincent de Paul had their refectory and adjacent chapel. After the diplomats moved out of it, the adjacent *palazzina* was refurbished for possible new arrivals.

Living with Sir D'Arcy was his English butler, John May, a London-born Cockney, who acted as majordomo of Sir D'Arcy's household. The relationship was not always smooth. On March 30, 1940, Sir D'Arcy wrote in his diary: "Bad morning. Very worried over finance … then John [May] lost his temper and shouted at me which is intolerable."[5] It was not to be the only time that John May and Sir D'Arcy exchanged angry words. Nevertheless, Sir D'Arcy described him in his unpublished memoirs as extraordinarily capable. Soon his duties would extend far beyond that of an ordinary butler.

On April 21, 1941, Tittmann relinquished his post in Switzerland and moved permanently to Rome. Now Myron Taylor's full-time assistant, Tittmann kept him and the US State Department abreast of developments in the Vatican. Taylor again visited Rome for two weeks of meetings with the Pope on September 9, 1941. The threat of bombing Rome was ever present. In his first audience with Taylor, the Pope cited a British Bomber Command statement that it was ready to bomb the city. The Pope warned that if the Vatican and other church property were struck, there would be a formal protest. Taylor passed this message to Washington to request the British government confine its targets to military and communications centers in Italy. After his two weeks of meetings, Taylor returned to the United States, leaving Tittmann in charge.

Things were moving fast. Italy declared war on the United States, five days after the Japanese attack on Pearl Harbor, Hawaii on December 7, 1941. Public opinion in Italy was at odds with this; many Italians had family members living in America.

On December 16, Tittmann moved into the second floor of the renovated *palazzina* at the Santa Marta Hospice. The ground floor was occupied by Kosta Zoukitches, the head of the Yugoslav Legation, and his wife, Betsa. By the end of September 1942, 13 chiefs of mission were residing in various apartments inside the Vatican, including eight delegations from Latin America; Brazil, Bolivia, Colombia, Cuba, Ecuador, Peru, Venezuela, and Uruguay, and these delegations resided in the Palazzo del Tribunale at the entrance to the Vatican Gardens. They moved in during the spring of 1942. Later that year the Nationalist Chinese Minister, Dr. Cheou Kang Sie, joined them. And so, as the war closed other diplomatic channels, the Vatican became the de facto diplomatic center for the Allies reporting on Italy.

Now housekeeping had to be arranged. John May was indefatigable and exceptional at finding scarce items in wartime Rome so Sir D'Arcy asked him to also get supplies for Tittmann. John May procured linens, chairs, and kitchen utensils for the apartment. Tittmann's secretary, Miss Nicolina Flammia, also moved in; and, until the American diplomats were removed from Italy, she was escorted daily between the Vatican and the US Embassy to bring back supplies, furnishings, and gossip from the now interned American diplomats. Other furnishings came from Americans who had left behind household goods when they had to suddenly leave Rome at the outbreak of the war. That included the sterling silver service and library from the family of Peter Tompkins.[6]

Tittmann paid his expenses with lire he obtained through the Vatican Finance Office. The US State Department deposited $1,500.00 each month into the J. P. Morgan Bank of New York which transferred it into a Vatican bank account. At an official exchange rate of 19 lire to the US dollar the amount was 28,500 lire a month. By the end of the war, the black-market exchange rate for dollars had risen to five times that, but Tittmann used only the official rate since it was illegal for diplomats to exchange money on the black-market.

Rent was free, but three times a year the diplomats gave the sisters 1,000 lire (less than $50) to cover hospice administrative costs. In addition, Tittmann paid utilities and salaries: his staff consisted of his chauffeur, Umberto (due to his wartime injuries Tittman required a car for even the shortest trips inside the Vatican); a married couple, Fani, the butler, and Velia, the maid; and later a chef named Ianni. Food was the major expense as supplies became increasingly scarce and more expensive.

The Fascist Italian government, encouraged by the Germans, complained about this newest Vatican arrival. Tittmann's exact diplomatic status was unclear so he requested that President Roosevelt give him the title of United States Chargé d'Affaires, in lieu of the absent Presidential Special Representative. This office would not require establishing formal diplomatic relations between the Vatican and the United States, nor political approval in Washington. Eventually Tittmann became Sir D'Arcy's closest colleague and they lunched together most days.

With America now with the Allies, Italian support for the war shrank rapidly. Taking advantage of this, President Roosevelt sent Myron Taylor back to Rome to meet with the Pope. His mission was to see if the Pope could be persuaded to get Italy to leave the Axis. Mussolini approved the visit and on September 17, 1942, Taylor flew to Rome via Lisbon. Inside the Vatican, he stayed in the Tittmann apartment. The Pope met with Taylor three times during which he again insisted that the Allies not bomb Rome. This may have been motivated by recent large-scale RAF bombings of northern Italian cities. Taylor departed Rome on September 28 without having accomplished much.

Eventually Tittmann's family joined him inside the Vatican. In 1940, when Tittmann had first returned to Rome, his wife, Eleanor, remained in Geneva but would visit him from their home in Geneva as their sons, Harold (Harold Tittmann III) and Barclay, were enrolled at a Swiss boarding school. In the summer of 1943, Eleanor was in Rome and the boys, now 15 and 11, took the train from Switzerland by themselves for a holiday with their parents in Rome. Train stations along the way had been bombed; there were delays, but the boys arrived safely. Because the Allied attacks on railways were increasing, it was no longer safe for the boys to return to Switzerland. Their new life was inside the Vatican in the very heart of a country at war.

It was difficult for diplomats to communicate with their home countries. New protocols introduced new red tape. Tittmann, scrupulously following Vatican guidelines, did not code his messages, but delivered them to the Vatican Secretariat of State in envelopes which contained plain texts of confidential telegrams and written reports. Delivery was timed for the twice-a-week diplomatic pouch to the Apostolic Nuncio in the Swiss capital. Tittmann's documents would be passed to the American Embassy in Berne where staff would encode the telegrams and cable them to Washington. Written reports went by airmail or by surface means. Confidential communiqués from Washington were telegraphed in cipher to Berne where they were decoded, typed, and forwarded to Tittmann via the Vatican pouch. Written reports which did not have to be decoded were handled in the same way. On rare occasions, his correspondence was routed via the Papal Nuncio in Lisbon.[7]

The large Vatican diplomatic mail pouches were sealed with tamper-proof lead seals. These secured the correspondence from the Vatican to its Papal *Nunciatures*, top-level diplomatic missions, and legations throughout the world – or so they thought! In reality, the lead seals were often broken and the contents read by the Italian intelligence services and passed to the Germans.

For his first three months of confinement within the Vatican in 1940, Sir D'Arcy had almost no communications with London. The British Foreign Office had offered Sir D'Arcy a secret radio transceiver, but he had refused. The Vatican had clearly stipulated that diplomats limit their reporting solely to Vatican issues; having a radio would imply that he was sending other intelligence, thereby compromising his position. So Sir D'Arcy, like Tittmann, and the other interned diplomats, communicated with his home capital via the Vatican diplomatic pouch. Unlike Tittmann, Sir D'Arcy used a cipher with a daily changing code to encode his reports before delivering them to the Vatican Secretariat of State. It was a tedious process but it was his only option. All other types of communications – phone, telegraph, and radio – were subject to interception by SIM, and passed to the Fascist police and German intelligence. Realizing that all his communications were subject to being monitored, Sir D'Arcy felt restrained in what he felt he could say.

In late summer 1942, Sir D'Arcy was sent an assistant: a former British Foreign Service officer, Hugh Montgomery. Montgomery had served as a secretary at the British Legation to the Holy See when Sir D'Arcy arrived in 1936. He left the diplomatic service soon after to study for the priesthood. Asked to assist Sir D'Arcy, Montgomery returned to Rome on September 11, 1942. Since he was accredited to the Holy See, a neutral country, he was granted permission to enter Italy and proceed inside the Vatican. He had the great advantage of knowing Vatican officials from his prior assignment and he spoke fluent Italian. Montgomery took over the coding, and assisted by Miss Tindall, Sir D'Arcy's secretary, the pair double-coded all of their telegrams using two different ciphers to ensure security. Montgomery slept and worked in the British apartment but took his meals in the refectory downstairs. In his time off Montgomery continued his studies for the priesthood.

Remarkably, Mussolini allowed Sir D'Arcy to return to England for consultations and home leave between April 8 and June 18, 1943. He traveled in a commercial aircraft from Rome to Seville, Spain, then to Lisbon and finally on to London. Although it was a routine home leave, it was urgent for Sir D'Arcy to travel to England to discuss how to get Italy out of the war and see what part, if any, the Vatican could play. While in London, he was knighted by King George VI.

Sir D'Arcy returned to Rome with new secret code books which, shortly thereafter, Livio Moratti, his Italian footman, surreptitiously photographed while Sir D'Arcy was out for his usual afternoon walk. There was so much to photograph it had to be done over two days. Why did Moratti take this chance to betray them? Was it for revenge, as Hugh Montgomery later suspected? More probably, Livio was a SIM asset and passed the photographs to SIM in return for a deferment from the Italian Army. Montgomery later wrote that it was strange that he and the others in the apartment, May and Tindall, knew nothing of it.

It is not known how or when Sir D'Arcy discovered the treachery, but there is a hint that he knew about the theft six weeks after he returned from London. On July 30, 1943, Sir D'Arcy told Cardinal Maglione, the Vatican's Secretary of State, that he doubted that his telegrams were secure and he suspected that his Italian footman was a SIM agent.

Being a clever diplomat, Sir D'Arcy used this suspicion to his advantage. Now convinced that everything he sent from the Vatican was being read by SIM, Sir D'Arcy included occasional false information to befuddle the Italians. On August 17, he used his new cipher when sending two cables protesting the indiscriminate bombing of Italian cities by the Allies. He was certain that the cables were read by SIM.[8] He was right.

From the very beginning of Mussolini's rule, SIM had been interested in Vatican diplomatic activities. In the 1930s the cipher section of the Vatican Secretariat of State had been penetrated by SIM. In fact, after the war, SIM revealed it had reviewed all Vatican cable and mail traffic and it had recorded some 8,000 radiograms from a nearby military listening post at Fort Boccea, an Italian military prison. SIM decoded at least 3,000 of these cables. When Italy subsequently changed sides, many SIM officers pledged loyalty to the Badoglio regime and refused to work for the Germans and Fascists and so fewer cables were read.

After the armistice and only for his most urgent dispatches, Sir D'Arcy may have had access to an unidentified clandestine radio transmitter hidden somewhere inside the Vatican. It was likely controlled by pro-Badoglio SIM agents.

Plain-clothes papal gendarmes, the gendarmerie, closely watched the diplomats, recording visitors' names and how long they stayed. The gendarmes, approximately 100 men, were all Italian natives and often former members of the Rome police forces who stayed in touch with their former colleagues. They worked only inside Vatican City, wore blue uniforms with red piping, and were responsible for internal security and surveillance tasks. When outside the Vatican, they had no policing powers, had to be unarmed, and were required to wear civilian clothes. The gendarmes mistrusted both the Fascists and Germans and, although their name-gathering was intensive, little of significance was ever reported by them.

Espionage is a house of mirrors and Kappler's operation was its reflection. SS-Chief Heinrich Himmler called the Vatican "a nest of spies" and he charged Kappler to penetrate the Vatican and break up the nest. Kappler was to unmask pro-Allied activities and uncover any Vatican peace feelers. He complied and became convinced that Sir D'Arcy and Tittmann were collecting military intelligence so he intensified his efforts and employed a number of agents to monitor them.

As early as 1939, Kappler had recruited Alexander Kurtna, an Estonian agent working for the Soviets. Kurtna had studied for holy orders at the Pontifical Russian Institute (*Russicum*) which trained priests for missions to the Soviet Union. The *Russicum* was a Catholic college dedicated to studying the culture and spirituality of Russia. Doubting his priestly calling, Kurtna quit his studies, and obtained a position as a researcher at the Vatican Archives where he remained until its closing after the September armistice. Because of his frequent trips from Rome to the now Soviet-occupied Estonia, Kurtna had been recruited by Soviet Intelligence to send information on the Vatican.

It was about then that Kurtna became a classic double agent. He was hired by Dr. Ferdinand Bock, the director of the Rome-based German Historical Institute, one of the cover organizations for the Nazi spy network. The Institute employed Kurtna to provide information on church relations with Russia. Kurtna's chief contacts were Monsignor Montini, the Vatican's under-secretary of state; Monsignor Martin of the Vatican Library; and Cardinal Eugène Tisserant (a French Gaullist), the director for the *Russicum*. He was well paid for this at 10,000 lire a month but his reports were regarded as superficial. Bock and Kappler were close so Kappler used Kurtna to feed false information to the Soviets with Bock's blessing.

Kappler's growing network added another spy in 1943 when Berlin sent SS-Obersturmbannführer Georg Elling to Rome. Elling, who had studied in Rome for the priesthood, spoke Italian and read Latin. He had joined the SS in 1933. Arriving unannounced from Berlin in early November 1943, he was to have diplomatic cover and be assigned as an assistant to Baron von Weizsäcker. Initially working out of Kappler's office, he was described by Kappler as fairly efficient.

Elling was introduced to a group of sources, diplomats and ecclesiastics who had been recruited by SS-Hauptsturmführer Eugen Haas and by a German professor, Joseph Mayer. Among the agents he monitored were: a man named Engelhardt, a librarian in the Oriental Institute; SS-Sonderführer Dr. Peter Scheibert, a special art expert; Ivan Kovacevic, a Croatian medical student; and an Italian journalist named Dr. Guadagni. Elling found their information and reporting unsatisfactory and inexact.

That being the case, Elling teamed up with Dr. Ludwig Wemmer, another agent accredited to the German Embassy to the Holy See. Dr. Wemmer was listed as a Scientific Academic Collaborator and the special advisor to Baron von Weizsäcker. He may have been the first SS officer assigned to the German Embassy at the Vatican. He was thought to be a personal spy for Martin Bormann, who in 1941 had succeeded Rudolf Hess as the head of the Nazi Party chancellery.

Elling, with his knowledge of ecclesiastical matters, produced a daily report on the Vatican Newspaper *L'Osservatore Romano*. He also wrote papers on Vatican finances; Vatican relations with other countries, particularly the Soviet Union; the attitude of leading cardinals in regard to the European situation and Germany; and the efforts of the Roman Catholic Church to expand to the near east.

Seeking other ways to penetrate Vatican secrets, Kappler devised what was called the Georgian Cloister Plan. Sometime in early 1942, the RSHA learned that a Georgian widow had died in Belgium and left her estate to endow a Georgian Seminary in Rome. Berlin saw the espionage value in such a seminary. The idea was to recruit young men from the Soviet Republic of Georgia who would study at the proposed seminary in Rome. The seminarians would provide information on the Vatican while in Rome and later be sent to Georgia as trained Gestapo agents to foment anti-communist activities including the creation of a Gestapo-funded Georgian Nationalist Movement to destabilize the Soviet government.

The widow's legacy, although large, was not enough to purchase a suitable property, so the RSHA added money to the bequest. The total available for the project was now 1,200,000 lire. A somewhat naive Georgian priest, Father Michael Tarchnisvili, was chosen to head the seminary as spiritual advisor. He was to be assisted by a lay administrator, Basilius Sadathierascvili, an SS agent who had befriended Father Michael. By 1943, a suitable Roman house was found and, unbeknownst to the priest, two of its rooms were set aside for the SS to house a radio transmitter. Kappler had SS-Sturmbannführer Haas meet with the priest and explain that the extra money, coming from an anonymous benefactor, would be available if Father Michael would pass on any interesting information that he came across. The priest balked but eventually capitulated.

To establish the seminary, Father Michael was required to submit a plan to Pope Pius XII who approved it, and property was purchased. Basilius, who was given 50,000 lire, went to Berlin to pick up six Georgian recruits and return to Rome with them. Once there, it was obvious that three of the men were unsuited for the priesthood and they were dismissed immediately. Two others admitted that they only came for the food and easy living. The plan was not working.*

Intelligence also came from unexpected sources. In 1942 Washington received a remarkable offer from a high official in the Papal Secretariat who wondered if the US would be interested in receiving firsthand information on strategic bombing targets in Japan. Although not officially acknowledged, this official was likely Monsignor Montini as it is known that he was a point of contact for the OSS Italian Desk in Washington headed by Earl Brennen, formerly of the US Embassy Rome. This information could be obtained, it was said, by an unknown representative of the Holy See in Tokyo. The offer was accepted.

The information arriving from Tokyo to the Vatican was passed to Dr. T. J. Kiernan, the Irish Republic Chargé d'Affaires to the Holy See.

---

* By March 1944 all the money was spent, the house renovations unfinished, and the project in disarray. The sixth recruit turned out to be a captured Soviet soldier who, after liberation, was turned over to a displaced persons organization. For his role in the plot, Father Michael Tarchnisvili was imprisoned in the Regina Coeli Prison; eventually released, he ended his days working in the Vatican Library.

Kiernan sent the information to Dublin and then it was sent on to London where it was received by Ricardo Mazzerini, an Italian anti-fascist émigré who sat on the OSS's Italian desk. He then transmitted it to Washington, using a special naval code. Once in Washington it was analyzed by an ex-Italian Royal Air Force colonel who had served as the Air Attaché at the Italian Embassy in Japan. Although this route took a few days it reportedly provided Washington with vital Japanese intelligence in the spring of 1943. It is thought that neither Tittmann nor Sir D'Arcy knew about this information channel. The project was codenamed the Vessell Project.[9]

The Vatican–Japan connection yielded important humanitarian information as well. In May and June of 1943, the Apostolic Delegation in Washington informed the US government that Vatican representatives had, on three different occasions, visited American and British POWs as well as civilian internees in camps across Japan. Seeing the prisoners' need, the representatives distributed foodstuffs, books in English and games to the Allied POWs. Red Cross lists from Japan were sent to the Vatican by radiogram. Interested Americans were enjoined to contact the Apostolic Delegation in Washington to seek information about their loved ones. On July 20, 1943, Tittmann sent to the US State Department the first of several long lists of American POWs held by the Japanese. In August 1943, the Holy See sent $45,000 to the Apostolic Delegate in Japan to be used for the relief of POWs, both civilian and military. It is not known who provided this money, but it likely came through Tittmann and Sir D'Arcy. The two diplomats would soon be called on to help POWs much closer to home.

8

Unexpected, but Welcome Help

As a consequence of the way war unfolded in North Africa, the Axis partners took Allied soldiers prisoner in increasing numbers. Both Germany and Italy had been signatories of the July 27, 1929 Geneva Convention. This Convention mandated the humane treatment of prisoners of war. At one time a stigma was attached to being captured; the man had let his country and comrades down. But World War I battlefield realities changed that perception. Thousands of soldiers in the trenches had been surrounded or bombed by aircraft; being a POW was no longer a personal disgrace. British servicemen were taught that, if captured, they were to regard themselves as still in the fight and that their duty was to escape. Being a POW was like being assigned to a new unit.

By the terms of the Geneva Convention, although not specifically required, prisoners could give name, rank, and serial number. If they refused to give their captors any additional information nothing could be done to them. They were allowed to keep personal possessions including helmets and gas masks. Arms and other military equipment had to be surrendered as well as horses and military papers. They were to be placed in permanent camps away from the front which were required to be dry, warm, clean, and sanitary. Freedom of religion was granted. Rations were to be equal with the holding power and they were to be provided with adequate clothing. Officers were to salute their equals or superiors in rank; they were not required to work. Enlisted men could be made to work as long as it wasn't dangerous, warlike, or for excessively long hours. Prisoners could correspond with their families and receive mail including food, clothes, games, and books. Prisoners who escaped and were recaptured could be held in solitary confinement for no longer than 30 days.

The POW guards were not the worst of the German military machine; diehard Nazi zealots gravitated to the SS and the concentration camps. Often POW camp commanders were older, retired military officers brought back on active duty to administer these camps. International law dictated that evaders, those military men who had never been captured and who entered into neutral countries such as Switzerland and Sweden, were supposed to be interned until the end of hostilities. Escapees, those military men who successfully escaped from a prisoner of war camp, were free to move on from a neutral country to their home country where they could again take up arms. It was an important distinction. Knowing this, many evaders, primarily downed airmen, invented fake POW escape stories so they could be returned to active duty. Contact for the ex-POWs in neutral countries was through the appropriate Allied Military Attaché. If an evader was captured in enemy territory, in theory all he had to do was declare his service identity to be treated as a POW. Naturally this applied to recaptured POWs. No safeguards applied to those who helped escapees or evaders. In Italy this usually meant deportation to Germany, imprisonment, and sometimes execution.[1]

As the prisoner population in the Italian camps swelled, guards found it hard to control them. The prisoners planned and executed escapes, and a number of them were successful. One result was a growing population of escapees in Italy trying to survive in hostile environments. Military planners had anticipated this eventuality and had put into place training programs for personnel who might be captured and then would be duty-bound to escape.

Few at that time knew that British Secret Intelligence Services (SIS) had begun efforts to assist in the repatriation of ex-POWs. SIS's best-known intelligence branches are MI-5, which collects domestic intelligence, and MI-6, which collects foreign intelligence. On December 23, 1939, the SIS had created a new Military Intelligence branch called MI-9, the British Escape Service. MI-9 was to support the repatriation of British servicemen who had escaped prisoner of war camps or otherwise were trapped in enemy-held territory. The active arm of MI-9 was given the cover name "A" Force. The force's missions in regards to escapees were:

a. To facilitate the escape of British POWs and return them to combat while making the enemy use manpower to act as prison guards
b. To maintain the morale of British prisoners of war in enemy prison camps
c. To debrief, collect and distribute intelligence obtained from escapees
d. To assist in the denial of intelligence to the enemy

All servicemen were given some basic instruction about what to do if captured, but unknown to most servicemen was that "A" Force, relying on World War I experiences, had set up five sections, christened B, D, X, Y, and Z, to solve different aspects of the problem.

Section B was responsible for liaison with other sections, branches, and services and the debriefing of returned servicemen. Escaped POWs and evaders could bring much intelligence back to friendly forces so all servicemen were trained to make mental notes of useful enemy information. Under no circumstances should they write information down for then they could be considered spies, and if caught with notes, they could be executed by the enemy.

Most ex-POWs or evaders who made it back to Allied lines were debriefed in theater by "A" Force officers. When intelligence was of high value, servicemen were flown to Section B in London for extensive debriefing before being reunited with their families.

Evasion training, Section D, was a high priority for "A" Force. The training provided information about escape services to a smaller section of British soldiers and airmen. Instruction booklets were produced and circulated outlining how to look like a national. For example, the French booklet told escapees in France to affect a tired slouch, to collect a bicycle, never to wear a wrist watch, to sling haversacks over the shoulder in the French manner, never to carry a walking stick, like the British, to get rid of army boots, to stay clean shaven, like the French, and to wear a beret. Men were told that village priests were likely to be helpful, which was true in both France and Italy.

Within every POW camp there was a hierarchy among the prisoners. The Senior British Officer (SBO) or the Senior American Officer (SAO) in each POW camp was responsible for the men as well as the planning and organizing of escape attempts. They were given guidance by Section X which directed the SBO to appoint officers and men to escape committees. An escape committee coordinated attempts to prevent one breakout from interfering with another. When all preparations were ready, the exact timing of escapes was based on cloud cover, weather conditions, time of year, and other factors.

The escape committee had to find the resources for those attempting escape; scrounging civilian clothes, obtaining money, and fabricating false documents. Communication was essential and the radio was the key to providing the SBO, the escape committee, and the men imprisoned with vital outside information. By the time of the Italian armistice, each camp in Italy had at least one clandestine radio receiver, often something improvised from rudimentary parts. Usually there were no radio transmitters because these active devices could be more easily discovered by the authorities.

"A" Force realized that not all servicemen had the psychological profiles necessary to escape. Successful escapees were men who were contrary, enterprising, adventuresome, and quick-witted. They were ready to take calculated risks and made decisions quickly. These individuals were not afraid to try something and they relied on luck. Others, willing to assist escapees, were more methodical and better suited for helping the risk-takers in the meticulous tasks of fabricating disguises, forging passes, and copying maps.

Escape-planning relied on acknowledging both of these personalities. Language proved to be a minor obstacle for those on the run. The Third Reich was so full of foreign laborers and other displaced persons that tram conductors and booking-office clerks took little notice of civilians with rough accents or imperfect command of German or Italian grammar and vocabulary. It would have been dangerous, however, to pretend to be a German soldier.

Getting information into the POW camps was difficult. To solve this problem, a simple system was developed in which code words would be embedded in letters sent to prisoners by fictitious relatives. The British "A" Force, Section Y, and its equivalent American MIS-X (see below), distributed unique codes to selected servicemen; these codes gave the men an innocent way of communicating with intelligence officers by using specific words or phrases in letters to and from fake family members.

British Major Guy Weymouth described how sensitive information was sent back and forth between "A" Force and the prisoners. In his book, *A.W.O.L.: In an Italian Prison Camp and Subsequent Adventures on the Run in Italy, 1943–1944*, Weymouth wrote:

> One interesting thing which exercised me quite a lot during my time in Capua [in 1943, POW Camp #66 was located north of Naples] was the sending of coded messages in the weekly letters to my parents. It was like this: whilst my battalion was in Scotland, two or three officers, including myself, were summoned to Brigade Headquarters and, in an atmosphere of strict confidentiality, were coached by the Intelligence Officer in the use of a simple code which could be employed in case any of us were taken prisoner, to send information about the enemy to Military Intelligence at the War Office. All letters sent home by a POW who was registered as "being in the know" would be intercepted by the Ministry's Intelligence staff before being forwarded, the recipient being completely unaware of any subterfuge.[2]

When an escape plan succeeded in freeing one or more men, they then had to evade recapture and survive. "A" Force's Section Z was charged with the development of escape tools such as magnetized razors which could be used as a compass, wire saws, and a small, easily concealed knife. In that time before the X-raying of packages was widespread, items were sent and distributed to POW camps in relief parcels. Maps were printed on easily concealed silk cloth and hidden in books and often board games. Specially made British versions of the board game Monopoly for example had silk maps and very flat tools inserted inside the playing board and sandwiched among the Monopoly money was actual currency. These special sets were marked with a dot in the No Parking square.

When "A" Force had gathered the names and locations of certain, pre-selected prisoners in a POW camp, Section Z would ship its special relief packages, meaning packages containing these escape materials. In 1941–1942, for example, 142 packages described as special, with escape equipment hidden inside, were sent. Also sent were 5,173 ordinary packages containing tobacco, useful for trade and barter. "A" Force's packages, appropriately postmarked, were sent under the aegis of sham organizations such as the Prisoners' Leisure Hours Fund, or by fake relatives. And local newspapers were used as packing material, thus sending news to the troops. In contrast, Red Cross parcels were never used to send escape equipment.

Section Z also developed a special kit for airmen in a small box to be carried in flight suits. It contained malted milk tablets, hard candies (boiled sweets), a bar of plain chocolate, matches, Benzedrine tablets for energy, Halazone tablets for purifying water, a water bottle, a magnetized razor, soap, needle and thread, and a fishing line. In theory, an air crewman could live for 48 hours on what was in the package. Occasionally aircrews refused to fly if the kits were not available.

The US counterpart to "A" Force was the Military Intelligence Service X (MIS-X), based on the British model, and set up by the OSS to deal with escape and evasion work. It has been described as the most secret component of US Military Intelligence during World War II. In February 1944, MIS-X produced a manual on Evasion, Escape, and Survival. Section C covered Italy and validated what the escapees in this book described as the conditions in Italy at this time. Not all US senior military officers wanted their troops to be briefed on activities to repatriate them. US General George S. Patton for one was no fan of such training until his son-in-law, John K. Waters, was taken prisoner in Tunisia.

Ignorance of current Italian history and of Fascism hampered the British in their work. Few British officers spoke Italian and they had trouble with the nuances of various political and partisan groups. Also, the British were in support of the Italian military, the king and Marshal Badoglio, and this was a point of contention with many of the left-leaning partisans (see Chapter 12).

Italian-Americans were recruited to work for the OSS and they resolved not to get involved in internal politics. For their part, the Italians seemed to prefer to work with the Americans since Italian-Americans spoke at least a dialect of their language. However, many of the Italian-Americans also had family connections with Sicily and so some Italians mistrusted them because of fancied, or real, Mafia connections.

After the declaration of the armistice, many Italian POW camp guards, like the soldiers servicing in regular units, simply walked away from their posts. Acting on orders from the British Eighth Army, the SBOs ordered that the men be restricted to their camps. All were sure that they would soon be liberated by the Allied troops, now landing in mainland Italy. Although these men were highly skilled and the Allies were eager to return them to active service, the order to remain in the camps was given as the military value of prisoners acting as improvised armed units was judged to be low: they had not trained together; there was a lack of weapons; and many POWs were not infantrymen but service personnel or aircrew. General Montgomery did not want the POWs sabotaging bridges or infrastructure that he needed to use to move his army north. Despite the order, as many as 50,000 POWs, following their Italian guards, walked away from their POW camps when they heard that British forces had landed at Salerno.

Allied escaped POWs now loose in Italy's cities and countryside had scant knowledge of the support systems which had been put in place for them and their daily reality was chaos. Active "A" Force repatriation activities were underway by September 23, directed by a British officer named Colonel Head. "A" Force personnel were usually drawn from British Airborne troops or other special forces and they divided Italy into two sectors. The first sector conducted repatriation activities within 50 miles of the front lines; the second operated further north.

The northern "A" Force Section component became operational on October 2, 1943. It was called SIMCOL, an anagram for Lt. Col. A. C. Simonds. It operated 50 miles north of the front lines and agents either parachuted in or were landed by boat along the coast. During the first year of operation, SIMCOL inserted nine teams. The teams carried suitcase-sized radios for communications and set up rat lines to bring escaped prisoners to Bari, primarily by sea, to rejoin Allied forces. A rat line was originally a maritime term referring to the hawsers which kept a ship moored to a pier. Rats were often seen moving on the line in single file and as most ex-POWS were moved singly the term was applied.

After landing in Italy, the British needed boats to evacuate escapees by sea. "A" Force was assisted by a small fleet of coastal boats detached from the Special Boat Squadron (SBS) nicknamed Popski's Private Navy and this small unit comprised six or seven men. It was headed by the same Major Popski who had set up Popski's Private Army, and entered the port of Brindisi on September 10. He was augmented by small boats of the Italian Royal Navy. This tiny unit operated out of the Adriatic ports of Termoli and Manfredonia, bringing out some 400 escapees between December 1943 and June 1944. It was not always successful, as on November 3, when Italian Motor Torpedo Boat (MTB) 33 struck and hit a mine near Pescara while transporting escaped British ex-POWs.[3] It is believed that most of the crew and ex-POWs were lost.

Nevertheless, "A" Force work was impressive. One pair of British soldiers, Lance Sergeant Peter Donald Phillips and Signalman Donald Stewart, was credited on their citations for the British Military Medal for returning 481 escaped POWs to Allied lines.

"A" Force teams also organized cells of Italians called "helpers" who passed escaped POWs from one cell to another along the rat lines. Italian recruits daily risked their lives, earning small amounts of cash to feed their families. Those who knew the mountains well smuggled escapees through German lines to the south to Allied-occupied Italy or led them to Switzerland or to the Balkans. By February 1944 there were an estimated 100 of these helpers across Italy. Escapees rarely knew that these friendly Italians were employed by "A" Force.

One "A" Force unit was commanded by an English officer known only as Colonel Jim, a tall, thin man with a handlebar mustache. He arranged for the repatriation of many Allied servicemen. Because many of his ex-POWs were black South Africans and British Army Indians who would be noticed in daytime, he moved his ex-POWs two at a time and at night. On one occasion an entire Sikh patrol that had been caught behind the lines — five men, wearing turbans — was successfully moved. Colonel Jim was assisted by these ubiquitous "A" Force Italian helpers, local farmers who fed and clothed the ex-POWs. The colonel's group numbered five men whose duties were interchangeable: guide, sentry, cook, messenger, and radio-generator operator. The latter was the hardest job because the generator was hand-cranked to produce power. Colonel Jim also collected intelligence and helped grow the local band of partisans.

Those POWs who could not make it to the coast would rely on both formal and informal Italian helpers as well as partisan groups to survive, and ultimately, many would then seek refuge in Rome and the Vatican itself.

With the outbreak of World War II, the Vatican's Holy Office assumed the responsibility to gather news about refugees, the newly displaced homeless, and missing persons. When Italy declared war in June 1940 and invaded British-held Egypt later that year, captured British and Commonwealth soldiers were moved to Italy to cut the cost of transporting food to feed them. As the number of POWs increased with the 1942 invasion of Greece, the Swiss Embassy, which oversaw British interests in Italy, commenced POW camp visits on behalf of the International Red Cross. For their part, the Holy Office also sent a Papal Nuncio, Monsignor Borgoncini Duca, to visit the camps. Duca spoke no English so Monsignor Hugh O'Flaherty, an Irish priest, was assigned to assist him.

Monsignor Hugh Joseph O'Flaherty was born in Killarney, County Kerry, Ireland, on February 28, 1898. From an early age, he wanted to be a priest. He studied at Catholic seminaries in Ireland where he was a distinguished athlete, a proficient boxer, and an avid golfer. A fierce Irish Nationalist, he was posted to Rome in 1922 to finish his studies and was ordained on December 20, 1925. O'Flaherty rose quickly in the hierarchy. He joined the Curia and worked for the Holy See, deepening his international experience by serving as a Vatican diplomat in Egypt, Haiti, Santo Domingo, and Czechoslovakia. In 1934, at age 36, he was appointed a papal chamberlain and made a monsignor.

Next, O'Flaherty was assigned to the Vatican's Holy Office in Rome which was responsible for the interpretation of Canon Law. While there he moved among Roman high society counseling on religious questions. Playing excellent bridge and golf, he was a frequent guest in the homes of wealthy Romans; he even taught Count Ciano to play golf at the Rome Country Club. At the Vatican, he resided at the German College (*Collegio Teutonicum*), where German Catholics had traditionally come to study, live, and meditate on their faith. It was run by a German rector with housekeeping by German nuns; there is even a German cemetery on the grounds.*

---

* On the wall opposite the entrance to the Camposanto Teutonico, the German Cemetery, is a plaque dedicated to Monsignor O'Flaherty. The plaque reads: "Monsignor Hugh O'Flaherty, born in Ireland 28.2.1898. Founder of the Rome Escape Line – Tireless defender of the weak and oppressed – Resided in this College 1938–1960 from where he saved over 6,000 lives from the National Socialists – died 30.10.1963 Buried in Cahersiveen, County Kerry, Ireland."

O'Flaherty and Monsignor Duca visited the more than 80 Allied POW camps spread around Italy with their tens of thousands of captured soldiers. Duca set a leisurely pace visiting only one camp a day. Not O'Flaherty; he kept a list of all the POWs he talked to, and often returned to Rome in the evenings to hand over his list so that the names could be broadcast on Vatican Radio to their home countries. The radio station was run by Father Filippo Soccorsi, a Jesuit priest, and it had five civilian radio technicians, at least two of whom were volunteer members of OVRA who passed on information concerning the POW visits to SIM.

These visits continued a Vatican World War I tradition of identifying prisoners of war. During that earlier world war, when Cardinal Pacelli, later Pope Pius XII, was working inside the office of the Secretary of State, he had maintained the Vatican's registry of prisoners of war and worked to implement papal relief initiatives. During his visits to the POW camps, Monsignor O'Flaherty had distributed thousands of English-language books. He evaded the official censors by giving the books to local priests who routinely administered to the POWs. O'Flaherty also sped up the distribution of Red Cross parcels for the soldiers. In this he had the full backing of the Swiss government. Many of the POWs would remember the kind Irish priest from the Vatican and vowed they would head to Rome and place themselves in his hands if they escaped from the prison camps. It was as a result of his visits that an embryonic network to help Allied servicemen was born inside the Vatican.

———

The primary broadcaster on Vatican Radio was Brother Robert Pace, a Maltese, a Christian Brother, and a British subject. Brother Robert was born to British parents in 1907 in Alexandria, Egypt but raised in Malta. In 1940 he earned a doctorate in European languages from the University of Naples and transferred to the Christian Brothers Mother House in Rome. He was attached to the Papal Secretariat of State where he served as secretary to Monsignor Montini.

An Italian, Montini was concerned about the fate and treatment of Italian POWs in Allied hands and he extended his concern to the Allied POWs in Italy. Brother Robert, who was multilingual, became the primary broadcaster on Vatican Radio, reading the names of thousands of POWs held in Italy. He broadcasted twice a day for several hours in three languages.

Both German and Italian officials were troubled by the broadcast of POWs' names. Further, O'Flaherty irked them by protesting the conditions of the Allied POWs in the Italian-run camps and their treatment in POW hospitals. Unsurprisingly, the Fascist government regarded O'Flaherty as a pest. Consequently, in November 1942, the Vatican released him from visitation duties and ended all such visits to the POW camps that Christmas. This was a remarkable bow to the Germans by the Vatican.

Meanwhile Brother Robert, with no new names to broadcast but still determined to help, spent his time at the Italian/German Military Hospital that had taken over the Christian Brothers Mother House in Rome. He attended to the spiritual and physical needs of the recovering wounded soldiers, regardless of nationality, passing out cigarettes and other small comfort items. From Italian Red Cross nurses, he obtained the names and addresses of Allied POWs being treated at the hospital. He then passed the names to the Vatican which forwarded them to the servicemen's home countries via papal nuncios.

9

Allied POWs Seek Freedom

A prisoner of war suddenly sees a chance to escape. He tells a guard he is late for duty, follows a water-fetching detail to a bend in the road, and slips out of a gate into a hedgerow where he hides until dark. He is in the mountains, dressed only in shorts and a light shirt, and has in his pocket one emergency ration bar. He is free; now how does he survive?

This was the experience of British Lieutenant John Furman who walked out of the Sulmona prisoner of war camp by claiming he was late for his work detail that was to fetch water from a nearby spring. Sulmona, approximately 120 miles due east of Rome, is a small but ancient town that even in Roman times had been a major hub for the roads between Rome and the Adriatic coast. It was famous for having been the home of the Roman poet Ovid after his banishment by the Emperor Augustus. Overlooking the camp in the mountains, there was an ancient shrine to Hercules.

Furman, a mustached junior British officer, had been captured in North Africa. He was first imprisoned at POW Camp #21 near the town of Chieti almost 50 miles east of Sulmona via winding, mountain roads. The camp was originally built for political prisoners and it now housed over 1,000 Allied officers and 250 enlisted men. He was one of more than 70,000 Allied prisoners then in camps scattered all over Italy. They came from all over the British Empire: Australia, New Zealand, India,

South Africa, and other places. Among them were 1,300 Americans, Free French, Greeks, and Yugoslavs.

The Italian *Comando Supremo* issued Secret Memo Number One on September 6, which clearly stated that every effort should be taken to prevent Allied POWs from falling into German hands. If it were not possible to defend the camps from the Germans, prisoners could be released. Italian troops were directed to assist the released POWs by giving them food and directions to Switzerland or to the Adriatic coast. A curious discrimination governed their release: only white prisoners would qualify for release as it was thought that non-whites would not blend in with the civilian population and would be easily recaptured by the Germans.[1]

According to Furman, the Italian guards at Chieti stayed at their posts because their commanding officer was following that order. The guards engaged in the subterfuge of wearing white coats over their uniforms in an attempt to convince German patrols that the camp was an insane asylum. The ruse did not work and at midnight on the night of September 19/20, the same 2nd Parachute Division that freed Mussolini from Gran Sasso took control of the camp.

Two days later, the Germans announced that the Chieti camp would be closed. Furman distinctly remembered that it was at 04:30 on September 22. The prisoners were to be taken by truck to the camp at Sulmona and then by train to camps in Germany. The transfer of the POWs was begun immediately.

The first group of 150 men was loaded into Italian Army diesel trucks, 20 prisoners and four guards in each, to embark on the two-hour trip to the new camp. The Sulmona POW Camp #78 was located three miles to the north of the town of Sulmona, outside the village of Fonte d'Amore. The Sulmona camp had actually been a POW camp during World War I when it housed Austrian prisoners of war. It had been reactivated at the start of World War II for enlisted men. While in use, more than 3,000 Allied officers and men passed through the camp.[*]

On the afternoon of September 23, Furman arrived at the Sulmona camp. Once inside he, and several other officers, made a cursory inspection of the guarded camp perimeter. Security had been tightened

---

[*] Several of the barracks and the sports field can occasionally be visited. Inside several of the buildings the POWs left graffiti which depicted unit crests and sometimes pin-up girls.

following the escape of ten officers the previous day. Furman saw that there was little water for bathing; however, while he was being trucked into the camp he had spied a spring which was called the Fonte d'Amore. The spring had an adjunct water trough about 150 yards away from the main gate and he saw German guards washing there with towels and soap. Furman had studied in Germany prewar and spoke excellent German. He addressed the guards in their native German, stating that, since the Chieti camp had had limited washing facilities, he requested permission for the prisoners to wash at the same trough. Remarkably the German guards allowed the prisoners out to wash in groups of ten or 12, under close guard of course. Apparently local women were amused to see the naked, white-bottomed soldiers splashing in the water trough. Furman also knew that regular access to the spring outside of the camp boundaries presented the best means of escape.

While Furman was thinking of escape a friend of his, then still en route from Chieti to Sulmona, actually broke free while being transported. He was Lieutenant William C. Simpson, a British Territorial (active reserve) Royal Artillery Officer. Simpson had been captured at Tobruk, along with 32,000 other defenders, on June 20, 1942. After a trip along the Libyan coast in a German truck, the Italians flew him to southern Italy and transferred him to Chieti where he became acquainted with Furman. Simpson, waiting to be transferred from the Chieti camp and wanting to escape, hatched a plan. Before boarding the truck for Sulmona, he switched identity cards with an enlisted man, reasoning that he would be less closely watched if he were with the other ranks.

As the truck left the main Popoli–Sulmona highway, making a right turn on the road to the camp, Simpson leapt from the truck unseen by the German guards. In his haste, he left his hoarded parcel of food and personal items behind. Luck was with him and that first night he was fed by sympathetic locals who also gave him a coverall to wear over his military uniform. From a distance, he might pass for an Italian railway worker. Simpson was now a mile northwest of the town of Sulmona. He had no idea what to do next.

The following day, September 23, Simpson encountered another escaped English officer, Captain Dennis B. Rendell of the 2nd British

Parachute Regiment. Captain Rendell had been captured at Oudna, Tunisia in November 1942 and transferred to a POW camp in Italy. Heading to the Sulmona railway station and hiding behind trees and bushes, they observed Allied soldiers being loaded on boxcars for Germany. The railway cars were parked on a siding near the Sulmona railway station. Suddenly the crack of a rifle sounded and Rendell saw a friend, Captain Jock Short, also of the 2nd British Parachute Regiment, shot and killed while attempting to escape.

Once more local Italians came to the rescue. Discovering the hiding soldiers, they took them away from the railroad and sent an Italian-speaking escapee to them. He was Private Joseph Pollak, a Czechoslovakian Jew who had fled his country in 1939, emigrating to Palestine. Later he joined the British Palestinian Pioneer Corps which was attached to the British Army in Greece. He had been captured by the Germans in 1941 and sent to the Chieti POW camp. A master of foreign languages, he spoke Czech, German, Hebrew, Greek, English, and Italian.

Pollak took Simpson and Rendell to Dr. Mario Scocco, a dentist in the Borgo Pacentrano district of Sulmona. Scocco was soon to be head of a local partisan group (see Appendix E for a list of Sulmona helpers) and he placed Simpson and Rendell with Angelo and Anna Carugno, on Vico Breve in Sulmona. Anna was short with a thin frame and wore metal-rimmed glasses. She was taller than Angelo and both were in their mid-fifties. They had two sons: one a POW of the English, the other hiding out in the mountains and soon to become a partisan.

At that time Borgo Pacentrano was an extremely poor part of town. Most of the tiny homes had only three rooms and an attic. The ground floor was for farm animals while the next floor had a kitchen with eating area and a bedroom. There was no running water and the bathroom was usually a bucket.

Soon after moving in with the Carugnos, Simpson and Rendell were introduced to US Army Air Force Captain Elbert L. Duke Dukate of Biloxi, Mississippi. Dukate was a well-built man, five feet eight inches tall, with wavy black hair. Before the war he had been a radio announcer for the Columbia Broadcasting System (CBS) radio network. Dukate had been on a bombing mission to the oilfields at Ploesti in Romania when his plane was hit. The plane made it as far as German-occupied Italy where it crash-landed and the entire crew was captured. Dukate was transferred to the Sulmona POW camp where, seizing the opportunity, he crawled under the wire to freedom. On the run, he was taken in by the Carabbia family who also lived on Vico Breve in the Borgo Pacentrano neighborhood.

Back in the Sulmona camp, Furman was still wrestling with how to make good his escape. It was on September 26 that he saw the working party leave camp to fetch water. On the spur of the moment, Furman ran after the detail, assuring the German guard that he was part of it and that he was simply late. It worked; he followed the detail right out of camp. Taking advantage of a bend in the gravel road, Furman slipped through a gate he had seen in a hedge on his earlier bathing trip to the spring; it led onto a field. He ducked through the gate, hid in the brush until midnight, then headed southeast for Sulmona.

Nights were cold in the Abruzzi Mountains in late September. Wearing only shorts and a light shirt and with only one emergency ration bar in his pocket, he was thoroughly unprepared. But like any Allied serviceman wanting to escape, when he saw an opportunity he took it. Opportunities to escape German-run POW camps were few and far between. It was a hair-raising flight, imagining Germans soldiers behind every bush, ready to pounce. After taking cover in a straw hut, he had to get help and soon.

It would come, again, from Italian civilians. As he moved toward the people on the road ahead, Furman practiced his Italian sentence: *Io sono un officiale Inglese prigioniero di Guerra, scappato del Campo Concentramento*, which means, "I am an English officer, prisoner of war, escaped from prison camp." He confronted two 14-year-old boys and spoke his line. It worked, and they took him home and their family sheltered him. They also sent for a bilingual escapee from Chieti to help him communicate; again it was Private Pollak.

Shortly thereafter and rounding out the group of escapees Furman met Henri Payonne, a small, dapper, and well-groomed Free French officer with wavy red hair and excellent English. He too lived in Borgo Pacentrano. Payonne was in contact with François de Vial, Vice Consul and Second Secretary at the French Embassy to the Holy See, who quietly looked out for the interest of French ex-POWs. Payonne may also have been a French member of "A" Force tasked to assist escaped prisoners. He lived with Roberto Cicerone, nicknamed *Pazzone* (crazy), an exceptional man who later joined the partisans led by Scocco and became his right-hand man.

Life for the ex-POWs in Sulmona settled into a routine of tension and boredom. Furman took Italian lessons but he suffered from chronic, explosive diarrhea. Eventually, English POW Dr. Hooper, the Sulmona camp doctor, was contacted during one of his occasional visits to Allied soldiers recovering in a hospital in the Sulmona Annunziata church complex. He sent Furman some much-needed medicine.

It occurred to Furman that the Annunziata Hospital patients, almost fully recovered, should be given the opportunity to escape before they were to be shipped off to internment in Germany. Furman presented his idea to Dr. Scocco and one of his dental assistants, Augustino, whose wife worked at the hospital. The hospital doctor, Dr. Romilde Semperlotti, and several women of the town agreed to help in the escape. The Carabbias and two other sisters, Iride and Maria Imperoli, smuggled in civilian clothes and soft-soled shoes for the POW patients. At 21:00 one night in early October, a half hour before curfew, nine POWs climbed down a rope made from bed sheets onto a side street. Only one remained, Lance Bombardier William D. T. McIntosh, who was not sufficiently recovered from a kidney stone operation. Of the nine who escaped, eight were quickly taken in by the townspeople.

The remaining soldier, Captain Gil Smith of 4th Royal Tank Regiment, was left in the street. He was suffering from severe eczema which caused large, open, weeping sores. Barely able to walk and extremely weak, he was such a sight that it was difficult to convince anyone to take him into their home. Two Vico Breve women, Marietta, a war widow in her twenties, and her mother, Maria, finally volunteered. Under their excellent care and with better food, his eczema substantially cleared up in two weeks.

The hospital escape infuriated the Germans who increased pressure on the townspeople. They lacked the manpower for a thorough search of the town which only fanned their frustration. Fearing detection, Dr. Semperlotti, who had played her role in the escape, fled to the mountains where she could help those hiding in the woods.

The ex-POWs were free but by no means safe. Living in fear, they nevertheless tried to live normally, even having parties. Furman, some other POWs, and several Italians attended one such party on the evening of October 15. At the party was Gino Ranalli, with whom Pollak lived, and two daughters from the house where two American pilots were staying, Captain Herbert "Herb" Perry, USAAF, and Glenn "Pat" Wilson, an American flying officer in the Royal Canadian Air Force (RCAF). Wilson had volunteered to join the Canadians and fight the Nazis prior to America's entry into the war. Other ex-POW attendees included Duke Dukate, Bill Simpson, and Dennis Rendell.

After an evening of much consumption of wine, the party broke up and the revelers went home. Just as his head touched his pillow, Furman heard a commotion down in the street – screaming and shouts of *Heraus!* (Come out!). It was a *rastrellamento*, a roundup. The Germans were scouring houses for laborers, any male capable of hard manual labor. Furman and several young Italian men ran outside and hid in a chicken coop. At first light, the Germans systematically searched each house and outbuilding on the block. Still in hiding, Furman heard Esterina, the woman with whom he was staying, call him. Thinking he was safe, he left the coop and bumped straight into a German soldier.

Again in custody, he was taken to an assembly point and marched along with 30 men of various ages, to a parking lot inside a compound. Wives, girlfriends, and relatives descended on the place, wailing. Believing the men were to be sent away, they had brought food and clothing packets which the Germans allowed them to pass through the iron gates of the compound. Gino Ranalli had been caught too. His mother and two sisters, Ada and Ida, had packages for him. Esterina also came. She told Furman that she had been terrified and had lost her head when she called to him.

More prisoners were brought into the compound including two unlikely looking Italians: the Americans Herb Perry and Pat Wilson. Eventually all were taken on buses to a work camp outside of the small town of Pescocostanzo, close to the front lines, some 20 miles south of Sulmona. Now a labor force, the men were herded into a hastily erected compound. A German sergeant major addressed them through an Italian interpreter, warning the men not to try to escape; for every man who escaped, ten would be shot. To mollify them, he promised them that if they worked hard they would be sent home when the work was finished. The men were taken to one of three large huts where they were to sleep. Sanitation was almost nonexistent and the latrine odor was everywhere. Inside the hut the men slept on straw, what little there was of it. A stove in the center of the room provided insufficient heat.

Dinner was soup, but there were no spoons. Women from Pescocostanzo threw small food parcels to their men over the wire fence of the camp. At dark the men were herded back into their huts. They tried sleeping but it was cold high in the mountains and, except for the straw, there was no bedding or blankets. More prisoner laborers arrived throughout the evening.

Early the next morning, each man got a piece of bread, some margarine, and a spoonful of jam. Some ersatz coffee quickly ran out. Then they were formed into working parties and marched to a tool depository where they were issued picks and shovels, arriving at the work site after walking about two miles. They were to work on what was called the Gustav Line, a German defensive barrier which was to stretch across Italy and eventually hold up the Allied advance for nine months. The men were directed to cut away part of a hill to form an anti-tank barrier. A heated discussion broke out among the prison laborers about whether to work hard or only seem to; some believed the German promise that they would be sent home when the work was done, but others felt it was just a ruse. So the believers worked hard and the skeptics pretended to work. No one believed that the Germans would shoot ten men for each escapee. As laborers they were simply too valuable a commodity.

Not all the German guards were Nazi zealots, something Furman and some of the others realized. So, taking a chance at another escape, Furman engaged two young Austrian soldiers, whom they called Hans and Fritz, in conversation. They told him they were draftees and wanted to desert to return home at the first opportunity. Hoping that assisting the escaped POWs might eventually benefit them, the Austrians offered help to Furman, Herb Perry, and Pat Wilson. They gave the men a map, a flashlight, cigarettes, and matches. They arranged that the three Allied soldiers, together with Gino Ranalli, would escape when the two Austrians were on guard duty. They successfully broke out of the camp one night at 23:00 and headed for the high mountains in the direction of Sulmona. Their plan was to return to their Italian hosts, obtain supplies, and then cross over to the Allied lines to the south. After some rough days in the mountains, they stumbled into Sulmona, much to everyone's amazement.

Back in his former quarters, Furman relaxed into old routines. But Esteria, the young woman who looked after him with her parents, feared another German raid and, to be safe, moved him into a tiny house at Vico Breve 6. Maria Santilli, who was in her mid-thirties, lived there with her husband, Cesidio Valeria, and their three sons: Vincenzino, nine, and two others aged seven and three. Rounding out the family was her 70-year-old mother-in-law, Nonna (grandmother). The family welcomed Furman warmly but his chronic diarrhea had returned and it caused him further distress because the family toilet was simply straw in the stable on the ground floor of the house.

Many other ex-POWs were now in that neighborhood, Americans, British, and French. Friends lived nearby, Rendell and Simpson across the narrow street, Gil Smith a few doors away and Duke Dukate around the corner. Next door lived an otherwise unidentified French officer named Robert; a large number of escaped POWs were being housed by the poorest of the poor and despite the clear risks.

During Furman's stint with the labor gang, Pollak had attempted to cross German lines to rejoin the Allies. He narrowly escaped recapture. Traveling with another soldier, they had been shot at and his companion was killed. Pollak was forced back to Sulmona. Alarmed at Furman's recurring diarrhea, Pollak took him to a young medical student who was able to find some sulfaguanidine that temporarily relieved it.

On his attempt to cross the lines, Pollak may have met Captain Jock McKee, one of the men sent by "A" Force from Bari as part of its repatriation mission. McKee arrived in Sulmona in October and was astonished to learn that there were some 1,000 escaped Allied POWs in the area. It was his job to persuade them to go south with him to Bari. It would be dangerous as they would need to cross enemy lines. But with the assistance of the Italian helpers, they could reach the southeast coast. He convinced only 23, the rest unwilling to give up their girlfriends and comforts, such as they were, in their meager dwellings of the Italian families they lived with.

Furman, in somewhat better health, often visited Gil Smith, whose eczema had healed. Iride and Maria Imperoli, who had helped with the hospital escape, often came to see Smith, and Furman resumed studying Italian with Ione, a young woman from the area. He also made rounds with Pollak visiting ex-POWs and distributing donated supplies to them.

It seems half the town was involved in helping the ex-POWs. Pollak persuaded some Sulmona friends to forge documents so the ex-POWs could move around the town. The town clerk supplied official blank forms. One of Furman's friends provided the necessary rubber stamps. This was Enzo, the brother of Furman's language teacher, Ione, and a fellow escapee from the Pescocostanzo labor camp. An unidentified photographer who lived in Vico Breve took the photos for the documents. Simpson's new identity, according to his forged ID, was Guglielmo de Cesare.

The bulk of the escapees lived in the immediate countryside but with little civilian transportation available their access to food and basic supplies dwindled. Dr. Scocco, Robert Cicerone, and Pollak brought more escapees into town from the countryside where it would be easier to supply them. BBC broadcasts back in June had urged escapees to head for neutral places like Vatican City. So, Pollak argued they should head to Rome, 120 miles to the west, and seek help from the Vatican, but most of the escapees considered it far too dangerous.

Following the chain of command established for POWs, Captain Rendell, the senior British officer, and Captain Dukate, the senior American, instead wrote the Vatican asking for advice and cash. Iride Imperoli carried the letters to Rome. Beautiful Iride was exceptional by Sulmona's standards: she was stylish, sophisticated, extroverted, highly intelligent, and very sure of herself. And her beauty caused envy, according to a friend, Franca del Monaco.[2] Before the war, Iride would come back from Rome with the latest fashions, and then design and make clothes for the women of Sulmona. During the war, she continued to visit Rome but now traveled via German military vehicle. Gossips said she hitched rides by sharing her favors with the soldiers but that was perhaps just jealousy.

It may have been the Frenchman Henri Payonne who told Iride to deliver the letters to French Vice Consul François de Vial at the Holy See. De Vial certainly passed the Rendell–Dukate letters to the Vatican's interned Allied diplomats, Sir D'Arcy and Harold Tittmann. De Vial also told her she could go see Father Benedetto at the International Capuchin College on Via Sicilia in an emergency.

The Vatican's reply, also carried by Iride, was devastating. In essence it told the POWs to avoid coming to Rome except as a last resort. The blow was softened somewhat by the enclosed 3,000 lire which was to be shared among the POWs in Sulmona. Although a modest sum in Rome, it was bounty in the countryside where a liter of wine cost 16 lire. The Vatican's letter also asked for the names, ranks, regiments, and next of kin of the escapees, so that their families could be notified. By providing that information, the escapees would also convince the Vatican of their authenticity and that would unlock future stipends.

Simpson and Rendell fulfilled the Vatican request, spending three days visiting the surrounding countryside obtaining names and other information from the ex-POWs. Noting that many of the men lacked adequate winter clothes and blankets, they turned to Guillermo (called William by the POWs, the English version of his name) Di Carlo for help. He was an English-speaking businessman and owner of a confectionary factory famous throughout Italy for *confetti*, sugar-coated almonds that were given out as favors to wedding guests. He introduced Simpson and Rendell to the Balassone brothers, wealthy Sulmona merchants. One of the brothers had been a major in the Italian Army and had obtained a large supply of Italian uniform articles and blankets. On Simpson's signature, he turned over the clothing. Simpson, Rendell, and Pollak were now responsible for billeting, feeding, and providing clothing for the escapees.

Iride, accompanied by Maria, her younger half-sister, returned to Rome. Armed with the list of escapees that Simpson and Rendell had gathered, she received 40,000 lire (about 100 pounds sterling) from de Vial, her Vatican contact, who himself had obtained it from Sir D'Arcy. Five days later the sisters returned to Sulmona with a large supply of pullovers and shirts they had purchased. It was an expensive but necessary addition to the escapees' wardrobes. They turned over the remaining 15,000 lire and, although not a lot of money for the large number of escapees, it helped. Simpson and Rendell kept the books, obtaining cash receipts from the men and the people who took care of them.

Things were improving somewhat and perhaps their guard was down. However innocent in intent, Pollak flirted with danger when he attended a festival on November 28 in Sulmona's Piazza Garibaldi Market Square. Taking a turn at a shooting gallery, he hit the target; there was a flash of light and he was rewarded with a photograph of himself taking the shot. In the photo he is standing next to two German soldiers who were observing his marksmanship. When Pollak showed the photo to Rendell, Smith, and Payonne, they all had to have a go and they too hit the target and had their photos taken with German soldiers. Di Carlo, their benefactor, was understandably disturbed at this recklessness.

Their luck was to be tested again, this time at Dennis Rendell's birthday party on December 5. The Americans Duke Dukate and Pat Wilson; British officers Gil Smith, John Furman, William Simpson, and Private Pollak; the Imperoli sisters (Iride and Maria); and the French officer named Robert all attended. The party was hosted by Angelo and Anna Carugno, who sheltered Simpson and Rendell. Pollak and the Frenchman left early, but the party became increasingly boisterous with much wine-soaked singing.

Suddenly there was incessant, loud banging on an outside door down the street. Harsh, guttural German commands rang out — the Sulmona-based German SS were on a house-to-house search. Tiny Vico Breve was surrounded. In a panic, the scraps of the party were cleared away and the Allied escapees headed for an attic hideaway. They scrambled into the attic through a trap door, pulling the ladder up behind them. They ringed themselves around the edges of the attic to reduce the likelihood of being shot if the Germans fired into the ceiling. Angelo and Anna climbed into their bed while Iride and Maria jumped into another, as though they were part of the household.

The house next door was occupied by Filomena, the wife of the local butcher, and her two children. The Germans burst into her house ransacking it. Filomena had hidden two British servicemen for a few nights, but thankfully they had moved on. The Gestapo man savagely interrogated Filomena, screaming at her. Speaking Italian, he called her a liar. She pleaded with him that there were no "English" in her house. Then the German turned to her eight-year-old daughter, Teresina. Furman recorded what the little girl said:

> "Two British prisoners? But that's silly. We live in this room. My mother cooks by the fire. Where could a bed be put down here? Come into the next room." [Furman then wrote that] I heard their footsteps retreat into the back room. Then Teresina's voice continued, quieter now, but still distinct. "You see my mother's bed takes up most of the space. I sleep in this little bed with my sister." She laughed, "When daddy's at home, there's no room for the four of us. Where could we put two British prisoners?"[3]

The Germans searched other houses in Vico Breve but found no one. Those hiding in the attic could hear every shouted German command echoing in the street. Sure that the Germans could hear their heartbeats, their terror knew no bounds. Then the German shouting stopped. The soldiers ran down the street from the top of Vico Breve, to form up and march away. The Gestapo had overlooked the one house where the escaped POWs hid! No one slept the rest of the night for fear that the Germans would return. Just before dawn, realizing that they could not stay where they were, the men, escorted by Angelo, descended to the tiny street. They went around the corner and through an unlocked door to the church of San Filippo where they climbed the squat bell tower, a temporary hiding place. Angelo promised he would send food and drink later. The men, looking out on the town's market square from the church's bell tower, could see that Germans appeared to be everywhere.

The raid was probably the result of an Italian informer, perhaps a local woman called Vera Cerrone. She was later described in an Allied Interrogation Report as aged about 24 with a height of about 152 centimeters (about 5 ft), peroxide blonde hair, gray eyes, and a very robust build but with only one arm. Vera had helped escaped Allied prisoners until losing her arm in a British RAF bombing raid on the Sulmona railway station. She then turned anti-British and was well known in Sulmona as an agent for the local Gestapo, known as the Pagan Unit after Oberleutnant Pagan, its commanding officer. Established in early 1944, it was this unit that conducted the Vico Breve raid.

Furman, with the others in the bell tower, needed to warn Pollak not to look for them, but he had no way to contact him. Angelo came with the promised food and drink and told them what they already knew, that the SS were everywhere and were camped out in the nearby market square. At midday, Pollak showed up, his false medical student identity documents having passed German scrutiny. Pollak convinced the men that they must leave Sulmona. Knowing from personal experience that it would be almost impossible to cross over to the Allied lines going south, he suggested that they make for Rome, regardless of the previous warning. All agreed.

At the railway station, Pollak found that one of the rare and irregularly scheduled trains to Rome was to leave at 18:00 that evening. They would have to catch it. Iride and Maria volunteered to make the journey with the men. With the two women, the nine would include Pollak, the only good Italian speaker, Furman, Simpson, Smith, Rendell, Dukate, and Wilson.

Residents of Vico Breve who heard of the escape plan collected the soldiers' meager possessions and kept a lookout for Germans. They gathered at Angelo and Anna's home. Maria Santilli and her husband Cesidio Valeri, Furman's hosts, their three sons, and Nonna were there to bid Furman and Wilson goodbye. Maria insisted on escorting the soldiers to the train station about a mile away. Furman learned later that the stress of the previous night's Gestapo raid had caused Maria to lose the baby she had been carrying. Climbing aboard the train, the party was shocked to see a horde of German troops also going to Rome on leave.

The train left, more or less on time. Iride, Maria, and Pollak purchased tickets onboard from the train conductor as was the custom. Unsurprisingly the conductor engaged in conversation with the pretty Iride. He explained that upon arrival in Rome, the German Railway Police (*Bahnschutzpolizei*) would closely examine each passenger's documents. The German Stadtkommandant had declared that any person entering Rome must have advanced permission as well as a permit to do so. Of course they did not have either.

The train lurched and stopped so often that the trip of 120 miles, normally taking five hours, lasted all night. German police checked documents at least twice as the small party anxiously feigned sleep. To their relief, their false identity cards were accepted. Shortly after passing through Tivoli, 20 miles southeast of Rome, the train screeched to a halt, three stops outside the city. It was first light. After a tense pause of about ten minutes the refugees decided they must leave the train and they did so theatrically, jumping out and waving goodbye to the other passengers and the German soldiers. Thinking that they could evade detection at a road checkpoint outside the city better than in the military confines of the Tiburtina railway station, they decided to walk.

After about a mile their suitcases became too heavy. Pooling their few coins, they paid a farmer to carry the baggage in his cart to a tram stop at the edge of the city. Then it started to rain. Now cold and wet, the party took shelter in a large garage with other people waiting for the rain to stop. From them they learned of a new threat: a checkpoint was only a few hundred yards up the road.

But there was no going back now. The rain stopped and Iride and Maria walked to the checkpoint to speak with the Italian policemen. Meanwhile Pollak told the sleepy German sentry a highly improbable story. He explained that they were all that remained of a family that had been bombed out of their house in Sulmona. On the invitation of their uncle, they were going to Rome to live with him. The German shrugged his shoulders, deferring to the Italian policemen, who believed the story. Documents were checked and again accepted. There was no mention of the authorization letter and permit to enter the city. The farmer's cart then made two trips to the tram terminus to deposit the intrepid travelers and their baggage.

It took several trams to get them to the city center and to the Albergo Vulcania on Via Cavour, where they checked in. The place, known to Iride, was in reality a brothel. There were no meals, but the rooms were luxurious, after the garish fashion of bordellos. There was plenty of hot water, much appreciated since in Sulmona they had had none. The nine were safe for now but they could not relax and it made them nervous when, following the standard procedure, they had to leave their identity documents with the concierge at the front desk.

10

Knocking on the Gates of Saint Peter's

The neutral status of the Vatican guaranteed it some protection during the German occupation of Rome; but its neutrality was merely a thin cloak. In fact the Vatican came to quietly condone and conceal an elaborate covert network on behalf of thousands of Allied escapees. These operations were carried out by a large cast of clerics, foreign diplomats, and petty functionaries. Underfunded and understaffed, this network nevertheless labored ceaselessly. It was gradually expanded despite the reluctance of Vatican officials to overtly take on the care and housing of these soldiers. Eventually it was christened the Rome Escape Line.

Albert E. Penny, a Royal Navy Submarine Petty Officer, was the first escaped POW to enter the Vatican for sanctuary. This was on October 5, 1942. Penny had escaped from Italian POW Camp #10, *Campo Acquapendente*, near Viterbo, a scant 40 miles north of Rome. Showing up at the Vatican, he simply told a guard he was English and was taken to Sir D'Arcy. Unwilling to turn him over to the Italians, Sir D'Arcy knew that he couldn't remain inside the Vatican for long, so a swap was engineered, Penny for an Italian POW. The negotiations took two months. While hiding inside the Vatican, Penny was jokingly referred to as the Military Attaché of the British Legation to the Holy See.

Finally, on January 3, 1943, Penny flew to Lisbon with a Vatican monsignor, who returned to Rome with an unidentified Italian service member. The Penny episode was the first known instance of Vatican diplomats assisting Allied military escaped POWs, but it would not be the last. Soon three more servicemen showed up and they too were exchanged for three Italian POWs. It was clear that these special arrangements could not continue if there were to be a large number of soldiers seeking Vatican sanctuary.

But come they did. POWs remembered kind Monsignor O'Flaherty's visits to their camps. It was natural that they should come to the Vatican to seek him out. On July 25, 1943, an Italian-naturalized British serviceman (name unknown) who had fought at El Alamein entered the Vatican. What started as a trickle with the walkout of guards and thousands of prisoners from camps following the September armistice threatened to become a flood. The stories of their interactions throw light on the characters of the players in this drama.

Four escapees who made the trek to Rome knocked first on the door of the British Embassy, but found it was closed. They then tried the Vatican. The men were Major John Munro Sym, Seaforth Highlanders; Captain Henry Judson Byrnes, Royal Canadian Army Service Corps; Captain I. Rowarth, Royal Engineers; and Sub-Lieutenant Ray Charlton Elliott, Royal Navy. Sym had fought at El Alamein in North Africa. Captured, he was taken to Calabria in southern Italy where he escaped and hid in a cave. After recapture he was put in a POW compound near Rome. Byrnes, who might have been a commando, had been captured in Sicily while riding in a jeep. Elliott was 20 years old, blonde, and nicknamed Goldilocks. He had been rescued at sea after his submarine had been sunk. Tittmann's oldest son, Harold III, in his diary for September 10, notes that the four simply walked into the Vatican and asked to see someone British.

When they walked into Saint Peter's, the Vatican gendarmes tried to throw the escapees out but they were rescued by Kosta and Betsa Zoukitches of the Vatican Yugoslav Legation. Sir D'Arcy requested permission for them to stay. It was granted and they were housed in the Vatican Gendarme Barracks, in the Oratory of Saint Peter's attached to the western side of Saint Peter's Basilica. They were, however, restricted to the confines of Vatican City. Rowarth, bored, often ignored this restriction. He went to the cinema, restaurants, public baths, or just rode around the city on trams and buses. On one occasion, claiming he was a Slovene, he spoke with a German officer. It is not known how long these extra-Vatican trips continued but it was certainly dangerous. According to young Tittmann, he and his brother, Barclay, talked to the men for hours, fascinated by their stories about the North African and Sicilian campaigns.

On September 14, two Royal Navy sailors arrived at the Basilica wearing Italian uniforms. Inside Saint Peter's, Sir D'Arcy's secretary, Hugh Montgomery, was pointed out to them. The sailors introduced themselves and Montgomery explained that Sir D'Arcy needed to obtain permission for them to remain. Sir D'Arcy asked Monsignor Montini to request Vatican hospitality from Cardinal Maglione. The request approved, Sir D'Arcy sent John May to stay with them until they could be escorted into the Vatican.

But they had not been cleared with the gendarmes at the gate, and a struggle ensued. Montgomery arrived at the Arco delle Campane just as the gendarmes were dragging the sailors down the Basilica's steps. Montgomery stopped them and called Sir D'Arcy on the telephone from the guardroom of the Swiss Guards, who were responsible for guarding the Pope and who, according to tradition, had to be both Catholic and Swiss nationals. Sir D'Arcy called Monsignor Montini and soon orders came from Cardinal Maglione: admit the two men. With Montgomery as escort, they re-entered the basilica and were billeted with the four others in the Gendarme Barracks.*

These two sailors, Sub-Lt. H. L. H. Stevens and Petty Officer A. S. Buxton, were both Royal Navy divers. They had been captured in Tripoli Harbor, Libya, while unsuccessfully trying to affix an explosive charge to the hull of an Italian ship to sink it to block the harbor entrance. They had been using a captured Italian *maiale* (pig), a mini-submarine. Visiting the ex-POWs on September 15, young Harold Tittmann reported that the men were well treated, had enough to eat, and lived in a big open room with a terrace.

The next group to show up in Saint Peter's Square was large: a total of 14 escaped British POWs, lucky to slip into Rome before German

---

* In addition to the 100 Swiss Guards there was a corps of Noble Guard made up of members of the black aristocracy, meaning those who owed their titles to the Pope. Befitting their aristocratic titles, no one had a rank lower than lieutenant. During the war, they acted as a personal bodyguard for the Pope and stood outside the papal bedchamber and escorted the Pope, from a distance, when he went for a stroll in the Vatican Gardens.

occupation tightened. Dressed in shabby uniforms, they stood around until an Irish priest offered to take them to a nearby religious college. Not knowing whom else to approach, the priest contacted Monsignor O'Flaherty who arranged for a former Vatican Gendarme, Antonio Call, to take the men under his wing. Call, a one-time corporal in the Pope's bodyguard, got permission from an Italian Carabinieri officer to house them in a nearby barracks.

Antonio Call also handled special requests from the interned diplomats and reported their movements to Monsignor Montini. For example, if an ambassador wanted a haircut outside the Vatican, he had to apply to Call, who requested a permit from Montini who sent it to the Italian Ambassador to the Holy See and then to the appropriate Italian Ministry. He could be allowed out for two hours, escorted by Italian police, and then handed back to Call.

Later, with the city firmly under German control, the 14 men could no longer be protected and the majority were recaptured and transported to Germany. But Call saved one or two by moving them to the Casa San Giovanni, on property owned by the North American College up on the Janiculum Hill near the Vatican. At the time the main campus of the North American College was located at the Casa Santa Maria near the Trevi Fountain where it remained until 1953. The college trained parish priests for the United States and Canada. Although most seminary students were sent home when war was declared, the Casa San Giovanni housed some Italian-American medical students until liberation. These men were joined by Allied servicemen and even a few Italians hiding from both the Fascists and the Nazis.

The men on the Janiculum were eventually joined by a few more escaped POWs, including one unknown Australian captured at Tobruk who entered the Vatican by simply following a car which drove through a Vatican gate on September 30, 1943.

Code words began to be used in the work of ex-POW assistance. A friend of Brother Robert's owned a Catholic bookshop near the Vatican on Via della Conciliazione and he called him, saying that he had two very special books for Brother Robert. This was a prearranged code to mean that he had two escaped POWs. At the bookshop

Brother Robert was introduced to two British officers, one of whom was a friend of his own brother. They requested help in returning to British lines or, failing that, getting into the Vatican. Temporarily stashing the two POWs in the bookseller's apartment, Brother Robert brought the problem to Sir D'Arcy, who offered to pay their expenses if a hiding place could be found. In the meantime, and to Brother Robert's delight, the bookseller had found a noble Italian family which had agreed to take care of the officers.[1]

The number of escaped Allied POWs now seeking asylum in the Vatican was so large that it issued orders to turn them away, forcibly if necessary. On September 17, 1943, Yugoslav Branko Bokun was approached by four Allied ex-POWs, two British officers, a Canadian officer, and an Indian sergeant. Bokun had been sent to Rome by the Yugoslavian Red Cross to inform the Vatican of the murder of Slavs by Ustaše Catholics in Croatian-operated concentration camps. Although he met with Pius XII, he accomplished little. Remaining in Rome, Bokun, posing as a Hungarian, worked at the Rome chapter of the International Red Cross. He took the four POWs to the Vatican but they were refused entry; neutrality had to be maintained, at least officially. So, Monsignor O'Flaherty and Brother Robert rose to the challenge and found billets for them across the city. It took all their contacts plus funds from Sir D'Arcy's personal resources. It was purely an ad hoc arrangement and lacked organization. Outside help was needed, so Brother Robert enlisted the aid of Mrs. Henrietta Chevalier, a Maltese widow, resident in the city. Other helpers were to follow.

Mrs. Chevalier was a 42 year old British citizen. Her husband had worked for a Roman travel agency but died shortly before the outbreak of the war. She lived with six of her family in apartment No. 9 on the third floor at Via Imperia 12, a five-story apartment block. Although not large it had two bedrooms, a dining room, a pantry, a tiny storage room, a bathroom, and a separate toilet. Her family consisted of five daughters ranging in age from nine to 21, two sons, and her mother. The youngest daughter had been sent away to live with Maltese nuns in Rome for safety and the eldest son, who was a British subject, had been arrested and sent to a camp in northern Italy. The eldest Chevalier daughter was Rosie; the three middle daughters were Gemma, slim, serious, and shy, Matilda, and Mary, aged 12.

Her second son, Paul, held diplomatic status because he worked and lived at the Swiss Embassy. There he routinely passed out Red Cross parcels and British Players cigarettes from the closed British Embassy to British subjects still in Rome and, increasingly, to ex-POWs needing assistance. Originally intended for interned British civilians, the parcels were sent out after Italy declared war on Britain. Now, many Allied soldiers survived on these British Red Cross food parcels. Swiss officials visiting British soldiers in POW camps told them they could collect such parcels if they came to Rome. Paul became his mother's chief ally and he increasingly helped ex-POWs in need.

In fact, Mrs. Chevalier's career helping escaped POWs began when Paul called her to say he was bringing home two books, now the standard code word for POWs. In this instance it was two escaped French POWs. Mrs. Chevalier, needing advice, turned to Brother Robert who arranged for Monsignor O'Flaherty to visit her. When O'Flaherty explained the danger to her, she shrugged it off and so their long collaboration began.

Besides Paul, she had other assistants. There was Milko Scofic, a Yugoslav medical student who lived on the same floor in her building. Scofic had been arrested in Yugoslavia and sent to a Serbian labor camp. He escaped and made his way to Ljubljana for a reunion with his two brothers. Obtaining false papers from his uncle, a former archbishop of Trieste, Scofic then moved to Rome to study medicine at the university. Mrs. Chevalier enlisted him to get medicines for sick or wounded escapees who had come to Rome. She also relied upon the building *portiere*, Egidio, and his wife, Elvira, who knew all the comings and goings of the building.

Brother Robert was now generally known to be a point of contact for those wanting to help ex-POWs. And the calls started to come in, each presenting a unique situation, such as the one that was brought to him by a friend, Mrs. Esmé Almagiá. She had learned that an escaped POW was hiding on a friend's farm and so contacted Brother Robert. She had to be careful in arranging a meeting because her grandchildren's French governess was having an affair with a German officer and he was a frequent guest in her home.

Brother Robert visited Mrs. Almagiá and learned that the POW was a black South African; moving him around under the eyes of the Gestapo and the Fascists would be dangerous. Mrs. Almagiá feared that her friend's Fascist neighbors would see the black man and turn them in to the Italian police.

Brother Robert would need a car and an Italian driver, neither of which he could afford, if he was to successfully move the POW. Sir D'Arcy provided the money and a friendly Italian police officer agreed to go with them to deal with German checkpoints. Informed that the South African was very tall, Brother Robert borrowed a black cassock and a hat from the tallest brother in the mother house, Brother Franciskus, who was, in fact, German.

Arriving at the farm, Brother Robert found the South African soldier hiding in a hay cart. The soldier was skittish at first, but was finally convinced that he was there to help him. The cart was moved to the front of the farmyard and the soldier donned the cassock over his uniform. Brother Robert put a prayer book in his hands, and told him to look cheerful. If anyone questioned him he was to reply, *Collegio Ethiopicol*, the Ethiopian College inside the Vatican. On the way into the city, the car was stopped at several German roadblocks but the Italian's police identification and Brother Robert's Vatican pass allowed them to pass.[2]

The drama was for naught. The South African ex-POW was hidden with another black soldier who, as Brother Robert later wrote, ran away with the wife of an Italian. The enraged husband informed the Germans about the two men with the result that both soldiers were recaptured and sent to Germany, never to be heard from again.

By mid-October, with the constant trickle of escaped POWs arriving in Rome, it was clear that the Vatican was silently condoning the activities of Monsignor O'Flaherty. So far Baron Ernst von Weizsäcker, German Ambassador to the Holy See, had not raised the issue, but Kappler had been informed of O'Flaherty's work through his spy network and had learned that Prince Filippo Doria-Pamphili, head of one of Rome's most ancient families, was supporting the monsignor's efforts.

Doria-Pamphili, an English-Italian friend of Monsignor O'Flaherty, had heard of his work with escapees and guessed that he would be short on cash. The prince had been educated at Cambridge, had a British-born wife, and was an ardent anti-fascist; he had even been imprisoned for conspiring against the regime. He invited O'Flaherty to his palazzo on Via del Corso, and, making sure they were not seen by his servants, the prince gave O'Flaherty 150,000 lire in cash, telling to come back when he needed more. This was dangerous for both men.

Hoping to catch them in the act, Kappler set a covert watch on the prince's palazzo. The trap was sprung when O'Flaherty next visited the prince, who this time gave him 300,000 lire. As O'Flaherty was leaving, a servant told the prince that the palazzo was surrounded by the SS, headed by Kappler himself. This might have been the end, but for O'Flaherty's astonishing reaction. Running downstairs into the cellar of the large palazzo, he looked for a way to escape.

As luck would have it, it was the day of the palazzo's winter coal shipment. A coalman stood in the courtyard above, sending bags of coal, one at a time, down a coal chute through a basement window into the cellar. O'Flaherty removed his cassock and stuffed it into an empty coal sack. Then he blackened his face and clothes with coal dust. He called to the coalman at the top of the coal chute that he was a priest and that he needed help. He persuaded the coalman to trade places with him. The man slid down the chute and O'Flaherty clambered up. The SS in the courtyard did not notice the change of cast, and O'Flaherty carried his coal bag out to safety, walking past the SS guards. They failed to notice that it was odd for a coalman to be carrying coal *out* of the palazzo courtyard.

Ducking into a nearby church, the monsignor cleaned up, donned his cassock, and was soon safely in his room at the German College. From there he called the prince and told of his escape. Prince Filippo informed O'Flaherty that, "Colonel Kappler is a very angry man. He spent two hours here and he said that if I happened to see you, I was to say that one of these days he will be entertaining you …"[3]

Eventually the prince, his wife, and daughter were forced to flee from Kappler, narrowly escaping arrest. The prince went into hiding in a monastery and grew a beard as part of his disguise. The princess and her daughter were safely hidden away by Monsignor O'Flaherty.[*]

———

Monsignor O'Flaherty remained in constant contact with Sir D'Arcy while a seemingly endless number of escapees came to Rome for help.

---

[*] After the war the prince was appointed the first mayor of liberated Rome.

To protect Vatican neutrality, Sir D'Arcy could not be seen to be actively helping escapees, but that did not apply to his butler, John May. Sir D'Arcy also enlisted the help of Count Sarsfield Salazar, of the Swiss Embassy who looked after things for the British Embassy and 25 other countries. So May, the monsignor, and the count joined forces, calling themselves "The Council of Three," and took on the huge task of organizing assistance to the escaped Allied POWs now pouring into Rome.

One of Count Salazar's Italian employees, Secondo Costantini, and his family managed the now closed British Embassy and still lived inside the building. Costantini passed out Red Cross parcels, clothing, and cigarettes to POWs who arrived at the embassy gate. He even allowed them to peruse English-language books in the library.

To house the numbers of Allied soldiers arriving, The Council of Three rented two apartments. The first, rented with the help of a communist partisan known only as Nebolante, was a luxury apartment across from the Opera in Via Firenze, just off Via Nazionale and very close to Termini, Rome's central railway station. It backed onto a hotel commandeered by the SS and was close to the Via Veneto area cordoned off by the Germans.

The second apartment was found by a Hungarian contact of the monsignor's, likely Nora Kiss, a Russian-speaking ballet dancer. It was on Via Domenico Cellini 4, in a fashionable new quarter of Rome, the Parioli district about a mile away to the north, and it was rented in the name of her Italian friend Ubaldo Cipolla – a name to remember.

Among the many remarkable stories of escapees is that of Lt. Colin Leslie, a member of the British Army's elite Irish Guards. Leslie had been captured in North Africa in March 1943, and transferred to Italy. He was moved from POW Camp #49 at Fontanellato near Parma to a local hospital on September 4, 1943. The Fontanellato camp held 500 Allied officers and 100 other ranks. After the armistice all 600 men walked away before the Germans arrived.

Well enough to make good his own escape, Leslie left the hospital and hid out in a cottage in the countryside with Italian farmers until mid-October. But with winter fast approaching, Leslie needed to find warmer quarters. Moreover, it was becoming increasingly difficult to avoid German patrols. So, on October 15, the farmers who were hiding him took him to a neighboring village in the vicinity of Parma, where he met Ristic Cedomir, a former Yugoslav Army lieutenant. Cedomir worked out of the Rome Office of the International Red Cross. Armed with official Red Cross papers, he was able to travel around the country, visiting POW camps and other refugee camps. On these trips, Cedomir also secretly distributed money and supplies to nascent partisans. If he couldn't contact his partisans, he promised to give the money to Leslie.

Cedomir returned to the village a few days later to say that the partisan he was to have met had been killed and so Leslie could have the cash. With the money, Leslie bought a new suit and smartened up. Posing as an Italian businessman he caught a train for Rome, sharing his compartment with some German soldiers. They ignored each other; perhaps the Germans didn't speak Italian and Leslie knew no German. He arrived in Rome early on October 20 with no contacts and nowhere to go, so he spent the day hiding in churches. When evening came, he went to find Cedomir at the office of the Red Cross which was in Via Sardegna in the restricted German-controlled hotel zone off Via Veneto.

Cedomir took Leslie to Count Salazar at the Swiss Embassy a ten-minute walk away and he arranged for Leslie to stay in the empty British Embassy which, for some reason, was not under German surveillance at that point. Monsignor O'Flaherty visited him there and, after about nine or ten days, took him to meet Sir D'Arcy and Tittmann in the Santa Marta hospice inside the Vatican, smuggling Leslie past the Swiss Guard in clerical garb.

Sir D'Arcy was looking for a military officer to be in charge of billeting, feeding, and caring for the swelling number of ex-POWs in Rome and the surrounding countryside. It is highly likely that Sir D'Arcy had been briefed on the activities of the British MI-9's "A" Force during his sojourn in London and it is also probable that he had been directed to create a more formal organization to provide ex-POW assistance. That would also start the cash flowing. Leslie might be just the officer to run the organization.

O'Flaherty and Sir D'Arcy tried to persuade Lt. Leslie to take the job, reside in the Vatican, and run what was shaping up to be the Rome Escape Line but he refused. Leslie was determined to get back to the war and feared that, once in the Vatican, the neutrality laws would intern him for the duration, even after Rome was liberated.

Having turned down the offer, Leslie was moved to the rented apartment on Via Domenico Cellini which he shared with a Yugoslav named Bruno Buchner. Buchner spoke good Italian and could move freely about Rome but was bellicose and his rants about killing Germans made Leslie nervous; he complained and was soon moved to an apartment found by another one of Monsignor O'Flaherty's helpers, Molly Stanley.

Stanley had come to Italy just after World War I to study Italian, and stayed on, working at odd jobs as a governess, secretary, and finally as the English teacher to the son of Vittoria Colonna, the Duchess of Sermoneta. Working with O'Flaherty, Stanley took money, food, and other items to wounded English POWs in Rome's military hospitals and to those interned in the Regina Coeli Prison. She often joined Monsignor O'Flaherty on his rounds. A couple walking in the street drew less attention than a man walking alone, so she acted as O'Flaherty's companion when he made his rounds in civilian attire.[4]

Lt. Leslie stayed at his new place for only a few days and then moved to new digs at the Casa San Giovanni on the Janiculum Hill, owned by the North American College. Monsignor Joseph McGeough, the American rector of the college, was in direct contact with Harold Tittmann and of course knew of Monsignor O'Flaherty's activities. McGeough had approved his tenancy because, at this point, this was the safest location to place escaped POWs and as Leslie had been told so many details of the Escape Line it was crucial that he was not recaptured and subjected to interrogation. It was the ideal place to stash him, and as a Guard's officer, he could be relied on to be in charge of the men hiding there.

The Casa San Giovanni was housing some 30 men when Leslie arrived: 15 American medical students of Italian heritage, eight British soldiers, three American servicemen, an Italian Air Force pilot, a South African priest, and several political refugees. Leslie needed help overseeing this motley collection of backgrounds and nationalities, so the Council of Three sent in Antonio Call, the former corporal from the Pope's bodyguard. Call, who often cooked for the ex-POWs, was just the man to keep a watch on them; and the escapees were said to remark that well-stewed beef became a familiar part of the diet.

Leslie wanted to let his wife know he was alive, so he wrote a check for five pounds sterling and had John May send it via diplomatic pouch to Leslie's bank in London. The amount was not important. It was his signature on the dated check that would convey his message. Mrs. Leslie was puzzled to be called to her bank in Palmers Green, in London, to verify the signature, but seeing his handwriting on the check in her hands, she knew he was alive.

That was not the only way that escapees were in contact with their families. A Signora Bruccoleri worked for the International Red Cross in Rome and letters for Allied POWs in Italy came through her hands. Monsignor O'Flaherty kept her apprised of the names of escapees he was sheltering in and around Rome and she pulled out those letters. Her daughter Josette would then deliver them to the monsignor.[5]

The danger of hiding escaped POWs suddenly escalated. Mussolini issued a decree on October 25, 1943 that called for the death penalty to anyone assisting escaped Allied prisoners of war. Shortly after this decree was issued, German authorities visited the Brancallone family farm outside of Florence; at one point the family had housed as many as 17 POWs. During the raid two escaped POWs were captured and Signor Brancallone was shot in front of his wife and daughters, the barn set on fire with the livestock in it and razed to the ground.[6] Those providing help did not scare easily, however, especially those at the Vatican.

For the ex-POWs, it took a certain élan, bravado, and even carelessness to forego the ignoble safety of captivity for the uncertainty of life on the run. A clear description of this type of person follows:

> One rapidly got used to the sight, shocking at first, of people in German uniform riding in trams, or going into shops; it was harder to get rid of the idea that every stranger, and particularly every official, was staring at one and regarded one's appearance as odd. The more one could adopt an actor's insouciance in the presence of strangers, the better ... One other attribute needs to be mentioned, next to the power of quick decision and hardly less important: luck. Unlucky escapers never got out of camps, unlucky evaders fell at the first fence, chance control from a passer-by in a country lane, or even at the ticket-office of a railway station. Lucky ones soared through difficulties that ought to have kept them pent: the sentry was asleep, or simply looking the other way; the wire fence had been inefficiently

put up; the train control never reached their carriage; the people to whom they appealed for help knew how to keep their mouths shut.[7]

The Council of Three still needed a leader. Sir D'Arcy found a possible solution in the form of a scribbled request for assistance from a British officer, signed, S. I. Derry, major. His story, like many others, was at once both unique and yet typical.

Major Sam Derry was a Territorial (active reserve) officer in the Royal Artillery and a veteran of the British Expeditionary Force in France. He had been evacuated from Dunkirk during the miracle of the little boats in 1940. Sent to North Africa in 1941, Derry was awarded a Military Cross for the way he employed his battery at the battle of the Omars during the British drive in Cyrenaica against Rommel's Afrika Korps in January 1942. Captured in February, he escaped, only to be recaptured with his surrounded garrison during the last-ditch defense line at El Alamein in July 1942. As it turned out, he was interrogated by the same Afrika Korps officer who had interrogated him during his first capture. That the German remembered him even though it was many months and more than 800 miles further away was itself extraordinary.

Flown to Lecce in southern Italy, in what he described as an ancient transport aircraft without parachutes, Derry was moved to a camp at Bari and then on to the Allied Officers Camp at Chieti, where he met Joe Pollak, our Czech private soldier. Pollak spent so much time talking with the Italian guards that Derry initially suspected him of being an informer. As a field-grade officer, major and above, Derry automatically became a member of the camp escape committee. In the late spring of 1943, after most of the senior officers had been moved to another camp, Derry found himself heading the committee. But there was no opportunity for escape and by the last week in September, Derry and the other POWs were moved to the Sulmona camp for staging to Germany via train. On the trains, field-grade officers rode in third-class carriages while junior officers rode in sealed boxcars. Derry's chance came just outside of Tivoli. He asked permission to use the lavatory; then, he neatly sidestepped a guard with a well-practiced rugby move, leapt from the train and found himself in the countryside, uninjured and free.

He had only the clothes on his back and no idea where he was. His vague plan was to head south, cross the German lines and join Allied forces. The Allies were now fighting their way north from Naples.

He cautiously spoke to an Italian family asking, in his broken Italian, for help. They fed him and invited him to spend the night. Knowing that if he were discovered in the house the family would suffer, he slept outside in a haystack. After a day's rest, he looked around and saw the mountains to his east. In the west he could make out the dome of Saint Peter's in Rome, about 15 miles away.

The Italian family told him that some other British ex-POWs were hiding nearby. Two farm boys took him to where a dozen soldiers were living in caves. Derry updated them on war news and promised he would return. When he came back the next day, there were two dozen soldiers. In time this number climbed to more than 50. The soldiers desperately wanted to get back across the German lines, 120 miles to the south. Derry had to figure out how they could.

These soldiers had escaped from Passo Corese Camp #54, located at Fara in Sabina, 30 miles northeast of Rome. It was a POW camp for 4,000 enlisted, other ranks, British, South African, and Gurkha soldiers – Nepalese who were enlisted to fight for the British, who had been captured at the surrender of Tobruk. Derry knew that leading 50 unarmed soldiers through enemy-occupied territory would mean certain recapture; he needed help.

Hoping that there were still British officials inside the Vatican, Derry, with the aid of a local priest, sent a note requesting assistance for his group of escaped POWs. In the rural areas of Italy, the local priests were very influential and often acted as intermediaries between POWs, partisans, and even Fascist forces and the Germans. The note was addressed to anybody English in the Vatican. Most importantly he signed the note, S. I. Derry, Major.

The fact that Derry was a senior officer caught the attention of Sir D'Arcy, who was still looking for an officer to run his growing ex-POW assistance effort. After three days, the village priest returned to the farm with 3,000 lire (equivalent to $50). Derry was delighted, signed a receipt, and then asked the priest to take another request to the Vatican for more money. Four days later, the priest returned with an additional 4,000 lire plus an invitation for Derry to visit his unknown benefactor in Rome.

Pietro Fabri, a local farmer who sold his vegetables in the city, gave Derry the perfect cover. Hiding in a load of cabbages, Derry safely lumbered in Fabri's horse-drawn cart to Rome. It was November 20, 1943. In the outskirts of the city he was taken to an apartment where he met a "small, greasy man of early middle age, wearing the long black cassock of a priest, who smiled toothily."[8] The priest was Don Pasqualino Perfetti. Derry's guide for the day was Aldo Zambardi who greeted him in English. Wearing an ill-fitting overcoat, flannel pants, and a hat, Derry left the apartment with Zambardi and boarded a tram filled with German soldiers and Fascist militiamen in uniform. Derry was nervous. He felt conspicuous because of his ill-fitting clothes, but no one noticed.

The pair got off near the Ponte Vittorio Emanuele II, crossed the Tiber with the looming bulk of the Castel San'Angelo to their right and the graceful dome of Saint Peter's to the left. With November came the cold, rain, and damp. Derry would have observed that the Tiber River was high and perhaps he may have even seen debris flowing down the river from the mountains, including trees, branches, and the occasional drowned pig. Seagulls would have been floating down from one bridge and, before reaching the next, turning to fly back to the previous bridge as if they were constrained to only one section of the river.

Turning left on the first major street, they proceeded down Via della Conciliazione towards Saint Peter's Square. After entering the piazza, they headed for the steps on the left side of the Basilica. The square was full of sightseeing German soldiers in uniform, as well as priests and nuns. They passed close by a tall priest who whispered "follow me," and he led them through the Bernini Colonnade and crossed to a building with "Collegio Teutonicum" (German College) written over the entrance. Fearing a trap, Derry froze. Then the priest introduced himself in English as Monsignor O'Flaherty and Zambardi disappeared.

Derry was taken up to the monsignor's room, given something to drink, some biscuits, and – most appreciated – the offer of a bath and a change of clothes. Later that morning he met John May and was served lunch by the silent German nuns who ran the college and who never acknowledged that O'Flaherty often had foreign visitors. He also met another visitor, Blon Kiernan, daughter of Dr. T. J. Kiernan, the Irish Republic Chargé d'Affaires to the Holy See, and his wife, Delia Murphy, a well-known popular singer, who were early supporters of Monsignor O'Flaherty. May returned that afternoon with an invitation to dine that evening with Sir D'Arcy.

In order to get to Sir D'Arcy's apartment inside the Vatican, one must go back into Saint Peter's Square and through the Arco delle Campane, passing Swiss Guards, now wearing war-service uniforms and not the colorful uniforms of yellow, slashed with red and blue, originally designed by Michelangelo. The trip called for a disguise, so Derry donned one of the monsignor's cassocks. Together the two set off. Once in Sir D'Arcy's top floor drawing room in the Palazzo Santa Marta, Derry was served a cocktail and offered cigarettes. He enjoyed them alone as the monsignor neither smoked nor drank. At last, Sir D'Arcy joined them and they all went into dinner where Derry ate fresh fruit and steak with mushrooms, grilled tomatoes, and other trimmings. It was followed by a creamy dessert, an incredible change from POW food.

After dinner Derry was told the latest war news. Rome was now just another German-occupied city. Without going into too much detail, they described the growing movement to help POWs and Sir D'Arcy's need for someone to head the new organization they had created to do this. Then Sir D'Arcy asked Derry if he would take on this responsibility, and Derry agreed to start immediately. Before taking over, Derry said he needed to return to the countryside to bring the men he had left up to date. The next day, wearing one of Sir D'Arcy's suits and a pair of his shoes – ironically made in Germany and marked "Unter Linden," Berlin's Fifth Avenue – he returned to the monsignor's room to change back into his old, ill-fitting clothes. His trip back to the countryside was a reverse of the one he made into the city. This time he and Fabri stopped at a *taverna* to drink wine which Derry paid for.

Back among the escaped soldiers, he placed the senior NCO in charge and gave him 50,000 lire to buy food and clothing from the local farmers. The money was also for insurance to guarantee that the *contadini* would continue to aid the escapees. Derry also set up a way to communicate with them. After spending another night in his haystack, Derry returned to Rome, once more amid the cabbages.

Pleased at having Derry accept the job, the prudent Sir D'Arcy nevertheless needed to be sure he was not someone who had assumed Derry's identity – a spy sent by the Gestapo. To do this, D'Arcy contacted England through a secret radio, and asked the local police to find Derry's father. It was to tell him his son was alive and more importantly to check out Derry's story. At his next meeting with D'Arcy, Derry realized that he was being gently interrogated, Sir D'Arcy asking him about his hometown and aspects of his life that only he would know.

We don't know precisely how Sir D'Arcy contacted the police in England. He probably sent his request to someone in the FMCR. The message would then have been sent to the newly established headquarters of the Badoglio government in Bari and passed to the British through official channels. However it was done, Sir D'Arcy received his answer in less than three days. His contact may also have been Monsignor Roberto Ronca of the *Pontificio Seminario Maggiore di Roma* at Saint John Lateran. Although it can't be verified, Ronca was supposed in some circles to be one of those responsible for the Vatican radio operations of SIM and its liaison with British Intelligence Inter Service Liaison Department (ISLD) throughout the German occupation. If so, that may have been one reason for the eventual raid on Saint John Lateran.

Certainly there seems to be evidence of multiple clandestine radios inside the Vatican. A wartime OSS report stated that a Vatican Radio operator simply had been bribed to make transmissions and that there were even two Italian military officers inside the Vatican with a British radio.[9]*

Cleared of all suspicion, Derry was now the head of the Rome Allied Escape Organization, the official name of the Escape Line. It came into existence on December 1, 1943 and its mission was simple: to expand on what the Council of Three (O'Flaherty, May, and Salazar) had accomplished and to build on that foundation of keeping the growing number of escaped Allied POWs out of German hands. Their aim was to ensure that the ex-POWs regularly received food, clothing, medical supplies, money, and, where possible, were moved to relatively safe coastal areas for evacuation by British forces. Derry was now an official "A" Force officer and in a post-liberation report of June 23, 1944, was listed as such in a report on American ex-POWs.

Major Derry relied heavily on O'Flaherty. They shared a room in the German College and spoke often. One day Derry was thanking the monsignor for being pro-British when O'Flaherty quickly disabused him of that idea. He had witnessed the Irish War of Independence (1919–1921) and had no love for the British. He explained:

Why am I helping you now? Well, I'll tell you, me boy. When this war started I used to listen to the broadcasts from both sides. All

---

* A radio, known as the Centro X transmitter, had been brought into the Vatican by Princess Ninì Pallavicini – see Chapter 11. After the war, Monsignor O'Flaherty took under his wing an 18-year-old Irish voice student. They met once a week for lunch in his room and on one occasion she noticed a large black box with earphones and a microphone in a corner. She quizzed the monsignor as to their purpose and he told her that he had used them during the German occupation to contact British Intelligence. See Walker, p. 289.

propaganda, of course, and both making terrible charges against the other; I frankly didn't know which side to believe – until they started rounding up the Jews in Rome. They treated them like beasts, making old men and respectable women get down on their knees and scrub the roads. You know the sort of thing that happened after that [the October 16, 1943 Jewish roundup]; it got worse and worse, and I knew then which side I had to believe.[10]

The monsignor had a Vatican identification card made with Sam Derry's own photograph but under the name of Patrick Derry. It said he was a Vatican researcher and a native of Dublin. His new birth date made him 11 years older so, at his new assumed age of 40, he would have been too old for Irish National Service. The card was backdated to January 15, 1943, when the real Derry was still in the POW camp at Chieti.

With his official Vatican ID, Derry visited the established billets. First he was escorted by the monsignor and later by other priests in the network, including Brother Robert. It was Brother Robert who introduced Derry to Mrs. Chevalier as he had the monsignor. Derry recalled:

> Father Claffey [an Irish priest working with Monsignor O'Flaherty] then took me to my next guide, the cheerful little Brother Robert Pace, who was to lead me to the home of his gallant countrywoman, Mrs. Chevalier, the first to provide accommodations for the Monsignor's escapers … Brother Robert led me through a couple of streets which, like so many in Rome seemed to be a mixture of the seedy and the spectacular … We turned into an entrance between two shops, climbed endless stairs, and rang the bell at an apartment door, which was opened by a vivacious and voluble little woman with bright dark eyes and a kind, motherly face … Mrs. Chevalier was expecting us, and she welcomed me as though I were a long-lost son. She ushered us in, and introduced me to the four British soldiers who were billeted with her … If Mrs. Chevalier realized that her life was in danger every minute she had a single escaper, let alone four, in her care, she gave no sign of it …[11]

Derry also wrote up his visits to other escapees and their billets in his vivid prose:

The course of the next few days followed the same pattern of scurrying about Rome under the noses of the enemy, but although I felt conspicuous in daylight, I knew that to be found on the streets after curfew would invite searching, and possibly a disastrous interrogation. I never became quite used to the sudden shock of finding myself walking among a group of German soldiers, or face-to-face with a couple of SS men as they emerged from a café, their jack-boots gleaming and the skull and cross-bones insignia leering hideously from their lapels; nor did I ever conquer the sense of loneliness that walked with me on the streets of Rome – for if the stranger in a strange land is always lonely he is never more so than when he dare not speak, even in his own language.[12]

Sir D'Arcy assigned three of the Vatican's permanently interned Allied servicemen as staff for Derry. They were Major Sym, Captain Byrnes, and Sub-Lieutenant Elliott. Having little to do, they had taken to hanging out in the office of Sir D'Arcy's secretary, Hugh Montgomery. Now put to work they immediately started to index the names of the ex-POWs being helped by the Escape Line. The records included the organization's expenditures, receipts and correspondence. It was prudent to track expenses for soon there would be huge sums of money flowing through the organization. In case of a German raid, however, the records had to be buried each evening in the Vatican Gardens.

Shortly after Derry came on board, the organization suffered a major blow: Count Sarsfield Salazar, the Swiss member of the Council of Three, learned he was under surveillance. Warned to restrict his movements lest he be thrown out of the country, he complied and in doing so lost much of his value to the organization.

Trust was essential to Derry's work and he tested all newcomers. One test case was that of Peter Tumiati, whom Derry met early on. Tumiati was a bilingual journalist and a British agent from "A" Force. Tumiati had been a political prisoner of the Fascists for years. SIM agents working inside of the Vatican may have told Sir D'Arcy and the monsignor to expect him. Tumiati arrived in Rome with 20,000 lire and contacted the monsignor, who introduced him to Derry. Derry was characteristically suspicious but the monsignor reassured him that he knew him well.

Nevertheless, Derry tested Tumiati. He sent him to Bari with a list of the 2,000 escapees that the organization was caring for in Rome and throughout Italy. John May microfilmed the list and had it baked in a small loaf of bread. After a few weeks, Derry heard an assigned code word broadcasted on BBC Radio and knew that the list had gotten through and that Tumiati could be trusted.

Late in November 1943, several more Allied soldiers turned up in Rome. Among them was D'Arcy Mander of the British Green Howards Regiment. He had been captured in the desert southwest of Tobruk and he arrived in Rome from the north.

While surrounded in the western desert on May 29, 1942, Mander, who spoke excellent German, interviewed a wounded German officer whose plane had crashed near his position. It was Lieutenant General (*General der Panzertruppe*) Ludwig Crüwell, commander of Rommel's Afrika Korps. While a POW himself General Crüwell would disclose information about the German V2 rocket program. This report caused the Allies to bomb Peenemünde and the developing facilities there, severely disrupting the V2 program.

The day he arrived in Rome, Mander met with a man known only as Franco. Franco's real name was Branko Bokun, the Yugoslav sent to Rome to inform the Vatican of the murder of Slavs by Ustaše Catholics in Croatian-operated concentration camps. Bokun worked with Ristic Cedomir at the Rome chapter of the International Red Cross. In this position, he traveled throughout Italy and France to pass money to Yugoslavian ex-POWs. His Italian was poor but his German was good so he conversed easily with Mander.

On his second day, Mander met Tug Wilson, a British captain, while he was waiting to see Captain Leonardo Trippi, the Swiss Military Attaché, and collect a Red Cross parcel. Wilson was a trained saboteur. Weeks earlier he had come ashore on a British submarine to demolish ammunition dumps and block a railroad tunnel. He missed his rendezvous, however, and instead made his way to Rome looking for sanctuary and a way back to the Allied lines. Arriving at the Vatican, he was thrown out by vigilant Swiss Guards. Monsignor O'Flaherty then set him up at the home of the Italian-named Nebolante, the same man who had rented the apartment on Via Firenze for the organization. Wilson wrote a letter to the Pope complaining about his treatment by the Swiss Guards and O'Flaherty was delighted to pass him the reply from a Vatican official, who apologized and suggested that he return to the Vatican at a more convenient time.

Later, Mander, and two traveling companions, Sandy Stewart and Jack Selikman, both South African officers, were billeted in the apartment at Via Domenico Cellini. Herta Habernig, an Austrian Jewess, lived there as well. Also a refugee, she cooked for soldiers. The number of ex-POWs living in the apartment was now 17.

Up at the North American College's Casa San Giovanni on the Janiculum Hill, another American was added to the mix when Raymond Downey, a B 26 Marauder pilot, moved in. He arrived at the Vatican on December 17. Downey was a US Army Air Corps major from the US Military Academy at West Point. Downey had been the commanding officer of the US 37th Bomber Squadron. While leading 18 Marauders on a mission to bomb a railway bridge four miles north of Todi, his plane was hit. Keeping it aloft until he was over Viterbo, he then crash-landed the plane, set it on fire, and split up his crew. Knowing that the Vatican was a neutral state, he decided to take his chances and head to Rome.

In his unpublished diary, Downey wrote that he and the others internees had to wear clerical robes when venturing outside. They were bored, passing the time reading, writing letters, and playing bridge and table tennis. But there were comforts: they could shower when they wanted and, despite food shortages, they certainly ate well. Downey wrote that they:

Had afternoon tea with an odd assortment of bread, cake, sandwiches and other junk – all good. Then I started shortening my cassock with needle and thread that I chiseled from Monsignor O'Flaherty. Got about a quarter finished when the grapevine came through that there was more cake in the other room.[13]

11

Official Military Resistance

The Italian armed forces had failed to defend Rome against the Germans, but military resistance to the German occupation grew rapidly. As we have seen, a pro-monarchy anti-fascist organization, the FMCR (Military Clandestine Front of the Resistance), swiftly came into being and swung into action. The FMCR comprised loyal officers and men from the Italian Army, Carabinieri, Navy, Air Force, and the Guardia di Finanza, the customs and financial police. In total, the FMCR would eventually have some 29,000 men, 12,000 of whom were active in Rome.

Acting as a conduit for information, the well-respected Italian SIM remained under the direct control of the *Comando Supremo*. It too was expressly loyal to the king and Marshal Badoglio and it played a significant role in anti-German military activities throughout the occupation of Rome. Although it was a joint staff organization, each of the three armed services (and the Carabinieri) maintained its own separate intelligence organizations. They were:

SIE – *Servizio Informazioni dell'Esercito* (Army Intelligence)
SIS – *Servizio Informazioni della Marina* (Naval Intelligence)
SIA – *Servizio Informazioni Aeronautica* (Air Force Intelligence)

Immediately after the king and Marshal Badoglio fled Rome, Badoglio started the process of reinvigorating SIM and using it to monitor what was going on in the city. He realized that, as he developed his relationship with the Allies, intelligence was his most valuable bargaining chip.

Needing to establish radio communication with the Badoglio government in exile, on September 10, or shortly thereafter, an Italian S-79 aircraft belonging to SIA flew five military officers from Littorio Airfield, the small urban airfield located along the Tiber in the north of the city, to Brindisi's Campo Casale Airfield. Although the officers had successfully dodged the Germans guarding Littorio, they were instead arrested and interned by the British when they landed at Brindisi.

When these Rome-based officers had cleared up who they were and convinced their captors of their good intentions, they met with the Italian SIM officers who had escaped with the *Comando Supremo*. Their goal was to establish a direct way to communicate with the Badoglio government. On September 13, 1943, Badoglio directed an Italian Army radio engineer, noncommissioned officer Giuseppe Baldanza, to fly from Brindisi to Pescara on the Adriatic coast, 100 miles east of Rome. Baldanza was a trained radio operator and he carried with him a new radio and secret codes for a Centro X transmitter, the new code name for the FMCR headquarters in Rome. Baldanza made his way overland from Pescara to Rome and this equipment was initially installed at the king's Villa Savoia. Now the loyal officers of the FMCR could communicate directly with the Badoglio government and the reestablished SIM headquarters in Brindisi at the new Italian *Comando Supremo*, now called Centro R.

Cooperation with the British grew rapidly and SIM headquarters in Brindisi also sent Captain Fabrizio Vassalli to Rome with secret codes supplied by the SOE to establish the so-named Rudder Link.[*] At 09:30 on September 19, 1943, the first direct message from Rome Centro X to Centro R was sent over the Rudder Link and passed to the British SOE "A" Force Brindisi station. This link was supervised by SOE agent Dick Mallaby in Brindisi and was the start of active SIM–SOE, and later SIM–OSS trilateral cooperation.

In response to continued SIM activities, on October 1, 1943, Mussolini's new Republican Fascist government formed a new intelligence organization called the Defense Intelligence Service (SID – *Servizio Informazioni Difesa*). It was controlled by Marshal Rodolfo

---

[*] Vassalli was eventually captured by the Germans and murdered on May 24, 1944. He was the cousin of Giuliano Vassalli, the socialist representative of the CLN who later became Italy's Minister of Justice.

Graziani, RSI (Fascist) War Minister. The emphasis for this new organization was counterintelligence and the detection of subversive elements. It worked closely with the Germans.

Most officers were drawn from SIM and the other service intelligence agencies, but they were mostly the victims of being in the wrong place at the wrong time. Most remained loyal to the Badoglio government and so efforts were lackluster.

***

Prior to the occupation Rome had been declared an Open City on August 14, 1943. The stumbling block to this was the paramilitary Royal Corps of Carabinieri. Prior to the armistice the armed Carabinieri had manned 60 local stations spread across the city.

When the Italians surrendered to the Allies on September 8, 1943, there were 11,000 Carabinieri on duty keeping order in Rome. Kesselring too declared Rome an Open City on September 11. Using that as an excuse, Herbert Kappler set about ridding the city of this armed police force.

The Carabinieri were traditionally fiercely loyal to the monarchy. As such, early in his dictatorship and well before war had broken out, Mussolini had established the National Public Security Police (PS – *Pubblica Sicurezza*) who owed their loyalty to him alone. This nationwide police organization fell under the jurisdiction of the Italian Ministry of the Interior. In Rome, as in every other province, it made its headquarters at the Questura, the central police station of the city. At its largest, the Rome force numbered about 10,000 men. The PS divided the city into 40 districts, each district headed by a *commissario* (inspector) or *vice-commissario*. Although they had distinctive uniforms, they usually wore civilian clothes. Normally they did not patrol the streets but responded to calls from loyal Fascists. They were not allowed to arrest military personnel and before the armistice they often came into conflict with the Carabinieri.

By October 1, the number of Carabinieri had shrunk to 8,000. Like the Italian soldiers who walked away from their posts, many Carabinieri simply went home. They were unwilling to work for a government hostile to their king. On October 6, the order came for all Carabinieri to report to their barracks the next day at 08:15. Arriving that morning, they were told to turn in their weapons and go home. They had officially been disbanded.

It was not enough to merely disband the Carabinieri. Kappler, using his own men and the PS, arrested 2,000 of them, mainly officers and noncommissioned officers. Many officers of the PAI (Italian Africa Police) provided advanced warning to some of their former Carabinieri colleagues which permitted them to escape the roundup. Those who were not so fortunate to receive advance notice were loaded onto trains at the Ostiense and Tiburtina stations, and sent to Germany. The last train headed north on October 10, 1943. Some 600 were to die in German concentration camps.

The reaction to this deportation was swift: those escaping the roundup formed the Carabinieri Clandestine Resistance Front (*Fronte Clandestino di Resistenza Carabinieri*). Its mission was to collect information and report it to the Badoglio government.* It quickly became the activist arm of the FMCR under the command of General Filippo Caruso and played an important role in the military resistance to German rule. Their agents would tip off factories about impending raids to arrest and deport their workers to Germany. Eventually, more than 9,000 Carabinieri joined the Carabinieri Clandestine Resistance Front.

Now that SIM, the FMCR, and the Carabinieri were working together, they needed additional communication resources. More Allied radio transmitters were sent to Rome to pass on the large amount of intelligence collected. These were nicknamed Victory Radios. In October 1943, the first SIM-OSS agents were recruited in Naples and were sent to Rome. The first OSS mission to Rome, called Rome One, comprised four men (their code names in parentheses) and they carried three radios with them:

Italian Cavalry Officer Clemente Mino Menicanti (Coniglio), Radio Vittoria 1
Italian Army Lieutenant Maurizio Giglio (Cervo), Radio Vittoria 2

---

* During the next three months, 12 of these Carabinieri were arrested and subsequently murdered. By the end of the war 2,735 Carabinieri had been killed and 6,521 had been wounded.

Italian Navy Lieutenant Paolo Poletti (Lepre), with an unnamed radio
Gino (Vittorio), a SIM radio operator who was to accompany Lepre
to the north

They carried three radios with them: Radio Vittoria 1, Radio Vittoria
2, and the unnamed radio carried by Poletti. This group crossed the
German lines on foot in the Matese Mountains, near the town of
Isernia, 60 miles northeast of Naples. Giglio led the way, followed by
Menicanti, Poletti, and Gino. Upon arrival in Rome, Menicanti and
Giglio contacted Montezemolo and commenced sending intelligence
to Brindisi. On October 16, 1943, SIM sent an Italian Army artillery
officer, Enzo Stimolo (codenamed Corvo – crow in Italian) to Rome
with additional Radio Vittoria equipment and spare parts.

Later, on December 10, the Badoglio government covertly announced
that Colonel Montezemolo was to be the liaison officer between the
royalist military underground in Rome and all other underground
organizations working in the capital. The 44-year-old Montezemolo
had fought for Franco's Fascist forces in Spain during its civil war and
had been decorated for action in North Africa but his family had served
the Italian royal house of Savoy for generations and he continued to
serve his king. He was chief of staff in Rome for General Count Giorgio
Calvi di Bergolo, recognized by the Germans as the Italian *Comandante
della Città Aperta di Roma*.

At a later date, Poletti returned across the lines with his radio and
was captured by the British. Because he had radio equipment with him,
he was immediately held as a spy and jailed on the island of Nisida, a
few miles along the coast to the west of Naples. He managed to escape
but in doing so was shot by the British guards. He was posthumously
awarded the Italian Silver Medal for Military Valor.

Despite this tragic incident the flow of intelligence quickly gathered
momentum. Radio Vittoria 1 made its first broadcast on November 18,
1943 with Vincenzo Converti (codenamed Enzo) as the radio operator.
Over time Radio Vittoria employed several radio operators and a Rome
Two Mission, including a second group of radio operators, was sent to
Rome by boat, but the details are not known.

In Rome, the FMCR directed operations to collect intelligence for
Centro R, now transferred to the larger city of Bari north of Brindisi.
Intelligence comprised all kinds of information and Centro X's radio

reports detailed German troop movements, minefields, ammunition dumps, and information on the arrests of prominent resistance people. The intelligence collected was shared with Allied intelligence agencies such as the OSS and SOE.

The key to success for Centro X radio transmissions was moving the radio. At one point Princess Ninì Pallavicini hid the Centro X radio in her Palazzo Rospigliosi-Pallavicini near Piazza Venezia. She was the daughter of Marchese Medici del Vascello, a former Fascist minister.* The attractive blonde princess also hosted CLN meetings at her palazzo and helped the Escape Line with food, money, and false papers. Eventually the radio may have been clandestinely moved inside the Vatican although as yet no concrete evidence to prove this has been discovered.

A third mission, Rome Three, was organized by Raimondo Craveri, son in law of Benedetto Croce. It left from the island of Corsica, which had been in Allied hands since October 4, 1943. The Corsican port of Bastia, codenamed Balaclava, became the east coast base to insert agents into the Italian mainland. Rome Three was dropped off by the Italian submarine Axum along the coast north of Rome. The team consisted of two sections of agents. One section was codenamed Siria and was made up of 2nd Lieutenant Arrigo Paladini, an Italian artillery officer, and a radio operator named Franco (codenamed Dama). Paladini maintained contact with the SIS, the Italian Naval Intelligence organization.

The other team, Iris, consisted of Captain Enrico Sorrentino (codenamed Nicola) and an unknown radio operator. The radio was called Darda and Sorrentino self-styled himself as General Mark Clark's personal representative. Both sections eventually arrived in Rome on December 6, 1943.

Radio communications were of paramount importance during the Nazi occupation of Rome and in fact throughout Italy. As we have seen, these communications networks were organized by SIM,

---

* The Pallavicini family had been extremely wealthy for years and the princess's art collection was extensive. It included Botticelli's *La Derelitta* (The Outcast), still on display at the palazzo.

British Intelligence, SOE (for both "A" Force and Number One Special Force) and the OSS. SOE had established Number One Special Force which was responsible for linking up partisan groups up and down the length and breadth of Italy and to do that, radio communication links were established and intelligence disseminated and resupply drops coordinated. Due to the extreme danger Special Force radios were moved frequently. The table lists the four most important clandestine radios known to have operated in Rome from September 1943 to June 1944.

Name	Operated by	Rome locations	Associated personnel	Notes
Centro X	FMCR in Rome to SIM (Centro R) in Bari	1. King's Villa Savoia 2. Saint John Lateran 3. Palazzo Rospigliosi 4. Possibily inside the Vatican and if so, used sparingly	Giuseppe Baldanza Col. Montezemolo Monsignor Roberto Ronca Princess Ninì Pallavicini	Active September 19, 1943 – Rudder Link direct from Rome to SIM in Bari
Vittoria 1	FMCR – SIM	Moved around Rome	Enzo Stimolo Vincenzo Converti Clemente Menicanti Major Malcolm Munthe Major D'Arcy Mander	Operational from November 1943 to March 17, 1944
Vittoria 2	FMCR – SIM	Moved around Rome; barge in the Tiber	Lt Maurizio Giglio Franco Malfatti Peter Tompkins OSS	Operational late fall 1943 to March 17, 1944
Unnamed Radio	Number One Special Force – SIM	All over Italy but in Rome Lousena didn't move the radio around	Major Umberto Lousena Major Sam Derry	Lousena arranged supply drops for partisans; Derry arranged pickups of Allied escapees

In addition, Allied intelligence organizations became adept at passing messages to spies and agents inside German-occupied Italy by means of coded personal messages broadcast as part of their news services. These broadcasts came from: BBC Radio London; Radio Bari (Italian Royalist); Allied Command Radio from Caserta; and later from US Fifth Army Radio.

Better, clandestine radio communications also ensured that the Allies could now more ably assist ex-POWs. A key task for this expanding organization was to better organize these ex-POW movements to the Adriatic for pickup. Major Umberto Lousena, an Italian Army parachute officer, SIM asset, and a British SOE Number One Special Force agent, was the connection. Lousena, with false papers, was able to move freely about the provinces of Lazio and Umbria, both close to Rome, so he and Major Derry became close collaborators. The two majors often met several times a week. Derry gave Lousena the names and locations of escaped POWs and Lousena distributed money and supplies. Further he passed on instructions on how to contact "A" Force rat lines to rejoin Allied forces. Once Major Derry was in place, he arranged at least three large pickups with Lousena that rescued 104 ex-POWs along the Adriatic coast.

Lousena, described as fearless, also arranged supply drops for both partisans and escapees. In the process Lousena brought back valuable information on German troop movements which he passed via his own secret radio transmitter to SIM. Occasionally Sir D'Arcy and Derry were able to send messages via this radio. The radio was to prove his downfall and in late winter, he was captured with it on a trip to northern Italy, because he unwisely did not change his transmission location.

In February 1944, "A" Force, working together with SOE's Number One Special Force, produced a status report on the disposition of the more than 70,000 Allied POWs in Italy:

50,000 had been taken to Germany

2,000 plus were on the run near the Gran Sasso Mountain, northeast of Rome

5,000 were near Venice

2,000 were near Padua, west of Venice

1,000 were near Belluno, in the Dolomite foothills north of Venice

1,000 were near Treviso, midway between Belluno and Venice
400 were in and around Rome
100 were in and around Florence
60 were in Slovenia, then part of Italy

Gathering these numbers required cooperation from other organizations, both in and out of Rome. "A" Force worked with a clandestine organization, the Allied Prisoner of War Assistance Service (*Ufficio Assistenza Prigionieri di Guerra Alleati*), a Milan-based group. It was organized by Giuseppe Bacigalupi, who, with his English wife and their helpers, sent more than 1,800 ex-POWs from as far away as Rome to safety in Switzerland. These rescues came at a heavy cost. Of the 359 people who helped Bacigalupi, six were executed, five were killed protecting ex-Allied POWs, three were permanently disabled, and 26 were deported to concentration camps in Germany where nine of them died. Another 48, including Bacigalupi himself, were imprisoned in Italy. By 1945, a total of 6,335 Allied military had been returned to friendly lines from German-occupied Italy by "A" Force personnel. This is a remarkable number when one considers that, upon occupying Italy, a high priority for the Germans was sending all Allied POWs to camps in Germany.

Among other organizations and groups helping POWs in Rome and in Italy, the Yugoslavs formed a huge contingent. After the Axis invasion of Yugoslavia in April 1941, thousands of Yugoslav soldiers became POWs. Like other Allied soldiers, the Yugoslavs walked out of their camps on Italian Armistice Day, September 10. Many Yugoslavs were taken in by *contadini* and, as the partisan movement grew, joined their mountain bands. Yugoslavs divided into two groups – the Yugoslav communists, and the Yugoslav royalists, like Ristic Cedomir who worked at the Rome office of the International Red Cross.

Cedomir told Derry about a number of POWs who had escaped to Switzerland in late December. Giannetta Augeri, who had lived in England for seven years, had paid smugglers more than 260,000 lire of her own money to help the men cross the border. Cedomir also said that the Fascist police had arrested 18 Italians who had helped over 600 Allied escapees in the Arda Valley, northwest of Florence. Cedomir blamed the escapees, who had been imprudent, and not the

Italians. It was from this area that many ex-POWs had made their way to Switzerland.

Another large Allied group was the Free French Mutual Aid Committee. It was directed out of Vichy France's Embassy to the Holy See and headed by First Secretary Jacques de Blesson and Vice Consul François de Vial. The two met frequently with Derry to coordinate activities and collect British funds. They also secretly sabotaged official French Vichy policies and circumvented the French Ambassador, Leon Bérard. Sometimes they shared workers such as don Pasqualino Perfetti, the former priest whom Derry met on his very first day in Rome.

12

Ciao Bella, Ciao – The Partigiani*

*Begin with the simplest acts, those that require only a few men,
for example; spreading four-pointed nails along the roads most
frequently used by enemy traffic (you should have a model nail, if
not we will send one); identify the local Fascist chiefs; put them
under surveillance to learn their movements and then attack them
pitilessly. Sometimes it is wiser to assassinate Fascist chiefs from
a town other than your own so as to confuse police searches. Cut
telephone lines. Where possible, provoke landslides to interrupt
the flow of traffic. String metal wires across roads to saw the heads
off the drivers and passengers of enemy motorcycles; these are all
actions that you can do with the scarce means at your disposal.*

Directive from the Central Military Committee
of the Italian Communist Party

Resistance wore three faces: it was a war of national liberation from
German rule; it was a civil war between Fascists and anti-fascists; and,
for others, it was a class war between capitalists and communists.
Resistance also took different forms; passive resistance included not

---

* *"Bella ciao"* (Beautiful, Goodbye), an Italian partisan song of World War II, was sung to inspire
Italians to rise up against the Nazis and join the partisans. Its lyrics say that "if I should die in
the mountains bury me in the shade of beautiful flowers so that those that pass by will know
that the partisan buried here is a flower of freedom."

reporting incidents, looking the other way when an event occurred, and work slowdowns by workers and bureaucrats. Active resistance was participating in forbidden strikes and demonstrations, and writing and distributing underground newsletters. Aggressive resistance, punishable by death, included assisting escaped or evading servicemen, intelligence gathering, sabotage, assassination, guerrilla warfare, and participation in full-scale armed liberation movements.

There were no partisans in Italy when the September armistice was signed but there were about 4,000 active anti-fascists. And so, despite the inherent dangers, the partisan movement was born. Partisans were motivated by a mixture of anger, patriotism, ideology, idealism, and self-interest – a perfectly understandable desire to avoid Fascist conscriptions and German labor roundups. The Italian population, and the people of Rome in particular, generally regarded the partisans with sympathy with the obvious exception of those committed to the Fascist cause. Many citizens would simply look the other way if they happened to see partisans engaged in clandestine activity.

There were at least 36 partisan bands in and around Rome and they came from all levels of Italian society: wealthy bankers and industrialists, middle-class professionals, factory and office workers, students, military personnel, artisans, *contadini*, local clerics. Notably some 3,000 Jews – spread all over Italy – which was almost ten percent of the entire Jewish population of the country, also acted as partisans.

Women played combative roles in the partisan organizations and some carried out armed attacks against the German occupiers. Other women were not under arms but helped slow down clerical work, and fed, clothed, and hid partisans, former Italian soldiers, Allied ex-prisoners of war, Jews, and political refugees. They were the primary message couriers and organized and distributed supplies, food, and money. Women also worked in hospitals and acted as go-betweens between prisoners and their families.

Although the partisans were represented by all political factions, undoubtedly the best-organized groups were the communists. Because they already had a political organization in place, they were able to rapidly form military squads. The communists established Garibaldi

Brigades which became the main strength of the resistance. By the end of the war there were 575 brigades all over Italy. It is believed that approximately 50 percent of all Italian partisans were communists or communist sympathizers recruited from the three leftist parties: the Action Party, the Socialist Party, and the Communist Party. Although they operated independently, in Rome they coordinated activities through a joint Military Council. They also shared weapons and tactics.

In Rome there was not a Garibaldi Brigade per se, but the communists divided Rome into sectors, each under a separate command so that if one group was taken out, the whole organization was not lost. One main sub-group – the Red Flag (*Bandiera Rossa*) – was hardline Trotskyite and it attracted mostly laborers and other working-class types. They were effective covert saboteurs and could call upon as many as 172 armed men for attacks divided into separate bands. They infiltrated key government ministries and intercepted messages sent to the Germans, created chaos in telephone communications, and falsified census reports for Mussolini's new military draft. A stunning example of this was an official report averring that 90 percent of Rome's population was female and all the males were either under 16 or over 80. There was even a Red Flag branch called Koba for the children.

The Red Flag launched its first major overt operation in Rome on October 22, with an attack on the Italian Fascist military base at Fort Tiburtina. The mission was to seize weapons. It was a disaster and 21 partisans were captured. The very next day 11 of them were executed at Fort di Pietralata.

Outraged by the executions of their comrades, a squad of Red Flag partisans undertook a truly audacious act. They learned that seven partisans from the Tommaso Moro band, members of Red Flag, were to be shot. They hatched a dangerous plan to hijack the truck carrying the firing squad, impersonate them, and free their comrades.

They had learned that the Italian Africa Police (PAI) were to execute the partisans so a Red Flag squad followed the truck taking the PAI from their sports complex barracks at Foro Mussolini, to Fort Bravetta, the Fascist military and police casern (barracks) in the northwest suburb of the city. Partisans, impersonating Germans in stolen police uniforms, set up a roadblock in a remote area along the route. They forced the PAI truck to stop by surrounding it with partisans in German police uniforms in front and blocked by other partisans in the rear. They then told the 20 PAI to strip. The fake Germans donned the PAI uniforms, abandoned the unclothed PAI men in a roadside ditch and drove to Fort Bravetta for the execution. The Fascist and German guards at the fort, expecting the PAI, waved them through an outer gate. They parked the truck outside the entrance of the thick-walled, star-shaped fort, formed up, and then marched into the fort's inner bastion.

A Catholic chaplain arrived to give the seven condemned partisans the last rites. The firing squad took its position. The SS observer, who was always present for executions, gave the command to fire. Instead, the firing squad turned its guns on the Germans, the SS man, and the Fascist guards and took them prisoner. The partisans quickly untied their comrades, then, using their new captives as hostages, made their way back to the PAI truck and roared out of the gate. They headed down the nearby Via Aurelia, not stopping until they reached the ancient Etruscan town of Cerveteri, northwest of Rome, and a secure hiding place far out of the city.

The man in charge of the daring action was Vincenzo Guarniera, whose battle name was Tommaso Moro. He distributed a sphinx-like warning in a leaflet in German and Italian which read: "Germans and Fascists, life in Rome will be more difficult; Signed Tommaso Moro, Partisan."

Eventually, Guarniera was decorated by General Mark W. Clark with a Bronze Star Medal, citing him one of the best men of the Fifth Army. The Red Flag was a clear threat to Gestapo authority, so it was penetrated by an Italian agent, Ubaldo Cipolla, the double agent who had rented an apartment for Monsignor O'Flaherty's escaped POWs.

It was during this time of turbulence that Carla Capponi, the university student who had rescued the injured tanker, met medical student Rosario Bentivegna. Capponi first saw Bentivegna, with another acquaintance, while he was riding a bus. They met when he later delivered documents to her apartment, a clandestine meeting place for the budding partisan movement. Bentivegna's first impression of Capponi was not good:

Carla herself was smoking a pipe. That bothered me a lot. What a show of snobbery! I thought. I did my best to mock her, to somehow offend her, not thinking that it had to do with the tobacco rationing and that a pipe was a way not to waste what was left in your cigarette butts.[1]

Despite first impressions Capponi and Bentivegna became a powerful team and eventually became lovers. The two joined a communist partisan organization called the Patriotic Action Groups (GAP – *Gruppi di Azione Patriottica*) in October 1943. GAP was modeled on the quasi-military French Maquis Resistance. It had been formed at the end of September 1943, pledging to carry out urban guerilla warfare to assassinate German and Fascist officials, expose spies, attack military headquarters, and destroy radio stations, railway hubs, war materiel, and moving columns of troops. The GAP leaders were often University of Rome professors, intellectuals, and idealistic middle-class students. GAP divided the city into eight zones for action. The ancient *centro storico*, the heart of Rome, was GAP Central. It was composed of four fighting squads called SAPs, Squads of Patriotic Action.

Each SAP had three or four members (men or women) and when more were needed to launch a specific attack, two or more squads would team up. Partisan casualties were heavy. In Rome more than 200 were killed by the Germans, 16 during partisan attacks, the rest after arrest and torture.

During their existence, the SAPs maintained secret arms depots called *santabarbaras*, after Saint Barbara, the patron saint of artillery. One *santabarbara* was at Via Giulia 23a. Another was at Via Pellegrino 82 in a bicycle shop owned (and still owned at the time of this writing) by the Collalti family. Eventually discovered, several Collalti family members would be arrested and died at the Nazi Mauthausen Concentration Camp. Another depot was at a villa on the west side of Rome beyond Saint Peter's owned by Prince Doria-Pamphili who enthusiastically remarked that he hoped it would blow up a lot of Germans.

Initially, the GAP partisans produced and distributed anti-German writings and propaganda. They recruited Bentivegna, Capponi, and two other GAP members – nicknamed Gappisti – Franco di Lernia and Lucia Ottobrini, to distribute a newspaper, *La Nostra Lotta* (Our Struggle), *the Journal of the University Students*, which urged University of Rome students to fight the occupiers.

One night, three SAPs spread out in central Rome to literally paint the town red, daubing anti-fascist graffiti over walls and buildings. Capponi, Bentivegna, and a Rodolfo Coari were on one team. They painted slogans on the side of the Vittorio Emanuele II Monument, the white wedding cake in the center of ancient Rome, garish red paint on the revered white marble walls. Next, they painted more slogans outside of the abandoned parliament building in Piazza di Monte Citorio and at the base of the Spanish Steps in the Piazza di Spagna. They ended up at the huge Piazza del Popolo where Capponi, standing on a boy's shoulders, painted a large red hammer and sickle on the upper part of the 20-foot-high base of the Egyptian obelisk.

Another squad was unlucky and was arrested that night and later that month, two of the squad's partisans would be executed by firing squad at Fort Bravetta, the primary Fascist execution site. Naturally, the Fascists painted over the graffiti with white paint, but the red was hard to cover and, almost like a portent of things to come, it tended to bleed through.

As partisan raids increased, the need for cheap weapons grew. One GAP partisan, Lindoro Boccanera, got an idea while hiding out in the Bersaglieri Regimental military museum at the Porta Pia city gate on Rome's east side. This was the site in 1870 where unified Italian troops entered the papal city and made it the capital of a united Italy. Boccanera noticed a World War I caltrop in a glass case and thought that it might be useful. A caltrop, he thought, could be a very effective weapon used to stop vehicles. It was made of two bent, heavy-duty nails sharpened on both ends and welded together. Three of the points formed the base while the fourth point stuck upward to puncture a tire. It was the same ancient Roman design Julius Caesar had used to disrupt mounted attacks.* When spread on a road, caltrops could flatten tires and cause a pile up when other vehicles rammed into the disabled first

---

*Actual Roman caltrops are displayed in the Archaeological Museum at Carnutum, outside of Vienna, Austria and in the City Archaeological Museum of Zagreb, Croatia. In the US these were called bobjacks. Union miners used them during strikes against coal companies who brought in scab, or non-union, labor in trucks.

vehicle. Then partisans could open fire on the halted vehicles. Partisans first used caltrops against German vehicles on October 10, 1943.

To mass produce the inexpensive caltrops, Enrico Ferola, a Trastevere blacksmith, worked nights at his forge to make more than 10,000 caltrops from a ton of iron that his assistants had recovered from bombed-out buildings.* It then became the mode for Roman kids to taunt German soldiers by crossing their fingers like the nails and chanting:

> How many points, how many points
> How many points has this nail?
> A point for me, a point for you,
> Four points for him.

The Germans declared that the possession of caltrops was a capital offense. Nevertheless, caltrops continued to be used in the hundreds, immobilizing many German motorized columns. Often, the roads leading out of the city were blocked for hours, giving Allied aircraft, looking for targets of opportunity, the chance to strafe the immobilized German vehicles. It was first erroneously believed, and was stated in Roman police reports, that the caltrops were strewn by Allied aircraft. These attacks caused the Germans to post the following:

> We are informed that if these acts of sabotage are repeated very grave measures will be taken against those who live along the roads and in the area where such acts are repeated. It is therefore absolutely necessary that the populace, in their own interest, cooperate with the authorities to facilitate the search and capture of those responsible.[2]

This is the first written record of a threat of retaliation against innocent bystanders and was in fact a war crime, recognized under international law since 1907.

Another inexpensive weapon used by partisans was the pipe bomb, called a *spezzone* – literally, "fragments." Celestine Avico, a World War I Italian Army captain, had been trained in making pipe bombs during

---

* In March 1944, Ferola was denounced and caught with 50 kilograms of caltrops. The Gestapo tortured him but he never revealed for whom he was making the caltrops. He was executed as part of the Ardeatine massacre (see Chapter 18).

the previous war and he supplied them to the partisans. He simply cut metal pipes into foot-long segments then packed TNT around a fuse and detonator and jammed them inside the pipe. The fuse would burn for ten seconds and, since TNT follows the path of most resistance, it would blow the pipe into shrapnel. It was to be used with devastating effect all over Rome.

General Kurt Mälzer replaced General Rainer Stahl as the new Stadtkommandant of Rome on November 1, 1943. He was overweight, dressed untidily, hid his baldness under a beret, and was described as looking older than his 55 years.[3] A drunkard, he imagined himself irresistible to women and he often referred to himself as the King of Rome. Consul Möllhausen, in charge at the German Embassy, felt that Mälzer was vulgar, repugnant, and utterly irrational. Nevertheless, Italian Fascists recognized him as the *Comandante della Città Aperta*, making his headquarters at the most luxurious hotel in Rome, the Hotel Excelsior on Via Veneto. Mälzer, an old comrade of Field Marshal Kesselring, made stopping partisan attacks a priority. He would prove to be an effective foe of the partisans, although not always successful. Meanwhile General Stahl was sent to the Eastern Front.

To welcome the new Stadtkommandant, on November 7, partisans celebrated the anniversary of the Soviet Communist Revolution at Piazza Fiume (northeast of Via Veneto) by throwing grenades near the German ORPO headquarters in Via Po. Another partisan demonstration in the open at Largo Ottavio Tassoni off the Corso Vittorio Emanuele II was broken up by members of the Fascist *Comando Squadre d'Azione di Palazzo Braschi* (the Palazzo Braschi Action Squad). A crowd had gathered, however, and the partisans escaped.

Not every partisan attack went off as planned. On November 18, Marshal Rodolfo Graziani, Mussolini's new Defense Minister, was to speak at a large assemblage of RSI officials at Rome's Teatro Adriano in Prati, the largest motion picture palace in the city and now a movie multiplex. Among the German dignitaries present was General Mälzer, a prime target. Partisans of GAP Central got into the theater early and planted a bomb under the stage with enough explosives to blow up half the theater, Mälzer, Graziani, and the audience with it. It was set to go off at 16:00 in the middle of Graziani's speech but it failed to detonate.

———

As November turned to December, the partisans – and the Gappisti in particular – increased their attacks on the Nazi occupiers. Seven GAP attacks were launched in rapid succession against Germans. The first took place on December 6, 1943, when Gappisti threw a pipe bomb into the Antonelli Trattoria, in Via Fabio Massimo. It was lunchtime and the trattoria was close to the German command post and barracks on Viale Giulio Cesare in the Pratti District. The bomb killed ten, six of whom were German soldiers.

The Wehrmacht had turned the *centro storico* (historic center of downtown Rome) into parking lots for military vehicles, reasoning that it was an area off limits to Allied bombers. But it was not off limits to partisans, so Capponi and Bentivegna zeroed in on the German vehicle park in front of the Rome Opera House (Teatro Reale dell'Opera). It was the evening of December 15. Strolling along as lovers, the two went to the Opera House plaza carrying two hidden pipe bombs. It was just before the 23:30 curfew and the performance was still going on. Capponi and Bentivegna placed a lit pipe bomb on a truck's gas tank and ran. The bomb exploded and the truck burst into flames. The resulting fire consumed several vehicles and wounded some German soldiers.

———

With Teutonic precision, every evening at 18:00, 33-year-old ORPO Sergeant Georg Johansen Schmidt belted his black leather dispatch case closed and exited the Hotel Ambasciatori on Via Veneto.* Although carrying highly classified documents, he was unescorted as he was in the

---

* The 1940s (and beyond) Hotel Ambasciatori, with the Fascist artwork on the façade, is now called the Grand Hotel Palace and is located across from the American Embassy. The current Ambassadors Hotel Palace, often called the Ambasciatori, is in the former US Embassy annex, further down Via Veneto.

secure and closely guarded German Headquarters Zone where senior Wehrmacht officers worked and lived in Via Vittorio Veneto's luxury five-star hotels.

Leaving the hotel, Schmidt turned right and walked half a block down Via Veneto across from the shuttered American Embassy, the Palazzo Margarita. Then he crossed the street where Via XXIII Marzo* entered Via Veneto, on his way to Via XX Settembre and the Italian Ministry of War, now occupied as a command center by the Wehrmacht.

And so, on the evening of December 17, 1943, Schmidt, in his police uniform and carrying his dispatch case, was easily recognized by the pretty women discretely shadowing him. Walking briskly, he covered two blocks and crossed the intersection at Via San Nicola da Tolentino. Suddenly, from ten yards, two shots echoed off the gray buildings and Schmidt fell dead in the southwest corner of the intersection.

Carla Capponi had killed her first German. Capponi, now using the code name Elena, was accompanied by her lover Rosario Bentivegna. She was covered by the team of Mario Fiorentini (codenamed Giovanni) and Lucia Ottobrini (codenamed Maria) who played the part of strolling lovers. Fiorentini was "a long-haired, romantic-looking, pale young man who was interested in poetry ... he was one of the most daring members of the GAP in Rome."[4] He was also a Jew. Lucia Ottobrini was a 20-year-old with a working-class background who was employed at the Treasury Ministry. She had immigrated with her family to France but returned to Italy in 1940. She had first met Fiorentini at a concert at the Teatro Adriano.

Schmidt had cried out as he fell dying: "*Mein Gott! Ich sterbe! Helft mir*" (My God, I'm dying, help me). Ignoring him, Capponi grabbed the dispatch case holding maps marked with the location of antiaircraft batteries surrounding Rome. The information was forwarded to FMCR contacts and sent to the Allies in the south, probably via radio.

But they were not done. Twice a week, German language films were shown to Wehrmacht soldiers at the Cinema Barberini, in Piazza

* Via XXIII Marzo, celebrating the date of the founding of Fascism, is now called Via Leonida Bissolati.

Barberini. This became a target on December 18, as two couples, Capponi and Bentivegna, and Fiorentini and Ottobrini, joined forces. As German soldiers exited the cinema at 23:15 and climbed into a waiting truck, Bentivegna rode up on his bicycle and hurled a one-kilogram pipe bomb into the back of the vehicle and raced off. At least eight soldiers were killed outright and 15 were wounded. Capponi and Ottobrini, the lookouts, were stopped and questioned as they walked together. Ottobrini explained in fluent German that they had just left two German soldiers with whom they watched the show. Believed to be Roman streetwalkers, they were released.

In retaliation for this attack, the German Stadtkommandant lowered the curfew from 23:30 to 19:00 hours. "The Germans chose to conceal their casualties … there was no reprisal as the Germans felt that the most important thing was to keep the city from realizing that there was a guerrilla war going on, and to protect the myth of their own invulnerability."[5]

The headquarters of the German High Command was in the Hotel Flora in Via Veneto. It was a billet for senior German officers and on the second floor it was the seat of the German War Tribunal where the Germans went through the motions of wartime legalities. They would drag arrested partisans before the tribunal for a 20-minute show trial with a predetermined guilty outcome. Emboldened by the successes with pipe bombs, four GAP members attacked the hotel on December 19, each throwing a pipe bomb through the ground floor windows of the hotel.

Two of the bombs detonated, severely damaging the lobby of the hotel. The other two were duds. Nineteen German officers and civilians were killed. More Germans and some civilians walking along the sidewalk in front of the hotel were wounded by flying glass. Additional damage was caused to the ground floor by bursting hot water pipes shooting water from the walls.

The attack had missed Field Marshal Kesselring who had been there that day but had left by 17:50, the time of the attack. People on the street were held for questioning. The German War Tribunal was moved to nearby Via Lucullo and, because the Germans believed that a bicyclist had thrown the bomb, the use of bicycles was banned throughout the city after 17:00.

––––––

The pace of partisan attacks gathered momentum. At midday on December 20, an attack was launched on the guard post below street level outside the Regina Coeli Prison as the German guards were being changed. Capponi and Bentivegna stood cover while Fiorentini tossed two pipe bombs from his bicycle into the midst of the German soldiers, killing seven and wounding 20. As Fiorentini fled, the Germans opened fire. He pedaled for all he was worth and, crossing the Ponte Giuseppe Mazzini in front of the prison, he scattered a troop of Fascist militia crossing the other way.

As reprisal for that attack, the Germans banned the use of bicycles altogether. The German Command declared:

> Pursuant to a new criminal attack by a cyclist committed yesterday in broad daylight against German soldiers the following is hereby ordered: from this moment on, without exception, the use of any bicycle anywhere in the territory of the Open City of Rome is prohibited. Transgressors will be shot without regard to who they are and without prior notice. The bicycle will be requisitioned with no right of compensation.[6]

Public transportation was unreliable and bicycle use was at an all-time high so this increased the duress on the public. In resourceful Roman fashion, citizens converted their bicycles into tricycles by adding a third wheel, sometimes from a baby carriage and absurdly small.

––––––

The Pension Caterina in an art deco building was the headquarters of the ORPO, and was located on the corner of Via Po and Corso d'Italia. On December 29, Bentivegna, Capponi, and two other Gappisti, after taking time off for the Christmas holiday, attacked it. The thrown hand grenade, however, only caused minor damage and broke some windows. As the partisans fled, they threw a second grenade which injured a policeman in the leg and two women passersby. Both women worked as telephone operators, one at the German headquarters in the Hotel Flora and the other at the Vatican.

General Mälzer responded to the increased partisan attacks by ordering Kappler and both the Fascist and German police to crack down on the partisans. Huge rewards were offered for turning in suspects. One reward was five pounds of salt, a commodity unavailable in wartime Italy. They also paid informants 5,000 lire for each partisan turned in. In war-ravaged Rome, this was a major temptation so there were many denouncements, and judgement was swift. As just one example, two brothers, denounced as anti-fascists, were arrested and imprisoned at the Regina Coeli Prison. The next morning they were taken to Via Tasso for interrogation and were brutally tortured. Later they were returned to the Regina Coeli where they died during the night.

The crackdown continued. Fascist and German police arrested 31 partisans during the month of December, most of whom were taken to Via Tasso. Notable was the arrest of Italian Lieutenant General of Artillery Vito Artale and a civilian, Ottavio Cirulli, who had hidden English POWs in his home. Other partisans, arrested while transporting weapons, were sent outside of Rome to a concentration camp at Castelfranco, Emilia, 200 miles from Rome but they eventually escaped.

Anti-government newspapers were a particular target. During one raid in Via Basento, east of Parioli, the Fascist police uncovered the printing press for the newspaper *Italia Libera*, the organ of the left-wing Action Party. They arrested seven partisans and found in the home a pistol, several hand grenades, a copy of the communist newspaper, *L'Unità*, as well as checks payable to the Italian Communist Party. In an apartment south of Saint John Lateran, a draft of the clandestine newspaper *L'Unità* was discovered along with a store of caltrops. Two partisans were arrested for possessing them. A Gestapo spy, Franco (Guido) Sabelli, captured a 17-year-old member of the Action Party. The youth tried to escape on the way to Via Tasso, and Sabelli shot him five times with his pistol. The youth died the next day at the San Giovanni Hospital.

Kappler, using his vast network of informers, started to identify key members of the GAP and had them arrested. Antonello Trombadori,

Left Bombs dropping to the west of the Tiburtina railway station, July 19, 1943. (NARA)

Above Photo taken three hours after this attack, to prove to the world that the Vatican and surrounding area was intact and not damaged. (NARA)

Below Although this photo was not taken until July 1944, it clearly shows the damage inside the San Lorenzo Basilica caused by the July 19, 1943 bombing. (NARA)

Damage to the Ostiense railway station. Note the Pyramid of Caius Cestius in the top center – this damage is probably from a springtime 1944 bombing raid. (NARA)

Damaged rolling stock in Rome. This photo was taken in June 1944 after the liberation of the city as can be seen by the American soldier standing in the ruins. (NARA)

Left German paratroopers, 6th Fallschirmjäger Regiment, fight in the western suburb of Montagnola on the way into Rome, September 10, 1943. The Italian reconnaissance vehicle was destroyed by the German antitank gun in the foreground. (Bundesarchiv, Bild 201-41-03-042, Fotograf(in): o.Ang)

Bottom left German paratroopers set up a 7.5cm gun in a parking lot in the Trieste quarter (eastern part of the city) after the battle for Rome, September 10, 1943. (Bundesarchiv, Bild 101I-304-0635-19, Fotograf(in): Funke)

German paratroopers prepare equipment during the battle for Rome, September 10, 1943. (Bundesarchiv, Bild 101I-304-0634-07, Fotograf(in): Funke)

A 1945 photo of the Pyramid of Caius Cestius, the center point of the battle for Rome. The US Army Signal Corps photo caption calls it "Saint Paul's Pyramid." (NARA)

A German soldier directs a shepherd at the White Line Border at Saint Peter's Square. (Bundesarchiv, Bild 101I-307-0752-21A, Fotograf(in): Funke)

Two German paratroopers collect weapons from
their former Italian allies of the Piave Division in
the Trieste quarter, Rome on September 10, 1943.
(Bundesarchiv, Bild 101I-304-0635-28,
Fotograf(in): Funke)

Field Marshal Albert Kesselring (left) speaks with
the German Ambassador to Italy Dr. Hans Georg
von Mackensen in Rome, September 1943.
(Bundesarchiv, Bild 146-1979-168-032,
Fotograf(in): o.Ang.)

Two Italian officers are led away by German paratroopers in Rome, September 10, 1943.
(Bundesarchiv, Bild 101I-304-0604A-27, Fotograf(in): Otto, Albrecht Heinrich)

A photo of the Gestapo Headquarters and prison on Via Tasso, taken on June 27, 1944. (NARA)

The partially inhabited prison and *Museo Storico della Liberazione* today. (Author)

SS-Obersturmbannführer Herbert Kappler, head of the Gestapo in Rome. (Reproduced with kind permission of Piero Crociani)

SS-Obersturmbannführer Eugen Dollmann's Rome residence identity card, dated October 6, 1941. Dollmann was SS-Chief Heinrich Himmler's man in Rome. (NARA)

Rome SS ABT III Headquarters at the Casino Massimo Lancellotti (in Villa Giustiniani Massimo) on Via Matteo Boiardo, behind Via Tasso prison headquarters. (Author)

Via del Portico d'Ottavia, the Ghetto's main street, relatively unchanged since 1943. (Author)

Portico d'Ottavia, where Jews were held prior to being loaded on trucks (it had not yet been excavated in 1943). (Author)

The Military College courtyard where Jews were held after the roundup. (Author)

Left A railway boxcar that according to Antonio Palo, director of the Disembarkation Museum, Salerno, Italy, was one of those used to transport Jews, POWs and others between 1943 and 1944. (Author)

Father Benedetto (right, with beard and robe), who helped French Jews in Rome. (NARA)

Pope Pius XII on June 21, 1944. (NARA)

Monsignor O'Flaherty, who started the Escape Line. (Hugh O'Flaherty Memorial Society)

Sir D'Arcy Osborne, British Ambassador to the Holy See, was another force behind the Escape Line. (Photo by Keystone/Getty Images)

Left Harold H. Tittmann, Jr.'s diplomatic credentials, dated March 10, 1940. Tittman was US Charge d'Affaires at the Holy See and was also behind the Escape Line. (Harold Tittmann papers, GTMGamms439, Georgetown University Library, Booth Family Center for Special Collections, Washington DC)

Brother Robert Pace, Escape Line organizer. This photo clearly shows the white bows that gave him his code name. (College Archives, Saint Mary's College of California)

POW graffiti of the 12th London Regiment at the Sulmona POW Camp #78 at Fonte d'Amore. (Author)

Right The Sulmona POW camp from a postcard, date uncertain. (Author)

Below The Sulmona POW camp today; modern garage doors have replaced the ones of the 1940s but the interiors are unchanged. (Author)

A second example of POW graffiti, less patriotic, at the Sulmona camp. (Author)

Tiny Vico Breve, Sulmona, where many escaped POWs were hidden. (Author)

Left The Fonte d'Amore spring and communal laundry used for bathing by POWs outside the camp. (Author)

Allied ex-POWs inside the Vatican. Those identified are: second from left, Captain Byrnes, RCASC; fifth from left, Hugh Montogomery. The boy is Barclary Tittmann, one of Harold Tittmann's sons. (*Museo Storico della Liberazione*)

This photo, taken on January 4, 1944, shows soldiers from the Hermann Göring Division displaying Giovanni Paolo Pannini's (1691–1765) painting of King Charles III visiting Pope Benedict XIV in 1746 in front of the Palazzo Venezia. This painting was owned by the Italian state and was therefore taken to Palazzo Venezia instead of the Castel Sant'Angelo where church-owned art was sent. (Bundesarchiv, Bild 101I-729-0001-23, Fotograf(in): Meister)

Above The Collalti Bicycle Shop, a partisan *santabarbara* (weapons depot). (Author)

Right The open window on the third floor (fourth floor in US) of this building was Mrs. Chevalier's apartment which housed numerous transient ex-POWs. (Author)

John Furman, Sam Derry, Henry Byrnes and Bill Simpson in a photo taken after the liberation of Rome while they all worked at the Allied Screening Commission. They have all been promoted, as illustrated by their rank insignia. (Hugh O'Flaherty Memorial Society)

Above The inner gate at the infamous Fort Bravetta execution grounds. (Author)

Right The Cinema Barberini, site of the December 18, 1943 partisan attack. This photo was taken in October 1945 when it was used as a US Red Cross Theater. (NARA)

The Regina Coeli Prison today, virtually unchanged in the last 70 years. (Author)

Left A group of Allied ex-POWs acting as partisans north of Rome, June 21, 1944. The group was led by an American Ranger, S/Sgt. Robert Taylor, the tall man in the picture. Taylor was listed as killed at Cisterna. Other partisans in this photo were from South Africa, Russia and Poland. (NARA)

Below The entrance to Vatican City used by the Escape Line for meetings with Derry and others. (Author)

Ristorante dell'Opera, used by Furman and Simpson after arriving in Rome, is now named Giglio after the symbol of Florence, the fleur-de-lis. (Author)

A Roman tram of the type often used by escaped POWs. (Tompkins-NARA)

The French Seminary which housed many ex-POWs. (Author)

The entrance to the Lucidis' apartment on Via Scialoja. (Author)

The Rome Opera. The box that is second to the right of the royal box, with the man leaning over, was the one used by the Lucidis and the ex-POWs during the New Year's gala performance on January 1, 1944. (Author)

Gino Bardi, head of an semi-official Fascist Party gang of thugs, the Banda Bardi-Pollastrini, trying to prove that Fascists love children. (Tompkins-NARA)

Palazzo Braschi, now a museum, was the base of the Banda Bardi-Pollastrini. (Author)

Above Rome Police Chief Pietro Caruso, seen here on trial in September 1944. (NARA)

Above Pietro Koch, leader of the special police unit Banda Koch. (Photo by: SeM/Universal mages Group via Getty Images)

Right Maurizio Giglio, the OSS agent who had control of Radio Vittoria 2. (Tompkins-NARA)

Above Palazzo Lovatelli, OSS agent Peter Tompkins'
Rome headquarters for six weeks.
(Author)

Left Tompkins peeking out from the tiny secret
doorway to the secret room in Palazzo Lovatelli.
(Tompkins-NARA)

Below Borin, Tompkins, Crespi, Mario (unidentified)
and Malfatti in the living room of their palazzo
apartment. In the 1960s Italian actress Sophia Loren
lived in the same apartment. (Tompkins-NARA)

commander of GAP Central, and several others had been arrested by the Gestapo; it was feared they would be forced to reveal the identities of their comrades. Locked in cells in Via Tasso, they refused to talk despite being severely tortured. The remaining members of the GAP decided that they needed to go into hiding so, on January 24, Carlo Salinari (codenamed Spartaco), one of the remaining GAP leaders, met with Bentivegna and Capponi in the ancient Café Greco, on Via Condotti, near the Spanish Steps. Seated among the late 19th-century splendor of the café over ersatz coffee, Salinari explained the changes: GAP Central would be temporarily dissolved and members would be sent to the suburbs.

The dispersal of GAP members began with Mario Fiorentini, Franco di Lernia, Lucia Ottobrini, and Guglielmo Blasi. Blasi was a petty thief, who in the eyes of the idealistic students represented the working class. They were sent to the Quadraro district of Rome in the southeast section of the city. The district lay along Via Tuscolana beyond the Porta Furba and the Aqua Claudia aqueduct on the way to Cinecittà. It was one of several quarters built on the extreme margins of Rome in the early 20th century.

Mussolini had ordered massive construction projects in the late 1920s and 1930s. The medieval buildings were torn down along Via della Conciliazione and Via dell'Impero (now Via dei Fori Imperiali). When their neighborhoods were demolished to make way for the new grand boulevards, artisans and workers were moved out of the central city to Quadraro, but their clients and jobs failed to follow them. The district's new two-story houses were poorly constructed and had no running water or electricity. Its inhabitants did not even consider it part of Rome and spoke of taking the tram to the city. The new residents were understandably mostly anti-fascist; Mussolini had only brought them the loss of their homes, war, poverty, and desperation. Most partisan factions had strong cells in this neighborhood and the Gestapo referred to the Quadraro neighborhood as a nest of vipers.

Franco Calamandrei, Maria Teresa Regard, and Francesco Curreli were sent north of Rome. And Bentivegna and Capponi were to be transferred from the *centro storico* to Centocelle, a working-class district also to the southeast of the city near Via Prenestina, not far from the Centocelle Airfield.

Capponi and Bentivegna had planned an attack for that evening, so Salinari allowed them to delay their departure. It was justified. The attack was to be on a German gas truck outside the church of Saint Peter in Chains (*San Pietro in Vincoli*), where in peace time Michelangelo's larger-than-life-sized seated statue of Moses was displayed. The church overlooked Via Cavour at the Borgia steps (*Salita Borgia*) where Pope Alexander VI's second son Giovanni Borgia was murdered one dark night in 1497. Two other partisans joined them and they waited for the gas truck that usually parked in front of the church to arrive. When it came, the four each threw a hand grenade, the blast and fire from which lit up the façade of the church, killing several German drivers. The four partisans escaped and Bentivegna and Capponi moved to the Centocelle district for the next month.

All that fall of 1943, the Germans poured men and supplies south to the Cassino front in an attempt to stall the Allies. Their convoys became major objectives for the partisans who relentlessly attacked Wehrmacht soldiers. German troop transports were blown up as they traveled south over roads and bridges mined by the partisans. But even simple actions could cause chaos. One night, road signs on three routes out of the city were removed by Gappisti along Via Casilina, Via Prenestina, and Via Tuscolana.

Destroyed railway lines and bridges cost the Germans dearly not only at the time of the blast but for some time after as repairs were attempted. Twenty-eight kilos of explosives were used by partisans to mine the Sette Luci Bridge at the 25-kilometer mark along the railway line Roma–Formia–Napoli. The bridge blew up at midnight, December 20/21, as a German train was crossing it, causing considerable loss of life and war materiel.

At about the same time, another partisan squad planted a 32kg mine on the railway line Roma–Cassino. This attack killed more than 400 men and wounded many others. German intelligence averred that both attacks had been the work of Allied parachutists. But Pino Levi Cavaglione, a prominent Jew and communist partisan, claimed credit for the partisans in a news sheet, saying: "No, you damned Germans, this time the attack did not come from the sky, or from English aviators. It came from us. From us who in this moment feel proud to be Italians and partisan and we would not change our tattered muddy and wet clothes for any uniform."

ALL ROADS LEAD TO ROME, 1943/1944

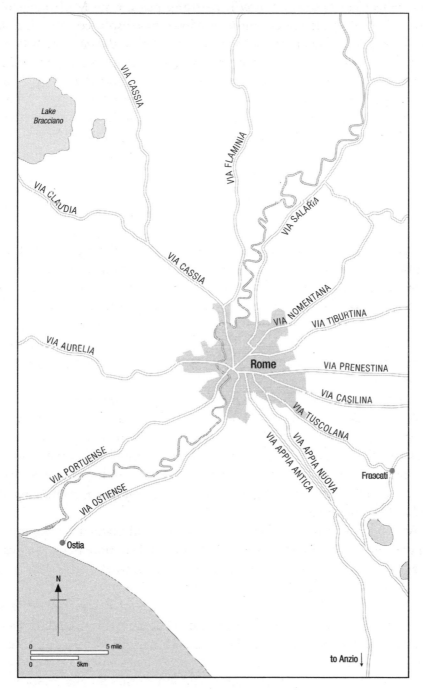

Communication was essential for the Germans so partisans cut telephone cables. On Via Tuscolana, they cut 330 yards of telephone cable. At Grottaferrata, a town about 20 miles southeast of the city, the Germans assigned a team of 20 men to stand guard over the telephone line to prevent further sabotage.

Partisan attacks were so numerous and successful that they could now be used as a threat to gain concessions from the Germans. After a partisan attack on the radio communications center at the headquarters of the VII German Parachute Regiment in the Ottavia quarter (west-northwest of the city), the Germans arrested 31 civilians. The partisan commander issued an ultimatum to the Germans: release the hostages within 24 hours or there will be attacks all over the city. To give teeth to the demand, the GAP mounted four attacks on German vehicles that night. The following afternoon, all the hostages were released. An SS officer, trying to put names to the formidable yet invisible partisan threat, interviewed the relatives of the hostages. Assisted by his Italian interpreter, he demanded to know who these communist bandits were. No one talked and the story of the German capitulation to the partisans was broadcast a few days later on BBC Radio London.

A group of Soviet ex-POWs had located south of the city. They had escaped from the German Todt Organization labor camp, the huge European-wide construction firm working on Wehrmacht fortifications. Attacking German soldiers, they were able to arm themselves and were originally supported by local farmers. At Cisterna, 30 miles southeast of the city, the Soviets blew up a German vehicle, killing five soldiers. Chased by a German armored car, the Soviets escaped thanks to the intervention of local partisans. After this attack, the Soviets moved from their hiding place in a grotto at Lake Nemi in the Alban hills to the Palestrina area 30 miles east of the city.

Throughout Rome there were constant attacks by partisans on German vehicles and convoys moving across the city. A Wehrmacht general's car was destroyed in Via Nazionale and other German vehicles were shot at. Many Germans were killed and wounded, harassed with bombs, hand grenades, caltrops, whatever was at hand. And indeed, the German occupation of Rome was severely hampered because of these attacks.

13

The Rome Escape Line

The innocuous-sounding Escape Line was a vital clandestine effort to aid escapees on the part of those working from within the protective walls of the Vatican. The redoubtable team of Monsignor O'Flaherty, Sir D'Arcy Osborne, Harold Tittmann, and Major Derry, plus a small band of priests, monks, and nuns, worked secretly to find billets, look after the needs of escapees, and pass them money provided by Sir D'Arcy and Tittmann. At risk, if the SS uncovered their work, was Vatican neutrality.

The invisible Escape Line operated everywhere. Those it helped blended into Rome's flow of daily life in sometimes unsettling ways as ex-POWs and their helpers rubbed shoulders with the enemy. Attending the Rome Opera on New Year's Day, 1944, was Adrienne Lucidi, a beautiful, dark-haired French woman. She was with her husband, Renzo, and four ex-POWs, Simpson, Furman, Pollak, and Hugh Fane-Hervey (MC), a British Army officer, who all lived with the Lucidis. They wanted to celebrate the New Year and going to the opera seemed the right way to go about it. Cultural performances continued throughout the war and the gala New Year's Day performance of the Rome Opera that early afternoon went on as scheduled. Certainly the Germans, as part of their desire for total control, wanted life in the capital to carry on, to appear normal, as if there was no war going on further down the Italian Peninsula.

On their way to the theater, the Lucidis and the four ex-POWs ran into Iride Imperoli and Henri Payonne. Iride was back in Rome from Sulmona and Payonne had come with her. It was a happy meeting. Pollak, Furman, and Simpson greeted them and Renzo Lucidi invited Payonne to tea and gave him his phone number. Then they all went into the theater.

Puccini's *Tosca* was being sung by a stellar cast: the great Italian soprano, Maria Caniglia, tenor Beniamino Gigli, and baritone Tito Gobbi, all artists of legendary fame. Simpson observed that the story of the opera resonated with the current climate in Rome:

> [It] was eerily evocative of our present situation. Rome, the locale of the historic plot, was dominated by local mercenaries of a foreign despot, Napoleon, a century earlier; the city trembled under the brutal command of its wicked police chief Scarpia [Kappler would now be that character's name].[1]

Beniamino Gigli (1890–1957) was the most famous Italian opera tenor of his age, sometimes called a second Caruso. He was a favorite of Mussolini, the Fascists, and the German opera lovers in Rome. He donated the painted ceiling in the church of San Roberto Bellarmino in Parioli, considered the Fascist Church of Rome. Ironically the church was also used by the Escape Line as a local center of operations to pass out money to ex-POWs.*

Simpson wrote later that he and Furman identified other ex-POWs in the theater as they peered over the railings. For, walking down the center aisle was Captain Pip Gardner, a recipient of the Victoria Cross and a former prisoner in the Chieti POW camp. He was with British Captain Tug Wilson. To the left in the orchestra seats (stalls) were Rendell and Dukate who waved when they saw Simpson and Furman. Adrienne and her group were in a box on the left side of the theater. Two boxes away was the Royal Box, in which sat a German general. A thin wall separated them from some other high-ranking German staff officers in their dress uniforms.

Simpson and Furman were unnerved by the presence all around them of German officers, so they took seats in the back of the box where they could not be seen. The Germans were not looking at them, however, but at the beautiful Adrienne.

One German officer was obviously smitten by the vivacious Frenchwoman for he could not stop admiring her. During the second

---

* The square in front of the Opera House is now named for Beniamino Gigli.

intermission, Adrienne plucked up her courage and asked the officer to autograph her program. It was a keepsake program for the first performance of the New Year, printed on parchment with gold embossed lettering and long silk cords, a real souvenir. Adrienne spoke to the officer in French. Charmed at her request, he said that it would be more appropriate if his general were to sign her program. He entered the Royal Box smartly, relayed Adrienne's request and returned to her with the signature of the general who had styled himself King of Rome and whose brutal crackdowns on partisans had taken many lives. And who, unbeknownst to himself, had escaped being blown up six weeks earlier at the Teatro Adriano – none other than German Stadtkommandant of Rome, General Kurt Mälzer.

Some sources, including ex-POW Simpson, say that General Eberhard von Mackensen was seated in the box. The general was second-in-command to Field Marshal Kesselring and later commander of the 14th German Army in charge of containing the Allied Anzio beachhead. But both ex-POWs Derry and Furman, writing closer to the event, say that the senior officer was Mälzer. There was also a rumor that Mälzer's signature was copied and used to forge passes but that has proven not to be true.

As we have seen, ex-POWs Furman, Simpson, and Pollak had arrived in Rome from Sulmona in early December. Checking into the Albergo Vulcania in the city center on Via Cavour was remarkably normal, no awkward questions about the size of their group or the men's shabby clothes. The group discovered that the hotel had no restaurant and they were all famished. Iride and Maria Imperoli set out to find food, returning soon, according to Furman, with an excellent hot meal in aluminum containers, apparently purchased without ration coupons. After eating, Pollak and Iride drove to the Vatican in a hired horse-drawn carriage (*carrozza*) to meet her Vatican contact, François de Vial, the French Vice Consul at the Embassy to the Holy See.

Pollak and Iride came back with important news: they had met Major Derry at the Vatican. Pollak said that Derry wanted to see Furman, whom he had known at the Chieti POW camp. Simpson volunteered to attend as well: if there was a possibility to help he would like to be included.

The next morning Furman and Pollak took a *carrozza* to Saint Peter's. It was broad daylight and, as they alighted at the piazza, they were observed by two German paratroopers who stood on permanent guard on the painted white line that separated Vatican City from the rest of Rome. But the German paratroopers were merely symbolic and did not interfere with most visitors entering the square.[*]

They were not stopped and, crossing the square, made for the left side of St Peter's Basilica. They went to the Swiss Guard post under the small arch and into an ante-room where they asked to see Monsignor O'Flaherty. As previously arranged Derry soon arrived beaming, glad to see his friend Furman.

The three walked along the south arm of the piazza and ducked through the Bernini Colonnade and, turning right, walked to an alley before the Holy Office, through an open gate, to the entrance of the German College, Derry's HQ. Ascending the staircase, Derry took Furman and Pollak to the room he shared with Monsignor O'Flaherty. But at the door he stopped and pulled Pollak aside and asked him to wait in another room.

While at Chieti, Derry had become suspicious of Pollak whom he had seen chatting frequently with the Italian guards. Could Pollak be an informer? Derry asked Furman how reliable Pollak was in Sulmona. Furman replied, "I think that Pollak is one of the most terrific chaps I've ever met."[2] Derry retrieved Pollak, apologized for his suspicions and had no further doubts about him.

Back in the monsignor's room, Derry explained how he had been recruited to run the Escape Line. He told them about Sir D'Arcy, Monsignor O'Flaherty, John May, and Count Captain Leonardo Trippi of the Swiss Embassy. He explained his function as coordinator for the organization, working closely with the monsignor's small band of priests, monks, and nuns, on behalf of the escapees, finding billets for them, looking after their needs and passing them the money provided by Sir D'Arcy and Tittmann. Sir D'Arcy had hoped that Derry, by relieving clerics and monastics of some of these responsibilities, would be able to shield the monsignor and his assistants – and the Vatican itself – from the risk of discovery by the SS, to preserve the appearance of Vatican neutrality. The Vatican, of course, was well aware of O'Flaherty's work

[*] Even today, it is Rome police who screen all visitors to Saint Peter's.

in aiding Allied ex-POWs but it could not acknowledge it. In keeping with Vatican City's status as a neutral country as per the Lateran Treaty of 1929, the Vatican was able to carry on humanitarian work, but aiding escaped POWs was far beyond that.

In turn, Furman told Derry about the others who had come to Rome with him and how they, with the help of the people of Sulmona, had distributed food, clothing, and the money provided by the Escape Line. Derry, who knew Simpson, was pleased to hear that he was eager to help. He then offered the three ex-POWs, Furman, Pollak, and Simpson, positions in the Escape Line organization and set about finding billets for them and the other men from Sulmona.

Meanwhile, Iride Imperoli enlisted François de Vial to help in finding clothes for the escapees. De Vial took one look at the country clothes worn by the men and knew they were not suitable for the city. He sent an elderly Frenchman and a hidden Jewish-German tailor to measure the men at the hotel. The next day, in groups of two, they were escorted to the Capuchin Monastery on Via Sicilia, the headquarters for DELASEM, the Hebrew Emigrant Relief Organization. At the monastery the monks provided clothing for the ex-POWs from Sulmona.

Simpson recalled that he went with a Yugoslav to a large department store where they picked out some clothes. He had only to sign for the clothing and no cash was exchanged. More likely Simpson, writing years later, confused picking up clothes from racks at the monastery with going to a department store.

The following day, Tittmann, who had obtained Monsignor Joseph McGeough's approval, moved the two Americans, Duke Dukate and Pat Wilson, and two of the British ex-POWs, Gil Smith and Dennis Rendell, to the Casa San Giovanni on the Janiculum Hill. Rendell had another reason to move: Iride had become too attached to him. That evening, at dinner with Iride and Maria at the Ristorante dell'Opera,* Furman, Simpson, and Pollak broke the news to Iride that Rendell, whom she thought of as her boyfriend, would not return to the hotel to be with her.

Don Pasqualino Perfetti, the ex-priest whom Derry had met on his first trip to Rome, was now working with de Vial. The next day

---

* Ristorante dell'Opera is now the Ristorante Giglio, not named after the famous World War II-era opera singer, Gigli, but the fleur-de-lis, the symbol of Florence.

Perfetti introduced Furman, Simpson, and Pollak to a young man who took them to his family home on Via Maranella in the distant suburb of Tor Pignattara, southeast of the city. They settled in, returning to the Vatican the following day to meet with Derry, John May, and Monsignor O'Flaherty.

Derry had false documents made for Simpson and Furman identifying them as Neapolitans. Because Naples was now in Allied hands, these identity cards could not be easily verified. Simpson was now Guglielmo del Monte and Furman was Giovanni Ferino. Furman easily passed for Italian when speaking with Germans and pretended to be an Italian Fascist. Because of his excellent German, Italians thought he was from the German-speaking part of Italy. Pollak kept his Sulmona ID, however, for with it he could pass as an Italian medical student, even with Italians.

False documents even came from the enemy. Baron Ernst von Weizsäcker, German Ambassador to the Holy See, regularly issued passes to Vatican staff who had legitimate reasons to be out in Rome after curfew. Slyly and at great risk to himself, John May filled out three bogus passes and slipped them into a pile being prepared by the Vatican Home Affairs Office for the Baron's signature. They were for Derry, Simpson, and Furman and were duly signed.

The first job for the three new Escape Line crew members was to run daily supplies to the two rented apartments on Via Firenze and Via Domenico Cellini. On December 11, after a simple lunch served in the monsignor's room by the silent German nuns, Furman, Simpson, and Pollak, with two of O'Flaherty's priests, made their first visit to Mrs. Chevalier.

When they arrived at the Chevalier apartment, the four servicemen living there were hiding in their beds, a standard procedure. Two were Royal Navy sailors off the British submarine HMS *Saracen*, sunk off the west coast of Italy six months before. The third was an antiaircraft gunner from Northern Ireland, and the fourth a British paratrooper sent behind enemy lines on a secret mission. He had not been captured and was therefore an evader. He had fallen ill, was cared for by Italians, and brought to Rome.

Over tea and cakes Mrs. Chevalier explained that hers was the collection point for food for both apartments. Her butcher, Giovanni Ceccarelli, gave her meat without asking for ration coupons. Bread, also without coupons, came from a friendly local baker. Money, of course, came from Derry, but originated with Sir D'Arcy, although she did not know that. It paid for the meat, bread, potatoes, fruit, and vegetables. Occasionally, sugar and other scarce foodstuffs could be had from the black-market. But, as Mrs. Chevalier complained, food was becoming more scarce and prices were rising daily. Simpson and Furman said they would try to get more funds from Derry.

Early the next day, the men picked up the food at Mrs. Chevalier's and took it by tram to the other escapees. From Mrs. Chevalier's, it took five different trams to get to both apartments. As the trio neared an apartment, their suitcases bulging with food, Pollak would go ahead to make sure the coast was clear.

The Via Firenze apartment, nicknamed the madhouse, was across from the Opera House on that street. Housing primarily enlisted men, a South African sergeant major named Neil G. Billet was in charge. There were five Yugoslavs (two communists and two liberals and a free Montenegrin); two English soldiers; two French soldiers (a Gaullist and a Marshal Pétain supporter); a Greek; an Australian; and another South African, P. L. Knox-Davis.

Most of the officers were billeted out in Parioli at the Cellini apartment. The British ex-POWs were: Major D'Arcy Mander, the senior officer in charge, Captain Dr. D. R. Macaulay, a Royal Army Medical Corps (RAMC) officer, and four other ranks. There were three South African officers: Sandy Stewart, Jack Selikman, and a dentist, Captain Marcus Kane-Berman. There was also a South African sergeant and a Yugoslav soldier, Bruno Buchner, whose Italian was so good that he would shop for necessities and whatever fresh fruit and vegetables could be found.

After three days of carrying food-filled suitcases, the trio realized that by hiring a horse-drawn *carrozza* they could make deliveries faster and it would be safer than riding trams encumbered with suitcases. They cajoled Derry for money and he agreed, so they hired a driver at 300 lire a day. He picked them up each morning at 10:30 near the Chevalier apartment. It no longer took two men to make the deliveries so, after a few days, Simpson and Furman split, one going to Via Firenze, the other to the Cellini apartment.

Often the pair would meet for lunch at the Osteria dell Orso (The Bear Hostelry), overlooking the Tiber, sitting upstairs and eating lunch with a view over the river. They were well known to the bartender,

Felix Oggione, who had previously worked at the Savoy Hotel in London. He was fully aware that these men were ex-POWs. Simpson and Furman would order schnapps as cover for any patrons who might be listening. But Felix, in on the ruse, would serve them their preferred drink, Scotch whisky or Gordon's English gin, from a prewar supply hidden under the counter. The proprietors of the Orso bought black-market food, so food coupons were not required.

The increasing numbers of foreigners meeting with Monsignor O'Flaherty concerned officials over the question of Vatican neutrality. They closed the gate leading from the street directly into a courtyard beside the Holy Office, and thence to the monsignor's rooms at the German College. It was hoped that this action would cut down on his visitors. Now every visitor to the German College had to wait at the Swiss Guard checkpoint at the Arco delle Campane while their host was called. John May arranged for visitors requesting to see the monsignor or Derry to be allowed to wait inside the Swiss Guard Room until either showed up. Not an ideal solution, but it was a necessary one. Not everyone knew of the gate closing that first day, and Pollak created a ruckus by pounding long and hard on it.

Expenses were rapidly increasing. Derry recorded that, by December 9, he had paid out 69,000 lire. Now, with additional help, and many more ex-POWs to handle, the total rose to half a million lire over the next four weeks. Sir D'Arcy was now handing out a hundred thousand lire a week. The British Foreign Office in London gave the Vatican bank a guarantee that it would cover any borrowing by Sir D'Arcy up to five million lire.

Not all supplies were paid for. There was a constant need for boots and shoes for the escapees. John May was able to get one or two pairs from helpful Swiss Guards, but more were needed. Two women at the Irish Republic Embassy to the Holy See, Blon Kiernan and her mother, Delia Murphy Kiernan, found a source – a Wehrmacht boot-repair depot backed onto their legation on Via dei Penitenzieri, mere steps from the Bernini Colonnade and the Vatican. The depot was closed during the night and was unguarded. Mother and daughter pilfered many pairs of boots, but not so many at one time as to be noticed.

Now relieved of trudging suitcases of food around the city by tram, Furman, Simpson, and Pollak still had a long commute from Tor Pignattara in and out of the city. Jacques de Blesson of the French Embassy to the Holy See introduced Simpson to a friend who knew someone who could help. This was how Simpson met Renzo Lucidi, who was at the New Year's performance of *Tosca*.

Lucidi was 38, half Danish, and half Italian. He was about five feet seven inches tall, stocky, but dapper with bright blue eyes. He had learned the hotel business in Paris where he had met the beautiful Adrienne. He had owned a small hotel in Venice, which he had to abandon because of his anti-fascist views. He moved to Rome to work as a film editor at Cinecittà, the Italian Hollywood, but that work disappeared when the film industry moved north with Mussolini. Adrienne had been a secretary in London and spoke perfect English in addition to her native French. She had an 18-year-old son, Maurice, by a previous marriage and a 12-year-old son, Gérard, with Renzo.

Learning of their long commute over lunch with Furman and Simpson, Renzo suggested that they and Pollak move into his apartment. The apartment was in a quiet neighborhood of four- and five-story apartment blocks a few streets north of Piazza del Popolo and between Via Flaminia and the Tiber. The arrangement was good for Lucidi as well, for their living allowances would help meet his expenses – he was unemployed and had been running through the couple's savings at a rapid rate.

On December 18, the three ex-POWs moved in. Lucidi said that the Germans had tapped all the phones in Rome so they should use the telephone only in an emergency. Asked about the other escapees from Sulmona, Simpson said that Rendell, Wilson, Dukate, and Smith were going stir crazy at the Casa San Giovanni North American College property up on the Janiculum Hill and they wanted to find a place in the city.

Adrienne contacted Père Meunier, the prelate in charge at the Pontifical French Seminary (*Pont. Seminarum Gallicum*) on Via di Santa Chiara, a street behind the 1st-century Pantheon built by Agrippa. The priest agreed to take the four in. They arrived at the seminary on December 22 but were not able to stay the night. And as we shall see, the day before, the Gestapo and the Fascist police had raided several Vatican properties in the city; Père Meunier feared the French Seminary would be next.

Searches were happening all too frequently. Somehow, Paul Chevalier had learned that the SS would search his mother's apartment building for an illegal radio transmitter that night. Warning his mother and the four soldiers staying there of the imminent search, they played a well-rehearsed drama. The Chevalier daughters each led the soldiers out of the apartment one at a time and tell-tale signs of their presence were hidden. Mrs. Chevalier set the table for the six family members and they waited for the Gestapo to arrive. Just after 19:00, Egidio, the *portiere*, told Mrs. Chevalier that the raid was about to start.

Then Paul heard the shouting and pounding on doors by the SS on the third floor outside the apartment. He opened his door and an SS man shouted in his face, "Wait! We're coming!" Then an SS officer and five SS men stormed in. They searched the apartment thoroughly then asked how many people lived there. Mrs. Chevalier calmly replied her four daughters, her mother, and herself.

After rummaging through a stack of phonograph records, and missing a forbidden British platter, they left. On the way out, the officer said, "Bravo" to Mrs. Chevalier who was not sure of his exact meaning but thought perhaps he was congratulating her on not getting caught. By 21:00 the family and the four ex-POWs sat down to their meal, safe for another night.

———

Meanwhile two more British ex-POWs had arrived in Rome in early December. They were E. Garrad-Cole of the RAF and British Army officer Hugh Fane-Hervey. Both men had been captured in North Africa and Garrad-Cole had been a POW for three and a half years. The two had escaped from a train rolling north toward Germany from Frosinone. Somehow, Fane-Hervey had secured an axe and with it he had hacked a hole in the end of the boxcar from which they could jump.

Garrad-Cole spent time in the Sulmona POW Camp #78. While on the run, he met a Number One Special Force British paratroop team — composed of a captain and three other ranks. They had been sent into the mountains to carry out acts of sabotage against the German lines of communication. Although they couldn't get him back to friendly lines, they gave him a map and some cash as well as intelligence on German troop positions. On the way into Rome he saw the wreckage of a POW train that was bombed while crossing a railway viaduct at Orte, 40 miles north of Rome. Many had perished, trapped inside the wreckage.

When Garrad-Cole and Fane-Hervey arrived in Rome they had gone straight to the Vatican. They waited in Saint Peter's Square until Brother Robert showed up. He then arranged to take them to the closed British Embassy to hide out. Their guide was Escape Line member Secondo Costantini, Count Salazar's employee whom we have already met in these pages, and the caretaker at the closed British Embassy. One of Costantini's duties was passing out Red Cross parcels in exchange for a chit (slip of paper) signed by Captain Trippi, military attaché at the Swiss Embassy. He got a package for each of the two soldiers and some cigarettes. There was also a stock of civilian clothing at the embassy and, most importantly, shoes and socks, which he gave the men.

Garrad-Cole and Fane-Hervey spent ten days inside the embassy, often taking meals with Costantini and his family. Brother Robert came several times to check on them and thoughtfully brought a better-fitting suit for Garrad-Cole, who was a large man. While exploring the embassy, the two ex-POWs stumbled upon its wine cellar, its grilled door tightly locked. They liberated several bottles of champagne by lassoing them with a loop attached to a pole which they passed through holes in the grill. They shared their catch with the Costantini family.

Believing that he and the embassy were being watched by the Gestapo, Costantini decided that the two soldiers should move. He called Brother Robert, who took them to the Lithuanian Seminary, past the Villa Torlonia, Mussolini's now-abandoned former residence on Via Nomentana. The pair stayed there safely for the next ten days. Although they could not go outside until dark, their boredom was relieved by the outstanding meals and the priest's excellent wine cellar.

The rector at the Lithuanian Seminary, like Père Meunier at the French Seminary before him, feared for the safety of his institution after the December raid on church properties. So, he asked Garrad-Cole and Fane-Hervey to find different accommodations. Brother Robert was called and he took them to the Lucidis' home where they met Simpson, Furman, and Wilson, who was visiting. The new arrangements split them up: Fane-Hervey would stay with the Lucidis and Garrad-Cole would go with Wilson to the French Seminary, which was once again open to the ex-POWs after being off limits for only a few days. Lucidi took photos of the new arrivals for identity cards. Lucidi slyly told Garrad-Cole that he was in contact with an unnamed organization that could pass on any information he obtained on the Germans. He was probably alluding to Derry's connection with "A" Force.

––––––

Success depended to a large extent on money. Tittmann was supplying money to Americans hiding at the Casa San Giovanni through Monsignor Joseph McGeough, head of the North American College. Monsignor McGeough did not want any recognition or personal publicity for the risks he took. He felt it was his duty to help those in need but it is clear he played a much bigger part in the activities of the Escape Line than has been acknowledged. His full contribution may never be known.

Originally, Tittmann had wanted to keep the American operation separate from the British, but he realized it was better to pool resources and work hand-in-hand with Sir D'Arcy and Derry. Tittmann received cash carried by Vatican couriers from Switzerland, and in loans from religious organizations, foundations, or even through special arrangements with Italian banks. According to Tittmann's dispatches to the State Department in late 1943 and early 1944, he disbursed over 170,000 lire through McGeough and Derry to American ex-POWs.

Funds for US ex-POWs were known as Authorization 90-1944. Tittmann passed 782,375 lire to Derry from December 19, 1943 to July 28, 1944. The cash was passed on ten different occasions in varying amounts. For his part, Major Derry listed 24 times he expended funds on behalf of American ex-POWs; the final total disbursement was 1,027,830 lire. At the official exchange rate that Tittmann was required to use, 19 lire to the dollar, the total cost was $54,096.32.* Tittmann wrote in his memoirs:

I had some 230 American escaped prisoners of war in constant touch with me through my own underground [in and around Rome] and at first I was sending them the necessary supplies through my own

* Note that by the time Rome was liberated, the black-market rate was five times as high or approximately 100 lire to the dollar.

channels. However, it gradually became apparent that it was simpler and more economical to use the efficient and much larger British organization for our prisoners as well. So for the last four or five months of the German occupation, the British organization was kind enough to serve the relatively few men that we had along with theirs. All that was necessary for me to do was to supply the cash which I was always able to produce.[3]

An increasing number of US airmen had begun to show up in Rome after their aircraft, shot up after bombing runs in central Europe, had to ditch over Italy. The Escape Line did its best to handle them, but the Americans apparently expected special treatment. They regarded their billets as sub-standard and they wanted more than the standard daily allowance of 120 lire per POW. Washington wanted the airmen to return to duty as soon as possible and it was suggested that perhaps the downed American aviators were having too good a time in Rome, and that because there was seemingly little danger of their being caught, they should make a greater effort to cross the lines and rejoin their units. Tittmann asked Derry to map out a safe route back to the front lines. Derry's frustrated reply was as follows:

I regret I am unable to give a route down to the lines, as ex-prisoners who have recently been dispatched on our recommended route have all returned. They state:

a. That it is practically impossible to obtain food when some distance from the lines;
b. That snow on the mountain slopes makes going very slow; and,
c. That they have seen several British ex-prisoners of war, especially Indians, dead on the mountains, apparently having died of exposure and/or hunger.

While I realize that it is the duty of all ex-prisoners of war to try and rejoin our forces at the earliest possible moment, I cannot help but feel it is exceedingly unwise to attempt to get through the lines.[4]

Indian and Arab Allied escapees were treated differently from other Allied ex-POWs. Because of their skin color, they would stand out in 1940s Rome, which had very few non-white residents. For their safety the Escape Line did not help them find billets in the city and these soldiers, as well as some white soldiers, were encouraged to remain outside Rome. Not only was it safer, it was cheaper to maintain soldiers in the countryside. If money could not be passed to them, they could chance a trip to the Vatican where they were given funds by John May.

There was another issue. Derry and the others of the Escape Line were concerned that the Muslim Indian soldiers could become susceptible to Nazi propaganda. The Germans had organized a campaign aimed at these Indian soldiers, urging them to join the Indian Volunteer Legion of the Waffen SS (*Indische Freiwillingen Legion der Waffen SS*), a separate Indian brigade. Although a very few soldiers responded, the vast majority remained loyal, even in captivity under the harshest conditions. The small Indian Volunteer Legion never saw action. Similar German efforts were made to recruit among Arab soldiers fighting alongside the British.

There were now 80, mainly British, American, and a few French, escapees in Rome to support. According to an account produced by Furman for an end-of-year audit, Mrs. Chevalier had handed out more than 500 British pounds' worth of lire between November 7, 1943 and January 3, 1944. That money paid for essentials and for Christmas presents as well. Molly Stanley, one of Monsignor O'Flaherty's helpers, organized a group of women volunteers to prepare small Christmas gifts for the 80 escapees. Each gift was accompanied by an English Christmas card. In honor of the season, Major Derry authorized an extra 20 lire for each escapee. Mrs. Chevalier's butcher, Giovanni Ceccarelli, hauled a large supply of scarce meats to her apartment which Simpson and Furman distributed to the other billets.

Christmas was festive despite the hazards of wartime Rome. At the Casa San Giovanni, after Catholic and Protestant Christmas services, the men sat down to a Christmas dinner of spaghetti, bread rolls, apples, chocolates, and wine. Simpson and some others spent Christmas dinner with the Galeazzo Pestalozza family. The old family governess of the Pestalozzas was an Englishwoman named Miss May, and she could not do enough for the POWs. She organized the festivities, complete with Union Jack flag decorations. Furman spent Christmas at the Lucidi apartment with Gil Smith, Dennis Rendell, Pat Wilson, and Duke Dukate, who all spent the night. Garrad-Cole and the others at the French Seminary were said to have spent a dull, bleak Christmas alleviated only by much wine. Monsignor O'Flaherty and Major Derry enjoyed a dinner of mutton and entertained lots of visitors at the German College that day and the next, Britain's Boxing Day.

For the two young Tittmann boys, life in the Vatican was unique. Jesuit fathers at Vatican Radio cast the boys, under assumed names, in roles for Vatican Radio's English-language children's programs. At Christmas, they were in a radio play where they spoke in French. As young Tittmann recalled, Monsignor O'Flaherty dined with the family fairly regularly and on one occasion presented him with a surprising gift:

> He [the monsignor] talked freely about his activities on behalf of the escapees, and when he mentioned that in addition to food and lodging, he provided them with weapons, I asked him, half seriously, to bring me a pistol the next time he visited us. A week later, O'Flaherty came to see us and presented me with a .38 caliber Italian Beretta pistol, the most spectacular souvenir of my Vatican days.[5]

In a benevolent gesture to the Christmas holiday, the jolly and fat Stadtkommandant, General Mälzer, extended the curfew by two hours – to 21:00 – for the three days beginning Christmas Eve. And, hearing that the British were giving a Christmas party for German POWs in England, Mälzer was not to be outdone. He asked the Swiss Embassy to round up 150 Allied POWs for a special Christmas Day dinner. The event was tightly controlled. At 15:00, six large buses brought British and American POWs into the city from the transit POW camp at Cinecittà, the studio, as the Germans called it.

First the prisoners attended a religious service at Santa Susanna on Via XX Settembre, the closed American Church of Rome. The press was on hand and broadcast the event on the radio. Not losing a chance to propagandize, the soldiers were then filmed to let the world see how well the Germans took care of Allied POWs. At the end of the service they were marched up to Via Veneto toward the Porta Pinciana, and there the soldiers sang the popular World War I song, "It's a long way to Tipperary." They were then escorted to the Hotel Regina dining room.[*] Their Christmas dinner consisted of Irish stew and potatoes with cake

[*] Now the Baglioni Hotel Regina at Via Veneto 72.

for dessert. Wine was on the tables. The Stadtkommandant himself stopped by and he gave each prisoner a pack of cigarettes. One German officer commented: "The British boasted that they would be in Rome for Christmas, well, they have been here." It was over by 18:00 and the prisoners were returned to internment at Cinecittà.

Escaped POWs wanted to improve their standard of living but needed additional money which they obtained in several ways. Roman businessmen, originally committed Fascists who had capitalized on Mussolini's government contracts, now saw that the Allies would eventually prevail so were only too willing to loan lire in exchange for a promise to repay in British pounds. Major D'Arcy Mander, using his expanding list of contacts, borrowed money from them and signed an IOU for it. An IOU signed by a British officer had value because, when liberation came, it would show that the lender had helped the Allies. Mander also had John May cash his checks from time to time to let his family, who had access to his accounts, know that he was in Rome. May was able to cash checks at the Vatican bank on the five million lire line of credit arranged by Sir D'Arcy and guaranteed by the British Foreign Office in London.

Pietro Nenni, head of the Italian Socialist Party, was a friend of Renzo Lucidi and member of the National Liberation Committee. He helped Furman and Simpson secure a separate 100,000 lire loan at the rate of 650 lire to the pound for ex-POW officers, who were able to cash checks against this amount. Nenni, later a postwar Italian political figure, was very sympathetic to the Allies as his daughter, Vittoria Daubeuf, had been arrested by the Germans and was later murdered at Auschwitz.

Furman, Gil Smith, Dennis Rendell, Pat Wilson, and Duke Dukate spent New Year's Eve at the Galeazzo Pestalozza's apartment where they "welcomed in the New Year in a spirit of gaiety quite unjustified by the circumstances."[6]

Holiday spirit did not halt Gestapo raids. Milko Scofic's apartment was raided during the first week in January. He was the Yugoslav medical student living in Mrs. Chevalier's building. The *portiere*'s wife,

Elvira, had warned Mrs. Chevalier of an impending raid but the raiding party went directly to Scofic's apartment and ransacked his room. Scofic, who had been on his way to class at the university, watched from the courtyard. They found nothing incriminating so the police made a perfunctory search of another apartment, where they also found nothing. Mrs. Chevalier was anxious because she had five Allied soldiers hiding in her apartment that day. They had gone out to the balcony and were ready to hang from it to avoid being seen but it wasn't necessary. Monsignor O'Flaherty visited the indomitable Mrs. Chevalier to ensure that she understood the danger, but she refused to abandon her boys.

With so many people now working to help the escaped POWs, Derry became understandably concerned about security. After all, civilians and priests were not trained for this kind of existence. It was unfortunately true that Monsignor O'Flaherty talked to everyone indiscreetly. John May was boastful, according to Sir D'Arcy's diaries, when he should have been silent. Count Salazar had already been forced to curtail his activities thanks to Gestapo surveillance and his assistant, Secondo Costantini, was also under surveillance at the closed British Embassy.

Civilian residents at the two rented Escape Line apartment buildings were well aware that Allied soldiers were being hidden there. Someone was bound to tip off the Gestapo. Those apartments needed to be closed and the men scattered across the city. Finding and transporting large amounts of food and supplies to ex-POWs was also becoming increasingly difficult. It was decided to distribute small amounts of cash to the men and their Italian hiders (*padroni*), and let them purchase what they needed on the black-market. Derry, with Sir D'Arcy's encouragement, issued to each member of their team a code name although most of the Italian helpers simply used their own first names.*

The plan was to have the escapees removed from Via Firenze and Via Cellini by December 31. The apartments would be kept for emergencies only. Derry found that this was not easy to implement. D'Arcy Mander, Dr. Macaulay, and the three South Africans, Marcus Kane-Berman (the dentist), Jack Selikman, and Sandy Stewart, all in Via Cellini, wanted to stay together. Mander, sure that he could find a new billet for them, won a ten-day extension from a reluctant Derry; otherwise they would have to go into other places singly or in pairs.

* See Appendix F.

Sergeant Major Billet, Sergeant Knox-Davies, and Private Archie Gibb (1st South African Division) also wanted to stay at their apartment on Via Firenze. Derry agreed, stipulating that they would continue to get cash but would have to find their own food and supplies. The others in Via Firenze were moved to other accommodations or to Via Cellini to await other billets.

———

A potentially damaging event at Sulmona now threatened the Escape Line staff. A note filled with desperation arrived at the Vatican on January 7. It was from Iride and was written after she had returned to Sulmona from Rome. It was an anguished plea for help:

> Dear Patrick [Derry], Yesterday at midday, I was arrested and I got the news that my mother, sister [Maria] and my baby, as well as Flora [Pacella] and her family and the famous "Dino" [Satriano] had been arrested and were in the hands of the German Command. We were betrayed by Captain Dick [Messenger] … who is not a Captain but a simple medical orderly who had divulged everything. They are here looking for Giuseppe [Pollak] and at all costs must take him … I begged Giuseppe to come to me because I am very sick, but I am guarded. I think the arrest of Giuseppe will be the saving of us all. I won't talk unless threatened that I endanger the life of my baby by not doing so – in which case I shall poison myself. I beg you however to save the lives of my baby and my poor mother … You must not believe that if they take Giuseppe that it is a betrayal – he is no interest to them – they only want to know who supplies the money and I repeat they will never know from me – I prefer death – I am only afraid Giuseppe may talk if he believes himself betrayed. Iride[7]

Dick Messenger was an otherwise unknown Australian soldier who had shown up in Sulmona claiming to be a medical officer. Furman and Gil Smith thought him rather coarse and not a doctor, but more likely a medical orderly. Nevertheless, they had accepted him and helped him settle in at Sulmona.

Furman and Pollak were summoned to the Vatican's Arco delle Campane guard post to discuss this major development. On New Year's

Day in Sulmona, a denouncement had resulted in the arrest of 40 Italians. All were charged with helping escaped POWs. The situation was dire. As we have seen, Iride had been in Rome but when she returned to Sulmona she was sent back to Rome to negotiate the exchange of Pollak (Giuseppe) for her family. By chance, Monsignor O'Flaherty was returning to his office from the steps of Saint Peter's Basilica when he saw Furman and Pollak arrive. He immediately took the pair to his room.

The Sulmona Gestapo suspected Pollak of supplying the ex-POWs with Vatican money. The fear was that Iride, who knew a lot about the organization, might talk to get her family released. She knew, for instance, that Sam Derry and Patrick Derry, the name on his Vatican Pass, were one and the same.

Iride was frantic. That morning she repeatedly called the Lucidi apartment, said she was back in Rome and demanded to speak to Pollak. Lucidi had given the number to Henri Payonne at the Opera and he had passed it on to Iride. Lucidi denied that Giuseppe, as she called Pollak, was there. Later the phone rang again and Adrienne answered it. It was Payonne, who apparently had remained in Rome, and who said that the men must leave immediately as there would be a raid. He added that under no circumstance should anyone meet with Iride because it was a trap.

Adrienne told Pollak, Simpson, and Furman to scatter. In her excitement, however, she forgot to tell them that Payonne warned them not to meet with Iride. The three dropped their things off at Via Cellini and Furman and Pollak rushed to see Major Derry. Simpson carried on his work of meeting with ex-POWs. Derry found that Iride's story was confusing and that they did not have a clear sense of what had actually happened in Sulmona. Pollak, not knowing of Payonne's suspicions, said he would find Iride and ask her what was going on.

Pollak went to Iride's pension and knocked on the door. When Iride opened it, he saw a man hiding in the shadows. He fled downstairs and into the courtyard but there was no exit. He was captured by two Sulmona Gestapo men. They had escorted Iride from Sulmona and now they took Pollak to Via Tasso for interrogation where he spent the night. The next day he and Iride were taken to Sulmona. More bad luck was to follow.

To protect the Lucidis, Simpson and Furman did not return to the apartment, but spent the night at Via Cellini. The next day, Saturday, January 8, the two left early on their morning routine to distribute money and check on the billets. They agreed to meet back at Via Cellini in the early afternoon.

Simpson arrived first and found that an American Air Corps sergeant named Eaton had been added to the roster. Eaton had suffered a severe blow to the head when his plane was shot down and he now believed that he was Adolf Hitler; he also screamed at times.

All were clearly distressed by Eaton's condition – especially Bruno Buchner the Yugoslav. Dr. Macaulay, the Royal Army Medical Corps doctor, told Simpson that Eaton needed immediate medical attention. Major Mander suggested Simpson have Brother Robert find a place for the injured airman in a hospital. Outside, on his way to telephone Brother Robert, Simpson ran into Furman returning to the apartment and he explained the situation to him.

Meanwhile the Gestapo had arrested another communist; it was the young man only known as Nebolante who had arranged the renting of the Via Frienze and Via Cellini apartments. To identify other communists, the Fascist police, acting for the Gestapo, approached his widowed mother and posed as her son's communist comrades. They informed her that the Gestapo would release Nebolante if he would take them to the apartments of other communists. Once there, they, his fellow communists, would ambush the Gestapo agents and free her son. But first they needed to search his apartment to see if he had any incriminating information and needed to verify the address. The widow fell for the ruse and gave the Gestapo Nebolante's apartment address.

The Fascist police, although not finding communists, struck pay dirt nonetheless. Captains Tug Wilson and Pip Gardner were discovered living in the apartment, as was Nebolante's aged, unnamed, cook. All three were taken to the Regina Coeli Prison where they joined Nebolante. Immediately Nebolante was severely beaten to extract information about the hiding of POWs, but he remained silent. The cook too was harshly interrogated – he broke, and agreed to lead two Italian plainclothes policemen to the Via Cellini and Via Firenze apartments.

At about 14:00 the cook rang the bell at Via Cellini in the correct coded sequence. The cook related that Nebolante's apartment had been raided by the Gestapo and while he was telling Furman about the capture of his boss and the two ex-POW officers, the Italian police pulled out their revolvers and rushed into the apartment with a half-dozen Gestapo men. All were arrested, including Herta Habernig, the Austrian-Jewish cook. Kappler was elated. Their raid had netted nine more ex-POWs. They missed catching D'Arcy Mander and two soldiers, Lance Corporal Thomas W. Dale (British) and Gunner Edward C. Jones (South African). Mander had been out looking for a new apartment; the others lived in the basement of the apartment house, which was not searched.

After a brief interrogation the men were packed into trucks while Habernig was put in an automobile to be transported to the Regina Coeli Prison. They were, however, allowed to take some personal items.

On the way to prison, Furman destroyed his false identity documents, his notebook with coded addresses and telephone numbers and his daily accounts. Hidden from the police by the other prisoners, Furman tore up the incriminating documents and pushed the shreds through a small hole between the side of the truck and the canvas cover. Then he stuffed 10,000 lire into a bread roll in his pocket.

Later the cook took the Fascist/Gestapo team to Via Firenze, where three South African soldiers, Sergeant Major Billet, Sergeant Knox-Davies and Private Archie Gibb, were captured – the three who had asked to stay.

After his arrest, Gibb, who had been with the 1st South African Division, wanted Derry to get word to his parents that he was a POW once again. It had been four years since Gibb had left for Abyssinia and he had not been home. He wrote a letter and the wife of one of his cellmates smuggled the letter out of the prison and gave it to an American girl working for Captain Trippi at the Swiss Embassy. She forwarded it to Major Derry. His letter to Derry describes the raid on the Via Firenze apartment:

The three of us who stayed in an apartment near the Opera [on Via Firenze] were arrested on Saturday evening about 6:30 [18:30]. The German SS carried out the job and true to their reputation it was all very dramatic. About ten of them came to get us and there was much running around with tommy guns, revolvers or rifles and one hell of a noise. I don't know what the neighbors thought. Someone

I'm afraid gave us away because our friends used our special knock to gain admittance. Still that probably was a blessing, since it saved them shooting the door... Anyway here we are in the Regina Coeli which reminds me of Sing-Sing on the Hudson River, which I was shown when visiting the States in 1938. It is pretty foul here and they split us up to make matters worse. After stripping us of money and cigarettes I was thrown into a cell with three Italians who don't speak English, unfortunately. The food is pretty grim and I'm getting tired of staring at the wall and wondering what I did to deserve this. How long we shall be here I don't know, but I have a feeling they will keep us here until they have satisfied themselves that we weren't involved in any bomb throwing jobs, the fools.[8]

While the raid at Via Cellini was in progress, Simpson had come back to the apartment and rang the buzzer. But it malfunctioned and the police inside had heard nothing. The *portiere* signaled to Simpson to flee and he ran up to the top floor of the apartment block and waited until the Gestapo left. He later made his way to tell Derry, but Derry had already heard of the raid from Lance Corporal Dale and Gunner Jones. They had fled to the Swiss Embassy during the raid and sent a message to Derry from there. Upon leaving the legation, though, both men were arrested by Italian police on Via Volturno across from Termini, Rome's central train station. Their false Italian papers were discovered and, according to the Questura's daily police report, they claimed that they had been in Rome for only 14 days. They were turned over to the German police.

Soon after the raid, Major Mander returned to the apartment and was arrested by two Gestapo men who had stayed behind. They told him to wait in an empty room until their officer returned. Alone, Mander quietly raised the *persiana* (roller shutter) and when it was high enough, he slid out over the window railing and dropped to the courtyard, 12 feet below. There, he saw Habernig's boyfriend, Cesare Coen. Together they exited to the street, unnoticed. It is unlikely that the two Gestapo men ever told their officer that they had captured another POW but allowed him to escape.

Mander and Coen went to the apartment of Nora Kiss, one of Mander's friends. She was a Hungarian ballet dancer who spoke Russian and eked out a living giving private dance lessons. After Mander and

Coen got to the apartment, Nora called her friend Ubaldo Cipolla, who came over right away. He was wearing his Italian SS uniform which was unsettling because the Italian SS was of course organized by the German SS and worked directly for Kappler.

Cipolla, whom we have already met, was a former Italian Army officer and had signed the lease for the Via Cellini apartment for Monsignor O'Flaherty. His father was a colonel in the Italian Army and it was through him that Cipolla was offered a post in the Italian SS. Cipolla was not a diehard Fascist, nor a communist; he was an opportunist. Before joining the Italian SS, Cipolla had reportedly asked Kiss if she thought it was a good idea. Kiss reasoned that at least they would know what was going on at Gestapo headquarters.

Mander, unaware that Cipolla was a double agent, thought that Cipolla, whom he called Daniele, worked for SIM. Later, Mander wrote that although he got no military information from Cipolla, he was warned in advance by him about Gestapo raids on apartments and roundups. Mander himself was not above suspicion. There were some who thought he might be a German spy because he spoke such good German and he had escaped the raid at Via Cellini.

These three raids had devastated the Escape Line's organization. First Pollak and Iride were taken to Sulmona. Then the line had lost Nebolante's apartment, followed by both clearing house apartments, and gone were Furman, 15 other escapees, and three civilian helpers.[*]

How to regroup? Simpson argued that, with both Furman and Pollak arrested, more help was needed. He recommended that Renzo Lucidi be brought in as an active player. Derry agreed. Simpson was upset about Furman's capture and annoyed with himself because he had left his briefcase in the raided apartment. Among other documents, it contained something of sentimental value, Adrienne's signed opera program.

---

[*]To recap, those arrested were as follows. Nebolante's apartment: Nebolante; the unnamed aged cook; British Captains P. J. Gardner, VC, MC and R. Tug Wilson, DSO. Via Cellini apartment: Dr. D. R. Macaulay, British, Doctor; Capt. M. Kane-Berman, South African, Dentist; Lt. J. Furman, British; Lt. W. B. Stewart, South African; Lt. J. Selikman, South African; Trooper W. Churchill, British; Gunner P. R. Hands, South African; Sgt. Robert H. Eaton, USA; Bruno Buchner, Yugoslav soldier; Herta Habernig, Austrian cook. Via Firenze apartment: CSM N. G. Billet, South African; Sgt. P. L. Knox-Davis, South African; Private A. Gibb, South African. From the basement Via Cellini apartment and found on the street: Lance Corporal Thomas W. Dale, British and Gunner Edward C. Jones, South African.

That day and the next, Monsignor O'Flaherty and his priestly network warned every billet in the city that their locations might be known by the Gestapo. The network had to exert extreme care not to jeopardize their hosts. The organization also changed the way business was conducted. Henceforth, one person would know of no more than the billets of half a dozen men.

The increasing loss of helpers further hampered Escape Line efforts. Concetta Piazza, who took money and supplies to POWs, was arrested. Her nickname was Midwife, probably because she nursed wounded and sick soldiers in Rome's outlying villages. In all, she supported 20 soldiers. Piazza was taken to the Regina Coeli Prison on January 8, just as she was finishing her rounds. It was assumed that she had been denounced to the Gestapo, but no evidence against her was ever produced. She carried no incriminating documents on her. Improvising, Piazza wrote a letter on prison toilet paper to Field Marshal Kesselring himself, explaining how she had also nursed Wehrmacht soldiers. The letter found its way to Monsignor O'Flaherty, who had it properly typed and sent to Kesselring via Michael MacWhite, the Irish Republic Ambassador to the Italian government. Her argument worked and Piazza was released a few days later.

Monsignor O'Flaherty was used to taking chances, even though he knew he was in constant danger. And so, when a glittery formal invitation to a reception at the Hungarian Embassy arrived on January 11, he accepted. There were not many guests, but among them were the German Minister to the Holy See, Baron von Weizsäcker, and from Berlin, Prince von Bismarck, head of the Italian section of the German Foreign Ministry. As the evening wore on the Baron approached the monsignor and said:

> My dear Monsignor, you know my private views and attitudes very well. Nobody in Rome honors you more than I do for what you are doing. But it has gone too far for all of us. Kappler is waiting in the hall, feeling rather frustrated, I am afraid. I am aware that he has made several ... informal ... and highly irregular attempts to capture you – which he should not have done. Now, I have told him that you will of course have safe conduct back to the Vatican tonight. But ... if you ever step outside Vatican territory again, on whatever pretext, you will be arrested at once ... The

Monsignor smiled at the Baron and replied "your excellency is too considerate. I will certainly think about what you have said … sometime."[9]

The pressure continued, this time from Monsignor Montini, who had obviously heard from the Germans. While O'Flaherty was not told to stop his activities, he was told to set a much lower profile. Years later, Monsignor O'Flaherty commented that he had had his knuckles rapped pretty hard.

Pressure also came from Baron von Weizsäcker, who had the rector of the German College tell Monsignor O'Flaherty that the visitor, known as Patrick Derry, who was staying in the monsignor's room, had to go. Sir D'Arcy provided the solution by secretly moving Derry to his apartment in the Santa Marta Hospice on January 12. Derry was safe but under virtual house arrest: he could no longer leave the building because, officially, he did not exist. His discovery would likely get the entire British Legation expelled.

14

Life under the Gestapo Boot – Raids, Roundups, Food, and Art

Now that the Carabinieri were gone from Rome, the Germans and their Fascist collaborators needed to maintain law and order in the city. The remaining police, the PS (the National Public Security Police) and the PAI, were considered inadequate. The answer to this problem came from the newly re-formed Republican Fascist Party (PFR – *Partito Fascista Repubblicano*) which had set up headquarters in the columned Palazzo Wedekind in Piazza Colonna. The piazza is pinned by the marble column erected by Roman Emperor Marcus Aurelius in AD 193 with the later addition of a bronze statue of Saint Paul on the top. Via del Corso, Rome's main street where horse races took place in Renaissance times, borders the piazza on the east side.

The PFR was nominally under the control of Guido Buffarini-Guidi, the Fascist Minister of the Interior in charge of Italian Fascist police forces. Buffarini-Guidi was a committed Fascist who had been fired from his post by Mussolini along with Count Ciano and the other Fascist ministers during the February 1943 cabinet shake-up. A close friend of Obersturmbannführer Dollmann as well as Himmler, Buffarini-Guidi returned to this post after Mussolini established the Salò Republic on September 23. Although he was the head of the Fascist anti-Jewish Office of Demography and Race, Buffarini-Guidi was known to have sold Aryanization certificates to wealthy Jews so they could evade arrest and deportation.

The PFR secretary was a diehard Fascist, Gino Bardi, the Fascist Commissioner General of the city. On September 18, Bardi formed a Special Police Unit made up of PFR volunteers and installed them in the now-vacant antique Palazzo Braschi. It had been empty since the fall of Mussolini and had once been the seat of the defunct Roman Federation of Fascists. The new unit was called the Palazzo Braschi Action Squad (*Squadre d'Azione di Palazzo Braschi*).

Bardi and his associate, Guglielmo Pollastrini – an ex-police sergeant expelled for violence and insubordination – headed this Action Squad, now commonly called the Banda Bardi-Pollastrini. It was a gang of 120 armed black-clad thugs in ten action squads whose mission was to rid Rome of anti-fascists, Jews, escaped Allied prisoners, and Carabinieri. There was no due process and they attacked anyone they chose. Palazzo Braschi, now the Rome City Museum, is a beautiful 18th-century building with a monumental marble staircase, spacious reception rooms, and ancient cellars that were part of the Roman Emperor Domitian's racecourse now covered by the Piazza Navona, humorously known as Rome's outdoor living room. It was in these cellars that the band imprisoned its victims who were held for ransom, tortured, and murdered. The Banda terrorized the city for the full 45 days it existed.

In retaliation for the horrible activities of the Banda, Gappisti partisans hatched a plan to assassinate Minister Buffarini-Guidi at Il Passetto, a restaurant where he often dined, close to the round end of the Piazza Navona, in a smaller piazza between Piazza Navona and the Tiber and so not far from Palazzo Braschi itself. They aborted the plan, however, fearing that it might backfire and that recently captured partisans might be killed in retaliation. Instead, four Gappisti attacked a group of swaggering Banda Bardi-Pollastrini thugs, and killed three of them as they exited Palazzo Braschi.

Banda Bardi-Pollastrini's undisciplined rampages reflected negatively on the German rule of the city and this sealed its doom. The Germans, in particular Kappler, Dollmann, and Consul Möllhausen, were fed up with being blamed for its excesses. The Banda had to be shut down. Acting with the approval of SS-General Wolff, the palazzo was raided on November 27, 1943 by a mixed contingent consisting of police assigned to the Open City, the PAI, and the PS. Forty members of the Banda including the leaders Bardi and Pollastrini were arrested and all sent to prison.

The police released the 24 prisoners found in the cellar of Palazzo Braschi and they uncovered a vast storehouse of loot worth millions of lire. The booty was in cash, jewels, furs, fancy clothes, motor-cars, and there was even a live cow. Announcing the raid, the Germans condemned these out-of-control Italian Fascists in a holier-than-thou fashion, as if they had not done the same themselves. Unsurprisingly the captured booty simply disappeared. Giuseppe Pizzirani replaced Gino Bardi as secretary and Fascist Commissioner General of the city. For the remainder of the German occupation, Palazzo Braschi was sometimes used as a depot and office space for units of the newly formed Italian SS, organized by the Germans.

Hardships increased under German rule for the ordinary citizens of Rome who did not have funds to spend in the black-market. By the middle of October 1943, six weeks into the German occupation, the price of eggs had risen almost ten times. Lemons now cost 56 centesimi (100 Italian cents to the lira) each. What was called bread was available but was rationed at 150 grams per day per person. It was now made with only a small amount of wheat flour and filled with rye and maize flour, dried chickpeas, mulberry leaves, and even elm tree pitch.

Some food could only be found on the black-market and sometimes there were even potatoes to buy. Olive oil – an Italian staple – could be purchased by the tenth of a liter and sugar by the half pound. Flour, rice, and lard were available, but were very expensive. Jam, milk, meat, and fish (fresh or preserved) were practically unobtainable, as were tea, coffee, and cocoa, unless one was prepared to pay a couple of thousand lire a kilo. A coffee substitute was made from barley, imitation tea of chamomile, lemon, blackberry leaves, or dried orange peel.

Anything edible would do. Fava (broad) beans and peas became main courses. Potato skins and other vegetable-leavings were used in soups. There was no pet food; feral cats were disappearing from the ancient Roman Forum as they were eaten by the populace. Cooking gas was cut off except for a few hours a day, so food was heated over improvised wood stoves. No dead tree or wooden park bench was immune from the wood hunters.

There was no butter, no fresh or canned fruit, and green vegetables were increasingly difficult to find. After being suspended on September 15, the weekly 100-gram meat ration was reinstated, but meat was rarely available. Mother Mary wrote in her diary that although everything was rationed, the rations never seemed to be found for purchase. For example, her convent was only able to buy half of its October pasta ration and none of its November ration.

At the end of the year it was customary for diplomats to send wrap-up reports. Michael MacWhite, the Irish Republic Ambassador to the Salò Republic, wrote about the food crisis in Rome on December 30:

> A census of the population has now been taken in Rome in order to force from their hiding places all those who are on the run of whom it is estimated there are one hundred thousand Italian soldiers, three thousand escaped prisoners of war and some hundreds of Jews. Only those whose names figure on the census page will get food tickets. The concierge of each house must keep a list of the names of the occupants on each floor posted up at the entrance so that in case of a raid the supernumeraries may be seized. Nobody can change his or her residence without having first obtained permission from the police ... The food situation is getting out of control. Due to cessation of rail transport and German requisition, commodities no longer arrive. So far, there has been no distribution for the month of November of butter, sugar, rice, etc. ... vegetables come from the neighborhood at present but as fighting approaches this source will dry up.[1]

Citizens scrawled graffiti around the city, which read: BREAD! BREAD! BREAD! – DEATH TO THE PEOPLE WHO ARE STARVING US.

The Pope opened soup kitchens and at least Mother Mary had ration cards while many in Rome had none. Help came from Dr. Ettore Basevi, the head of the State Printing Office in Piazza Verdi. Basevi was a captain in the Guardia di Finanza and was secretly a member of the FMCR. He stole a large amount of watermarked paper from the State Printing Office and set up a press to produce false documents on the blank official paper. He was prolific, printing over 85,000 census receipts (a necessary document), 50,000 identity cards, 33,000 convalescent permits, 23,000 military discharge papers, 15,000 *soggiorno* permits (permission to live in Rome), and 3,000 German Todt Organization passes. Jews were given 1,000 Catholic baptism and marriage certificates, ration cards, and various other documents. Basevi's false ration cards let thousands of illegals eat when food could be bought.

Basevi was helped by his girlfriend, a German-Jewish woman, Lily Marx, an expert forger in her own right, who produced identity documents in the German Gothic script. Marx acted as the go-between for Basevi and Major Derry, delivering documents and receiving cash in return. The cash was always given to her in a shoe box in a public place. Basevi's money came from both Sir D'Arcy and the FMCR. Basevi was arrested in January 1944 and sent to the Regina Coeli Prison which temporarily caused the suspension of printing activities. His eventual fate is not known. Soon others were found to carry on his work as later Rome police reports mention the arrest of another group making false ration cards which included another member of the State Printing Office. Thanks to Monsignor O'Flaherty, Marx was appointed the Chancellor of the Haitian Legation to the Holy See which gave her diplomatic status. In that position Marx was able to continue as the editor of the FMCR's daily bulletin.

Electricity was rationed by zones, each zone being without power two nights a week. When the power was on, it was sporadic and unreliable. Light bulbs, when they worked at all, put out only a feeble light. Candles were of the poorest quality. Carbide (acetylene) lamps were in use, often with disastrous results, causing fires, occasionally burning out entire apartments. The acetylene lamp was made up of two tin cans. The top can dripped a tiny amount of water on calcium carbide lumps in the bottom can, causing a chemical reaction that produced acetylene gas. It was flared off with a lot of smoke. After the war, apartments where these lamps were used had to be repainted.

Water was rationed throughout the city and available only on certain days and for a limited time; Romans quickly learned to fill containers and bathtubs to store this precious commodity. Many of the public fountains still worked but there were long lines to get water from them.

New clothing was unavailable. Frayed collars were turned inside out, and often a contrasting piece of material sewn over them. This quickly became a wartime fashion. There was a synthetic fabric made from milk casein (a milk protein) that became smelly when wet while soles for shoes were made of compressed cardboard due to a lack of leather and were not very sturdy in water.

The few buses that continued to run were converted from diesel fuel to *gassogeno*, a gas produced by burning charcoal in a specially adapted wood stove welded to the back of the bus. The ticket conductors stoked the fire. Often these buses did not have the power to make it up the fabled hills of Rome and passengers would be asked to get out and push. In the winter they usually did, but in the spring it was easier, and less sweaty, to simply continue on foot.

Trams, being subject to the frequent power outages, were increasingly unreliable; additionally, thieves, risking electric shock, would steal the overhead copper wires to sell, since copper had become quite valuable. Bicycles were banned, but Romans were able to use three- and four-wheel modified bicycles, although there were no rubber replacement tires or tubes. Existing tires and tubes were so patched that there were patches on patches.[2]

Shortly after taking control of the city, the German military government of Rome ordered the confiscation of all private vehicles in the city. As we have seen, they set up a separate command under Köhler to oversee this and to reissue the cars to the Gestapo and others.

The deprivations suffered by Rome's citizens were not shared by the German elite who were living the good life. For a privileged few, mainly those Nazi collaborators still driving cars, whose women were well dressed, wearing furs, and attending the opera and the theater, life in Rome was good. General Mälzer gave an entertainment at the Hotel Excelsior on Via Veneto – the *Komiker Kabarett*, a show seen in the Nazi capital – directed and organized by a producer especially brought in from Berlin. In Rome, the show featured Italian actors and singers, elaborate refreshments and plenty of fresh flowers for the ladies. Mother Mary, aghast at this excess, wrote: "They're losing men by the hundred in Italy and by the thousands in Russia, but the *Komiker Kabarett* must go on. One wonders if that sort of revelry by night is inseparable from war."[3]

The Germans exerted increased pressure on the Italians to step up their arrests of Jews who had avoided the earlier roundups. On December 1, 1943, Buffarini-Guidi issued Police Order Number Five requiring Italian police to arrest Jews whenever they encountered them. Jews were sent to concentration camps, their property confiscated, sold, and the proceeds supposedly used to help Italians who were homeless because of the Allied air raids. The police reaction to these orders was slow and confused; there were orders and counter orders about who to arrest and when they were to be arrested.

In his severity, Marshal Graziani (Mussolini's Defense Minister) also ordered the shooting of deserters and draft dodgers. General Mälzer supported this with an ordinance calling for a death sentence for anyone in violation of the order to report for military service. This also applied to the labor service call up of men between the ages of 16 and 60. The military inspector of labor, Italian Army Engineer General Francesco Palladino, started a Nazi-like Todt Organization for the voluntary recruitment of workers. Despite the threats, he had negligible results.

As noted by Mother Mary, in the first week of December, the German government of Rome ordered all *portiere* to post a list of their buildings' residents near the front doors. They were held responsible for failure to list everyone residing in their building. Severe punishment was promised, including the confiscation of food-ration cards.

A plot to kidnap the Pope was again on some minds in the German High Command. Early that December, SS Obergruppenführer Wolff, head of the SS in Italy, had met with Hitler and had argued against the plot. He reasoned that the Pope was the only one with real authority in Italy and that kidnapping him would provoke extreme negative reactions in Rome, throughout Italy, and among the numerous German Catholics. Wolff believed that the Pope could be very useful to Germany in the future and any temporary advantage to the Reich in taking the Pope would not be worth it. Hitler agreed. Hearing the rumor that the Germans were threatening to remove the Pope from Rome, Tittmann cabled Washington:

> The Vatican seems to be convinced that the Germans realize they
> would have more to lose by removing the Pope than by allowing him

to remain here even though he may fall eventually under exclusive influence of Allies and to feel that for the time being the only danger is that a sudden outburst of anger against the Church on part of Hitler himself might overrule the wise counsels of those who have the long-term interests of Germany at heart ...[4]

The Germans had reason to believe that the Pope was at least neutral to them. They were getting good press from the Vatican newspaper, *L'Osservatore Romano*, which published an article thanking the German troops for respecting the Vatican and the person of the Pope. And back on October 29, Vatican Radio had announced that: "The Holy See confirms that German troops have respected the Roman Curia and Vatican City and welcomes the assurance given by the German Ambassador as to the future."[5]

The Pope, in a December 29 meeting with Tittmann, expressed his fears that Soviet successes on the Eastern front would lead to the spread of Godless communism in Western Europe. Tittmann saw that the Pope's chief worry was the looming communist threat. This anxiety was repeated in a memo to Berlin reporting a private audience between the Pope and Baron Ernst von Weizsäcker, Germany's Ambassador to the Holy See. Weizsäcker quoted the Pope as having expressed alarm at the left-leaning political situation in Rome and in northern Italy and reportedly he said that we fear the worst if Germany finds herself forced to evacuate those regions.

On December 8, 1943, Mussolini ordered the creation of a National Republican Guard (GNR – *Guardia Nazionale Repubblicana*). While technically not a police force, it was created to replace the Carabinieri and the original blackshirts and to enforce Fascist ideology. Some Carabinieri were inducted and some forced into the new organization if they were considered reliable by the Fascists.

The GNR was a direct descendant of the original blackshirts, the Volunteer Militia for National Security (MVSN – *Milizia Volontaria per la Sicurezza Nazionale*) organized by Mussolini in the 1920s. By 1943 there may have been as many as 20,000 blackshirts throughout the country. Some men were formed into military units, such as the

Centauro II Division, which was one of the Italian forces surrounding Rome at the time of the armistice. MVSN men wore either black uniforms or civilian clothes and were also known as the Milizia.

In Rome, the GNR headquarters were at the Mussolini Caserma in Prati, not far from the apartment where Rosa Guarnieri Carducci was murdered back on October 7. The MVSN also maintained several important special militias to watch over the railways (*ferrovie*), mail and telegraph offices (*postelegrafica*), and sea ports (*portuaria*). One unit, Battaglione M (for Mussolini), was permanently stationed in Rome at Piazza Sonnino in Trastevere. Originally, Battaglione M was an elite unit of the MVSN. It fought in Tunisia, Russia, and the Balkans among other places before it was absorbed into the GNR. The GNR was hampered by scant resources and it was in direct conflict with Rodolfo Graziani's new army for recruits.

There was another military unit in the city. Prince Junio Valerio Borghese, sometimes called the Black Prince because of his pro-Fascist views, was an Italian Navy captain from one of the oldest and noblest of families.* He reorganized the Italian Navy's Decima MAS (*Decima Flottiglia Motoscafo Armato Silurante*, the Armed Torpedo Motorboats of the 10th Light Flotilla).

The new Decima MAS, based in La Spezia and now without most of its motorboats and midget submarines, became a land-based, naval commando unit and gained a reputation for being especially adept at apprehending, torturing, and murdering partisans. Its ranks grew to almost 15,000 men. Decima MAS maintained a propaganda office in Rome and stationed the Barbarigo Battalion nearby. Borghese placed the battalion at the disposal of the SS and the German Army, where it fought at Anzio and it was highly praised by the Germans.[6]

The terrorizing of ordinary Roman citizens enduring life under occupation now gathered pace. Minister Guido Buffarini-Guidi, still

---

* Borghese was a very interesting character. After the war he served three years in prison for his activities fighting for the Fascists. Later he became a prominent hardline, neo-fascist politician and even planned a 1970 coup which was discovered. He fled to Spain where he died a few years later.

looking to expand his control of the city, decided that Rome needed a citywide network of police informers ready to denounce neighbors and settle old scores. He created a new Special Police Unit (*Reparto Speciale di Polizia*) to do this. It was commonly referred to as the Banda Koch after their leader, Pietro Koch. The Banda was paid for by Buffarini-Guidi, but was controlled by Kappler.

Koch had arrived in Rome in December 1943, and was described as a "suave, gentle-mannered man, 26 years old, with brilliantine black hair, a short, trim mustache, and a refined vocabulary. He would not touch his victims without gloves."[7] Koch had served in the Army but had been discharged in 1939 for insulting a senior officer. Although he styled himself *Doctor* Koch, he did not have even a high school diploma and it was said that he had been expelled for masturbating in the presence of female classmates. His specialty was tracking down and torturing anti-fascists. His was as sinister a character as one could imagine in the world of Fascist horrors.

Koch made his headquarters on the fifth floor of Pension Oltremare, Via Principe Amedeo, a few blocks from Rome's central train station, Termini. Neighbors complained of hearing the screams coming from his victims. Koch's torture methods involved alternately applying scalding hot and freezing water, all under bright lights, as well as piercing victims' penises with pins.

Koch's informer network included Ildelfonso Epaminonda Troya, called don Ildelfonso, a former monk from Tuscany. Don Ildelfonso would say a Mass in the morning and then report to Koch. Another was a man called Alfredo, who enjoyed playing the pension's piano while victims were being tortured. One of Koch's men was assigned more or less permanently to the tobacconist's shop across the street from Mrs. Chevalier's apartment. Koch was convinced that there was an illegal radio transmitter somewhere in the neighborhood. The surveillance made life difficult for the ex-POWs under Mrs. Chevalier's care.

Koch was especially keen to test the Holy See's reaction to violations of its institutions outside the territorial limits of the Vatican City. Many of these institutions existed without extraterritoriality status but were recognized by the Lateran Treaty as belonging to the Vatican. At the time, such buildings in Rome were provided with a sign in German and Italian which read: "This building serves religious objectives and is a dependency of the Vatican City. All searches and requisitions are prohibited."

During the evening of December 21, the Banda Koch raided three Vatican institutions sheltering refugees, anti-fascists, former military officers, labor leaders, draft evaders, and Jews. The Gestapo was present in the form of an observer, SS-Hauptsturmführer Erich Priebke, the chief of counterespionage.

The first raided was the Lombard Seminary (*Seminario Lombardo*), in the Piazza di Santa Maria Maggiore, close to the Basilica, housing 110 refugees. The building was surrounded by 50 policemen and Koch, and about a dozen others, burst in. Some refugees escaped over a fourth-floor bridge to the next building and one refugee even played dead by lying in a coffin, but was unfortunately resurrected. Some of the younger men, posing as seminarians, were tested by don Ildelfonso, who had them recite Latin texts to see who the true seminarians were; those who could not were arrested.

The second site to be raided was the Pontifical Institute of Oriental Studies, which housed 20 refugees and was located next door to the Lombard Seminary. It included the Russian Institute (*Russicum*), which had been formed to bring Roman Catholicism back to the atheist Soviet Union. There Koch's men were responsible for much looting and destruction. They left at 07:00 the next morning, taking 18 prisoners with them.

The third institute raided that night was the Roman Seminary (*Seminario Romano*). It was adjacent to the Basilica of Saint John Lateran but, unlike the basilica, it did not have extraterritorial status. It was located inside the Lateran Pontifical University and was the primary hiding place for 200 of the anti-fascist elite, including CLN President Ivanoe Bonomi and the heads of four of the six coalition partners. There were also 55 prominent Jews there. Other refugees included Mario Badoglio, the son of Marshal Badoglio.

After the raid on the seminary the 90 refugees who had evaded discovery fled, remaining on the streets of Rome until they found new hiding places. Those taken prisoner were sent to the Regina Coeli Prison. The Vatican protested verbally, but because it had no direct relations with the Salò Republic, there was no office through which the Vatican could directly protest so the vast majority were not released.

Just before Christmas, General Mälzer published a list of new offenses for those living in the city. They were divided into three categories by degree of punishment. An offense in the first category — harboring escaped

POWs, owning a radio transmitter, and not fulfilling labor obligations – was punishable with execution. Second category offenses – any contact with escaped POWs, printing or publishing news derogatory to the Axis forces, assisting with radio transmissions, and taking photographs out-of-doors – were punishable with hard labor for life. The third type of offense got the perpetrator a 20-year prison term for failing to notify authorities of a change of address.[*]

Roman aristocrats played uncertain roles under the German occupation. Kappler believed that many were responsible for spreading anti-German propaganda. Since the armistice, the Gestapo had arrested six aristocratic women including Princess Virginia Agnelli of the Fiat family. However, on the night of January 26, the women escaped by squeezing under a fence at the makeshift prison at San Gregorio al Celio, formerly a Vatican college across from the Palatine Hill and near the Colosseum. Obersturmbannführer Dollmann was furious when he learned of their escape. He had already given orders that the Duchess of Sermoneta, lady-in-waiting to the Queen of Italy, the last high-profile, pro-monarchy aristocrat still openly living in Rome, was to be sent north the very next day.

Dollmann did not like Vittoria Colonna, the Duchess of Sermoneta, because she did not receive him in her palazzo. Prewar she had written a book, *Things Past*, which Dollmann had translated into German for a Munich publishing house in 1938, without her permission. Moreover, he had spread the word that he had been lavishly entertained by her and that they were close friends – and he included this in his autobiography. None of it was true.

According to the duchess, she was placed under house arrest on January 28 at her Palazzo Orsini. Knowing the intricate layout of the palazzo, she slipped through the warren of rooms and escaped to the Spanish Embassy inside the Palazzo Borghese, a harpsichord-shaped building in central Rome. There she learned that her property was forfeit to the nation and her furniture was to be sold at auction. Joined

---

[*] In Italy residents were and still are required to register their address with the local civil authorities.

at the embassy by her maid, she returned to the Palazzo Caetani, on Via delle Botteghe Oscure, halfway between the Largo di Torre Argentina and the Vittorio Emanuele Monument. The palazzo, her first marital home, was somewhat modest by Rome palazzo standards but it was here where the two women hid out for the next four months in a tiny room, their only egress to the outside, the rooftop.

For the Escape Line, a high-ranking British officer became a top priority to find a suitable billet. On January 13, Brother Robert was told by Sir D'Arcy that an ex-POW general had arrived in the city. British Major General Michael Denman Gambier-Parry had been the general officer commanding the British 2nd Armoured Division. He was captured at Mechili, 170 miles east of Benghazi, Libya, in April 1941, and had been held in a senior officer POW Camp #12, at Castello de Vincigliata, near Florence. He escaped after the Italian armistice.

The information had come from an unusual source, the Greek Freedom or Death underground movement. The Greeks, taken prisoner during Mussolini's invasion of Greece, had also escaped during the Italian armistice and they were taking care of 92 escaped Greek soldiers. The leaders were Major Evangelos Averoff and acting Sergeant Theodore Meletiou. They contacted the Rome Escape Line in early December 1943.

Derry was astonished to learn that an elite band of British ex-POWs was being hidden near Arezzo, 120 miles northeast of Rome. The group consisted of three generals, an air vice-marshal, and four brigadier generals. Derry gave Meletiou 10,000 lire for the general officers and suggested that, although all of them could not be hidden in Rome, perhaps one could. Derry, swamped with work, promptly forgot about his suggestion.

Acting on this, the Greeks escorted General Gambier-Parry and an English woman, Mary Boyd, to Rome. Mary Boyd had helped many Allied soldiers in the Arezzo area, dispersing funds through Meletiou from the Escape Line. The general, dressed in rags, and without money, was in desperate need of assistance. Meletiou was given 20,000 lire for his needs and, through his contacts in the black-market, got the general suitably outfitted.

Gambier-Parry, now the highest-ranking British officer escapee in Rome and a rich prize were he to fall into German hands, required special housing. Brother Robert knew an English-born woman, Signora di Rienzo, who he mistakenly thought was the daughter of Lord Strickland, fourth prime minister of Malta. She lived with her husband not far from the Colosseum. In renovating their apartment, the di Rienzos had built a secret room which would be ideal for hiding the general. Brother Robert described the secret room this way:

All the rooms in the apartment were on one side of a corridor except one which was completely partitioned away from all the rest by walling off an entrance door … The only passage from the secret room was through a toilet which was reached by means of a narrow plank, something like a springboard six feet long, and one end of which could be placed on the window sill overlooking the courtyard three floors below … The General used to spend his days alone in the secret room which, incidentally, was the best furnished room in the house; he would do a lot of reading and typing. His breakfast and lunch were slid across the plank when no neighbor was looking and a servant girl would cross over to do the cleaning. When it was completely dark the General would balance himself across and join the family for the social part of his stay, having his dinner with them and listening to the news until about midnight. On Sundays he would spend the whole day with the family and Brother Robert would meet with him then.[8]

After he settled in, General Gambier-Parry wanted to know how the Escape Line operated and, in a note to Major Derry, asked him to explain the setup, in particular the chain of command.

Derry replied that although he tried to maintain military discipline, it was pretty much impossible; occasionally one or two of the soldiers got out of line. He said there was no real chain of command and he and Monsignor O'Flaherty shared the work. He deferred to the general, as the senior Allied military officer in Rome, inviting him to take over, but the general declined. According to Derry:

In fact, the General's letter brought home to me, I think for the first time, the strangeness of this organization, in which soldiers and priests, diplomats and communists, noblemen and humble working folk, were all operating in concord with a single aim, yet without any clearly defined pyramid of authority.[9]

Kappler was desperate to supply laborers to build fortifications to contain the Allied landing at Anzio, an Allied operation designed to bypass the impressive German fortifications and leapfrog Allied amphibious forces closer to Rome.* At 10:00 on January 31, 1944, abandoning the concept of Italian-only raids, he led the largest *rastrellamento* for forced labor of able-bodied men between the ages of 18 and 70. He commanded 1,500 men from the SS, Wehrmacht soldiers on leave, the National Republican Guard (GNR) as well as local Roman police. Armored cars and machine guns sealed off a vast area in the *centro storico*. The zone stretched from Piazza Independenza, to Termini Station and down Via Nazionale. Men were summarily snatched off the streets, buses, and trams.

In a few hours, at least 2,000 men had been taken to the ORPO Barracks at the Macao Caserma at the Castro Pretorio. Although some were sent to factories in Hanover, Germany, at least 800 men were sent to work on the fortifications on the perimeter at the Anzio front where many would be strafed and wounded by Allied aircraft.

In its dedication, the SS mistakenly arrested Rome's newly appointed Fascist Chief of Police, 44-year-old Pietro Caruso, a Neapolitan. Caruso had been sworn in that morning at the Questura on Via San Vitale. Wanting to observe the roundup operation, he walked the short block to the nearby Via Nazionale where he was arrested by an SS patrol along with every other adult male they encountered. The error was soon detected and Caruso was released with effusive apologies.

Although successful in terms of numbers taken, the January 31 Via Nazionale roundup had a disastrous effect on occupied Rome. People were now too afraid to go out on the street. Shops closed and the city appeared abandoned. A joke ran that half the people of Rome were hiding in the homes of the other half. Field Marshal Kesselring reacted

---

* See Chapter 16 for further information.

by again ordering the manhunts involving German police and soldiers to stop.

The next day, on February 1, unfazed by his arrest by the SS, Pietro Caruso mounted his own raid. He hoped to find 200 men for labor service with a combined force of Banda Koch men and his own police. Caruso raided suspected partisan locations, including the *santabarbara* bomb factory at an apartment on Via Giulia which, at that point, contained 70 kilos of explosives. An Italian Gestapo agent, Giovanni Pastore, had given Erich Priebke the location and the information was passed on to Caruso. He arrested the bomb factory's chemist, Gianfranco Mattei, who was severely tortured. Mattei found a poisonous cleaning agent in the bathroom at Via Tasso and used it to commit suicide rather than reveal any information. But Caruso did learn where the Action Party's underground newspaper *Italia Libera* was produced and he shut it down.

Meanwhile Escape Line member Furman and the others arrested continued to be held in the Regina Coeli Prison. The prison was protected by two sets of massive gates and guarded by Fascist police. Furman described the effect of the prison:

> [It had an] enormous, glass-roofed, circular hall from which corridors radiated in all directions. The same massive, iron gates barred the way into, or out of, each of these corridors. The grim, deathly silent, electrically charged atmosphere was overpowering. My heart sank within me. This was a tomb. There could be no escape.[10]

The prison had seven branches and Furman was in the third, the branch administered by the Germans which held the POWs, Italian political prisoners – communists, socialists, and partisans – aristocrats, Jews, and anyone suspected of plotting against German authority. Women were also held in this branch. The seventh branch was reserved for German AWOL (absent without leave) soldiers or soldiers who had committed crimes. The other branches were administered by the Italians and held civilians, most accused of civil offenses.

Furman wrote that the prison reminded him of a 1930s American prison movie, where the cells reached up to the sky, tier upon tier. The stairs and walkways were constructed of open ironwork to enable the guards to monitor the prisoners' movements.

Sandy Stewart, an ex-POW taken from Via Firenze, was the first one to be interrogated, by a Gestapo sergeant major who used a female Italian translator. When it was Furman's turn, he allowed the guards to find 2,000 lire in small bills but his 10,000 lire hidden in the bread roll was not found. Anything that could be used to hang himself was taken away: belt, tie, and shoe laces. His confiscated personal effects were placed in a small bag with his prisoner identification information.

Furman had been separated from the other POWs and was in a cell, ten feet long by eight feet wide, with three Italian civilians. He was given a pallet, two blankets, a sheet, a washbasin, a plate, mug and spoon. A bucket served as the toilet. For privacy, they fixed the sheet on the wall to shield the bucket when in use. During the evenings prisoners conversed from cell to cell and Furman was able to talk to Captains Tug Wilson and Pip Gardner who told him the story of their capture.

The prison day started at 06:30. An orderly with a watering can allowed each prisoner to fill his washbasin. The floor was swept and the latrine bucket taken out. At 07:00 ersatz coffee was provided and at 09:00 bread was passed out, 150 grams for each man. It had to last all day. At noon, there was a thin vegetable soup, supplemented twice a week with horsemeat. Sometimes there was a small piece of cheese. In the evening there was another cup of ersatz coffee. Every week prisoners were allowed to receive two parcels of food from outside. That supplemented the prison fare and helped to make the evening meal. An hour of exercise per day in a high-walled narrow court was scheduled but took place infrequently.

Inside the prison, the prison barber ran the black-market. Anything could be obtained from him for cigarettes or cash. For example, Furman wanted to pass 1,000 lire to the South African lieutenant Jack Selikman who did not get the money, but did get 1,000 lire worth of cigarettes instead. Thus the barber took his cut. Through the use of bribes, the Escape Line smuggled food, clothing and money to incarcerated Allied servicemen.

After about ten days, Eaton, the American airman, no longer had fits and his head injury seemed much improved and he was far more subdued. Furman got him some extra rations, mostly bread. Furman also saw the Austrian cook, Habernig, and spoke to her on one occasion.*

Beatings and torture were conducted at night. Although the POWs were not usually tortured, the Yugoslav Buchner and the communist Nebolante were both severely beaten. Buchner had his teeth extracted. He was, however, able to get a note out to Monsignor O'Flaherty and, against all good sense, the monsignor visited him in prison. Although Buchner had suffered much, he wanted to reassure the priest that he had revealed nothing but the barest of information. Nevertheless, the Escape Line was pretty sure he had compromised them all. A few days later, Buchner was executed.

Prison routine was broken one day as cries of celebration sounded throughout the prison. News had filtered in of the Allied landings at Anzio on January 22. The hardnosed German guards were sent to the Anzio beachhead, summarily replaced by ordinary soldiers, many coming directly from their hospital beds for prison duty. Convinced that Rome might soon be captured, the new guards were easier on the prisoners. This improved situation lasted only a few days, until the old hardline German guards returned.

From the beginning of the war, the Vatican had expressed concern about protecting the patrimony of the Church – the buildings, artworks, antiquities, and literary treasures – both in Rome and throughout Italy. Much contentious debate concerned the 6th-century Benedictine Abbey of Monte Cassino. In September, due to the invasion of mainland Italy, irreplaceable works from the churches and the state museums in Naples, including some of the most important ancient artifacts from Pompeii, were taken from the city during the night of 6/7 September. Church property went to Monte Cassino, the artifacts from Pompeii were sent to the town of Teano, 15 miles south of Cassino; Moved were 100 crates with 413 paintings. Surely the war would bypass the abbey.

---

* Habernig was later sent back to Austria where she was tried and sentenced to five years' imprisonment. At the end of the war she returned to Rome where she lived for the rest of her life. The fact that she survived suggests that she successfully hid her Jewish identify.

It quickly became apparent that the Abbey of Monte Cassino was the linchpin in the strongly reinforced Gustav Line which blocked the Allied advance toward Rome. The Vatican, through Cardinal Maglione, voiced its concerns on October 25 in an official communication to Tittmann, written in formal diplomatic French requesting that all possible consideration be given to preserving the Benedictine Abbey of Monte Cassino. At the same time, the Vatican asked the Germans not to fortify Monte Cassino. On November 7, Sir D'Arcy received a note from Vatican officials quoting a German communication which stated that Monte Cassino would *not* be occupied by German troops.[11] It seemed the abbey was safe.

Nevertheless, a German officer, Lieutenant Colonel Julius Schlegel, of the Hermann Göring Division, claimed to be worried about the artworks stored at the abbey. Unbeknownst to the Germans, in addition to the abbey's treasurers and the artifacts, art, and manuscripts from Naples, the manuscripts and relics from the English poet John Keats and his friend Percy Bysshe Shelley had been placed in three boxes and moved from Rome to the abbey in December 1942. These boxes were joined in May 1943 by an additional three boxes and a special zinc-lined crate containing the sacred relics of the Patron Saint of Naples, San Gennaro. Due to fear of an invasion of Sicily, the Ancient Greek coin collection from Syracuse was hidden in the abbey by June of that year.

Other art crates were sent to the abbey but were too large to be easily hidden and so it was acknowledged that they were at the abbey. The first of this art moved from Teano, arriving on June 15, 1943, consisted of 60 cases of ancient artifacts from the Naples Archaeological Museum, including gold, glass, gems, and ivory. Sometime on September 6 or 7, 100 more cases containing 413 paintings from the state museums of Naples and another 87 cases containing more of the best from the Archaeological Museum, including the Pompeian bronzes and ancient Roman jewels, arrived at the abbey.

On October 14, Schlegel visited the abbey and convinced the abbot to let German soldiers remove the art stored there. Three days later two German trucks arrived with packing materials and wood to construct additional crates for the treasures. As part of the moving of the materials, he also convinced the abbot to authorize most of the monks and a great number of civilians who were taking refuge in the abbey to relocate to Rome. These monks hid the smaller and unacknowledged materials

Tompkins hides his files in the cellar of Palazzo Lovatelli. (Tompkins-NARA)

SS-Hauptsturmführer Erich Priebke. (EN Archive)

The swimming barge across from the Naval Ministry on the Tiber River where Giglio hid Radio Vittoria 2. (Tompkins-NARA)

Italian African Police (PAI) on parade. (Tompkins-NARA)

American and other Allied POWs march down Via dell' Impero (Via dei Fori Imperiali), Rome, February 1944. (Tompkins-NARA)

A photo of the B-26 Marauder "Little Chum" attacking the Tiburtina Railway Marshalling Yard in March 1944, taken from another bomber. The Vatican can clearly be seen in the lower right of the image. (NARA)

Above Bomb damage in Rome with the graffito "*Opera dei Liberatori*" ("work of the liberators") painted on a destroyed house, circa March 1944 (Bundesarchiv, Bild 101I-476-2094-17A, Fotograf(in): Rauchwetter)

Left The only known photo of Teresa Gullace, who was killed when caught up in a protest as she was trying to deliver a food and clothing parcel to her husband, who had been rounded up for forced labor. (*Museo Storico della Liberazione*)

TERESA GULLACE

Right The Antica Birreria Peroni Restaurant where the partisans had lunch before the Via Rasella attack on March 23, 1944. (Author)

The *santabarbara* where the partisans put together the Via Rasella bomb was in the basement of this building. (Author)

The *Il Messaggero* newspaper office where Carla Capponi waited prior to the Via Rasella attack. (Author)

Palazzo Tittoni on Via Rasella almost immediately after the explosion. (Bundesarchiv, Bild 101I-312-0983-15, Fotograf(in): Koch)

German police and naval commandos from the Italian Decima MAS Barbarigo Battalione round up civilian suspects from the Via Rasella attack in front of the Palazzo Barberini. (Bundesarchiv, Bild 101I-312-0983-03, Fotograf(in): Koch)

The building at the corner of Via Rasella and Via del Boccaccio immediately after the attack. Bullet holes can still be seen on the building today. (Bundesarchiv, Bild 101I-312-0983-24, Fotograf(in): Koch)

The garden of the Via Tasso annex in the Villa Giustiniani Massimo where those to be murdered were herded onto trucks prior to being taken to the Ardeatine Caves. (Author)

An official Italian Army photo of Colonel Giuseppe Cordero Lanza di Montezemolo. (*Museo Storico della Liberazione*)

The reprisal victims at the Fosse Ardeatine. (Tompkins-NARA)

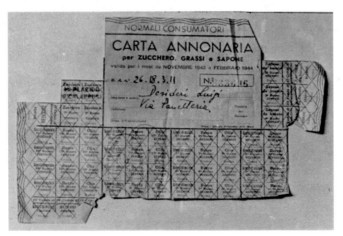

Left A Rome ration card. In March 1944, food shortages in Rome had become so acute that the city had only a two-to-three-day supply of food. (Tompkins-NARA)

DECLASSIFIED
Authority NND 867125

QUESTURA DI ROMA

Ore 18

218

Div. _____ N. _____

Roma _____ 194__

Risposta a nota N. _____   OGGETTO:

del _____ 194__   _____

Il Capo Guardia delle carceri di "Regina Coeli" consegnerà al Tenente
Tunnat della Polizia Germanica, che ne ha fatto richiesta, i sottono-
tati detenuti ristretti in codeste carceri a disposizione di questa
Questura:

1°) Bussi Armando		26°) De Micco Cosimo	
2°) Albertelli Pilo		27°) ~~Sargirio Tommaso~~	
3°) Mancini Enrico		28°) Nubili Edoardo	
4°) Norma Fernando		29°) Ferola Enrico	
5°) Fondi Edmondo		30°) Intrecialagli Mario	
6°) Baglivo Ugo		31°) Giglio Maurizio	
7°) Bendicenti Donato		32°) Mastrogiacomo Luigi	
8°) Fabbri Renato		33°) Bucciani Franco	
9°) De Giorgio Carlo		34°) Foschi Carlo	
10°) Bernabei Elio		35°) Ottaviani Armando	
11°) Lotti Giuseppe		36°) Imperiali Costantino	
12°) Leonelli Cesare		37°) Sepe Gaetano	
13°) Buttaroni Vittorio		38°) Viotti Pietro	
14°) Bucci Umberto		39°) Troiani Eusebio	
15°) Renzi Egidio		40°) Canalis ~~Salvatore~~	
16°) Eluisi Aldo		41°) ~~Lori Cipin~~	
17°) De Marchi Raule		42°) ~~Terracina Leone~~	
18°) Medas Giuseppe		43°) ~~Terracina Pellegrino~~	
19°) La Vecchia Gaetano		44°) ~~Terracina Alberto~~	
20°) Gallarella Antonio		45°) ~~Sermoneta Giacomo~~	
21°) ~~Piacentini Vittorio~~		46°) ~~Di Castro Emanuele~~	
22°) Annaruni Bruno		47°) ~~Di Veroli Davide~~	
23°) Bucci Bruno		48°) ~~Bianco Sud Angelo~~	
24°) Benati Nino		49°) ~~Moscati Ettore~~	
25°) Pierleoni Romolo		50°) Grieco Ennio.	

Caruso's original list of those to be murdered at the caves and the subsequent mark-up of the
substitutes. (NARA)

The SD form letter sent out on April 10, 1944 to the families of those murdered at the caves.
(Harold Tittmann papers, GTMGamms439, Georgetown University Library, Booth Family Center for
Special Collections, Washington DC)

Left The Ponte di Ferro (Iron Bridge, now renamed the Ponte dell'Industria) where ten women were murdered on April 7, 1944 for trying to get bread to feed their children. (Author)

General Kurt Mälzer hugs babies and passes out bread in a publicity attempt to reverse anti-German sentiment during the food shortages. (Tompkins-NARA)

Left An undated SS roundup. (Tompkins-NARA)

Lieutenant Thomas Peter Welch in his tank destroyer (tiny head figure on left, the author's uncle) directs fire on a hidden German machine-gun nest at Porta Furba, Rome, June 4, 1944. (NARA)

Sergeant Nowak is one of the soldiers standing in the lead vehicle in this famous photo of M-10 tank destroyers driving around the Colosseum on the morning of June 5, 1944. (NARA)

Allied troops flood the Piazza Venezia, June 5, 1944. (NARA)

Right Left-behind German troops captured in Piazza dell'Esedra (now Piazza della Repubblica). (NARA)

Below American troops march down Via Veneto, June 5, 1944. The Hotel Excelsior is on the right. (NARA)

American troops march across the Piazza del Popolo, June 5, 1944. (NARA)

Partisans surround a fascist during the liberation, June 5, 1944. (NARA)

Left Monsignor O'Flaherty greets General Mark Clark at Saint Peter's Square, June 5, 1944. (Photo by Popperfoto via Getty Images/Getty Images)

Below Partisans march across one of the Tiber bridges in front of the Italian Naval Ministry, June 5, 1944. (Tompkins-NARA)

Professore Attilio Ascarelli, with clipboard, working to identify the victims of the Fosse Ardeatine massacre. (NARA)

Dr. Carretta, the former director of the Regina Coeli Prison, in the Tiber on September 18, 1944, just before he was drowned by civilians who mistook him for Caruso. (NARA)

A Monument Man instrumental in returning Moses by Michelangelo to the Saint Peter in Chains church on November 24, 1944. (NARA)

General Kurt Mälzer on the right, notably thinner, arrives for his war crimes trial, November 18, 1946. (NARA)

Left Pietro Caruso, former police chief of Rome, is executed at Fort Bravetta on September 22, 1944. (NARA)

Bottom left Commemorative plaques which can be found all over Rome in front of the homes of Jewish residents whom the Gestapo sent to concentration camps. These plaques are called *Stolpersteine* in German (stumbling blocks). (Author)

Monsignor O'Flaherty receiving the US Medal of Freedom from US General John C. H. Lee in Rome after the war. He was also honoured by the British government, receiving a CBE in 1945. (Hugh O'Flaherty Memorial Society)

The author with US Cardinal William W. Baum at the Basilica di SS Giovanni e Paolo, September 1983, for a Mass for US Cardinal Terrence J. Cooke, vicar for the US Armed Forces, who was unwell. (American Embassy Rome, Author's collection)

Above Three Italian Fascist propaganda posters: "Good blood remains true", "Wellbeing, join the Todt Organization", American plane bombing children; and an Italian Communist Party propaganda poster: "Unite against the Nazi-Fascist Assassin." (*Museo Storico della Liberazione*)

Next page Rome and environs, 1944: this is a portion of the Italian Campaign battle map belonging to US Brigadier General William Cary Crane. (Reproduced with the kind permission of his grandson, W. Carey Crane III)

mentioned above with their personal effects and, on October 30, the Keats and Shelley artifacts were returned to Rome and to the little museum, the Keats-Shelley Memorial House, at the base of the Spanish Steps. The San Gennaro relics and the Syracuse coins were smuggled out with some of the abbot's personal effects and were stored at Saint Paul Outside the Walls where they remained until the end of the war.

Schlegel promised to move the larger 187 cases to the Vatican, and these were divided into two groups, those that belonged to the Roman Catholic Church and those that belonged to the Italian state. By November 3, 1943, all of the art had been moved to the Villa Marignoli in Colle Ferretto, a huge country estate outside the town of Spoleto, 60 miles northeast of Rome, and an area which was less likely to see action. Schlegel also had another agenda. He wanted to find important artworks for Reichsmarschall Hermann Göring's personal collection. It was reasoned that the Hermann Göring Division had the right to compensation for their efforts in transporting the works of art.

The art objects stayed in Spoleto for about a month where they remained intact. Because the press had started to demand to know the whereabouts of these treasures, the German removal actions were documented and announced at a press conference at the Quirinale Palace in Rome. This event was for the neutral press from Switzerland, Sweden, Spain, and Portugal and was held on November 25. At that time, German Baron Bernhard von Tieschowitz, an art historian, had been sent from Paris to Rome to set up a Kunstschutz, a bureau organized for the Protection of Art in countries occupied by the Reich. In France, his organization had identified and confiscated Jewish-owned artworks and sent them to Germany. Von Tieschowitz explained the precautions that the Wehrmacht and Schlegel had taken to safeguard the artistic treasures of Monte Cassino. While in Rome, he got Field Marshal Kesselring to sign a decree declaring ruins and religious monuments off limits to German soldiers. Posters to that effect were displayed at various sites.[12] Von Tieschowitz also developed a plan to move the art to the Vatican, since it was unlikely to be bombed.

That plan was put into effect on December 8, described as a cold but sunny day when the rescued Monte Cassino church-owned treasures were ceremoniously turned over to Vatican control by the Stadtkommandant of Rome, General Mälzer. The ceremony was witnessed by the neutral press assembled along with several dozen invited guests outside the Vatican's Castel Sant'Angelo. This public display was intended to contradict British propaganda that the Gestapo was stealing priceless art treasures and to show the world that Germany was making every effort to protect Italian cultural property. It was a major photo opportunity and effective propaganda.

The ceremony began dramatically as 12 or 14 trucks crossed the Tiber River over the Ponte Sant'Angelo, pulling up outside the Tiber gateway to the Castel. There, under the watchful eye of Colonel Schlegel, German soldiers uncrated one of the paintings and a medieval scroll to exhibit to the press. Mother Mary, apparently an eyewitness, wrote: "Anyway, here are the treasures in countless cases and boxes: archives, manuscripts, books, pictures, engravings and illuminated missals. There are about a hundred thousand volumes in all, not counting the manuscripts."[13] Later, a poorly attended dinner was held at the Hotel Excelsior to celebrate the turnover. Nine days later, the artworks were moved from Castel Sant'Angelo to the closed Vatican Museum.

The Fascist Ministry of Education, responsible for Italian art and antiquities, had moved to Padua. A former director of the ministry, Marino Lazzari, entered into an agreement that December with the Vatican which stipulated: "The Vatican will welcome all artworks that you will deem necessary to store in the rooms of its picture galleries."[14] As Mother Mary recorded in her diary, the Roman aristocracy started to donate their ancient family archives to the Vatican Library. They felt that their papers would be safer there than in their palazzi and eventually be cataloged and made available to researchers.

On January 4, the cache of books and artwork that earlier had been moved from Italian state museums in Naples to Spoleto, were driven to the Palazzo Venezia by members of the Hermann Göring Division. The 31 (or, according to some, 40) trucks containing 172 crates of paintings and more than 600 crates of books from the National Library of Naples were unloaded and, as reported in the Questura's daily report, General Mälzer gave another luncheon at the Hotel Excelsior. Shortly thereafter, the books were sent to the University of Rome for safekeeping.

It soon became apparent, however, that not all the treasures had been returned to Italian hands. Two trucks, with 15 crates, had left Spoleto with the German convoy but did not arrive in Rome. They were Schlegel's birthday present for Reichsmarschall Göring. The truck's cargos included Pompeian bronzes, ancient Roman jewelry from the Naples Archaeological Museum, and several paintings, including Titian's voluptuous reclining nude, *Danae*, just Göring's taste.*

The concern for preserving cultural artifacts was shared by the Allies. By January 1944, the Allied forces had developed special maps to preserve art works:

> A grid was superimposed on maps that were provided by the Army Map Service, the National Geographic Society, and the Library of Congress, and the exact location of an important building [cultural or artistic] was highlighted. The little white circles that identified a monument or a cluster of them, on the [so-called Helen] Frick Maps were the result of thousands of questionnaires on monuments and art collections and their whereabouts that the committee sent to art historians, archaeologists, and architects around the country [US].[15]

Helen Clay Frick (1888–1984) was an American philanthropist and art collector who cataloged her father's art collection which eventually became the Frick Collection in New York City. These map plots were accomplished by the American Council of Learned Societies and its committee for the protection of European Art at the Frick Art Reference Library in New York. The library was closed to the public from July 15, 1943 to January 4, 1944 so that this task could be accomplished. This question of preserving art and ancient artifacts reached the highest echelons of power and, when the maps were ready, General Eisenhower issued the following order to Allied forces:

> Today we are fighting in a country [Italy] which has contributed a great deal to our cultural inheritance, a country rich in monuments

---

* American troops found the 15 crates at the end of the war in a salt mine near Alt-Aussee in Austria. They had suffered only minor damage. The controversy was not over. After the war Countess Maria Josepha Gani, the wife of General von Senger, turned over correspondence to the British Imperial War Museum which claimed that Schlegel's rescue was really planned as a theft and it was only due to von Senger contacting Kesselring and pointing out the negative consequences of the proposed theft that both collections were not sent to Germany.

which by their creation helped and now in their old age illustrate the growth of the civilization which is ours. We are bound to respect those monuments so far as war allows ... If we have to choose between destroying a famous building and sacrificing our own men, then our men's lives count infinitely more and the building must go. But the choice is not always as clear-cut as that. In many cases the monuments can be spared without any detriment to operational needs. Nothing can stand against the argument of military necessity. That is an accepted principle. But the phrase "military necessity" is sometimes used where it would be more truthful to speak of military convenience or even of personal convenience. I do not want it to cloak slackness or indifference ... It is a responsibility of higher commanders to determine through AMG [Allied Military Government] Officers the locations of historical monuments whether they be immediately ahead of our front lines or in areas occupied by us. This information passed to lower echelons through normal channels places the responsibility on all Commanders of complying with the spirit of this letter.[16]

A debate on the relative value of human life versus art raged. Archbishop Lang of Lambeth in the United Kingdom wrote declaring that Rome was not like any other city and should be spared the ravages of war. This started a row in *The Times* of London, in which A. A. Milne, the author of *Winnie-the-Pooh*, the popular children's book, and a World War I veteran, responded that Allied soldiers' lives should not be sacrificed to save Rome. And Mollie Panter-Downes, the London correspondent for the *New Yorker* magazine, wrote that a military advantage was worth a Michelangelo fresco.

15

An American Boy Scout OSS Spy in Rome

But to go behind the enemy lines and live for long periods like a hunted beast requires a certain flair, even a little madness, a large measure of Boy Scout loyalty and patriotism, a stout heart, an alert brain, and, I think, a remarkable self-assurance approaching the point of swagger and carelessness – all based on one's belief that one's own keenness, wile, intelligence, wits, and luck are superior to those of the enemy. Knowing Peter [Tompkins] well, I think he was justified in this belief.[1]

Peter Tompkins was born in the United States but his parents took him to Europe at an early age. He was educated in Italy, Switzerland, France, and England, and he spent much of his school holidays in Rome, so he knew the city well. While living in Rome, Sir D'Arcy acted as his godfather. His family was also close to the Tittmanns and, as mentioned earlier, Tittmann borrowed the Tompkins family silver and books for his apartment inside the Vatican. Because the Florentine dialect was the first Italian Tompkins learned, he passed as a well-educated Italian. He studied at Harvard, Columbia, and the Sorbonne in Paris, but never graduated from any of them.

In 1939, at age 20, he returned to Rome and found work as a war correspondent for the *New York Herald Tribune* and several European newspapers. He broadcast the start of the war in Europe from Rome for the American Mutual Radio Network. Limited to reporting only the Fascist side, he went to Greece after the Italian invasion and wrote of the war from the British lines. Eventually he found himself in North Africa working as a news editor for Allied Forces Headquarters in Algiers. It was there that he joined the OSS.

Tompkins landed with the first wave of troops at Salerno on September 9, 1943, when the Allied Fifth Army invaded mainland Italy after the September armistice. There he debriefed refugees in the city and recruited men to go behind the lines and report on German troop movements and potential targets. Shortly after landing, the OSS received two urgent requests to use their behind-the-lines contacts to obtain critical pieces of Axis technology.

On September 11, 1943 the USS *Savannah* (CL-42) was hit by a German Fritz X, a radio-controlled glider with a 435-kilo warhead that had been launched from a Dornier Do 217 bomber. The *Savannah* lost 197 crewmen and another 15 were wounded when the bomb penetrated the number three turret and exploded in a magazine. The cruiser was able to get up steam and made for Malta where four trapped sailors were freed from a watertight compartment.

This was the second recorded time that a Fritz X was used. The first occasion was against the Italian Navy ship (Regina Marina), *Roma*, on September 9, 1943 as it was near Sardinia en route to Malta. Admiral Carlo Bergamini and 1,392 officers and men went down with her.

A few days after the *Savannah* was hit, the British battleship HMS *Warspite* was crippled by a similar bomb and also forced to withdraw to Malta for emergency repairs. As well as sustaining serious damage, nine crew members were killed and 14 wounded. The attack on the *Savannah* was the first time such a weapon had been used against the US Navy. The OSS, believing that some of these radio-controlled gliders were stored at Italian air bases, launched a major effort to get a sample of this weapon and any Italian engineers who had worked on it.[2]

To the US Navy, the second piece of technology was even more important. US Naval Intelligence was keenly interested in bringing Carlo Calori, a professor at the University of Bologna and an Italian naval officer, to Washington DC. Calori had designed a torpedo for the Italian Navy that was so effective the Germans ordered 12,000 of them. They were used with deadly effect on Allied convoys to Murmansk.

At the time, the US Navy's torpedo was fitted with a contact fuse that frequently failed. Calori's torpedo used a proximity fuse that could explode under a ship without touching it. Although various parts of the torpedo had been found at captured Italian Navy supply depots, the Navy needed Calori to develop countermeasures and build a better US torpedo. Calori was willing to leave Italy and, after eight attempts, the OSS successfully smuggled him out on January 3, 1944 and whisked him to Washington. How much, or if, Tompkins was personally involved in these two foreign materiel operations is unknown.

During the battle for Salerno, Tompkins worked with SOE British Major Malcolm Munthe. Munthe was the son of Swedish author Axel Munthe, who wrote the remarkable book, *The Story of San Michele*, about his experiences building his villa on the Isle of Capri. In 1940, Malcolm Munthe had been in Finland supplying weapons to partisans during the war with the Soviet Union. After the fall of Naples, on October 1, 1943, both Tompkins and Munthe were responsible for training Italians to work as agents behind the lines. Munthe was subsequently made head of Number One Special Force and became responsible for sending arms to partisans. On Christmas Eve 1943, he was ordered to coordinate all his future operations with SIM and informed that the Number One Special Force would confine its activities to the Adriatic. However, Munthe was told to maintain radio contact with the FMCR in Rome. In general, the OSS and the SOE got along well with each other, but the OSS put a greater emphasis on espionage.

Once OSS cells were established in Italy, they regularly transmitted information about German strategic and tactical planning, identified military targets for Allied aircraft raids, and coordinated requests for supplies and arms for the partisans. Although they acted independently, the OSS and the SOE often shared information.

After Salerno, Tompkins moved to Naples where he identified, vetted, and oversaw the training of Italian volunteers, many of them former military officers. These OSS operatives had been recruited from a resistance group called the Organization for Italian Resistance (ORI – *Organizzazione della Resistenza Italiana*) founded by Raimondo Craveri, the son-in-law of Italian Senator Benedetto Croce, a longtime opponent of Fascism. Craveri's recruits were apolitical but anti-fascists and eventually were to work closely with local resistance groups from the entire Italian political spectrum. Craveri's men, now working with Tompkins, were trained and given false identities. Ultimately, they would be parachuted or smuggled by boat and submarine into occupied Italy. Once in enemy territory, they were to link up with anti-fascist organizations to collect and transmit military, economic, and political intelligence.

Soon the OSS had agents and 12 clandestine radio transmitters throughout German-occupied Italy but there was a chronic shortage of qualified radio operators. Tompkins learned that there were nine idle Italian Navy submarines in Naples harbor, each with two qualified radio operators. He offered the men a monthly salary and a death benefit of $5,000 to join the OSS and go behind enemy lines.

Under the cover of a Luftwaffe air raid on the port of Naples, the Italian radiomen defected to the OSS. Tompkins got them into US Army uniforms and billeted them in his headquarters, a dilapidated Neapolitan palazzo on Via Francesco Crispi. After their training they were sent behind the German lines to establish additional OSS cells and, once in position, they started to transmit valuable information.

About a week before Operation *Shingle*, the Allied landing at Anzio on January 22, 1944, General William "Wild Bill" Donovan, the founder of the OSS, visited Tompkins in Naples. Before dinner Donovan told Tompkins that he needed a man in Rome prior to the coming invasion. This agent would be the head of the OSS in Rome, responsible for representing the OSS to the CLN and other resistance organizations. It was an important assignment for a 23-year-old and Tompkins readily volunteered. He scrambled to get ready.

Tompkins was given the temporary rank of major, high enough to deserve respect, but not so high as to make others question his suitability because of his youth. He procured two false identities from his Naples contacts. For the first identity, to be used to get into Rome, he gave himself the alias of an imaginary brother of a titled friend, Roberto Berlingieri. Fascists and Germans were still impressed with titles and he knew enough about the family whose name he was using to pass as a relative. Once in Rome, he would discard the first identity and assume the second with a less noble name. The second set of false papers was sewed inside his spare shirt.

Tompkins traveled light, fitting all his spare clothing into one small bag. He made sure that all his clothes were Italian, including a pair of handmade shoes he had recently purchased on the Island of Capri during a brief stop there. In addition to Italian lire, he carried 300 British gold sovereign coins that were accepted currency anywhere in the world. His spy equipment consisted of secret radio ciphers and the crystals to produce certain wavelengths, a Beretta 9mm handgun and, much to his later regret, a Minox miniature camera.

He knew that, some months earlier, SIM had inserted several clandestine radio transmitters with FMCR Italian military officers in Rome. The caretaker of one of the radios, Radio Vittoria 2, was Italian Security Police Lt. Maurizio Giglio who would be his main point of contact.

Tompkins left his Naples headquarters on January 20 with no goodbyes. He took with him Bene, an otherwise unidentified but resourceful Italian assistant who had already crossed the German lines several times. Bene's nickname came from the Italian phrase *va bene*, meaning OK. They headed for the Allied-controlled Naples airfield at Capodichino and boarded OSS General Donovan's converted B-25 Mitchell light bomber for an unescorted flight to Corsica. The island was now in Allied hands, having been abandoned by the Germans. The plane landed on the east coast of the island at Borgo Field not far from Bastia.

Bastia had become a useful point of departure for agents. Several days before, during the night of January 17/18, 1944, an OSS clandestine team was inserted along the coast of mainland Italy. It consisted of an engineer named Morris, a woman agent, Vera Vassalle, and others. They departed Bastia for the Italian Maremma coast, landing at the 115-kilometer marker of Via Aurelia, north of Rome. They had with them explosives, 13 radio sets, a large amount of money, maps, and other equipment.

Once in an OSS safe house west of Bastia, Tompkins met six other agents who were also making the run to the Italian coast that night but on different missions. One of these agents was Dr. Beltramini, an elderly man, who was with Miss Wanda Malvezzi, his one-legged companion. They were to go to Milan with two men, Prini and Barelle, their radio operators. In Milan the group was to split up and conduct separate missions. The other two agents, an Italian couple, Lt. Mario and Carmela Cernia, were going to Rome. They were trained saboteurs and carried plastic explosives to blow up bridges and other infrastructure. Tompkins considered mixing these three missions together a major breach in protocol and a security threat since their missions were so different.

After a tasteless C-rations lunch, Tompkins checked his equipment. The agents then piled into two cars and drove to the port of Bastia, arriving at the quay shortly after dark. The operation was called the *Third Richmond Seaborne* Operation. Awaiting them were two captured Italian Navy motor torpedo MAS (*Motoscafo Armato Silurante*) boats, now under the command of a Royal Navy officer. Embarking on the two boats they headed due east, the small convoy skirting south of the island of Elba, and made for a beach off the Italian mainland, about 15 miles north of the ancient Etruscan city of Tarquinia. Cutting the engines when they spotted a solitary light, they drifted slowly to within a mile of the beach, then they climbed into rubber dinghies, and paddled ashore in a thankfully quiet surf.

After the eight agents got out of the dinghies, two other men climbed in. One was Oreste Lizzadri (code name Longobardi), a Socialist Party leader from Rome. He was going to Italian government headquarters in Bari to meet with Marshal Badoglio. The Rome CLN (National Liberation Committee), believing that Badoglio and the king had deserted them, was against joining the royalist government, and it was critical that their view be expressed. Badoglio now realized that he needed the support of the members of all anti-fascist factions so he had called a meeting for January 28. Lizzadri was to represent the Rome CLN. The second man to board the dinghy was an unnamed Italian electronics engineer who had helped the German Navy to develop the German Fritz X, the radio-controlled glider.

From the beach, Tompkins and the others climbed into two horse-drawn carts, driven by the unknown men who met them on the beach, and slowly made their way to a safe house a few miles down the coast. Turning at a fork onto the main coast road, the carts stopped at a car parked along Via Aurelia. The agents piled into the car which followed the leisurely horse carts to the safe house. The original plan was to take the saboteurs to Viterbo where they would take a train to Rome. Not the best idea, since a car arriving at the railway station in the middle of the night would attract unwanted attention.

Tompkins had not been expected. He found it difficult to convince the driver to take him and Bene directly to Rome but the 20,000 lire he put in the driver's hand swayed him. He and Bene were allowed to accompany the saboteurs. A young man, known only as T, a courier between the safe house and Rome, also went along. Apparently the group of agents going to Milan was left behind.

Tompkins settled in for the circuitous drive to Rome. First they went south along the coast road to Tarquinia and then turned inland to Viterbo. It was a large car, now filled with a mixture of seven – spies, saboteurs, and drivers. The car was stopped at several Fascist roadblocks along the way, but after their documents were checked, it was passed through. The driver had papers from the German Embassy and his assistant's papers were from the Fascist National Republican Guard (GNR). Nevertheless, the tension was palpable.

At Viterbo, 40 miles north of Rome, the car turned onto Via Cassia for the final sprint into the city. Crossing the 1,700-year-old Roman Bridge, the Ponte Milvio north of the city, it sped down tree-lined, ancient Via Flaminia. Just before dawn, Tompkins' car entered Rome through the city gate at the Piazza del Popolo, a Wehrmacht parking lot, complete with the Egyptian obelisk with the 20ft-high base which still had traces of a large red hammer and sickle, painted on it several months before by Carla Capponi, the GAP partisan.

In the piazza, the car angled off to the left of the two identical churches, taking Via del Babuino to the base of the Spanish Steps. At the now silent *Fontana della Baraccia* (boat fountain), Tompkins, Bene, and T got out of the car and climbed the now-deserted steps to the church of Trinità dei Monti. Reaching the small square at the top, Tompkins turned to the right and headed down Via Sistina to an address where he would meet someone from the FMCR. He was way too early: the building was still locked.

Settling in was hard for Tompkins, and in fact, he was to move three times on the day of his arrival, January 21, 1944. Everywhere he saw the ubiquitous presence of the 1,700 men of the Italian Africa Police (PAI) in their tropical helmets.

Realizing he couldn't hang around Via Sistina for long, Tompkins told T to wait for his contact and pass the information to Bene. He then told Bene where to find him in the central medieval quarter of Rome and then crossed town alone to hide with a couple who used to work for his family.

Several hours later, Bene showed up and told him a man would call for him in an hour. Soon a short, well-dressed OSS agent named

Edmondo Di Pillo showed up driving a small Fiat 500 car, called a *Topolino* (little mouse).* Tompkins was driven to Di Pillo's home in the new and fashionable Parioli quarter, not far from the now-abandoned Escape Line's Via Domenico Cellini apartment. He was in time to have lunch with his family. Now Tompkins got down to business.

After a few phone calls, a young Italian police lieutenant arrived in full uniform, and was introduced as *Cervo*, meaning "stag" in Italian. He was Tompkins' contact and had control of Radio Vittoria 2. A friend of Di Pillo's, Cervo's real name was Maurizio Giglio, an auxiliary member of the 400-man cavalry section of the Metropolitan Police (*Polizia Metropolitana*), who were uniformed traffic police.

Giglio had been a second lieutenant in the Italian 187th Infantry Regiment, had served with distinction in the Greek Campaign, and later fought the Germans at the Porta San Paolo on September 10, 1943. Afterwards, he went to Naples and was part of the local citizens' uprising called the Four Days of Naples. He was then recruited by the OSS and, as we have seen, returned to Rome with one of the Victory Radios. Giglio and Paolo Poletti (codenamed *Lepre* – hare), an Italian Navy lieutenant junior grade, had made the trip together. They carried radio crystals, ciphers, and the clandestine radio in a large suitcase to Rome. Once there they set up Radio Vittoria 2 and Giglio joined the Rome Mounted Police unit with the help of his father, a Fascist police commissioner in Bologna and part of the notorious OVRA organization that spied on anti-fascist Italians.

Shortly thereafter, a young SIM agent with an aristocratic manner arrived at the Di Pillo apartment. He was Baron Franco Malfatti, a former SIM intelligence officer on Marshal Badoglio's staff and a member of Pietro Nenni's Socialist Party. He compiled military intelligence and sent reports via Giglio's Radio Vittoria 2 to SIM and the Badoglio government – intelligence which was then passed to the Allies. Malfatti, who spoke excellent German, ran a German bookstore called Domus on Via Veneto across the street from the Hotel Excelsior in the German-occupied luxury hotel zone.

Two more men showed up and Tompkins told the group about the coming Allied landing, not disclosing the place or time. He needed to know what sabotage equipment and weapons were available and what they could do to impede the Germans while preventing the destruction

---

* *Topolino* is also the Italian name for Disney's Mickey Mouse.

of key city infrastructure. It was agreed that early the next morning Tompkins would meet with several more Rome operatives.

Still uneasy, Giglio decided it would be safer for Tompkins to leave Di Pillo's apartment in Paroli and stay with his family in the Prati district, very close to the Vatican. Who would suspect an enemy agent to be hiding in a Fascist policeman's apartment? So, for the third time, Tompkins moved. Giglio took him to the apartment he shared with his mother and sister where he spent the night of January 21. Malfatti came for dinner and the three of them talked through the night. During the discussions, Giglio agreed to put Radio Vittoria 2 at Tompkins' disposal.

Giglio, appalled at the poor quality of Tompkins' false identity documents, told him he needed new ones. In the interim, Giglio gave him the red-and-yellow arm band of a voluntary police auxiliary to stuff into his pocket in case they were stopped.

That morning, the pair sped down Via del Corso on Giglio's motorcycle, heading for the meeting place inside a small gray house on Via d'Aracoeli, a tiny street on the left side of the Vittorio Emanuele II Monument in Rome's center. Malfatti met them there, and Giglio introduced Tompkins to Clemente Mino Menicanti, codenamed Coniglio (rabbit), an Italian cavalry officer, and to his radio operator, Gino (codenamed Vittorio). Menicanti was a small man with piercing dark eyes. Both OSS agents worked closely with SIM and had control of Radio Vittoria 1. Also present was Giuliano Vassalli, the Socialist Party representative of the CLN.

When Tompkins woke up that morning, he did not know whether the invasion of Anzio had taken place. The Rome radio morning news broadcast said nothing about it and he could hear no sound of military activity south of the city. Despite his uncertainty, Tompkins again said that an invasion was imminent and that his mission was to disrupt German communications and their avenues of retreat, while safeguarding bridges, utilities, and other infrastructure. Menicanti agreed to these actions, but Tompkins distrusted him.

One reason for Tompkins' mistrust of Menicanti was that he had been sent to Rome by Captain André Bourgoin, an OSS agent and former member of the French *Deuxième Bureau*, the French Military Intelligence Service. The French had had a longstanding relationship with SIM but Tompkins, who knew Bourgoin, thought him unreliable and believed the rumors that he had been compromised by German agents as far back as World War I.

Giglio told Tompkins that Menicanti was using OSS funds to further right-wing causes and often described himself as General Mark Clark's (US Fifth Army Commander) personal political representative for German-occupied Italy. Furthermore, Tompkins knew of another OSS Agent, Enrico Sorrentino, another Bourgoin recruit, who also claimed to be the Chief Political Agent in Rome of General Mark Clark.

As they left the meeting, Tompkins saw a column of German trucks loaded with paratroopers rushing southward through the city, probably on its way to the Anzio beachhead. This confirmed for him that the Allies had, indeed, landed.

Shortly after arriving at Giglio's apartment, Giuliano Vassalli, the Socialist Party representative representing Sandro Pertini, the Socialist Party leader who had been arrested and was being held at the Regina Coeli Prison, showed up. The Socialist Party was a proletarian movement guided by intellectuals, which included both anti-Stalinist and pro-democratic members. Vassalli informed Tompkins that CLN's leaders had accepted Tompkins' bona fides and eagerly looked forward to meeting the new American agent to receive directives from the Allied command. A second meeting was set for that afternoon.

Before the meeting, Giglio handed Tompkins a document dated January 19, prepared by the Rome Questura. The report was a listing of German-occupied facilities spread across the capital and revealed that only 1,500 German troops were currently stationed in the city. The report detailed the locations of headquarters, command posts, car parks, food depots, hospitals, and psychiatric wards. It had already been sent to the Allies.

He also gave Tompkins details about Colonel Giuseppe Montezemolo's clandestine military organization, the FMCR. Montezemolo, loyal to Badoglio, had recruited members from the Carabinieri, the Italian Navy, and other traditionally monarchist elements of the former Italian armed forces and elements of the various police organizations. Montezemolo, as we have seen, was an aristocrat and a selfless and religious person who had disapproved of partisan activities in Rome as he feared German reprisals. Colonel Montezemolo was the liaison officer between the royalist military underground in Rome and all other underground organizations working in the capital.

The members of the CLN military committee traveling singly with armed guard escorts arrived for the afternoon meeting. One of the first to arrive was Riccardo Bauer, a representative of the Party of Action, an anti-monarchist group, supported by intellectuals and university students. It was also anti-clerical and anti-communist. The last to arrive was Giorgio Amendola of the Italian Communist Party. Representatives from three other parties – the Christian Democrats which were supported by the Roman Catholic Church; the numerically insignificant Liberals; and the Labor Democrats – apparently did not attend.

Tompkins, aware of the political differences of the men representing the various parties, opened the meeting by making it clear that he was only interested in military, not political, matters. The agenda centered on the question of maintaining Rome's infrastructure during the period of German retreat and Allied arrival. The military committee of the CLN had an agreement with Colonel Montezemolo about safeguarding essential buildings and the water, electricity, gas, radio, and telephone services. From the Island of Capri, Tompkins had seen the time-delay German demolitions of infrastructure in Naples and wanted to avoid that devastation in Rome.

Toward the end of the two-hour meeting, Giglio gave Tompkins an urgent message from Captain John Croze, a Franco-American officer at the OSS detachment now on the beach at Anzio. It pleaded for knowledge about enemy troop movements toward the beachhead. The message also said that the Allied occupation of Rome would be delayed and there would be no Allied airborne landing in the city.

16

A Stranded Whale

I had hoped that we were hurling a wildcat onto the shores,
but all we got was a stranded whale.

Winston Churchill

Suddenly everything changed. At 05:30 on January 22, 1944 an alarm sounded and was flashed to the German command. It screamed: *Alarm! Feind beiderseits; Nettuno gelandet* (Alarm! Enemy landing each side of Nettuno). Operation *Shingle*, the Allied landing 30 or so miles southwest of Rome at Anzio and Nettuno, had begun. Anzio is a small town and a traditional summer resort for Roman citizens. The Roman emperor Nero was born there. Next door was Nettuno, a larger town with a fortified medieval center and a small castle.

By October 1943, it had become clear that the Allies were going to have a long slog up the mountainous Italian Peninsula and through the formidable German fortification of defenses known as the Winter Line, the most significant of which was the Gustav Line. With great foresight, General Eisenhower had ordered that some landing craft, scheduled for the landing in Normandy in late spring 1944, be held back for a possible amphibious landing in Italy to outflank the Germans. The Anzio landing involved 250 combat-loaded ships of all description from six Allied navies. A partial listing of Allied forces included: the British 1st Infantry Division; the British 2nd Special Service Brigade; the British 2nd Commando Battalion; the US 3rd Infantry Division; the US 504th Parachute Infantry Regiment; the US

509th Parachute Infantry Battalion; and the US 6615th Ranger Force, known as Darby's Rangers.

To maintain surprise, there was no massive pre-invasion bombardment at Anzio. Instead at 02:00 two British assault ships launched an intense, ten-minute barrage firing 1,500 five-inch rockets. Immediately after the barrage, British Commandos and American Rangers landed to secure the landing beaches and take out defenses of which there were few. After the Rangers captured the town of Anzio, they moved on to the nearby coastal town of Nettuno, setting up roadblocks and killing the few German sentries who challenged them.

During the winter, the Germans had evacuated most of the civilians living along the coast at Nettuno and Anzio. Thousands of mines had been laid and routine coastal patrols monitored the beaches for signs of invasion. Ironically, the day before the invasion, these patrols were curtailed due to a shortage of soldiers for this type of duty, a costly mistake.

Both Anzio and Nettuno were dominated by a large Renaissance villa on a hill covered with pines and evergreens. The villa belonged to the bachelor Prince Stefano Borghese, a relative of the Black Prince Junio Valerio Borghese. Stefano Borghese had been made mayor of the two towns by the Germans. He had been permitted to remain with a small retinue of servants, probably because he allowed the Germans to conduct training exercises on his estate. The prince owned most of the land around the two towns. He was immediately captured by the Allies and kept as a prisoner for 24 hours at Ranger Headquarters at the Anzio Paradiso Casino. After seeing the Royal Palace at Caserta just outside of Naples, the Rangers could not believe that he was a prince since his home was so modest in comparison.

Hearing of the invasion, Kesselring invoked *Case Richard*, an emergency plan to bring as many troops as rapidly as possible to where they were most needed. Among the first German troops to respond were the men who guarded Kesselring's headquarters at Monte Soratte, 25 miles due north of Rome. These troops brought with them their company of Tigers and established a German HQ at Albano about 16 miles south of Rome. They were ordered to secure the railway station at Campoleone, 12 miles further south on the main Rome–Naples line. From there the Germans made a reconnaissance toward Aprilia, about five miles further south of the railway station and about ten miles north of Anzio. Elements of the Hermann Göring Division, resting outside of Rome, were activated and within two hours were on the road to the beachhead. Additional troops from northern Italy moved south that evening. Even German soldiers recuperating in Rome hospitals, including the venereal disease clinic, were sent to the new front lines.

Inside Rome there was panic. The German High Command declared the entire province of Rome a military operational zone. Germans and Italian Fascists prepared to flee the city. Obersturmbannführer Kappler expected the Germans to pull out shortly. He had orders to destroy utilities, government buildings, and other infrastructure so he placed explosives all over the city and was ready to set them off; but the partisans discovered their locations and so they were quickly defused.

The morning of the Anzio landings, Obersturmbannführer Dollmann was summoned from his bed to meet with Field Marshal Kesselring, who was worried that there might be a popular uprising in the city. Dollmann reminded him of the calm reaction of the Romans to the German takeover in September and, perhaps cynically, said there was nothing to worry about. General Mälzer, on the other hand, feared the worst and proclaimed Martial Law, adjusting the citywide curfew down to 17:00 hours.

Meanwhile Maurizio Giglio had given OSS Agent Peter Tompkins the urgent message from the OSS detachment at Anzio, pleading for intelligence about enemy troops moving toward the beachhead. For their part, the partisans were not interested in collecting intelligence; they wanted to fight and kill Germans. Nevertheless, Tompkins convinced them to concentrate on developing the information requested.

Giuliano Vassalli agreed to have more than 100 of his people track German traffic moving toward the beachhead and report back to him.

The other organizations agreed to route the intelligence they collected to Malfatti's bookstore on Via Veneto where it would be passed on to Tompkins. Their efforts bore fruit. By the end of the day, Malfatti brought updated reports to Tompkins at Giglio's apartment and, that evening, Malfatti, Tompkins, and Giglio broadcast the following detailed report on Radio Vittoria 2:

Night 22 to 23: intense southbound traffic through Rome, out Via Appia [Nuova]. All available German units in a radius of 90 kilometers north of Rome have been ordered south. Special units have been formed from various headquarters and offices in Rome. 610 vehicles transited. Noted: 3 battalions of parachutists, elements of 90th Panzer Grenadier Division, five divisional artillery groups. Road followed: Appia Antica, Albano, and Anziate.

The next day's report described more German traffic flowing through Rome, giving additional specifics:

Panther and tiger tank units, two 88mm groups, and two battalions of motorized infantry. Units of the 29th and 3rd Panzer Grenadier Divisions reported transferred from Garigliano front towards Beachhead. Units of the Hermann Göring Division moved towards Albano and Beachhead ... Armored units and artillery concentrated at S. Palomba and Lanuvio astride Albano-Anzio road on perimeter of Beachhead ... Trenches and field defenses were thrown together just south of Rome at the Porta S. Paolo on Ostia Road. Machine guns and artillery turned towards the city. German Headquarters in Corso Italia protected by German and PAI armored cars ...[1]

During these first days of the invasion, Allied headquarters addressed the citizens of Rome in radio broadcasts as follows:

From Allied Command stop The hour has come for Rome and all Italians to fight with all means possible and with all their strength stop Refuse to work for enemy on railways or elsewhere stop Sabotage wherever possible.

The partisans held open meetings in the streets. The partisans Sandro Pertini and Giuseppe Saragat* and five others were released from the Regina Coeli Prison on January 24, thanks to falsified release documents prepared by the prison's night doctor.

Partisan groups stepped up actions to support the invasion. The committee of Roman Youth of the Christian Democrats passed out leaflets at the University, encouraging renewed acts of resistance. The clandestine newspaper *Italia Libera* ran a banner at the top of each page, saying: "This is the moment we have waited for! Men and women of Rome arise," while an extraordinary edition of the Communist paper *L'Unità* urged an insurrection and called the people of Rome to arms.

While the American and British armies were landing on the Anzio and Nettuno beaches, two GAP partisans bombed a German refreshment stand outside Termini Station. Maria Teresa Regard and Guglielmo Blasi, wearing a captured German uniform, walked into the refreshment stand and Regard, who had concealed a pipe bomb in her purse, lit the fuse and ran. The bomb exploded, killing or wounding 30 German officers and men.[†]

Major Derry over at the Vatican heard of the landing within an hour or two of the invasion. He could see and hear evidence of the battle on the southern horizon from Sir D'Arcy's roof. Derry had a dilemma: should he send all his escaped Allied POWs to the invasion beaches, some 37 miles away; or, believing that the Allies would reach the city in a day or two, should they stay put? Opting for the latter, he would come to regret his decision, for during the first two days of the landing, many ex-POWs could have easily rejoined the Allied lines and, in fact, a few left their hiding places and managed to become repatriated.

Later that day, Mrs. Kiernan, the wife of the Irish Republic Chargé d'Affaires, visited her friend Otto Christian Archibald, Prince von Bismarck. Prince von Bismarck had been the German envoy to the King of Italy (1940–1943) and now he headed the Italian section of the German Foreign Ministry in Berlin (1943–1944). In that capacity he was a frequent visitor to Rome and Mrs. Kiernan asked him whether he thought the Germans would defend Rome or retreat from the city. The prince told Mrs. Kiernan that they would abandon the city.

---

* Both Sandro Pertini and Giuseppe Saragat would later become presidents of Italy.
† The location is now the site of a McDonald's restaurant.

Reportedly, Derry sent this information via an Italian SIM clandestine radio, probably via Italian Major Umberto Lousena's radio, to British Intelligence.

Monsignor Montini was briefed on the Anzio landing by Emilio Bonomelli, the manager of the Pope's summer villa Castel Gandolfo, 14 miles from the city.* Bonomelli had seen the landing through binoculars and described the Allied fleet as being made up of hundreds of ships, easily visible from the heights of the castle. He also reported that Allied aircraft were overhead attacking moving German columns.

To ensure the invasion's success, the Allies had to interrupt the flow of German military materiel to the south so Allied Air Forces increased their bombing efforts. There was a corresponding increase in partisan saboteur activity. Mines, incendiary bombs, and phosphorous grenades were used against German vehicles, both moving and parked. During one night, hundreds of caltrops were strewn along the roads, blocking many German vehicles. The stalled convoys were strafed by Allied aircraft and attacked by partisans, resulting in dead Germans and captured supplies, although many partisans were also killed or wounded.

In addition to German convoys carrying troops or war materiel, infrastructure and telephone lines were also attacked by partisans. Parked trucks were attacked near Saint John Lateran, the Roman Forum, the Trevi Fountain, and in Piazza del Popolo, often used by the Wehrmacht as a parking lot.

Partisans also blew up two and a half miles of road on Via della Magliana. The damage blocked the road for two weeks, interrupting the movement of German supplies for the Anzio front from the nearby Ostiense railway yard. At the Ostiense station itself, railway workers together with partisans from Garbatella blew up parked boxcars loaded with German war materiel on two occasions.

The Tiburtina railway station, on the east of the city, saw a lot of partisan action. There, two partisans attacked a train in an attempt to capture the food supplies on board. After shots were exchanged with

---

* In 1953 Bonomelli wrote a book in which he discussed caring for refugees, especially Jews, on the papal property.

the Germans, the train caught fire, burning all the vital provisions. On another occasion, partisan Michele Bolgia, a socialist and railway worker at the Tiburtina station, impetuously opened the sealed wagons of a train loaded with prisoners, including some Jews, and released them. He was caught, imprisoned at Via Tasso, and later shot. And for a second time, the German refreshment stand outside of Termini Station was bombed. Often documents were taken during these attacks; one even gave the location of minefields at the Centocelle Airfield.

In retaliation SS arrests of partisans continued. Due to the efforts of Armando Testorio, a Fascist spy who may have worked for Kappler and was eventually tried for treason and shot after the war, a number of partisans, students, and workers were imprisoned by the SS. They included Aldo Finzi, a leader of the Democratic Labor Party, a Jew, and a former vice-minister in Mussolini's cabinet. Finzi had gone into hiding outside of Rome after the German takeover, but was denounced and taken. Others arrested at that time included a music maestro, two members of the FMCR, three members of the Red Flag, a member of the Action Party, and a Carabinieri.

Nevertheless, partisans also made a major dent on Fascists and the SS spy and informer network in Rome. As many as ten Italians in the service of the SS were assassinated by partisans on the streets and even while riding in trams across the city or preparing to flee Rome.

For example, Armando Stampacchia, the police inspector of Centocelle, was killed at his home in Piazza Ragusa near Tuscolana Station in the southern part of the city. Stampacchia was a rabid Fascist who displayed absolute loyalty to the party. He had boasted that he had no fear of partisans and could move with impunity without an escort anywhere in the quarter. He had personally rounded up Jews and civilians evading the obligatory draft. The reward for information about his murder was set by the Gestapo at 200,000 lire.* Another Fascist, unnamed, who bragged about asking to have the honor to be part of an execution squad shooting partisans, was assassinated on a tram headed to Tor Pignattara. Two senior Fascists were also eliminated by the GAP,

---

* After the liberation of the city, the partisan Scifoni was arrested and accused of the premeditated homicide of Stampacchia. After two years in prison it was judged that this action occurred during a military operation and he was released.

one an executive of the Fascist Committee of Tor Pignattara, and the second a secretary of the Roman Fascists Federation.

On January 23, a Sunday, SS-Obersturmbannführer Dollmann wanted to see the situation for himself, so he, his dog, Lupo, and his chauffeur, Mario, drove toward Anzio. They saw no Allied columns racing toward the city. However, he noted the hastily improvised contingent of German soldiers, hauled out from the Rome military hospitals, that was formed up to march south. He realized that there was little to prevent the Allies from driving straight to Saint Peter's. Reportedly Dollmann was heard to say that the Americans had put up their tents, said their prayers, had a good meal, and then lost a unique occasion to capture Rome.

SS-Obersturmbannführer Kappler, guessing that valuable intelligence was being sent to the Allies at Anzio, struck back. On January 25, he arrested Colonel Montezemolo, seriously curtailing the activities of the pro-monarchist FMCR. It is likely that an informer turned in Montezemolo to steal the money that he had received from the Badoglio government to finance the organization. Later Kappler would declare that his most important success during his time in Rome was the capture of Colonel Montezemolo and the consequent disruption of the FMCR. The sweep that netted Montezemolo included at least 22 members of the FMCR and some civilian partisans, including a medical doctor, a lyric tenor, a lawyer, and a printer.

Montezemolo had spent the night of January 24/25 at Palazzo Rospigliosi at the invitation of Princess Ninì Pallavicini who, as we have seen, was an active supporter of the FMCR and even hid the clandestine Centro X radio transmitter in her palazzo. After Montezemolo's arrest, the Gestapo must have known that the princess was helping the resistance. At this, the princess turned her palazzo over to the church for use as a convent while Monsignor O'Flaherty smuggled her into the relative safety of the German College. There she worked for the Escape Line. As a trained calligrapher, she forged ration coupons and other documents. The Gestapo put a huge bounty on information leading to her arrest, but she was never pried from her German College hideout. Among the items it was believed that she brought into the Vatican was SIM's Centro X radio which, it is believed, was used sparingly, to transmit only the most important messages to SIM headquarters.

That Giglio had control of Radio Vittoria 2 was well known to Montezemolo. Tompkins feared that Giglio could be implicated. Tompkins also deduced that, with Montezemolo's arrest, Kappler now knew of his presence in Rome, so it was decided to move him once again from Giglio's apartment. They need not have worried. Montezemolo staunchly resisted Kappler and Priebke's efforts to break him in the torture chambers of the prison at Via Tasso. Kappler was even reported to have been impressed by Montezemolo's courage during the horrific torture inflicted on him by his Gestapo tormentors.

Montezemolo's arrest convinced Tompkins that, in the event something unforeseen should happen, he should tell Sir D'Arcy and Tittmann that he was in Rome and working undercover and he discretely did so. Tompkins' contact with the Vatican was indirect and maintained through Franco Malfatti's uncle, a distinguished diplomat and at that time Chargé d'Affaires for the Sovereign Military Order of the Knights of Malta to the Holy See headquartered on the Aventine Hill, south of the Circus Maximus.

———

Shortly before the Allied invasion of Anzio, in view of a renewed danger to the priests, several ex-POWs, including Gil Smith and newly arrived RAF pilot Garrad-Cole, mentioned previously, had been asked to leave their hiding place at the French Seminary in Rome. The pair moved to Via Casilina in the southeastern outskirts of Rome. Their new hosts were a retired Italian Army colonel and his wife. It was quiet but remote, requiring a long tram ride to the city. While there, they heard of the Allied landing on January 22 and briefly considered trying to get to the friendly lines. Garrad-Cole wrote that during a trip into the city, he saw German reinforcements pouring south:

> It was a depressing sight to stand in Via dell'Impero [now Via dei Fori Imperiali] and watch columns of tiger tanks passing through with the German crews squatting on the top of their vehicles, waving to the crowds that gathered on both sides of the roads … It used to give me an enormous kick to watch the waves of American Flying

Fortresses come over. Occasionally we saw an aerial [dogfight] between the escorting Spitfires and any German F.W. 190s that dared to try to interfere with the bombers.[3]

At the end of January, Garrad-Cole saw that many more German aircraft were overflying Rome, suggesting that things were heating up. Then he and Gil Smith sighted an ammunition train parked on a siding on the mainline track to Monte Cassino close to where they were staying. They gave the specifics to Renzo Lucidi who forwarded it to the Allies; several days later the train was blown up. The men liked to think it was due to their report.

It was assumed – by the Germans, the Allies, and by Winston Churchill himself, who had put forward the original proposal for the Anzio landings – that the Allies would quickly move from the beach, secure the overlooking Alban Hills, and put the entire Gustav Line in jeopardy while opening the road to Rome. But the leader of the invasion, US General John P. Lucas, was cautious. He felt he had to consolidate his beachhead position first. General Lucas also thought that he did not have enough troops to hold both the beachhead and the hills overlooking it. This cautiousness allowed the Germans crucial time to gather their forces to stem the Allied tide. Instead of leapfrogging German fortifications and streaming into Rome, the Allied forces became trapped on the beaches of Anzio.

The deteriorating strategic situation for the Allies was still largely unknown in Rome itself. Tompkins' hideout for the next week was a dressmaker's shop on Via Condotti, the most fashionable shopping street in central Rome, where he occupied a tiny bedroom. Malfatti brought him information reports to organize for forwarding to the Allies. Giglio also visited. Despite the exceptional meals, Tompkins asked Giglio to find him a place large enough to spread out maps and to better edit the intelligence reports.

Shortly thereafter Giglio arranged a hasty transfer to take Tompkins to his new hideout in the Palazzo Lovatelli. The palazzo lies on a quiet street not far from the Palazzo Venezia and the Jewish Ghetto. Tompkins had known the palazzo as a boy, having played there with a friend in the same first-story room which was to become his hideout. The palazzo had served as the headquarters for the Rome branch of the Italian National War Veterans Organization and was a seat for the local Fascists. Now practically empty, it made an excellent headquarters.[*] It was owned, ironically, by Princess De Seta-Pignatelli who was an ardent Fascist. She was a relative of Princess Enza Pignatelli Aragona Cortes who had first told the Pope about the Jewish roundup. Princess De Seta-Pignatelli had crossed the German lines to Naples as a Gestapo agent. Her husband had accepted the position of Fascist Party Secretary for the Republic of Salò but was now on his deathbed in a Rome hotel. Her son, Emanuele, and daughter, Maria Salata, often stayed at Palazzo Lovatelli.

Tompkins and Giglio were let in by the 20-year-old Maria Salata who did not share her parents' Fascist views. In the sitting room, Giglio showed Tompkins a moveable panel which hid a small trap door to a secret bedroom with two beds and a heavily curtained window. Since the apartment had occasionally been used to hide escaped Allied POWs, Tompkins was passed off as another escapee. After Giglio left, Maria introduced him to the two men hiding in the apartment, Palatine Count Baldo Secco-Suardo and his friend, Italian Air Force officer Lele Crespi. He was Maria's boyfriend and a doctor in civilian life. She used the apartment to occasionally hide the two men from labor and military roundups. Crespi had a typewriter, an incredibly rare commodity in Rome.

Malfatti arrived and he and Tompkins agreed to let his three hosts in on their work. Crespi and Secco-Suardo were told and both were eager to help; Maria was informed that they were gathering intelligence but was not given any details. Now Tompkins could spread out his maps and track the action. In the event of a raid, they practiced ridding the apartment of any sign of their presence within 60 seconds. They also found a place in the cellar to hide equipment, files, and weapons.

---

[*] During a search of the Palazzo Lovatelli on the internet, the author found a photograph from the 1960s of the same interior room used by Tompkins. Standing in front of the fireplace was the famous Italian actress Sophia Loren. The palazzo now hosts high-end art auctions on the floor above Tompkins' apartment.

A few days after moving into the new headquarters, Giglio rushed into the apartment, yelling, "It's all over, I've been caught." During the night of February 3/4, Pietro Caruso, the new police chief of Rome, and Pietro Koch, head of the Banda Koch, had organized a raid at the Basilica of Saint Paul Outside the Walls.

The raiding party comprised 120 men, units of the National Public Security Police which included Giglio and don Ildelfonso, the Banda Koch's ex-monk. The midnight raid began with don Ildelfonso's ruse of knocking on the door and claiming he was fleeing from the Germans and he needed help. Once admitted, the police pushed in with him. As he had during a December 1943 raid, he used Latin to separate actual clerics from those in hiding.

It was brought to Caruso's attention that Giglio was taking pictures during the raid using the Minox miniature camera that Tompkins had brought from Naples. The camera was confiscated and Giglio sent home, Caruso keeping the camera as a souvenir. The pictures had no intelligence value but Giglio had put himself at risk by drawing attention to himself.

Not sure what to do, Tompkins told Giglio to go to his father who was visiting Rome for a few days and tell him about the raid. When Giglio returned to his squadron he complained that a camera belonging to his father had been taken by a plainclothes policeman and he had to have it back. He took it with him only to test it out. At least for a while the story was believed.

The San Paolo raid netted almost 100 fugitives. Included was Italian Air Force General Adriano Monti, four other Italian military officers, 20 NCOs and soldiers, two fugitive policemen, ex-Carabinieri, nine Jews, and 48 labor draft evaders. They were all sent to a German concentration camp.

The raiders confiscated four heavy-duty trucks, a car, a Wehrmacht motorcycle, 6,000 liters of gasoline, and a vast array of military hardware, hand grenades, rifles, side-arms, gas masks, and army cots. At 10:00 the next morning, the raiders walked out with food (prosciutto hams, salamis, and cheeses), thousands of yards of fabrics and many fur coats. The raid violated the sanctity of extraterritoriality and Monsignor Montini protested. But the prisoners were not released. Many averred later that the Vatican's reaction to this unprecedented raid was to order refugees to be turned out by any religious institutions holding them. However, courageous churchmen all over Rome refused to expel their hidden refugees. Nevertheless, on February 5, refugees who had returned to hiding inside the seminary of Saint John Lateran left to seek other places to hide.

───────

Despite the raid intelligence gathering continued. Tompkins' main task was counting German military traffic moving on the principal roads around and through Rome. It was difficult and especially dangerous during curfew, and he relied heavily on Giuliano Vassalli's Socialist Party members. In order to monitor the roads 24 hours a day, at least 50 people were needed to provide coverage at different times and places. They noted details of every vehicle that passed, including type, contents, insignia, kind of troops, and the type of any gun being transported.

Tompkins sent all this information to the Allies via Radio Vittoria 2. On February 4 he reported that the Germans had a new strategy to avoid Allied air raids while moving supplies and men. Trucks traveled almost exclusively by night, in columns of 15–20 vehicles, each about a kilometer apart. This reduced their losses even during daylight because, while US aircraft bombed towns and villages during daylight hours, they rarely attacked individual trucks.

Tompkins recommended bombing bypass roads and freight yards instead of towns and villages, saying it was essential to maintain constant attacks on bridges, overpasses, and other such choke points as they were harder to repair than roads and such raids did far less damage to civilians. For the partisans, he asked for air drops of fuses, detonators, and timing devices disguised as pencils which could only be obtained from the OSS or British SOE. Tompkins also said that the Germans had easily broken the Allied air-to-ground code because the Allied pilots continued to use only the first cipher, of 31 available daily. The Germans were reading all of their communications. It was as if the pilots were transmitting in the clear.[4]

Tompkins' network also included, as part-time informers, farmers coming in from the countryside who gave details of German concentrations, minefields, gun emplacements, gasoline dumps, and progress on local fortifications; hospital workers, who gathered details from injured soldiers about where and when they were wounded; doctors, who went to villages to tend wounded civilians, bringing back useful details; and even children, while playing in the fields near German long-range guns like Anzio Annie, the immense 270mm railway gun, who would tell their parents what they had seen and the parents would pass it on.

As word of Tompkins' activities became known among the partisans of Rome, volunteer agents would approach him, not all of them helpful. One was an unidentified Italian engineer nicknamed "the colonel." Secco-Suardo, Tompkins' helper at the Palazzo Lovatelli, held a daily liaison meeting with him, but his information was not considered reliable. The colonel was later captured by the Gestapo, but his fate is not known.

Another volunteer agent was British Major D'Arcy Mander who had escaped from the raid on the Escape Line's Via Cellini apartment. Tompkins referred to Mander as "the cousin." Mander later wrote:

> I had been sending messages to Allied HQ by means of a heterogeneous collection of organizations in which I had no very great confidence and of which I was sure the Allies could not have had a very high opinion. But all this changed dramatically with the arrival of Pietro (I never discovered his surname) and it was Pietro who rousted me out rather than the other way round. He told me that he had been sent to Rome to establish a *Centrale*, literally a telephone exchange but in fact it was an organization using a number of wireless sets which moved around in Rome and transmitted messages to the Allies.[5]

Mander described Pietro as short, stocky, a regular Italian Army artillery captain from northern Italy. He was in fact Clemente Menicanti, codenamed Coniglio, the man whom Tompkins mistrusted. Menicanti had initially contacted Mander through Ubaldo Cipolla, the double agent known to Mander as Daniele. Mander must have been referring to sending messages via Radio Vittoria 1. The British codenamed Mander "Volunteer." He eventually got Daniele to tell him who was to be left behind and later claimed he broke the entire stay-behind German network after the liberation.

Mander sent a message via Radio Vittoria 1, proposing that he bike to Anzio and rejoin the army. He was told to stay in Rome and continue his good work. Mander later wrote that his contact with the FMCR was makeshift and tenuous:

> As I got around I met people who supplied me with all kinds of information. I knew a chap who gave the details of all the rail traffic passing through Rome. I met Italian officers on the run and I had one living on nearly every main road in and out of Rome and they kept watch for me and reported all military convoys. And of course, there was Daniele [Ubaldo Cipolla] ensconced in the German security Headquarters. I didn't want to hide and be walled up as some POWs were, I wanted to be active and do something to help, and I was able to send a lot of varied information to the Allies, and also helped other less fortunate prisoners living in the mountains outside Rome.[6]

Mander may have given himself too much credit for creating this vast reporting network; he was unaware of Tompkins' reporting; and in any event it was SIM that had organized the whole thing. Clearly the British wanted to have a source of intelligence inside Rome that was not dependent on Tompkins and so they encouraged Mander. While Mander may have felt that he was a key cog in the intelligence machinery of Rome, Tompkins had a different take:

> As for the British, an escaped POW major [Mander] who was so anxious to be of assistance to us and who wished to file through us the intelligence he was able to collect, I found myself in a very unhappy position. Bluntly, the chances of his collecting anything which we did not already know or which could be of timely importance were very limited. But this I could not possibly tell him, as it was clearly the only thing which kept up his morale and his sense of being useful; so I undertook to have his messages picked up at regular intervals. To have him with us would have been impossible, as our salvation in case of a raid, or disaster, was to stick to our false identity cards and play them for all they were worth – for which a perfect knowledge of the language was essential. Above all I didn't want him to know the extent of our own espionage network, which was becoming so precise in its

mechanics that it would have been folly to endanger its security for any reason other than one essential to our work. We were too big and too well organized to risk endangering our network by the addition of minor sources.[7]

Raw intelligence was brought to Domus, Malfatti's Via Veneto bookstore. There Malfatti sorted the information and sent it on by courier to Tompkins at the Palazzo Lovatelli several times a day. It was never passed direct, but through multiple hands so that the beginning and end of the information train was never known. Tompkins evaluated and prepared the information for transmission:

The completed cables, written on thin tissue paper, were then tightly folded and carried by special messengers, inside their socks, or slipped through a ring on their finger where it could be easily swallowed. They took the messages to a man waiting at a prearranged rendezvous a few blocks away. This man, who didn't know who I was or where I lived, carried the message across town to meet another man at another prearranged rendezvous who in turn took it to wherever the radio station happened to be hidden. Thus, the central messenger knew neither where the message came from, nor where it went to. If they caught the radio there would be absolutely no way they could trace the message back to me – and vice versa.[8]

Tompkins also kept a diary which Franco Malfatti arranged to be sent regularly every week to a friendly cleric inside the Vatican for safekeeping. In his entry for February 14 Tompkins wrote:

The German High Command has decided to make a supreme effort towards a rapid elimination of the beachhead, not only to have a victory exploitable for internal reasons of prestige, but so as to establish the tactical premise for further operations on the southern Front. It is thus hoped to bring about a change in Italian public-opinion and make it possible to implement Hitler's order to maintain the present line at all costs. The German offensive against the beachhead cannot be sustained for long; and the opinion is expressed in German military circles that either the Allies are thrown back into the sea in two or three days or the situation may turn the other way. Lack of gasoline is obliging the Germans to long hauls on foot and to use pack animals to draw artillery. Nevertheless, there is still movement of German troops southward ... The Spezia-Rimini [defensive] line, on which the German units in northern Italy were based, has been almost completely stripped in order to send men and equipment to the southern front. The interruption of the railways has absorbed all German vehicles for logistic necessities; furthermore many German gas dumps have been destroyed by recent air attacks.[9]

Tactical intelligence was sent directly to the OSS unit at the Anzio beachhead or to US Fifth Army Headquarters in Caserta via Radio Vittoria 2. Based on this information, targets were selected and bombed and strafed by Allied aircraft. Tompkins wrote: "To begin with we received far more information than we could possibly file. [Tompkins noted it was a huge plus that he] ... had experience gained from drafting innumerable messages in cables as a foreign correspondent, cable desk editor, and intelligence officer."[10]

Radio Vittoria 2 reported increased traffic heading south through Rome on February 15. The next day, Tompkins reported that a major 14th Army German offensive against the beachhead would be coming within the next 24 hours. His team had observed 230 freight cars loaded with war materiel, 50 troop transports, 100 cars loaded with horses, 11 Mark VI panzers, and six medium panzers. This report scored a major intelligence success:

> The Germans have deployed their forces to form two powerful spearheads of heavy tanks and armored vehicles with which to break through from each flank of the beachhead with the purpose of: (1) cutting the beachhead in two, laterally, thus surrounding a large part of the defending troops: (2) inhibiting the fire of Allied naval guns who would be unable to distinguish between their own troops and the Germans. At the same time pressure is to be maintained along the center of the front to permit successful attack from the flanks.[11]

It was Tompkins' biggest intelligence coup but Mander also claimed that the same reporting was his most important message. Mander had received his information during a meeting with an unidentified friend, probably Menicanti, in the Hotel Eden, a German officer hangout, just off Via Veneto. Tompkins' report went to the Americans, Mander's to the British.*

———

Radio Vittoria 2 transmitted twice a day. Tompkins would get requests for more information, thanks for useful information passed on and, occasionally, a report of what actions had been taken. Special descriptions of German military insignia were sent to enable the careful tracking of individual Wehrmacht units. Over six weeks, 98 single-spaced typewritten pages of information were sent. Tompkins had a suitcase full of files hidden in the cellar of his headquarters at Palazzo Lovatelli. Files were titled: order of battle, insignia, antiaircraft gun locations, gun emplacements, minefields, gas and ammunition dumps, counterespionage, relations with partisans, and political information. Tompkins plotted much of this information on his map. Although he moved the radio around frequently, Tompkins described one of his radio's most secure locations this way:

> As a place from which to operate the radio, Cervo [Giglio] had made a clever arrangement with the caretaker of one of the many river boats [actually a barge] along the Tiber (complex wooden buildings on floating pontoons used during the summer as swimming and boating clubs, but largely unused during the winter except for their locker-room and shower facilities) where the caretaker was only too happy to make a little extra money renting out the cabins and closing an eye to what went on inside – their fame as places of homosexual assignations being well known throughout the city. This particular river boat was almost opposite the Italian Ministry of Marine [Naval Ministry] from which radio signals were bound to be emitted and which I was inclined to believe would add cover rather than draw attention to our own weak signal in case of triangulation.[12]

---

* Years after the war, Tompkins saw his original reports at the US National Archives and compared them with Field Marshal Kesselring's troop dispositions. He was pleased with how accurate they were. At the time, with the exception of a few congratulatory messages, he had no way of verifying his reporting for accuracy. Official OSS documents record that more than 500 messages had been received from Radio Vittoria 2.

The barge was moored near the Ponte Risorgimento at the corner of Piazza Monte Grappa, but the radio transmitter was moved periodically to hinder potential triangulation by the Germans. Although the Abwehr had triangulation gear, Kappler later claimed that he did not have access to this equipment although he had requested it.*

———

Much of Tompkins' best and most relevant information came from Ottorino Borin, an Italian officer and OSS and SIM agent assigned to Rome's Open City organization. Borin was a young man from Alto Adige, a region of Italy where both German and Italian are spoken. He acted as liaison between Domenico Chirieleison, the Italian Open City Commander, and General Mälzer, the German Commander. In the course of his duties, he obtained information for the Tompkins team on German troop movements, and pending Gestapo police actions. Importantly he acquired false Open City Organization papers for the Tompkins team.

Tompkins kept detailed expense accounts in the event that some of his OSS colleagues would question his efforts. He was spending money on intelligence from socialist and communist sources and he was right to account for every lira. One expense listing was *Cognac per Frühling*, which translates in German-Italian as cognac for spring. However, it was in fact for SS-Scharführer (NCO) Frühling who was stationed at Via Tasso. Tompkins said that there was virtually no government office in the city in which they did not have someone planted. For example, contacts in hotels reported German officer and troop check-ins and, among other things, filed reports on their morale.

Tompkins complained about Allied propaganda that seemed set on aiding the enemy. He wrote that the broadcasts to Italy by Fiorello La Guardia, the New York City Italian-American mayor, were politically naive; they were spoken in incomprehensible Italian, and they failed to grasp the reality of the situation. The BBC commentator, nicknamed

---

* Apparently it was not the only Tiber barge in use during the occupation. Some sources relate that 20 Yugoslav ex-POWs hid on a bathing barge below the Castel Sant'Angelo where they fished at night and sold their catch every morning.

Colonel Stevens, made broadcasts that were monotonous, but at least they broadcast jazz.

At the same time, Tompkins' organization set about distributing the latest news around Rome. They edited a daily sheet of collected news items from Radio Bari, Radio Moscow, and Radio London. These were passed on to individuals or included in clandestine publications. The news sheets were distributed by young women in churches, on streetcars, in theaters, and on street corners. It was risky work.

Tompkins also uncovered a planned German deception: large numbers of wooden decoy panzers and guns were being mocked up at the Cinecittà film studio. The decoys would masquerade as deployments of actual German assault units when placed at strategic spots at the center of the front in order to deceive Allied observers.

Kappler was also busy in the battle for the Anzio beachhead. SS-Hauptsturmführer Eugen Haas devised a sabotage plan. His first idea was to release rats contaminated with deadly bacteria on the beach but Kappler realized that the rats could also infect Wehrmacht soldiers and so rejected the idea. A second idea was to send a team to blow up the Anzio HQ of Generals Alexander and Clark but bad weather and rough seas repeatedly postponed the plan to infiltrate the beachhead. When the attempt was finally launched several weeks later – to coincide with a huge German attack on February 29 – one of the saboteurs, Michele Coppola, a secret resistance fighter, forced the boat to land and the conspirators to surrender.

It was probably due to Tompkins' reporting that, in early March, the Allies again bombed the rail yards in the San Lorenzo district east of Rome, and around the Ostiense train station. Tompkins had reported increased rail activity in and around Rome. At the Ostiense station, for example, his team had counted 28 freight cars full of munitions; at the Littorio station several trainloads of supplies; and, six miles north of Rome near Via Salaria, more than 70 open railway cars, mostly carrying light panzers and armored cars. Mother Mary wrote of the Allied bombing:

> Tuesday March 14th. This morning we had the most terrible air raid that we have had since they began on July 19th. It took place between 11:30 and 12:30; waves of heavy bombers came over and dropped tons of explosives on and around the Tiburtina, Prenestina and San

Lorenzo stations. All of these are clearance points for war materiel: weapons, ammunition, petrol and oil bound for the Anzio front in trains or stored in sheds near them. The stations, goods yards, railway tracks and vans were completely wrecked, but the damage to civilian dwellings and the casualties were appalling. Bombs fell in streets where queues were lined up for water from emergency pipe lines, and simply wiped out entire groups. One woman was beheaded by the blast; the body of another was blown onto a telegraph wire where it hung until, the confusion having subsided, firemen came with ladders and removed it.[13]

The bombing stymied Tompkins because his observers were busy finding housing for their bombed-out families. For several days, he had no complete road counts of the German traffic on Via Ostiense.

Tompkins' diary entries reveal the vast organization he was supervising, hundreds of people in the strangest positions, gathering libraries of assorted information, and involved in a lot of varied situations with never a dull moment. It is worth noting author Robert Katz's evaluation of what Tompkins and his team accomplished:

> The remarkable work of the full-fledged spy network, overcoming deadly intramural intrigue, has received only spotty recognition and remains largely a tale of unsung heroes. They played a pivotal intelligence role in the battle to save the beachhead from extinction. Tompkins' long-classified mission report to Donovan explains that the network drew enormous energy mainly from the spirit of resistance rather than from conventional sources. It was a model of an inspired undercover apparatus probably unique in the annals of espionage, all the more so as an operation of the agency that would become the CIA. Tompkins' report stands as a rare tribute from the Allied side to the partisan operations, above all, but also to the people of Rome.[14]

Also on March 14, Clemente Menicanti (codenamed Coniglio) was arrested. It was a major victory for the Gestapo because he controlled Radio Vittoria 1. He divulged information over the next few days leading to the arrest of 47 members of Tompkins' network. They were taken to Via Tasso for interrogation and torture. The entire network was compromised. Enrico Sorrentino, the self-styled Chief Political

Agent in Rome of General Mark Clark, was also arrested. He sold out Arrigo Paladini who gave us the description of Erich Priebke's torture methods. Another was Lt. Eugenio Arrighi, arrested as he was preparing the charges to blow up a train. Arrighi identified the man who denounced him by leaving a message on a wall of his Via Tasso prison cell, a drawing of a rabbit (*coniglio*).

One of those arrested escaped by wrestling a gun from his Gestapo interrogator, hitting him on the head, and calmly walking out of the prison. Via Tasso had recently been fortified with barbed wire and machine guns. Tompkins wanted to storm the prison and release all the prisoners and he thought that precision bombing of the prison might work, but nothing was done.

Also arrested was Vincenzo Converti (codenamed Enzo), the Radio Vittoria 1 operator. Hearing of Converti's arrest, on March 17, 1944, Giglio decided to retrieve Radio Vittoria 2's clandestine transmitter from the barge on the Tiber River and was caught, the transmitter in his hands. Giovanni Scottu, Giglio's military orderly, who was awaiting his boss with a motorcycle and sidecar, was also arrested.

Later, Scottu gave Tompkins a report of what had happened. He and Giglio had been taken to Koch's headquarters in the Pension Oltremare. On the top floor they were interviewed separately by Koch. Scottu had denied knowing Giglio because he knew he was involved in patriotic activities, his words for partisan activities. Under interrogation and torture, Scottu admitted that he was Giglio's orderly. Thus commenced six excruciating interrogation sessions during which pistols were pointed at their mouths and they were ordered to talk.

During a fifth torture session, Scottu said he was placed naked on a wooden frame with his back against a wool carder. A heavy bar placed across his chest was clamped down, pressing his body against the raised nails of the carder, thus puncturing and ripping his skin. Koch's men applied steel points to his temples and drew them slowly together with a steel band. They demanded to know the names of Giglio's collaborators, but Scottu remained silent, probably because he simply did not know them. Reportedly Scottu's testimony may have been completely made up and, although he was taken into custody, he was never tortured and may have even participated in the physical abuse of Giglio.[15]

After his torture sessions, Giglio had lost several teeth and was bleeding heavily from his mouth and nose. Suffering violent blows to the neck as well as electric shock, he was returned to his cell covered in blood.

One of the interrogators in these sessions was the man who initially denounced Converti, Francesco Argentino, also known as Walter di Franco (or by other aliases, Walter de Rossi or Franco di Walter). A former Italian SIM officer, Argentino had been Giglio's friend. Arrested during the February 1 labor roundup conducted by Caruso and the Banda Koch, Argentino had convinced Koch that he could provide information on partisans and intelligence units in Rome. His offer was accepted and, as a turncoat, he joined the Banda Koch, eventually becoming Koch's deputy.

Amid these crises, Tompkins again had to move. After more than six weeks at Palazzo Lovatelli, he relocated to an apartment owned by Secco-Suardo. Safety forced the pair to change trams several times to reach Piazza Pitagora in Parioli. Constantly looking over their shoulders, they walked the mile to a new apartment in Via Ruggero Fauro. Once inside, they fell into a deep sleep. Later that afternoon, Malfatti arrived with depressing news confirming that the radio operator Vincenzo Converti had indeed betrayed Giglio.

To lift their spirits, a party was in order. It would confirm their cover stories that they were worthless playboys, always ready for fun. Franco Malfatti organized a curfew party where the guests were to spend the night. There would be eight guests: Tompkins, Secco-Suardo, Crespi, and Malfatti, two girls, and two other friends, one a gay man called Emanuele, who was invited "to give verisimilitude to the party and confuse the police in case of a raid."[16]

Tompkins was in the kitchen making toasted ham sandwiches and omelets for the guests. Liquor was flowing, and, as the party livened up, the men called for more girls. Malfatti, who had a pass to travel around Rome after curfew, went to the city center to pick up another girl. And the other girl called a friend who lived nearby – on the same street – to come over. The friend asked if she could bring along her German companion and Tompkins, Crespi, and the girl left the apartment to fetch them. Ever cautious, Tompkins tucked a long slim kitchen knife into his coat.

His caution was well placed, for he had no idea into what sinister waters their innocent curfew party had just sailed. Arriving at the friend's house, they were ushered into a large room where another party was in full swing. Tompkins quickly realized it was the home of Italian film star Laura Nucci, and her husband, a well-known racketeer, Nazi collaborator, and a self-styled baron. A naked woman, presumably Laura, was sprawled on a couch, covered in furs, and with a German officer holding her hand. Tompkins later wrote that, "One look into her eyes was enough to tell me she was doped."[17]

For introductions, Crespi chose a plausible and spontaneous alias for Tompkins, one of the aliases he had first used when he came to Rome, Roberto Berlingieri, an old and dear friend. The Berlingieri family was known in Rome and by some at this party. Roberto, it was explained, was a distant relative, and that seemed to work.

The German officer rose, clicked his heels, and introduced himself. His name meant nothing to Tompkins at the time. To him he was only an unidentified SS captain. Yet Tompkins was aware that he was being stared at both by the captain and the faux baron. He calmed his nerves by dancing with one of the women after which he guided everyone, including the half-naked actress, down the street and back to his party.

Back in his kitchen, Tompkins again made omelets, one of which he prepared for the SS captain, who ate it with relish. When he finished, the Nazi officer went back to fondling the actress and drinking huge amounts of brandy. A card game, *chemin de fer*, was being played, and it helped Tompkins to keep his cool. He later said that, in his anxiety, he had made a stupid language mistake, which fortunately went unnoticed.

Malfatti returned with two girls, having been delayed on his trip downtown and stopped twice by PAI policemen. In his excellent German Malfatti struck up a conversation with the SS captain about conditions on the Anzio beachhead. At last the faux baron and the SS officer, again clicking his heels, left, towing the actress behind them. It was four in the morning.

With the German gone, the party flared up briefly but then most of the revellers fell asleep by the light of the dying fire. It was close to noon when they awoke. The house was a mess. Tea with black-market sugar helped ease their hangovers. And they replayed their party. Crespi worried that Tompkins, drunk, had acted and danced like an American so that others would see through him. Malfatti said that, on his way out, the SS captain had asked who Tompkins really was and that he accepted the explanation that Tompkins was a no-good playboy who only cared about gambling and women.

Now Malfatti told the astonished Tompkins that the man who had eaten his omelet was in fact SS-Hauptsturmführer Erich Priebke, the Gestapo officer who had the job of uncovering and eliminating enemy agents like Tompkins. Malfatti had encountered Priebke when he had been held at Via Tasso after being denounced as a Badoglio agent. Lacking evidence, he had been released. He also told Tompkins that Priebke had been the SS officer who had arrested Count and Countess Ciano (Mussolini's daughter) and had given her jewelry to Donna Lola Giovanelli Berlingieri for safekeeping; Berlingieri was the very name that Crespi had used for Tompkins that night, and that it had been that connection that sparked Priebke's interest.[18] It was as though Priebke and Tompkins, hunter and prey, had brushed against each other in the dark, the pungent whiff of menace and helplessness not sensed by either. Now he knew who his guest had been, Tompkins knew they must vacate the apartment immediately.

Tompkins now had no access to a radio, both Radio Vittorio 1 and 2 having been shut down and their operators arrested. His backup plan was to contact Italian Major Umberto Lousena. But he too had been arrested and taken to Via Tasso. Lousena, it will be recalled, was a conduit between British Major Sam Derry of the Allied Escape Line and escaped POWs outside the city. Lousena used his radio, supplied by Number One Special Force, to coordinate partisan supply drops but it had been located by an Abwehr triangulation device because he had failed to move it from place to place.

Even if Lousena had not been arrested, Tompkins may have not been able to send a message via his radio. For some reason the Number One Special Force had ordered its men in Rome not to relay any messages from Tompkins. Tompkins did not know this and it has never been explained. According to Kurzman there were perhaps three reasons for the prohibition against relaying messages from Tompkins. One was they had been told Tompkins was a fraud, but since he and Munthe were friends this is unlikely; the second reason was it only trusted information from pro-Badoglio sources, very plausible; and the third potential reason was SOE felt it was in competition with the OSS, which was also very plausible.[19]

With no access to a radio, Tompkins could no longer report to OSS headquarters. In danger himself, now he needed to disappear. But before that he had to let his headquarters know why Radio Vittoria 2 had been off the air since March 16, 1944. He wrote a short message and sent it to D'Arcy Mander via a team member, Ottorino Borin of the Open City organization. Mander, he hoped, would send the message. But Mander's contact, Manicanti, had been arrested so Tompkins' message went nowhere. Tompkins had to make his exit in silence.

The descriptions here of the partisan attacks against Germans and Fascists, their installations and facilities, represent only a small sample of what was going on. A spectacular partisan attack and its repercussions will come later in our story. The Germans seemed powerless to subdue the partisans. Nor were reprisals taken against the Romans in general for partisan attacks during those first six months. If individual partisans were apprehended during an attack they would be arrested, tortured, and often put to death, but innocent civilians, with the obvious exception of Jews, were largely left alone. However, as tensions continued to rise, that was set to change.

17

No Roman Holiday

The key to advancing on Rome from Anzio was the capture of the German-held Italian town of Cisterna di Latina. The town was critical to the control of Italian State Highway Seven, following the course of the ancient Via Appia which runs through Cisterna to Rome. Cisterna was four miles from the 3rd Infantry Division lines, the outer defense of the Anzio perimeter. A major US attack had been planned to start at midnight, January 30, 1944. It was spearheaded by the 1st and 3rd battalions of Darby's Rangers who moved out across the fields and followed drainage ditches toward the town. The Rangers' mission was to capture Cisterna, cut Highway Seven, and move to capture the Alban Hills.

The 4th Ranger Battalion, to the left of the other two battalions, was to move up Cannon Company, its integral anti-tank company equipped with four M3 75mm gun half-tracks. Cannon Company would stay on the road running from the tiny village of Conca inside the lines to Cisterna, before crossing into what the Rangers called Jerryland, at a crossroads named Isola Bella for the nearby local village, two miles south of Cisterna. The 7th Infantry was to the left and the 15th Infantry was to the right, both regiments ready to move as far as the Alban Hills overlooking the beachhead. The 4th Rangers were augmented by two Sherman tanks and a section of tank destroyers from Lt. Tommy Welch's 1st Platoon, B Company, 601st Tank Destroyer Battalion (TD BN).[1] Once taken, other elements of the 3rd Infantry Division were to enter Cisterna.

Intelligence reports had mistakenly assessed Cisterna as being lightly held. Unbeknownst to the Rangers, the Germans had heavily reinforced the town and its environs that evening because it was to be the staging area for German forces readying for a major attack. The Germans, alerted to the Rangers' movement toward Cisterna, held back. The Rangers were falling into a trap.

On the move, the 4th Ranger Battalion ran into a roadblock and suffered heavy, sustained fire from houses, farm buildings, and concealed German locations. Although supported by tanks and TDs, the Rangers were in a running fight. By 04:00 they had not reached Isola Bella on the way to Cisterna, and they never would.

As the sun rose, the 1st and 3rd Rangers were caught out in the open, about 800 yards from Cisterna. The Germans hit them hard, trapping both Ranger battalions. Completely cut off, they could neither advance nor retreat. It was a disaster. These two Ranger battalions suffered more than 400 casualties, and approximately 600 of them were taken prisoner. Only six Rangers from the 1st and 3rd battalions made it back to friendly lines. Darby's Rangers never recovered from this attack and were evacuated from the beachhead.

The character of the Rangers can be summed up in the description of one of its men who was captured. He was 1st Lt. William L. Newman, 3rd Ranger Battalion, Baker Company. Ranger T/5 James P. O. O'Reilly of Baker Company said of Newman:

He was a little fellow with big thick glasses. But boy he loved a fight ... He never would send his men where he wouldn't go. And there was never a place, however hot, that he would hesitate at going. That's the kind of guy he was.[2]

Late the next day, the surviving Rangers, now prisoners of war, were moved to a large warehouse about ten miles north of Cisterna. After a day and a half, the soldiers were moved again, closer to Rome, to what Lt. Newman described as "an old interurban [trollycar] roundhouse, well wired and well protected as far as guards and machine guns were concerned."[3] It was probably located near Cinecittà. There they joined other POWs, British, Canadian, and French Colonial troops. Newman wrote about his new POW status:

Being captured was quite a shock to all of us because we had been able to visualize very graphically the idea of being badly hurt, or perhaps even being killed, but the idea of being taken prisoner was something that none of us had considered at all.[4]

After remaining in the roundhouse for the better part of two days, Newman and approximately 700 other POWs were loaded onto trucks and taken to the center of Rome. There they were marched around the Colosseum, down Mussolini's new triumphant road, Via dell'Impero, to Piazza Venezia, then along the Corso Umberto (now Via del Corso) and right onto Via del Tritone where they remounted the trucks that had brought them to the city. Ignoring the Geneva Convention's prohibition of photographing POWs for propaganda, the Wehrmacht took movies and still pictures of the forced march. POW soldiers made the V for Victory sign and shouted in broken Italian that in two or three weeks they will enter Rome. Later the trucks loaded with POWs were driven about 30 miles to Passo Corese Camp #54, the POW camp near Fara in Sabina, northeast of Rome.

The Germans paraded captured troops around the Colosseum again on February 14. Mother Mary recorded that Romans joked that the Allies said they would come to Rome and here they are. Lieutenant Simpson wrote of a widely published photograph of a captured detachment of Scottish infantrymen with the caption: "The famous Gordon Highlanders reach Rome ... as Prisoners of War!"[5]

The Germans had sent Ranger Newman to the Passo Corese camp, then on to the POW camp at Laterina, Camp #82, northwest of Arezzo in Tuscany. Newman escaped by first removing his rank insignia and slipping in with a group of enlisted men, knowing they had already been counted and were ready for the trip to Germany. Moving away from that group, he hid in a truck inside a maintenance shed until lunch. While the guards were eating, he hopped over the fence and with a lot of help from some friendly Italians he made it to Rome. According to Newman, five other Rangers escaped from Laterina POW Camp. They were PFC James Anderson; Cpl Pasquale D'Amato; PFC Harry Pearlmutter; Captain Charles Shunstom (who disappeared); and Lt. Gerald C. Simons. Simons joined a British group fighting with the partisans, was wounded, and died on the operating table after undergoing interrogation.

In Rome, Ranger Newman made his way to the Vatican and contacted the Escape Line. In his memoirs Newman later wrote about Lt. Simpson:

> By the time I arrived there, Rome was his oyster. If you wanted a tailor you asked Lt. Simpson; if it was a boot maker you needed, Lt. Simpson would produce him; change in billets, cigarettes, wine – Lt. Simpson was your man. He wished no praise; he did not even seem to care for appreciation of his work ... He felt that it was his duty as an officer and gentleman ...[6]

Four days after arriving in Rome, Simpson took Newman to lunch at the Casina delle Rose, located a few hundred yards inside Rome's central park, on the grounds of the Villa Umberto, now called the Villa Borghese. It was dangerously close to Via Veneto and the German Command area of Rome. Newman's account of the restaurant and the lunch shows his verve:

> The Casina delle Rose is in the fine park called Umberto, right on the edge near the section of the old Roman wall, a lovely place. Everybody would walk in; Simpson was talking in English to me, of course, not loudly or shouting. We walked up to the bar and Simpson talked first in Italian to the bartender and then in English. The bartender spoke English – perfect English; in fact, he had lived in New York for a long time, and kicked himself for ever going back to Italy. We would buy a drink and he would buy a drink. We bought some cigarettes. The bartender had saved cigarettes for Simpson, at a heavy price. Then we went into the dining room. We ordered a meal and only five tables away sat two German officers, with close cropped hair, trying to look as fierce as they could. I sat there looking right at them. We had a good meal, got up and left with no trouble at all. Then I was taken on to my new billet.[7]

Newman soon met other Escape Line helpers, including Adrienne Lucidi, who helped him get a new suit of clothes. He was able to cash checks of $400 on his account at the Wabeek State Bank in Detroit to supplement the 3,000 lire he had received from the Escape Line. Later he learned that his checks never reached the bank; he had hoped that they might have been a way to let his family know he was still alive.

Newman easily settled into life as an escapee in Rome. He took Adrienne Lucidi to lunch at the Casina delle Rose to thank her for getting him the suit. At an adjacent table sat four German officers, including, as Adrienne told Newman, Kappler, the head of the Gestapo in Rome. Newman could feel Kappler's eyes on him, studying him and, when he left his table to make a telephone call, Newman feared he had been caught. A friendly waiter came over and whispered to Newman in English that Kappler was on a routine call. When they got their coats to leave, Newman was tempted by something he saw. He later wrote about that moment:

> Even more amusing is the fact that all four of them [the Gestapo officers] hung their Lügers in the check room with their hats; same theory as the old western practice of checking the revolvers with the bar-keeper. There was no one in the check room and I had an overpowering desire to take the Lüger of the chief of the Gestapo as a souvenir, but finally conquered this desire when I realized that the Jerries would simply wreck the Casina delle Rose if this happened.[8]

The accidental seating of enemies next to ex-POWs in Italian restaurants was not only bizarre but drew unwanted attention. The German Ambassador complained of one incident that made headlines, and his complaint made its way through the Swiss Ambassador to the Vatican and to Sir D'Arcy. The story was that two British ex-POW officers were having lunch at Ascenzio, one of Rome's best restaurants, now long since closed. They had a lot to drink and became loud, and were drawing attention to themselves. Seated nearby was Bruno Spampanato, the editor of the Roman newspaper *Il Messaggero*, the most virulently Fascist of Rome's daily newspapers and the government's mouthpiece.

Spampanato recounted his experience in a bitter editorial about the affront of ex-POWs dining out in Rome. The headline read, *Rome Starves while British Escaped Prisoners Gorge*. The article castigated the deluxe restaurants of Rome for being "meeting places of the vicious, the black-marketer, the war profiteer, the shirker and the escaped British prisoner."[9] In reaction, General Mälzer closed some establishments, to the annoyance of his own officers, who dined at the same restaurants.

Monsignor O'Flaherty was pleased that the escapees had enjoyed their outings and that it bothered the Germans so much.

On one occasion, Simpson was waiting for Furman in a bar, probably the Orso, when a group of German officers entered in the company of a hulking figure, who Simpson recognized as none other than Max Schmeling, the famous German 1936 Olympic heavyweight boxing champion. Schmeling had been drafted into the Luftwaffe as a paratrooper and had been wounded in the battle for Crete. For the rest of the war, he entertained German troops with goodwill boxing tours. Simpson, speaking reasonable Italian and pretending he was an Italian Fascist, struck up a conversation and invited them all for a drink. They ended up singing songs around the piano. The Germans had such a good time that they invited Simpson for lunch, but he begged off, not wanting to tempt fate any more that day.

The more POWs taken by the Germans, the more escapees there were. In February, Major Derry added 338 names to his roll, bringing his total to 2,591 known ex-POWs throughout Italy. This was not counting recaptures, flights into Switzerland, and the few successful returns to Allied territory.

Derry's policy was still to get escapees out of the city as soon as possible. The countryside was safer and it cost less to support men there. Although some Italian *padroni* made the hiding of escapees a business, they were the exception. Many, however, agreed to take only officer escapees, thinking that they would be better behaved than enlisted men. Derry promoted several of the men temporarily to officer status to suit this preference. In February, the number of escapees in Rome rose from 84 to 116 despite Derry's efforts to send them out of Rome. More men often arrived in one day than were sent to the countryside.

Luck played a major role in the daily lives of Roman citizens but on March 3, 1944, it had run out for one woman. She was Teresa Gullace, a 37-year-old working mother of five with a sixth child on the way. Her husband and several hundred others had been taken two days earlier for forced labor for the Todt Organization. They were being held at the Italian military casern on the corner of Viale Giulio Cesare and Via Fabio Massimo in Prati. Standing outside the casern, she could see her husband in one of the open windows. Gullace was there with her 14-year-old son, Umberto, to deliver a food and clothing parcel to her husband.

GAP partisans had called for a major demonstration to protest the roundup at the casern that day. Hundreds showed up, mostly women, including Carla Capponi, back from her exile at Centocelle. Gullace found herself in the middle of the protesters. The Gappisti protesters threw leaflets into the air calling for action against the German occupiers. They were addressed to the women of Rome. Defending the barracks was the 10th Company of the 3rd Battalion of the SS Police Regiment Bozen (*Polizeiregiment Bozen*).

Intent on delivering her parcel, Gullace broke through the German police cordon, and again and again tried to throw it to her husband. A German police corporal mistook her actions and grabbed her. He shot her in the throat and Gullace died with her husband watching from his window. They allowed him to accompany his wife's body in the ambulance as she was taken away.[*]

Capponi, enraged at the murder, pulled out the brand-new Beretta 9mm pistol she had lifted from a Fascist soldier's holster on a tram. She was not fast enough to kill the soldier that murdered Gullace – it was another partisan, Guglielmo Blasi, who shot the corporal, wounded two militiamen, and fled.

But Capponi was close to Blasi when he fired, so it was she who was arrested and dragged into the casern by two Italian Fascist policemen. Marisa Musu, Capponi's partisan friend, quickly grabbed Capponi's pistol from her pocket and instead slipped into its place a fake membership card of the Fascist group Honor and Struggle (*Gruppi d'Onore e Combattimento*). It was found on Capponi in the interrogation room at the casern. Capponi explained to the Italian police lieutenant that the Honor and Struggle group was there to control the protesters in case they got unruly. He believed her and perhaps also fell victim to her flirting when she told him he could return the card in person later. She was released.

[*] This incident was dramatized in Roberto Rossellini's 1945 film masterpiece *Open City*.

Marisa Musu was a 19-year-old chemical student at the university. She was born in Mulhouse, France and so spoke German and French. She was part of a special GAP Central female squad that included Carla Capponi, Lucia Ottobrini, and Maria Teresa Regard. Her quick-thinking actions undoubtedly saved Capponi's life that day.

Partisans retaliated for Teresa Gullace's murder by targeting a Fascist procession in Via Tomacelli, near Augustus' Altar of Peace (*Ara Pacis*) in central Rome a week later, on March 10. Built in 9 BC, the altar had been excavated and reconstructed by Mussolini in 1938. That morning, 200 Fascists gathered in front of the National Association of Invalids and the Maimed of War (*Associazione Nazionale Mutilati e Invalidi di Guerra*) at the Piazza Adriana next to the Castel Sant'Angelo on the Tiber River. They were to celebrate a hero of the Risorgimento (the unification of Italy), Giuseppe Mazzini, head of the 1849 Roman Republic, by marching to the the Vittorio Emanuele II Monument. The Fascists were from the same Honor and Combat Group of the GNR, the new blackshirts, whose fake membership card Capponi had used to get out of trouble after Gullace's murder.

Their route took them through Piazza Cavour, past the ornate high court of Italian Appeals, down Via Vittoria Colonna, across the Tiber over the Ponte Cavour and onto Via Tomacelli, near the restored Ara Pacis. While they marched they chanted a Fascist song: "To arms, we're fascists, terror of the communists" (*All'armi, siamo fascisti, terror dei comunisti*).

Four partisans attacked the procession where Via Tomacelli passes the tiny Piazza di Monte d'Oro and the Largo degli Schiavoni near Caesar Augustus' 1st-century round tomb, a fairly open spot with few bystanders. The four threw hand grenades killing three Fascists and wounding several others. The partisans escaped unharmed although a reward of a half million lire was offered for information. General Mälzer subsequently banned public marches as well as street demonstrations and restricted Fascist gatherings to indoor venues.

Food shortages continued to plague the city. Though it was now March, people were still waiting to buy their November rations. Shortages in Rome had become so acute that the city had only a two-to-three-day supply of food. People collapsed and died in the streets. The Germans rescinded their prohibition on importing food into the city, but it was only available on the black-market.

Vatican soup kitchens were now feeding 100,000 people a day. Those who had money paid one lira per meal. Rome's middle class was hardest hit; they were neither poor enough for Vatican charity, nor rich enough for the black-market. The Vatican increased its food convoys. To avoid being bombed the tops of Vatican vehicles were painted in the papal colors of white and gold. The paint job failed to protect the convoys, however, since the markings were impossible to see from an aircraft.

Tittmann recorded nine Vatican food convoy attacks between February 15 and April 29, 1944 when an Allied air attack struck a 52-vehicle Vatican convoy bringing food into the city (see Appendix B). Tittmann questioned whether the Vatican, by bringing food convoys to feed Rome, was breaking the Allied blockade. If the food were confiscated and used by the Germans, the Vatican could be accused of a non-neutral act. But in the end Tittmann acknowledged the humanitarian need was too great, so he didn't interfere.

The Vatican sought alternative ways to bring in food; for example it suggested that ships flying the papal flag could sail from Genoa to Ostia and then barge the food up the Tiber. The Germans would not agree to the plan unless 70 percent of any food brought by ship would be turned over to the Wehrmacht and the idea was soon abandoned. The Argentine and Spanish governments offered to send flour to starving Rome if a way could be found to bring it into the city. The Germans had confiscated most of the trucks in Rome to transport supplies to their troops at Cassino and Anzio so the Swiss suggested parachute drops into the Vatican Gardens. Sir D'Arcy feared that mobs would attack the diplomatic corps and even the Pope to get inside the Vatican to the air-dropped food.

The German solution to the food problem was to reduce the number of mouths to feed. This meant removing all refugees, students, and the unemployed. According to the Rome daily police blotters, the Germans carried out more roundups and deportations, sending refugees from the south to northern Italian cities in special trains.

Food was now so expensive that Simpson and Furman agitated for an increase in the daily allowance per escapee. Derry, as head of the Escape Line, increased the allowance from 120 lire to 133 lire per day. With

American troops at Anzio, US Army "C" rations were showing up in the black-market in Rome. According to the author Romagnoli:

> Unbelievable were the contents of the brick-shaped, carefully wax-papered cardboard boxes … tin can of soup, one of vegetables, one of meat, a small tin of butter, crackers, a chocolate bar, toothpicks, a pack of ten cigarettes and waterproof matches … Around these goodies alone we could have built a Christmas package … the ultimate luxury? Toilet paper had been for years, unobtainable on our markets; we imagined that only royalty and cardinals were privileged to its use.[10]

And still the ex-POWs came to Saint Peter's. On February 28, 1944 young Tittmann wrote that an unidentified British sergeant approached the Vatican gate and was allowed to remain. He was followed by three more servicemen on March 15, 1944. Young Tittmann again noted in his diary that Tech Sgt. B. L. Scalisi, an American, together with a British serviceman, Warrant Officer P. J. Grimmer and another American, S/SSgt. A. P. Brodniak, climbed a telephone pole outside of Vatican City and jumped over the wall. They roamed around the Vatican but were eventually found and locked up at the Santa Marta Tribunale, near the guest house. Scalisi came from Louisiana and was the top gunner of a flying fortress. He had flown 14 missions and shot down two German planes. Brodniak was from New Jersey and was a waist gunner who had flown 13 missions and also shot down a German plane. Both had been shot down over Terni on January 14, 1944 and had hooked up with Grimmer. Remarkably they were allowed to stay.

Their good luck may have had something to do with a tragedy that struck the Escape Line organization the same day. Sub-Lieutenant Elliott, who had been helping with the Escape Line paperwork, died during the early morning hours of that same day, March 15, 1944. Elliott had become disoriented during one of his repeated nightmares about his escape from his sinking submarine. Sometime during the night, he rushed from his bed at the Vatican Gendarme Barracks, jumped through a window, and fell three floors to his death.

It is now time to again take up the story of Lt. John Furman, who had been held in the Regina Coeli Prison since early January. In prison Furman had befriended Giorgio Giorgi, an Italian Air Force pilot who had been arrested for partisan activities. Giorgi was able to send notes out of the prison and through him Furman wrote to Major Derry several times. On January 25, Derry received a note from Furman. Written in haste, the note was passed in a book borrowed from Giorgio. Furman wrote:

> I have just had notice that all British prisoners are leaving here [Regina Coeli] within the next 2 or 3 hours … I know you will see my wife and Diana [daughter] when you get back. Would you also ask Bill [Simpson] to remember me to all our friends here who have been so kind to me. And would you greet our Irish golfing friend [O'Flaherty] for me and also John [May] who made me such an excellent dish of porridge [to cure his diarrhea] not so many days ago …[11]

As the prisoners were marched into the prison courtyard for their journey northward, the German officer in charge assured them they would be shot if they attempted to escape. Furman carried 3,000 lire with him, again concealed in a loaf of bread. This money would pay dividends later. Passenger trains were not frequently running out of Rome, so the Germans loaded the men onto a modern bus with comfortable seats and they were driven to the nearest working railhead, 90 miles away. German soldiers on their way home on leave from the Italian front stood guard.

The first stop was the Passo Corese POW Camp #54, near Fara in Sabina, 30 miles northeast of Rome. There, the bus waited to pick up two British officers captured on the Anzio beachhead. The ex-escapees rigorously questioned the two new arrivals about the progress of the war. The new officers were amazed by the civilian dress of their comrades from Rome and were reluctantly convinced they were Allied servicemen.

The bus drove through the towns of Rieti and Terni north of Rome, the bad roads, pockmarked from frequent bombings, reducing their speed to five miles per hour. Then the bus broke down and had to be towed by two oxen. Once in a village, the POW-filled bus was pushed into a large garage and locked in for the night. In the morning the men were herded into an open truck that took them through Spoleto, depositing them outside the little village of Pissignano, 66 miles almost due north of Rome, where the Germans had established a POW transit camp, Campello sul Cliunno Camp # 77.

Most of the camp's prisoners were from an American infantry battalion. Furman described them as raw soldiers. They had been sent into the line to launch an attack to cross the Rapido River on the Cassino front. It was their first and only taste of combat and reportedly they were captured without firing a shot.

After the expected interrogation, the Rome POWs were separated by rank. The enlisted men, Sergeant Major Billet, Sergeant Knox-Davies, and Privates Hands and Churchill, were sent to live in a tent, while the officers went to a long wooden building. It was strange for the Rome men to be separated now they had bonded through their common experiences.

Furman met a friend from his days at the Chieti camp, Lt. J. S. Johnny Johnstone, of the Royal Engineers. He was a six-footer with blonde hair and blue eyes. Furman, Tug Wilson, Pip Gardner, and Johnstone formed a syndicate to plan their escape from the camp but it proved impossible.

They were marched to the train station on January 30, where they were given bread and a small tin of meat and told that these rations had to last until they reached Germany. The POWs had to surrender their boots and shoes so they would be barefooted if they did escape. The men paired themselves into escape teams: Furman and Johnstone; Wilson and Gardner; Jack Selikman and Marcus Kane-Berman; Sandy Stewart with an unidentified South African; Sergeant Major Billet with Sergeant Knox-Davies; and finally, Privates Hands and Churchill. They had two knives among them; Johnstone had a superb jack-knife, and Hands an old, and very dull knife.

They may not have known it at the time, but Furman and the others were lucky to be moved that day. A few days earlier, on January 28, 1944, more than 1,100 British, South African, and American POWs were being moved by rail from the Passo Corese POW Camp #54. The train's route took it over a railway bridge at Allerona in Umbria, outside Orvieto, 65 miles north of Rome. As it was crossing the bridge, the American 320th Bomber Group attacked and shot up the train. It stopped in mid-bridge. The German guards fled, leaving the POWs locked in their boxcars. The Bomber Group, unaware that Allied soldiers were on the train, continued to drop bombs and caused several of the cars to tumble into the river, killing about half of the men.[12]

Furman's train consisted of standard European boxcars and, every two or three wagons, one was topped by a turret. The cars were furnished with two bales of straw for bedding and there were two petrol cans for latrines. Each wagon had small ventilation holes, most of which were blocked. Without some type of a tool, escape was impossible and the guards were ready to fire at any POW who tried.

While boarding his train, Furman noticed a rusty iron bar lying alongside the tracks. He was still struggling with diarrhea and said he needed to relieve himself. The guards acquiesced. He squatted near the iron bar, threw his jacket over it and completed his task, returning to the boxcar with the bar barely concealed in his coat.

In order to escape, two things were necessary: the train must be in motion so that its noise would cover any sounds, and it must be nighttime so the guards could not see to shoot. The first night the train remained on the siding; the second night the train started up, moving north. Furman, with his iron bar and Johnson's knife, and with the help of Sergeant Major Billet, carved a hole in the car's wall, big enough for a man to crawl through. During one stop they were almost caught: a guard saw knife scratch marks on the wall and demanded the knife. They gave him private Hands' dull knife and assured the guard there would be no more escape attempts.

But the hole was almost finished. It opened out between the railway cars so the men, once outside the car, could ride the train buffers while waiting for the train to slow down; then they would jump. Furman, Johnstone, Selikman, and Kane-Berman were to be in the first group of four to escape through the hole. Billet, Knox-Davies, Hands and Churchill were to follow. By being in groups of four, two could jump from either side of the train at the same time.

At last, the train slowed down to about 25 miles per hour and the men hanging between the boxcars jumped. They were shot at but, after a bit, the train picked up speed and it went on. Furman heard someone in the brush and thought it might have been Billet, but he was not able to find him. He ran into Johnstone back along the track and some Italian railway workers pointed out a path. The two escapees took off and several hours later found themselves miles from the train line, with bare feet. Wilson, Gardner, and Stewart were not able to jump and they spent the rest of the war in Germany. The fate of the other men is not known.

Furman and Johnstone had been carried far north. They were in fact close to the Swiss frontier. Their clothes were lightweight, wrong for the end of February, and they were hungry, thirsty, and tired. At a farmhouse they were given breakfast. They bartered an English blanket for shoes and walked to the village where they found warmer, if ill-fitting, clothes for the raggedly dressed Johnstone. A local anti-fascist barber improved their appearance considerably with a shave and wash up.

There were three choices: go to Switzerland, go to Yugoslavia, or return to Rome. Furman, now speaking good Italian, wanted to return to the city. With his 3,000 lire he saw to their needs, and purchased supplies and, for transportation, two ancient but serviceable bicycles.

They moved south over the next two weeks, avoiding Germans, blackshirted Fascists, large cities, roadblocks, and guarded bridges. In one place, they had their bicycles repaired and were given a *Touring Club Italiano* guide book for central Italy, complete with maps and descriptions. They bicycled through Modena, avoided Bologna, but took the Bologna–Pistoia road.

Outside of Pistoia, they had to stop to repair the broken forks on Johnstone's bike. Avoiding Florence and traveling through the countryside, they arrived at Siena. Then they took the road to Saint Quirico d'Orcia and on to Viterbo and shortly thereafter arrived in the Rome suburb of Monte Mario. There, a friendly farmer told them that they could take the tram directly into Rome as the tram was not regularly searched.

After 400 miles, they were almost there. Knowing that bicycles were forbidden in the city, they gave them to a local priest at Monte Mario. They hopped on the tram and half an hour later, they were back in Saint Peter's Square. A message was sent to Monsignor O'Flaherty and he and Furman were reunited. Furman's memoirs record the tremendous welcome he received. O'Flaherty said: "In the name of God, it's good to see you back, John. You're paler and thinner, but you're all in one piece. This is surely a happy day for all of us."[13] It was February 14, 1944; Furman had been off the streets of Rome for five weeks.

The Monsignor led Furman and Johnstone to an apartment building on Via dei Penitenzieri, just steps from the Vatican white demarcation line where two Irish priests, Fathers Claffey and Tracy, took care of them. They luxuriated with hot baths and a good lunch. Later, O'Flaherty returned with one of his suits for Johnstone. Then they re-entered Saint Peter's Square to meet Simpson and Lucidi. Johnstone was astonished to see Simpson elegantly attired and not the scruffy lieutenant he had known in the Chieti prison camp. Lucidi took charge of Johnstone and they left. Shortly thereafter, Simpson and Furman left. They would all meet later at the family apartment of the POW supporter Galeazzo Pestalozza.

Over the next few days, false documents were prepared for the two new arrivals, and Simpson brought Furman up to speed. He said that Derry was now holed up at Sir D'Arcy's apartment inside the Vatican. John May had arranged that all messages and reports were to be exchanged in the Swiss Guard Room. Simpson acknowledged that this made sending messages more difficult but not impossible.

It didn't take long for Furman to be back working full time with the Escape Line. There was much to do. Complicating things was the fact that Fascists were now enthusiastically rounding up all able-bodied men for labor details on the fortifications south of Rome. As a sign of the times, captured American cigarettes from Anzio were everywhere.

Furman was anxious to see his old friend Derry but the best O'Flaherty could do was to let Furman wave at Derry across the courtyards from his room. Eventually Princess Ninì Pallavicini, now living at the German College, smuggled Furman into Sir D'Arcy's apartment. The princess was going to a party at the Santa Marta Hospice. Placing Furman in the middle of the partygoers, she walked him past the Swiss Guards and into Vatican territory.

After a few days, Furman left the Pestalozza apartment and was taken to an apartment on Via Buonarroti, not far from Santa Maria Maggiore. There he stayed with the Giuliani family, headed by 60-year-old Romeo, his wife, three daughters (Ione, Maria, and Lucia), and two sons, one of whom was away and the other, Gino, although only 18 years old, was eager to help and soon became Furman's assistant.

Without the two large rented apartments on Via Firenze and Via Cellini, the work of Furman and Simpson in distributing money and finding billets for escapees became increasingly more difficult. Gino

Giuliani, Furman's new assistant, and his friend Memo spread out in the city to find billets. Meanwhile, ex-POWs continued to flood into Rome to be taken under the wing of the Escape Line.

In an attempt to break out from the Anzio beachhead Allied bombing intensified. Nowhere from Rome to Anzio was safe from Allied bombs. Castel Gandolfo, the summer residence of the Pope, was bombed at least ten times by Allied aircraft. The first attack, on February 1, 1944, killed 17 nuns and injured many others. The Apostolic Delegation to the United States of America protested the bombing in a letter dated February 2, underscoring that those sheltering in the Papal Gardens included the entire civilian populations of the towns of Albano and Castel Gandolfo, more than 6,000 refugees, men, women, and children. A third raid, on February 10, killed more than 400 people within the castle grounds. The Pope's order that the Castel be opened to refugees allowed them to stay in the Hall of the Swiss Guards, the Throne Room, the Napoleon Room, and even his private apartments.

Italian outrage at the bombings failed to consider that the Wehrmacht had used the main square in front of the Pope's palazzo as cover for its repair shops. The Germans assumed the square would be safe from Allied attack. Other bombing raids took place on February 13, four times in April, and twice in May.

The Vatican had another problem at Castel Gandolfo. A young lieutenant of the Grenadier Guards, Lt. Paul Freyberg, had been captured at Anzio on February 7. He was the son of General Bernard Freyberg, VC, and Commander of the New Zealand Corps. It had been General Freyberg who had repeatedly requested that the Abbey at Monte Cassino be bombed, believing it to be a key German position on the Gustav Line. On February 9, Lt. Freyberg escaped and was helped by some friendly Italian farmers, including one who had lived in America and spoke English. In the chaos after the second bombing, he was given civilian clothes and shown the way to the castle. He arrived several days later and, seeing the sign designating the castle as extraterritorial, he climbed over the wall. Although he should not have been allowed to stay, because he was the son of General Freyberg, he was permitted. It was clear that he could not remain there for long.

After talking over the Freyberg problem with Monsignor O'Flaherty and Sir D'Arcy, Vatican officials decided to bring the lieutenant inside the Vatican. An exception was being made for this son of a senior officer because his recapture would have been a German propaganda coup. He was smuggled inside the weekly supply vehicle that ran between the Vatican and the castle. On its way into Rome the vehicle was stopped but, hidden in a false compartment and covered by produce, the lieutenant made it safely to the Vatican. It was his 21st birthday and Derry threw a party for him at the British Legation with the help of John May, who did wonders organizing refreshments.

As soon as was feasible, the remaining Castel Gandolfo refugees were moved to Vatican institutions throughout the city. Young Tittmann wrote in his diary that 40 cows were moved from Castel Gandolfo as well, and were bedded down in a storage area under the Vatican Museum.

The Allies finally bombed the ancient Abbey of Monte Cassino on February 15, 1944, destroying it. Its abbot, Gregorio Diamare, was rescued by German troops after the bombing and he was sent to Rome. Baron Ernst von Weizsäcker, German Ambassador to the Holy See, intercepted Abbot Diamare as he was being brought into the city, on February 18. Exhausted, dirty, hungry, and thirsty, the elderly abbot was forced to sign a statement saying that the abbey was not being used as a German observation post and was compelled to go on the radio to be interviewed. The abbot is supposed to have said to a fellow Benedictine monk, "The Lord willed it, and it was a good thing for the salvation of Rome."[14] Later an official of the Holy See later admitted, "It is revealing no secret to say that the Vatican exploited the disaster of Monte Cassino to obtain respect for Rome from the belligerents."[15]

The destruction of Monte Cassino had stimulated an anti-Allies atmosphere and the Allied Vatican diplomats were from this point criticized openly by Vatican officials. Despite the abbey's destruction the German front remained unbroken.

———

Police raids were constant and struck to the heart of the Escape Line. In early February, Simpson was meeting one night with a Polish saboteur (codenamed Raffaello) and Major Fane-Hervey in the Lucidi apartment, when the place was raided. The door resounded with banging fists and the ex-POWs went into play-acting mode. Lucidi pushed the Pole into bed with the housemaid and told Simpson to act like Lucidi's half-witted nephew. Fane-Hervey hid in the back. The Gestapo had come for Lucidi's 18-year-old French stepson, Maurice, whose name had been found on a list given them by a detained University of Rome professor. The Gestapo took the young man to Via Tasso after which Simpson and Fane-Hervey quit the apartment. What happened to the Pole is unknown.

The next day Lucidi went to Via Tasso to secure Maurice's release. This visit attracted the unwanted attention of the Gestapo and, the day after, he too was arrested. François de Vial vouched for father and stepson as being French citizens and they were released. But for now, the Lucidi apartment was off limits to the organization.

For the third or fourth time, Mrs. Chevalier's apartment was raided while another five escapees were in hiding there. Four were British (Martin, Flood, Stokes, and O'Neill) and one a South African soldier (Matthews). One evening, a lame 17-year-old neighbor boy only known as Giuseppe rang her doorbell.* She did not know him but instinctively felt she could trust him. The boy had a senior contact inside the Questura and told her that the police were going to raid her apartment shortly. The five soldiers stuffed personal belongings in their pockets, hugged Mrs. Chevalier and her daughters goodbye, and were out in a flash. They were accompanied by Paul Chevalier who felt it was better to leave with the others.

At the start of curfew, the police came demanding to know who lived there. She replied that only the family lived here and that there was barely room for all of them. The policeman said that he had been informed that many men, including British POWs, had been seen coming and going. She asked, innocently, where she would put them.

The policemen replied that someone must have passed false information and inquired if Mrs. Chevalier had any idea who might do such a thing? She thought for a second and then mentioned that her Fascist neighbors had lately been getting a lot of visitors. Needless

---

* Tompkins (p. 283) also describes being helped by a young man with a limp named Eugenio who was extremely "conscientious and willing to work." This causes the author to wonder if Giuseppe and Eugenio were the same boy.

to say, she could barely conceal her smiles as the police ransacked her neighbor's apartment for almost an hour.

Major Derry sensed the danger and moved the five soldiers to the home of Mrs. Chevalier's butcher, Giovanni Ceccarelli, on Via Appia Nuova. No more escapees were to be billeted at the undaunted Mrs. Chevalier's apartment.

———

Floyd J. Dumas, of the 45th Infantry Division, was a draftee from New York State, who had seen action in Sicily, Salerno, and Anzio. He had been at Anzio for three weeks, guarding the Mussolini Canal, when he and several others were captured in mid-February. First they were taken to Cisterna, where they were required to bury German dead. Then they were moved to Cinecittà, used as a German POW camp. During Dumas' time there, he was fed a thin soup made of greens, sometimes with horsemeat. Every fifth man was given a loaf of black bread to be divided among five men. Unsurprisingly diarrhea was rampant.

The prisoners were housed in the huge Sound Stage Five at Cinecittà. After a week or ten days, two prisoners had made a hole in the fence. Undetected, they escaped during a daylight American bombing raid. Dumas and an unidentified British soldier also decided to take a chance and slipped out of the hole, covered by other POWs. They were still inside the camp but hid out in a scenery storage room. When a heavy rain started that evening, the pair breached the outer fence while the perimeter guards took shelter.

The soldiers found refuge with an Italian couple at an isolated farmhouse. After they were fed and dried out they moved to a second, but abandoned, farmhouse some distance away. The Englishman wanted to return to British lines and so they parted. Shortly after, Dumas heard a shot and believed that the other soldier had been recaptured or worse. Dumas, still in uniform and needing food, decided to go to try his luck in a nearby Rome suburb. Friendly Italians gave him civilian clothes and allowed him to remain. They also told him about another escaped Allied POW, a British Army Indian soldier, who spoke both English and Italian. Dumas joined him and they continued to be fed by their Italian neighbors. After about a month, by now the middle of March, the Germans raided the suburb but they escaped detection. Dumas had heard that the Vatican often helped escaped Allied soldiers find billets in Rome and the Indian soldier agreed to take him there. As previously explained the Escape Line gave Indian soldiers money but let them find their own accommodation.

At the Vatican, Dumas was told to return in three days and look for a man wearing a black raincoat and holding a newspaper. At the appointed hour, he approached his contact. It was one of Monsignor O'Flaherty's priests. After a trip of about an hour on public transportation, Dumas was admitted to a convent where he and the priest were fed. The next day he was introduced to a Scottish ex-POW with whom he was to stay.

The Scotsman was Bill Robb from Aberdeen. He had been captured at Tobruk but escaped from a train on the way to Germany. Leaping from the moving train, he had broken his leg. After two weeks at the convent, they were moved to Via Vetulonia where they hid in a fifth-floor apartment under the care of Signora Capisoni, a woman whose Italian officer husband was missing in action. Since money was tight, the soldiers went to the Swiss Embassy to request cash. At the embassy they met with Captain Leonardo Tripp who gave them some money on their signatures. Dumas returned to the embassy three more times and obtained the lire equivalent of $108.12.

After a couple of weeks, two more ex-POWs were brought to the apartment. One was Bob Schultz from Pennsylvania and the other an unidentified South African. Schultz was subsequently caught in a German roundup on the streets of Rome and sent to Germany. Taking a chance of being recaptured, Robb and Dumas often went to the countryside to purchase food at the suburb of Tor Sapienza. On one occasion the pair was stopped on a trolley but in the confusion avoided recapture. As the German crackdowns increased, the pair decided to move to the countryside. There they lived with a family, sleeping in an outbuilding and only occasionally going into Rome.[*]

---

[*] Eventually Robb and Dumas fell in with a group of six Italian partisans who operated out of a cave. The two soldiers joined in their attacks on isolated groups of German soldiers. At liberation, the pair marched into the city with soldiers of the US 88th Infantry Division. They were then sent to Naples and Dumas returned to the States.

Pope Pius XII was to celebrate his fifth year on the Throne of Saint Peter and he would commemorate it with a speech, on March 12, in Saint Peter's Square. He requested that the Allies not bomb the city that day. Since the request had been made with little advance notice, Sir D'Arcy may have sent the request via the SIM-controlled, secret Centro X radio, now inside the Vatican. As an outside event, security for the Pope's speech was tight – 100 Swiss Guards blocked the steps and the entrance to the Basilica. There were more than 200,000 people in Saint Peter's Square, and the skies over Rome remained clear all day. Mother Mary noted in her diary that there were no German soldiers in the crowd for they had been forbidden to attend.

After several weeks in hiding, Major General Gambier-Parry was quite bored. Monsignor O'Flaherty asked Brother Robert to bring him to the Vatican for the papal event. The Pope began speaking promptly at 15:30. After platitudes, he made a direct appeal to both sides to save Rome from ruin. As he gave the papal blessing, red banners appeared near the central obelisk in the square and partisans in the crowd threw leaflets in the air. There were sustained shouts of "Down with the Germans" and "Long live peace." Mounted Roman police rode into the crowd to disperse the celebrants and other police fired shots in the air.

Major General Gambier-Parry saw all this from the Vatican's *Terrazzo delle Dame*, one of the outside terraces on top of the Bernini Colonnade reserved for diplomats to the Holy See. There he had joined Monsignor O'Flaherty and stood with the Roman nobility and aristocracy to watch the Pope. Neither Sir D'Arcy nor Tittmann attended, fearing their presence would call attention to themselves. The German diplomats were there in force, however. Major General Gambier-Parry was introduced to Prince von Bismarck and Baron von Weizsäcker as an Irish doctor. He so impressed the prince, who was again visiting from Berlin, that he was invited to call on him.

Derry was understandably annoyed that O'Flaherty had exposed himself and General Gambier-Parry to possible arrest, so he sought a place for the general where he would be safe and not so confined. He therefore arranged for the general to become a patient at the hospital of the Little Sisters of Mary, nicknamed the Blue Nuns, in the quiet Roman neighborhood of San Stefano Rotondo on the Caelian Hill.

Until the liberation of Rome, General Gambier-Parry safely strolled its gardens.

———

Brother Robert was now taking care of 60 ex-POWs, giving them food, clothing, and money. On March 16, 1944, he made a trip out of the city on Via Aurelia; his destination was a small landholding next to the grounds of the Good Shepherd Convent, about a half hour's walk from the Vatican. He was there to pick up four escaped POWs and their two Italian guides. The Good Shepherd Convent was the mother house of the Sisters of our Lady of Charity of the Good Shepherd (*Suore di Nostra Signora della Carita del Buon Pastore*).

He was well known to the nuns of the convent and so he rang the bell at 07:30 and asked to cut across the convent's back garden to collect four escaped POWs who were hiding in a chicken coop next door.

Because it was a cool morning, the convent Reverend Mother wanted to offer the men something warm to drink. She sent a nun to see if they would accept, but by then all seven men were inside the coop, including one who was unwell, and she could not get their attention. When the nun retraced her steps to the convent, she saw a German soldier on the other side of the fence, then more soldiers; and she heard a pistol shot as the Germans surrounded the coop.

Brother Robert and the others were marched out, put into a truck, and taken to Via Tasso Prison. The sick soldier could barely keep up. Three of the arrested soldiers were Americans (Ashton, Cain, and Schoenke), and the British soldier was C. W. Gamble of the Royal Fusiliers. The four POWs were taken to the Regina Coeli Prison and later sent to Germany.[16] Brother Robert and the two Italians, Andrea Casadei and Vittorio Fantini, were extensively questioned.

Knowing they were in deep trouble, the captives expected to be tortured with little chance of being released. Repeatedly, Brother Robert said that he had received a request from a village priest to guide two people to an address in Rome and had agreed to render this small service to a brother in the Church. He said that he was well known to the German staff at the military hospital and asked to send a message to his superior and to the hospital commander. The hospital commander asked that he be returned to them as soon as possible. He was released after one day in prison, and warned that he was likely to be rearrested for further questioning.

It was time for Brother Robert to disappear, and thus, the Escape Line lost one of its most valuable members. Brother Robert recorded his story in a third person voice, writing that when he was arrested:

> He was carrying a small notebook with very thin paper on which were written many names of helpers with their addresses and phone numbers, including Mrs. Almagiá. While the truck in which they were conveyed headed to Gestapo Headquarters, Brother [Robert] was able to swallow the pages of the notebook. Mrs. Almagiá has since always made a joke of this sending him every Christmas a notebook with the words, "Lest we forget – hope you will never have to eat this one!"[17]

Meanwhile, the Marchesa Ripa di Meana, cousin of Colonel Giuseppe Montezemolo (the FMCR Resistance leader), had visited Dollmann on March 19 to plead for the colonel's release. She had known Dollmann even before the war as he had lived in her family's pension while studying in Rome. Dollmann said that the matter was out of his hands and there was nothing he could do. The same day, she also met with the Pope and pleaded for his intercession, also to no avail. Her vain efforts were to have tragic results for Montezemolo.

Italians were war-weary and, pointedly, German-weary. Nor were they too happy with the Allies. The Rome populace no longer wondered when the Allies were going to break out of Anzio and liberate them. A new militant spirit of resistance to the Germans in Italy was rising. In northern Italy, general strikes rippled throughout the industrial regions, especially Turin and Milan. Strikers wanted fewer work hours and increased rations for their families. These were the first labor strikes in German-occupied Europe. It was not a good sign for the German occupiers.

18

The Order Has Been Carried Out

March 23, 1944, dawned clear and bright with the azure blue sky that countless artists visiting Rome have tried to capture. It was an ideal day to celebrate the 25th anniversary of the founding of Fascism, March 23, 1919. The weather was also perfect for another Allied bombing raid on the city, but the bombs didn't fall that day. Instead it was the day of Rome's most spectacular partisan attack.

That morning, American OSS agent Tompkins learned that his key agent, Maurizio Giglio, was being held in the Fascist Banda Koch prison within their Pension Oltremare headquarters. Tompkins decided to blow up the pension with 80 pounds of dynamite and free Giglio. He was set to act on March 25, but, as it turned out, he was to be two days late.

The Badoglio government in Allied-occupied Italy had urged Giorgio Amendola, the Communist Party leader, to launch a major attack against the German occupying forces. Later, partisan Mario Fiorentini explained the rationale for the attack:

Among the objectives that we wanted to accomplish was that the Wehrmacht was not invincible; we wanted to show them that they were not the rulers of Rome, that there was a hostile population. We had to attack their lines of communication, their movements, the transit of their vehicles, their parked trucks, their commanders, and in particular to show that they were not safe in the city; we wanted to prove that in fact it was an open city.[1]

The partisans' first idea was to attack the Via Tasso Prison and release its prisoners. It would have required three GAP squads to arrive at the prison from different locations at the same time. In the end the partisans felt that the prison was too well guarded.

Fiorentini then suggested an ambush of the fully armed SS police company that every afternoon like clockwork marched stridently from one end of the city to the other. This parade by the German occupiers managed to infuriate half the city and terrify the other half while reminding her citizens that Rome was indeed an occupied city.

The attack would involve hiding a 12-kilo bomb in a rubbish cart along the route of march. A partisan disguised as a street sweeper pushing his cart, ubiquitous throughout Rome, always seen but never noticed, would detonate the bomb. The logistics included finding a cart and uniform, making the bomb, loading it into the cart, then pushing it inconspicuously halfway across Rome. More than 40 German soldiers would be killed and 335 Romans would die because of this attack and the widely condemned German reprisals.

The target was the men of the SS Police Regiment Bozen. This regiment was made up of Italian citizens from South Tyrol, formerly part of the Austro-Hungarian empire, which had become a part of Italy post-World War I. After the armistice Hitler had occupied the largely German-speaking region in September of 1943. The men were mostly farmers from near the town of Bozen and were World War I veterans. They were called *optors* because they had opted to become German citizens and had joined the German police regiment.

The Bozen men had come to Rome after Kappler requested additional SS police units. The Germans sent the 3rd Battalion of the regiment to Rome on February 15, 1944. It was a 500-man battalion, divided into three companies. The 9th Company was deployed to the south of the city; the 10th Company was spread across Rome; and the 11th Company was in training. SS-General Karl F. Wolff commanded the police force; but, when it reached Rome, it was assigned to Kappler. In reality, it was under the direct supervision of Stadtkommandant General Mälzer.

The Bozen men had the mission to enforce law and order in the city. They were equipped with light infantry weapons, including machine pistols and hand grenades. In addition to small arms training, they were taught crowd control and other police duties. The unit's German officers despised their men because they considered them rustics from the rural countryside of South Tyrol. According to their officers, they lacked the proper martial spirit and so they subjected the men to a harsh training regimen.

The target of the partisan bombing was the 11th Company. A contingent of 160, they were German-speaking, mostly middle-aged men, optors who chose to serve. The company was barracked at the Ministry of the Interior, the Palazzo Viminale near the Opera. Every morning it would march to a shooting range near Ponte Milvio, to the north of the city across the Tiber. After the day's training, at the same time every day, the company would march through Rome singing. One of its songs was a popular German Army World War I marching version of "*Hupf, Mein Mädel*" (Skip, My Lassie). Originally a dance song, the new German version was strident and intimidating, especially when sung by a fully armed company of police. Ironically, this was an American Tin Pan Alley tune composed in 1908 and originally called "Yip I Addy I Ay" which bears a slight resemblance to "Take Me Out to the Ballgame." It was said that the men themselves resented being forced to sing while marching through the city.

The usual route back from the training grounds took them across the Ponte Milvio, down Via Flaminia, south on Via del Babuino to the Piazza di Spagna, next on Via Due Macelli which becomes Via del Traforo, and finally, around 14:00, they turned left on Via Rasella.

This then was the time and place chosen for the attack planned by the Gappisti of the Central Rome Patriotic Action Group. True comrades, these partisans were bound together and Carla Capponi later wrote of the stress of this comradery:

We were a very close group, understand, tight knit. They put you together, you do actions together, you study together, have emotions together, there's living matter in it, you are involved with all your feeling. There is fear, there is courage, there is danger, there is death before you, you see it, and you yourself give it. This wears you out and you need a human relationship. The relationship with my family, for me closed completely.[2]

GERMAN AND PARTISAN ROUTES TO VIA RASELLA, MARCH 23, 1944

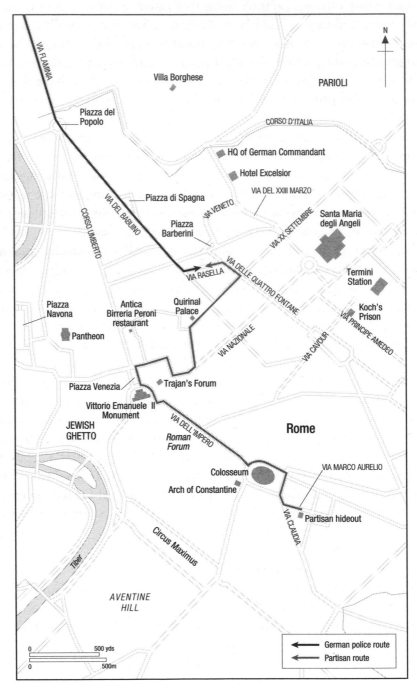

Getting the explosives and making the bomb were the keys to the operation. Capponi obtained 12 kilos of explosives from an FMCR Italian Army officer. She took them to a cellar *santabarbara* in a small apartment building in Via Marco Aurelio, a five-minute walk south of the Colosseum in a quiet neighborhood where GAP member Duilio Grigioni was the *portiere*. An older man, he had participated in clashes with Fascist blackshirts even before Mussolini's 1922 March on Rome. The cellar also provided a refuge where the young Gappisti often spent the night.

Giulio Cortini, a university-trained chemist and self-taught bomb maker, supervised packing the bomb materials. He was an assistant in the physics department of the University of Rome. It was a difficult and dangerous job, made more so because he had to do it in a dark, damp basement with limited lighting. His wife, Laura Garrone-Cortini, a literature student at the university, helped him prepare the explosives and fuses.

Carla Capponi and Carlo Salinari, the GAP commander and an assistant professor of literature at the University of Rome, staked out the target area and the route the Germans used. They were assisted by Franco Calamandrei, the GAP vice commander who had a law degree from the University of Rome, Fiorentini, who had had the idea for the bombing, and medical student Rosario Bentivegna. Salinari chose Via Rasella as the best place for the attack. Via Rasella was a quiet, two-block-long street intersected a third of the way up the hill as it climbed from Via del Traforo to Via Quattro Fontane to the 16th-century Palazzo Barberini. Not a major thoroughfare, it was an ideal location for the attack as the Bozen Company used it to march in formation back to their barracks.

Who should have the honor of lighting the fuse? Salinari suggested Guglielmo Blasi, but Capponi objected believing that Blasi would be too hesitant. She suggested Bentivegna and Salinari agreed. Because Fiorentini's uncle lived nearby, neither he nor his longtime girlfriend, Lucia Ottobrini, a 20-year-old employee at the Treasury Ministry, could play a part in the attack for fear of being recognized.

Raoul Falcioni, a taxi driver and the most audacious member of GAP, hunted for and found a garbage cart parked in front of the Colosseum. During the night of March 22, he took it to the *santabarbara*. Blasi stole a street sweeper uniform for Bentivegna to wear. All was ready to go.

City authorities, fearing disruptive demonstrations for the 25th Anniversary of Fascism, decided to curtail celebrations. That morning there had been a Fascist church service at 09:00 in Santa Maria in Via (Saint Mary on the Way) located one block east from Via Corso. It was easy walking distance from Piazza Colonna and the Rome Fascist headquarters in Palazzo Wedekind. A larger planned outdoor celebration was moved indoors to the Chamber of Corporations on Via Veneto after outside demonstrations were forbidden following the partisan attack on March 10, near Augustus' Altar of Peace. It was felt that an elaborate display of Fascist pomp and ceremony while Rome was starving was inappropriate.

The Chamber of Corporations was an apt choice. Mussolini did not immediately abolish the Italian Chamber of Deputies, analogous to the United States House of Representatives, but had directed his handpicked Fascist Grand Council to select the candidates to be elected. Eventually, elections were eliminated and the deputies were appointed. The name Chamber of Deputies was changed to the Chamber of Corporations, and the deputies titled *Consiglieri* (advisors). They met in a newly constructed Fascist building with a frieze depicting various types of economic activities.

To avoid midday crowds and any possible counter-demonstration, the movement of the SS Police Regiment Bozen back to its barracks was delayed by two hours. The partisans knew nothing of this delay. So before noon, four of the partisans, Capponi, Bentivegna, Cortini, and Garrone-Cortini, ate an early lunch at the 1906 Antica Birreria Peroni restaurant in Via di San Marcello. Wood paneling and frescos decorated the walls, but the partisans would not have noticed the ambiance. Their waiter, a friend, refilled their plates twice with a potato stew, only charging for one serving. Knowing what they were about to do did not blunt their appetites; they were hungry and ate quickly.

The four left the restaurant to pick up the bomb at the *santabarbara*, a half an hour walk away. They hurried down Via dell'Impero, around the Colosseum, up Via Claudia, and then turned left on Via Marco Aurelio to the cellar. Bentivegna donned his dark blue street sweeper uniform, complete with old socks, ruined shoes, and a street sweeper's hat with a black visor. He carried the 12 kilos of explosives up the cellar stairs to the street and placed them in his garbage cart along with another six-kilo bomb, separately fused. The municipal two-wheeled, two-handled trash cart was heavy. The cart had a rectangular metal box divided into two compartments each with a lid. Bentivegna would prop the lid open with a small piece of wood so the fuse would have oxygen to burn. Cortini and Garrone-Cortini stayed behind at the cellar to clean up after the bomb making.

Bentivegna started his solitary trek to Via Rasella, pushing his bomb-laden cart, past the Colosseum, down Via dell'Impero, and into the Piazza Venezia. He was sweating profusely from nerves and exertion. Falcioni, Blasi, and Capponi followed at a safe distance. It was early afternoon. At the Palazzo Venezia, Blasi and Capponi broke off on their way to Via del Tritone. They passed the Trevi Fountain, now devoid of water, its famous statuary protected by wood and sandbags. Bentivegna labored up the steep hill to the abandoned Royal Quirinale Palace followed by Falcioni.

Outside the palace, he was stopped by two actual street sweepers. Who is he, what is he doing in their area, and, what is in the cart? Bentivegna said he was pushing cement. Believing instead that it was black-market prosciutto in the cart, the two men let him pass, but only if he would agree to sell them some of his prosciutto later. Falcioni nervously watched from a distance and breathed easier when he saw Bentivegna move on.

Bentivegna moved up Via del Quirinale. Reaching the intersection with the four fountains, he turned left on Via delle Quattro Fontane. With gravity's help, the cart rolled downhill and he turned it to make a second left onto Via Rasella across from the Palazzo Barberini. One third of the way down the street, he stopped in front of the rundown Palazzo Tittoni at number 156. Fittingly, this was where Mussolini had lived in the 1920s when he was first in Rome. Now the building was semi-abandoned. Bentivegna left his cart in the middle of the street, to force the Bozen column to divide in two as it passed around it. Bentivegna was on time. The column was expected to arrive at 14:00; at least that was when it usually got there.

Once in view, it would take the police column 90 seconds to reach the cart. Bentivegna went over the plan. Calamandrei was on the south side of Via del Boccaccio and when the Germans turned the corner and started up the street, he was to give the signal to Bentivegna to light the fuse by lifting his hat. Then he would cross the road in front of the German company and escape down Via del Boccaccio to Via del

Tritone. Bentivegna would then move to the cart, light his pipe and place it where it would light the fuse. As the column marched closer, he would prop up the lid with the wooden stick. After the fuse was lit, he had 50 seconds – the time it took the fuse to burn – to walk slowly up Via Rasella, turn the corner to the right onto Via Quattro Fontane, and escape. While he waited, he swept the street, betraying by his ineptitude that he was no regular street sweeper.

By this time, Capponi had arrived on the scene with four 45mm Italian Army Brixia mortar shells which had been converted into hand grenades. She had covered them with a raincoat which Bentivegna would put on over his street sweeper's uniform when he got to Via Quattro Fontane after lighting the fuse. She handed the grenades to Fernando Vitagliano, at 18 the youngest member of the GAP. Vitagliano went to the steps on Via Boccaccio leading up to Via dei Giardini.

Capponi stood in front of the *Il Messaggero* newspaper office on the corner of Via del Tritone, and, to avoid suspicion, feigned reading the afternoon edition of the newspaper which had just been posted outside. The lead story that day was about the eruption of Mount Vesuvius near Naples.

Pasquale Balsamo, a 19-year-old student, acted as lookout. Waiting at the Piazza di Spagna and not seeing the Bozens, he made his way to Via Rasella where he joined Vitagliano and Falcioni. The three positioned themselves on Via Boccaccio at the base of the steps leading up to Via dei Giardini where Silvio Serra, another partisan, would join them. After the bomb went off they were to throw the hand grenades into the side of the German column. Then they were to escape up Via Boccaccio. Their route took them up the steps to make a right turn on Via dei Giardini and race down the steps at the end of the road and then turn left into the unfinished tunnel on Via del Traforo, now crammed with bombed-out refugees. The tunnel's interior was like a gypsy encampment into which they could easily disappear.

Salinari, the GAP commander, would direct the attack from the lower Via Traforo which allowed him to shift personnel to support the others. Two more partisans, Marisa Musu, the 19-year-old chemical student who had previously saved Capponi's life, and Ernesto Borghesi, a medical student who was a sergeant in the Italian Military Medical Corps, acted as lookouts and messengers and provided the back up. Another partisan, Francesco Curreli, was across from the *Messaggero* office.

THE VIA RASELLA ATTACK, MARCH 23, 1944

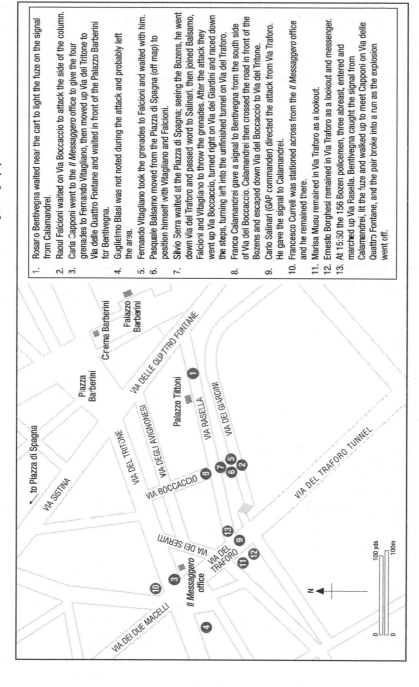

1. Rosario Bentivegna waited near the cart to light the fuze on the signal from Calamandrei.

2. Raoul Falcioni waited on Via Boccaccio to attack the side of the column.

3. Carla Capponi went to the *Il Messaggero* office to give the four grenades to Fernando Vitagliano, then moved up Via del Tritone to Via delle Quattro Fontane and waited in front of the Palazzo Barberini for Bentivegna.

4. Guglielmo Blasi was not noted during the attack and probably left the area.

5. Fernando Vitagliano took the grenades to Falcioni and waited with him.

6. Pasquale Balsamo moved from the Piazza di Spagna (off map) to position himself with Vitagliano and Falcioni.

7. Silvio Serra waited at the Piazza di Spagna; seeing the Bozens, he went down Via del Traforo and passed word to Salinari, then joined Balsamo, Falcioni and Vitagliano to throw the grenades. After the attack they went up Via Boccaccio, turned right on Via dei Giardini and raced down the steps, turning left into the unfinished tunnel on Via del Traforo.

8. Franco Calamandrei gave a signal to Bentivegna from the south side of Via del Boccaccio. Calamandrei then crossed the road in front of the Bozens and escaped down Via del Boccaccio to Via del Tritone.

9. Carlo Salinari (GAP commander) directed the attack from Via Traforo. He gave the signal to Calamandrei.

10. Francesco Curreli was stationed across from the *Il Messaggero* office and he remained there.

11. Marisa Musu remained in Via Traforo as a lookout.

12. Ernesto Borghesi remained in Via Traforo as a lookout and messenger.

13. At 15:50 the 156 Bozen policemen, three abreast, entered and marched up Via Rasella. Bentivegna caught the signal from Calamandrei, lit the fuze and walked up to meet Capponi on Via delle Quattro Fontane, and the pair broke into a run as the explosion went off.

Francesco Curreli was a fascinating individual. Originally a Sardinian shepherd, he had embarked on an odyssey of looking for work which took him to France, Algeria, and Spain, where he fought for the Republican cause in an all-communist regiment until he fled to France ahead of General Franco's troops. He was placed in a French concentration camp and eventually repatriated to Italy where he was immediately arrested. After some time in prison he was released and fought at the side of the Sardinian Grenadiers during the battle for Rome. Then he joined the GAP.

Silvio Serra was the farthest-placed lookout, at the corner of Via Condotti and the Piazza di Spagna. From there he could see the Bozens marching down Via del Babuino. After spotting them, he was to go down to Via del Traforo, pass word to Salinari, and join Pasquale Balsamo, Raoul Falcioni, and Fernando Vitagliano, who would be ready to throw their hand grenades.

Capponi still lingered at the *Messaggero* office – so long that she was accosted by two plainclothes policemen, bodyguards of the paper's editor and director, Bruno Spampanato. They asked why she was hanging around and why she had a raincoat on such a beautiful day. She told them that she was waiting to return her boyfriend's raincoat to him. The bodyguards were making Capponi nervous. With the small Beretta pistol in her purse, she could easily shoot them and escape. She had murdered before, but knew that firing her gun would jeopardize the entire operation.

After a few minutes, she saw what she thought was the signal from one of the lookouts and she slowly walked up Via del Tritone toward Via Quattro Fontane. But she had misread the sign. The Bozens were now more than an hour late and still were not coming! One of the *Messaggero* bodyguards followed her to Via Quattro Fontane, but luckily she saw a friend of her mother's outside the Palazzo Barberini's iron gates. She crossed the road and chatted with her. After her mother's friend left, the bodyguard approached her and asked where her boyfriend was. Thinking fast, Capponi said that he was at the male-only officers' club inside the palazzo which she could not enter. She just had to wait for him to come out. The suspicious bodyguard hung around waiting to see if the boyfriend would exit the palazzo.

The Bozens were now an hour and a half late. What to do? The anxious partisans considered calling off the attack. Twelve of them surrounded Via Rasella and all the routes in or out of the street. Three times Bentivegna thought he had seen the signal and had lit his pipe, but they were false alarms. Finally, at 15:45, Balsamo went to him and whispered that if the SS police regiment didn't show up in the next ten minutes the attack was off.

To complicate things, a delivery truck with building materials turned into Via Rasella. Alarmed, Bentivegna went to the driver and told him to leave. The partisans wanted no civilian casualties. One look at the shabbily dressed Bentivegna with his posh accent and the driver drove on. Bentivegna then sent the Palazzo Tittoni's ancient and nosy *portiere* who had come out to see about the truck back inside.

After an interminable wait, the Bozen column finally entered Via del Traforo. Major Helmuth Dobbrick, the commanding officer, accompanied the formation and had his car pull ahead as they approached Via Rasella. Another German officer, Lieutenant Wolgast, nodded to the major as he drove by and called for a song. As they turned onto Via Rasella the men started to sing "*Hupf, Mein Mädel.*"

Roman children, like most children, loved a parade, and a gaggle followed the Bozen policemen marching and singing through the city. Fortunately, the children had a ball with them, which Vitagliano kicked away, sending the kids after it and to safety.

Meanwhile Bentivegna, his rubbish cart strategically standing in the middle of Via Rasella, was ready to light his pipe for the fourth time. He was almost out of tobacco. Absentmindedly sweeping the street, he saw Capponi at the Palazzo Barberini gate. She had just shooed away two boys who were playing in the gardens of the palazzo.

Suddenly the police came into view, almost two hours late. The 156 men of the 11th Company of the 3rd Battalion, Police Regiment Bozen entered Via Rasella three abreast, singing. It was 15:50. An advance patrol with submachine guns at the ready led them. It would take about two minutes for the column to reach the top of Via Rasella.

Calamandrei lifted his hat. Bentivegna, seeing his signal, relit the pipe and put it into the box, lighting the fuse. He left his cap on the trash cart, the signal that the fuse was lit, and strolled up the street. He had 50 seconds to get to the top of the road and meet Capponi.

As he turned the corner, Capponi threw him the raincoat and they broke into a run.

Bentivegna slipped the raincoat over his street sweeper outfit. They were not out of danger. The *Messaggero* bodyguard ran after the couple but a bus appeared, separating him from the partisans. Suddenly a thunderous blast roared through the street, rocked buildings, blew out windows and pushed the moving bus off the street and onto the sidewalk. The bodyguard vanished.

Immediately Bentivegna heard three Brixia mortar grenades explode – the fourth was a dud. Raoul Falcioni, Fernando Vitagliano, Pasquale Balsamo, and Silvio Serra had acted. Some of the policemen's grenades went off, adding to the din and chaos.

Twenty-six Bozen policemen were killed immediately by the blast and more would soon die of their wounds. The dead and wounded – more than 100 – littered the pavement. The bomb had also killed two Italian civilians, a 13-year-old boy, Piero Zuccheretti, and a 48-year-old man.

The blast left a ten-foot-wide hole in the street and no trace of the trash cart. A ruptured water main spewed water; a flood of water mixing with blood ran down the street.

The unwounded Bozen men fired wildly at the windows along Via Rasella, believing the bomb to have been thrown from an upper story, killing another Italian. It was Annetta Baglioni, a 60-year-old maid in Palazzo Tittoni, who had rushed to her window to see what had happened only to be caught in a burst of gunfire. She died slumped over a third-floor windowsill of the palazzo.

The bombing almost involved M. de Wyss, the female Swiss journalist/diarist:

> I am still shivering. In the Via Rasella there lives a photographer who develops all my films. I was quietly going to him this afternoon and had just approached the street when there was a terrific explosion, then screams and yells. Then wild machine-gun fire made me spin round and run for my life, while out of a corner of my eye I saw Germans catching people who tried to escape. I doubled like a hunted hare and stopped only in the Piazza di Spagna. A boy about twelve stood near me, panting. He told me that he had been caught already but had ducked under a German soldier's arms and slipped away.

He didn't know what had happened. He was in the street playing. Then a terrific explosion threw him on to the pavement. He heard shouts, groans, machine-gun fire and saw people running away and did the same.[3]

The response by the German military authorities, including the Gestapo and Fascist police, was swift. Kappler was called immediately and he rushed to the scene, taking with him four SS men: Domizlaff, Schütz, Clemens, and Kahrau. He took command and stopped the wild firing into the buildings on the street.

Earlier, General Mälzer had been lunching with Kappler at the Hotel Excelsior, nearby on Via Veneto, and he too showed up, drunk. Dollmann and Consul Möllhausen heard the explosion from the Fascist commemorative ceremony being held at the Ministry of Corporations, also on Via Veneto. They too rushed to the site, along with Buffarini-Guidi, Mussolini's Interior Minister, and Pietro Caruso, the head Fascist policeman in Rome. Caruso's driver, Erminio Rosetti, drove them. A Fascist policeman, Rosetti had pulled his pistol and was running toward Via Rasella when police arriving on the scene, thinking him a partisan, shot him in a hail of bullets in Piazza Barberini.

General Mälzer, in a drunken rage, demanded revenge for his slaughtered *Kameraden*. The bodies of the dead were being lined up on the sidewalk. Mälzer roared and ordered the entire city block be blown up and that every man, woman, and child who lived in the street itself executed. Consul Möllhausen tried to calm Mälzer, but Mälzer turned on him and screamed, "This is the result of your politics! Now everything will change! I don't care. All these houses will go up in the air, even if the diplomats fire me tomorrow!" Mälzer said he was going to let Field Marshal Kesselring know that Möllhausen was obstructing his authority.

News of the massacre was quickly relayed up the chain of command. Möllhausen telephoned Kesselring's Monte Soratte Headquarters but he was not there. Möllhausen gave the details to Kesselring's chief of staff, Colonel Dietrich Beelitz, who then telephoned the details to the OKW (*Oberkommando der Wehrmacht*) in Berlin. For Hitler, it was another blow on a day of bad blows.

Hitler was already fuming about the Hungarians because they wanted to end their alliance with Germany, an Italian-like betrayal. Also, that day, Allied aircraft from Italy had bombed Bavaria. From his Eagle's Nest at Berchtesgaden Hitler saw the glow in the sky over Munich as the result of firebombing. He reacted to the news of bombing with predictable rage. He demanded that all the residents of Via Rasella be shot and all the houses along the street destroyed.

At the scene of carnage, the Germans looked for the guilty. Domizlaff and Clemens searched houses on the street for the attackers. Various forces – the SS, the Guardia di Finanza, the PAI, and the Decima MAS – arrived and broke into houses and shops on Via Rasella, arresting everyone. The German dead now numbered 32. Reprisals would soon follow.

In no time more than 100 people had been dragged out of their homes and shops and were standing along the wrought iron fence in front of the Palazzo Barberini. The arrested included a man in bed with the flu; an 18-year-old student; a dentist and his patients; and, most unlikely, Donna Bice Tittoni, a former Italian senator's octogenarian widow and the owner of the Palazzo Tittoni. Soon the total number arrested rose to more than 200 people. They were turned over to the Fascist police who, after taking them into custody, released most of them.

Dollmann had an idea that would generate maximum positive publicity for the Germans: bring the families of the dead Bozen men to Rome for a Requiem Mass celebrated by the Pope. Dollmann presented his idea to Karl F. Wolff, head of the SS in Italy, who agreed to fly to Rome the next day to discuss it with Kesselring. The city of Rome was to pay monetary reparations.

Dollmann changed into civilian clothes and called on Father Pancrazio Pfeiffer at the Vatican. He was the Abbot General of the Salvadorian Order and often acted as an unofficial Gestapo liaison to Pope Pius XII when either the Pope or Kappler had issues. During the occupation, Father Pfeiffer would be sent by the Vatican to Via Tasso to see Kappler about any matters concerning priests or of Vatican interest. Kappler reportedly hated him; nevertheless, he often was able to obtain the release of prisoners from the Regina Coeli or Via Tasso prisons.*

Dollmann and Pfeiffer were both Bavarians and they got along well. Dollmann told Pfeiffer that Hitler was beside himself with

---

* There is now a short street named for Pancrazio Pfeiffer located just outside the Bernini Colonnade on the left side of Via della Conciliazione, Via Padre Pancrazio Pfeiffer.

rage and suggested that the Pope request a postponement of any reprisals. He then outlined his idea for the Requiem Mass, adding that Kesselring and the Pope could speak on the need for peace and calm. Pfeiffer gladly agreed to report it to the Vatican as an alternative to a German reprisal for the attack. It is important to note that when Dollmann spoke to Pfeiffer the extent of the German reprisals had not yet been decided.

Kappler and General Mälzer telephoned General Eberhard von Mackensen, commander of the 14th German Army, and the brother of the former German Ambassador to Italy, Hans Georg von Mackensen, in hope of speaking with Kesselring at the Anzio beachhead, but he was not there. Mälzer asked Kappler how many prisoners were then on death row or who could be executed for crimes against the German government. Kappler said he thought he had about 200 death candidates (*Todeskandidaten*). Then orders came from Berlin at 19:30: for every German, ten Italians must be shot. That would be 320 men. And the reprisal must take place within 24 hours.

Kesselring was not at the Anzio beachhead as he later claimed during his war crimes trial; he was in northern Italy. This is based on the fact that he personally gave the go-ahead for the murder of 16 OSS saboteurs, all wearing uniforms, on March 26. The saboteurs had launched boats from Corsica and landed near La Spezia on March 22 to destroy a railway tunnel along the Ligurian Coast in Operation *Ginny*.[4]

———

Kappler got busy. He did not have enough *Todeskandidaten* to reach the goal, so he telephoned Rome's Chief of Police, Caruso, and demanded 50 names. He then called Pietro Koch and told him to empty his prison at the Pension Oltremare and give him a list of names and offenses. Kappler promised Consul Möllhausen, who was uneasy about selecting reprisal victims arbitrarily, that he would personally review each name three times before he added it to the list. Kappler, he claimed later, felt there should be no injustices.

During the evening the death total rose to 33 and Kappler increased the reprisal number to 330, in accordance with Berlin's ten-for-one formula. That decision would have personal consequences for Kappler later. Eventually, nine more Germans died in hospital, raising the total to 42; these nine had died after the executions, though, so Kappler did not add more names.

Berlin told Kappler that he could meet his quota by adding Jews to the list. Many Jews were turned in by Celeste Di Porto, a Jewish turncoat, later earning the name the Black Panther. She was just 18 years old, beautiful, and known by her nickname, Stella (Star). She met Fascist collaborators at the Trattoria il Fantino in the Jewish Ghetto, on a tiny street behind the larger Da Giggetto restaurant. Vincenzo Antonelli, a member of the German-organized Italian SS, was Celeste's lover. On the night of the bombing, March 23, Celeste and Antonelli went prowling for Jews to fill Kappler's list.

They asked Giovanni Cialli Mezzaroma, the leader of a Fascist band from Via della Scrofa, to help with the roundup. He had been a former World War I artillery captain and later a member of OVRA. Pietro Caruso and Kappler had allowed Mezzaroma and his band of a dozen thugs to shake down citizens and arrest partisans and Jews, with no official supervision. They routinely were paid 5,000 lire for each Jew arrested.

Their roundup method was simple: Celeste would see a man in the street that she knew to be Jewish, and greet him, thereby identifying him to Mezzaroma's band. Then they would seize him and, if he denied being Jewish, Celeste would pull his pants down to show he was circumcised. They took any arrested to the Regina Coeli Prison.

Celeste was responsible for the arrest of one third of the 77 Jews who were to be executed. When she discovered that her brother had been taken, she exchanged him for a famous Roman-Jewish prizefighter named Lazzaro Anticoli. Before the racial laws, he had fought under the name *Bucefalo*, Bucephalus, the name of Alexander the Great's horse. Anticoli wrote on the wall of his Regina Coeli prison cell, "I am Lazzaro Anticoli, called Bucefalo, the prize fighter. If I never see my family again, it is the fault of that bitch, Celeste Di Porto. Avenge me."[*]

The Pension Oltremare Prison held Maurizio Giglio and his orderly, Giovanni Scottu. They were ignorant of the bombing, but seven or

---

[*] His graffito can still be seen today. Celeste di Porto continued to denounce Jews until the liberation of Rome. Notably on April 1, 1944, she was responsible for the arrest of four Jews, who were sent to the Regina Coeli, while their homes were ransacked and more than one million lire worth of goods were stolen.

eight Banda Koch men rushed into their cell screaming and demanded to know what they knew about the attack. Then they beat the prisoners. Giglio's friend Walter di Franco was among them. He had joined the Banda Koch and he delivered a savage kick to Giglio's groin. Giglio cried out, "Judas!" Then another kick to his kidney and he repeatedly shrieked, "Mamma! They've killed me!" He was then taken to Regina Coeli Prison and Scottu followed later.*

Kappler worked through the night at Via Tasso, which was strangely silent because no one was being tortured. By early morning his list was still short with only 223 names. Among them, only four of the men had received death sentences, ten came from suspicious houses on Via Rasella, 17 had been given long-term sentences of hard labor, and 57 were Jews. Kappler also chose those Italian military officers who were members of the FMCR. He considered these men particularly dangerous. He expanded his list with political prisoners, especially communists, partisans, and more Jews. Many of these, Giglio for example, had been Tompkins' agents or helpers of the Escape Line.

Police Chief Caruso was slow compiling his list of 50 names. He was well aware that the Allies were advancing and that his own neck might be on the block when they arrived and sought out active supporters of the Fascist regime for punishment. At 08:00 he woke the Interior Minister, Buffarini-Guidi, in his suite at the Excelsior Hotel and asked for advice. He wanted to get specific orders so he could shield himself against Allied accusations later. Buffarini-Guidi was not specific and told Caruso to give the Germans whomever they wanted, since being Germans, they will take them anyway. Caruso returned to his office and slowly worked on his list.

The honor of carrying out the executions was first fittingly offered to Major Helmuth Dobbrick, commander of the 3rd Battalion. His men could enact revenge for the deaths of their comrades. Dobbrick balked at the idea. His battalion was made up of religious old men, who were also superstitious. They would simply refuse to do it and he said no. General von Mackensen was requested to send German troops from the beachhead to carry out the executions. He too refused; he didn't want

---

* Scottu eventually married an American woman but was never let into the US because he had tuberculosis.

his front-line troops to become executioners. The executions devolved upon Kappler's men.

Killing them was one thing; disposing of the dead bodies was another. It had to be done outside of Rome. One of Kappler's men, SS-Hauptsturmführer Gerhard Köhler, came up with the perfect site. There were caves off the old southern road to the town of Ardea – the Ardeatine Caves – close to the catacombs of Domitilla just outside the Roman walls. They were formed from a soft rock used in construction known as *pozzolana*. The Gestapo knew of the caves because the partisans had hidden stolen vehicles in them. The caves were abandoned and could be sealed off after the executions. It was the ideal location.

Believing that they were being sent to Germany, the condemned prisoners at Via Tasso were rousted from their cells at 14:00 and were taken out through the back door of the prison and into the garden of the Casino Massimo Lancellotti. There they were jammed into butcher-shop meat trucks, 50 at a time, unobserved from the street. Even so, it would take several trips to assemble all the prisoners at the caves. As the operation commenced, Caruso had still not provided his list.

The SS man in charge of the executions and the first to arrive at the caves was Hauptsturmführer Carl-Theodor Schütz. He had a dozen SS officers, 60 SS men, and a Wehrmacht soldier, 73 in all, to execute the prisoners. When Kappler arrived, he addressed the men reminding them that the Führer himself had issued the order. He added if any soldier refused to kill a prisoner, he would be shot.

SS-Hauptsturmführer Erich Priebke stood by as the trucks were unloaded, ready to check names off his list. A deserter from the Romanian Army named Rudi assisted Priebke as interpreter. The men, whose hands and ankles were bound, were formed in groups of five. As each prisoner was asked his name, Priebke crossed it out. Then the man, escorted by a German, was taken into the caves to be shot. Kappler ordered the officers to shoot a prisoner each as an example to the lower-ranking SS men.

Schütz passed out rounds of ammunition and then he, Kappler, and Priebke each shot a man in the first group. SS-Obersturmführer Reinhold Wetjen told Kappler that he could not kill in cold blood. Kappler suggested that they both fire together and Wetjen agreed.

Each took a prisoner into the caves and, firing simultaneously, killed them. It was Kappler's second execution. SS-Scharführer Günther Amonn also had scruples about executing bound prisoners but Schütz ordered him into the caves to carry out the order. Amonn recalled the scene vividly:

> I raised my gun but I was too afraid to shoot. The four other Germans fired one shot each into the backs of the necks of the other prisoners, who fell forward. Upon seeing the state in which I was another German pushed me out of the way and shot the prisoner I had been detailed to shoot.[5]

After this, Amonn fainted.

Those who were about to be shot were not silent. Don Pietro Pappagallo, the vice rector of the Basilica of Saint John Lateran, had been active in a group that helped Italian soldiers, Jews, and Allied ex-POWs find refuge and obtain false papers. Facing death, he performed his final sacerdotal duty by blessing all those who would be executed with him. Don Pappagallo not only gave the last rites to the condemned, but he could be heard shouting: "Long live Italy! Long live liberty!"

And there was General Simone Simoni, 64 years old and retired. The general had been tortured with a blow torch at Via Tasso and now, enraged at the mass execution, he too shouted "*Viva Italia*," and other encouragements to rally the others.

According to American author Robert Katz, only one man escaped the massacre, an Austrian deserter, Josef Raider, sentenced to death. He did not count as one of the reprisal victims. Raider had been tied to don Pappagallo but the rope had broken. Pappagallo then untied Raider and he escaped up and over the bank. He was later recaptured at the site by two SS men who did not return him to the others waiting to be shot. He alone escaped the massacre.[6]

It would be a long afternoon. Kappler issued cognac to his troops the effects of which made the operation even messier. Drunken soldiers fired off-center, missing the nape of the neck, the most efficient execution spot. Possibly because of this, one or more victims survived the execution and were left in the pile of corpses. After the cave was sealed, one wounded prisoner apparently crawled some distance from the pile to die. An unidentified SS noncommissioned officer gave an eyewitness account of the killings:

> The prisoners had their hands bound behind their backs. Their feet too were tied so that they could move only with very short steps or jumps. They were picked up and thrown into the lorries [trucks] like baggage. Many of them had signs of ill treatment on their faces and some had lost their teeth. Out of curiosity, I went in the caves and watched the execution of about sixty hostages. They were made to kneel in a row of from five to ten, one behind the other. SS men, stepping behind the rows discharged their guns into the necks of the victims. They died quietly, some crying "long live Italy!" Most of them were praying ... An old man, whom I learned to be General Simoni, was speaking words of encouragement to all the rest ... I came away because I felt I was going to be sick.[7]

Kappler was vexed at Caruso's failure to deliver his 50 men. So, at 16:30, he sent a squad under SS-Obersturmführer Heinz-Josef Tunath and SS-Scharführer Willi Kofler to the Regina Coeli Prison to get more prisoners. Eleven men were standing in the courtyard awaiting their release. Asking no questions, Tunath rounded up the unlucky men and loaded them into a German truck. Caruso arrived ten minutes later with his list. None of those taken by Tunath were on the list. Tunath spared the lives of 11 men on Caruso's list with his action and condemned those who took their place (see plates section).* And, in his haste, Tunath had taken 55 men, five more than was required.

Meanwhile, at 15:00, General Wolff's plane had landed at Viterbo Airfield, north of Rome, where he was met by Dollmann. Together they drove to Monte Soratte to present to Field Marshal Kesselring their proposal of a Requiem Mass as a substitute for reprisal, but they were too late, the executions were in progress, and Kesselring was still in northern Italy. The reprisal could not be stopped.

At 20:00, after the executions were over, the Germans blew up the entrance to the caves, sealing within it 335 corpses, five more than the formula of ten-for-one demanded. The dead ranged in ages from

---

* The author obtained a copy of the list at the US National Archives. It is chilling to see the 50 names listed, 11 of which were crossed out and their replacements written in.

15 to 75. The five extra men brought by Tunath saw the massacre so they had been killed too. This was to have severe consequences for Priebke many years later. After the cave entrance was blown, Kappler suggested that the soldiers get drunk and they did.

The executions did not satisfy the Germans' lust for revenge. There were still further steps to be taken. Himmler planned to round up all the communists and suspect elements together with their families from the most dangerous sections of the city and deport them. It was to be organized immediately. That evening, Karl F. Wolff, Eugen Dollmann, Herbert Kappler, and Consul Eitel F. Möllhausen met in Wolff's suite at the Excelsior Hotel to decide on how to proceed. Kappler recounted to the others the details of the execution at the caves and then they discussed Himmler's plan for deportations.

Kappler was unenthusiastic; Dollmann was stunned. He and Möllhausen pointed out that the logistical difficulties in rounding up such numbers were insurmountable. Möllhausen is said to have described how such a gigantic operation would look: "Hundreds of thousands of persons marching north on foot ... carrying their possessions, with the weaker ones falling along the way ... The supply roads blocked, the troops endangered."[8]

Nevertheless, were the deportations to be carried out, the group meeting in Wolff's suite needed assurances that Pius XII would not publicly condemn the plan. At one in the morning, Dollmann telephoned Himmler, urging him to authorize the German Ambassador to the Holy See, Baron von Weizsäcker, to explain the deportation plan to the Pope. Himmler knew that when the Pope heard what the subject of the meeting was to be, he would not even grant an audience. Himmler postponed the deportation; however, Kappler was to plan for it, just in case.

When Field Marshal Kesselring returned to Rome and heard of the plan, he dismissed it; it made no military sense and, in any case, he did not have enough troops to carry out the deportation.

The next day, the German government of Rome issued an Official Communiqué on the Via Rasella attack and the reprisal which had taken place:

On the afternoon of March 23, 1944, criminal elements executed a bomb attack against a column of German police in transit through Via Rasella. As a result of this ambush, thirty-two men of the German police were killed and several wounded. The vile ambush was carried out by *comunisti-badogliani* [Badoglio Communists]. An investigation is still being made to clarify the extent to which this criminal deed is attributed to Anglo-American involvement ... The German command has decided to terminate the activities of these villainous bandits. No one will be allowed to sabotage with impunity the newly affirmed Italo-German cooperation. The German Command has therefore ordered that for every murdered German ten *comunisti-badogliani* criminals be shot. This order has already been carried out.[9]

The massacre site was discovered the day after the event by don Fernando Giorgi, a Salesian monk, and a few of his brothers from a nearby monastery. On the morning of March 25 they crawled down a hole in the ground and saw bodies and were assaulted by the stench and flies. They reported the horror to their superiors; word reached Kappler that the site had been found and his execution chamber discovered. He ordered his men to seal the entrance again; however, this blast opened a new hole in the cave's roof, releasing the reek.

Locals complained to Caruso about the stink and the Fascist police chief ordered garbage to be dumped there to disguise the smell! The SS returned a third time to close the new opening but could not. It was the Friday before Palm Sunday and the massacre site began to be venerated as a shrine. People spontaneously came, cleared away the garbage, and left flowers. The Germans installed an off-limits sign at the caves in a final attempt to cover up their atrocity.

On March 26, the GAP defended the Via Rasella action in a communiqué claiming responsibility for the attack and stating, in part, that it was the duty of all Italians to shoot the enemy without hesitation, at any time. They called their actions against the Nazi-Fascists acts of war which would stop only with the liberation of Rome from Nazi occupation.

The Italian Communist Party issued a flyer justifying Via Rasella, saying the best of their comrades gave their lives. It ended with, "Long

Live the Communists! Long Live Russia! Long Live Stalin!" The CLN, after some deal-making, reluctantly agreed to take responsibility for the attack along with the GAP. The Badoglio government soon joined others in declaring that the Rasella attack was a legitimate act of war and the partisans were adjunct soldiers fighting at the side of the Allies.

Most Romans, impatiently waiting for the Allies, reacted negatively to the attack and expressed the view that there was no point in killing a few Germans when the Allies would soon push them out of the city. The Via Rasella bombing was unjustified, went the argument, and it was the partisans themselves who were responsible for the deaths of the 335 victims of reprisal.

The Vatican newspaper, *L'Osservatore Romano*, in careful and ambiguous language appealed to all Romans to refrain from acts of violence one day after the German announcement. It read:

> In the face of such deeds every honest heart is left profoundly grieved in the name of humanity and Christian sentiment. Thirty-two victims on the one hand; and on the other hand three hundred and twenty persons sacrificed for the guilty parties who escaped arrest ... We call upon the irresponsible elements to respect human life, which they can never have the right to sacrifice, to respect the innocence of those who are their fatal victims, from the responsible elements we ask for an awareness of their responsibility toward themselves, toward the lives they seek to safeguard, toward history and civilization.[10]

As can be seen from the above, the numbers were wrong; but the statement was enough to convince the Germans to continue the fiction that Rome was an Open City, a propaganda effort to bolster their claim that they were protecting Rome and its population. During a meeting with the editors of Rome's newspapers, the German Ambassador to the Italian Fascist government (RSI), Rudolf Rahn, referenced Via Rasella and Ardeatine, affirming that:

> It is well that the communists and the Badogliani know that it is not possible to resolve the situation with an attack. The clandestine maneuvers to sabotage German Forces are destined to fail and cause the loss of blood while provoking the Italian people.

Investigations continued. Pietro Koch learned that a man, codenamed Paolo (Bentivegna), had lit the bomb on Via Rasella. He offered a reward of 1.8 million lire for his capture, the highest reward offered for any partisan during the occupation of Rome.

The day after Easter, the Germans began notifying the families of those executed at the caves. The text of the printed form letter was in German. The letter was dated April 10, 1944 under the letterhead of *Der Befehlshaber* (commander) *Der Sicherheitspolizei u. des SD in Italien E.K. Rom*. It stated that (for example): "Maurizio GIGLIO died on March 24, 1944. Personal belongings, if any, may be recovered at the office of the German Sicherheitspolizei in Via Tasso 155, where they are being held." Although the letter was not translated into Italian, the Via Tasso return address was enough to know what the letter meant. Jewish families never received death notices because they were in hiding and had no fixed addresses. The letter was signed by SS-Hauptsturmbannführer Borante Domizlaff.*

Later, Giglio's parents published a notice in a Rome newspaper requesting that their friends neither call nor send messages of condolence.

The Fascist authorities were so out of touch with the events in Rome that they announced that the execution had taken place at the Colosseum, a misstatement that made its way into some official US Fifth Army reports. After the massacre site was identified, common usage changed its name from the Ardeatine Caves to the Ardeatine Graves (*Fosse Ardeatine*).

The victims came from all walks of civilian life, including: 33 professional men, six students, one priest, one diplomat, 37 office workers, nine artists, 71 businessmen or shop owners, nine farmers, 37 artisans, 49 workers (railway, waiters, etc.), and four whose professions are not known. Seventy-seven of them were Jewish. Sixty-four were military: 47 from the Army or Carabinieri, 11 from the Air Force and six from the Navy. Many had been members of the FMCR and included officers, NCOs, and other ranks. The youngest victim was 15-year-old Michele

---

* The author obtained a photocopy of the death notice for Emanuele Caracciolo from the Georgetown University Tittmann papers where Domizlaff's name is clearly visible.

di Veroli, who was murdered with his father. The Red Flag partisans lost 60 members.

Twelve OSS operatives were executed. Many had been caught with incriminating notes on their persons while counting vehicles for Tompkins. The OSS losses were deeply felt. Tompkins' assistant, Franco Malfatti, told him on March 25 that they had shot Cervo (Giglio) and 11 of their men. Tompkins mourned their loss, but he reasoned that it would have been a release for Giglio who had been undergoing unbearable torture. Tompkins feared his own exposure less now. And he had reservations about the Via Rasella attack and its consequences, as noted in his diary:

> Our first reaction was that there was no point in killing thirty nondescript German MPs! Why hadn't whoever was responsible for the attack risked his courage against Via Tasso, or picked off Kappler and his gang of butchers? Now there was no telling what the German reaction might be; certainly it boded no good for the underground in the city. What saddened us even more was to contemplate the beauty and precision of the attack, the organization of which appeared to have been damned-near perfect![11]

A woman was also an unintended victim. Although her tragic story only came to light in 1994, it was reported that 74-year-old Fedele Rasa had been out near the caves around 17:00 that day, picking chicory for dinner, when she was hit by a stray bullet. Perhaps she did not hear the gunfire or the guttural commands of the Germans. She was taken to the hospital by the Germans in one of the same meat trucks that brought prisoners to be shot; she suffered a fatal cardiac arrest two days later.

A listing of all 335 men murdered is available elsewhere;[12] however, those who are mentioned in this book are recorded below:

Anticoli, Lazzaro (26, the Jewish prize fighter), denounced by the Black Panther
Bernardi, Lallo (38, laborer), a helper of Monsignor O'Flaherty
Casadi, Andrea (31, carpenter), arrested with Brother Robert Pace
Fantini, Vittorio (25, pharmacist), arrested with Brother Robert Pace
Ferola, Enrico (42, blacksmith), forged the four-pointed nails

Finzi, Aldo (52, former Secretary for Home Affairs), for helping Russian ex-POWs

Giglio, Maurizio, Lt. (approximately 23, OSS agent), arrested with Radio Vittoria 2

Lousena, Umberto (39, Italian Army major), radio operator for Number One Special Force/Derry

Montezemolo, Giuseppe (42, Italian Army colonel), of the Clandestine Military Front

Pappagallo, Pietro don (55, priest), vice rector of the Basilica of Saint John Lateran

Roazzi, Antonio (46, chauffeur), a helper of Monsignor O'Flaherty

Simoni, Simone (63, Italian Army general), shouted encouragement to the prisoners

Vittorio, (codenamed Gino, last name and age unknown), radio operator for Radio Vittoria 1

In the complex scenario of the German occupation of Rome – its plots and counterplots, and the survival, despair, suffering, and solace of the people – the March 23 partisan attack at Via Rasella and the massacre at the caves the next day by the Germans stand as the most dramatic and brutal events perpetrated throughout that dark time.

19

The Roman Spring of 1944

An escaped POW risked recapture, torture, even death. Yet they escaped to run the gamut of Rome's streets patrolled by Germans to find safety with the Escape Line. Such was the case of Joe Pollak, the Czechoslovakian Jew and a key member of the Escape Line, whom we met earlier in these pages. It will be recalled he had been recaptured and returned to Sulmona.

Renzo Lucidi was surprised in early March to answer his phone and hear Pollak's voice. Knowing only one place to go, he had returned to the apartment on Via Domenico Cellini, thinking it was safe. It wasn't; Ubaldo Cipolla was living there. The apartment raid in January had rendered it useless to the Escape Line. Derry suspected Cipolla of being a Gestapo double agent. He was right.

Pollak told Lucidi that on New Year's Eve more than 40 men and women of Sulmona had been arrested for helping Allied ex-POWs. They had been denounced by an Australian medic named Dick Messenger. The local Gestapo had arrested Messenger who was drunk and celebrating the New Year. After he sobered up and the Gestapo promised him good treatment if he would identify the people who were aiding escaped soldiers, Messenger agreed and led the Germans to houses where he knew Allied soldiers were living. Because of this, the Germans arrested Dr. Scocco, the Balassones, Flora Pacella and her elderly parents, Maria Imperoli and her mother, and others. Then the Germans threw Messenger in jail with those he had accused.

When Pollak arrived back in Sulmona, he and Iride were confined in the same prison with the Sulmona helpers. Pollak urged Messenger to explain to the Germans that he only randomly pointed out Sulmona people to escape punishment and that they were innocent. Messenger did so but was not believed. Shortly thereafter, the Fascist authorities took all of them to Bussi, 12 miles from Sulmona, and then on to the nearby town of Civitaquana for trial. On February 14, 1944, five Sulmona helpers were sentenced to death.

Four of the Sulmona prisoners escaped from the Civitaquana jail during a stormy night. Some of the others were sent to Germany. Pollak and Messenger, as foreigners, were turned over to the Germans and sent to L'Aquila where Pollak was identified as a Jew, a Czech, and a citizen of the Third Reich. He was locked in isolation, thrown into a freezing cell with no blankets, beaten, and given little food. He contracted pneumonia, coughed up blood, and was denied medical attention. The Gestapo called him a spy, a traitor, and a dirty Jew.

Pollak was recognized by a recaptured British officer as he was led into the courtroom for his trial. The officer, who had been with him at Chieti, convinced the German colonel in charge of the local Military Tribunal that Pollak was an escaped POW. Remarkably, that distinction saved him from the firing squad. Pollak and Messenger were sentenced to be deported to a POW camp in Germany.

While waiting at L'Aquila railway station for a train bound for Germany, the RAF bombed the station and, in the chaos, Pollak escaped. He and another unidentified British ex-POW hitched a ride to Rome in the back of a truck. Outside the city, the truck was stopped at a roadblock by two German soldiers. Hearing the commotion, Pollak jumped from the truck and hid beneath it. His companion was captured but Pollak hung to the underside of the truck as it drove away. He dropped off before it entered the compound of a German casern. The amazing escape ended with Pollak dusting himself off and, as he was still in civilian clothes, he walked into the city to find safety at the Cellini apartment.

Pollak was seriously ill, so ill that his friends thought of sending him to Switzerland for treatment, but he said no. Lucidi took a change of clothes to Via Cellini for Pollak and moved him to Simpson's billet in the Parioli district, with Flora Volpini, a former Italian film star.

By mid-March, to the chagrin of Kappler, the Escape Line was big business. In the last three weeks, the number of escapees throughout Italy had risen by 800 to 3,423. In Rome, the number of escapees had increased to 180. Black-market clothing expenditures rose from 107,000 lire in January to 157,000 lire in February to 187,000 lire in March. By this time many Allied ex-POWs had made their way to Switzerland or joined bands of Italian partisans fighting in the mountains.

Escaped British POW Garrad-Cole was enjoying the good life in Rome; but one day in mid-March he found himself running for his life from the German police. He was spotted from a window of the Lucidi apartment by US Ranger 1st Lt. William L. Newman who heard shots being fired and, of course, looked out. There was the well-dressed Garrad-Cole with Germans at his heels heading for the Lucidi apartment.

Garrad-Cole had been staying with Gil Smith at the French Seminary but they were not happy there. Monsignor O'Flaherty found a new place for them at a fashionable address in Parioli. Their new hostess was a marchesa from northern Italy, an anti-fascist. In his memoirs, Garrad-Cole identifies her only as Christina. The marchesa took a shine to Garrad-Cole and had him fitted for a suit of finest prewar British wool by a tailor on Via XX September. She also paid for a smart pair of shoes, a top coat, and a black homburg hat. When his suit was ready, Garrad-Cole and Christina celebrated with pre-lunch cocktails at the bar in the Grand Hotel then went on to the Osteria dell'Orso for lunch.

The Orso was their favorite place. On another occasion after lunch at the restaurant, they boarded a tram back to Christina's apartment. Garrad-Cole noticed uneasily that a pair of German policemen on the tram seemed to be taking too much interest in him. He said goodbye to Christina and got off at the next stop followed by the Germans. As he later recounted the episode:

> Frantically I tried to form a plan of escape. When I had left Christina on the tram I had not noticed where we were. But now I realized that I was at the Porta del Popolo, walking down Via Flaminia. And I was greatly relieved, for I knew the area well. The Lucidis lived nearby.[1]

The policemen quickly covered Garrad-Cole's 20-yard lead, accosted him, and demanded to see his papers. "*Nix est buono*," they said in fractured Italian – the papers were no good. Garrad-Cole understood only one other phrase, Via Tasso, the Gestapo prison. And off they went back toward the Piazza del Popolo. Garrad-Cole thought, it is now or never. He tripped one of the Germans and struck him as he fell. As he ran away, the other policeman got off several shots, firing wide.

Garrad-Cole outran his pursuers and, rounding a corner, turned on Via Scialoja to the Lucidis' apartment building. He bounded up the small flight of steps into the entrance hall. In the foyer, he turned right and hid in an apartment doorway around the corner. His two pursuers rushed past the doorway and he was able to race up the stairs to the Lucidi's fourth-floor apartment and knock.

Renzo Lucidi opened the door and realized what had happened because he had heard the shots in the street. He signaled Garrad-Cole to go to the roof where he was able to squeeze himself onto the top of the building's elevator car. Lucidi then ran downstairs and turned off the power to the elevator.

Garrad-Cole could hear the Germans in the apartment-block stairwell and the *portiere* shouted, "You have just missed him. He ran out the back." The Germans saw a five-year-old boy playing with his ball outside the apartment, Giuseppe Gessi. They asked him if he had seen anyone run into the building. Little Giuseppe said "no!"[*]

An hour later, Lucidi deemed it safe enough to bring Garrad-Cole down from the elevator roof. From his apartment Lucidi sent his 12-year-old son, Gérard, to scout for Germans. When he returned saying the coast was clear, Newman, the silent witness to the drama, and Adrienne Lucidi descended to the street where they casually walked, arm-in-arm. Lucidi feared that Garrad-Cole's elegant attire would attract attention, so he switched Garrad-Cole's expensive top coat for his own modest one and substituted his brown trilby hat for Garrad-Cole's homburg.

Then young Gérard and Garrad-Cole went into the street, turning left and sauntering the two blocks to the Tiber River. They passed

[*] As told to the author by Signore Giuseppe Gessi in October 2015. He remembered the Lucidis and an English colonel had occupied the ground floor apartment for about six months after the liberation. Upon departure, the colonel, who was probably Sam Derry, now promoted, gave Giuseppe a British pith helmet and a swagger stick, both now lost. As the Allies pursued the Germans north, the American Red Cross set up a doughnut and coffee trailer on the nearby Via Flaminia. Giuseppe, more than 70 years later, still remembers the doughnuts he was given.

groups of Germans searching for the escaped POW. Gérard, knowing well the game they were playing, kept up a lively chatter, and, taken for father and son, they were ignored. It had been a close call for Garrad-Cole and Newman.

It was now necessary for Garrad-Cole to change his appearance. The police had confiscated his documents so they now had his current photo. Garrad-Cole grew a mustache, combed his hair differently, and started to wear glasses. With the mustache grown out, pictures were taken for a new identity card. Christina found him a place to live on Via Aurelia Antica outside the city. It was a place of isolation and he stood the solitude for a while but when he was too restless and bored, he would go into Rome, again risking capture. Once while strolling down Via Veneto, Garrad-Cole narrowly missed running right into Field Marshal Kesselring. Such was the life of an escapee.

An escapee with a medical emergency faced a Hobson's choice between his life and freedom. A US Army Air Corps aviator with severe head injuries sustained when he bailed out of his plane desperately needed surgery. To help him, the Escape Line again went to Mrs. Chevalier's neighbor, Milko Scofic, whose University of Rome professor of neural surgery agreed to operate. An ambulance, probably from the Vatican, took the wounded airman to the San Giovanni Hospital. Two military medical orderlies there became suspicious and asked the surgeon who the patient was. The doctor lied, saying the patient was a high-ranking Fascist Party member who had been injured in an air raid. The operation was successful and the flyer was returned to his billet on Via Aurelia. Scofic crossed the city daily to check on his recovery.

Private Norman I. Anderson, of the Cameron Highlanders, was another case. He chose not to be treated for acute appendicitis if it meant surrendering to the Germans. Anderson had become ill while hiding near Subiaco, a hill town 40 miles south of Rome and the site of a Benedictine abbey. Brother Robert, who was contacted, urged Anderson to be treated by the Germans. He refused, saying he would rather die first.

Thankfully he did not die. Instead Monsignor O'Flaherty arranged for a friend to operate on Anderson. Professor Albano was a distinguished surgeon with Rome's Regina Elena Lazzaretto Hospital.* The wards were crammed with Anzio beachhead wounded – from both sides. The question was how to transport Anderson? Dr. T. J. Kiernan, the Irish Republic Chargé d'Affaires, had a car with diplomatic plates and Father Buckley and Brother Robert borrowed it to take Anderson to the hospital. Albano operated while they waited. Later, Anderson was taken to Mrs. Chevalier's apartment which was now only for emergency use. Once again, her medical student neighbor Milko Scofic cared for the recuperating soldier.

Mrs. Chevalier's 17-year-old neighbor, the lame boy Giuseppe who had warned her of an earlier raid, played an increasingly important role with the Escape Line. A week after Anderson's operation, he rang Mrs. Chevalier's doorbell and told her there would be another evening raid. Fearing that her phones were tapped, Mrs. Chevalier sent one of her daughters to Monsignor O'Flaherty who called Dr. Kiernan's wife and told her to get the car somehow; our friend must be moved in a hurry! Anderson was sped to the Casa San Giovanni where Monsignor McGeough had Lt. Colin Leslie care for him. Anderson regained his health in a month.

Now that young Giuseppe had firmly established his bona fides with the Escape Line, he told John May that his information about the raid had come from Giuseppe Pizzirani, a senior official in the Questura, the Rome police headquarters. Pizzirani had replaced Gino Bardi of the now defunct Banda Bardi-Pollastrini as Fascist commissioner general of the city. He routinely had access to the German police schedules which listed all projected raids. The Gestapo raids were coordinated with the Italian police in written reports called Daily Orders. These specified where and when a raid would take place. They were tightly guarded, but could be clandestinely copied. John May could buy the Daily Orders from Giuseppe at 1,000 lire each.

Even with this advance notice, there was not much time for a runner to warn of an impending raid from the moment a copy of the Daily Order was received to the curfew, which now fell at 17:30. Contacting

* Fleming says the doctor was named Urbani.

the Escape Line billets would be dangerous. Public transportation was unreliable and almost nonexistent. Further, only four people knew where all the billets in the organization were: Monsignor O'Flaherty, Major Derry, Lt. Bill Simpson, and Captain Henry Byrnes, the Royal Canadian Army Service Corps officer who kept the Escape Line records.

Simpson would have to find one of the cooperating priests to warn the billets of an impending raid. In the event no priest was available, Simpson and Furman would have to do it. Giuseppe also told Major Derry that the police had learned that the Escape Line was using priests as contacts and so they disguised Gestapo officers as priests to locate escaped POWs.

Giuseppe said that Pizzirani had offered, for a price, a way to prevent recaptured POWs from being deported to Germany. He could simply cancel the required official police paperwork. He would do this for 50,000 lire each.[2] It is not known whether Pizzirani was paid to obtain the release of any POWs in this way.

Kappler, ever more frustrated, tried to cripple the Escape Line by attacking the cleric who had set it up – Monsignor O'Flaherty. He took two SS men with him to the Vatican control line – the white painted control line dividing the Vatican on one side from Rome on the other – which was manned by two German paratroopers who carried submachine guns. It was just after 08:00 one morning in mid-March. Kappler called his men's attention to the steps of the Basilica of Saint Peter in the far-left corner. Standing there was Monsignor O'Flaherty, as usual, waiting for escaped Allied ex-POWs, disaffected Wehrmacht soldiers, Jews, or anyone else desperate to get away from the Gestapo.

Kappler ordered his SS men to go to the basilica the next day, bring the monsignor out by force, take him across the control line, and, thereby, out of Vatican sanctuary. Then they were to take O'Flaherty into a side street and shoot him while he was trying to escape.

Giuseppe again came through and told John May of Kappler's plot. May devised a counterplot. He warned the monsignor that evening, and when Kappler's SS men entered Saint Peter's Basilica the next morning to carry out the assassination, they were accosted by four Swiss Guards who surrounded them and escorted them outside. The men crossed the piazza, turned left, and passed under the Bernini Colonnade, then immediately passed under the *Passetto di Borgo*, the above-ground covered passage that earlier popes had used to flee the

Vatican apartments to safety in the Castel Sant'Angelo. This brought them out onto the little Piazza della Città next to the *passetto*, and outside of Vatican territory, where the guards released the SS men to a group of Yugoslavs who, hating Germans, severely beat them.

This was not the first time the Swiss Guard had assisted the Escape Line. On at least two previous occasions the Guard had helped smuggle individuals into the Vatican. Early on, Prince Carracula, one of the monsignor's first supporters, learned that Obersturmbannführer Kappler had planned a raid on his palazzo. He was provided with a Swiss Guard uniform and he entered the Vatican during the changing of the guard. On a second occasion, Mita Colonna di Cesarò, a friend of Vittoria Colonna, the Duchess of Sermoneta, had been arrested by Pietro Koch. The mother of Mita, Colonna di Cesarò, induced Pietro Koch to accept a 100,000 lire bribe to release her. She was, however, still in danger and Monsignor O'Flaherty arranged to smuggle the young woman into the Vatican. John May managed to borrow a Swiss Guard uniform and, during the changing of the guard at midnight, Mita changed into it under the Bernini Colonnade and at the right moment she joined the soldiers marching into the Vatican through the Arco delle Campane.

One cleric, however, received no warning that his life was in danger. Don Giuseppe Morosini was the spiritual advisor of the Fulvio Mosconi Band of partisans affiliated with the FMCR. The priest had helped the partisans with clothes and food, and even hid their weapons. He also passed on military information. Don Morosini had obtained the schematic plan of the German forces at Monte Cassino from an Austrian captain in the Operation Office of the Wehrmacht. He gave the plans to his FMCR contacts and they passed them on to the Allies. Betrayed to the Germans by an unknown Gestapo spy for 70,000 lire, he was arrested while returning home with a former student in Via Pompeo Magno (Prati), several blocks from the Vatican. When the Gestapo searched the priest's apartment, they found weapons and a radio transmitter set he had hidden for the partisans.

Don Morosini had been in custody since the beginning of the year. Often, he was taken from his cell in the German wing of the Regina

Coeli Prison, to be questioned for the names of partisans. He was severely tortured but never broke and gave up nothing. He was condemned to death after a trial at the German Tribunal on Via Lucullo, a farce lasting 20 minutes. He might have been killed in the caves massacre, but his name had not been on Caruso's list. Pope Pius XII interceded on his behalf, begging for leniency, but Field Marshal Kesselring denied the request. Reportedly his case was even brought to the attention of Hitler, but that is not certain.

His execution by firing squad was set for March 29, 1944, at Fort Bravetta. Don Morosini was given permission to say Mass for a last time before his death. To their astonishment, he turned to the firing squad of PAI policemen who were about to shoot him and he blessed them. The order was given to fire, but Morosini's act of forgiveness had so unnerved his executioners that their aim was off, either by accident or on purpose. Morosini fell wounded and another priest administered extreme unction, the last rites. As he lay dying he is reported to have said: "It takes more courage to live than to die" (*Ci vuole più coraggio per vivere che per morire*). A German, likely SS-Scharführer Pustowka, who was on hand during executions, gave the *coup de grâce*.[*]

At a time when Derry was having trouble getting money and supplies to the escapees in the northern part of Italy a solution presented itself. Monsignor O'Flaherty told Furman that he had been contacted by Evangelos Averoff and Theodore Meletiou of the Greek Liberty or Death organization – the same men who had brought Major General Gambier-Parry to Rome.

The two Greeks had obtained a car from a leading Fascist who could read the writing on the wall and now wanted to help the Allies. He not only had a car, but the papers and gasoline ration coupons that went with it. The Greeks drove to Milan and, with names and locations provided by Derry, passed out more than 100,000 lire, many pairs of boots and much-needed clothing to Allied soldiers. In three weeks they covered more than 2,000 miles and brought back critical information on

[*] Don Giuseppe Morosini was memorialized in Roberto Rossellini's Film in 1945, *Roma, Citta Aperta* (Rome, Open City). The actor Aldo Fabrizi played the role of don Morosini.

partisan activities that Derry passed on to Number One Special Force. Of most value to the Escape Line, the Greeks brought back an updated list of escapees together with home addresses and military organizations.[3]

The German occupiers of Rome never ceased to demand the Allies recognize Rome as an Open City. On March 26, Sir D'Arcy reported to London a *Messaggero* newspaper article which published a communiqué from the German Command of Rome. The article, as he summarized it, reported that the Germans declared that the only soldiers inside the city were those Germans and Allies recovering in hospitals, escaped POWs, or German police assigned to maintain order. It went on to say that the German Command, in light of the continued bombing of the city, retained the right to abandon their scrupulous respect to the characteristics of the Open City. Necessary transportation of supplies and German soldiers on leave were said not to be moving through the city and Rome was declared to be off limits to German soldiers as was the Vatican. It concluded by stating that these actions were taken solely to benefit the Roman population regardless of the negative effect on German military forces.

Rome was of course not an Open City and there were still military targets to attack. Sir D'Arcy again complained to the Foreign Office that the renewed bombing of Rome by the Allies was counterproductive. The destruction of civilian targets and the loss of life were not justified for the meager military results, he wrote. Deaths from Allied bombing now numbered over 5,000. More than 11,000 people had been injured, figures that may be too low. His opinion was shared by others.

The propaganda war continued when the head of the German press office at the German Embassy in April invited a dozen journalists to see that Rome was indeed, as they claimed, an Open City. They were taken for a lightning tour of the city accompanied by German officials, following a prepared and carefully guarded route.

Conditions were actually frightful. "Swollen by Refugees" was the subject of an official note that MacWhite, the Irish Republic Ambassador to the Salò Republic, sent to the Irish government on April 3. He said that of Rome's more than one million inhabitants, a quarter were refugees. Many had been bombed out of their homes by Allied bombers south of the city. On the streets of Rome, a sarcastic graffito read: "Allies hold on! We'll be there soon to liberate you."

Threats to the Escape Line's work came not only from the outside. Derry had mounting evidence that it was being betrayed from within and his suspicions had centered on don Pasqualino Perfetti. He was the unkempt former priest whom Derry met in November on his first trip into Rome to meet Sir D'Arcy. Young Giuseppe told them that Perfetti was working for the Gestapo. In a routine raid, Perfetti had been arrested by Pietro Koch, who had him beaten and tortured until he agreed to work for him. Derry had sought to distance the Escape Line from Perfetti but, because he continued to work with François de Vial, at the French legation to the Vatican, Perfetti had an in and knew many details about the organization and was dangerous.

Young Gino Giuliani casually mentioned to Furman, who was still staying at the Giuliani apartment, that he knew Perfetti. Furman recognized the name and fearing to be found he immediately left the billet. Furman and Pollak (now in relatively good health) quickly made the rounds of billets to warn the escapees that they might be compromised. After a few days, nothing had happened so Furman returned to the Giulianis on April 5.

Two days later, Furman was invited to an all-night birthday party for one of the daughters of a widow who had helped him find temporary housing. This was the night that the Giuliani apartment was raided. Both father and son were arrested by Banda Koch policemen. Romeo Giuliani was released, but his son, Gino, was kept by the infamous Dr. Koch. Under torture, young Giuliani talked. Furman and Pollak, when they heard this, anxiously checked on the billets that were in danger of being raided, but they were too late. Gino had identified the places where he knew ex-POWs were hiding to Banda Koch men as they drove around the city. They raided six of the billets and captured *padroni* and 21 Allied soldiers. On April 11, Furman gave Derry the details of what he knew and who had been taken:

> The situation is now a little clearer but I'm afraid the clearer it gets, the blacker, if you know what I mean. Nearly all the lads known to

Gino have been taken, so it is quite clear that Gino spilled the beans. All were taken on Saturday night between 1 a.m. and 5 a.m. … Memo [a friend of Gino] was also taken on Saturday night, but I learn he has been released. He thinks however that he is being tailed. I shall try to make contact with him if it can be done safely.[4]

Five days later, Furman wrote Derry again saying his earlier list had been incomplete. He had expected to meet with an ex-POW, at his padrone's place of business, but the man did not show up because he and the padrone had been arrested and taken to the Regina Coeli Prison. The padrone's wife visited the prison and was told by her husband that he had seen Gino Giuliani, badly beaten up with his head swollen up like a pumpkin. He had been transferred from the Pension Oltremare. He also told her that all those who had been arrested had been questioned about the English lieutenant, Furman.

A few days later, Furman met Memo, Gino Giuliani's friend, at the Giuliani apartment. Memo confirmed that Gino had been savagely tortured with most of his teeth knocked out. He had given the police Furman's description, down to his clothes and the Fascists had told Gino that Furman was a spy and he would be shot on sight. Furman immediately changed his look by cutting his mustache and dying his natural ruddy-brown hair jet black.

Some prisoners were luckier than Gino Giuliani. A French captain named Martin had also been arrested and severely beaten that day in Banda Koch headquarters at the Pension Oltremare. But Martin escaped from a fourth-floor window by shimmying down a drainpipe and dropping into the courtyard. The exit was through the main entrance where there were several tough-looking Banda Koch policemen. Martin coolly walked out unchallenged, even though he was bloodied and his clothes disheveled. Perhaps his Gallic *sang froid* had given him a cloak of invisibility, or was it just luck?

———

After the capture and execution of Maurizio Giglio, Tompkins was sure that the Gestapo knew he was an American OSS agent with the codename, Pietro. He was right. The Gestapo even had a prewar photo of him from his Rome correspondence days. Tompkins asked Tittmann whether he could move into the Vatican, but was told that it was not safe – German spies were monitoring everyone inside the Vatican. So Tompkins adopted the name he had used when he had been introduced to Priebke, Roberto Berlingieri.

Franco Malfatti thought that Tompkins could join the Italian Africa Police (PAI), using his alias as a cover. An interview was set with the PAI commander, a colonel thought to be sympathetic to the Allies as were many PAI officers, for March 31. Tompkins told him he was an Italian Air Force major who knew details about Axis aircraft development. He said he had to hide in Rome and wait for the Allies who wanted to speak to him. It worked.

For those like Tompkins who had OSS money to spend, food could be bought and an Easter holiday could be celebrated in style. Prior to his short stint in the PAI and courtesy of the black-market, Tompkins' Easter lunch consisted of roast beef, *foie gras*, roast chicken, hearts of lettuce, ricotta-filled cannoli, Bordeaux wines, and an excellent old bottle of Barolo – he ate like a king.

Tompkins began his enlistment with the PAI on April 10 but it would last only four days. He reported to the PAI barracks at the Marble Stadium at the Foro Mussolini, fronting the Tiber River in the northern part of the city. His induction was typical of the military; filling out multiple questionnaires and long-winded interviews with noncommissioned officers. His physical examination literally threatened to expose him. Tompkins, like many non-Jewish Americans, was circumcised, whereas in Italy, only Jews were. Was he not Berlingieri as he had claimed to be? He improvised an excuse: a venereal infection had caused him to have the operation. With eyebrows raised, his story was accepted and he was outfitted in an ill-fitting tropical-style uniform complete with pith helmet. He was to be assigned to a squad under a PAI lieutenant who had agreed to give him plenty of free time to continue his work.

During his days in the PAI, Tompkins enjoyed the good white bread reserved for the police. In fact he spent most of his time drinking wine at the outdoor canteen and doing perfunctory drills at which he was inept. Four days later, the lieutenant who was to look after Tompkins was arrested and the colonel who had endorsed the enlistment, fearing he would be next, told Tompkins to desert.

Tompkins' associates from the Palazzo Lovatelli, Crespi and his gay friend Emanuele, had moved into Secco-Suardo's apartment during that same four-day period. They continued to hold parties believing that, even if they were rounded up for the labor gangs, the Fascists would release them. Playboy partygoers and homosexuals were normally released as they were judged unsuitable for forced labor.

Tompkins was frustrated with the mess in which he found himself. He needed new orders, supplies, and money. He had had no recent communications with the OSS in Caserta. He had no radio and many of his operatives had been arrested. He decided to cross the lines and make for OSS headquarters at Caserta. Through his Open City contact, Ottorino Borin, he got an Italian police car registered to the Open City. It had papers and fuel authorizations. On May 1, Tompkins left Rome with Malfatti, Crespi, Secco-Suardo and their friend, Emanuele. It was to be a unique journey across Italy to the Adriatic.

Before he left, Tompkins made sure that the OSS knew that Menicanti had tried to undermine his work. He deposited a full report with Tittmann and Sir D'Arcy at the Vatican through Franco Malfatti's uncle, the Chargé d'Affaires for the Sovereign Military Order of the Knights of Malta to the Holy See. In the event of his death, the report was to be released to the OSS.

The OSS, in the meantime, had not heard from Tompkins and needed to know what was going on in Rome. An agent was landed on the Adriatic coast to investigate. This was Prince Raimondo Lanza di'Trabia. He and two radio operators had been dropped off beyond German lines by a British speedboat. British Agent di'Trabia had a forged pass signed by Generalarbeitsführer von Kurtschmann, a high officer in the Todt Organization. Di'Trabia and his team were given a staff car in which they drove to Rome. Once there, however, they were unable to contact any remaining OSS men because Tompkins had left and Menicanti had been arrested.

Tompkins and his four men crawled across Italy in their car, stopping at small hotels. They moved cautiously because they were often surrounded by German troops and Fascists. Tompkins soon realized that they would not be able to cross the lines without a local guide. Failing to reach the Allied lines, they gave up and returned to Rome on May 12. They brought with them some food and, lashed to the top of the car, a butchered pig, still bleeding.

20

Prelude to Liberation

Rome was starving, people were dying. The hospitals were full of the sick and malnourished. Since February 1944, no pasta ration had been available for purchase and 90 percent of the city's food was available only on the black-market, centered on Tor di Nona, the site of a medieval prison between Via dei Coronari and the Tiber, but the food prices there had increased ten times since November. To make matters worse, on March 26, General Mälzer ordered the daily bread ration be reduced from 150 to 100 grams per person. It was seen as another reprisal for the Via Rasella attack.

Revolt was brewing, especially among women trying to feed starving children. Communist women partisans took up the call first and distributed leaflets urging housewives to demand bread and food and to demonstrate. Due to these leaflets, demonstrations by women spontaneously broke out at bakeries throughout the city. It started when women waiting to buy their daily ration of bread formed a long line at the Tosti bakery (*panificio*) in the Appio quarter on April 1. After waiting two hours, they were told that the bread distribution would be late. Incensed, they began screaming that the real reason for the delay was that there wasn't even Mälzer's 100 grams per person to distribute.

The two Fascist militia guards on duty called for help. They told the women there would be no bread distributed until reinforcements arrived. After another long delay, the reinforcements came and the women were shoved into three lines. One woman shouted at one of the guards and was forcibly removed. The enraged crowd rushed the bakery door and the Fascist militia fired into the air. The women fought their way inside. There was the black bread to be distributed and, adding to their outrage, they found a large supply of white flour to be baked for the Germans. Order was restored at last and the bread distribution commenced.

A few days later, on April 6, another demonstration was organized at the Arrigoni bakery at Via Borgo Pio 126. Each day at the same time, a truck came to take Arrigoni's bread to the Fascist militia casern a few blocks away in Viale Giulio Cesare. They always took, without paying, five or six loaves of bread. They said it was to test the quality, but in reality they were stealing it for themselves. At least when the Germans came to the bakery they were polite and paid for what they took.

Two Fascist militiamen always rode with the truck for protection. Local partisans living next door to the bakery vowed to protect the women in case the demonstration became violent. The truck pulled up in front of the bakery as expected. As the bread was being loaded, women surrounded the truck and would not let it move. They grabbed the guards and threw them to the ground immobilizing them. Others pulled the driver from the cab. They broke into the truck and grabbed bags of fresh white bread and spilled them onto the street. Suddenly free from his captors, one of the guards pulled his pistol and fired shots into the air. The women dispersed. Some accounts of this demonstration erroneously claimed that one of the guards was killed by a partisan. However, the guard had only been injured in the crush and was taken to hospital by the baker.

The Panificio Angelo Arrigoni was founded in 1930 and served the Borgo, at the time one of the poorest and most crowded neighborhoods in the city. It has provided bread for every pope since that time. When bread rationing started, there was never enough to feed all and it could only be sold in return for coupons and cash. To obtain the raw flour, the baker had to present the collected coupons at a city depository. Being sympathetic, the baker, Erminio Arrigoni and his wife, Maria, often gave bread to those who needed it and, to make up the shortfall, they purchased additional flour on the black-market.

Erminio was in the Italian Army. His unit (unknown) was stationed in the vicinity of EUR until his regiment was sent to Russia. However, as a city baker he was ordered to remain behind. It saved his life, since most of the men sent to Russia never returned. Nevertheless, Erminio had to report to an army casern during the day and return to Borgo Pio in the evening to start the bread making. During the winter of 1943/44 the bakery produced a lot of hot water since much of the bread was steamed during the baking process to make the crust hard. At the end of the baking day, at about 13:00, small boys from the neighborhood would come to the bakery and fill containers with hot water. They then distributed this water to those neighbors who had small children or were elderly and needed the hot water for bathing, it being the only hot water available in the neighborhood.[1]

The next day, April 7, women and children again raided another bakery, this time in the Ostiense neighborhood. They had learned that it had a large supply of bread and flour. The crowd rushed the door and burst into the unguarded bakery. The baker passed out bread and flour to placate them; the women didn't know he had called the Germans, which led to a horrific outcome.

Germans, some say they were regular Wehrmacht soldiers, arrived and blocked the escape route: the bridge next to the bakery called the Ponte di Ferro (Iron Bridge, now renamed the Ponte dell'Industria). The women tried to flee but were trapped. The Germans seized ten of them, lined them up on the bridge facing the river and machine-gunned them all. The ten bodies remained on the bridge all day, their blood coloring the flour which had spilled from their sacks, red. It took years to discover the identities of the victims because they were refugees whose presence had not been registered by the authorities.

Another killing was of Caterina Martinelli, a mother of seven children, who took part in a raid on a bakery in the Tiburtina quarter of the city on May 3. She was shot dead by a PAI policeman standing guard. In her arms were a loaf of bread and her last-born child. Such tragedies were repeated as bread shortages and raids on bakeries took place throughout the city.*

Partisans coming to the aid of the starving populace raided the Centocelle Airfield, liberating a significant amount of food, which was distributed among the poorer families of Quadraro. General Mälzer was photographed passing out bread and hugging children in a publicity

---

*Other raids on bakeries occurred in Via Candia, in Via Leone IV, in Piazza S. Maria Ausiliatrice, in Via delle Cave, and in Via Camilla. Often the women broke in, overpowered the bakers, and took many kilos of bread and flour.

attempt to reverse anti-German sentiment. Mother Mary's diary caught the true picture:

> Partly for propaganda, partly to prevent food riots, and partly because the people were starving, General Mälzer, commander of Rome, has ordered rice, flour and bread to be distributed free in the poorer parts of the city, where the people are in an ugly mood. For instance, no German dares to go alone in the Trastevere. That district, the Garbatella and the Testaccio were the ones chosen. The lorry carrying the food was accompanied by a crowd of Italian and German journalists and camera men, and the papers published columns of praise of General Mälzer's generosity. They did not mention the fact that he is one of the "black-market kings" into whose pockets pass large sums gained in illicit traffic in food and tobacco.[2]

According to some witnesses, after the photos were posed, German soldiers snatched the bread away again. Sir D'Arcy wrote to London on April 25 of the apocalyptic effects of the Roman famine:

> I cannot too strongly emphasize that unless we can within the immediate future either ourselves provide for essential supply of flour to Rome or enable the Vatican to do so we shall be inviting a catastrophe by which the sole beneficiaries will be the Germans who, by their demilitarization of Rome, can claim to have divested themselves of the responsibility ... Famine, with all its terrible unknown consequences, is now hanging over the city of Rome. The population, swollen by refugees, is now destitute of all resources. The only way to supply Rome is by lorry. It cannot be believed that the Allies wish to deprive the population of this ultimate means of subsistence.[3]

The Escape Line's food expenses for all of Italy in May increased to more than 2,750,000 lire ($350,000). At least 250,000 lire came from Tittmann, the rest from Sir D'Arcy. The money was used to help the 164 escapees in Rome and the more than 3,500 in the countryside who were scattered around in groups of three to ten (or more) in more than 32 different locations.

The Escape Line list grew by 300 names at the month's end. The Germans, still anxious to recapture the ex-POWs, filed a complaint with the Vatican with at least a limited effect. When Baron von Weizsäcker formally complained that several religious orders were actively aiding Allied escapees, three priests – Fathers Borg, Madden, and Buckley – were confined by the Vatican to their religious houses. Brother Robert was still in hiding and Monsignor O'Flaherty was restricted to the German College and the Vatican. This made it too risky to collect signed receipts from ex-escapees for monies expended, so that was suspended. And Pollak was again seriously ill.

With the Escape Line caring for over 3,900 Allied soldiers scattered throughout Italy it was a constant challenge for them to thwart German attempts at recapturing them and they sometimes failed. The German policy toward recaptures outside of Rome was changing: instead of sending them to Germany, they were executing them in direct violation of the Geneva Convention.

Monsignor O'Flaherty received a letter from a country parish priest detailing one such execution. The Germans had recaptured four escaped Allied soldiers. The priest gave them the last rites before they were shot. One of those executed – an unidentified soldier – was allowed to write a letter home and that letter was enclosed in the priest's note to the monsignor with the request that he forward it to the soldier's family. The letter read:

> Dear Mother, Father and Family. This is the last letter I will be able to write as I get shot today. Dear family, I have laid down my life for my country and everything that was dear to me. I hope this war will be over soon so that you will all have peace forever. Goodbye. Your ever loving soldier, son and brother, Willie.[4]

The Escape Line was further weakened by losing the support of the Swiss legation. The Gestapo and the Fascist police were arresting escapees who went to the legation for assistance: food, money, cigarettes, clothes, and Red Cross parcels. The Swiss immediately informed the Escape Line that they could no longer help. Major Derry explained the problems in a note to Lt. Colin Leslie at the Casa San Giovanni. Leslie and the men were in the most secure place in Rome, but they were bored and out of touch with the action. Derry's note captures their frustration:

We have had a very black time recently; eight chaps have been shot in the country (some forty kilometers north of Rome)… and three of Golf's friends [Golf was Monsignor O'Flaherty's code name; his three friends were Fathers Borg, Buckley, and Madden] have had to go into strict hiding. Most of the denunciations have been due to a semi-padre [Don Pasqualino Perfetti]; fortunately, he did not know anything about your position – although we are of the opinion that they will not raid places like yours. Added to these black times, a lot of our boys have been going about contrary to orders, and some have been getting drunk. I think the waiting is getting them down (but it is slowly getting us all down). However, I am still full of optimism, personally, in spite of all. There is definite evidence that the Huns have pulled out a hell of a lot of their heavy stuff. I only hope the recent activity points to them pulling out too.[5]

Furman volunteered to supply the escapees in the surrounding countryside. Major Derry warned him to be careful as the country boys know all the tricks. He added that they will give false names and numbers; they will say there are four men at a site when there are only two. They will not give money to their *padroni* but spend it on drink. He also cautioned Furman to look out for stool pigeons – Germans dressed as escaped POWs with official British Army pay books who would trap the helpers.

A few days later Furman, in his new clean-shaven look, with slicked-back hair, was making deliveries of money and black-market American cigarettes to his escapees. He was in a tram in Prati, near the Teatro Adriano, his pockets bulging with the cigarettes and a small notebook where he kept records of his deliveries. Unwisely, he wore a small Union Jack pin under his lapel.

German police often conducted so-called blitz raids on trams, random stop-and-search actions. Furman's tram was stopped and surrounded. Men were taken out the front door; women and children remained seated. Furman, near the front of the tram, was startled by a man suddenly pushing past him. Using the distraction, Furman plopped down next to a woman, tore the incriminating pages of information from his notebook and stuffed them into her shopping basket.

Two German policemen and two National Republican Guard (GNR) officers were interrogating the men most of whom loudly protested that they were loyal Fascists, they had high-level Fascist connections, they were a friend of Mussolini, or any such story. This did no good if their papers were not perfect. Furman showed his legitimate Vatican identity card, with Baron von Weizsäcker's signature, together with an accompanying document that stated that he was employee of the Vatican Office of Technical Services. Furman affected boredom and said nothing. It worked. After a brief lecture from the police, he was allowed to go, the only one of five or six men to be released from that tram.

Fascist police continued their apartment raids. For some time, five of Mrs. Chevalier's former guests had been billeted with her butcher, Giovanni Ceccarelli. When Fascist police raided his apartment without warning, Ceccarelli pushed his five guests out onto his small balcony. After a thorough search, a policeman asked what was behind the curtain over the balcony window. "Only the balcony," replied Giovanni and, to deflect his attention, he offered the policeman a drink. "Sure," replied the policeman, "I'll just check the balcony first."

Ceccarelli's hand probably trembled as he poured the wine. The policeman came back in saying that there was not much of a view. They drank and he left. Ceccarelli closed the door, wondering what had become of the five men and he rushed to the balcony to see them climbing down from the apartment above on the stepladder he always kept there.

———

By late spring 1944, it was obvious that the Germans could no longer hold Rome, so preparations for the stay-behind network accelerated. Kappler had explosives hidden in gardens and parks around Rome, including the Germany Embassy, for later use by saboteurs. Locations included a park at Monte Mario, at Viale Guido Baccelli, the grounds of the Villa Umberto, and in some ancient tombs along Via Appia Antica. Supplies included plastic explosives and fuses.* The stay-behind effort was overseen by SS-Sturmbannführer Haas, and SS-Hauptsturmführer Priebke was put in charge of obtaining radios, organizing radio operator

---

* With liberation, the German Embassy was closed, the doors locked and secured with lead seals, and put under Swiss protection. It was then learned that explosives might have been hidden there. Fearing a detonation, the Swiss permitted Allied demolition experts to search the premises, resulting in the discovery of many important documents as well as explosives.

training, and radio security. These agents were to communicate with a German colonel, codenamed, Falco (hawk), who spoke multiple Italian dialects. Falco was actually several people. This coded character allowed the Germans to have as many Falcos as needed.

Kappler assigned G. Cipolla (his first name is unknown), the father of the previously mentioned Ubaldo Cipolla, to coordinate the stay-behind effort. Saboteurs were divided into four groups, each identified with a code letter. Section F, with five agents, was under the younger Cipolla. Section G, with 12 men, was under a man named Grossi and its mission was to penetrate and report on the black-market. The head of section H, with six men and three women, was Eugenio Flandro; his specific tasks are unknown, but he may have been responsible for sending couriers and sabotage agents through Allied lines. Section K, which had eight men and one woman, was led by German agent Georg Elling inside the Vatican.* Kappler's Dutch mistress, Helene Louise Ten Cate Brouwer, was also designated as an independent stay-behind agent.†

In Rome the roundups continued and the largest of these – some 2,000 men – was ordered by Kappler as a reprisal a week after three German soldiers had been killed by a partisan band on April 10. The roundup swept through the Quadraro district. The district lay along Via Tuscolana on the way to Cinecittà. Most partisan factions had strong cells in these neighborhoods which had led to the Gestapo dubbing the Quadraro neighborhood a nest of vipers.

One partisan band was led by a mere 17-year-old, Giuseppe Albani, called the hunchback of the Quarticciolo (*Il Gobbo*).‡ He styled himself a Robin Hood, stealing food to feed the poor. On April 10, Gobbo and his band were dining with others in the Trattoria da Giggetto near

---

* See Chapter 7.

† After the fall of Rome, Brouwer surrendered to the Allies on June 6, 1944, and for several weeks she worked for them. When she demanded that she be allowed to cross the German lines as a spy for the Allies, she was refused permission and became hysterical. Judged to be unstable and therefore untrustworthy, she was arrested and sent to England for interrogation.

‡ After the war Albani produced fake certificates for former Fascists to prove that their Fascist activities had been performed under the auspices of his partisan band. Reportedly, Rome Opera tenor Beniamino Gigli obtained such a certificate.

Cinecittà (not the same trattoria as at the Ghetto). Three German guards from the nearby POW transit camp at Cinecittà entered the trattoria and Gobbo and the others killed them.* Kappler's reaction was total and brutal and, on April 17, he unleashed a massive civilian roundup at Quadraro.

The SS, backed up by Wehrmacht troops and paratroopers on leave from the Anzio beachhead, surrounded the Quadraro district. The raid began at 05:00. An eyewitness described the chaos of the assault, the women crying, the mothers fleeing with their sons, and wives with their husbands. Men of all ages were snatched from their homes and taken to the transit camp at Cinecittà.

It was the largest-ever roundup of civilians. Kappler called it Operation *Whale* (*Unternehmen Walfisch*). Of the more than 2,000 men taken, 947 were judged fit for work and sent to Germany; 350 never returned. The Germans congratulated themselves. General Mälzer called it a good job. The same evening, Kesselring used the Roman newspapers to say that he was forced to arrest communists and their supporters in the Quadraro in retaliation for the murder of his soldiers at the trattoria on Easter Monday.

After this raid, *rastrellamento* became a daily occurrence. The absence of young Italian men on the streets made the Allied escapees stand out. The only good thing was that there were more empty seats on the trams, when they ran.

Roundups based on information from arrested partisans were devastating. The 40-year-old partisan and thief Guglielmo Blasi, who had participated in the attack on Via Rasella, had continued his secret life of petty crime. Blasi was captured during an attempted robbery in which two Fascist policemen were killed. Caruso personally interrogated Blasi who quickly broke down and gave him names and other details of GAP operations. With Blasi's names, Caruso initiated other roundups.

The first arrested were Franco Calamandrei and Carlo Salinari, the GAP commander. Blasi tricked them into meeting him at the Colosseum

---

* According to the Open City Police report of April 26, two members of Gobbo's band were later arrested in connection with the attack.

at 10:00 in the morning. Then he contacted Raoul Falcioni saying he had an important message from Bentivegna and needed to speak with him and Duilio Grigioni, the *portiere* at the *santabarbara* at Via Marco Aurelio. Both were captured by Banda Koch men. Then Silvio Serra was arrested. The captured Gappisti were all taken to the Pension Jaccarino on Via Romagna 38, at the corner of Via Sicilia. Although all five – Calamandrei, Salinari, Falcioni, Grigioni, and Serra – were tortured, Koch failed to pry any information from them about the GAP organization.

The Pension Jaccarino was Pietro Koch's new interrogation center and prison. Unlike his previous location, it was a separate building with high walls and a deep cellar so that the neighbors could not so easily hear the screams. Koch and his Banda enjoyed comfortable furnishings, a wine cellar, and an ample supply of coffee. Koch slept in the honeymoon suite and retained the kitchen staff. The chief punishment room, called the hole (*buca*), was windowless. There was also the coal cellar (*carbonaia*) and an attic (*soffitta*), both without lights and stinking of feces. The cleaning staff quit, complaining that there was too much blood to clean up.

Calamandrei boldly escaped the pension by asking to go to the bathroom where he squeezed himself out through a small window. He was able to warn those not yet arrested about the roundup.

Salinari was in the same cell as Falcioni and the two plotted to kill Koch. Falcioni, pretending to repent, convinced Koch that he had regretted working with the Gappisti and wanted to join Koch's Banda. It worked, and as a former taxi driver, he was taken on as Koch's personal driver. Other Banda Koch members doubted his sincerity though and they convinced Koch to throw Falcioni back into prison.

Others denounced by Blasi had escaped before they could be arrested. Mario Fiorentini was sent to Monti Tiburtini and Fernando Vitagliano hid out in Rome. His hiding place became known, and when Banda Koch members broke into his apartment in the middle of the night to arrest him, he shot two of them and fled, wounded. He randomly knocked on a door and explained to the old woman who opened it that he was a partisan. She took him in, dressed his wounds and gave him a bed.[*]

---

[*] By May 1945 the number of partisans had grown to more than 225,000 of which 35,000 were women. Of note, 63,000 partisans had been killed either in battles or in Gestapo or Fascist prisons and 33,000 had been badly wounded. See Wihelm, p. 97.

Because of the success of roundups based on Blasi's denouncements, partisans Carla Capponi and Rosario Bentivegna were ordered on May 5 to move to Palestrina, a town southeast of Rome, to make contact with the large number of escaped Russian POWs. Their mission was to organize the local partisans and the Russians for joint anti-German operations. It was thought that the Germans would retreat along Via Casilina once the Allies broke through and they had been sent in anticipation of that retreat. Germany had been sending Soviet soldiers captured on the Eastern Front to work in Italy on German fortifications. The Germans underestimated the resolve and toughness of these Russians, however, for many escaped and they soon constituted a threat to German troops in Italy.

The Russians acquired arms and attacked Germans convoys in the Palestrina area as they moved between Rome and the front. Aleksej Nikolaevich Fleysher, son of a noble White Russian family who had converted to communism, was their leader. He was helped by Father Dorotheo Bezchectnoff, a Russian priest, the Communist Party's Red Flag organization, and the Escape Line who provided funds for 400 Soviet escapees living in and around Rome, some of whom fought with the partisans. In one spectacular attack, they ambushed and killed 12 Wehrmacht motorcyclists and blew up a fuel truck. This drew the attention of Allied aircraft which repeatedly bombed and strafed the whole area. After that, the German troops eschewed vehicles in favor of marching along the highway. But this made them easy targets for the Russians who attacked and captured them.

Determined to carry out the mission, Capponi struggled against starvation and illness. She was sick, spitting up blood from a lung infection and suffering from cramps brought on by not drinking enough water. She and Bentivegna pushed a bicycle loaded with grenades and revolvers and it took ten hours for them to go the 20 miles to Palestrina. In Palestrina, they contacted the local partisans and moved with them down Via Casilina toward Valmontone, 25 miles east of Rome, to meet up with the Russians, about 140 of them, and their Italian girlfriends.

The Russians had hidden 47 German prisoners in a cave, including a complete Red Cross Unit: a doctor, nurses, and a large supply of medicines. A fight broke out between partisans and Russians over the medicines and in the squabble, both groups left Bentivegna and Capponi alone to guard the Germans. After three days in the heat and with no food, Bentivegna collapsed. The German prisoners were about to overcome Capponi when the Russians returned with food and apologies.

———

With the Allies seemingly stalled and the liberation of Rome on hold, Simpson believed that they should get as many ex-POWs out of Rome and across the lines as soon as possible. He was painfully aware that German collaborators were out and about in Rome and dangerous to his work but he nevertheless fell into a trap laid by two Greek-Italians named Giorgio and Dino. They had told Dukate, the American airman, they could arrange transportation for ex-POWs to cross the Allied lines at Anzio and only needed 150,000 lire to hire a boat. Dukate told Simpson and he was interested.

Dukate and Simpson met with Giorgio and Dino at a little basement trattoria on a quiet street off Via Flaminia, a mile north of Piazza del Popolo. Dukate and Simpson lingered past the curfew and had to spend the night at the men's apartment. Before leaving in the morning, Simpson arranged to meet them again that afternoon at the same trattoria.

Simpson outlined their proposal to Major Derry, who approved it. Meanwhile, at Rompoldi's bar in Piazza di Spagna, Dukate told Dennis Rendell, Pat Wilson, and Gil Smith about the plan. Bill Simpson joined them and after the meeting he and Dukate took the tram running up Via Flaminia to the trattoria. They overstayed the curfew again and agreed to spend the night with Giorgio and Dino. They had made a fatal mistake. Giorgio and Dino were Gestapo collaborators and had deliberately caused the men to remain out after curfew.

The Gestapo stormed into the apartment shortly after curfew on April 18, and arrested Dukate and Simpson. Bundled into a car, they were taken to the Regina Coeli Prison. Simpson had the false Vatican identity card given him by Monsignor O'Flaherty on him. It was in the name of William O'Flynn, an Irish researcher at the Vatican Library. This was to cause both confusion and missed opportunities.

At the prison, Simpson (under the name of O'Flynn) protested: he was only there because of the curfew; he knew none of the other men there. He said he had to go to work the next day and there would be trouble with the Vatican if he was late. The police contacted the Vatican and learned that there was indeed a priest named O'Flynn, but no civilian called William O'Flynn. They locked Simpson in a cell on the third floor of the German-run third arm of the prison. He was neither interrogated nor tortured.

The Escape Line was hatching plots to release Simpson from prison. Derry knew that Simpson was using his false name, O'Flynn, in the Regina Coeli. He also knew that his recapture was the Gestapo's highest priority as they had identified Simpson as one of the most important of the ex-POWs operating in Rome. Derry and Furman feared that if the Germans knew they had Simpson they would torture him until he broke and exposed everyone. They had to free Simpson.

A friend of Mrs. Almagiá, Wehrmacht Sergeant David Yorck, was enlisted to help. Yorck was a titled German nobleman, Graf von Wartburg. He had an American wife and children back in German Silesia. Yorck had been a banker before the war and had traveled in high social circles. He was anti-Nazi and had turned down a Wehrmacht commission. He had no intention of returning to Germany until after the war. Yorck, not knowing that Simpson's pseudonym was O'Flynn, went to the Regina Coeli and asked to see Simpson. When his real name was called, Simpson, of course, did not answer. He knew what the Germans would do if his cover were blown.

Desperate, Furman toyed with an idea of Adrienne Lucidi's. She thought that Ubaldo Cipolla, who they now knew was an Italian SS officer and a double agent, would want to avoid trouble with the Allies after liberation by proving his usefulness to them now. He was in fact willing to help but the fatal flaw in the plan was again Simpson's name and his alias. Cipolla was to go to the prison and ask for two prisoners to be released – Simpson and a Captain John Armstrong. Armstrong was not involved in the Escape Line but was a British officer with the SAS and therefore would have been at much higher risk than Dukate.

Cipolla convinced the Germans that the plan was good for them too, that releasing these prisoners to him would further ingratiate him with the British. In doing so, he would also be more valuable later to the Germans as a stay-behind agent. So Cipolla went to the prison and there was provided with a list of names of British prisoners to choose from. Of course, Cipolla found neither Simpson nor Armstrong so he picked two British names at random, one a British army private named Smith and the other, a civilian named Mr. Leslie, interned since the start of the war.* The two were released to Cipolla but were of no use to the Escape Line.

Simpson needed money and he requested 10,000 lire in a letter that he smuggled out. Derry received the request and sent the money, but Simpson never got it. Nor did he get Derry's accompanying letter that warned him that the Italians at least knew that his alias was the fictitious Irishman, William O'Flynn. When four British paratroopers disappeared from the prison on May 21, it was thought they had been sent north to German POW camps. Simpson and Dukate thought that they, along with other POWs, would be next.

———

With Simpson in custody, the Gestapo increased its assault on the ex-POWs. Mrs. Chevalier was alarmed after the Gestapo had grilled Egidio, the *portiere* at her apartment. She rarely phoned Monsignor O'Flaherty but called him now to warn away anyone who might come, even though she no longer provided a billet for ex-POWs. Nevertheless, a British soldier named Martin and an American sergeant named Everett, both escapees, did indeed turn up at Mrs. Chevalier's. She quickly sent them away but not fast enough to prevent the Germans from seeing them leaving the apartment house. The Germans chased them through the alleys near the apartment but did not catch them.

This episode made it clear to Mrs. Chevalier that she was no longer safe. It was time for her and her family to go. One by one she sent her daughters off to a friend's house, each leaving at different times and walking in different directions. She was last to leave. Two days later the whole family resettled on a farm outside the city.

Trying to safeguard those in his care in this worsening time, Derry issued contingency instructions. If ordered to leave Rome the ex-POWs were to be prepared to head for the ancient catacombs, just outside of the city. Derry's instructions included detailed descriptions on how not to get lost inside the ancient labyrinths.

The mood and tensions of the time are precisely delineated in the preserved Escape Line documents such as one Derry memo written on April 23. It was to be read to all the ex-POWs in Rome:

* He may have been the Leslie Ingram mentioned in the Escape Line notes, see Appendix F.

The facts are:

1. A large number (over 40) ex PW [1940s version of POW] have been retaken in the last few weeks in Rome. Of these, 28 were recaptured as a result of denunciations, and 16 have been picked up on the streets (of these 16, three were picked up in a drunken condition).
2. Current propaganda in Rome is that the Allies will not arrive before the autumn. This is strong propaganda when coupled with the food shortage and with the static condition of the bridge-head and Cassino fronts.
3. The Fascists and the German SS have been, during the last four weeks and still are, far more active in the respect of the rounding up of Allied ex PW than any time since the armistice.

These facts point to the following conclusions:

1. Fascist gangs, working in collaboration with the Gestapo, are out to make a name for themselves by rounding up all ex PW in Rome.
2. The work of finding billets, paying padroni, contacting and supplying our men is more difficult than before.
3. The longer men remain cooped up in-doors, the more desperate becomes their attitude of mind and stimulated by a drink or two, the more likely they are to take ill-advised action.

In view of the foregoing, I regret to have to issue the following instructions:

1. No more ex PW are to be billeted in Rome. Any arriving in the city will be given financial assistance and advised to return to the country.
2. Ex PW must on no account leave their billets unless they receive warning of an imminent raid. THE PRACTICE OF GOING FROM ONE BILLET TO ANOTHER TO VISIT FRIENDS MUST CEASE FORTHWITH.
3. If forced to make a run for it, ex PW must leave Rome and hide out in the country. Dashing to another billet only compromises additional people.

4. A lump sum of 6,000 lire per man for the month of May will be
   given to you. This is for maintenance for May, and should allow
   for some ready cash in an emergency. In some cases, the lump sum
   may be paid to ex-PW. In other cases it will require to be paid in
   installments, as some of the boys would convert cash into assets of
   a more "liquid" character.

German intelligence was on the whole reliable, but mistakes were made. In one instance, the Gestapo misidentified a Dutch priest, Father Anselmo Musters, as a British colonel and the head of the Escape Line.

Father Musters had been fingered by an unidentified "V-Mann" spy recruited by the SS and working inside the Vatican. The V-Mann had the priest trailed by the Gestapo when he left the safety of the Vatican. Spotting the tail, he headed straight to the close-by Basilica of Santa Maria Maggiore for sanctuary.

A high column topped by a bronze statue of the Virgin Mary stands before the steps just in front of the basilica. There the Gestapo men blocked Father Musters' entry and demanded his identity papers. He was without his documents so he raced up the short flight of steps to one of the five bronze doors into the basilica. As he entered, the German struck the priest on the back of his head. A Palatine Guard stationed at the door dragged the half-conscious priest inside. When he came to, Musters telephoned Monsignor O'Flaherty who told him to spend the night inside the basilica where he would be safe. He was not.

The Gestapo, certain that Father Musters was an English colonel masquerading as a priest, surrounded the basilica. Six men, led by SS Hauptsturmführer Gerhard Köhler, ignoring Vatican extraterritoriality, charged into the basilica. Later, the Germans justified their illegal action by saying that by leaving the Vatican, Father Musters had forfeited his immunity to arrest. They hauled the priest out of the basilica and dragged him down the steps. A Gestapo policeman struck him again on his head with a submachine gun. They took him to nearby Via Tasso.

SS-Hauptsturmführer Karl Wolff, not to be confused with the SS head in Italy, Karl F. Wolff, was the head interrogator at Via Tasso and he went to work. Priebke and Carl-Theodor Schütz were also present. Father Musters was shown a chart of the Escape Line organization which was quite accurate, indicating the depth of knowledge the Germans had on the organization. Musters later revealed that he was afraid that he would inadvertently confirm its accuracy.

The interrogators had no luck at breaking the priest, so they brought in Helene Louise Ten Cate Brouwer to question him. Brouwer was a Dutch national, an SS agent, and one of Kappler's mistresses. Also present at the interrogation was Dr. Ludwig Wemmer, an SS officer assigned to the German Embassy to the Holy See and the special advisor to Baron von Weizsäcker. Wemmer was able to get von Weizsäcker to placate the Vatican over the arrest. The Gestapo interrogated Father Musters for three weeks then gave up and left him for two more weeks in a lightless cell. They eventually sent him north on June 3 on the Gestapo omnibus along with the German female secretaries who worked at Via Tasso. When it reached Florence, Father Musters slipped off the bus and escaped. He made his way across the shifting battle lines and when he returned to Rome it was a liberated city.

Things were about to change. In late May, the Allies began their breakout from the Anzio beachhead. The Allies had been steadily reinforcing their troops since the original landings and now had more troops than the Germans who surrounded them. The tide of war in Italy was about to irrevocably turn.

Pietro Koch, like many others, was now looking for insurance against future indictment. Koch, who had made more than 400 arrests during his tenure in Rome, planned to leave with the Germans when they left the city. However, he was concerned about leaving his mother and wife behind. Therefore, Koch sent a man to visit Monsignor O'Flaherty requesting safety for his relatives. In return, he promised to leave the monsignor's friends in the Regina Coeli Prison when the Germans departed.

Naturally suspicious of Koch's offer, O'Flaherty requested the immediate release of both Simpson and Armstrong. But the alias problem again stymied the effort. When their names were called out again, neither man replied. Simpson had not received the note telling him to answer to his real name, and Armstrong, thinking it was a trap, also refused to answer. Meanwhile Monsignor O'Flaherty fulfilled his side of the bargain and contacted Koch's wife and mother, but they refused his help to leave the city.

———

At the end of April, 1944, Mario Badoglio, son of Marshal Badoglio, who had been hiding inside the Basilica of Saint John Lateran, was betrayed, arrested, and taken to Via Tasso. He had on him a letter he had written to his father saying that he was going to cross the lines to the Allies. Berlin thought this was significant and ordered that Kappler send him to Berlin so Priebke and Haas were given the job to escort the prisoner to the German capital. When they returned on June 3, they found the city in chaos and their fellow Germans preparing to flee.

At Long Last, Liberation

The vast Allied attack on Rome was imminent as the armies of the United Nations, as the Allied forces in Italy were often called, massed for battle. During the long winter and spring, they had been reinforced by fresh troops and now were superior in number and equipment to the Germans. For their part the Germans had no more troops to send to Italy, so the balance had undeniably shifted in the Allies' favor. The German fallback position, the Gothic Line, in the mountains north of Florence, was almost complete. It was now obvious that Germany would soon abandon Rome and the occupiers' idea was to salvage whatever they could. Meetings were held, agreements reached, deals struck and, while they awaited the attack, the Germans continued their repressive policies.

Although he lacked the authority to negotiate, SS-General Karl F. Wolff nevertheless came to Rome to seek a way to save the city from destruction and broker some kind of deal. At his request, Dollmann arranged a secret meeting with the Pope on May 10. Wearing a tight-fitting civilian suit, courtesy of Dollmann, Wolff was accompanied by Father Pancrazio Pfeiffer, the unofficial Gestapo liaison to Pope Pius XII.

They met for an hour and spoke German, in which the Pope was fluent. Playing on the Pope's fears of communism, Wolff offered to broker a compromise peace between the Germans and the Allies. This effort was his own initiative and it was questionable whether he could pull off such an agreement.

The Pope was more interested in the terrible conditions at the prison on Via Tasso and asked, as an act of good faith, that the Gestapo release

Giuliano Vassalli, the socialist leader. Wolff promised to review the conditions at the prison and to see about Vassalli. At the end of the meeting the Pope told Wolff he would never voluntarily leave Rome. As Wolff took his leave he demonstrated his continued loyalty to the Third Reich by clicking his heels and giving the Nazi salute, Heil Hitler! He simply couldn't help himself.

Meanwhile, the Germans continued to look for laborers for the Todt Organization and workers to be sent to Germany. During May, there were at least three roundups, one in conjunction with the German order to evacuate Castel Gandolfo; a second at Ostia; and the third on Via Aurelia. Partisan resistance to the roundups, re-energized by the coming Allied invasion, was intense and successful. Many of the laborers never made it to Germany. Two Gappisti blocked a train filled with workers being sent to Germany at the Casilina railway station in southeast Rome and freed all the men. Other partisans, helped by railway workers at the Tiburtina station, derailed a second train that carried 300 prisoners, enabling many to escape.

By this time, Caruso had organized a special squad to round up any remaining Jews. On April 12, 1944, a group of 157 Roman Jews arrived at Fossoli (near Verona). One of those was Piero Terracina, a 15-year-old boy who was taken on April 7 as he sat down with his family for the Passover meal. Although they had false papers, two local informants sold out the entire family, mother, father, and three siblings. All were taken to the Regina Coeli Prison and then sent to Fossoli. Piero was quickly separated from his family at Auschwitz and was the only one to survive.[*]

On May 13, 400 more Jews were taken from the Regina Coeli Prison. Old men, women, and children, were marched to the ground floor of the prison and loaded on trucks and sent to Fossoli, 215 miles north of Rome. By the middle of May there were too many Jews at the concentration camp so the Germans put them all on a train to Poland.

---

[*] In his later years, Terracina devoted his life to telling the story of the Holocaust. His death at 91 was reported in the Obituaries Section of the *Washington Post* in the Sunday, December 15, 2019 edition. In response to this article, on January 4, 2020, *Washington Post* reader Larry L. Goldstein wrote that three brass *Stolpersteine* (stumbling blocks) are located in front of Via del Temple #4 to mark the last residence of three members of his extended family who were killed at Auschwitz. More than 70,000 of these ten-inch-square markers have been placed in more than 1,200 cities and towns all over Europe. They are often encountered in Rome.

While the exact number is not known it was more than 1,000 people. On the way, the train stopped in Verona to add three further wagons which contained 163 more Jews, many of whom were reportedly British nationals. The train traveled to Munich's Ostbahnhof, the train station on the east side of the city used to transfer Jews to extermination camps in the occupied Reich. From there the train went to the Bergen-Belsen concentration camp in Germany and then moved onward to Birkenau in Poland for labor selection. A total of 486 men and 70 women were selected for work details and the rest were exterminated.

The Allied move on Rome was called Operation *Diadem*, a multi-pronged attack whose objective was to destroy the enemy south of the city. Preparation had started more than two months earlier. Field Marshal Harold Alexander, Supreme Allied Commander Mediterranean, thought the most important prong was that of the British Eighth Army advancing up Via Casilina. In order to do this the greater part of the British Eighth Army, under Lieutenant-General Sir Oliver Leese, was shifted from the Adriatic to the Cassino front under great secrecy. This would give the Allies the superior forces necessary to move up the Liri Valley in conjunction with the breakout at Anzio. The Eighth Army would start the attack first and, when successful, the Fifth Army would head east from Anzio and cut off the retreating German forces.

The British Eighth Army was an army of diverse forces. In addition to British troops, the rest of the Empire was represented by Canadians, Indians, South Africans, and New Zealanders. There were also divisions of Free Poles and reconstituted Italian troops. Earlier in North Africa, the Eighth Army had included Australians but they had been called home to protect Australia from a potential Japanese invasion.

French General Alphonse Pierre Juin was the commander of the French Expeditionary Corps. The French Corps now consisted of four divisions: two Moroccan, one Algerian, and one French. Juin had long argued that his corps, with many mountain fighters from North Africa, could proceed through the Aurunci Mountains facing Monte Cassino, 60 miles to the south of Rome, and capture the 3,000-foot peak of Monte Maio. From there they could catch the Germans off guard south and west of the Liri Valley. Frenchmen saw

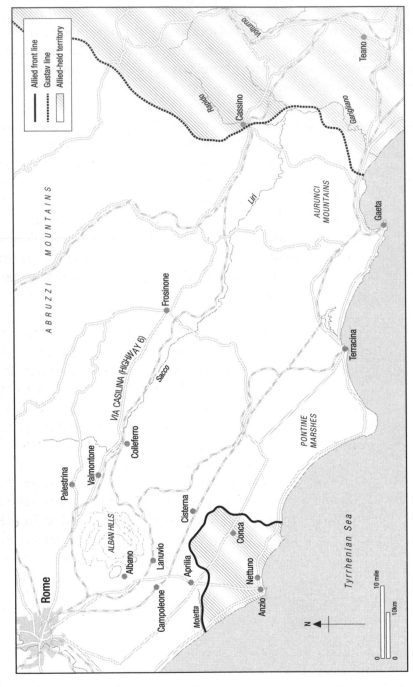

STALEMATE ON THE ITALIAN FRONT, SPRING 1944

Allied front line
Gustav line
Allied-held territory

Volturno
Teano
Rapido
Cassino
Garigliano
Liri
AURUNCI MOUNTAINS
Gaeta
ABRUZZI MOUNTAINS
Frosinone
Terracina
Sacco
VIA CASILINA (HIGHWAY 6)
PONTINE MARSHES
Colleferro
Valmontone
Palestrina
Cisterna
Conca
ALBAN HILLS
Lanuvio
Aprilia
Nettuno
Tyrrhenian Sea
Albano
Campoleone
Moletta
Anzio
Rome
N
10 mile
10km

this as the first step in recapturing their homeland. Unfortunately some of the North African forces merely looked forward to reaping the spoils of war. As they spread up and over the mountains, Moroccan troops raped at least 2,000 women including girls as young as 11, grandmothers, and some young boys. Later an unnamed Italian recorded their behavior:

> We suffered more during the twenty-four hours of contact with the Moroccans than in the eight months under the Germans. The Germans took away our goats, sheep and food, but they respected our women and our meager savings. The Moroccans flung themselves upon us like unchained demons. They violated, threatening with machine-guns, children, women, young men, following each other like beasts in rotation; they took our money from us, they followed us into the village and carried off every bundle, our linen, our shoes. Even those of their officers who tried to intervene in our defense came under their threats.[1]

The French troops, as agreed, would break through the mountains, but there was competition between rival Allied generals, in this case General Mark Clark's US Fifth Army and Lieutenant-General Sir Oliver Leese's British Eighth Army. Each wanted the honor of being first to enter Rome. The rivalry and questions were thought to have been put to rest when British Field Marshal Alexander gave the order that the primary objective was to cut off the German retreat from Cassino along Via Casilina; Rome was a secondary objective.

At the end of May, Tompkins, now back in Rome, wrote in his diary of hearing a Fifth Army radio broadcast from the beachhead. The speaker was giving the people of Rome a pep talk and telling them to be patient. Tompkins, cut off from radio access, was frustrated at hearing that six clandestine Allied radios that had been captured by the Germans were being used by them for counterintelligence and to feed false information to the Allies. On May 29, Mother Mary wrote:

> The sounds of war continue to echo around us day and night, but unusually, continuous pounding of guns in the Alban Hills begin to be heard about mid-day. The electric current for such buses and

trams as remained to us was cut off this morning, so one has to walk or not go at all. It is really better for all to stay indoors, especially the men.[*][2]

Simpson, still imprisoned, could see that things were changing by May 31. Crack SS guards were replaced by ordinary Austrian soldiers at Regina Coeli Prison; and the routine became sloppy. The prisoners were encouraged by the distant firing they could hear from the hills south of the city. Simpson wrote that the Austrian guards called out the names of 200 young men and boys whom they believed were being taken to work on Wehrmacht Gothic Line fortifications north of Florence. Their fate is not known.

All over Rome the sound of heavy guns was heard and Allied dive bombers could be seen from the rooftops of the Vatican. German resistance had been weakened. Reportedly, since May 23 and the start of the Anzio breakout, the Wehrmacht's 14th Army had lost 75 percent of its manpower killed, wounded, or captured and most of its equipment. There was no stopping the Allies now.

The transition from a status quo to chaos was rapid as entities and factions acted and reacted separately without reference to each other or to a plan or to a presumption of normalcy. Order toppled as the Allies, the Germans, the Vatican, the Italian governments, the partisans, the diplomats, the Escape Line, all moved in their own directions. With these disparate elements initiating actions in isolation, it may be clearer to the reader if events were presented day by day:

JUNE 1, 1944

The night sky glowed red from the direction of the Alban Hills. A mysterious fire also burned out Pietro Koch's new torture prison at the Pension Jaccarino. The four arrested GAP Central partisans incarcerated there – Raoul Falcioni, Duilio Grigioni, Carlo Salinari, and Silvio Serra – were transferred to Kappler's Via Tasso Prison. Meanwhile, German

---

[*] Scrivener notes that the Germans had taken the city buses for troop transport. By mid-March, the manager of the Rome Tram and Bus Company reported that 434 out of 713 trams remained serviceable, and only 128 out of 661 buses were still in the city. See Scrivener, p. 142.

senior officers stacked their baggage in the foyers of the grand hotels along Via Veneto.

Old people collapsed in the streets, starving. The Pope pleaded with the Allies to bring food into the city along with an advance governing party. The Allies agreed to the food but not the advance party.

Over in the Borgo, near the Vatican, the people were so starved for food that something remarkable occurred. As the Germans left the city, one of their horses became lame and had to be shot. Within five minutes the entire carcass was gone and even the blood from the poor animal was sopped up from the street.

Reportedly Hitler said Rome was a place of culture and must not be a scene of combat operations. But no one knew for sure if the Germans would defend the city. Later Major Derry wrote his thoughts on the deteriorating situation in Rome:

> Beyond the city the sound of battle was already audible, but Furman and the other escapees could only guess what would happen next. They could see German columns being withdrawn from the battle line, and much heavy equipment moving steadily northward, but for all any of us knew the Germans were still prepared to stand and turn the Eternal City into a second Stalingrad, defending it street by street, until nothing but ashes remained.[3]

Bruno Spampanato, the editor of the Roman newspaper *Il Messaggero*, called on the citizens of Rome to defend their sacred city against the multi-racial horde of Anglo-American soldiers. Not a single Fascist responded to the call to take up arms.

JUNE 2, 1944

The Supreme Allied Commander sent a message to his commanders with the code word "Elephant": the liberation of Rome was imminent. On the same day Rome was bombed for the last time. The Allies were less than ten miles from the outskirts of the city and the liberation of the city appeared to be merely hours away.

That morning John May ran excitedly into Derry's office exclaiming that a British officer was on the radio link between Castel Gandolfo and the Vatican. Derry got on the radio and gave the surprised officer a detailed report of what was happening inside the city, including the exact placement of Wehrmacht anti-tank guns. In his turn, the officer told Derry that Valmontone, south of Rome, had been captured.

In a radio address, the Pope said, "Whoever raises a hand against Rome will be guilty of matricide to the whole civilized world and in the eternal judgment of God."[4] Partisan factions honored the Pope's plea that there be no insurrection in Rome.

General Wolff had left the city. After his meeting with the Pope, he went to Karlsbad, Germany, to take the waters. Kappler honored General Wolff's pledge to the Pope and released the socialist leader Giuliano Vassalli to Father Pancrazio Pfeiffer.

General Clark's US Fifth Army's orders, moving toward Rome, were purposely vague. He wanted to take advantage of the expected German withdrawal; however, on what seemed to be his own initiative, Clark divided his forces and sent several divisions directly north to Rome while he sent the US 3rd Division to Valmontone to cut off the Germans. There they ran into heavy resistance. The Germans had ordered an all-out effort until their largely intact 10th Army could retreat along Via Casilina. It was now streaming up the highway, saved to fight another day. Had General Clark sent his entire command to Valmontone, he might have cut the highway and entrapped the entire German Army.

Although the German Army had escaped, the Allies still had a successful day. The German line had collapsed and was in retreat from the Alban Hills toward Rome. Upon reaching the highway, the US 3rd Infantry Division handed over its positions around Palestrina to the French and started its sweep into Rome. From the Anzio beachhead, a live GI band broadcast swing music.

JUNE 3, 1944

Thousands of Germans were flowing through Rome. There were continuous streams of German trucks, panzers, and long-range guns pouring along Via dell'Impero, heading north. The noise of the German withdrawal could be heard all over the city under the full moon. A long line waited to cross the ancient Ponte Milvio on Via Cassia Antica. The retreat lasted well beyond noon as can be seen in a series of photographs taken from the heights at the Pincio Park overlooking the Piazza del

Popolo. An Italian Catholic priest, Monsignor Giovannetti, wrote about the German withdrawal:

> The soldiers were retreating orderly, but they looked spent and humiliated. They had requisitioned anything with wheels, private cars, horse-drawn taxis, even oxcarts with the oxen. It was an interminable procession. Some were marching with huge, overstuffed backpacks, carrying their weapons in their hands. The people stood by and watched them saying nothing. A few boys offered them something to drink. Soldiers, who for nine months had fought with valor against a superior enemy passed by, showing all the signs of a terrible battle. How many of them still believed in the promise of Hitler's Thousand-Year Reich?[5]

In the morning, the Germans blew up fuel and ammo dumps at Fort Tiburtina, the Macao Barracks, and the Verano cemetery. The Fiat works in Via Manzoni and three railway yards were also blown up. Partisans and other patriots, however, saved many public buildings. Other partisan formations did what they could to hinder the German retreat, actively collaborating in the liberation of Rome. Rearguard German troops engaged in firefights on roads leading out of the city which were increasingly clogged with German vehicles in retreat. Many vehicles were simply abandoned.

The partisan attacks netted hundreds of German prisoners as well as a notable amount of war materiel. At Monterotondo, the former *Comando Supremo* Headquarters just outside of Rome, partisans and Russian ex-POWs assaulted a German command post and, in fierce combat, captured more than 250 Germans, killing and wounding many.

A GAP squad attacked a German truck during the night, at the nine-kilometer marker of Via Trionfale, north of the city. It was carrying men and ammunition. They killed 14 German soldiers during a brief firefight. Along the Via Cassia and Via Flaminia retreat routes, German soldiers mixed with GNR soldiers, Fascist commissioners, prefects, and inspectors; the hierarchy of Fascist Rome were in flight. At 18:00 Allied dive bombers attacked the German columns and Via Flaminia and Via Cassia were visions of hell, repeatedly bombed and strewn with the wreckage of innumerable vehicles. The attacks lasted about an hour and were also visible from the Vatican.

On the way out of the city, the Germans sabotaged the telephone exchange, silencing all of Rome's telephones. They also damaged the water and electric supply distribution systems. And at Fort Bravetta, the Gestapo had PAI policemen shoot six partisans from the FMCR. This brought the total executed at the Fort to 77 during the nine months of German occupation.

Civilians were not safe. A German patrol abandoned an armored car which had broken down as it retreated near the large ancient city gate, the Porta Maggiore. The soldier in charge threw a hand grenade into the car, ignoring the crowd of civilians in the vicinity. The resulting fire ignited munitions which exploded, killing 30, mostly women and children.

Tompkins wrote in his diary that, although the Germans declared that the line from Valmontone to the sea was still holding, the rumor was that the Germans would clear out that night. He also wrote there was no news of the fate of the prisoners in the Regina Coeli Prison. OSS agent Franco Malfatti hoped to get prisoners released from Via Tasso by guaranteeing that the 15,000 wounded Wehrmacht soldiers could recover in local hospitals and they would not be badly treated, but nothing happened immediately.

Tompkins had a plan to round up all the senior Italian Fascist collaborators but the Allied radio from the beachhead broadcast their names which allowed them to flee north with the Germans. According to CBS news journalist, Eric Sevareid:

In the morning, again we drove around the eastern slopes of the lovely green hills, past mutilated Valmontone ... and as we progressed it began to dawn upon us that the German defenses were falling apart so fast that we would be in Rome within hours. The air was charged with excitement, with savage triumph and obscene defeat. German vehicles were smoldering at every bend of the road, and dead Germans lay sprawled beside them, their faces thickening with the dust sprayed over them by the ceaseless wheels that passed within inches of the mortifying flesh. Shells were screaming over in both directions, but in the general frenzy not even the civilians paid them much notice. By wrecked gasoline stations, in the front yards of decapitated homes, flushed Americans were shoving newly taken prisoners into line, jerking out the contents of their pockets and jabbing those who hesitated with the butt ends of their rifles. A child was vigorously kicking a dead German officer, until a young woman shoved the child aside and dragged off the man's boots. Infantry of the Third Division were arriving in trucks, and their General Iron Mile O'Daniel, jumped from his jeep before it had stopped and in stentorian voice shouted the orders for their de-trucking and deployment. One of our tank destroyers ahead burst into flames, and shells began falling nearer.[6]

Field Marshal Kesselring reiterated that Rome was an Open City. At 16:00 hours, Kesselring called Hitler and briefed him about the situation. Uncharacteristically, Hitler had not insisted on a fight to the death for Rome and gave the field marshal permission to abandon it. Both he and Kesselring considered Rome to be no longer of strategic or tactical value. Although it probably pained Hitler to cede anything to the Allies, he balanced that against the powerfully negative propaganda were Rome to be damaged or destroyed. Fifteen minutes later Kesselring called General von Vietinghoff and informed him that the Führer had decided that no fighting was required within the city itself or in the surrounding area.

Tittmann wrote of a tank battle at Lanuvio, 25 miles away to the south, which he watched from the Vatican rooftop with binoculars. He watched the tanks move in and out of the dust and smoke that obscured the main action from view. It was the last serious resistance put up by the Germans in the Rome area.

They looted civilian shops, including the hardware store in Piazza Fiume near the closed British Embassy. The soldiers packed everything carefully. The Germans left the big hotels in good order, ready for their next guests: all linens clean and intact, the restaurants with all their plates and cutlery.

On his way out of the city, Dollmann visited Kesselring's headquarters at Monte Soratte to say goodbye to the field marshal and then he, his driver Mario, and his faithful dog, headed north. Later, Derry learned that the Number One Special Force had sent four Italian radio operators north with the Germans and Fascists to send back intelligence. Meanwhile Pietro Koch was being bribed by a Roman family to release its relatives. The family was busy counting out the one and a half million lire ransom, but he fled before he could collect it.

Some prisoners were taken away with the Germans. At 20:00 the Gestapo loaded 30 of their most important Via Tasso prisoners into two trucks, 16 on the first and 14 on the second. Driven by lower-ranking SS members, the first truck broke down and those 16 men, including four GAP partisans, Raoul Falcioni, Duilio Grigioni, Carlo Salinari, and Silvio Serra, were taken back to Via Tasso where they were liberated a few hours later.

The second truck, escorted by four German and two Italian SS men, drove north along Via Cassia on its way to a concentration camp in Germany. It stopped for the night at the 14-kilometer marker at La Storta on Via Cassia, a former way station. Anxious to avoid capture by the Allies, the guards had their prisoners stay in a garage on a nearby estate.

In a remarkable twist, the partisans took hostages. A partisan commander went to the Via Tasso Prison to tell SS-Hauptsturmführer Carl-Theodor Schütz that he had taken four of their women. He said his partisans would release them, when all the Tasso prisoners were released. Schütz capitulated and released 40 badly beaten prisoners, who, dressed in rags, began their painful shuffle home.

Field Marshal Kesselring, in a bid for time, ordered Ambassador Weizsäcker to meet with Monsignor Montini that evening. The ambassador asked the Vatican to get the Allies to hold off on their attack on the city; he said it was to save the city but in reality it was a ploy to allow more time for the Germans to escape.

At 21:00 the BBC read a communiqué from General Alexander saying the Fifth Army had broken through all along the line from Valmontone to the sea. The Alban Hills, visible from Rome, were entirely in Allied hands.

Although, in accordance with Hitler's orders, the bridges of Rome were left intact, Field Marshal Kesselring had some wired for demolition, including the Ponte Cavour in front of the Justice Ministry, in case of a fighting withdrawal.

To ensure calm in Rome, General Mälzer, the self-proclaimed King of Rome, attended, as he had planned, a gala evening performance at the Rome Opera House of Verdi's *Un Ballo in Maschera*. At midnight, Tompkins sent a man to see what the Germans on Via Veneto were doing and he learned that General Mälzer was back from the opera, stinking drunk, and babbling in French. The German HQ was preparing to leave, but it was complete chaos. At the Vatican, young Tittmann wrote in his diary:

> We did not sleep well during the night of June 3, because of the noise generated by the retreating German troops. One of the main roads to the north of Rome, Via Aurelia, passed by the Vatican walls close to Santa Marta. Because of the Allied air attacks, the Germans moved their heavy equipment primarily by night. Some German vehicles would take a wrong turn up a dead-end street not far from us, resulting in much shouting and grinding of gears. Unable to sleep, I went to the roof of the main Santa Marta building to view the German trucks and panzers moving north ... One could tell that the Germans were lacking motor transport, for they were extensively using horses to draw wagons and every kind of contraption you could think of. Some were even on bicycles. They had stolen all Rome's horse drawn cabs. They also used horses to pull their artillery. One felt rather sorry for them; they looked so young. Some were tired and dirty, but others looked perfectly fit. Not all Germans had managed to steal a horse or a bicycle, for there were long columns of them marching. Those were the ones that really looked exhausted. Some had to carry machine guns on their shoulders. They looked terribly depressed. Some stopped right below me and sat down on some grass. Others bought filthy lemonade from a little stand, also right below me. I must say the Romans were very kind to them, although they were immensely relieved to see them leaving. They gave the Germans drinks and cigarettes. It is in the character of Romans to be kind to everyone in trouble.[7]

JUNE 4, 1944

A long column of cars, buses, and trucks formed up in Via Veneto as Germans and others departed the city under the cover of darkness.

The SS drove away in trucks, stolen automobiles, and an omnibus.* Kappler was the last to exit Via Tasso, leaving behind the large portrait of Hitler in the reception room. In abandoning Via Tasso, the SS tried to destroy evidence of atrocities. They carried incriminating documents out of the prison and set them on fire while other documents were thrown out of the windows.

These papers might have been lost to history were it not for a former Rome police inspector, detective, playwright, master of disguise, and author. Often called the Sherlock Holmes of Italy, Giuseppe Dosi (1891–1981) lived nearby and was then working as a photojournalist for EIAR, the Italian National News and Radio Organization. Dosi had rushed to Via Tasso to see what was being done with the prisoners incarcerated there. Instead, he found documents floating on the street, many only half-burned. Realizing that the documents must be saved, he and a German-Swiss Wehrmacht soldier who had gone AWOL and had been hiding with him scooped up the scorched papers. They took them to Dosi's apartment by wheelbarrow, making several trips to move the lot. Significantly, the records included prison registers, receipts, copies of the German War Tribunal deliberations, correspondence, and a list of the 77 Jews murdered at the Fosse Ardeatine.

Those fleeing included Rome's Italian governing officials. Not all got away. Police Chief Pietro Caruso fled in the early hours in a ministry-owned Alfa Romeo driven by Corporal Franzetti. The car slammed into a tree outside Viterbo in the early daylight as Franzetti was dodging a strafing aircraft. Caruso's leg was fractured and he was taken to the local hospital where local partisans arrested and held him until he could be turned over to the Allies.

---

*At the German Embassy, the Germans left behind a document that listed all the SS men in Rome and in which vehicle they were to leave Rome. These 27 vehicles included 15 passenger cars (PKW – *Personenkraftwagen*): Fiat 500 (Topolino), Fiat 1100, Fiat 1500, Fiat III, a military version of the Fiat 2800 C, two Lancias (one a Ballia), a Lazarett Druenn (a French Simca?), a Mercedes, two Porsches, a Rome police car, and three other unidentified cars. There were 12 miscellaneous German Army vehicles or trucks (LKW – *Lastkraftwagen*) including: a communications van (*Funkwagen*); a mobile kitchen (*Küchenwagen*); four MG LKW Schütz, machine gun-equipped trucks with the designations Hines, Juge, ON, and Mun; a military liaison vehicle (*Verbindungst Miliz*); two motorcycles; two otherwise unknown vehicle types (with the markings K.E. and Ivagea) and a passenger bus (*Omnibus*).

At 06:30 Italian General Roberto Bencivegna left his hideout inside the Vatican to take military and civil control of Rome, a responsibility given him by the Badoglio government.

Via Tasso SS guards, whose truck was stopped on Via Cassia, murdered their prisoners at La Storta that morning. With the Allies fast approaching, there had been an argument among them whether they should continue on with the prisoners, free them, or shoot them. The decision was to take the 14 prisoners to a wall and execute each with a pistol shot to the head. Writing of this incident later, author Simonetti reported that Kappler had sent a motorcyclist to La Storta ordering the execution, although this is considered unlikely. Among the 14 executed were: British Army Captain John (Gabriel) Armstrong, who was a British No. 1 Special Service Force officer and whose real name was Adler Gabor; Lt. Eugenio Arrighi, Tompkins' agent who had identified his denouncer by drawing a rabbit (*coniglio*) on the wall at Via Tasso; Bruno Buozzi, the Socialist Trade Union leader; Vincenzo (Enzo) Converti, the radio operator who betrayed Maurizio Giglio; Edmondo (Topolino) Di Pillo, who had fetched Tompkins on his first day in Rome; and Enrico Sorrentino, the self-stylized personal representative of General Mark Clark who had sold out Arrigo Paladini. Three days later, local inhabitants recovered the cadavers of what were the last victims on a long list of murders committed by the Gestapo during their nine-month occupation of Rome. The battle for Rome was almost over.

Meanwhile, order broke down at the Regina Coeli Prison as first the Austrian guards fled, and then the Italian guards followed them. One of the prisoners took charge; an unknown Italian Army major had other officers unlock cells. With Simpson's help, they searched for Allied soldiers, and found 16. The Italian major then prepared for an orderly departure of the prisoners. He was not sure that troops guarding the outside of the prison would not mow down prisoners as they left, but reasoned that the troops were unlikely to fire on women so they were let out first. The next contingent was the Allied soldiers, then Italians in small manageable groups. Although many Germans were still around, they ignored the prison break. And Simpson, resuming his role of Escape Line officer, found billets for the Allied soldiers for the night. By noon there were reportedly hundreds of ill-clad groups of men and women wandering away from the Regina Coeli. Although he was not specifically mentioned it appears that Duke Dukate was part of the group of Allied soldiers who left the prison.

Simpson kept an American soldier with him, a young GI, who later described himself as a bookie from Brooklyn. He was still dressed in his khaki uniform. He had been taken prisoner on June 2 during heavy fighting south of Rome near Velletri and put in a POW camp outside of Rome. That morning he had been sent to the Regina Coeli. The pair walked past several vehicles loaded with Wehrmacht rearguard soldiers who ignored them.

The streets were crowded and Simpson was weak. They took a horse-drawn *carrozza*, one of the few that the Germans had not commandeered, to Mrs. Almagiá's apartment on Via Stanislao Mancini. There Simpson found Fane-Hervey and the German count, David Yorck. Yorck, taking advantage of the chaos of the German evacuation, had deserted from the Wehrmacht.

After liberation, Vittoria Colonna, the Duchess of Sermoneta, ran into Yorck, whom she had met before. She noticed that he was now in civilian clothes and on very cordial terms with a couple of British captains. She reportedly said that at first she was speechless when he came up and claimed acquaintance, then recovered her voice and said: "You were dressed very differently last time I saw you!" He laughed and told her he had been working for the Allies all the time.

The Lucidis' apartment on Via Scialoja was only about 200 yards away from Mrs. Almagiá's, and when Simpson arrived there, it was a homecoming. A thunderous greeting erupted as he reunited with Lucidi, Adrienne, Pat Wilson, Dennis Rendell, Pollak, and John Furman.

Partisans stepped up their attacks on the fleeing Germans and felled trees along the road, blocking Via Cassia for a few hours. Tompkins' diary recorded the conflicting details of that day:

From six-thirty this morning all bridges were being guarded by Germans with tanks and machine guns. The Caserma Mussolini in

Prati, evacuated by the Battaglione M [Mussolini], was sacked by women and children. At ten the Germans distributed food at the Macao barracks. Two mines blew up and wounded some women. The Quadraro has been evacuated and the Germans have put artillery in it. 155mm have been placed in the Fort Trionfale, and I believe the Fort Boccea, to hit the Cassia north of Rome. Between seven and eight, in front of Rubinati [a ristorante] on Via Flaminia, the Germans were distributing food. Battaglione M passed in trucks and shot into the crowd, killing three women. At the 1st Infantry barracks women are reported to have fired rifles. This morning three Communists occupied a depot of food at Via P. Valle, but abandoned the place without a fight upon the arrival of the PAI. At Ponte Milvio, early this morning, the Germans collected about a hundred young men who were milling around and marched them off, covering them with automatic weapons.[8]

General Alexander ordered Allied aircraft to drop leaflets urging citizens to protect the city's infrastructure from German destruction: water, electricity, gas, railways, telephone, telegraph, and radio communications. They asked the people to conserve their food supplies, to identify where mines were placed, and to remove from the roads all obstacles, barricades, and other obstructions. It was Sunday and the Allies needed to move through the city without hindrance or delay; the populace must ensure that.

Radio broadcasts all that day blared: "Citizens of Rome, this is not the time for demonstrations. Do what we tell you and continue with your daily work. Rome is yours. Your job is to save the city ... Ours is the destruction of the enemy ... The future of Rome is in your hands." How many heard the broadcast is not known; bombing had left much of Rome without electricity and there were few battery-powered radios.

Anti-fascist reprisal was in the air. There was looting, especially of known Fascist-owned shops. In front of the Quirinal Palace, an unidentified man – probably a Fascist – was shot and stripped naked. Two dead Germans lay outside the English Church on Via del Babuino.

In his diary, Tompkins recorded that at 08:00, Germans were still pouring through Rome, pushing carts, stealing cars if they could, or just on foot. The populace was in the streets watching, as it would a parade. It was hot. Cafes were open and doing a brisk business. Fleeing

Germans were selling typewriters at 1,000 lire each and cars, perhaps inoperable, from 25,000 to 40,000 lire. Germans with vehicles refused to allow the disdained Italian National Republican Guard (GNR) to ride with them.

Tompkins, intent on doing what he could, took charge and issued orders. He had no instructions, no radio, but he plowed on nevertheless. He sent an official order to General Umberto Presti, head of the PAI in Rome, and to Open City Commander General Domenico Chirieleison, to take charge of public order, and to employ their forces to prevent sabotage to buildings and public utilities; to arrest and intern German and GNR deserters; and to prevent civilians from leaving the city.

He wrote his orders on paper headed United States Office of Strategic Services and used official military language. Tompkins signed them OSS Officer Commanding Rome Area. To add authenticity to his letter, he affixed a special OSS rubber stamp which he had prepared for such an occasion. Both Presti and Chirieleison immediately complied with his orders. He did not know if anyone else was issuing orders but figured it was the only thing to do in such a case.

American troops were fast approaching the southern limits of the city, with General Robert T. Frederick's joint American–Canadian First Special Forces Brigade, also known as the Devil's Brigade, in the lead. The brigade was advancing cautiously up Via Casilina and was being harassed by Wehrmacht snipers left behind as well as a few Nazi panzers. Incongruously, at 08:30 the bells of a tiny white church started to ring out. Was it to celebrate the liberation of the city? Was it a warning? Neither of these; it was to announce a wedding which was described by the US Army *Stars and Stripes* newspaper two days later:

> Pretty soon a handsome well-dressed young couple came down the middle of the highway with an entourage of half a dozen neatly garbed young people. Nothing not even a global war was going to keep lovely Agnese Gotti and stalwart, smiling Marcello Traolo from going through with their June wedding ... After graciously pausing to pose for a battery of war photographers, the bridal party proceeded through a field in the direction of the liveliest machine gunfire.[9]

To protect property and individuals the PAI fired on looters. Tompkins noted that by 14:15 the PAI had altered its uniforms by removing the

M, for Mussolini, insignia and replacing it with the Italian Army *stellette*, or five-pointed stars. By 14:25 the electricity was temporarily on and Romans were able to listen to the BBC and General Alexander's order to save the city. Fear of a possible takeover of the city by the communists led to an attempt to rein in the partisans. They were ordered to wait for specific instructions before taking to the streets, a direction that was too late in coming and would have been ignored anyway. The partisans had played a vital role in resisting the German occupation and they had their own ideas of how to proceed.

That afternoon, an incident of high drama took place on the outskirts of the city, near the area where the morning wedding party celebrated:

> General Frederick, like everything else on Highway Six [Via Casilina], was standing still when a jeep carrying [General] Mark Clark and II Corps Commander, General Geoffrey Keyes, pulled up beside him. Clark, just down from the Alban Hills, the prize now so close, wanted to know what was holding things up. A welcome distraction then arose as one of the photographers traveling in Clark's entourage drew attention to the reflector studded blue highway sign just beyond them. It read ROMA. It was in fact a city-limit marker on the Casilina, approximate at best, but if you were reading it you were probably not in Rome, whereas if you were looking at the blank reverse side, you might be. It was awe inspiring, in any event, and, in a flash, so to speak, a famous photo was taken. Then Clark turned to Frederick and said, "Golly Bob, I'd like to have that sign in my command post." Frederick himself went to retrieve what was now a museum-class artifact but at that moment a German sniper, with three generals in his crosshairs, cut loose.[10]

The sniper missed. The three generals were uninjured and General Robert T. Frederick retrieved the sign for Clark. Frederick's Devil's Brigade's mission was to get into the city, get to the bridges, and keep the retreating Germans from blowing them up. They did secure the bridges, but there were casualties, including General Frederick who, leading his troops from the front, was wounded and his half-track driver killed. Historians of the First Special Service Force noted: "Frederick had been hit three times that day. Added to his six previous wounds, he could now lay undisputed claim to being the most-shot-at-and-hit general in American history and he was finally willing to concede his mortality."[11]

———

Not far away, Lt. Thomas Peter Welch, commanding a tank destroyer section from the 601st Tank Destroyer Battalion, encountered fighting on the way into Rome. Welch was on Via Tuscolana. Shortly after passing through the arches of the Aqua Claudia aqueduct at the Porta Furba, a hidden machine-gun nest opened fire. Stopping his destroyer, he returned fire, an action that was caught on film and later published in the Army's *Yank* magazine, a World War II publication. Just after that picture was taken, a US Army Engineer bulldozer arrived and dumped a load of dirt on the machine-gun nest, burying the German defenders.*

US troops knew they were close to occupying the city when they received instructions on how to conduct themselves while in Rome. Operations Instructions Number 33 marked "Secret," from Headquarters 3rd Infantry Division, dated June 4, 1944, was written by General Iron Mike O'Daniel. It noted the 3rd had been designated to garrison the City of Rome and set out the following rules:

> Troops will refrain from associating with civilians until further instructions are issued on the subject. At this time acceptance of gifts such as alcoholic beverages is prohibited.
>
> While passing through ROME and its suburbs and while occupying ROME care will be taken not to commit overt acts or be misunderstood with the civilian population. Care will be exercised to prevent unnecessary bloodshed.
>
> We are envoys of our country and must endeavor to create a favorable impression. As we act so acts our army in the eyes of the Romans.

———

*With the help of the *Museo Storico della Liberazione*, Via Tasso, Rome, the author found the exact spot where the picture of his uncle, Lt. Tommy Welch, was taken. This is because there is a preserved ancient Roman water storage pressure tank for the Aqua Claudia aqueduct just inside the Porta Furba. It is visible in the photo.

The people of this country respect force and dignity. Be firm without being overbearing, be courteous without being too familiar. We are conquerors and must act like conquerors, therefore dignity is necessary. When in doubt as to what action to take, men will be instructed to consult the officer in charge.

Be alert and on the job at all times until the moment comes for relaxation. When that time comes you will be notified.[12]

Gunfire still spattered here and there in the city's neighborhoods. A band of 40 Germans atop the Palatine Hill fired on anyone trying to climb it. At 18:00, Rome police units announced a curfew from house to house because electricity was sporadic.

Irish Dominicans at the Basilica of San Clemente, near the Colosseum, heard a commotion outside like wheels grinding. It was about 20:00 and, going out to investigate, they saw a line of American tanks drawn up close to the church walls. The Allies were finally here! The fathers invited the soldiers in for wine and cold-water showers, one of the few places in Rome with natural running water.

Pollak was sent to meet advancing Americans not far from the Basilica of Saint Paul Outside the Walls. There he convinced them that there were friendly partisans about and, by preventing a skirmish, he was even credited with saving the city's gas works.

Brother Robert left his hiding place inside the Vatican to check up on his old billets across the city.

German traffic around the Piazza del Popolo had fallen off by 21:00 and the two 88mm anti-tank guns guarding the retreat were hitched up and removed. The Grand Hotel was where everyone seemed to be going, including American journalist Eric Sevareid. British soldiers, ignoring General Clark's order that only Americans were to be allowed into the city, sneaked into Rome that first evening. Their entry at the Grand Hotel created a sensation as the shout went up that the English had arrived at the Grand Hotel (*Gli inglesi stanno al Gran Hotel*). A German sniper atop the hotel was waiting.

Garrad-Cole, the British ex-POW, needed to report to someone – he felt he was still on duty. He asked an American Army colonel in the street to whom he should report, but suddenly the sniper shot at them and they dodged for cover. As the sniper was being dealt with, an Italian woman went into labor in the middle of the street. The colonel sent for a doctor but the baby arrived before the ambulance. Then, to answer Garrad-Cole's question, he made a few radio calls, and told him to report the next day to the Villa Umberto (Borghese) Park where an Allied interrogation center was to be set up. Another British ex-POW, D'Arcy Mander, described the scene:

> We went upstairs to give the news to the Bassianos [where he was staying]. Marguerite as an American was wild with joy, and I went out on the roof-garden by myself for an unforgettable moment. The great bell of the Capital began to toll and its deep notes boomed out across the night; the roofs and cupolas of Rome were bathed in moonlight that transformed them into a dream city carved out of pearl-grey stone. Then, one-by-one, shutters began to open and there were dark heads silhouetted against golden light: I could hear voices called to each other. The Americans have arrived! Rome is free ... The Germans have gone! *Evviva! Evviva!* [Hurray] From all the windows came the sound of clapping hands, and then down in the streets the rush of people running, running, running, for the Romans had poured out of their houses regardless of the blackout and the curfew, and were going off to look at the Americans.[13]

Ranger Newman, still in the French Seminary, wrote in his memoirs:

> That night I went to bed and I said, "I'm not going to run out on the streets and get shot after waiting this long to get back." But about three in the morning the Frenchmen run in and kiss me on both cheeks and hug me and say, "Put on your uniform! The Americans are here!" I wanted to say, "Well, darn it, I'll go see 'em in the morning." But I reluctantly put on my uniform and out we sally and they take me to the Americans. It is one lone G.I. lost in the middle of Piazza Venezia ... The Jerries did leave a small rearguard in Rome to keep our boys from just ripping on through the town after them and there had been a pretty good scrap about four or five o'clock in the morning – Monday morning that would be. I sallied forth to see our boys and all the Romans were happy and cheering and our stuff began coming in. First, of course, the infantry and a few tanks and then later the big stuff.[14]

Newman ran into some Special Service Force soldiers and told them he was an escaped Ranger officer. They then took him to see Brigadier-General Frederick. The heavily bandaged general told Newman about the fight over the Tiber bridges, adding that it had been pretty fierce. According to Newman's description, the general was full of scratches and nicked all over. There was even a bullet hole through his glove. Newman accompanied the general out of the city to deliver the Roma sign full of bullet holes to General Mark Clark's staff. Then General Frederick took Newman back to Anzio with him. Along the way, the general had his driver stop at a particular place and asked Newman if he knew where they were. He did not. But how could he when it was the totally flattened town of Cisterna, the Rangers' original objective, and the place where he had been captured?[15]

JUNE 5, 1944: LIBERATION

The first liberating American soldier to enter the Vatican was not a diplomat or a general. The first American to enter the Vatican did so by accident, unintentionally, perhaps ignorant of what he was truly doing, yet nonetheless he entered the very heart, one might say the soul, of the city.

Charles W. Phallen was a technical sergeant, a member of A Company, 601st US Tank Destroyer Battalion. The wounds he had suffered at Anzio had healed and he was driven north from Naples. He was eager to rejoin the battalion and his company. At battalion headquarters, Phallen was given a jeep and told to go find his unit. It was the night of June 4/5. Knowing his company was somewhere up ahead, he gunned his jeep into the darkness. Dawn and still no luck, he was now driving through the deserted streets of Rome. He was alone, a single soldier in a jeep. He had crossed the Tiber River and found himself in the middle of Saint Peter's Square.

He knew full well where he was and, fearing he might never get another chance, he parked his jeep, jumped out, and ran up to the huge doors of the great basilica. Amazingly, they were unlocked so he pushed one open and peered into the depths of Saint Peter's. As Phallen started to leave, two soldiers, strangely uniformed, called to him from his left side. As he went over to them, they asked if he were an American. When he said yes, they said that the Holy Father, Pope Pius XII, had not yet met an American soldier and wanted to greet him. Phallen, astonished, was then escorted by them up the stairs into the Papal Apartments where he spoke with the Pope. After about five minutes the audience was over, and his escorts took him back to his jeep. Phallen got in and drove away, eventually rejoining his company.[16]

———

Among the left-behind German snipers active in the city that early morning, one at the Colosseum was eliminated by a burst from the 50-caliber machine gun mounted on Rudy Larson's M-10 Tank Destroyer. Larson was a staff sergeant with the 601st Tank Destroyer Battalion. He rationalized his firing at the ancient structure by saying that the Colosseum had so many holes in it, he figured a few more would not make any difference. Larson and Sgt. Nowak found out at about 02:00 on June 5, that they were to lead the battalion's early morning entry into Rome at daybreak, at approximately 05:30. Sgt. Larson later wrote:

> I was one of the first in the city and I won't forget it for a long time. It was in the very early morning hours that we rolled in there. Had little difficulty at that stage and in no time at all people were swarming out of their houses and lining the streets. By the time we got near the center of town the crowds were so large we had difficulty in moving … Everyone was clapping their hands and cheering and shouting "Bravo Americans!" They swarmed around us trying to shake our hands, and many of the pretty Senoras were trying to get near the soldiers to kiss them. But we all fought bravely to prevent that, as you can imagine. Many brought us wine until we were as hilarious as the Romans themselves. We probably didn't look much like conquering heroes. I hadn't shaved for about a week, was filthy dirty and bleary-eyed from lack of sleep, for in the two or three days before that I had had only a couple hours sleep.[17]

By 08:00 the streets of Rome were filling with parading, shouting, flag-waving Romans. One US sergeant, John A. Vita, a signal corps photographer, had promised his Italian-born mother that he would climb up on the balcony in the Piazza di Venezia, where Il Duce used to harangue the crowds, and outdo Mussolini. His imitation was performed to the delighted roars of the crowd gathered below – many of whom had doubtless seen the real thing themselves. Vita shouted to them: "Vincere! Vincere! Vincere!" (Win!) and he cajoled the crowd in pidgin Italian.

Young Tittmann was watching American jeeps roll by the Vatican wall at the Santa Monica guest house. He later wrote:

> A jeep stopped briefly before us, and we shouted welcoming words in English to its occupants. Obviously surprised, one of the soldiers asked us who we were. When he learned we were Americans, he reached in the back of the vehicle, pulled out a carton of cigarettes, a box of Hershey bars, and a copy of *Time* magazine, which he proceeded to toss over the wall in our direction. This was our first, happy contact with American soldiers.[18]

However, violence continued to erupt as partisans attacked fleeing Germans north of the city. At 10:00, partisans ambushed a German column of six trucks, three automobiles, and several panzers. A 19-year-old boy, Felice Rossi, blocked one of the panzers, throwing two hand grenades. He then tried to block a second tank, but was shot in a burst of fire from the Germans. Another boy was killed as the partisans fought on Via Salaria. He was 13-year-old Ughetto Forno, an invalid's only son. With his companions, he prevented the Germans blowing the bridge over the Aniene River. The last member of the Roman resistance to fall was Pietro Principato, killed by a Fascist sniper at Tor Pignattara.

A tragic incident occurred on the steps near Trajan's Column, close to Carla Capponi's apartment. What remained of the local Rome Carabinieri, the PAI, and the Guardia di Finanza, had all been mobilized to keep order in Rome. Anyone with a weapon was to be arrested. Guardia di Finanza Lieutenant Giorgio Barbarisi, while on patrol, started to peel a partisan poster from a wall. He was seen by Rosario Bentivegna. Tempers flared, they argued and Bentivegna shot and killed him. Tragically, both men were on the same side. A US military policeman declared the shooting to be in self-defense and he let Bentivegna go home to be with his parents.

The grand entrance of the American liberators into Rome on the morning of June 5 was actually confused and anticlimactic. When General Clark entered the city to receive the surrender no one actually knew where or if a surrender ceremony was to take place. Someone suggested the mayor's office at the Campidoglio, the ancient heart of the Roman capital. But Clark's aides and drivers didn't know how to get there and so the little convoy of jeeps meandered around city streets, lost. They finally arrived at Saint Peter's where an American priest from Detroit was found. He and Monsignor O'Flaherty welcomed the general. In the crowd of excited Romans surrounding General Clark's lead jeep was a boy who knew the way and he led the convoy back across the Tiber and to the Campidoglio on his bicycle.

The general arrived to find the building locked. There was no one to surrender the city to him. Such a squandered opportunity but General Clark was undaunted. He addressed the accompanying press saying that he had just called a meeting of his corps commanders and declared that this was a great day for the Fifth Army and for the French, British, and American troops of the Fifth Army who made this victory possible. He omitted acknowledging General Leese's Eighth Army and the overall theater commander, General Alexander. Such slights are unwelcomed by military egos and both were furious. It was not unusual behavior for Clark, however, and some said it was vintage one-upmanship.

That day, Giuseppe Dosi, the ex-police detective who saved the Via Tasso documents the day before, was at the Campidoglio when General Mark Clark arrived to receive the surrender of the city. Dosi, who spoke English, German, French, and several other languages, explained to General Clark and other Fifth Army officials that he had salvaged the documents from Via Tasso. On the spot, Clark made him a special investigator for the US Army Counter Intelligence Command.

Showboating over, the Allies set about restoring water and electricity and bringing food supplies to the starving Romans. Derry saw the need for vehicles and obtained the use of Prince von Bismarck's abandoned and smartly ostentatious, polished aluminum Heinkel motor car for Sir D'Arcy. Sir D'Arcy, however, requested something less glitzy and Derry found him a Mercedes, keeping the Heinkel for himself.

The work of the Escape Line was by no means over with the liberation of Rome. Finding new billets for themselves, Simpson, Furman, Derry, Byrnes, and Meletiou moved into an apartment vacated by departed

Fascists. It was on the ground floor of the Lucidi apartment building at Via Scialoja 18 and it served as the Escape Line headquarters for the next six months.

Celebrations were still in order, and that night the Escape Line threw a bash at the Grand Hotel. The Orso Bar posted a sign announcing that it had been used by escaped British POWs during the occupation. It later became an Allied officers' club.

In the miasma of wartime, deception can mean survival. "Accept nothing and no one on face value" was the Escape Line's unofficial motto. Major Derry had had his suspicions of a man he called Jack S. (his last name is not known). Although his father was Italian, Jack was British, born in London, and had routinely loaned Brother Robert his car. Eventually Jack was imprisoned in Regina Coeli where he was beaten. With the liberation, he had emerged alive. Major Derry nevertheless had always restricted Jack's access to and knowledge of the Escape Line. He was proven right in the end when it became known that Jack had collaborated with the Germans, broadcasting propaganda to British troops in Italy under the moniker, the Cockney Broadcaster of Rome. Jack was not punished with prison, but was never allowed to return to England.

Michael Stern, a reporter for the North American Newspaper Alliance, was seeking interviews with German brass or at least those close to them. He discovered Dollmann's residence in the Pension Jaseli-Owen near the Spanish Steps where he was told that Dollmann had fled. Stern next asked how he might find Dollmann's girlfriend, who he thought might give him information. The landlady took him into Dollmann's bedroom and pointed to the double bed he had shared with Mario. No girlfriend, no interview.

According to Eric Sevareid, young women rode in trucks throughout the city calling the people to go to Saint Peter's at 18:00 to hear the Pope lead a ceremony of thanksgiving for the liberation of Rome. More than 100,000 people packed the square. Many Allied soldiers in battle dress attended. Sevareid reported that the Vatican was feeding more than 300,000 people in the city every day. When the Allied Military Government arrived, they joined the Pope's efforts in providing food to the starving populace.

Garrad-Cole was in that crowd at Saint Peter's and later he went to the Grand Hotel for drinks. Dressed in mufti (civilian clothes), he was refused entrance to what had been taken over as an Allied officers' club by two American Military Police (MPs). A few minutes later he met two RAF officers, Group Captain Duncan Smith and Wing Commander Barry Heath. They chatted and he convinced them that he in fact was an RAF officer. In their celebratory mood, they vouched for him, and he entered the Grand Hotel bar with apologies from the MPs.

Rome was free, but many pro-Allied Italians were not there to celebrate. During the nine-month German occupation, almost 10,000 Italians had been killed throughout Italy. They were partisans, laborers, former military members, Jews, and ordinary citizens. And Romans continued to die, ironically now at the hands of the liberators. An American Army truck taking supplies north to the rapidly advancing Allied front accidentally struck a priest outside the Bernini Colonnade at the Vatican, running over and crushing him.

Epilogue

To many, perhaps most Americans, the most important date of World War II is June 6, 1944, the Allied Invasion of Normandy. But the news of that pivotal invasion was not known to the editors of the *Stars and Stripes* newspaper's Mediterranean edition. They had put their paper to bed the night before, having taken over the *Il Messaggero* office. Instead, it was filled with news of the successful capture of Rome by the Allies. Of course, news of the Normandy Invasion spread quickly and it blotted out the heroic efforts of so many and also dimmed General Mark Clark's glow of triumph. If the noise of its celebration was drowned out by Normandy, put it down to the vicissitudes of history.

With Rome's liberation came an enormous responsibility of ministering to a wide range of people, including Escape Line ex-POWs. On liberation day, June 4, the Escape Line was caring for 3,925 men all across Italy. Of this total: 1,695 were British, 896 were from South Africa, 429 were Russian, 425 Greek, and 185 American. The remaining men were from 20 other Allied countries including 28 from the neutral Irish Republic. Those in Rome and the surrounding area were handed over to military authorities for debriefing first in tents in the Villa Umberto (Borghese) and later in offices set up for the purpose. After debriefing, the men were sent to Naples for fresh uniforms and other gear. Most were then returned to their home countries, but if they were only recently captured, they were returned to their units. Major Derry, who would continue to work for the Escape Line, met with a senior British intelligence officer from "A" Force who debriefed him on his activities.

Celebrations popped up everywhere. General Clark ordered a victory parade through the city on June 7, insisting that Sir D'Arcy and Mr. Tittmann join him on the reviewing stand at the Porta Pia.

Scottish bagpipers honored the British participation in the liberation. Pope Pius XII gave an audience to the Allied press corps which included women wearing slacks, the novelty of which scandalized many at the Vatican. The next day a memorial ceremony for the Jews who had been deported, exterminated, or otherwise lost was solemnized at the Rome synagogue. It was also attended by Jewish-American soldiers.

Vittoria Colonna, the Duchess of Sermoneta, was finally free to leave her hiding place. High on the list of her priorities of restoring normalcy to life was the retrieval of her sterling silver tea service from a bank vault where it had been placed for safe keeping. Arriving at the bank alone, she realized she could not possibly carry the service through Rome's celebrating throngs. She approached an American Army captain with her dilemma, saying: "I have an English officer coming to see me today, and I do need my tea set."[1] The officer ordered his sergeant to deliver her and her silver to her palace and to be back in 20 minutes.

Liberated Rome was filled with GIs and the US 3rd Division *Daily News* gave practical advice to soldiers about spending their money in the Eternal City:

> Members of the 3rd Division will soon be on the streets of Rome with money in their pockets. Rome, one of the great cities of the world, will offer most everything possible to spend that money for. After four months on the Anzio beachhead, the Third's doughboys will have plenty of money to spend and plenty of inclination to spend it. At least those who haven't fallen victim to the poker wolves. Our price standards will be new to the Roman citizens. If we refuse to pay more for anything than we would in the States, we won't have to pay any more for it. Prices, in other words, will be just what we make them. If the dough foots, loose under the bright lights for the first time in months, fail to show restraint in their spending prices on everything will sky rocket and black-markets will flourish. Don't rob yourself. Remember, the natives wise up fast.[2]

Many soldiers took guided tours of the city. For the first time in months, they could relax. According to Lt. Ed Josowitz of the 601st Tank Destroyer Battalion:

> Rome was clean, beautiful, full of lovely girls and it had hardly been touched by the war. Of course, there was at least one jerk in

every company who looked at the Colosseum and said, "Boy! We sure bombed the hell out of that place." On the 6th, there came the tremendous, electrifying news of the Normandy Invasion! Hope ran high in Rome that day and the vino flowed freely. There were trips to the Vatican and to less holy places.[3]

Sgt. Rudy Larson of the 601st also recorded his impression of the Eternal City:

Rome itself was surely a treat to those of us that had spent those long months at the little Anzio beachhead. There we had experienced almost constant danger, lived like rats in a hole, and saw nothing but dirt and destruction. Now here in Rome we saw a city beautiful beyond all expectation, little touched by war, and streets filled with well-dressed people, pretty girls, flags waving and banners hastily put up, saying "Welcome to the Liberators." And best of all we felt like we had finally accomplished one of the primary jobs that we had been working on for such a long time. And when we heard of the invasion of France, well you can just about imagine what a boost our morale got with the two events so close together. Wish you were over here to see some of the sights of Rome. There surely is plenty to see in the city, especially if you've studied Roman history. I wish I had remembered more of it ... And besides ancient Rome there also are beautiful modern buildings, memorials, hotels, apartments, business houses, etc. The average American surely knows little of how the other half of the world lives. It's just a shame that a war is necessary to bring this about.[4]

Lt. Thomas Peter Welch, also of the 601st, described these first heady days of occupation:

Things really ran riot in Rome the first two days. A good time was had by all. I made my headquarters the Grand Hotel, a really lush spot. I went to the Vatican and saw the Pope as well as Saint Peter's, which is really lovely.[5]

Not everyone was pleased with the American occupation or the behavior of GIs fresh from battle. Sir D'Arcy complained to the British Foreign Office that he thought the discipline of American troops guarding the city was not good. He also said Roman women's eager rush to meet Americans was a public scandal. The Vatican issued a formal complaint about the morality of the troops. Harold Tittmann wrote that the Vatican sent him a note on June 10 suggesting that Allied troops be kept outside the city. Exceptions were made for those concerned with maintaining order, feeding the population, and providing technical services.

More troublesome was the request from someone in the Vatican that said the Pope hoped that "colored" troops would be stationed in the outskirts of Rome. The Allies found this potentially embarrassing. The note added that the Holy See had nothing against "colored" soldiers but hoped that the request could be honored.[6] One rationalization for this racist attitude was that the request may have been a reaction to the large number of reports concerning French North African soldiers raping Italian women on the way to Rome. In response, General Alexander, with Sir D'Arcy's help, convinced General Clark to reduce the number of troops in the city and, as an immediate result, the US 3rd Infantry Division orders to garrison in the city of Rome were rescinded.

At liberation, the SD's stay-behind network quickly collapsed because its agents lacked professionalism. Within the first week of Allied occupation, more than half of Kappler's stay-behinds had been arrested. Once an SD agent was identified, he led them to others. Panic seized those in hiding. One agent, reading that agents were to be shot, smashed his radio. Others claimed, as mitigation, that they had helped shelter escaped Allied POWs. In Ubaldo Cipolla's case, it had been true. But as more followed suit, the claim of having helped ex-POWs, only helped confirm to Allied Intelligence that those making the claim were, in fact, German agents.

The Abwehr's stay-behind network in Rome was more successful than Kappler's. The Abwehr had placed 18 Italian and German stay-behind agents. Some Abwehr agents reported directly to Field Marshal Kesselring. As an example of its importance, when the German Wehrmacht captured Allied infiltrators or suspected spies, they were handed over to the Abwehr first and only later passed to Kappler.

One Abwehr agent, Wehrmacht Oberleutnant Helmut Haeusgen, had been quite successful. He was interviewed by British Headquarters,

15th Army Group, on June 23, 1945, and in its report, it was said that Haeusgen claimed that of the seven stay-behind radio-equipped agents in Rome, two stations, Riga and Zeno, went on the air in end of May, 1944, and both regularly transmitted information on Allied troop and vehicle movements through the city two or three times a week.

The Vatican also requested the removal of antiaircraft batteries and that Rome now finally be declared an Open City. The guns were removed but the Allies, like the Germans, needed to move supplies and materiel through Rome, so they did not hypocritically declare Rome an Open City.

Rome was free, but the war continued. A captured German document issued by Field Marshal Kesselring, *Operations against Partisans*, dated July 20, 1944, spells out these Wehrmacht efforts:

> The partisan situation in the Corps rear area continues to be a serious menace to the fighting troops and supply services. The fight against partisans must therefore be conducted with maximum severity. The good nature and credulity so common among German troops must be suppressed by continual instructions … Every act of violence must be immediately punished … Where partisans exist in considerable numbers, hostages will be taken from among the local population (relatives or able-bodied sympathizers) and will be shot in the event of acts of violence … In cases where soldiers are shot at from villages, the village will be burnt down … The following will be shot at once, anyone assisting the criminal, treacherous partisans by giving them food or lodging, or by carrying military messages … the old principle holds true that it is better to act and make mistakes than to do nothing … [7]

The effort of identifying the bodies of those murdered at the Fosse Ardeatine began after the liberation of Rome, and was headed by Professor Attilio Ascarelli, an Italian forensic expert. He took on the difficult task with the assistance of US Fifth Army personnel. Identifications were based on articles of clothing or the contents of pockets. One method Ascarelli used was to separate prisoners based on the condition of their hands, office workers from laborers. Initially, 12 corpses were unidentified; however, DNA analysis is slowly reducing that number. In the more than 70 years that have passed, the names and occupations of the 335 victims are still incomplete (see also p. 446).

Maurizio Giglio, the Italian police lieutenant and OSS agent, together with the other 334 victims of the massacre, is buried in a public memorial at the Fosse Ardeatine, which can be visited along Via Ardeatina. Giglio is also honored with the naming of *Polizia Caserma Maurizio Giglio Medaglia D'Oro V. M.* (Police Barracks Gold Medal, for Military Valor) on Via Guido Reni north of Piazza del Popolo. There is also a street named after him in the La Giustiniani suburb north of the city. He is not the only victim so honored as there are many plaques spread around the city that commemorate the men killed that day. One that stands out is the plaque that is on the apartment house where Colonel Montezemolo lived around the corner from the Lucidis.

Controversy swirling about the bombing and the reprisal may never be settled. One question was, if the partisans carrying out the attack had surrendered to the Gestapo, would the massacre have taken place? Field Marshal Kesselring was asked during his postwar trial in 1946 whether he thought to ask the Roman people to turn over those responsible in lieu of the ten-for-one reprisal. He responded that now in more tranquil times and after two years have passed, it would have been a good idea; but he didn't do it.

Almost 50 years later, at his Rome trial in 1995, Hauptsturmführer Priebke kept the controversy alive by averring that the Germans had in fact wanted the partisans responsible for the attack to turn themselves in and there would have been no reprisals if they had. Further, he claimed that the Germans had announced this on Radio Rome and broadcast the message through the streets via loudspeakers mounted on vehicles. Contemporary evidence is lacking to substantiate his claim and, although widely believed by many Italians to this day, it appears not to be true.

It has also often been claimed that the partisans should have known that in a German reprisal, people randomly taken from the streets of Rome would be executed. Partisans would not have assumed that, however. During the first seven months of the German occupation partisans were tortured and shot by Germans when captured in some act, but, until Via Rasella, Germans had never massacred randomly rounded up civilians in Rome as a reprisal.

Within a few months, the Italian theater of war became a backwater, a backwater commanding half the resources it had at the liberation of Rome. Nevertheless, the Italian front still required the presence of many Allied and Axis soldiers. With the major focus of the war on Normandy and France, three full, highly experienced US combat divisions, the 3rd, 36th, and 45th, and the four French divisions, were pulled from Italy. On August 15, together with other Allied troops, they were landed near San Tropez in a new "D-day," Operation *Dragoon*, the invasion of southern France.

Major Derry, Furman, Simpson, Byrnes (the Canadian Escape Line bookkeeper), and the Greek Theodore Meletiou were asked to volunteer to continue their work from Rome. There were still many POWs in the northern part of Italy. They now worked openly with officials from the British MI-9 POW "A" Force organization and its American counterpart, MIS-X.

Continuing its work but changing its name, the Escape Line became the Allied Screening Commission. They also took on a new task: sorting the claims of those who had assisted the Escape Line. Its staff grew to over 200 workers who investigated more than 90,000 claims, and paid out more than 1,000,000 pounds sterling in compensation to those Italians who had fed and sheltered escapees. They also presented more than 75,000 official Certificates of Merit signed by Field Marshal Alexander.

On September 14, 1944 Sir D'Arcy sent the British Foreign Office a letter praising the Italian people:

> I take this opportunity to record my admiration for, and gratitude to the numberless Italians, mostly of the poorest class in the country districts, who displayed boundless generosity and kindness to our men over a long and trying period; it must be remembered that, in so doing, not only did they refuse the financial rewards for the denunciation of British prisoners of war which the Germans offered and which would have been a fortune to them, but they also showed magnificent abnegation and courage in sharing their few clothes and scanty food and, above all, in risking their lives and the lives of their families and friends in disregarding the increasingly severe German injunctions against harboring or helping British prisoners. A number of them indeed were shot by the Germans. We owe a debt to the Italian people in this respect that should not be forgotten and cannot be repaid.[8]

In addition to cash and certificates, they assisted these recognized helpers in finding jobs; aided in the early repatriation of the sons and husbands who were being held as prisoners of war by the Allies; allowed admission to British hospitals for their sick; transported separated families from one part of Italy to another; and gave them other preferential treatment. The Allied Screening Commission ceased its existence on September 30, 1947.

Among foreign countries whose POWs were assisted by the Escape Line and who therefore owed money, the first to repay the British for their expenses was the Soviet Union. At the time the Germans fled the city, the Russians were afraid that they would be rounded up and taken away with them. Derry thought that it would be better for the Russians to escape and he honored their urgent request to pay off their *padroni*. Derry had paid out over 120,000 lire (400 pounds sterling) with the quip "I hope Stalin pays us back!" And payback came, over 25,000 pounds sterling.

Three months after the liberation, there was a triumphant exhibition of 48 salvaged masterpieces of art at the Palazzo Venezia; among the works displayed was *Circe Turning Ulysses' Companions into Pigs*, by Renaissance master Dosso Dossi (1490–1542). The curator pointedly hung the painting over Mussolini's old desk in the Sala del Mappamondo (world map room) in the palazzo.[9]

US Army Special Services set up a recreation facility in Rome at the Foro Mussolini, now renamed the Foro Italico. There, GIs were able to book tours of the city and arrange to visit the Vatican. Today the Foro Italico retains the original modern obelisk at the main entrance to the complex which reads "Mussolini Dux."

Allied officers, like German officers before them, stayed on Via Veneto. Eric Sevareid reported that the US Army infantry officers had one brothel and US Air Corps officers another. Military police kept the two groups separate. Ernest DeWald authored a *Soldier's Guide to Rome* in which he suggested walking tours for the GIs. He was one of the US Monument Men stationed in Italy and a former professor of art and archaeology at Princeton University.

Mussolini continued the fiction of an independent Fascist Republic but his time was soon over. On April 28, 1945, near Lake Como, Mussolini was executed by partisans. He was shot in a walled garden in the village of Giulino di Mezzegra at 16:10. His body and those of his mistress Claretta Petacci and several others were hung upside down from a lamp post at a Milan gas station.

Also that April, 1945, SS-Obergruppenführer Karl F. Wolff and SS-Obersturmbannführer Eugen Dollmann traveled to Switzerland to arrange a separate peace on the Italian front. They were unsuccessful. Their efforts succeeded, however, in making the Russians believe that the British and Americans were trying to form a separate peace with the Germans so they could form a new alliance against the Soviet Union.

It was time to recognize sacrifices and award loyalty. The Teatro Adriano held a ceremony for those who had helped the Allied POWs during their sojourn in Rome on May 24, 1946. More than 700 were in attendance. There were representatives of the United Kingdom, the United States, South Africa, and France as well as a select core of special Italians who were brought up on stage and each presented with a Certificate of Merit. They were all toasted at a reception. Derry and Furman should have been there but were unable to attend because they had been sent back to London to continue their work with MI-9.

Except for the bombing, Rome had remained almost intact during the war and what damage had been done by the Germans leaving and the Allies arriving was quickly cleared away. Once again church bells rang the hours and called the faithful to prayer. The azure blue skies were no longer filled with bombers flying over the city. Romans embraced the Allies, especially the Americans. After the war thousands of GIs came to Rome and some stayed for years. American bars, serving drinks with ice, proliferated. If one was wealthy enough, a large American car could be purchased and seen attempting to navigate Rome's narrow, ancient streets. For a while Cinecittà became Hollywood on the Tiber. Coca-Cola was available everywhere. Even up until the 1980s there was a newspaper, the *Rome Daily American*, originally published by former members of the US military paper the *Stars and Stripes*.

What happened to our leading characters after the liberation of Rome?

THE ALLIED SERVICEMEN

Evangelos **Averoff**, the founder of the Greek Freedom or Death resistance group, was presented with the Order of the British Empire. In 1956 Averoff was appointed Foreign Minister of Greece.

Major Sam **Derry** was awarded the British Distinguished Service Order for his work with the Escape Line. His book, *The Rome Escape Line, Primary Source Edition*, came out in 1960.

Floyd J. **Dumas** of the 45th Infantry Division and the Scottish soldier, Bill **Robb**, stayed in contact and even got together once after the war after Robb moved to Canada. This might have been the end of the story but, in May 1947, Dumas received a letter from a US Army captain demanding that he pay back the $108.72 (2,000 lire) he received from the Swiss Embassy. Robb contacted his congressman and an article appeared in the *Washington Star* newspaper on May 20, 1947, "Dunning GI on Escape Cash." The paper contacted the War Department and was told the request for reimbursement was a mistake. This is the only case known where an individual ex-POW was requested to reimburse money given him during their hiding in Rome.[10]

Lieutenant John **Furman** was presented with the Military Cross. In 1956, by then a lieutenant colonel, he published his book, *Be Not Fearful*.

RAF officer E. **Garrad-Cole** wrote that shortly after liberation he helped make a short British Army film about POWs who had hidden in Rome. Duncan **Smith**, the RAF officer who got him into the Grand Hotel, offered his jeep to take him to Anzio and fly him to Naples. There he was joined by escapee Pat **Wilson**. Then Garrad-Cole flew from Naples' Capodichino Airfield to Algiers, Casablanca and finally to England on a route that took him far to the west, away from the Bay of Biscay, to avoid Luftwaffe fighters. The plane landed at Saint Mawgan in Cornwall where he took the train to London. It was June 21, 1944. In 1955, by then a wing commander, he published his book, *Single to Rome*.

Captain D'Arcy **Mander** was awarded a Distinguished Service Order in 1944 for his Rome espionage work and in 1987 published *Mander's March on Rome*. He died at age 91.

1st Lieutenant William **Newman** wrote the first book about the Escape Line and it was called *Escape in Italy*, published in March 1945. In a signed copy purchased by the author were carbon copies of a 1946 exchange of letters between Monsignor O'Flaherty and the lieutenant. The monsignor wrote Newman that he was the Irish priest who met him at the house of Paolino.* O'Flaherty had read about the book in an English newspaper and requested a copy.

Private Joe **Pollak**, the Jewish-Czech soldier, is known to have stayed in touch with Iride Imperoli. He opened a leather goods shop in Rome and married Angela Liberatore from the Abruzzi Mountains.

Captain Dennis B. **Rendell** of the 2nd British Parachute Regiment remained in the army and had a very successful career. He ended up as a brigadier and was appointed Provost Marshal, one of the most ancient of Crown appointments and eventually was appointed Aide-de-Camp to the Queen from 1975 to 1977. At the end of his long service, he was awarded an OBE (Order of the British Empire).

Lieutenant Bill **Simpson** was presented with the Military Cross and in 1996 his book, *A Vatican Lifeline*, was published. The jacket says that he received the US Medal of Freedom and the Silver Cross of the Order of George I of the Hellenes.

OSS agent Peter **Tompkins** was back in Washington DC by November 4, 1944 and in danger of being drafted as a private in the US Army! The OSS arranged for him to be returned to Europe. Immediately after the war, Tompkins applied for a postwar position with the OSS in Switzerland, but he did not get it. An OSS man named Scamporino did not like Tompkins and would not recommend him. Tompkins' work in Rome is greatly underappreciated and "has never received proper credit for the cool competence he displayed in keeping the few frail threads of governmental continuity from snapping that day."[11] He wrote *A Spy in Rome*, about his time in Rome and *Italy Betrayed* about the battle for Rome. In January 2007 Tompkins died in Shepardstown, West Virginia.

Sam **Derry**, Bill **Simpson**, John **Furman**, and Renzo **Lucidi** were reunited in Rome for the June 4, 1984, 40th anniversary of the liberation of Rome. It was the last known time that they were together. The author participated in these events serving as the Assistant US Naval Attaché at the American Embassy. Unfortunately, he did not know their story at that time and did not meet them. Also at the ceremony were many of

---

* Paolino was a helper of the Escape Line and his apartment was used as a temporary billet for arriving escaped POWs. Eventually he was captured but he had managed to hide five ex-POWs behind a small door (hatch) in his basement apartment.

the surviving partisans of Rome; *Stars and Stripes* Sgt. Bill Mauldin, the famous World War II GI cartoonist, and many Allied WWII veterans. The mayor of Rome presented a commemorative medal to each of the participants, including the author.

THE CLERGY

German Bishop Alois **Hudal** stayed on in Rome, eventually moving to a deluxe villa at Grottaferrata outside the city. It was rumored that the money for his lifestyle came from helping ex-Nazis relocate to South America as part of ODESSA (Organization der Ehemaligen SS-Angehörigen), the Organization of Former SS Members. It is not certain that ODESSA was the actual name of this organization but there certainly was such a group even if by another name. Among those he helped was Erich Priebke. Hudal was asked to resign from the German College in 1952 and was barred from the Vatican.

Monsignor Hugh **O'Flaherty** expanded his efforts to help thousands of Italian POWs communicate with their families. Many Italian soldiers had been captured in North Africa when the Italians surrendered in 1943 and had been taken to POW camps in South Africa. General Alexander arranged for a plane to fly the monsignor there to set up a network of Catholic priests to facilitate his work. Later the monsignor flew to Jerusalem to arrange the transfer of foreign Jews in Italy to Palestine.

Monsignor O'Flaherty was made a Commander of the British Empire, awarded the Silver Medal from the Italian government, and presented with the US Medal of Freedom with Silver Palm. O'Flaherty's *New York Times* obituary of October 31, 1963, reprinted part of the citation, which read:

> For exceptionally meritorious conduct in the performance of outstanding services to the Government of the United States in Italy between March of 1942 and June 1944. His untiring energy and efforts, often at the risk of his own life and his unfailing devotion to the cause of freedom were exemplified in the concrete aid given to so many prisoners of war.

Monsignor Giovanni Battista **Montini**, Vatican Under-Secretary of State to Pope Pius XII, later became Pope Paul VI, 1963–1978.

Brother Robert **Pace** was made a member of the Order of the British Empire and a Knight Commander of the Maltese Order of Saint George in Carinthia. In his third person biography, Brother Robert Pace recorded: "Brother Robert was rightly proud of the honor but never stuffy about it: he would in later years remind those who mentioned it that the *notorious* [author's italics] Beatles received the same honor."[12]

After Rome was liberated, Brother Robert continued to help American POWs. In June 1945 he contacted the Special Counter Intelligence (SCI) Unit Rome to ask the imprisoned Kappler if he knew the fate of three missing American enlisted men. The authorities interrogated Kappler who did not recall these men but suggested that, if they were captured in Rome, they would have been sent to Cinecittà.

In 1952 Brother Robert, after several years in the United States, became a naturalized US citizen. In 1964/65 he lived in the Rheem Valley, California where Frank Billecci served as his secretary and driver at *Lasallian Digest* office in the late 1960s.

As stated in the introduction, the author and his wife, Patricia, met Billecci in Naples more than 40 years ago and showed him around the ancient sites of the *Campi Flegrei* outside of the city of Pozzuoli. He contacted the author in 2014 and suggested that Brother Robert's story needed to be told. While serving in Washington DC, Brother Robert suffered a stroke, returned to California in 1968, and, on December 3, 1970, died at age 63 at Stanford University Hospital in California.

Fathers **Borg** and **Maden** were made members of the Order of the British Empire and Father **Buckley** and four other priests, **Claffery**, **Gatti**, **Lennan** and **Treacy**, were also specially commended by King George VI.

Israel **Zolli**, Rome's chief rabbi at the time of the German occupation, was eventually allowed to hide inside the Vatican after being refused assistance by some of his fellow Jews. He worked at the Vatican Library until liberation. He caused great consternation among the Jews of Rome by converting to Catholicism on February 1, 1945.

DIPLOMATS

Albrecht (Teddy) von **Kessel** was arrested on June 5, 1944 together with Baron Ernst von **Weizsäcker**. As duly accredited diplomats and because the Vatican was still officially neutral, they were allowed to move into the Vatican Hospice of Santa Marta on July 8, 1944. On April 11, 1945, von Kessel terminated his status as first secretary to the German Embassy to the Holy See and offered his services to the Allied forces to design and develop educational programs to be broadcast to Germany. Von Kessel was released on October 5, 1946 and a note in his file avers he was a plotter in the 1938 assassination attempt on Hitler.

Sir Francis Godolphin D'Arcy **Osborne**, the British Minister to the Vatican, inherited the title of the Duke of Leeds in 1963. As he never married and had no children, the title ended with him. Sir D'Arcy died on March 20, 1964 in Rome and he chose to be buried in Rome's Protestant Cemetery. His 1943 knighthood was the recognition for his diplomatic efforts in Rome.

Harold H. **Tittmann**, Jr., the American Chargé d'Affaires at the Holy See and Sir D'Arcy's close friend and confidant, served as US Ambassador to Haiti and later to Peru. He compiled his notes into a book that was finished by his son, Harold H. Tittmann III (quoted in this book as young Tittmann). The book was *Inside the Vatican of Pius XII: The Memoir of an American Diplomat during World War II.* Tittmann died in December 1980 and his book was published in 2004.

Baron Ernst von **Weizsäcker**, German Ambassador to the Holy See, moved into the Vatican Hospice of Santa Marta in the quarters vacated by Sir D'Arcy on July 8, 1944. Sir D'Arcy was told to delay his departure as long as possible so that he could observe von Weizsäcker and the Japanese Special Envoy to the Vatican, Ken Harada. He resented these orders as he felt it was an abuse of Vatican hospitality.

Other German staff at the Holy See moved into the Santa Marta Guest House:* a male secretary named Sigismund von Braun, who was a member of the Gestapo; a young Gestapo woman named Charlotte Rahlke; Attaché Bruno Buyna; and an SS man named Papst, described in Allied reports as the head of a German Information Service (GIS, an American Army term), who took his radio inside the Vatican. Herr Swichtemberg, a Gestapo man described as the first usher at the now closed Germany Embassy to the Holy See on Via Piave, was allowed to stay there.

---

* The Santa Marta Guest House was replaced by a newer, hotel-like structure. It is now known as the residence of the current Pope, Francesco, who refused to reside in the Apostolic Palace.

ESCAPE LINE CIVILIAN HELPERS: NON-ITALIAN

Mrs. **Chevalier** was awarded the British Empire Medal. One of her daughters, Gemma, married Corporal Kenneth Sands, one of her boys, an escaped British POW.

John **May** returned to England and slipped into obscurity.

Milko **Scofic**, the Yugoslav medical student, eventually married an art student who, during the occupation, drew sketches and caricatures of Allied escapees in the cafes and restaurants of Rome. She became famous as the actress Gina Lollobrigida. During the war, she often hid escaped Allied ex-POWs.

Molly **Stanley** was specially commended by King George VI.

GERMANS

(See also Appendix C for the complete SS list in Rome.)

SS-Hauptsturmführer Johannes Max Hans **Clemens** (1902 –1976), one of the first on the scene at the Via Rasella attack, left Rome on May 12, 1944 and transferred to Lake Como where he was nicknamed the Tiger of Como for his aggressiveness against enemies of the German occupation. By May 1945, he was a POW. He was tried with **Kappler** and sentenced to time in prison. After that, Clemens was recruited in Germany by British MI-6 and worked for the ex-Abwehr General Reinhard Gehlen at the postwar German Federal Intelligence Agency, *Bundesnachrichtendienst* (State Information Service). Subsequently charged as an agent of the German Democratic Republic (DDR) and the Soviet KGB, he was tried and sentenced to ten years for spying for the East but was released for health reasons after five years.

Eugen **Dollmann** escaped prosecution for war crimes. In November 1947 he was recognized by his old lover Mario exiting a theater in Rome. Dollmann was there for Kesselring's war crimes trial. In 1956 he published a book called *Call Me Coward* (later published as *Nazi Fugitive*) which describes his life after the war including, remarkably, an escape from an Allied POW camp, not unlike the other accounts described in this book. His second book was published in 1967, *The Interpreter: Memoirs of Doctor Eugen Dollmann*, a fascinating, if self-serving and not totally accurate, read. He later offered his services to various western intelligence organizations but was never hired. He died in Munich in 1985. Mario then claimed to have been a communist partisan all along.

Obersturmbannführer Georg **Elling**, due to his diplomatic immunity, was the logical control point for the post-occupational spy network. However, things fell apart at liberation. Elling was not on the list to enter the Vatican and he was not an enthusiastic stay-behind agent. He asked to be repatriated to Germany two days after the Allied liberation of Rome. Double agent Alexander **Kurtna** was to have become Elling's clandestine radio operator after training at the German Embassy Radio School, but at liberation he too fled Rome with the rest of the Germans. He left Elling with two radio codes, 100 Swiss francs, and five gold pieces with a total value of 25,000 lire.

Wilhelm **Harster**, head of police activities in Italy, was convicted of war crimes and was implicated in the deaths of 104,000 Dutch Jews, including Anne Frank.

Herbert **Kappler** was tried as a war criminal after the war and was sentenced to life imprisonment. He was charged with murder, not for all of the 335 executed at the caves, but rather only for the ten he added on his own initiative after the thirty-third soldier had died, and for the five additional men mistakenly taken from prison who were executed because they were witnesses to the massacre. He was kept in the Regina Coeli Prison with five other Rome SS men: Clemens, Domizlaff, Quapp, Schütz, and Wiedner. Eventually all, except Kappler and Clemens, were acquitted. It was adjudged that the others were only following orders. Kappler, serving a life sentence in the seaside fortress of Gaeta, Italy, maintained a correspondence with these men and others including Haas. On July 15, 1949 Kappler received a letter from Priebke, then living in Buenos Aires, Argentina. This exchange of correspondence lasted through the 1950s. Several times he mentioned that he was sent books by a former Gestapo agent, Princess De Seta-Pignatelli, who owned the Palazzo Lovatelli. On February 3, 1949 he wrote Monsignor O'Flaherty for the first time and after that his only visitor was the monsignor. In March 1959, O'Flaherty baptized Kappler into the Catholic Church.

Soon after, Kappler, long divorced from his first wife, married a German woman he had been corresponding with in prison, Anneliese. His new wife smuggled him from the Rome hospital where he was being treated for cancer on August 14, 1977. She picked up her son at the Grand Hotel and they drove all night to Austria and then into Germany. An apocryphal story circulated that she had carried him out in a suitcase but that has proven to be false. Kappler died shortly after reaching Germany. His funeral was attended by many Nazis who bade him farewell with the Nazi salute.

Field Marshal Albert Konrad **Kesselring** was sentenced to death for war crimes, mainly relating to the massacre at the Ardeatine Caves. The sentence was commuted to life imprisonment and he was eventually released. Kesselring died in Bad Wiessee, Germany in July 1960. He wrote an autobiography, one of the few German generals of World War II to do so. It was called *A Soldier to the Last Day* (*Soldat bis zum letzten Tage*).

Richard Raiber, a University of Delaware Ph.D. candidate, wrote *The Anatomy of Perjury: Field Marshal Albert Kesselring, Via Rasella, and the Ginny Mission*, a convincing study of Kesselring that revealed that he was not the ideal German soldier he appeared to be. He had in fact covered up his involvement in the murder of 16 OSS men in military uniform by claiming he was at the Anzio front and was not informed of the executions while in fact he was in northern Italy and knew all about it. Raiber was posthumously awarded a Ph.D. for his comprehensive research.

General Kurt **Mälzer**, the self-appointed King of Rome, was sentenced to death for his role in the Ardeatine massacre. The sentence was later commuted to life in imprisonment in Werl Prison in North Rhine-Westphalila, Germany, where he died in 1952.

SS-Hauptsturmführer Erich **Priebke**, like many of his comrades, was likely helped by ODESSA, or a group with similar aims, and fled to Argentina after the war. Using his own name, he freely traveled to Europe and brazenly visited Rome on one occasion. Priebke was eventually discovered in San Carlos de Bariloche, Argentina, a resort in the Andes, where he had lived since 1954. In Bariloche he had worked as a waiter until he opened his own food store, the Vienna Delicatessen.

On May 5, 1994, a US television program, ABC News Prime Time Live, broadcast a story about Priebke noting he was alive and living in Argentina. Researchers for the story found him listed in a declassified US Navy Intelligence document which had a vague reference about a still-wanted second-in-command of the Gestapo at Via Tasso. He was interviewed by the American reporter Sam Donaldson and he freely, and perhaps foolishly, admitted that he was the wanted war criminal. In 1995 Argentina extradited Priebke to Italy where he was tried and convicted for his role in the Ardeatine Cave massacre. Returned to Rome, he gave his pretrial deposition at Fort Boccea where he had sent prisoners to be shot. He was sentenced to 15 years in prison along with SS-Sturmbannführer Eugen **Haas**, head of German counterintelligence in Rome.

Priebke was given a second trial due to public demonstrations about his light sentence. During that time he was held under house arrest. Priebke died in Rome on October 11, 2013 aged 100. It is not known what happened to Haas.

SS-Hauptsturmführer Carl-Theodor **Schütz** (1907–1985) was the first head of ABT IV. After Rome, he was sent to Forlì and later Merano. By May 1945, he was a POW and he was tried with Kappler and the others (Clemens, Domizlaff, Quapp, and Wiedner) but was acquitted. In 1952, Schütz was recruited by ex-Abwehr General Reinhard Gehlen, the co-founder of the postwar German Federal Intelligence Agency, the *Bundesnachrichtendienst*. Along with Clemens, he was subsequently charged as an agent of the German Democratic Republic and the Soviet KGB.

SS-Hauptsturmführer Otto **Skorzeny** was nicknamed "the long jumper" after successfully rescuing Mussolini. He had a long career in special operations which may have included an unsuccessful plot to capture Allied leaders during the Big Three Tehran Conference. During the Battle of the Bulge he led a special German unit outfitted with American uniforms and equipment and who spoke English. After the war it was claimed that he was part of the German ODESSA group formed to aid former Nazis, if in fact such an organization existed.

SS-Obersturmführer Heinz-Josef (Heinrich) **Tunath** (Thunath) was the officer who transferred the prisoners to be executed from the Regina Coeli Prison to the Ardeatine Caves. He was not on the list found at the German Embassy so was not in Rome at liberation and was believed to be in Berlin. After some time in the German capital, from January 1944 until 1945, he joined Skorzeny's SS Jaeger Battalion 502 in a Special Task Force in Italy. He was captured at Verona in April 1945 and after the war he was recruited by the German Federal Intelligence Service.

Karl F. **Wolff** was sentenced to 15 years in jail for war crimes and died in 1984.

ITALIANS

Donato **Carretta** was the victim of a miscarriage of justice just after Pietro Caruso's verdict for war crimes was announced. A mob outside the Palace of Justice mistook Carretta, the former head of the Regina Coeli Prison, for Pietro Caruso. The incensed mob grabbed him and threw him into the Tiber. As Carretta struggled to stay afloat, young men struck him on the head with oars and he drowned. One irony in this tragedy was that Carretta had been called to testify against Caruso. In his testimony at the trial he said that he received telephone orders from Caruso ordering him to provide the 50 men demanded by Kappler for reprisal against the Via Rasella bombing. He said he was told that they would be sent to labor camps in the north, and he even returned their personal belongings prior to their being loaded on the trucks, which subsequently helped in their identification. While Carretta was, in a sense, not innocent, he was at least not the worst. He had often assisted the prisoners by allowing extra food parcels to be given to them and he permitted more contact with their relatives.

Pietro **Caruso**, the notorious Roman police chief, was arrested when Allied troops captured Viterbo, to the north of Rome. Caruso had with him a small fortune in watches, jewelry, British pound notes, and Italian lire. He was tried for his unlawful raid on Saint Paul's Basilica, the roundups he performed at the behest of the Germans, the arrest of anti-fascists and Jews, the looting of private homes and most of all for providing the names of Italians to be murdered at the Fosse Ardeatine. He was sentenced to death in September 1944, and was shot on June 5, 1945, at Fort Bravetta, where he had sent so many others.

Giuseppe **Dosi**, the Rome ex-police detective, who saved the incriminating Via Tasso documents, was awarded the US Medal of Freedom. Later he brought Italy into the International Police Organization, INTERPOL. The records that he saved were instrumental in the prosecution of Kappler, General Mälzer (second Stadtkommandant of Rome), and Ernst Baron von Weizsäcker (German Ambassador to the Holy See) for war crimes. They were also helpful to Professor Attilio Ascarelli as he identified the victims of the massacre.

Pietro **Koch**, the Banda Koch leader, made good his escape, ending up in German-controlled Florence. He was later placed in charge of a new prison, a torture palace, in Milan, the so-called Villa Triste (Villa of Sorrows). He was eventually captured, tried and shot at Fort Bravetta on June 5, 1945, the same day as Caruso.

Iride **Imperoli** married a man named Colaprete and had two more children, Salvatore and Giancarlo. She stayed in Sulmona.

Celeste Di **Porto**, the renegade Jew called the Black Panther, who identified Jews on the street for the SS, was arrested and sent to the Regina Coeli Prison. Eventually she was interrogated by a US counterintelligence official. She told the story that she was a victim of the Germans and had actually helped many Jews escape. Perhaps because she was such a beautiful young woman, she was believed and released. Next she hitched a ride to Naples with an American GI in a jeep. There she became a high-priced prostitute but was spotted by two Roman Jews and rearrested. She was returned to Rome and tried for her crimes and sent to prison.

Baron Franco **Malfatti**, one of Tompkins' key helpers, served as the Italian Ambassador to France for several years.

THE ROMAN PARTIGIANI (PARTISANS)

110 partisans were killed at the Ardeatine Caves (see Chapter 18); 55 were shot at Fort Bravetta during the German occupation, 14 at La Storta, ten at Fort Boccea, and nine during their incarceration at Fascist and German-run prisons such as Via Tasso and Regina Coeli. Seven were sent to concentration camps in Germany and did not return. In total during the German occupation of Italy, there were 1,183 recognized Red Flag partisans and they suffered 186 deaths and 137 deportations.[13]

Pasquale **Balsamo** was a 19-year-old student. After the Via Rasella bombing, he was arrested while attempting to assassinate Benito Mussolini's eldest son, Vittorio Mussolini. With him were Fernando **Vitagliano**, Marisa **Musu**, Ernesto **Borghesi**, and another newly recruited partisan, Franco **Ferri**. Balsamo was taken to the Regina Coeli, but sympathetic police officials transferred him to a psychiatric hospital where he stayed until liberation. Upon release, he joined the Partisan Cremona Brigade and was with Silvio Serra when Serra was killed. After the war he became a journalist and for many years was the editor of the weekly *Italian Automobile Club* magazine. He was presented with an Italian Bronze Medal and a War Cross.

Rosario **Bentivegna**, the partisan street sweeper in the Via Rasella attack, and his lookout and longtime colleague, Gappista Carla **Capponi**, married on September 20, 1944. The next day Bentivegna went to lead partisans in Yugoslavia where he contracted malaria. Bentivegna admitted shooting Guardia di Finanza policeman Sottotenente Giorgio Barbarisi and he served 18 months in prison. After the war, Bentivegna finished his medical studies and received numerous decorations from Italy, Yugoslavia and the Soviet Union. In 1968–1969 he was in the Greek resistance against the rule of the colonels running the government at that time. He was assisted by his daughter Elena. In 1996 he wrote *Operazione Via Rasella, verità e menzogne: protagonisti raccontano* (*Operation Via Rasella, truth and lies, the protagonist speaks*). He died in 2012.

Guglielmo **Blasi** was the turncoat and informer who betrayed his former comrades. He fled north with Koch, and was returned to Rome in 1945 where he was tried for the murder of an Italian Socialist Party member and sent to prison for 15 years. He died in 1964.

Ernesto **Borghesi** was a medical student who was a sergeant in the Italian Military Medical Corps and served at the Celio Military Hospital in Rome. During the attempt to assassinate Benito Mussolini's eldest son, Vittorio Mussolini, he engaged in the shootout but was captured and sent to the Regina Coeli Prison. At his German Military Tribunal trial, his defiance so enraged the Germans that they arrested his parents and wife and all were kept in Via Tasso until liberation.

Franco **Calamandrei** was the GAP vice commander. He was arrested with Salinari. His warning to others of Blasi's denouncement resulted in many leaving the city and evading capture. He was awarded both Silver and Bronze Italian medals. After the war, he was the London and Beijing correspondent for the Italian Communist newspaper *L'Unità*. He was later elected senator in the Italian parliament.

Carla **Capponi**, as a result of her partisan activities, remained in poor health for the rest of her life. Nevertheless, after the war she became a successful journalist and later served in the Italian parliament as a representative of the Italian Communist Party (PCI). She was presented a Gold Medal by the Italian government. Bentivegna and Capponi had a daughter, Elena (Carla's partisan code name), but divorced in 1974. Her book, *Con Cuore di Donna* (With the Heart of a Woman) was published in 2000, the year she died.

Giulio **Cortini** was an assistant in the physics department of the University of Rome and head of the GAP bomb-making team. He finished his studies after the war and worked with nuclear energy. He refused all interviews and never wrote his memoirs.

Francesco **Curreli** was a Sardinian shepherd. After the war, he returned to Sardinia and by chance ran into another ex-partisan, Antonello Trombadori, who convinced him to return to Rome and become the head of the security at the Communist headquarters on Via Botteghe Oscure. Curreli died in 1966.

Raoul **Falcioni** was a taxi driver and the most audacious member of the GAP. After the war Falcioni returned to being a taxi driver. He died in 1961.

Mario **Fiorentini** was the student who rode his bicycle and threw hand grenades in the Regina Coeli Prison attack. After the liberation of Rome, he went to North Africa for OSS parachute training. He was dropped into northern Italy as the leader of a partisan insertion team but was captured and imprisoned in Milan until liberated on April 25, 1945. He received three Italian Silver Medals and awards by the British SOE and the American OSS.

Laura **Garrone-Cortini** was a literature student at the university and Giulio Cortini's wife. She worked at the University of Naples library and died in 1996.

Duilio **Grigioni** was the *portiere* of the building on Via Marco Aurelio which housed the *santabarbara* near the Colosseum. After the war he stayed on in his job as the *portiere*. He died in 1960.

Marisa **Musu** was a 19-year-old chemical student at the university. She was arrested with the group that tried to assassinate Vittorio Mussolini and was sent to the Regina Coeli Prison and released on June 4. She became a journalist for *L'Unità*, the Italian Communist Party newspaper and traveled to Vietnam, China, and Mozambique. Later she became an activist for the Palestinian cause.

Lucia **Ottobrini** was 20 years old and employed at the Treasury Ministry. Although she participated in many GAP attacks in the city and was awarded a Silver Medal after the war she remained a private person, preferring not to speak of her partisan activities.

Carlo **Salinari** was the GAP Central Commander and an assistant professor of literature at the University of Rome. He organized the Via Rasella attack and was the on-scene commander. After the war, he edited a communist cultural magazine. He was proposed for a Gold Medal by the Italian government, but was awarded two Silver Medals instead. He died in 1977.

Silvio **Serra** was recruited for GAP by his friends **Balsamo** and **Falcioni**. A literature student, he paid for his studies by working in an auto workshop taken over by the Germans. After liberation, he joined the 28th Garibaldi Brigade, a partisan unit which fought with the new Italian Army (with Pasquale Balsamo). He was killed in a hail of machine-gun bullets on April 10, 1945. Serra was posthumously awarded a Gold Medal.

Fernando **Vitagliano** at 18 was the youngest member of the GAP. He wanted to fight in the mountain branch but Falcioni persuaded him to join GAP Rome. After the war Vitagliano married, had two children, and became a businessman. He was posthumously awarded a Silver Medal for valor in 1985, a few months after he died.

Because partisans shared their lives under such intense pressure, many of them married, like Rosario Bentivegna and Carla Capponi. They included: Maria Teresa Regard and Franco Calamandrei; Lucia Ottobrini and Mario Fiorentini; Marisa Musu and Valentino Gerratana; and Antonello Trombadori and Fulvia Trozzi.

OF NOTE

American author Robert **Katz** did extensive research and published three key books on the period. First was the 1967 title *Death in Rome*. This book was controversial in Italy as many felt it unfairly laid the blame for much of what happened at the Ardeatine Caves at the feet of the Pope. He was sued by the late Pope's sister, Princess Pacelli, but was eventually cleared of defamation charges. In 1969 Katz published *Black Sabbath* which detailed the expulsion of Rome's Jews.

Robert Katz co-authored the screenplay for the 1973 film *Massacre in Rome*, based on his book. Richard Burton played Kappler with Marcello Mastroianni as Father Pietro, an invented character. The film was criticized for being overwhelmed by its stars, but it presents a mostly accurate account of the massacre. By 2003 much new World

War II material had been released by the Vatican and other archives. Katz published *The Battle for Rome* that year, updating much of what was in *Death in Rome*. Robert Katz died on October 20, 2010 at Montevarchi, Italy.

In 1955 the *Museo Storico della Liberazione* at the former Gestapo Headquarters on Via Tasso was opened and the torture cells preserved for all to see. The museum remains controversial and, shortly before midnight on November 23, 1999, a bomb was thrown against the museum door. Fortunately, no one was injured.

———

The search for the remaining names of the Fosse Ardeatine victims continues. In April 2020, Dr. Alessia Glielmi informed the author as this book was going to press, that another victim had been positively identified using advanced scientific research. His name was Marian Reicher, a Polish Jew, born on February 7, 1901 in Kolomyia, Poland. It is not known how he came to Rome. Eight victims remain unidentified, but the search goes on.

Endnotes

CHAPTER 1: BOMBING THE CRADLE OF CHRISTIANITY

1 Portelli, *The Order Has Been Carried Out*, p. 78.
2 Sermoneta, *Sparkle Distant Worlds*, p. 198.
3 Tittmann, *Inside the Vatican of Pius XII*, p. 146.
4 See Tittmann p. 147 for the full letter from the Pope to the President.
5 De Simone, *Venti angeli sopra Roma*, p. 110, translated by the author.
6 Tittmann, pp. 162–163.
7 This information was taken from the Italian language book by Silveri and Carli, *Bombardare Roma*, summarized and translated back into English by the author.
8 Tittmann, p. 165.
9 Tittmann, p. 164, author's translation.
10 De Wyss, *Rome Under the Terror*, p. 42.
11 Tompkins, *Italy Betrayed*, p. 19.
12 Tompkins, *Italy Betrayed*, p. 19.
13 Mussolini, *The Fall of Mussolini*, p. 71.
14 De Wyss, p. 48.

CHAPTER 2: THE FRANTIC EFFORT TO LEAVE THE AXIS

1 De Wyss, p. 83.
2 Tittmann, p. 183.
3 De Wyss, p. 86.
4 Raiber, *The Anatomy of Perjury*, p. 35.
5 Katz, *Battle for Rome*, pp. 11–12.
6 Comments adapted from a footnote in Kurzman, *The Race for Rome*, p. 67 and were noted as coming from an unnamed senior Vatican official.
7 For the full story of Dick Mallaby, see Barneschi, *An Englishman Abroad*.
8 Tompkins, *A Spy in Rome*, p. 147.
9 Tompkins, *A Spy in Rome*, p. 168.
10 Tompkins, *A Spy in Rome*, p. 175.
11 Brey, *The Venus Fixers*, p. 20.

CHAPTER 3: THE FORMER ALLIES SQUARE OFF

1 Barneschi, in the book's photo section from the Professor Gregory Alegi Archives.

2 Tompkins, *Italy Betrayed*, p. 212.
3 Tompkins, *Italy Betrayed*, p. 218.

CHAPTER 4: WAR IN A MUSEUM – THE BATTLE FOR ROME

1 Katz, *Death in Rome*, p. 42.
2 Scrivener, *Inside Rome with the Germans*, p. 4.
3 Sermoneta, p. 208.
4 Scrivener, pp. 6–7.
5 De Wyss, p. 110.
6 Sermoneta, p. 209.
7 SCI Unit Z, Memo Subj: *Otto Lechner*, September 8, 1945.
8 Scrivener, p. 28.
9 Munthe, *Sweet is War*, p. 169.

CHAPTER 5: THE GESTAPO IN ROME – KAPPLER, ESPIONAGE, AND SABOTAGE

1 The biographical notes were based on Kappler's First Interrogation Report. It was classified Top Secret with the file designation CSDIC/SC15AG/SD 18. The author had access to copy number 25, dated June 8, 1945. Many of Kappler's comments in this debriefing were self-serving.
2 Simonetti, *Via Tasso*, p. 167, translated by the author.
3 Allied Force Headquarters, Office of the ACOS G-2; Subject: Summary and Appreciation for the Activities of EINSATZKOMMANDO ROM, SIPO und SD, dated January 13, 1945, p. 10, paragraph 53.
4 Katz, *Battle for Rome*, pp. 297–298.
5 *La Nostra SS Italiani*, 1944, is a booklet describing the organization.

CHAPTER 6: FIRST THEY TAKE THE JEWS

1 Katz, *Black Sabbath*, pp. 216–217.
2 Zuccotti, *Under his very Windows*, p. 68.
3 Zuccotti, *Under his very Windows*, p. 69.
4 Newman, Louis Israel, *A "Chief Rabbi" of Rome Becomes a Catholic*, p. 113.
5 See Debenedetti, *October 16, 1943*, entire volume and Thomas, *The Pope's Jews*, p. 197.
6 Katz, *Death in Rome*, p. 82.
7 *Centro di Documentazione Ebraica Contemporanea* (Center for Contemporary Jewish Documentation).
8 Zuccotti, *The Italians and the Holocaust*, p. 177.
9 Zuccotti, *Under his very Windows*, pp.158–159; also Cornwell, *Hitler's Pope*, p. 303.
10 See Zuccotti, *Under his very Windows*, pp.159–160.
11 Kurzman, p. 77. Susan Zuccotti in *The Italians and the Holocaust* writes that this letter was written by Hudal at the urging of the Pope, see p. 129.
12 Kurzman, p. 78.
13 Email, Archivio Storico Romaebraica, October 16, 2018.
14 Zuccotti, *The Italians and the Holocaust*, p. 135.
15 Weisbord and Sillanpoa, *The Chief Rabbi, the Pope and the Holocaust*, page number unknown.
16 Blet, *Pius XII and the Second World War*, p. 165.
17 See Zuccotti, *Père Marie-Benoît and the Jewish Rescue*, p. 175.

CHAPTER 7: THE VATICAN NEST OF SPIES

1 Chadwick, *Britain and the Vatican*, p. 90.
2 Chadwick, p. 98.
3 Chadwick, p. 97.
4 Tompkins, *Italy Betrayed*, p. 12.
5 Chadwick, p. 97.
6 Tittmann in a letter to his wife Elly, dated January 17, 1942.
7 Tittmann in the preliminary draft for his book, p. 201.
8 Chadwick, p. 260.
9 Smith, *OSS: The Secret History*, p. 84.

CHAPTER 8: UNEXPECTED, BUT WELCOME HELP

1 This information has been adapted from Foot and Langley, *MI-9 Escape and Evasion 1939–45*, pp. 18–20, 23.
2 Weymouth, *A.W.O.L.*, p. 31.
3 Bragadin, *The Italian Navy in World War II*, p. 344.

CHAPTER 9: ALLIED POWS SEEK FREEDOM

1 This is taken from *Le Operazioni delle unità Italiane nel Settembre–Ottobre 1943*, p. 64.
2 The author sat down with Signora del Monaco in October 2015.
3 Furman, *Be Not Fearful*, p. 77.

CHAPTER 10: KNOCKING ON THE GATES OF SAINT PETER'S

1 Kneale, *Brother Robert*, pp. 9–10.
2 Kneale, pp. 11–12.
3 Gallagher, *The Scarlet and the Black*, p. 57.
4 Adapted from Gallagher, pp. 48–49.
5 See Fleming, *The Vatican Pimpernel*, p. 70.
6 Mander, *Mander's March on Rome*, p. 72.
7 Foot and Langley, pp. 26–27.
8 Derry, *The Rome Escape Line*, p. 32.
9 This was taken from an otherwise unmarked NARA OSS document, Enclosure A: *Report on Visit to Rome with two Couriers from PARMA CLN* and NARA OSS document, *Report covering the Activities of OSS Special Detachment G-2 5th Army in Italy*, undated, pp. 31 and 57.
10 Derry, p. 56.
11 Derry, pp. 59–60.
12 Derry, p. 61.
13 Quoting from the diary, Walker, *Hide & Seek*, p. 90.

CHAPTER 11: OFFICIAL MILITARY RESISTANCE – NO NOTES

CHAPTER 12: CIAO BELLA, CIAO – THE PARTIGIANI

1 Katz, *The Battle for Rome*, p. 90.
2 Katz, *Death in Rome*, p. 88.
3 Kurzman, p. 121.
4 Portelli, p. 59.

5 Portelli, p. 106.
6 Katz, *Death in Rome*, p. 128.

CHAPTER 13: THE ROME ESCAPE LINE

1 Simpson, *A Vatican Lifeline '44*, p. 82.
2 Derry, p. 75.
3 Tittmann, p. 189.
4 Derry, p. 118.
5 Tittmann, pp. 189–190.
6 Furman, p. 114.
7 Furman, p. 121.
8 January 11: letter to the Escape Line from Archie Gibb, 1st South African Division, from Regina Coeli Prison, see Appendix F.
9 Gallagher, pp. 119–120.

CHAPTER 14: LIFE UNDER THE GESTAPO BOOT – RAIDS, ROUNDUPS, FOOD, AND ART

1 Fleming, p. 92.
2 Adapted from Romagnoli, *The Bicycle Runner*, pp. 151–156.
3 Scrivener, p. 63.
4 Kurzman, pp. 82–83.
5 Hapgood and Richardson, *Monte Cassino*, p. 51.
6 See Kurzman, p. 143.
7 Kurzman, p. 138.
8 Kneale, pp. 13–14.
9 Derry, p. 115.
10 Furman, p. 128.
11 Hapgood and Richardson, p. 77.
12 Hapgood and Richardson, p. 68.
13 Scrivener, p. 68.
14 Brey, p. 25.
15 Brey, p. 47.
16 As quoted by Brey, pp. 83–84.

CHAPTER 15: AN AMERICAN BOY SCOUT OSS SPY IN ROME

1 From Tompkins, *Spy in Rome*, Introduction by Donald Downes, p. 9.
2 Bragadin, p. 328.

CHAPTER 16: A STRANDED WHALE

1 Tompkins, *Spy in Rome*, pp. 74–75.
2 Trevelyan, *Rome '44*, p. 62.
3 Garrad-Cole, *Single to Rome*, pp. 100–101.
4 Tompkins, *Spy in Rome*, p. 119.
5 Mander, p. 125.
6 Mander, p. 115.
7 Tompkins, *Spy in Rome*, p. 122.
8 Tompkins as quoted by Katz in *Battle for Rome*, p. 177.
9 Tompkins, *Spy in Rome*, pp. 134–135.
10 Tompkins, *Spy in Rome*, pp. 125–126.

11 Tompkins, *Spy in Rome*, p. 148.
12 Tompkins, *Spy in Rome*, p. 127.
13 Scrivener, p. 134.
14 Katz, *Battle for Rome*, p. 175.
15 See Katz, *Battle for Rome*, footnote 9, page 378.
16 Tompkins, *Spy in Rome*, p. 182.
17 Tompkins, *Spy in Rome*, p. 183.
18 See Tompkins, *Spy in Rome*, pp. 179–185, for a fuller description.
19 Kurtzman, p. 266.

CHAPTER 17: NO ROMAN HOLIDAY

1 See Failmezger, *American Knights*, for the story of this famous tank destroyer battalion and a detailed discussion of their part in the Ranger attack on Cisterna.
2 Black, *The Ranger Force*, p. 267.
3 Newman, p. 2.
4 Newman, p. 1.
5 Simpson, p. 105.
6 Newman, p. 27.
7 Newman, p. 28
8 Newman, p. 31.
9 Furman, p. 182.
10 Romagnoli, p. 189.
11 Furman, p. 140.
12 See Dethick, Janet Kinrade, *The Bridge at Allerona – 28 January*, lulu.com, 2018.
13 Furman, p. 175.
14 Hapgood and Richardson, pp. 221–228.
15 Hapgood and Richardson, p. 241.
16 Derry, pp. 171–172, muddled this story, having Brother Robert captured at a Rome apartment house while turning over the escapees. The story related in Scrivener, pp. 138–140 appears to be correct.
17 Kneale, pp. 14–15.

CHAPTER 18: THE ORDER HAS BEEN CARRIED OUT

1 Simonetti, p. 245, author's translation.
2 Portelli, p. 112.
3 De Wyss, p. 204.
4 See Raiber.
5 Trevelyan, *Rome '44*, p. 225.
6 Katz, *Battle for Rome*, p. 250. Only Katz and Simonetti discuss the escape of Raider.
7 Kurzman, p. 185, footnote.
8 Kurzman, p. 192.
9 Katz, *Death in Rome*, p. 178, which he found in the *Messaggero* newspaper of March 25, 1944.
10 Kurzman, p. 190.
11 Tompkins, *Spy in Rome*, p. 206.
12 See, for example, https://it.wikipedia.org/wiki/Eccidio_delle_Fosse_Ardeatine#Vittime.

CHAPTER 19: THE ROMAN SPRING OF 1944

1 Garrad-Cole, p. 112.
2 Fleming, p. 143, as quoted from a document held at the British National Archives.

3 Derry, p. 154.
4 Furman, pp. 199–200.

CHAPTER 20: PRELUDE TO LIBERATION

1 As told to the author by Angelo Arrigoni, the current owner and son of Erminio.
2 Scrivener, p. 187.
3 Trevelyan, *Rome '44*, pp. 250, 264.
4 Derry, p. 197.
5 Derry, p. 198.

CHAPTER 21: AT LONG LAST, LIBERATION

1 Trevelyan, *Rome '44*, p. 277.
2 Scrivener, p. 187.
3 Derry, p. 216.
4 Trevelyan, *Rome '44*, p. 305.
5 Katz, *Battle for Rome*, p. 310, from the diary of A. Giovannetti.
6 Sevareid, *Not so Wild a Dream*, p. 408.
7 Tittmann, pp. 208–209.
8 Tompkins, p. 337.
9 The *Stars and Stripes* newspaper, Mediterranean, Italy edition, June 6, 1944, p. 2.
10 Katz, *Battle for Rome*, pp. 316–317.
11 Adleman and Walton, *The Devil's Brigade*, p. 218.
12 Author's collection, original from the US National Archives.
13 Sermoneta, p. 265.
14 Newman, pp. 44–45.
15 Newman, pp. 46–47.
16 Dr. Charles W. Phallen, in his nineties, and interviewed by the author, died in March 2015.
17 Letter supplied by Col. Lars Larson, US Army Retired.
18 Tittmann, p. 210.

EPILOGUE

1 Sermoneta, p. 298.
2 3rd Division News Sheet, author's collection from the US National Archives.
3 Josowitz, *Informal History of the 601st Tank Destroyer Battalion*.
4 Sgt. Larson letter, courtesy Col. Larson.
5 Author's collection.
6 Silveri and Carli, p. 43, author's translation.
7 Appendix "B" to Fifth Army G-2 report No. 349, Translation of Captured Document: HQ I Parachute Corps, Operational Order No. 838/Secret, 20 July 44, Subject: *Operations Against Partisans*.
8 Chadwick, p. 300.
9 Brey, pp. 211–212.
10 Adapted from an oral statement by Dumas and published in Rozell, *The Things Our Fathers Saw*.
11 Adleman and Walton, p. 258.
12 Kneale, p. 18.
13 Osti Guerrazzi, *Tedeschi*, p. 90.

Acronyms

ABT	German, *Abteilung*, section
AK	German, *Aussenkommando*, local command
AMT	German, *Amt* (plural *Ämter*), bureau
CLN	Italian, *Comitato di Liberazione Nazionale*, National Liberation Committee
DELASEM	Italian, *Delegazione per l'assistenza agli emigranti Ebrei*, Hebrew Emigrant Relief Organization
EK	German, *Einsatzkommando*, task force
FMCR	Italian, *Fronte Militare Clandestino della Resistenza*, Military Clandestine Front of the Resistance
GESTAPO	German, *Geheime Staatspolizei*, Secret State Police (ABT IV in Rome)
GNR	Italian, *Guardia Nazionale Repubblicana*, National Republican Guard
LKW	German, *Lastkraftwagen*, truck
MAS	Italian, *Motoscafo Armato Silurante*, Navy motor torpedo boats
MC	Military Cross, a British decoration
MG Schütz	German, MG LKW is a machine gun-equipped truck
MVSN	Italian, *Milizia Volontaria per la Sicurezza Nazionale*, Volunteer Militia for National Security (blackshirts)
ODESSA	German, *Organization der Ehemaligen SS-Angehörigen*, Organization of Former SS Members
ORPO	German, *Ordnungspolizei*, uniformed Order Police
OSS	Office of Strategic Services, American intelligence organization
OVRA	Italian, *Organizzazione per la Vigilanza e la Repressione dell'Antifascismo*, Organization for Vigilance and Repression of Anti-Fascism, the Italian Gestapo
PAI	Italian, *Polizia dell'Africa Italiana*, Italian Africa Police
PCI	Italian, *Partito Comunista Italiano*, Italian Communist Party
PKW	German, *Personenkraftwagen*, passenger car
POW	prisoner of war; 1940s version of the acronym was PW
RAF	Royal Air Force (British)
RCAF	Royal Canadian Air Force
RCASC	Royal Canadian Army Service Corps
RSHA	German, *Reichssicherheitshauptamt*, Reich Main Security Headquarters
RSI	Italian, *Repubblica Sociale Italiana*, Italian Social Republic aka Salò Republic

SA	German, *Sturmabteilung*, storm section (shock squad)
SD	German, *Sicherheitsdienst*, security service (ABT VI in Rome)
SIM	Italian, *Servizio Informazioni Militar*, Military Intelligence Service
SIPO	German, *Sicherheitspolizei*, Security Police, also referred to as the Gestapo
SIS	Secret Intelligence Service, British intelligence organization
SOE	Special Operations Executive (British)
SS	German, *Schutzstaffel*, Protection Squad
USAAF	US Army Air Force
V-Mann	German, *Vertrauensmann*, agent, literally a "trusted man"
VC	Victoria Cross, Highest British and Commonwealth Military Award
X-MAS	Italian, Decima MAS, *Decima Flottiglia MAS*, Armed Torpedo Motorboats of the 10th Light Flotilla, a special naval commando unit

Appendices

APPENDIX A: CHRONOLOGY

1889: Italy established Italian Somaliland

1895–1896: Italy defeated in the 1st Abyssinian (Ethiopian) War

1912: Italy established a protectorate over Libya

1915: Italy joined the WWI Allies; 600,000 Italian soldiers died

1918, Nov 11: WWI ends; the seeds of WWII are planted in Italy and Germany

1918–1922: Crushing Italian recession and unprecedented levels of unemployment and unrest

1919, Jun 28: Versailles peace treaty signed: Italy received little, Italian Navy restricted

1922, Oct 22–29: Mussolini's March on Rome

1922, Oct 31: Mussolini becomes Prime Minister of Italy

1929, Feb 2: Lateran Treaty with the Vatican signed

1935–1936: 2nd Abyssinian War; Italy conquered Ethiopia and "finally" had her empire

1936–1939: Italy sent troops to support General Franco during the Spanish Civil War

1937: Mussolini made a triumphal visit to Germany

1938: Hitler visited Rome; Italian government banned Jewish children and teachers from schools

1939

Jan 5: Italians published the Racial Purity Law

Mar 2: Cardinal Pacelli elected Pope (Pius XII)

Apr 7: Italy invaded Albania

May 22: Germany and Italy signed the Pact of Steel

Sep 1: Germany invaded Poland

Sep 3: Britain and France declared war on Germany

1940

May 10: Germany invaded the Netherlands

Jun 4: 340,000 British and French troops evacuated from Dunkirk

Jun 10: Mussolini declared war on France and England

Sep 10: Italian Air Corps joined the Luftwaffe in the Battle of Britain

Sep 13: Italian Tenth Army invaded British-held Egypt from Libya

Oct 28: Italy invaded Greece

1941
Feb: German Field Marshal Rommel formed Afrika Korps to aid the Italian Tenth Army
Apr 6: Germany invaded Greece to rescue the Italian Army
Nov 12: The British Royal Navy attacked the Italian Battle Fleet at Taranto
Dec 7: Japan attacked Pearl Harbor, Hawaii
Dec 10: Italy declared war on the United States

1942
Jul: Italian Eighth Army sent to the Soviet Union to fight with the German Wehrmacht
Nov 8: Allies landed in North Africa
Nov: Germans and Italians occupied Vichy France

1943
Jan 14–24: Casablanca Conference, principle of unconditional surrender announced
May 13: Axis forces defeated in North Africa
Jul 10: Allies landed in Sicily
Jul 19: Mussolini met with Hitler; Rome bombed for the first time
Jul 25: Meeting of Fascist Grand Council, Mussolini received vote of no confidence
Jul 26: Mussolini deposed by the king, Italian Marshal Badoglio told to form a government
Aug 14: Marshal Badoglio declared Rome an Open City
Aug 17: Germans abandoned Sicily to the Allies
Sep 3: British Eighth Army invaded mainland Italy; Italian armistice signed in secret
Sep 8: News of the Italian armistice is publicly announced
Sep 9: Allies landed at Salerno; Germans battled Italians for Rome
Sep 10: Germans occupied Rome
Sep 12: Mussolini rescued from Gran Sasso
Sep 23: Mussolini declared the Italian Social Republic, the so-called Salò Republic
Sep 26: SS Rome chief Kappler demanded the Jews of Rome hand over 50 kilos of gold
Oct 1: Allies entered Naples after a four-day citizen revolt; city's infrastructure destroyed
Oct 3: Germans abandoned Sardinia and Corsica
Oct 4: Hitler ordered resistance south of Rome; Gustav Line built with conscripted labor
Oct 7: Nazis rounded up Rome Carabinieri
Oct 13: Royalist Italy declared war on Germany
Oct 16: The Gestapo roundup of Rome's Jews
Oct 18: First partisan attack on German troops in Rome
Nov 5: Vatican City bombed
Dec 10: Partisans bombed Hotel Flora in Rome
Dec 18: Partisans attacked the Cinema Barberini
Dec 20: Partisans attacked the Regina Coeli Prison
Dec 21: Fascists and the Gestapo raided Church institutions in Rome

1944
Jan 22: Allies landed at Anzio
Feb 15: Allied air raid destroyed the Abbey of Monte Cassino
Mar 12: The Pope delivered his fifth anniversary address in Saint Peter's Square
Mar 23: Partisans attacked SS police unit in Via Rasella
Mar 24: 335 Italians executed at the Fosse Ardeatine
May 11: Allied Operation *Diadem* commenced the drive to Rome
May 23: Operation *Buffalo*, the breakout from the Anzio beachhead, commenced
May 25: US II Corps broke through the Gustav Line and met US troops from Anzio

Jun 4: American troops entered Rome
Jun 5: Rome liberated
Jun 6: D-Day, Allies landed in Normandy

1945
April 28: Mussolini executed near Lake Como

APPENDIX B: THE BOMBING OF ROME AND ENVIRONS

Chapter 1 covered the first bombings of Rome but the city was bombed multiple times. Details for these attacks, listed below, have been compiled from information provided by multiple sources. Every attempt has been made to make this as accurate as possible but the author has had only partial access to US Army Air Corps bomb damage assessment reports. The number of victims is given when known but is subject to interpretation. The Allies intentionally bombed Rome only during daylight hours in order to avoid damage to the Vatican and other buildings in the historic center of the city. In that they were largely successful. Flares, leaflets, and only an occasional bomb were dropped during the night. It is estimated that Allied bombing caused 4,000 deaths and injured 9,000. The total may have been higher. On April 5, 1944, the *Giornale D'Italia* claimed in a headline: "… the victims of the Liberators, five thousand killed and more than 11,000 wounded. Most of these victims were killed in their own homes. It cannot be forgotten that Rome has offered up its blood, pain and destruction."

1943
May 4/5: Overnight the British RAF dropped leaflets over Rome which asked Italians to sue
     for an honorable peace; otherwise Rome will become a battlefield.
July 18: From 00:15 the RAF dropped leaflets that Rome would be bombed the next day.
July 19: Rome was bombed. The targets were the San Lorenzo and the Littorio railway
     marshalling yards, and the Littorio and Ciampino Airfields. Collateral damage occurred at
     the Policlinico and the Basilica of San Lorenzo; 1,486 people were killed and 2,000 injured.
August 13: The same targets were struck again. At least 380 people were killed.
September 9: The German Luftwaffe dropped bombs near the University of Rome to stop
     Italian troop movements to the north of the city. There were multiple victims.
September 16: A German vehicle column was strafed in the Magliana quarter, south of the city.
October 1: Unknown aircraft dropped flares at night over the city.
November 1: Near the town of Colleferro, 31 miles southeast of Rome on Via Casilina, the
     main supply route for the Wehrmacht to Cassino was bombed.
November 5: At 20:10 an unidentified aircraft dropped five small bombs on the Vatican. It
     may have been the idea of Roberto Farinacci, a leading Fascist (with the encouragement
     of the Rome SS), to knock out Vatican Radio. The Vatican administration building, the
     mosaic factory, and the Bernini stained-glass windows in Saint Peter's were damaged.
November 11: The Vatican was bombed by an unidentified aircraft but there was no damage.
     Tittmann recalled that a small plane called the "Black Widow" would from time to time
     drop small bombs on the city, as a reprisal against anti-fascists.
December 15: Via Casilina at Colleferro was bombed by the Allies.
December 19: Colleferro town was bombed and at least 19 civilians were killed.
December 23: The southern part of the city was bombed; several factories were lightly damaged.
December 28: After the Allies decided to land at Anzio, the bombing of Rome's military
     targets resumed. Bombs, including using incendiaries, were dropped and 75 civilians were
     killed.

1944
January 13: At midday, 80 B-17 Flying Fortresses escorted by P-38 Lightnings flew over
the city to bomb Ciampino, Centocelle, and Guidonia airfields. They were attacked
by German Messerschmitt Bf 109s and machine-gun projectiles landed in the Vatican
Gardens. Young Tittmann wrote in his diary:

*On January 13, as I was coming out of the Vatican Radio Station at noon following my
lessons, I heard the sound of many motors. Looking up, I saw formations of American
bombers over Rome, escorted by twin-tailed Lockheed Lightning fighters flying directly over
the Vatican. The Lightnings were then attacked by German fighter planes, and I witnessed
a number of dogfights, with clearly audible machine gun firing. I heard something strike
the soil near me, and later learned that several cannon shells had exploded within the
Vatican, fortunately without injuries or damage.*

Tittmann and his wife, Eleanor, saw a P-38 shot down near the Vatican and later learned
that the Germans had captured the pilot. A German Bf 109 was shot down after it was
attacked by three P-38s and a parachute was seen. At 13:15 there was a second wave of 50
B-26 Marauder medium bombers but they were not met by German fighters as German
airbases had been damaged and they could not rearm or refuel.
January 19: At 12:30, the Quadraro quarter was heavily bombed. Young Tittmann wrote that
he counted at least 150 aircraft.
January 20: At 12:45, 50 aircraft bombed the southeast of the city; 128 civilians were killed.
January 21: In preparation for the landing at Anzio and to slow men and supplies on their
way to the Monte Cassino front, targets along the east and southeast were bombed.
January 23: At 19:30 young Tittmann wrote that he heard an aircraft pass over the Vatican
and that it crashed outside the Vatican walls and there was an explosion.
January 27: The Allies bombed the town of Albano in support of the Allied beachhead at
Anzio.
February 1: Bombs were dropped on the Pope's summer residence at Castel Gandolfo;
17 nuns were killed and many others injured.
February 10: The Allies again bombed Castel Gandolfo; more than 400 people were killed.
February 12: In the morning, bombs were dropped on Santa Maria Maggiore and Saint John
Lateran. According to Mother Mary:

*Last night British planes flew over the city. German planes rose to meet them, and there
was a duel in the air. One big bomb fell in Via Mecenate, not far from the Colosseum, and
hit a private nursing home, the Clinica Polidori, wrecking a large part of it and killing
the surgeon who directed it.*

February 13: Young Tittmann wrote that flares were dropped over the Vatican and one landed
on the roof of the Pope's palace. Bombs were also dropped on Castel Gandolfo. Over
the next several days, a concentrated effort was launched to cripple the rail movement of
German reinforcements and materiel to the Cassino and Anzio fronts.
February 14: Between 09:30 and 11:00 the 12th US Air Force bombed the railway
marshalling yards at San Lorenzo, Ostiense, and Tiburtina. Stray bombs hit a police
commissary west of Trastevere and nine people were killed. Dogfights between German
and Allied fighters were observed all over the city.
February 15: Between 10:00 and 11:00 the Rome railway marshalling yards were again
bombed. On the eastern side of the city two people were killed and errant bombs around
the Tiburtina yard caused damage. Sir D'Arcy reported that, across the city, 30 people
were killed and 600 injured. A Vatican food convoy and the Villa Bianca Clinic were

attacked. It was on February 15 that the Abbey of Monte Cassino was destroyed by Allied bombers.

February 16: Seven waves of US B-17s and British Wellington bombers attacked the Ostiense and Tiburtina railway marshalling yards. Stray bombs fell in Trastevere, killing five. Errant bombs hit the Central Market on Via Ostiense to the south. Sir D'Arcy reported that during the air raid 80 were killed and 150 injured.

February 17: In the morning, 500lb bombs were dropped over the Portonaccio quarter and vias Tiburtina and Prenestina. The San Lorenzo Railway Marshalling Yard was again hit.

February 20: A radio message was intercepted from a German train hauling men and supplies to the front saying that the Allies had bombed the Poggio Mirteto railway bridge near Rieti.

February 20–26: Allied naval aircraft repeatedly bombed Cisterna on the Anzio beachhead.

February 25: A Vatican food convoy was attacked near Lake Bracciano.

From March 3 through March 18, 1944, an intensive air bombardment of Rome transportation infrastructure was underway. The purpose was to cut off supplies and reinforcements to the Cassino and Anzio fronts. German military traffic through Rome had increased threefold since the landing at Anzio. According to Katz in *The Battle for Rome* (p. 190), the Swiss correspondent for the *New York Times* described the traffic through Rome this way:*

> On the Ponte Milvio, which is perpetually clogged throughout the hours of darkness, down the Via Flaminia and the Corso in the heart of Rome proper, the stream pours in unending waves of tanks, motorized artillery and trucks loaded with munitions which filter through the maze of streets to disappear in the Pontine Plains [to Anzio] or southward to the escarpments of Cassino.

This drive by the Allied 12th Air Force to disrupt rail, road, and other communications was somewhat successful in hampering German resupply but supplies continued to flow at a substantial rate as the Wehrmacht had top priority. Food and supplies to the city of Rome were greatly disrupted.

March 1: A Vatican food convoy was attacked near Velletri. During the evening (19:59) a lone Wellington bomber inadvertently flew over Rome. It was flown by British RAF Flight Lieutenant (Captain) McCurry who lost altitude while on a bombing mission to the Anzio beachhead. It was a cloudy night and the pilot became disoriented. McCurry clipped a tree on the Janiculum Hill, very close to the Vatican and attempting to gain altitude, he jettisoned his bombs but his plane struck a building. He was killed instantly. There was damage to the Oratory of St Peter's attached to the west side of the basilica. A Vatican workman was killed and three others wounded. The cynical people of Rome

* Although speculative and Katz does not say so, it is possible that the Swiss correspondent for the *New York Times* was in fact M. de Wyss. Her access in Rome would have been easier as the representative for this major American newspaper.

believed the bombing to be the work of Fascists to create resentment against the Allies. The British, embarrassed by the incident, did not admit to the bombing but noted that the pilot was a Roman Catholic and would not have intentionally bombed the Vatican.

March 2: Along Via Ardeatina bombs were dropped on German convoys with many victims.

March 3: From 11:04 to 12:37, 120 aircraft overflew the Tiburtina and Ostiense railway marshalling yards in three waves. The air raid shelter in Via Tiburtina was hit, killing 364. At the Ostiense station some of the 28 freight cars full of explosives ignited. The city gas utility near the station was the main target but some bombs landed near Monte Testaccio and at the Porta San Paolo. The ancient masonry between the gate and the Pyramid of Caius Cestius collapsed. There was a direct hit on the Protestant cemetery which damaged the graves of the English poets Shelley and Keats and houses collapsed in the nearby Via Ostiense. There was a fire at the Central Market. In Via Pellegrino Matteucci, the Salomone printing factory was destroyed, burying 250 workers in the rubble. The Atena Publishing House in Via del Gazometro was hit and 34 civilians were killed. The Viale del Campo Boario and Piazza Vittorio Bottego were hit and at the Fiorentini factory 189 people were killed. The stained-glass windows of Saint Paul Outside the Walls shattered. This attack was the opening salvo of a three-week-long major bombing campaign by the Allies to curtail the German ability to move men and supplies through the city. It was so extensive that Pope Pius XII wrote to President Roosevelt to complain.

March 7: At 10:45 two US 12th Air Force bomber waves flew over the Garbatella quarter and the Ostiense and Trastevere railway marshalling yards. In the northeast of the city a train was hit which resulted in 60 deaths. East of the Tiburtina station 15 civilians were killed. In the Ostiense area 22 civilians died in an air raid shelter and six more in the surrounding area. A children's nursery school on the Aventine Hill was hit but there were no reports of casualties.

March 8: At 11:00, southeast along Via Tuscolana at Porta Furba, eight civilians were killed. To the northeast in Via di Valle Melaina, the Breda factory (manufacturer of small arms and ammunition) was bombed. A US B-17 Flying Fortress was hit flying over the Miglio quarter. Ten US airmen parachuted to safety. They were all captured.

March 9: Near the Divino Amore Sanctuary district along Via Ardeatina, a German column was bombed and strafed with 30 trucks destroyed.

March 10: The areas around Piazza Bologna and the Tiburtina Railyard were bombed by US B-17s and B-24 Liberators; 76 civilians and six soldiers were killed and two American planes downed.

March 12: The Pope requested that Allied aircraft refrain from bombing Rome on this day as thousands gathered in Saint Peter's Square to hear his fifth anniversary address.

March 14: Three waves of US B-17s and B-24s escorted by fighters bombed the eastern edge of the city. The primary target was the Tiburtina station but bombs fell to the east and west of the station and more than 40 were killed, including 11 clergy. The second raid was an armed reconnaissance mission in which 49 civilians were killed when a US aircraft hit and destroyed a German column. The third wave was over the San Lorenzo Railway Marshalling Yard and the Verano Cemetery was again hit. On Via Prenestina an air raid shelter was destroyed and at least 130 German soldiers and 300 civilians were killed. The total for the day was many as 800 killed and 2,000 wounded. There was a dogfight at 10,000 feet between a British Spitfire and a German Fw 190. At least 400 rounds were fired by the Spitfire and spent shell cases and bullets fell into the city. Two women on the ground were killed by stray machine-gun bullets. One was the wife of an Ambassador to the Holy See from one of the neutral countries.

For a two-month period that spring (March 14 to May 20) Allied Air Forces flew 4,807 sorties against Rome.

———

March 17: At 07:45 the Open City police report noted that an antiaircraft projectile fell inside the Vatican and wounded four workers unloading a truck; a Vatican food convoy was attacked near Narni and one of the drivers killed.

March 18: At 15:00 more than 20,000 people camping out in Piazza Saint John Lateran sought refuge in the basilica when the air raid started. A three-year-old child was crushed in the crowd. The gigantic Italian Macao Barracks used as a Wehrmacht staging area at the Castro Pretorio (the site of the ancient Roman Praetorian Guard barracks) was the target. The planes missed and the Policlinico was hit again; thirty were killed and many wounded. The bombing caught people off guard since it took place in the afternoon and not during the usual morning hours. At least 60 people were killed and 2,000 wounded.

———

March 24 saw the start of Operation *Strangle*, a major effort to interdict German supplies north of the city. This operation accounts for the lack of bombing in Rome during April. It was largely successful in damaging the Wehrmacht's ability to resupply its troops; however, it also damaged Vatican food convoys. Because the Wehrmacht had established major repair facilities at the Pope's summer residence at Castel Gandolfo, it was repeatedly bombed as can be seen below. Railway marshalling yards, railway lines, and bridges were constant targets.

———

April 10: A Vatican food convoy was attacked near Lake Bracciano where three refugees in one automobile were wounded and a child killed.

April 12: A Vatican food convoy was attacked near Trevi where two Vatican automobiles were destroyed by four Allied aircraft.

April 15: A Vatican food convoy was attacked at Acquasparta between Terni and Todi; the driver and a priest were killed and, subsequently, two others died of their wounds.

April 16: A Vatican food convoy was attacked when it stopped at a church near Trevi.

April 19, 21, 23 and 28: Bombs were dropped on Castel Gandolfo.

April 29: A 52-vehicle Vatican convoy bringing food into the city was attacked.

May 1: Young Tittmann was awakened that night by a large number of German aircraft heading in the direction of the Anzio beachhead. An antiaircraft barrage was visible from his window.

May 2: The Magliana quarter was bombed.

May 4: The Quadraro quarter was bombed.

May 5 and 9: Bombs were dropped on Castel Gandolfo

May 12: 730 US B-17s and B-24s bombed Field Marshal Kesselring's headquarters at Monte Soratte. It was the largest heavy bomber force used by the newly reorganized 15th Air Force for a daytime raid up to this time.

May 25: As part of the Anzio breakout to interdict German reinforcements to their rapidly collapsing defense lines, there were multiple air raids over the city starting at 06:00. US B-17s and B-24s flew over all major roads heading in and out of the city. The Monte Mario quarter on the heights in the northwestern part of the city was bombed, and 15 were killed on the Ponte Mammolo bridge over the Aniene River in the eastern part of the city.

May 28: From 06:00 to 21:00 there were multiple Allied raids on the roads exiting the city.

May 29: For the second consecutive day, a 07:00 raid caused huge destruction in the Magliana and Quadraro quarters. A tram was hit on Via Tuscolana and two people were killed.

May 30: Reflecting the Allied advance, at 08:00 retreating German forces heading out of Rome were bombed and strafed.

May 31: At 08:40 a three-wave air raid occurred. The area around Trastevere was hit and vehicles at Grottarossa on Via Flaminia were machine-gunned.

June 1: The southeast quarter of the city was bombed and 24 people were killed.

June 2: US B-24s flew over the roads leading to the north and northwest of the city. Eight German trucks carrying ammunition were hit and exploded. At Tor Sapienza five civilians died under the rubble of a warehouse.

June 3: 18 US B-24s damaged German trucks on Via Casilina.

APPENDIX C: *AUSSENKOMMANDO ROM DER SICHERHEITSPOLIZEI (SS-GESTAPO) UND DES SICHERHEITSDIENST (SD)* – THE AK ROM

Below is a listing of personnel assigned to the AK Rom during the German occupation of Rome. They include the SS, the Gestapo, the SD, civilian employees, agents, and collaborators. It is partially based on a transportation list found on the floor inside the German Embassy in Rome after the liberation. The list was a current personnel roster which had been annotated in pencil with vehicle assignments for the flight from the city. Many other documents were used to flesh out the names and provide additional information. Alternate spellings are in parentheses. SS ranks and the individual functions of those listed are noted when known.

While many of the personnel mentioned here are not mentioned elsewhere in the book, it is important to list each known individual as a record of their participation in the Nazi occupation of Rome. Under each ABT officers are listed first and other ranks (enlisted) second. All uniformed SS were required to participate in the Fosse Ardeatine massacre; those absent from Rome at the time are noted.

Two tables of SS ranks and their British and American army equivalents for those assigned to the AK Rome follows:

SS Ranks (officers)	British	American
SS-Obersturmbannführer	Lieutenant Colonel	Lieutenant Colonel
SS-Sturmbannführer	Major	Major
SS-Hauptsturmführer	Captain	Captain
SS-Obersturmführer	Lieutenant	1st Lieutenant
SS-Untersturmführer	2nd Lieutenant	2nd Lieutenant

SS Ranks (enlisted)	British	American
SS-Sturmscharführer	Regimental Sergeant Major	Sergeant Major
SS-Hauptscharführer	Sergeant Major	Master Sergeant
SS-Oberscharführer	(not applicable)	Technical Sergeant
SS-Scharführer	Staff Sergeant	Staff Sergeant
SS-Unterscharführer	Sergeant	Sergeant
SS-Rottenführer	Corporal	Corporal
SS-Sturmann	Lance Corporal	(not applicable)

Note: SS-Obersturmbannführer Eugen Dollmann, SS-Chief Heinrich Himmler's man in Rome, was not assigned to the AK Rom. Another pre-armistice agent assigned to Kappler was a man named Heymann, a journalist of the *Münchner Neueste Nachrichten* (Munich's Latest News). Additionally SS-Hauptscharführer Otto Lechner was a special undercover agent for Kappler. Sent from Berlin he initially shared an office with Priebke. He attempted several undercover missions, none of which succeeded.

SS Headquarters Section marked STAB (staff) on the original document (at Via Tasso):

SS-Obersturmbannführer Herbert Kappler headed the SS in Rome and later moved to
    Maderno, Italy. He is known to have shot at least two men during the Fosse Ardeatine
    murders.

SS-Hauptsturmführer Gerhard Köhler was the Rome administration officer. It was Köhler
    who recommended the abandoned quarry tunnels along Via Ardeatina as the site of
    the massacre. In May 1944 he assumed duties as the head of ABT IV, probably on a
    recommendation from Berlin's troubleshooter, Clemens. Leaving Rome with his wife,
    Doris, he was assigned as liaison to the Italian naval commando unit, the Decima MAS.
    Allied reports described him as a drunk.

SS-Hauptsturmführer Herbert Wuth did odd jobs for Kappler and ran agents for the
    Gestapo. He left Rome with Kappler and was later assigned to Gorizia where he remained
    until May 1945. Kappler reported he was killed by Yugoslav partisans before the end of
    the war.

Fräulein Schwartzer (Swarzwer) was Kappler's secretary and was described as efficient as well
    as officious. She befriended double agent Alexander Kurtna and removed his file from the
    Gestapo office to shield him from Kappler. She was engaged to marry SS-Oberscharführer
    Enrico Perathoner.

ABT I: Long Range Radio Communications Section (*Funker*) (Via Tasso and Villa Wolkonsky):

SS-Obersturmführer Stephen Unterweger was an engineer and the SS signals officer assigned
    to Kappler's staff. He was in Rome from September 1943 through March 1944 when he
    retired to civilian life.

SS-Sturmscharführer Kessels was a clerk and the cashier in Via Tasso. He rode with Kappler
    out of Rome, perhaps carrying SS funds, and was later killed by partisans in Milan.

SS-Unterscharführer Schauer rode the *Funkwagen* (the German mobile radio communications
    van) from the city.

SS-Unterscharführer Stemmer rode the *Funkwagen* from the city.

SS-Rottenführer Boehm was responsible for the training of post-occupational agents in the
    use of radios and he drove the *Funkwagen* from the city. He was one of those punished for

selling goods on the black-market. He eventually joined Haas at the SS-Aussenkommando IDA (not otherwise identified) near Parma and later was transferred to Bozen.

SS-Rottenführer Grasshoff, like Boehm, was sent to a German military prison in Verona for black-market activities but he too was returned to Rome. He manned the radio transmitter for the SD's Italian network and worked out of the German Embassy.

Fräulein Hoffman was a radio operator and Kappler's mistress. She ended up in Maderno with Kappler and eventually he found her an apartment in Berlin.

Fräulein Löwenstein-Conti was an ABT I telephone operator. She ended up in Bologna.

ABT III: General Political and Economic Intelligence (Villa Giustiniani Massimo):

Officers:

SS-Hauptsturmführer Borante Domizlaff was in charge of the German Propaganda Information Office. It was he who signed a form letter to relatives informing them that their loved one had died on March 24, 1944, at the Ardeatine Caves. Noteworthy is the fact that his wife committed suicide after the massacre. He was on leave outside Rome at the liberation and wound up in Verona. By May 1945 he was a POW of the Allies.

SS-Obersturmführer Reinhardt Wetjen was Domizlaff's assistant in the propaganda office. Wetjen balked when ordered to shoot a man at the Ardeatine Caves until Kappler escorted him inside and made him carry out the order. Eventually he ended up in Bologna.

Other ranks:

SS-Hauptscharführer Paul Huber was an interpreter who worked in ABT I and III. He left Rome with his wife, Dolores, and a person named Zofe. Later he was sent to Lake Como.

SS-Hauptscharführer Martin Lösch (Loesch) had been sent to Rome from Berlin in 1942 with the mission to establish direct links between Berlin's agents in Rome. He ended up in Verona.

SS-Scharführer Günther Amonn (Amann) prepared military reports on information and acted as liaison with Kesselring's headquarters for military intelligence exchanges. He later claimed that he refused to shoot his assigned prisoner at the Fosse Ardeatine.

SS-Scharführer Victor Gasser worked in ABT I, III, and IV. He was the driver of the designated Military Liaison Vehicle (*Verbindungsdienst Miliz*) and was later sent to Verona and Genoa.

SS-Scharführer Willi Kofler (Koffler in Italian documents) was sent by Kappler with Tunath to the Regina Coeli Prison to get Caruso's selected prisoners for the massacre. After the liberation, he was assigned to Florence and Padua.

SS-Scharführer Pretz was responsible for providing economic reports for Domizlaff.

SS-Scharführer Vonter ended up in Brescia in May 1945.

SS-Scharführer Karl Wiedner ended up in Forlì and Genoa and was tried after the war with Kappler and four others but was acquitted.

SS-Sonderführer (specialist) Durst was mentioned by Kappler as being in ABT III.

SS-Sonderführer Rausch was responsible for infusing the German spirit into Italian propaganda.

SS-Sonderführer, known only as di Brunico, otherwise unknown.

SS-Sonderführer, known only as di Merano, otherwise unknown.

SS-Sonderführer Vonier may have been confused with Alexandra Vonier, see below.

Alexandra Vonier was a female interpreter and together with her child left Rome prior to liberation and ended up in Brescia.

Italians, Germans, and others who worked in ABT III, were listed as agents or otherwise were closely associated – some mentioned in the Domizlaff debrief. Many of these also worked with ABT IV and ABT VI:

Alwens was a civilian correspondent in Rome of the German newspaper *Volkischer Beebactor* who was recruited through a Dr. Siebert for ABT III. Eventually he left Rome for Turin and worked for the German Embassy.

Bewley, Charles, an Irishman, wrote reports on Vatican society gossip for Lechner. One report, dated June 3, 1943, was discovered in the Tittmann papers. It was called *Activities of Diplomats of Enemy States at the Vatican; Ciano and the English Ambassador at the Vatican Mr. Osborne*. It provided only insignificant details.

Bock, Dr., was the civilian head of the German Institute in Rome, an informal arm of the SD which provided information on academic questions.

Borch, von, was the civilian head of the Press and Propaganda Section of the German Embassy in Rome. He later went to Fasano.

Engelhardt was a librarian in the Oriental Institute.

Fuchs, Professor, was an SS-Untersturmführer in the Waffen SS and liaison officer between Kesselring and the Italian War Ministry in Rome. He passed information on the corrupt conditions of the Italian armed forces. Before the war, he had been an archaeologist in Rome.

Fuchs, Oberinspektor of the Wehrmacht in Rome, controlled permits for driving vehicles and reported on efforts of Italians to obtain permits for their vehicles.

Garulli, Guido, a gentile who lived in the Ghetto, was a source for Jewish information.

Guadagni, Dr., was an Italian journalist.

Hartmann, German police colonel, worked for Dollmann from December 1943 to June 1944. He gave the SD information about the organization of the Italian police.

Hiltebrandt, Dr., was a civilian and the author of books on Italy and Rome. He provided the SD with information on Italian life and culture and left Rome for Merano in January 1944.

Hoppenstädt, Professor, was the chief of a German Institute near the Spanish Steps. He left Rome for Merano in January 1944.

Kovacevic, Ivan, was a Croatian medical student.

Mayer, Professor Joseph, a German, was a recruiter for SS-Hauptsturmführer Eugen Haas.

Pagnozzi, private secretary to Italian Chief of Police in Rome, was one of Kappler's informers on various Italian ministries. He fled to Switzerland.

Pastore (Pastori), Giovanni, was an Italian agent handler who discovered the GAP's *santabarbara* on Via Giulia.

Prinzing, Professor, was the head of the German Academy in Rome and acted as a liaison officer to the German Embassy and Mussolini and his ministers. He took credit for helping formulate the Salò Republic. He thought so highly of himself that he would only speak to Kappler.

Sachs, Consul, was at the German Embassy and a former POW who had been exchanged because he was wounded.

Sadathierascvili, Basilius, was an SS agent for the Georgian project.

Scholz, SS-Untersturmführer Hans Eberhard, was an author and poet and a special war correspondent in Rome for the magazine *SS Standarte Kurt Eggers*. He went to France in June 1944. The magazine was an SS propaganda effort which publicized the actions of Waffen SS combat formations. Kurt Eggers had been a war correspondent and editor of the SS magazine *Das Schwarze Korps*. He was killed while reporting near Kharkov, Russia.

Schulz, Wehrmacht Major Ahoi, claimed he had a special mission from Reichsmarschall Göring to follow black-market activities and to deal with them in the interest of the Reichsmarschall. He provided information on economic questions in Rome.

Vinatzer, Dr., was a civilian lawyer who gave information to the SD on legal issues in Rome.

Wangenhelm, SS-Untersturmführer Reichsfreiherr von, wrote for the *SS Standarte Kurt Eggers* magazine in Rome and reported on cultural matters. He went to Finland in June 1944.

Wemmer, Dr. Ludwig, was the Scientific and Academic Collaborator accredited to the German Embassy to the Holy See.

Wodtke, Dr. Klaus, was originally the German liaison officer to the Italian Ministry of Justice and a member of the International Law Commission. After the armistice he volunteered to remain in Rome and work in ABT III. He was responsible for escorting saboteurs to the Netherlands for training. He was inept, fired, and returned to Germany in mid-October 1943.

ABT IV: The Gestapo (*Geheime Staatspolizei*), the most important ABT in Rome (Via Tasso):

Officers:

SS-Hauptsturmführer Carl-Theodor Schütz (1907–1985) was the first head of ABT IV. He attended the two-week PAI Italian Colonial Police School in February 1942 and was sent to Naples in September 1943. He moved to Rome later that month. He was responsible for ABT IV personnel and he directly oversaw all interrogations, conducting the most important ones himself. He received and counted out the 50 kilos of Jewish gold demanded by Kappler and was the commander of the firing squads at the Fosse Ardeatine. He was sketched by an Italian prisoner artist inside Via Tasso who remarked that he had eyes like a hyena – a remark he treated as a compliment. Described as a drunk, he was replaced by Köhler, probably as the result of a recommendation by Clemens.

SS-Hauptsturmführer Johannes Max Hans Clemens (1902–1976) joined the SS in Dresden, Germany in the 1930s. In 1943, he worked in the Italian section at RSHA Berlin. He was sent from Berlin to Rome in March 1944 to put Rome in order, administratively. At the Ardeatine Caves massacre, he was responsible for leading the first group of prisoners into the caves.

SS-Hauptsturmführer Erich Priebke, the second in charge of the Gestapo, murdered two men at the caves. Leaving Rome, he ended up in Bozen in May 1945. Originally detained by the Allies, he was passed from one POW camp to another. Eventually he was released and, shortly after, fled to Argentina.

SS-Hauptsturmführer Karl Wolff (Wulff) was in charge of counterespionage and was the primary Via Tasso interrogator. He likely acted as liaison to Rome police organizations for ex-POW affairs. He left Rome on May 22, 1944 and was last seen with a man known as Regus, otherwise unknown.

SS-Obersturmführer Heinz-Josef (Heinrich) Tunath (Thunath) joined the Kripo (*Kriminalpolizei*) in 1939 in Hanover, Germany. He was the officer who transferred the prisoners to be executed from the Regina Coeli Prison to the Ardeatine Caves, and he was responsible for bringing five extra men from the prison. He was captured at Verona in April 1945 and after the war he was recruited by the German Federal Intelligence Service.

SS-Untersturmführer Brandt was in the political and counterespionage sections and was assigned to focus on identifying partisan groups. He worked closely with Perathoner. He ended up in Roncegno (Trento) and later Bozen.

Other ranks:

SS-Sturmscharführer Max August Banneck (Bannek) worked with SS-Hauptsturmführer Karl Wolff on counterespionage and was present at torture sessions. He was responsible for tracing food hoarders and may also have been the head of the Jewish section.

SS-Sturmscharführer Breer left Rome in the kitchen truck.

SS-Sturmscharführer Lange, otherwise unknown.

SS-Sturmscharführer Martin Engmann was in the counterespionage section and ended up in Brescia and Marzano.

SS-Sturmscharführer Hans Gassner was in the Jewish section and often acted as an assistant to Kessels. He was on leave and not in Rome at liberation.

SS-Sturmscharführer Schrieber was in the Jewish section.

SS-Hauptscharführer Casteiner, otherwise unknown.

SS-Hauptscharführer Walter Hoffmann was the office quartermaster; he was last known to be in Verona.

SS-Hauptscharführer Walter Hotop was an interpreter, a torturer, and worked in the anti-Badoglio and counterespionage sections. He was later sent to Brescia and Bozen.

SS-Hauptscharführer Hübner, otherwise unknown.

SS-Hauptscharführer Rudolf Huhn worked under Priebke in the White Russian minority section.

SS-Hauptscharführer Joseph (Hermann) Matzken was an interpreter and was later sent to Bozen, Parma, and Feltre.

SS-Hauptscharführer Johannes (Hans) Quapp ran Via Tasso Prison. He worked in the anti-Badoglio and anti-communist sections. He ended up in Parma and was later seen in Reggio Emilia. After the war he was tried with Kappler but was acquitted.

SS-Hauptscharführer Wilhelm Schlemm was in the counterespionage section and ended up in Forlì.

SS-Hauptscharführer Kurt Schütze was in the confiscated goods section and also worked in ABT VI. By the end of the war he was known to be in a hospital in Karrersee, South Tyrol, with psychiatric problems.

SS-Hauptscharführer Paul Seidel was in the anti-communist section and ended up in Reggio Emilia.

SS-Hauptscharführer Steinbrink was in the counterespionage section.

SS-Hauptscharführer Süptitz ran the garage at Via Tasso. He drove the omnibus from Rome and was later sent to Verona.

SS-Hauptscharführer Paul Wagner dealt with persons with counterfeit documents and was in the counterespionage section. He was sent to Bologna and to Forlì.

SS-Hauptscharführer Wedemann was head of the anti-communist section.

SS-Hauptscharführer Heinrich (Karl) Weismann was in the political section and ended up in Forlì.

SS-Oberscharführer Heinrich Bodenstein worked in the anti-communist section.

SS-Oberscharführer Franz Braun, otherwise unknown.

SS-Oberscharführer Ebner, otherwise unknown.

SS-Oberscharführer Juengling was the cook at Via Tasso and was later sent to Forlì.

SS-Oberscharführer Enrico Perathoner was an interpreter, a torturer, and a V-Mann (undercover agent). He was an Italian citizen from Alto Adige (South Tyrol) but chose German citizenship in 1939. He worked undercover inside the Todt Organization and later, together with Brandt, he was assigned to focus on finding partisan groups. He ultimately went with Kappler to Madero and Merano. He was engaged to marry Fräulein Schwartzer, Kappler's secretary.

SS-Oberscharführer Riedrich, otherwise unknown.

SS-Scharführer Frühling was the OSS source supplied with cognac. On the Rome vehicle personnel list, he was assigned as a guard for the omnibus and he ended up in Verona.

SS-Scharführer Hermann Grüb was the warden for the German branch at the Regina Coeli Prison. He was later killed at Forlì.

SS-Scharführer Oekermann (Ökermann), otherwise unknown.

SS-Scharführer Philip was on the personnel list and was assigned as a guard for the omnibus.

SS-Scharführer Pustowka escorted condemned prisoners to Rome execution sites.

SS-Unterscharführer Dettmering (Deitering), otherwise unknown.

SS-Unterscharführer Kaspar was an interpreter in the partisan section.

SS-Unterscharführer Rudolf Preusser, otherwise unknown.

SS-Unterscharführer Karl Reinhardt was sent to Bozen.

SS-Unterscharführer Ruepp was an interpreter for SS-Hauptscharführer Wesemann in the political section.

SS-Unterscharführer Schifferegger was mentioned by Kappler but is otherwise unknown.

SS-Unterscharführer Sottopera was an interpreter and torturer and was involved in arresting Allied POWs. This may be another name used by Enrico Perathoner.

SS-Unterscharführer Ullmann was on leave and not in Rome at liberation.

SS-Schütze Prieve was a co-driver of the *Funkwagen* (communications van).

SS-Sturmann Alexander Keusch was a cipher clerk.

Italians and others who worked in ABT IV, some of whom left Rome with the Germans; some may have been members of the Italian SS:

Miliani, an interpreter.

Battopera, otherwise unknown.

Birger, an interpreter, otherwise unknown.

Bisotti (Bisetti), an interpreter.

Perelli, an Italian agent handler.

Pistolini, otherwise unknown.

Ruta, Renato, an interpreter, was an Italian with a German mother and wife. He worked in a travel agency at the Rome Termini Station.

Von Wageningen, Noels, was a Dutch national and interpreter. He was a V-Mann and also worked as a receptionist at Via Tasso. He was not trusted by Kappler.

ABT VI: The SD – Espionage and Sabotage Section, headquartered at the Villa Wolkonsky and the SS barracks in a villa on Viale Rossini:

Officers:

SS-Sturmbannführer Eugen Haas was the head of ABT VI, the SD, responsible for organizing and dispatching agents, the training of post-occupational agents, and the sabotage school. Reportedly Haas sometimes posed as a German officer with Allied sympathies in an effort to locate Allied POWs in hiding in Rome. He ended up at the SD Aussenkommando IDA at a villa near Parma. He killed two men in the Fosse Ardeatine murders.

SS-Sturmbannführer Hammer was sent to Rome from Berlin to help train saboteurs. He did not get along with Kappler and was returned to Berlin after a short time.

SS-Obersturmführer Baldoni was a former Italian SIM officer and turncoat. He had been assigned to Centro A, the Monterotondo secret headquarters for the *Comando Supremo*, and was likely a member of the Italian SS.

SS-Obersturmführer Schuberning was part of the sabotage training team. He later joined Haas and was sent to SS-Aussenkommando IDA near Parma. In May 1945 he and Haas tried to escape to Salzburg, Austria.

SS-Untersturmführer Dr. Peter Scheibert rode with Haas out of the city. He was a civilian lecturer at the University of Rome and collaborated with the Vatican in the protection of works of art and their safekeeping in the Castel Sant'Angelo.

Other ranks:

SS-Hauptscharführer Herbert "Fritz" Meyer was an agent recruiter and counterespionage man. He briefed penetration agents before they left on their missions. He was on leave and out of the city at liberation, eventually ending up in Verona.

SS-Oberscharführer Manfredo Agostini was a Tyrolean who was an interpreter and assistant to Haas who also ran agents to penetrate Allied lines. He went with Haas to the SS-Aussenkommando IDA near Parma.

SS-Oberscharführer Birkner was a wireless transmitter operator who was sent to the Eastern Front in January 1944 as punishment for black-market activities.

SS-Oberscharführer Ganzenmueller was a wireless transmitter operator last known to be in Bozen in May 1945. He may have been the Mueller, a former boxer who was responsible for torturing a young man with his bare hands, at Via Tasso. On one occasion while listening to Chopin's Prelude No. 15 (*Raindrop*), he broke into tears at the beauty of the music.

SS-Oberscharführer Alexander Sergant (Sergeant) was Kappler's second batman and rode the kitchen truck out of Rome. He went with Kappler to Maderno. He was Flemish by birth and had emigrated to Morocco, where he joined the French Foreign Legion. He was captured by the Germans in the battle for Tunis. Taken to Italy he escaped with other Allied soldiers at the armistice and eventually made his way to Rome where he was arrested by the Gestapo. Although accepted into the SS, he and Kappler had a falling out. On May 19, 1945, he was captured by partisans and interrogated because of his involvement with the SS.

SS-Scharführer (or Sonderführer) Dr. Norbert Meyer (Meier or Mayer) trained saboteurs and helped to organize the post-occupation network; he ended up in Verona.

SS-Unterscharführer Wilhelm Fritz Kahrau was Köhler's secretary. After leaving Rome, he returned to Germany in June 1944.

SS-Rottenführer Dapra was an interpreter and assistant to Haas. He accompanied Rome sabotage students to the Belgrade Sabotage School.

SS-Sturmann Reinisch was Kappler's first batman (personal assistant) and a wireless transmitter operator. He was sent to the Eastern Front in January 1944 as punishment for black-market activities.

SS-Sturmann Rinkh was a wireless transmitter operator and was sent to the Eastern Front in January 1944 as punishment for black-market activities.

Italians and others who worked in ABT VI, the SD, many of whom left Rome with the Germans; others were stay behind agents. Information is from various sources:

Beretta, otherwise unknown.

Breyer, otherwise unknown.

Brinkmann, otherwise unknown.

Brouwer, Helene Louise Ten Cate, a Dutch national and Kappler's mistress. She was a stay-behind agent.

Cipolla, G., the father of Ubaldo Cipolla, was the coordinator of the stay-behind agents.

Cipolla, Ubaldo, was a one-time member of SIM, a member of the Italian SS, a double agent and the head of Section "F" of five stay behind agents.

De Mauro, otherwise unknown.

Elling, SS-Obersturmbannführer Georg, head of Section "K," with eight men and one woman; he was to be left inside the Vatican.

Flandro, Eugenio, the head of section "H," with six men and three women stay behind agents.

Gold, SS-Sturmführer Hugo, otherwise unknown

Grossi, Frau, was a secretary and interpreter for Kappler and Schütz. She went to Forlì.

Grossi, the head of Section "G," with 12 male stay behind agents.

Kagteiner, SS-Hauptscharführer Otto, interpreter.

Kurtna, Alexander, was an Estonian agent working for both the Soviets and the Gestapo; a stay behind agent.

Loos, SS-Sturmbannführer, also worked in ABT III and IV.

Monico, a secretary.

Negroni, Dr. (alias Bianconi), was a recruiter of agents and ran the sabotage school.

Nusser, an interpreter.

Preisegger, Fräulein, Rome employee.

Pretting, SS-Scharführer Franz, also worked in ABT III and IV; he was sent to Forlì.

Pusto, went to Forlì, otherwise unknown.

Rainharst, SS-Obersturmführer, otherwise unknown.

Scarpato, Federico (Fritz), an interpreter who ran many Italian agents.

Scharzer, otherwise unknown.

Sreer, otherwise unknown.

Stacul (Stackul), an interpreter who went to Forlì and then Verona.

Veronesi, engineer, went to Forlì.

Von der Schulenburg, Werner, was editor of the SD-funded bilingual publication *Italien*.

Van Solt, (Fräulein), was an SD employee.

Wenner, SS-Obersturmführer Eugen, otherwise unknown.

The following names were found on several different lists. Some were SS and others civilians. It is not known in which ABT they served:

Christian, SS-Hauptscharführer, also mentioned positively by Kappler.

Ender, otherwise unknown.

Gaute, otherwise unknown.

Knobloch, otherwise unknown.

Leidel, SS-Hauptscharführer, otherwise unknown.

Schrems (Schremy), SS-Obersturmführer, worked in Berlin on the Arab effort. Kappler mentioned that he saw him in November 1943 when he visited Rome.

Sommer, otherwise unknown.
Wiendner, SS-Scharführer, otherwise unknown.

APPENDIX D: VATICAN EXTRATERRITORIALITY AND EXPROPRIATION

The listing that follows has been adapted from the introduction by Carlton J. H. Hayes to Jane Scrivener's book *Inside Rome with the Germans*. The book was published in 1945 and it accurately reflects the status of these places at the time of the German occupation of Rome. Churches and institutes not owned by the Vatican did not have this special status.

Vatican buildings which enjoyed extraterritoriality:

Major basilicas:

- Saint John Lateran and all connected buildings, *Basilica di San Giovanni in Laterano*, Piazza di San Giovanni in Laterano
- Saint Mary Major and all connected buildings, *Basilica di Santa Maria Maggiore*, Piazza di Santa Maria Maggiore
- Saint Paul Outside the Walls and all connected buildings, *Basilica di San Paolo Fuori le Mura*, Via Ostiense

Other basilicas/churches/convents and monasteries:

- Basilica of the Twelve Apostles, *Parrocchia Santi XII Apostoli*, Piazza dei Santi Apostoli, 51
- Church and convent of Saint Onofrio on the Janiculum, *Chiesa di Sant'Onofrio al Gianicolo*, Piazza di Sant'Onofrio, 2
- Church of Saint Michael and Magnus, *Chiesa Santi Michele e Magno*, Borgo Santo Spirito 21/41

Palaces (buildings)/hospitals/headquarters:

- Baby Jesus Pediatric Hospital, *Bambino Gesù ospedale pediatrico*, Piazza di Sant'Onofrio, 4
- Saint Calixtus building, *Palazzo di San Callisto*, Piazza di San Callisto
- Chancery building, *Palazzo della Cancelleria*, Piazza Palazzo della Cancelleria, 68
- Castel Gandolfo, Pope's summer residence and farms, *Palazzo Pontificio*, Piazza della Libertà, Castel Gandolfo
- Datary building, *Palazzo della Dataria*, Palazzo della Dataria, 96; the Datary was part of the Roman Curia which investigated candidates for papal benefices – permanent church appointments; it was abolished by Pope Paul VI in 1967
- Holy Office, *Palazzo del Sant'uffizio*, Piazza del Sant'uffizio, adjacent to Vatican City
- Jesuit Headquarters and Retreat House, *Curia Generalizia della Compagnia di Gesù*, Borgo Santo Spirito, 4
- Propagation of the Faith, *Propagazione della fede*, Piazza di Spagna

- Raphael's House (now destroyed), *Palazzo Caprini*, was between Via delle Conciliazione and Borgo Santo Spirito, in Via Scassacavalli
- Vicariate, *del Vicariato*, traditionally in Piazza di San Giovanni in Laterano, 6; however, Hayes says that it was in Via della Pigna

Colleges/institutes/seminaries/universities:

- Augustinian College of Santa Monica, *Ordine di Sant'Agostino*, adjacent to Vatican City across from the Holy Office
- German College, *Collegio Teutonico*, located adjacent to Vatican City to the left of Saint Peter's
- Romanian College and Seminary, *Pontificio Seminario Romano Maggiore*, Piazza di San Giovanni in Laterano, 4
- Ukrainian Pontifical College of Saint Joseph, *Pontificio Collegio Ucraino di San Josaphat*, on the Janiculum Hill
- Urban Pontifical University for the Propagation of the Faith, *Pontificio Università Urbaniana De Propaganda Fide*, Via Urbano VIII, 16

Note: Casa San Giovanni, the North American College property on the Janiculum, was not listed as having had extraterritorial status but it is likely that it did.

Property of the Holy See free from expropriation (not able to be taken over legally by the Germans or Fascists), but without extraterritorial status:

- Saint Andrew, *Sant'Andrea della Valle*, Corso Vittorio Emanuele II
- Saint Apollinaris two buildings, *San Apollinare*, Piazza di Sant'Apollinare, 49
- Archaeological Institute, *Istituto Pontificio Archeologico Cristiana*, via Napoleone III, 1
- Buildings attached to the Basilica of the Twelve Apostles, *Parrocchia Santi XII Apostoli*, Piazza dei Santi Apostoli, 51
- Biblical Pontific Institute, *Pontificio Istituto Biblico*, Piazza della Pilotta, 35
- Basilica of Saints Ambrose and Charles on the Corso, *Basilica dei Santi Ambrogio e Carlo al Corso*, Via del Corso, 437
- Pontifical Gregorian University, *Pontificia Università Gregoriana*, Piazza della Pilotta, 4
- Lombard Pontifical College and Seminary, *Pontificio Seminario Lombardo*, Piazza di Santa Maria Maggiore, 5
- Pontifical Oriental Institute, *Pontificio Istituto Orientale*, Piazza di Santa Maria Maggiore, 7
- Russian Pontifical College and Seminary, *Pontificio Collegium Russicum*, Via Carlo Cattaneo, 2A
- Convent and Retreat House of Saints John and Paul, *Convento dei SS. Giovanni e Paolo*, Piazza dei SS. Giovanni e Paolo

APPENDIX E: THE PEOPLE OF SULMONA, 1943–1944

Thousands of escaped Allied POWs throughout Italy were given life-saving assistance and support from local people. These Italians gave freely of their often meager resources, putting themselves at considerable risk. In and around the small Abruzzi town of Sulmona, there were as many as 100 ex-POWs to hide, feed, and clothe. Most had escaped from the POW concentration camp #78 (*Campo di Concentramento Prigione di Guerra #78*). The following alphabetical listing of Sulmona helpers will illustrate the extent of their support to the escaped Allied POWs.

The named Italian Sulmona helpers:
Alicandri-Ciufelli, Concezio, a doctor who helped plan the hospital escape.
Antonangeli, Ida, arrested New Year's Eve, 1943.
Autiero, Carlo, collaborator of Dr. Scocco and helped with the hospital escape.
Balassone, Angelo, arrested New Year's Eve, sentenced to be deported to Germany.
Balassone, Antonio-Loreto, arrested New Year's Eve, sentenced to death but survived.
Balassone, Assunto, helped Captain Dennis Rendell, 2nd British Parachute Regiment.
Balassone, Giacomo, arrested New Year's Eve, sentenced to be deported to Germany.
Balassone, Paolo, Italian Army major with access to Italian uniforms and blankets and gave
    them to the escapees. He also obtained documents for the POWs. A member of the
    armed partisan band Scocco, he was arrested on New Year's Eve and sentenced to death.
    One of the Balassone brothers died in prison in Germany, but it is not clear which one.
Bellei, Francesco, helped Henri Payonne, a Free French officer.
Bianchi, Arturo di Umberto, helped Lieutenant William Simpson.
Bolino, Giuseppe, arrested New Year's Eve and sent to the Regina Coeli Prison in Rome.
Cantelmi, Santa
Carabia, Esterina, the widow of an Italian Air Force pilot who had three children and helped
    USAAF Captain Elbert Dukate and British Lieutenant John Furman.
Carracini, Umberto, arrested New Year's Eve.
Carugno, Angelo, husband of Anna.
Carugno, Anna, wife of Angelo; together they hid Lieutenant Simpson and Captain Rendell.
Cicerone, Roberto, Scocco's right hand, helped Henri Payonne.
Cipolletti, Dante, arrested New Year's Eve and sentenced to death.
D'Alessandro, Armando, a member of the armed partisan band Scocco.
D'Angelo, Lucia
Di Carlo, Guillermo, owned a Sulmona confectionary factory and was a major benefactor to
    the escapees.
Di Censo, Domenico, arrested New Year's Eve.
Di Cesare, Mario, a railway clerk and an "A" Force helper.
Di Girolame, Alfieri, arrested New Year's Eve.
Evangelista, Giuseppe
Ferri, Paolino, the town clerk of Sulmona who helped with documents; he was arrested on
    New Year's Eve.
Ferri, Pina
Ginnetti, Maria, worked in the hospital laundry and with her daughter helped with the hospital
    escape. She hid and fed hospitalized British Lance Bombardier William D. T. McIntosh.
Imperoli, Iride, unmarried with a child named Lorenzo. She carried money and letters back and
    forth to Rome and helped with the hospital escape. She made the train trip to Rome with
    the Sulmona ex-POWs. Arrested on New Year's Eve, she returned to Rome to entrap Pollak.
Imperoli, Maria, half-sister of Iride. She helped with the hospital escape, made the train trip
    to Rome, and was arrested on New Year's Eve.

Imperoli, mother of Iride and Maria, arrested New Year's Eve.

Lanca, Ida, wife of Amedeo Liberatore.

Liberatore, Amedeo, a member of the armed partisan band Scocco and a guide for POWs in the mountains; he was arrested on New Year's Eve.

Marcantonio, Vincenzina, arrested New Year's Eve.

Marcone, Loreto, a member of the armed partisan band Scocco.

Masciangoli, Paolina, arrested New Year's Eve.

Mestica, Guido, arrested New Year's Eve.

Miccolis, Mario di Giovanni, a member of the armed partisan band Scocco. He helped Lt. Furman and Henri Payonne.

Mocellin, Consiglia, helped an English officer named Bernard Rosen.

Pacella, Flora, arrested New Year's Eve.

Pacella, Gaetano, father of Flora, arrested New Year's Eve.

Pacella, mother of Flora, known as Genoveffa Treonze-Paolilli, arrested New Year's Eve.

Pietrorazio, Alberto, a member of the armed partisan band Scocco who helped USAAF Captains R. J. Gardiner and F. B. Hawkins. Through him, other POWs obtained access to Major Balassone and his storehouse of uniforms and other supplies.

Pistilli, Vincenzo, barber and member of the armed partisan band Scocco, helped Henri Payonne and was involved in the hospital escape. He was arrested on New Year's Eve.

Ranalli, Ada, older sister of Gino Ranalli.

Ranalli, Gino, a friend and helper of Pollak; he was arrested on New Year's Eve.

Ranalli, Ida (17), younger sister of Gino Ranalli who helped Lt. Furman.

Riccitelli, Giovanna

Santilli, Maria, wife of Cesidio Valeri, helped Lt. Furman and Flying Officer Wilson.

Satriano, Dino, Italian military lieutenant, arrested New Year's Eve and sentenced to death.

Schettini, Carmine, a doctor who helped Simpson, Furman, and Pollak.

Sciubba, Dr., police inspector (*Commissario di Pubblica Sicurezza*).

Scocco, Dr. Mario Vittorio, a dentist. He and his wife had two daughters and he was head of the local resistance, the armed partisan band Scocco. He was arrested in May 1944.

Semperlotti, Romilde, a medical doctor who helped plan and organize the hospital escape, after which she went to the hills to join the partisans to provide medical assistance.

Silvestri, Pasquale

Silvestri, Domenico

Tirabassi, Francesca, helped Captain Rendell.

Tirimacco, Carmine "the Brigand," the brother-in-law of Balassone, helped Lt. Furman and Captain Rendell. He was the supplier of fruit and vegetables to the POW camp and was a member of the armed partisan band Scocco.

Trasunto family, lived outside the town and sheltered Lt. Simpson in their farmhouse after he leaped from the truck taking him to the POW camp.

Valeri, Cesidio, the husband of Maria Santilli.

Vecchiarelli family

Sulmona people, unidentified or only known by their first names, who helped ex-POWs:

Agostino, an elderly man and his hospital worker wife who helped with the hospital escape

Anna and her sister helped Lt. Furman. She sometimes had a small boy with her.

Concita, sister-in-law to Carmine Tirimacco
Enzo, brother of Ione, escaped from Pescocostanzo and produced rubber stamps for ID cards.
Filomena, wife of a town butcher. They had two daughters, one named Teresina (8) who spoke up to the Gestapo. They helped two unidentified British soldiers, one known as Sandy.
Ione, sister of Enzo and a teacher friend of Maria Imperiali who taught Lt. Furman Italian.
Marietta and her mother, Maria, who took in Captain Gil Smith and helped cure his severe eczema. Maria was described as an angel but had a bad eye that some considered evil.
Medical student with two sisters who furnished medicine for the ex-POWs.
Peppino, a former Italian Army officer who spoke French, helped Lt. Furman.
Photographer who lived in Vico Breve and took photos for POW documents.
Women who lived in a house on the outskirts of Sulmona where they sheltered Captain Perry and Flying Officer Wilson.

Italians who collaborated with the local Sulmona-based Gestapo run by SS-Obersturmführer Pagan.
This unit employed paid informers to denounce escaped Allied POWs.
Cerrone, Vera "without the arm" (*Vera senza braccio*), denounced Sulmona helpers.
Del Signore, Antonio, denounced Mario di Cesare to Obersturmführer Pagan's section on April 23, 1944. After interrogation and a beating, di Cesare was released for lack of proof.
Del Signore, Vincenzo, was a member of the armed partisan band Scocco but later became a Gestapo agent; probably related to Antonio Del Signore.
Filippi, Bruno, worked with Antonio Del Signore to help arrest Mario di Cesare.

APPENDIX F: ESCAPE LINE NOTES

Escape Line documents are on microfilm at the US National Archives, College Park, Maryland (see bibliography). It is amazing that any records survived since many were written on scraps of paper and buried each night. To make the microfilm, many documents were originally photographed at distorted angles and had dark spots. The author only imaged those that were typewritten and legible and then photoshopped them to improve readability. The majority of the documents were receipts for cash, food, clothes, or personal articles.

The key to understanding these précis below is that Major Derry decided that each member of the team member should have a code name. Interestingly, Bill Simpson, John May, John Furman, Joe Pollak, and Harold Tittmann never used code names and often Monsignor O'Flaherty and Sir D'Arcy used real names instead of code names in their notes. The code names below are mentioned in the following pages:*

---

* Other code names assigned but not mentioned in the notes that follow: Bishop – Giuseppe Gonzi, an Italian National; Dutchpa – Father Anselmo Musters, a Dutch priest who was captured and tortured; Emma – Count Sarsfield Salazar, Swiss Embassy; Eyerish – Father Claffey, an Irish priest; Fanny – Father Flanagan, an Irish priest; Horace – Father Owen Sneddon, a New Zealand priest and Vatican Radio broadcaster; Midwife – Concettà Pazza, an Italian district nurse; Rinso – Renzo Lucidi's code name, taken from a popular brand of washing powder; Sailor – Father Galea, an Irish priest; Schoolmaster – Fernando Giustini, an Italian national; Uncle Tom – Father Lenan.

- Barney – Captain Henry Judson Byrnes, Royal Canadian Army Service Corps
- Edmund – Father Madden, a very popular priest with the ex-POWs
- Golf – Monsignor O'Flaherty, an Irish priest
- Grobb – Father Aurelius Borg, a Maltese priest
- Mario – Theodore Meletiou, a Greek national
- Mrs. M – Mrs. Chevalier, a Maltese national living in Rome
- Mount – Sir D'Arcy Osborne
- Patrick – Major Sam I. Derry, name changed to Toni when he moved inside the Vatican
- Sek – Secondo Costantini, an Italian employee of the Swiss Legation
- Spike – Father John Buckley, an Irish priest
- Till – Hugh Montgomery, a British subject and secretary to Sir D'Arcy
- Toni – Major Derry's second code name after he moved in with Sir D'Arcy
- Whitebows – Brother Robert Pace, a Maltese priest, whose code name refers to two white ribbons worn on the collar by members of the La Salle Teaching Order

Chronological Escape Line Notes:

1943:
September 8 [earliest correspondence]: Letter from an 80-year old man to Sir D'Arcy that Germans had recaptured escaped English prisoners from the Passo Corese POW Camp #54.
November 11: Golf to Hugh Montgomery that villagers are passing Allied soldiers through the German lines and some have now safely crossed.
December 6: a memo from Mrs. Maud Mary Sermanni, a British widow and clerk in the British interest section of the Swiss Embassy. She went with Secondo Costantini to a village near Rome to visit ex-POWs. She was met by a South African soldier and an Italian woman and introduced to more than 100 men. She reported that in three local villages there were about 450 men and they were in need of medicines.
December 27: Till to Patrick about ex-POWs in the countryside near Lake Bracciano where food is scarce and the men are actively being sought by Germans.

1944:
January 1: Patrick to Mount that two ex-POWs have returned to Rome after escaping a second time. They got within 500 yards of the British lines and in evacuated Italian mountain villages they found the bodies of Allied soldiers who had likely died of starvation.
January 4: Mount to Golf forwarding a list of Allied ex-POWs who the Badoglio government has passed through the lines in small groups. It noted that a thousand ex-POWs are in the Viterbo and Castelli Romani districts. There are also 350 men at Villa Vallelonga in the Sulmona area who are armed and acting as a military formation. Barney wrote a note that although we are in contact with Sulmona, we have heard nothing about such an organization.
January 8: Mount wrote that three British officers, a German deserter, and an Italian guide are being hidden at the church of *Santa Maria Sopra Minerva*, near the Pantheon.
January 11: Toni passed to Golf a list of ex-POWs to receive money. Ristic Cedomir was to be given money for his excellent work. There is a chance that John Furman [now captured] had on him a receipt signed by Mrs. M in her right name which the Gestapo could use to find her.

January 11: Golf to Toni wondering when Hugh Montgomery was going to find a place for the General [Major General M.D. Gambier-Parry, MC].

January 11: Letter to the Escape Line from Archie Gibb, from the Regina Coeli Prison, which described the raid on Via Firenze as quoted in the text.

January 11: Letter to Sir D'Arcy explaining that the Head of the British Interest Section at the Swiss Legation, Dr. Sommaruga, had a visit from an Italian general [probably Roberto Bencivenga] whom Badoglio has appointed commandant of Rome. Sommaruga was shown a secret message which detailed the Rome underground government and that Montezemolo was his chief of staff. The Italian general is ordered to have nothing to do with political parties and to confine himself to military activities. He is to organize the safety of the city and when the Allies arrive he is to hand over the city to them. The general asked for detailed plans of German fortifications around Rome. He also related gossip that German women are giving tea parties as they prepare to leave Rome as at least 30 German administrative personnel are scheduled to depart Rome by January 20.

January 12: Golf to Toni about sending radio messages to South Africa for the next-of-kin of escaped POWs. The letter noted that Major Mander was placed in a good home but is never there and the occupants think he is a German spy. Brother Robert has calmed them down. An American plane fell outside of Rome yesterday; one aviator was killed and another parachuted to safety, but he was denounced and sent to Forte Boccea.

January 13: Golf to Toni about a Russian priest reporting Russian ex-POWs in hiding at the Legation of Siam [Thailand]. Mrs. Tittmann gave Toni a parcel for an American who landed near Viterbo; John May will provide boots. Spike wants to bring six American sergeants to Rome so asked that Toni speak to Monsignor McGeough about the Casa San Giovanni.

January 16: Golf to Toni reporting that some ex-POWs have arrived in Switzerland. Mander brought back some documents from the raided Cellini apartment including Borg's [Grobb] famous note [not explained] to Buchner, and John Furman's and Joseph Pollak's identity cards and photos. Mander tells others that he is a German interpreter for the British and does not work for the POW organization but will do anything for them.

January 19: Toni to Mount concerning Father Sneddon and Brother Robert who work for the Vatican Information Bureau but are without Vatican identity cards. He said that as British subjects they need cards signed by the Germans.

January 19: Tittmann to Toni that South African Archie Gibb is asking for money. The American airman Eaton is being held in separate quarters because of his illness. As a result of revelations by Buchner, two monsignors, one a Maltese and the other a Scot, are in danger of arrest [meaning Brother Robert and Monsignor O'Flaherty].

January 21: Golf to Toni that the French are speaking against Pollak to protect Iride; Golf is sure she would have spoken sooner than Pollak. Buchner has given away a good number of secrets and says that Golf runs a political organization. Brother Robert is coming this afternoon to see about the senior officer [General Gambier-Parry].

January 24: Golf to Toni that Colin Leslie knows Mander well and the reason he wants to contact Derry is so he can collect another decoration [award].

January 25: Toni to Mount that the organization [Number One Special Force] is feeding and clothing some ex-POWS, but their interest is in organizing armed bands. These armed bands need money and have asked for it on the grounds that they have helped ex-POWS. Toni believes the number of ex-POWs helped is limited.

January 31: Golf to Toni that a friend of Major Umberto [Lousena] called and left a list of ex-POWs and requested shoes and clothes. He notes that Bill Simpson is not pleased with the officers at the French Seminary as they are not anxious to pay for anything.

He added that General [Gambier-Parry] believes it is better to leave his brother officers [ex-POW generals] where they are. Spike wants to bring some Americans to Rome and has spoken to Mrs. Tittmann [evidence that she was actively involved] to prepare Monsignor McGeough.

February 2: Toni to Bill [Simpson] that some new boys may be drawing money from two sources.

February 2: Grove Johnson gave a letter to Sir D'Arcy that three ex-POWs threatened a woman for not helping enough and if she does not do more, they will report her to the Germans.

February 3: Toni to Mount that a Russian priest [Father Dorotheo Bezchectnoff] has been found to help Russian ex-POWs. To date, Toni has given them 38,000 lire but is worried that if more Russians show up he will have to make other arrangements.

February 4: Golf to Toni that Mander is bringing in five ex-POWs and wants money and food. A young Irish priest was arrested yesterday for giving a cigarette to an American soldier [during the POW march around the Colosseum]; blackshirts took him to Regina Coeli, Rome has a new Rome Police Chief [Pietro Caruso] and he has begun arresting Jews.

February 6 [?]: Golf to Toni that he gave 10,000 lire for the men at Viterbo with the armed partisan band. The Jew [Cipolla] with the big dog staying at the Cellini apartment called and wants to get a receipt for some money that Mander was supposed to give to them. Golf said he had nothing more to do with this business. He will ask Mander about all this. Tittmann gave 3,000 lire for the American pilot at Viterbo.

February 7: Golf report to Toni that five ex-POWs have gone across the lines at Nettuno. Monterotondo is getting difficult since the Russians brought down a German plane and shot five German soldiers.

February 10: Golf to Toni in which he noted the January 28 bombing of the railway bridge at Allerona in Umbria, outside Orvieto and passed on that:

The Germans during the week left a train of British and American troops on a bridge outside Aquapendente [at Allerona near Orvieto] during an air raid; the train was first at a station and was brought out to save the bridge; people say about three hundred prisoners were killed by the Flying Fortresses; one got away, an American named Hubbard; this news was given me by an Italian flying officer and was confirmed by that young Yugoslav who was one of the wounded. I am giving Hubbard's home address to Tittmann.

Mander came in this morning and gave 5,000 lire to Brother Robert for some prisoners who he said were in grave danger and needed to be warned. Golf told Brother Robert not to go.

February 11: Golf to Toni that one of the Italian secret service crowd [SIM] was in today asking for information about Mander; they have been following him and say that he is moving in German circles. They had his name written as Derry Mander.

February 15: Golf to Toni that an Italian captain who visited this morning is a chief of one of the partisan bands. He has a brother in Regina Coeli who has given the British prisoners his home address. Golf met one of Brother Robert's guides who knows Mander and he asked for John Furman's identity card. On Sunday night Golf heard a British spy was arrested so it must be one of the ex-POWs. Madden has picked up a young Italian-American soldier [PFC George Frasca] and Golf passed the name to Tittmann. He has an uncle in Rome but will not go there as he is a Fascist. Golf wondered if they would not be able to pick up the two bikes left by John Furman outside of Rome yesterday. He also noted that when money is sent to the prison it should be in small bills since it is very difficult for the prisoners to get a thousand lire bill changed. He added that they must get more overcoats to hide the prisoners when they are being moved across the city.

February 15: Commendatore Marcello Piermatteri, a Verano Cemetery Superintendent, to Brother Robert with a list of 47 British and American soldiers buried at the cemetery. Eventually they will be moved to a new section, Riquadro Numero 14 Bis. Four more men were due from the new German Heldenfriedhof [Hero Cemetery] at Tor di Quinto. He will meet with two priests to discuss final layout for the new section but for now he has had marble pieces inscribed with names and some ivy plantings. Father Martin, Catholic, and Pastor Comba, Protestant, attend to the spiritual care.

February 16: Golf to Toni that Madden visited an American who had been captured at Nettuno. Tittmann has been asked to put him on the hill [Casa San Giovanni]. Green [unidentified and un-located] and other American aircrew members are anxious as one of their men is wounded and in a civilian hospital. Watched by one German, the others are intent to rescue him.

February 17: Tittmann to Toni about four unknown airmen buried at Verano Cemetery that he believes are British or Canadians because they crashed in a bomber at 23:00 hours [7 Feb according to *Giornale d'Italia*]; two articles of their clothing have Canadian markings.

February 18: John Furman to Toni who wrote that he is OK again and able to get back to work.

February 21: Toni to Golf that he was sorry to hear about the girl [Herta] in Regina Cœli Prison. He will try and send her small sums of money.

March 1: Tittmann to Barney that a message arrived in Rome on February 28, that 300–400 ex-POWs are living as refugees in the town of Le Cese [Aquila, 11 kilometers from Avezzano] and the town itself has only 1,000 inhabitants.

March 9: Toni to Tittmann with the names of four US ex-POWs. Ten other US ex-POWs are coming to Rome and asked him to convince Monsignor McGeough to put them at Casa San Giovanni.

March 14: Tittmann to Toni with a list of Americans including several flying officers.

March 14: Toni to Golf that the Germans have brought 200 women into Rome for undercover work, but can't believe the Germans would go to that trouble to recapture ex-POWs.

March 15: Golf to Toni that some soldiers say that officers take the good billets and reserve Mrs. M's place for themselves. Golf noted that Italian authorities are making some food parcels available but to hide that it is done officially, they have the Vatican food kitchens make the distribution. Golf sent 2,000 lire, two pairs of socks, a shirt and a *golf* [a sweater] to the American [Ranger] Newman who came a few days ago.

March 20 [?]: Golf to Toni about two Egyptian soldiers who escaped a work detail at Frascati.

March 20 [?]: Archie Gibb wrote to Toni that on January 8, he, Neil [CSM N.G. Billet] and Knox [Sgt. P.L. Knox-Davis] were arrested because of a gross betrayal to the SS [see January 11 letter from Archie Gibb]. Shortly after the Anzio landing, he saw them when they were sent to Germany from Regina Cœli Prison. He was not taken because there was no room in the truck and after several more weeks he was moved to the Cinecittà prison camp. A few days later, he escaped back to the city as he still wore civilian clothes. He fixed himself up in an apartment with wireless [radio], books and a good companion in Major Cummings [no further information]. Yesterday he spoke to an officer who was in the same boxcar as Neil when they left for Germany [probably Johnstone] and related the story of Furman's escape. Note on the bottom states that Derry was annoyed with Gibb because he collected 3,000 lire from him, 2,000 lire and a new suit from the Swiss, and 1,440 lire from Simpson all at about the same time.

March 21: Golf to Toni noting that three Americans will arrive this morning and will need socks, boots and shirts and that Edmond is getting an apartment for them. Brother Robert let me down this morning; he was to come at 8:45 and I kept everyone waiting for him. [Author's note: Brother Robert had been captured that morning.]

March 22: Golf to Toni with an enclosed letter from the General [Major General Gambier-Parry] who intends changing his billet.

March 23: Golf to Toni about the two Egyptians to whom he gave 1,000 lire each. Golf gave a suit to one of the boys at the Oratory of St Peter's [staying at Gendarme Barracks] who then had a walk to see the piazza of Saint Peter's and was nearly arrested.

March [?]: Toni to Mount with the names of six escaped POWs near Monte Terminillo who were shot and killed by Fascist Troops of Battalion M [GNR]. He included a note to Barney not to report this to London until confirmed. This information was passed on by a Lt. Stone, an Australian officer in charge of a group near Rieti, who reported that 400 ex-POWs, captured at Anzio and Cassino, were killed and 200 wounded on a railway bridge bombing attack at Orvieto on 28 January. Some POWs escaped and arrived in Montebuono [Rome] area [see February 10 entry]. Russians at Monterotondo shot down a German plane and then got into a firefight with Germans in which five ex-POWs were killed. Toni advised the priest helping the Russians [Father Bezchectnoff] that money was not to be used for arms and that the organization [Escape Line] takes a poor view of this type of attack.

April 3: Golf to Toni that the Germans have complained about the Swiss so Sek was warned not to speak to ex-POWs and not to give them money or clothes. Since then, Trippi has stopped all payments, Golf arranged for Sek to slip money into their pockets; not talking to them but winking. He reported that Secondo Bernardini from Pisoniano [east of Rome] has been shot by the Germans for sheltering POWs; please inform Whitebows. Included was a list of nine POWs at Regina Coeli; including John Armstrong and a civilian named Leslie Ingram.

April 4: John Furman to Sam Derry in which he mentions Barclay and McBride, both six footers with round red faces and blonde hair. Going through Rome with them he felt like a man walking with a Union Jack in each hand.

April 5: Edmund to Toni that ex-POWs are going out and getting drunk. One man, when drunk, tells everyone he is English. The host family is very concerned. Edmund asked Toni to write a letter ordering them to stay indoors and quit drinking.

April 19: Edmund to Toni that three of his men had been retaken. They were caught coming out of a beer shop. Edmund asked for a letter for another soldier named Keegan who gets drunk, shouts his name as well as Golf's and Toni's, and talks about an organization in the Vatican that helps ex-POWs and pays him 120 lire a day.

April [?]: Notes: Recently a man outside Rome presented himself as a British captain responsible for ex-POWs. He was a German agent provocateur. An American ex-POW [Frasca] may have applied to the police for Italian Republic citizenship, stating that his mother was Italian. To prove his good faith, he stated that he was prepared to give the police the names and locations of all ex-POWs whom he knows to be hiding in Rome. We may be doing this man an injustice but until we are able to prove his good faith toward us, we must warn you to be on the alert against him.

May 1: Edmund to Toni that our friend S.P. [John Sperni, a British Journalist working for Derry] has been taken in a raid and may have talked since the SS have been back to his wife and asked all about me. There were two ex-POWs taken with him, Keegan in a drunken condition. Edmund wrote about a man named Ball who returned to his billet against our wishes and threatens to tell the SS everything if send him away again as he is in love with the daughter of the house. Edmund says he can't move about freely and asked what the SS may know about him. He mentioned a woman with two children whose money was taken by the SS and he gave her 2,000 lire. He asked Toni if he really believes the Allies won't be there until autumn and if so he will go to Anzio.

May 11: Till to Toni about three American ex-POWs who have been staying at Castel Gandolfo for the past two months. He sent them 1500 lire for the month and 500 lire for clothing.

May 27: Edmund to Toni passing information about Sperni who, with the help of the Swiss, convinced the Germans that he was a British subject. He was taken to Via Tasso for a month, fed a so-called soup once a day, kept in a dark cell and beaten and interrogated several times but never said anything. He has been moved to Regina Coeli Prison and will be sent to Germany. His wife was also interrogated and was asked if she knew Sir D'Arcy, Monsignor O'Flaherty and Father Madden.

May 28: From Colin [Leslie] to Toni asking for information about his 24th Guards battalion as he intends to set out for them immediately and see if he can be of some use, even temporarily.

APPENDIX G: VISITING KEY SITES IN ROME TODAY

There are many places discussed in this book that should be visited. Two of the most important are the *Museo Storico della Liberazione* at the former Gestapo Headquarters on Via Tasso and the Fosse Ardeatine memorial cemetery. In addition, many of the Rome restaurants featured in this book can still be visited for a meal or drink, although not necessarily recommended by the author. They include:

- Antica Birreria Peroni restaurant, near Piazza Venezia, where the partisans lunched before the attack at Via Rasella
- Café Greco, on Via Condotti, where with Bentivegna and Capponi met with the GAP commander
- Casina delle Rose, now called Casa del Cinema, in the Villa Borghese Park, where the ex-POWs often dined, sometimes with the Gestapo
- Da Giggetto, in the Ghetto, where Kappler often dined
- Passetto restaurant, the site of a called-off partisan attack and the favorite restaurant of Fascist Minister Buffarini-Guidi
- Restaurante dell'Opera, now called del Giglio, where the escaped POWs first ate when they came to Rome
- Osteria dell Orso (The Bear Hostelry), along the Tiber, a favorite hangout for the Escape Line, recently closed after being converted into an expensive nightclub
- Scarpone, Dollmann's favorite and secluded restaurant behind the Janiculum Hill.

Hollywood and Cinecittà did not neglect these events. Immediately after the war these stories started to be told on film. Here is a partial listing by date:

Open City, 1946 – The Nazi occupation of Rome

Il Gobbo, 1960 – The Hunchback of the Quarticciolo

Two Women, (La Ciociara), 1960 – Sophia Loren won the Best Actress Oscar for her role in this film; she was the first foreigner to do so.

L'oro di Roma, 1961 – Roman Gold, the story of the Jewish gold collection

Von Ryan's Express, 1965 – Escaped Allied POWs on the run

Massacre in Rome, 1973 – The attack on Via Rasella

The Scarlet and the Black, 1983 – The exploits of Monsignor O'Flaherty

Captain Corelli's Mandolin, 2001 – The German execution of Italian soldiers at Cephalonia in September 1943

I Nazisti a Rome, 2007– Key images from Insituto Luce's vast collection of World War II materials

Pius XII, Under the Roman Sky, 2010 – An uncritical look at Pope Pius XII during the war.

———

The Benedictine Abbey of Monte Cassino was rebuilt in the 1950s and its treasures, which had been stored at the Vatican, have long since been returned. But there was a so-called second battle of Cassino, a battle against malaria. Shell holes and bomb craters filled with water were ideal for mosquitoes to breed and for malaria to run rampant, which it did. Even those making a brief stop at the rebuilt Cassino train station often contracted the disease. An Italian friend, retired Admiral Giuseppe Mazzoli, is from the Cassino area and told the author that many died of malaria in the years after the war. War and pestilence, hand in hand throughout history, lingered in this manner to bedevil the ancient town of Cassino, Rome itself, and all of Italy.

Bibliography and Resources

Note: German and Italian language materials were read and in part translated by the author.

BOOKS

Aarons, Mark, and Loftus, John, *Unholy Trinity: The Vatican, the Nazis and the Swiss Banks*, St. Martin's Press, New York, 1991

Adleman, Robert H., and Walton, George, *The Devil's Brigade*, Naval Institute Press, Annapolis, MD, 2004

Adleman, Robert H., and Walton, Col. George, *Rome Fell Today*, Little, Brown and Company, Boston, 1968

Allen, William L., *Anzio, Edge of Disaster*, E. P. Dutton, New York, 1978

Alvarez, David and Graham, S. J., Robert A., *Nothing Sacred, Nazi Espionage Against the Vatican, 1939–1945*, Frank Cass, Portland, OR, 1997

Annussek, Greg A., *Hitler's Raid to Save Mussolini: The Most Infamous Commando Operation of World War II*, Da Capo Press, Cambridge, MA, 2005

Antonucci, Silvia Haia, editor, *Anatomia di una deportazione*, Guerini e Associati, Milano, 2010

Antonucci, Silvia Haia, and Procaccia, Claudio, editors, *Dopo il 16 ottobre, gli ebrei a Roma tra occupazione, resistenza, accoglienza e delazioni (1943–1944)*, Viella, Roma, 2017

Atkinson, Rick, *The Day of Battle*, Henry Holt and Company, Inc., New York, 2007

Barker, A. J., *The Rape of Ethiopia 1936*, Ballantine's Illustrated History of the Violent Century, Ballantine Books, Inc., New York, 1971

Barneschi, Gianluca, *An Englishman Abroad: SOE Agent Dick Mallaby's Italian Missions, 1943–45*, Osprey, Oxford, UK, 2019

Battistelli, Pier Paolo, and Crociani, Piero, *World War II Partisan Warfare in Italy*, Osprey, Oxford, UK, 2015

Bentivegna, Rosario, *Operazione Via Rasella, verità e menzogne: [protagonisti raccontano]*, Editori Riuniti, Rome, 1996

Berger, Sara, editor, *I signori del terrore*, Cierre edizioni, Verona, 2016

Black, Col. Robert W., *The Ranger Force*, Stackpole Books, Mechanicsburg, PA, 2009

Blet, Pierre S. J., *Pius XII and the Second World War*, Paulist Press, Mahwah, NJ, 1999

Bokun, Branko, *Spy in the Vatican, 1941–45*, Praeger Publishers, New York, 1973

Bosworth, R. J. B., *Mussolini's Italy: Life Under the Fascist Dictatorship, 1915–1945*, Penguin Books, New York, 2006

Bragadin, Marc Antonio, *The Italian Navy in World War II*, US Naval Institute Press, Annapolis, MD, 1957

Brey, Ilaria Dagnini, *The Venus Fixers*, Farrar, Straus and Giroux, New York, 2009

Buckley, Christopher, *The Road to Rome*, Hodder and Stoughton, London, 1945

Camposano, Raffaello, editor, *Giuseppe Dosi, il poliziotto artista che inventò l'Interpol italiana*, Quaderno II, Roma, 2014

Cappellari, Pietro, *Lo sbarco di Nettunia e la Battaglia per Roma*, Herald Editore, Roma, 2010

Capponi, Carla, *Con Cuore di Donna*, Saggiatore, Milano, 2000

Casavola, Anna Maria, *7 Ottobre 1943, La Deportazione dei Carabinieri romani nei Lager nazisti*, Edizione Studium, Roma, 2010

Caviglia, Stefano, *Alla scoperta della Roma Ebraica*, Intra Moenia, Napoli, 2013

Chadwick, Owen, *Britain and the Vatican during the Second World War*, Cambridge University Press, New York, 1988

Clark, Lloyd, *Anzio: Italy and the Battle for Rome 1944*, Grove Press, New York, 2006

Cooke, Philip and Shepherd, Ben H., editors, *Hitler's Europe Ablaze: Occupation, Resistance and Rebellion during World War II*, Skyhorse Publishing, New York, 2014

Cornwell, John, *Hitler's Pope: The Secret History of Pius XII*, Viking, New York, 1999

Corvo, Max, *The OSS in Italy 1942–1945*, Praeger, NY, 1990

Crociani, Piero, *La Polizia dell'Africa Italiana (1937–1945)*, Ufficio Storico della Polizia di Stato, Roma, 2009

Dams, Carsten, and Stolle, Michael, *The Gestapo: Power and Terror in the Third Reich*, Oxford University Press, Oxford, 2014

Dank, Milton, *The French against the French: Collaboration and Resistance*, J. B. Lippincott Company, New York, 1974

de Wyss, M., *Rome Under the Terror*, Robert Hale Limited, London, 1945

D'Este, Carlo, *Fatal Decision: Anzio and the Battle for Rome*, Harper Perennial, New York, 1992

Dear, Ian, *Escape and Evasion: Prisoner of War Breakouts and the Routes to Safety in World War Two*, Sterling, New York, 1997

Debenedetti, Giacomo, *16 Ottobre 1943*, Notre Dame, Ind., University of Notre Dame Press, 2001

Derry, Sam, I., *The Rome Escape Line: Primary Source Edition*, W. W. Norton and Company, New York, 1960

Dollmann, Eugen, *The Interpreter: Memoirs of Doktor Eugen Dollmann*, Hutchinson, London, 1967

Dollmann, Eugen, *Nazi Fugitive: The true story of a German on the Run*, Skyhorse Publishing, New York, 2017

Edsel, Robert M., *Saving Italy: The Race to Rescue a Nation's Treasures from the Nazis*, W. W. Norton & Company, New York, 2013

Failmezger, Victor, *American Knights*, Osprey, Oxford, 2015

Fargion, Picciotto, *L'occupazione tedesca e gli ebrei di Roma: documenti e fatti*, Carucci, Roma, 1979

Fermi, Laura, *Mussolini*, University of Chicago Press, 1961

Fleming, Brian, *The Vatican Pimpernel: The Wartime Exploits of Monsignor Hugh O'Flaherty*, The Collins Press, Wilton, Cork, Ireland, 2008

Foot, M. R. D. and Langley, J. M., *MI-9 Escape and Evasion 1939–45*, Little Brown and Company, Boston, 1980

Forczyk, Robert, *Rescuing Mussolini: Gran Sasso 1943*, Osprey, Oxford, UK, 2010

Furman, Lt. Col. John, *Be Not Fearful*, Anthony Bond, London, 1959

Gallagher, J. P., *The Scarlet and the Black: The True Story of Monsignor Hugh O'Flaherty, Hero of the Vatican Underground*, Ignatius Press, San Francisco, 2009

Garrad-Cole, Wing Commander E., *Single to Rome*, London, Allan Wingate, 1955

Gilbert, Michael, *The Danger Within*, Rue Morgue, Boulder, 2007

Greene, Jack, and Massignani, Alessandro, *The Black Prince and the Sea Devils: The Story of Valerio Borghese and the Elite Units of the Decima MAS*, Da Capo Press, Cambridge, MA, 2004

Hapgood, David, and Richardson, David, *Monte Cassino*, Congdon & Weed, New York, 1984

Haupt, Werner, *Kriegsschauplatz Italien*, Motorbuch Verlag, Stuttgart, 1977

Head, Louis, *Dancing in the Dark: Escape and Evasion in Croatia during the Second World War*, Writers Club Press, New York, 2002

Hibbert, Christopher, *Anzio: The Bid for Rome*, Ballantine Books, New York, 1970

Hymoff, Edward, *The OSS in World War II*, Ballantine, New York, 1972

Jackson, W. G. F., *The Battle for Rome*, Charles Scribner's Sons, New York, 1969

Josowitz, First Lt. Edward L., *An Informal History of the 601st Tank Destroyer Battalion*, Pustet, Salzburg, Austria, 1945

Kappler, Herbert, *Lettere dal carcere, 1948–1950*, Maurizio Edizioni, Rome, 1997 (written in German, translated into Italian)

Katz, Robert, *The Battle for Rome*, Simon & Schuster, New York, 2003

Katz, Robert, *Black Sabbath*, Macmillan, New York, 1969

Katz, Robert, *Death in Rome*, Macmillan, New York, 1967

Klinkhammer, Lutz, *Diplomatici e militari tedeschi a Roma di fronte alla politica di sterminio nazionalsocialista*, Deutsches Historisches Institut Rom, Rome, forthcoming

Klinkhammer, Lutz, *Die abteilung "Kunstschutz" der Deutschen Militärverwaltung in Italien, 1943–1945*, Perspectivia.net, Band 72, 1992

Klinkhammer, Lutz, *Stragi naziste in Italia: la guerra contro i civili (1943–44)*, Donzelli Editore, 1997

Kloman, Erasmus H., *Assignment Algiers: With the OSS in the Mediterranean Theater*, Naval Institute Press, Annapolis, Maryland, 2005

Kneale, Brendon, *Brother Robert Pace Biography*, self-published, circa 1960s

Kurzman, Dan, *The Race for Rome*, Doubleday, New York, 1975

Landwehr, Richard, *Italian Volunteers of the Waffen-SS, 24 Waffen-Gebirgs-Karstjäger Division der SS and 29 Waffen-Grenadier-Division der SS, italienische Nr. 1*, Siegrunen, Glendale, OR, 1987

Lodi, Marco, *La Resistenza a Roma (1943–1944)*, Brigati, Genova, 2011

Ludwig, Emilio, *Colloqui Con Mussolini* (translated from the German to Italian), Mondadori, Milan, 1932

Macadam, Alta, *Blue Guide Rome*, tenth edition, Somerset Books, London, 2010

Macintyre, Ben, *Rogue Heroes: The History of the SAS*, Crown, New York, 2016

Majanlahti, Anthony and Osti Guerrazzi, Amedeo, *Roma Occupata 1943–1944*, il Saggiatore, Milano, 2010

Malaparte, Curzio, *The Skin (La Pelle)*, New York Review of Books, New York, 2013

Mander, D'Arcy, *Mander's March on Rome*, London, Allan Sutton, 1987

Manzari, Giuliano, *I Servizi Segreti Alleati a Roma*, publisher and date unknown

Marinucci, Rosalba Borri, Faraglia, Maria Luisa Fabilli, and Setta, Mario, *E si divisero il pane che non c'era*, Edizioni Qualevita, Torre di Nolfi, 2009

Marzilla, Marco, and Mori, Alessandra, *Roma 1943–1944 ieri & oggi*, Herald Editore, Roma, 2007

Masson, Georgina, *The Companion Guide to Rome*, Fontana/Collins, UK, 1970

McConnon, Aili, and McConnon, Andres, *Road to Valor*, Broadway Paperbacks, New York, 2012

Mogavero, Giuseppe, and Parisella, Antonio, *Memorie di Quartiere, Frammenti di storie di guerra e di Resistenza nell' Appio/Latino Latino, e Tuscolano 1943–1944*, Edilazio, Roma, 2007

Molinari, Maurizio, and Osti Guerrazzi, Amedeo, *Duello nel Ghetto, la sfida di un ebreo contro le bande naifasciste nella Roma occupata*, Rizzoli, Milano, 2017

Morton, H. V., *A Traveler in Rome*, Dodd, Mead & Company, New York, 1957

Munthe, Malcom, *Sweet is War to Them that Know It Not*, Sickle Moon Edition, Denmark, 2012, originally published by Duckworth, London, 1954

Mussolini, Benito, *The Fall of Mussolini*, translated by Frances Frenaye, Farrar, Straus and Company, New York, 1948

Newman, Louis Israel, *A "Chief Rabbi" of Rome Becomes a Catholic*, New York, Renaissance Press, 1945

Newman, William L., *Escape in Italy*, University of Michigan Press, Ann Arbor, MI, 1945

Nisbett, Alfred, *Always Tomorrow: Sempre Domani*, Athena Press, London, 2008

Olivieri, Alessandra, *Messi al Muro, I manifesti Conservati nel Museo Storico della Liberazione*, Granatiere, Roma, 2011

Orna, Joseph, *The Escaping Habit*, Leo Cooper, London, 1975

Osti Guerrazzi, Amedeo, *Tedeschi, Italiani ed Ebrei, Le polizie nazi-fasciste in Italia 1943–1945*, forthcoming

Paladini, Arrigo, *Via tasso: carcere nazista*, Istituto poligrafico e Zecca dello Stato, Rome, 1986

Parisella Antonio, editor, *The Museum Narrates: The Liberation of Rome from the Nazi Occupation*, Gangemi Editore, Rome, 2018

Pezzetti, Marcello, editor, *16 ottobre 1943, La razza nemica*, Gangemi Editore, Rome, 2018

Pezzetti, Marcello and Berger, Sara, *La razza nemica, la propaganda antisemita nazista e fascista*, Gangemi Editore, Rome, 2017

Piscitelli, Enzo, *Storia della resistenza Romana*, Editori Laterza, Bari, 1965

Pompeo, Augusto, *Forte Bravetta*, Odradek, Roma, 2012

Portelli, Alessandro, *The Order Has Been Carried Out*, Palgrave Macmillan, London, 2007

Raiber, Richard, *The Anatomy of Perjury: Field Marshal Albert Kesselring, Via Rasella, and the Ginny Mission*, University of Delaware Press, Newark, DE, 2008

Reid, Howard, *Dad's War*, Bantam Books, New York, 2003

Rocca, Gianni, *L'Italia Invasa 1943–1945,* Oscar Storia, Mondadori, Milan, 1999

Romagnoli, G. Franco, *The Bicycle Runner: A Memoir of Love, Loyalty, and the Italian Resistance*, St. Martin's Press, New York, 2009

Rozell, Matthew A., *The Things Our Fathers Saw: The Untold Stories of the World War II Generation, Volume IV: Up the Bloody Boot: The War in Italy*, Woodchuck Hollow Press, Hartford, NY, 2018

S. K., *Agent in Italy*, Doubleday, Doran & Company, Garden City, NY, 1942

Salwa, Ursula, and Wanderlingh, Attilio, *Roma in Guerra, dal Fascismo al il Conflitto*, Intra Moenia, Naples, 2011

Scrivener, J., *Inside Rome with the Germans*, Macmillan, NY, 1945

Sermoneta, Vittoria [the Duchess of Sermoneta], *Sparkle Distant World*, Hutchinson & Co., London, 1947

Sevareid, Eric, *Not So Wild a Dream*, Athenaeum, NY, 1976

Silveri, Umberto Gentiloni, and Carli, Maddalena, *Bombardare Roma, Gli Alleati e la 'citta aperta' (1940–1944)*, il Mulino, Biblioteca Storica, Bologna, 2007

Simone, Cesare de, *Venti angeli sopra roma*, Mursia, Milan, 2013

Simonetti, Fabio, *Via Tasso, Quartiere generale e carcere Tedesco durante l'occupazione di Roma*, Odradek, Rome, 2016

Simpson, William C., *A Vatican Lifeline '44*, Sarpedon, New York, 1996

Smith, Richard Harris, *OSS: The Secret History of America's First Central Intelligence Agency*, University of California Press, Berkeley, CA, 1972

Smith, Ruby Simon, *Wine, Cheese, & Bread: A POW's Story of Survival in Italy*, Wood Burner Press, Austin, Texas, 1998

Spataro, Mario, *Dal caso Priebke al Nazi Gold, Storie d'Ingiustizia e di Quattrini*, Settimo Sigillo, Rome, 1999

Spataro, Mario, *Rappresaglia, Via Rasella e le Ardeatine, alla luce del caso Priebke*, Settimo Sigillo, Rome, 1996

Stern, Michael, *An American in Rome*, B. Geis Associates, New York, 1964

Sullivan, Mark, *Beneath a Scarlet Sky*, Lake Union Publishing, Seattle, Washington, 2017

Sweet, Col. Russell H., General Staff Corps, Chief, Captured Personnel and Material Branch, US War Department, Military Intelligence Service, *MIS-X Manual on Evasion, Escape, and Survival*, Washington DC, February, 1944

Thomas, Gordon, *The Pope's Jews: The Vatican's Secret Plan to Save Jews from the Nazis*, Thomas Dunne Books, St. Martin's Press, NY, 2012

Tittmann, Harold H., Jr., *Inside the Vatican of Pius XII: The Memoir of an American Diplomat During World War II*, Doubleday, New York, 2004

Tompkins, Peter, *A Spy in Rome*, Simon and Schuster, New York, 1962

Tompkins, Peter, *Italy Betrayed*, Simon and Schuster, New York, 1966

Trevelyan, Raleigh, *The Fortress: A Diary of Anzio and After*, Buchan & Enright, London, 1985 (reprint of 1956)

Trevelyan, Raleigh, *Rome '44*, Viking Press, New York, 1981

Waagenaar, Sam, *The Pope's Jews*, Open Court Pub. Co., LaSalle, IL, 1974

Walker, Stephen, *Hide & Seek: The Irish Priest in the Vatican Who Defied the Nazi Command*, Lyons Press, Guilford, Connecticut, 2011

Weisbord, Robert G. and Sillanpoa, Wallace P., *The Chief Rabbi, the Pope and the Holocaust*, Transaction Publishers, New Brunswick, NJ, 1991

Weymouth, Major Guy, *A.W.O.L.: In an Italian Prison Camp and Subsequent Adventures on the Run in Italy, 1943–1944*, Tom Donovan, London, 1993

Whiting, Charles, *Gehlen: Germany's Master Spy*, Ballantine Books, New York, 1972

Wilhelm, Maria De Blasio, *The Other Italy: The Italian Resistance in World War II*, W. W. Norton and Company, New York, 1988

Williamson, Gordon, *The SS: Hitler's Instrument of Terror*, Zenith Press, St. Paul, Minnesota, 2004

Zuccotti, Susan, *The Italians and the Holocaust: Persecution, Rescue, and Survival*, Basic Books, Inc., New York, 1987

Zuccotti, Susan, *Père Marie-Benoît and the Jewish Rescue*, Indiana University Press, Bloomington, Indiana, 2013

Zuccotti, Susan, *Under his Very Windows: The Vatican and the Holocaust in Italy*, Yale University Press, New Haven, CT, 2000

Books by unknown Italian authors

4 Giugno 1944, Roma libera, Ed UP, Rome, 2004

Ten Years of Italian Progress, printed in Italy by the E.N.I.T (Italian State Tourist Department), Edizione Inglese, Milan, 1933 XI [11th Year of Fascism] (booklet in the author's collection)

da Carcere a Museo, Museo Storico della Liberazione, Via Tasso: Official Italian Government Publication, 2013

La Nostra SS Italiani, courtesy of Lutz Klinkhammer of the Deutsches Historisches Institut in Rom, 1944

Le Operazioni delle Unità Italiane nel Settembre–Octtobre 1943, Ministero della Difesa (formerly Ministero della Guerra), Stato Maggiore dell'Esercito, Ufficio Storico, Roma, 1975

Books by unknown German authors

Der Deutsche Kommandant von Rom, Kriegstagebuch für die Zeit 10.9–31.12.1943 (the German
Commandant in Rome, War diary for the period September 10, 1943 to December 31,
1943). Photocopy from the Bundesarchiv – Militärarchiv in Freiburg, Germany:
October 7, 1943
October 10, 1943
October 17, 1943
December 4, 1943
December 15, 1943
December 18, 1943
December 25, 1943
Faschismus in Italien, Bibliothek Susmel I, Katalog der Brochüren, Deutsches Historisches
Institut Rom, 1988
Faschismus in Italien, Bibliothek Susmel II, Katalog der Periodoca, Deutsches Historisches
Institut Rom, 1988
War diary of 3rd Panzergrenadier Division for September 1943, photocopy from the
Bundesarchiv – Militärarchiv, Freiburg, reference RH 26-3/11

BRITISH REPORTS

AFHQ, EXP. Det. G-3, J.I.C.A. G-2, June 8, 1943, subject: *Italian Police Organizations
(based on conversations with an Italian deserter)*, copies to Washington and London
How to Become a Spy: The World War II SOE Training Manual, British SOE, Skyhorse
Publishing, New York, 2015
Interrogations of Italian Nationals concerning German Activities in Rome, from the Public
Record Office (National Archives) at Kew, London

MISCELLANEOUS ITEMS

Georgetown University Library Special Collections Research Center: the Tittmann, Harold
H., Jr. Papers: ID GTM.GAMMS439: Date [bulk] 1940–1945: Date [inclusive] 1939–
1988: Extent: 4.5 Linear feet Total: 9 boxes
Documents from the Dosi collection at the *Museo Storico della Liberazione, Procedimento
Penale, contro Caruso, Pietro, Roma, 18 Settembre, 1944*
National Catholic Welfare Conference, letter to President Roosevelt of September 15, 1942

Period maps

BGEN. William Carey Crane Battle Map of Rome, Drawn by CIU and War Office, Photo
lithographed by War Office, 3rd edition, December 1943

Internet

Resistance in Rome a Chronology (Resistenza a Roma una cronologia), by Pavia, Aldo, a month
by month summary of partisan activities and German and Fascist reactions as of July
19, 2016 was culled from many sources. A printout was forwarded to the author by Pier
Paulo Battistelli. The author and his wife Patricia translated the 40 or so pages, condensed
them into a monthly summary adding other material and then placing the information
throughout the book.
www.dalvolturnoacassino.it/asp/tesoro-di-montecassino.asp

NEWSPAPERS

Brown, Emma, "American Writer Chronicled War Massacre in Italy," *Washington Post*, October 24, 2010

Langer, Emily, "Erich Priebke, 100, Nazi War Criminal Involved in Massacre," *Washington Post*, October 13, 2013

Unknown, "War Hero, Brother Pace Dies at Stanford," *Oakland Tribune*, December 4, 1970

Unknown, "War Resistance Hero bro. Robert Pace Dies," *Oakland Tribune*, December 5, 1970

Unknown, "Brother Robert Paces Dies at 63," *San Francisco Chronicle*, December 5, 1970

US ARMY PUBLICATIONS/BOOKLETS

3rd ID, *Operations Instructions Number 33*, Special Instructions for the Occupation of Rome, June 4, 1944

If you should be CAPTURED these are your rights, War Department Pamphlet No. 21-7, May 16, 1944, US Government Printing Office, Washington, 1944

Rome, A Soldier's Guide, compiled and published by Information & Education Section, HQ, MTOUSA, circa 1944

Road to Rome, Salerno, Naples, Volturno, Cassino, Anzio, Rome, issued by Lt. General Mark Clark, USA

US Army-associated newspapers

The *Stars and Stripes* newspaper, Mediterranean, Italy edition, June 6, 1944, Vol. I, No. 174, Tuesday, June 6, 1944

US NATIONAL ARCHIVES AND RECORDS ADMINISTRATION

Escape Line documents are on microfilm at the US National Archives, College Park, Maryland. They are listed under the heading, *The Record of Allied Force Headquarters (AFHQ) 1942–1946*, (see the Analytical Guide to Combined British-American Records, p. 82, the AFHQ Relief Organization contained in RG 331 Records of Allied Operational and Occupation HQ WWII contained in Reel 32 M Box Number 284). Documents scanned by the author in July 2016.

Allied Force Headquarters, G-2: 0GBI-389.704-B/1 January 13, 1945, Subject: *Summary and Appreciation of the Activities of Einsatzkommando Rom, SIPO and SD*

Appendix "B" to Fifth Army G-2 report No. 349, Translation of Captured Document: Von Hoffman, Chief General Staff HQ I Parachute Corps Operational Order No. 838/Secret, 20 July 44, Subject: *Operations against Partisans: Order No. 2* (translated from the German)

HQ Allied Armies in Italy; AAI/1403/1/GSI (b) May 25, 1944, Subject: *The Sicherheitsdienst*

HQ Allied Central Mediterranean Force; ACMF/1403/1/G (1b) March 1944, Subject: *Organization of German Intelligence in Italy*

Kern, Robert Bruce, *Sergant* (sic), *Alexander, Captured SS Personality*, May 24, 1945

NND 867125: Angleton, James H., *Report of Visit to Ardeatine Caves*, August 21, 1944 HQ 2677th Regiment OSS (Prov) APO 534

NND 877190: Unknown, *Italian Operations (OSS) August 1st, 1943 to May 1944*, undated

NND 917144: Amerman, Harry Lee, *Crossing of Enemy Lines by four purported Allied Officers, May 25, 1944*, May 26, 1944

NND 974345: Bourgoin, H. E. A., *Names of Agents (OSS) Killed or Missing*, pages four and five, February 8, 1945

No identifying information; Subject: *Further Interrogation of Helene Louise Ten Cate Brouwer*

No identifying information; Subject: *Ferruccio Furlani, Sabotage Considerations*

Questura di Roma, *List of names to be turned over to Lieutenant Tunath of the German police*, March 24, 1944 (in Italian)

Schutt, Willard A., *Investigation of Activities as Escaped POW* (Frasca), June 23, 1944

Spingarn, Stephen, *Sergant* (sic), *Alexander, Captured SS Personality*, May 29, 1945

HQ 15 Army Group, CMF: CSDIC Reports (Combined Service Detailed Interrogation Centre)

CSDIC/CMF, Jun 26, 1945 Subject: *Eighth Detailed Interrogation Report on SS Sturmbannführer Huegel, Dr. Claus*

CSDIC/CMF/SD 9, May 28, 1945 Subject: *First Detailed Interrogation Report on Rittmeister Graf Thun-Hohenstein* (Hohenberg)

CSDIC/CMF/SD 10, May 29, 1945 Subject: *First Detailed Interrogation Report on SS Sturmbannfeuhrer Domizlaff, Dr. Borante*

CSDIC/CMF/SD 64, Aug 29, 1945 Subject: *First Detailed Interrogation Report on SS Oberstumbannfeuhrer Elling Georg*

CSDIC/SC/15AG/SD/3, May 19, 1945, Wedeking, R. V., Subject: *First Interrogation Report on Col. Helffrich, Otto*

CSDIC/SC15AG/SD 18 (copy number 25) dated June 8, 1945 Subject: *Kappler's first Interrogation Report*

CSDIC/SC/15AG/SD 24 (copy number 6) dated June 28, 1945 Subject: *Aufklärungszeit Kommando Süd West* (FAK 150)

OSS documents

Caggiati, Alessandro, *Report on Visit to Rome with two Couriers from Parma, CLN*, November 28, 1944, Folder 193 OSS

Italian Desk, OSS, *Abwehr Organization in Italy*, September 28, 1943

Poczta, Andre, *Report Covering the Activities of OSS Special Detachment G-2, 5th Army in Italy*, undated

OSS X-2 Branch Headquarters Washington DC, *Abwehr Organization in Italy*, September 28, 1943

Peter Tompkins records on his OSS Mission and his photos of Rome

SCI (Special Counter Intelligence) reports

SCI Unit Z; Memo Subject: *Otto Lechner*, Sep 8, 1945

SCI Unit Z; Memo No. 603 Subject: *Eugen Haas*, Feb 25, 1945

SCI Rome; SCI/Rome/730/0003 Subject: *SD Personalities Rome*, June 14, 1944

SCI Rome; SCI/Rome/730/159 Subject: *SD Personnel (AMT VI in Rome and Berlin)*, July 27, 1944

SCI/730/56; Subject: *Notes on Obersturmbannführer Herbert Kappler*, June 24, 1944

SCI/730/166; Subject: *SD Agents* (salvaged from Via Tasso), July 20, 1944

SCI/876/6; Subject: *SD Sabotage Course*, July 22, 1944

SCI NA 770/4 335/11; Subject: *SS SD Bologna*, Aug 14, 1944

SCI/240/241 A; Subject: *Ruta Renato*, Sep 23, 1944

SCI/730/481; Subject: *Names of SS Personnel found in Documents taken from the German Embassy, Rome, June 1944*, Sep 16, 1944

Index

Note: Page locators in **bold** refer to maps.